ANNETTE H. TOMARKEN

THE SMILE OF TRUTH

The French Satirical Eulogy

and Its Antecedents

PRINCETON UNIVERSITY PRESS

Copyright © 1990 by Princeton University Press

Published by Princeton University Press, 41 William Street,
Princeton, New Jersey 08540

In the United Kingdom: Princeton University Press, Oxford

Library of Congress Cataloging-in-Publication Data

Tomarken, Annette H., 1938-
The smile of truth : the French satirical eulogy and
its antecedents / Annette H. Tomarken.
p. cm.
Includes bibliographical references.
ISBN 0-691-06791-0 C

1. French literature—16th century—History and criticism.
2. Satire, French—History and criticism. 3. Eulogies—History and
criticism. 4. Satire, Latin (Medieval and modern)—History and
criticism. 5. French literature—Foreign influences.
6. Renaissance—France. I. Title.
PQ239.T66 1990   840.9′003—dc20   89-10882

This book has been composed in Linotron Aldus

Princeton University Press books are printed on acid-free paper
and meet the guidelines for permanence and durability of the
Committee on Production Guidelines for Book Longevity of the
Council on Library Resources

Printed in the United States of America by Princeton University Press,
Princeton, New Jersey

10 9 8 7 6 5 4 3 2 1

Frontispiece: From Helius Eobanus Hessus, Podagrae ludus (Mainz: J. Schoeffer, 1537),
reproduced by permission of the Österreichische Nationalbibliothek, Vienna.

Designed by Laury A. Egan

For My Family and Friends
IN GRATITUDE

Contents

Preface

"There is nothinge so incredible, but by artificiall handelynge maye bee made probable: nothinge so rugged and rustye, but by Eloquence maye bee poolyshed (and as it were glitteringly burnished)," asserted Thomas Newton, the translator of Cicero's *Paradoxa stoicorum*.[1] This remark manifests the faith in the transforming and persuasive power of rhetoric that was shared by the many Renaissance writers who composed mock encomia or satirical eulogies inspired by works such as Cicero's paradoxes, and, most importantly, by the writings of Lucian of Samosata.

Lucian was one of the most popular Greek authors rediscovered during the Renaissance. From the fifteenth century onwards, editions, translations, imitations, and adaptations either of the complete works or of individual satires appeared all over Europe. Classical scholars have long recognized that certain Lucianic works belong to a particular class of satire with its own distinctive nature and aims, the paradoxical encomium. Practiced by Greek and Roman writers, the satirical eulogy fell out of favor during the Middle Ages and regained its popularity in the late fifteenth century, in large part because of the renewed interest in Lucian.

At its height, this genre appealed to most major Renaissance authors, from Erasmus, Rabelais, and Ronsard to Du Bellay, Ben Jonson, and Shakespeare. The mock eulogies of these writers have received considerable critical comment in recent years—from Barbara Bowen, Rosalie Colie, Walter Kaiser, C.-A. Mayer, Christopher Robinson, P. M. Smith, and others— but far less attention has been paid to the dozens of less-famous writers of this same period who composed often significant mock encomia. The "Hymne de la Surdité," the "Eloge des Dettes," and Berni's *capitoli* on the plague did not spring into being *ex nihilo* and were far from being the isolated productions of a few men of genius. By tracing a broader picture of the development of this genre from the early Renaissance to the early seventeenth century, we may shed new light on some familiar masterpieces and reassess some little-known or neglected works.

Although the chief focus will be on French writing, consideration will also be given to Neo-Latin mock encomia, to Italian Bernesque poems, and to some German and a few related English works, analyzed primarily from the point of view of the French examples. Since Spanish works of this type do not seem to have influenced French encomia, they will not be discussed. Although the amount of available material makes it impractical to consider all instances, I have sought to show that several works rarely accorded more than a ritual mention by scholars repay more careful attention. Since many of these are not available outside specialized rare book libraries, I have included some description to help the reader to determine the validity of my interpretations.

My aim is to suggest that a better historical understanding of this kind of writing leads to new interpretive insights and to new ideas concerning the relationship between the mock encomium and other forms. Because of the elusive nature of irony, certain mock encomia have proved hard to classify; familiarity with the conventions and traditions of the genre permits more accurate classification and a better understanding of the complexity of the texts.

But first, two matters of definition need to be clarified, the notion of genre and that of irony. I use the terms *genre, type,* and *kind,* but not in the sense of a fixed form or of an essentialist definition of the sort often assigned to tragedy. A less rigid notion of genre is both necessary and historically justifiable: as Colie puts it, "Confusion underlay all Renaissance genre-theory, even the simplest."[2] In fact, the terms *subgenre* or even *countergenre* would be equally applicable. What is referred to is a type of writing widely and consistently recognized by its practitioners as belonging to a particular kind, having few inflexible rules but nonetheless remaining distinct from other kinds of writing. As Heather Dubrow explains in her discussion of genre, "Certain literary forms are associated with a great many conventions and others with only very few and very loose rules."[3] Of the latter type, the mock encomium is marked by a degree of praise variable in intensity, and by a degree of satire or irony that can vary from the merely playful to the overtly satirical. Since the works can range in length from a page to an entire volume, in verse or in prose, they constantly risk being absorbed by or impinging upon other genres or subgenres, such as the blason, the epitaph, and the paradox. Thus, their Renaissance titles vary, from "louange" and "encomie" to "blason" and "épitaphe," but they are linked by various types of internal references that serve as signals to interpretation and classification.

These clues to reading are presented in various ways, some quite oblique, as when Du Bellay announces, echoing the end of one of Lucian's mock encomia, that he does not wish to disguise a fly as an elephant. Alternatively, they may consist of lengthy lists of famous predecessors whose authority makes acceptable the imitators' seemingly frivolous endeavors. A way of alerting readers to an ironic overall intent that was adopted by both Erasmus and Philibert de Vienne was to drop the playful mask and insert passages of direct satire. A fourth technique, that of exaggerating the hyperbole to underscore the difference between topic and language, was employed by Lucian in the *Muscae Encomium* and by many Renaissance animal-praisers. All these intertextual references and clues became quite conventionalized as the sixteenth century progressed.

The second matter of definition in this study concerns what is meant by irony. As Norman Knox and others have shown, the concept of irony was a fluid one in the sixteenth century. Deriving primarily from Cicero and Quintilian's definitions, it frequently referred to the rhetorical trope of inversion, saying the opposite of what was intended, but it could also be used to describe a sustained posture of the type associated with Socrates. Mock encomia use irony in both these ways and may also incorporate the occasional passage of nonironic criticism mentioned above. In general, however, the more detached posture typical of the ironist is preferred. The justification for my flexible definitions of genre and irony lies ultimately in the worth of the resulting interpretations.

In addition to retaining a fluid sense of genre and of irony, I have also followed recent critics like H. K. Miller and Mayer in using the terms *satirical* or *mock eulogy* and *ironic* or *paradoxical encomium* as roughly equivalent. Other critics employ the term *mock-epideictic* to indicate the display aspect of the pieces, their resemblance to public defenses delivered in a court of law. Seeing these works in relationship to one another, as their authors most definitely did, understanding how they manipulate and reflect the past history of the genre, we arrive at a far richer reading of each encomium. Furthermore, it becomes evident that the historical awareness so often voiced by the genre's practitioners actually modified the later development of the form.

My first chapter considers Lucian and the classical mock encomiasts regularly cited during the Renaissance. Following the topics of works by Lucian, modern critics have found it convenient to divide the mock encomia into three groups related by subject: vices or vicious ways of life, diseases, and, finally, small animals or insects. Crucial to the Renaissance revival of this genre was Erasmus, whose influence, as chapter 2 shows, was both direct, in the *Moriae Encomium*, and indirect, in his translations of Lucian. Erasmus's efforts were imitated by numerous Neo-Latin writers anxious to practice the new genre, who are examined in chapter 3. Before turning to the French mock encomia, the central focus of the study, I consider some related Italian works influential in France: the Bernesque *capitoli*, the *paradossi*, and the *sermoni funebri*. The three remaining chapters, on the French encomia, consider the vice, the disease, and the animal encomia. The chapter on French animal praises demonstrates how in some instances the genre moved towards parody, while in others it managed to maintain the delicate ironic balance that marks the best paradoxical eulogies.

The historical perspective called for by so many mock eulogists enables us to appreciate the subtlety of this type of writing. Concurrently, however, it permits us to understand the changes in the genre in the seventeenth century. Studied from an exclusively historical point of view, the genre has frequently been denigrated, as when Arthur Stanley Pease, an early commentator, remarked that "whimsical or paradoxical declamation has had a long, if not a highly exhilarating history."[4] Those like Colie who are interested in individual works by major writers have been more enthusiastic.[5] By including in my interpretations the perspective suggested by the works themselves, I hope to reassess the importance both of the best individual writings and of the genre as a whole in literary history.

Since this study is likely to be read chiefly by scholars familiar with French, I have not provided translations of French citations. For citations in Latin and Italian within the text I have provided translations in square brackets immediately after the passage cited. To avoid lengthening the text unduly, I have not provided translations for citations in footnotes. Except where otherwise indicated (for classical works and for the *Moriae Encomium*, for example), all translations are my own. In citations from Neo-Latin and Renaissance French printed works, I have followed the current practice of distinguishing between the letters *i* and *j* and between *u* and *w*. I have also followed the recent critical practice of adding the acute accent to final tonic *e* in French citations (but not to the feminine or plural forms); distinguishing *là* from *la*, *où* from *ou*, *à* from *a*; adding the grave accent to words such as *très*, *près*, and *poète* (except where the word *poete* was spelled as *poëte* in the original); and the cedilla to words such as *ça*. If these works were cited from nineteenth- or twentieth-century editions, I have retained the modern editors' spelling of words. Decisions about which accents to add (or delete) from foreign citations are still not standardized: my goal has been internal consistency and readability.

Latin contractions have been expanded and Renaissance accents on Latin omitted. In the Italian citations (other than modern editions), I have added accents to *più* and distinguished *è* from *e*.

Acknowledgments

O felicem me! omnia debitorem!
ROBERT TURNER

When a long and complicated book has taken many years to complete, the number of friends and colleagues to whom the author is indebted grows. In the course of rereading familiar works and tracking down little-known or neglected ones, I have been aided by the help and advice of many people both in the States and in England. They know the debt I owe them and, I hope, the gratitude I feel. In England, the first thanks go to Klaus Mayer, then at Bedford College, London, who long ago encouraged me to work on the satirical eulogy. As teacher, friend, and adviser, he was a tower of strength. At Birkbeck College, London, I benefited from the wise counsel of David Ross and from the expert "outside readership" and encouragement of Michel Blanc. In later years, the comments of Ian McFarlane on my Neo-Latin chapter and of Michael Screech on the Erasmus section provided many fresh insights. Pauline Smith of the University of Hull gave help with the Lyons "blasons" analysis, and Graham Anderson provided the latest information on Lucian studies while I worked in the summers at the University of Kent at Canterbury. Franz Quadlbauer of the University of Kiel sent me photocopies of hard-to-find early texts. The years of research at the British Library were made easier by the help and kindness of Ian Willison. Most recently, Agnès Béhar carefully checked citations from rare works at the Bibliothèque Nationale.

In the United States, the range of indebtedness widens to include John Dutra of Miami University's Classics Department, corrector of my readings of strangely printed Renaissance Greek; Peter Pedroni, in French and Italian at Miami, who checked my translations of Italian citations; and Carl Schlam in Classics and Harry Vredeveld in German, both at Ohio State University, generous readers and commentators on the first three chapters of the work. I am grateful also to the editors of *Bibliothèque d'Humanisme et Renaissance, Symposium, LittéRéalité*, and *Fifteenth Century Studies*, as well as to French Forum, Publishers, who published some of my earlier writings on paradoxy and permitted me to cite passages from certain of these essays. William Heckscher at Princeton University and Robert Baldwin of Connecticut College kindly shared with me their writings on Rennaissance fly and flea works.

To the College of Arts and Science and to the Alumni Affairs Office of

Acknowledgments

Miami University (in particular, to former Vice President for Alumni Relations, Douglas Wilson) I am grateful for a Summer Research Grant and for other travel grants that enabled me to attend conferences and conduct my research. My friends in Langstroth Cottage at Miami gave help beyond the call of duty.

I was fortunate in the readers the Press selected for my manuscript; these scholars gave me the wherewithal to revise the book in ways of which I hope they will approve. To Joanna Hitchock, Deborah Tegarden, and Robert Brown of Princeton University Press, my thanks for their cooperation and encouragement. Julie Marvin was a patient, creative, and supportive copy-editor.

To my mother, brother, and family, thank you for so many summers of encouragement and support in England. To Emma, my daughter, thank you for always believing I would finally revise the book enough times to satisfy even myself. I would like dear friends Stephanie and Michael Shea in New York and Monique and Bernard Labbé in France to know that their hospitality and kindness over the years were beyond price.

Without my husband, Edward Tomarken, this book would never have been finished at all. With humor and determination—and willingness to do the housework—he helped me through the last months of juggling disks, checking accents, and renumbering footnotes. His "other perspective" saved me from many an overeasy generalization, and his long experience in modern literary theory opened up new possibilities for interpretation and speculation.

A combination of indebtedness and originality marks most satirical eulogies. The indebtedness of the present study is outlined above: my hope is that its originality may become apparent below.

THE SMILE OF TRUTH

ONE

The Satirical Eulogy
in Antiquity

Ridentem dicere verum / quid vetat?
HORACE

ORIGINS AND EARLY DEVELOPMENT

Although the writings of Lucian were the most influential in the later development of the satirical eulogy, many other classical writers, both Greek
and Latin, composed similar works, which were also mentioned by Renaissance imitators. Mock encomia began to appear in the fifth century B.C. and
attracted the attention of practitioners and theoreticians alike. The techniques that evolved were gradually codified in treatises that were to influence Renaissance practice.[1] The genre flourished in both Greek and Latin
and continued to appear in the Byzantine period, but fell into disuse in the
Middle Ages. The early encomia and the origins of the genre have been
analyzed by Theodore C. Burgess, Adolf Hauffen, Pease, and other scholars
whose discussions have provided the basis for a number of more recent
studies dealing primarily with Renaissance encomia.[2] Thus, the English
vogue for the satirical eulogy, Erasmus's fondness for Lucian, Ben Jonson's
use of paradox in drama, and Lucian's importance for the Renaissance in
general have all been investigated.[3] In this chapter, I shall concentrate on
those classical theories and encomia which were to be most influential during the fifteenth and sixteenth centuries.[4]

In general, classical writers from Aristotle on divided rhetoric into three
kinds: deliberative, judicial, and epideictic. The encomium, whether serious
or ironic, belongs to the third category, the term *epideictic* being used to
refer to the oratory of praise and blame and of sophistic display. In some
instances, such pieces were composed for delivery as speeches at public ceremonies (hence the name *panegyric*, from the Greek *panegyris*). In the case
of the *epitahios* or funeral oration, they were delivered at the annual public
ceremonies for those killed in battle during the previous year. In yet other
instances, they were used by the sophists as demonstrations of literary and
rhetorical skill, models of technique for their students to imitate and listen-

[3]

ers to admire.[5] Thus, both Greek and Roman students of rhetoric learned to compose laudatory speeches, ἐγκώμια in Greek and *laudes* or *laudationes* in Latin, or their opposite, *vituperationes*, ψόγοι in Greek. The subjects of laudations and vituperations might be gods, heroes, rulers or other persons, as well as cities, rivers, countries, mountains, or even, on occasion, humbler topics such as animals, plants, and smaller inanimate objects. The use of pro and con writing for training in rhetoric and in the development of forensic skills was also prominent during the Renaissance, when authors such as Lando and Estienne produced contrasting encomia designed to enlighten and challenge readers by abrupt changes of attitude.

A number of recent studies have analyzed the significance of the idea of praise in early Greek literature.[6] As Dio Chrysostom puts it: "Homer praised practically everything—animals, plants, water, earth, armour, and horses; in fact it may be said that there is nothing which he failed to mention with praise and honour. At any rate, there is only one out of all the characters in his poems about whom he said harsh things, namely, Thersites, and even Thersites is called a 'clear-voiced speaker.' "[7] The serious encomium usually followed a recognizable pattern, traces of which persist in its sixteenth-century counterpart. Burgess describes a typical pattern for the praise of a person, and encomia on other topics follow a similar plan. After the *prooemion*, or introduction, often a profession of inadequacy before so splendid a subject, the ancestry of the person praised is discussed, with flattering reference to his native city or country. His birth, the omens and dreams preceding it, his youth, deeds, and profession are all recounted in their prescribed place. Virtuous deeds of war and peace occupy an important position, as do comparisons between the hero and classical predecessors. Finally, the *epilogos* sums up what has been said before the concluding prayer.[8]

The paradoxical encomium seems to have been a natural, playful extension of the serious encomium, "a result of that tendency to sheer display which was likely to mark epideictic speeches of all kinds."[9] It did not arise at some late date in the history of classical writing, but early on. Alcidamas, Polycrates, and Gorgias, some of the earliest exponents of the mock-epideictic style, were among the celebrated orators in the great flowering of Greek city-states. By considering the varied reasons for the classical popularity of this genre, we may better understand its Renaissance vogue.

First, the paradoxical encomium provided a pleasant means of varying the customary topoi of panegyrics: praising the unpopular or the despised was a sure way to gain attention. The unexpected element in such works, their thwarting of normal audience expectations, would serve to enhance the humor of the speeches and provide a novel form of entertainment. Aristotle stated that men desire to prove paradoxes in order that they may, if successful, be considered clever, and Lucian, centuries later, may have had the genre in mind when he attributed to Aristippus the statement that "many men have on many occasions forgone discussion of the topics best and most advantageous to us and have embarked upon other subjects from which they think they bring themselves renown, although to their audience their words are of no profit."[10]

Other critics have pointed out that the genre may have found ready acceptance because it overlapped on occasion with other genres. There is, for example, a paradoxical element in many Greek comedies, and passages of playful or burlesque praise were common in Aristophanes. The self-praise by Poverty in *The Plutus* is an oft-cited example of such writing.[11] The presentation of mock encomia within a larger, different literary framework was thus an early development and was to reappear in the Renaissance in the works of Rabelais, Ben Jonson, and others. The mock encomium bore some resemblance to the nondramatic form of the description or portrait. In addition, paradoxical encomia often resembled scientific monographs on plants and animals, so much so that from the title alone it is often difficult to determine the exact status of some works. Pliny, our main source of information on authors of these latter treatises, states that Themiso wrote on the plantain (25.80), Pythagoras on bulbs (19.94), Moschion on the radish (19.87), Phanias in praise of the nettle (22.35), and Diocles on the turnip (20.10). Typical of his brief references is the following: "It would be a long task to make a list of all the praises of the cabbage, since not only did Chrysippus the physician devote to it a special volume, divided according to its effects on the various parts of the body, but Dieuches also, and Pythagoras above all, and Cato no less lavishly, have celebrated its virtues."[12] Most of these medico-botanical studies were probably not laudations in the rhetorical sense, although they may be what Quintilian has in mind when he mentions that eulogies have been written on sleep and death as well as on certain kinds of food.[13] Many sixteenth-century authors had no qualms about classifying medical works together with literary ones; accordingly, Cato, Themiso, and Pythagoras are frequently cited in prefaces to paradoxical encomia.[14] The freedom to use either verse or prose in such compositions was also much exploited during the Renaissance, as were the close links between the epitaph and the speech of praise or blame.

Finally, the chief advantage of such writing is its apparent harmlessness: although increasingly used for satirical and thus more dangerous purposes, it could be passed off by authors as a mere game or exercise, at worst a "momentary lapse."[15] Most famous of such defenses is that by Erasmus, seeking to forestall criticism of the *Moriae Encomium*. Although such strategies might be transparently disingenuous, easily penetrated by contemporary readers, they permitted authors to avoid the most aggressive moments of confrontation and could readily be linked to the modesty topos that was so frequent a part of the *prooemion* of laudations.

Despite this early and lasting popularity, the genre was not without its critics, some of whom were extremely outspoken. In addition to the relatively mild criticisms by Aristotle and Lucian quoted above, the following comments, each from a different period, are typical. They are taken from Isocrates (436–338 B.C.), Polybius (202–after 120 B.C.) and Philodemus of Gadara (ca. 110–ca. 40–35 B.C.). Although Isocrates himself composed mock encomia, he asserted elsewhere that there was no virtue in defending something which others did not care to support: "While on famous subjects one rarely finds thoughts which no one has previously uttered, yet on trifling and insignificant topics whatever the speaker may chance to say is entirely original."[16] Polybius, on the other hand, focused on the risks of moral corruption in the young. Timaeus, he says, praised Sicily as extravagantly as do boys at schools of rhetoric who try to eulogize Thersites or censure Penelope. These sophistic games, he remarks sourly, have given young men such depraved ideas that they pay no more attention to beneficial studies, such as ethics and politics, preferring to spend their time "in the vain effort to invent useless paradoxes."[17] Finally, the poet and Epicurean philosopher, Philodemus, dwelt on the intellectual frivolity of such writing: "They say that men are turned to virtue by their encomia, and dissuaded from vice by their denunciations. But the sophists by their praise of Busiris and similar characters, persuade men to become villains. . . . Not only do they fail at times to praise anything useful, but they frequently praise bad things, and by lavishing praise on matters of small account they incline us to treat all subjects lightly."[18]

Despite these criticisms, which were to be echoed in the Renaissance, mock encomia continued to be composed by both major and minor orators attracted by the freedom and variety of the genre. The earliest such works concentrated on legendary or historical figures, but the range of topics soon increased. After Gorgias's fifth-century praise of Helen came Polycrates' reported writings on mice and on pebbles. Following Gorgias, Isocrates wrote on Helen and Alcidamas on death. Alcidamas also praised poverty and, trying to improve on Polycrates' treatment of the theme, defended the mythical and inhuman Egyptian king Busiris. The writers employ the various methods of praise noted by the theorist Aristides—the exaggeration of meritorious features, the suppression of undesirable ones, favorable contrasts with something else, and the clever turning of an unpleasant fact into a pleasant one.[19] Thus, Polycrates' encomium on mice dwelt upon their service to the Egyptians in gnawing the bowstrings and shield handles of invading enemies, while Philostratus, praising hair, gave examples of long-haired heroes at Troy.[20] Appion's praise of adultery recounts the love affairs of Zeus and other gods, and Libanius stresses the good parentage of Thersites, ugliest of the Greeks who fought against Troy. But for all their diversity of individual arguments, the overall pattern for these playful or "adox-ographic" works remains that of the serious encomium, and their subject matter can conveniently be grouped under the three broad headings of vice, disease, and animals.[21]

To the class of eulogy devoted to vices or bad habits belong the praise of negligence by Fronto and of adultery in the Pseudo-Clementine homilies.[22] Among encomia on vices embodied in a given individual are four praises of Thersites, encomia of Busiris by Polycrates and Isocrates, and vindications of Helen by Isocrates and Gorgias. Well known vituperations are those of Penelope (mentioned by Polybius) and of Achilles and Hector by Libanius.[23]

The second category, the encomia on disease, is exemplified by that on the quartan fever by Favorinus. In addition, Plutarch mentions works on vomiting and fever, while, in describing a young poet who had composed encomia on gout, blindness, and deafness, Philostratus (A.D. 170–ca. 244), makes Apollonius sarcastically advise the youth to extend his efforts further: " 'And why not of dropsy too,' said Apollonius, 'for surely you won't rule out influenza from the sphere of your cleverness, since you are minded to praise such things?' "[24] Whether or not the pieces referred to here actually existed, they show clearly Philostratus's awareness of the disease eulogy. Insomnia was eulogized by Fronto, and we know of works on old age, death, and poverty that are probably philosophic and consolatory, rather than paradoxical. In the same group one can place eulogies on external physical defects or peculiarities. Here, the presence or absence of hair was a popular topic, probably because beards, the distinguishing mark of certain Greek philosophers, could readily be exploited in satire. The best known of these works, by Synesius, bishop of Cyrene, was also popular during the sixteenth century.

The third group of encomia, although customarily associated with small animals and insects, can be conveniently extended to works on larger animals and to pieces on various aspects of the natural world. It is also frequently related to the tradition of the animal epitaph, a tradition in which the Renaissance followed chiefly Catullus, Martial, and the writers of the *Greek Anthology*. Dio is said to have written on the parrot, and Isocrates refers to eulogies on the bumblebee. Fleas, gnats, and lice proved a challenge to even the most skillful orators. Eulogies of plants have already been mentioned: in them and in the encomia on inanimate objects the satirical element is reduced to a minimum, often to a kind of gentle badinage. The majority of these pieces were known to the Renaissance only by name or as brief descriptive references (for example, the eulogy on salt mentioned by Plato); they could not, therefore, provide later writers with more than points of departure, instances of what could be and probably had been done within the limits of the genre.[25]

LUCIAN'S SATIRICAL EULOGIES

In Lucian, on the other hand, imitators found a body of satires that included mock encomia belonging to each of the categories described above. The use by many modern critics of a tripartite, topical grouping of these works is probably due to the dominant influence of Lucian as a model in all three areas.[26] He was to exercise both a direct influence, by way of the numerous Renaissance editions of his writings, and an indirect one, in that famous later eulogies, such as Erasmus's *Moriae Encomium*, so obviously owed much to him. For the sixteenth century, Lucian was without doubt the principal source of paradoxical encomia. We may therefore turn to Lucian's satirical eulogies before considering other similar works regularly mentioned in the sixteenth century.

The *De Parasito* is Lucian's longest encomium, although some scholars have questioned that he is in fact the author.[27] Similar reservations have been expressed with regard to the *Podagra* and the *Muscae Encomium*.[28] However, during the Renaissance all three works were generally accepted as by Lucian. In any case, doubts as to authorship did not at that time necessarily prevent suspect writings from being printed alongside unquestioned productions. Some works that have since been proved beyond all doubt to be spurious, such as the *Philopatris*, were accepted as genuine by many humanists.[29] We may therefore consider together all encomia that Renaissance publishers presented as by Lucian.

In the *De Parasito*, a parasite or professional sponger, Simon, praises a way of life generally scorned, defending it as the best of all possible lives. In composing this dialogue, Lucian seems to have had a twofold aim. First, he sought to parody the Platonic dialogue by using its methods on an apparently absurd subject. Second, he wished to formulate a general attack on parasites. Accordingly, he presents a parasite who inadvertently confesses his faults while imagining he is defending himself. Simon becomes what Christopher Robinson has labeled a "self-denouncer," and his narrative takes the form of a "récit-aveu."[30] The inside witness, then, is a representative of a given group who extols and defends his opinions in such a way as to provide the wary reader with a more balanced and "normal" picture.[31] Much is gained in dramatic impact by this indirect manner of presentation; Erasmus was to exploit it most effectively in the *Moriae Encomium*, where Folly is the "self-denouncer."

Lucian frequently criticized the hangers-on of rich men; his attack on those who took salaried posts in great houses, for example, was so virulent that in old age, after accepting a government post, he felt obliged to write an apology for the earlier work.[32] His *Timon* also contains numerous insults directed at false friends and self-seeking flatterers.[33] Expressed indirectly, the attack in the *De Parasito* creates a very different effect. The parasite dialogue parodies the methods of Plato, and Simon has been seen as in many respects a caricature of Socrates, "un 'négatif' de Socrate."[34] The dialogue is also related to the battle of words between philosophy and rhetoric, during which the competing systems of education sought to discredit and disprove their opponents' beliefs.[35] Some of these attacks are known to us: the Peripatetic philosopher Critolaus (early second century B.C.) debated Diogenes the Stoic on the subject of rhetoric and philosophy. Testing rhetoric according to the Stoic definition of an "art," he proved, to his own satisfaction at any rate, that it was not one.[36]

In the form of a discussion concerning the nature of parasitism, Lucian presents a similar debate. When mocked by Tychiades (a name Lucian uses elsewhere for a persona expressing views he himself probably held), Simon agrees to explain why he is so proud of his profession.[37] He proposes to show that parasitism fulfills at every point a current definition of an art, being "a complex of knowledges exercised in combination to some end useful to the world" (4, 247). First he considers the "knowledges" required to be a successful parasite: "First of all there is testing and deciding who would be suitable to support him, and whom he could begin to cultivate without being sorry for it later" (4, 249), a difficult science, for, as Euripides said, "In men, no mark whereby to tell the knave / Did ever yet upon his body grow." The parasite must also know "how to talk appropriately and to act in such a way as to become intimate and show himself extremely devoted to his patron" (5, 249). At banquets, he must "go away with more than anybody else, enjoying greater favour than those who do not possess the same art" (5, 249). He needs knowledge of food and wine, the better to enjoy banquets. Obviously, his skills, constantly exercised, are not allowed to molder away in some remote corner of his mind. When he comes to the second part of the definition of art, which states that the "knowledges" need to be directed to some worthy end, Simon sidesteps the issue: "I, for my part, cannot discover that anything in the world is more useful than eating and drinking, and in fact without them it is impossible to live at all!" (7, 251). Poor Tychiades can answer no more than "Quite so" to this confident manipulation of facts. Following up the point gained, Simon shows that parasitism "is not the same sort of thing as beauty and strength, so as to be considered a gift, like them, rather than an art" (8, 251). Simon finally convinces Tychiades that parasitism is indeed an art by comparing it with helmsmanship and with horsemanship, occupations requiring as much skill as that of the sponger. When Tychiades is still reluctant to yield, Simon defines parasitism for him more precisely as "that art which is concerned with food and drink and what must be said and done to obtain them," with pleasure as its goal (9, 255). Here, rather than in the virtue sought by the Stoics, lies what should be our aim in life. Too busy worrying about metaphysical questions to find peace of mind, Epicurus merely filched this end from parasitic and failed to achieve it even then. Tychiades' protestations weaken until he comes to agree that parasitic is indeed the highest of all the arts, since eating and drinking, regarded by other men as the reward of their labors, are viewed by the parasite as his chief professional goals. Listing famous heroes of antiquity who were parasites, Simon waxes lyrical on the subject of the high moral qualities needed to make friends with rich men and gain access to their tables. Quoting "wise Homer," he claims that the life of a parasite is indeed happy since "he alone . . . 'neither planteth a plant with his hand nor plougheth, but all, without sowing or ploughing,' supply him with pasture" (24, 271).

Pushing the argument to the limit, Lucian next has Simon claim that parasitic excels even those arts such as philosophy which are commonly acknowledged to be the greatest. Many philosophers, the wily sponger explains, have become parasites, but parasites have never yet become philosophers. For Simon this truth proves the superiority of his profession, not the weakness of human nature. In war, parasites make better warriors than philosophers, worn out with too much study, while in peacetime the parasite is a truly social being, athletic and entertaining. Having no wife to make him jealous, nothing to be angry at, no possessions whose loss can trouble him, he is free from the baser passions of the rest of mankind. Tychiades' last jibe is to ask whether a parasite will not be distressed by lack of food. Simon's reply to this question will be remembered by Erasmus in his colloquy *Pseudochei et Phyletimi*: "You fail to understand, Tychiades, that a priori one who lacks food is not a parasite. A brave man is not brave if he lacks bravery, nor is a sensible man sensible if he lacks sense. . . . the parasite is a parasite because he has food at his command."[38] The end of the dialogue, however, turns on Simon as much as on the once condescending and now chastened Tychiades. For Simon has created not only an admirer but a pupil, that is, a potential rival for the security and protection of the great and rich. "Hereafter," says Tychiades, "I shall go to you like a schoolboy both in the morning and after luncheon to learn your art" (61, 317). Caught up by the natural human desire for self-justification, Simon has been so convincing in his own defense that he has endangered his social situation. The paradox of parasitism is thus never resolved. The agile argumentation makes it abundantly clear that parasitism cannot be objectively proved to be vicious. Tychiades may be Lucian's mouthpiece, but his creator here leaves his representative vanquished by an obviously amoral opponent. As Rabelais was to show in the "Eloge des Dettes" in the *Tiers Livre*, all of us are in some way dependent upon one another, for food, protection, recognition, or service. Lucian's conclusion points beyond itself to the world outside the self-contained circle of the dialogue, where most men scorn parasites, despite what this inside witness may suggest. The unwary reader risks being maneuvered into a verbal corner, becoming an orator's dupe even as Tychiades becomes a parasite's parasite. Fortunately, the abrupt and comical ending suggests the need for a broader perspective than that of either Simon or Tychiades. The parasite wastes precious "sponging" time justifying his existence in terms of a system of values he professes to scorn. His interlocutor enters so completely into the logical framework of the argument that he is finally unable to return to the larger social world where the parasite is generally held to be less admirable than the man who creates and sustains an independent way of life, having some values and aims above and beyond his own personal interests and physical well-being.

Cunningly, the sponger has made a seeming virtue out of the lack of any provable depravity: this tendency of the vice eulogy to hover on the edge of the moral and the amoral or immoral helps explain the preference of most mock encomiasts for less serious vices as topics for encomia. A sustained encomium of rape or murder would involve outright falsehood instead of the balancing between truth and falsehood, the literary and the literal, that marks the best paradoxical encomia. Serious crimes are usually treated in works describing specific legendary or historical individuals, such as Busiris or Nero. In these pieces, the game involves the careful selection of facts and their adaptation or revision for more favorable presentation, rather than moral acceptance or rejection of specific deeds. Few were the criminals about whom nothing positive could be said, even if praise had to be lavished in the form of compliments concerning ancestry or place of birth. Nonetheless, authorial anxiety about possible misreading seems to have been at its most acute in the vice eulogies. Gorgias pointed out that what he had said in praise of Helen was only a joke, and Isocrates had to be careful not to praise the honorable Theseus at greater length than Helen, the professed subject of his encomium.[39] Similarly, in the Renaissance, Erasmus was as eager to remind his readers of his serious intent in praising Folly ("my praise of Folly is not altogether foolish") as Rabelais was to call attention to *Gargantua's* "sustantificque mouelle."[40] After the first edition had perhaps left some doubts in his readers' minds, a less well known encomiast, Christoph Hegendorff, even went so far as to compose a eulogy on sobriety to be published with subsequent editions of his encomium on drunkenness.[41]

The most overtly satirical of Lucian's paradoxical encomia, the *De Parasito* was frequently referred to by later writers wishing to defend a seemingly indefensible (*inopinabilis*) cause. In addition to the imitation of the dialogue's central paradoxical idea, interest in Lucian also led to the resuscitation of his favorite secondary themes. Thus, Lucianic jokes about the inability of the various philosophical schools and religious sects to agree among themselves, about their uncouth appearance, disreputable conduct, and failure to live up to their lofty claims of virtue reappear in the *Moriae*

Encomium and *Dialogues* of Erasmus, often extended or updated to apply to quarrels between contemporary scholastic or religious groups.[42]

Another satire which may appropriately be discussed in conjunction with the parasite dialogue is Lucian's *Rhetorum Praeceptor* (A professor of public speaking). This dialogue presents an inversion of the usual method of training orators, such as that described by Quintilian. Many would-be speakers under the Antonines, it seems, hoped for an easier road to success. Some found it, "for as success in those days, especially in the case of the Greeks, was far less a matter of persuading juries and swaying deliberative assemblies than of entertaining audiences with oratorical display, it could be attained readily by meretricious methods which, in so far as they were capable of being taught at all ('natura enim non docetur,' says Quintilian), could be taught quickly."[43] The *Rhetorum Praeceptor* is not in fact a dialogue, but a monologue within a monologue. We never hear the "professor's" interlocutor speak in his own voice; what we read is a second speech set within the first teacher's advice. The framed speech is presented as being "spoken" by a proponent of the easy way to fame as a public speaker. It is important to remember this difference between the *Rhetorum Praeceptor* and the *De Parasito*. The parasite gradually elaborates a self-defense that convinces Tychiades to change his entire way of life. The speaker in the *Rhetorum Praeceptor* is presented as a man who has learned public speaking the hard way, through years of toil and study of the best writers, but who offers, with considerable cynicism and self-irony, directions concerning the way he himself has not taken. The *arriviste* orator's words are formulated and spoken, not by the man himself, but by a narrator who scorns him. Although the idea of praising the generally despised is thus common to both these Lucianic speeches, the manner of presentation is very different.[44]

The professor begins by addressing a pupil described as eager to acquire glory by way of rhetoric but reluctant to spend long years laboring to obtain his heart's desire. Promising to facilitate this process, the teacher first paints an attractive picture of an allegorized Rhetoric, a lady escorted by Wealth, Repute, and Might, surrounded by "Compliments, resembling tiny Cupids" (6, 141). The high mountain upon which this Venus-like personage reclines can be scaled in one of two ways, a narrow, thorny track taken by a few brave souls including our speaker, or a broad, flower-fringed path, gently sloping and easily travelled. Each path up the mountain has a guide. At the foot of the narrow, difficult path is a virile, tanned, alert man whom the speaker, with overt irony, urges us to avoid, since he might persuade the student that hard work, learning, and an investment of money in one's studies are necessary, or that such antediluvian writers as Demosthenes and Aeschines are worth imitating. Barry Baldwin points out that these rejected qualities are exactly those recommended to Lucian by Paedeia in the *Somnium*.[45] We can therefore feel reasonably confident that Lucian's sympathies lay with this first guide.

The primrose path has quite a different guide: "If you turn to the other road, you will find many people, and among them a wholly clever and wholly handsome gentleman with a mincing gait, a thin neck, a languishing eye, and a honeyed voice, who distils perfume, scratches his head with the tip of his finger, and carefully dresses his hair, which is scanty now, but curly and raven-black" (11, 149). Whether or not the individual satirized in this vivid portrait is the second-century rhetorician Julius Pollux, as some critics have asserted, the passage is remarkable for its detail and humor.[46] The character's vanity, effeminacy, and affectation become more apparent in the interpolated speech:

> "Prithee, dear fellow, did Pythian Apollo send you to me, entitling me the best of speakers, just as, when Chaerephon questioned him, he told who was the wisest in that generation? If that is not the case, but you have come to me of your own accord in the wake of rumour, because you hear everybody speak of my achievements with astonishment, praise, admiration, and self-abasement, you shall very soon learn what a superhuman person you have come to." (13, 151)

The requirements listed by the "second" speaker are few but significant. Ignorance is the first prerequisite: "Modesty, respectability, self-restraint, and blushes may be left at home, for they are useless and somewhat of a hindrance to the matter in hand" (15, 155). A very loud voice, singing delivery, and "a gait like mine" are "sometimes sufficient in themselves" (15, 155). Gaily-colored or white clothing, a reputation for being a ladies' man, and vociferous supporters constantly in attendance complete the outward appearance of the splendid being. As to rhetorical training, the pupil, having paid special attention to the graceful set of his cloak, must "cull from some source or other fifteen, or anyhow not more than twenty, Attic words, drill [himself] carefully in them, and have them ready at the tip of [his] tongue— 'sundry,' 'eftsoons,' 'prithee,' 'in some wise,' 'fair sir,' and the like" (16, 155–57). He must scatter such expressions in his discourse, regardless of appropriateness or comprehensibility, never bothering to read "either that twaddling Isocrates or that uncouth Demosthenes or that tiresome Plato" (17, 157). Undaunted by solecisms, the ambitious speaker should invent new and ugly words to prove his talent, seek to attract students eager to defend him, and be overt in his scorn for rivals. His private life should be utterly depraved: fornication, cheating, gambling, and lying are all permissible. Even if not famous as a good man, he should at least be pointed out in the streets as a wicked man, a fate preferable to anonymity.

In the last section of the second speech, the satire has been pushed to the limit, since not only must the new-style orator scorn the traditional virtues of hard work, patience, and dedication to ideals, together with the social qualities of tolerance, loyalty, and politeness, but he will also soon find that the dividing line between easy fame and notoriety is fine. If he desires only fame, by any means, then criminal methods may prove just as effective as virtuous ones. We are then brought back by Lucian to the original image of Lady Rhetoric on the Mountain, and to the idea that the same summit is to be attained by two opposing routes. At this point in the work (25, 171), the encapsulated speech ends, the main speaker promising his silent listener that by following these rules he will surely be successful. Incapable of courting Rhetoric by the new method, he determines to stand out of the newcomer's way, although not without a parting jibe: "It is not by your speed that you have defeated us, through proving yourself more swift of foot than we, but because you took the road that was easy and downhill" (26, 171).

The paradox in the *Rhetorum Praeceptor* is complex. The disillusioned old-style speaker has provided a brilliant portrait of the newcomer's *modus operandi*, using an irony so blatant that if the young listener follows the advice and goes to the teacher of the easy way, that, we feel, is where his morals and intelligence best fit him to be. But the frame for the work remains the speaker who represents stern old values and training. We realize that the upstart orator is in reality constantly working in reference to the industrious one, exerting all his ingenuity to find ways of bypassing or simulating the good. He does not form a different and original method, merely a crude imitation of the old. He fakes the classical quotations, the references to hallowed authors, the innovations in style and vocabulary, the subtle delivery, and sensitivity to audience that the older speaker would have developed in the course of years of patient study and practice. Nonetheless, it is the old-fashioned orator who is performing this clever impersonation: he can comprehend and toy with every aspect of his imaginary rival, so much so that some critics have forgotten that the text is a complex monologue, not a dialogue. The subtlest paradox here is thus the fact that the man trained in the old school is best able to understand the new, to demonstrate its methods and reveal its flaws. The disgruntled "solid scholar" is at his most lively and convincing when acting out the role of his despised rival. Once again the listener or reader is forced to make some judgments that lie outside the explicit content of the work, as he did when deciding upon the real worth of parasitism. The very form of the *Rhetorum Praeceptor* suggests that the good orator can incorporate an understanding of the bad orator while the latter, although constantly entwined with the good, is unable to function separately and find an entirely new vehicle of expression.

This ironic praise of a way of life scorned by Lucian was to inspire several important Renaissance works, most notably Du Bellay's "Poëte Courtisan" and Philibert de Vienne's *Philosophe de Court*. The "rhetor" figure and Simon, although fictional creations, are related to the historical or legendary figures eulogized in some encomia. Lucian's contribution to the latter form is his pair of speeches, *Phalaris I* and *Phalaris II*, self-defenses by the cruel tyrant Phalaris, who claims to be a thoughtful respecter of the gods, anxious only that his offering to them not be scorned because of unjust rumors they may have heard about his life and conduct. Lucian can thus plausibly remind his hearers of Phalaris's respectable family connections and background. But he goes much further, pushing the limits of credibility. One of Phalaris's most notorious crimes concerned Perilaus, the inventor of a lethal torture instrument in the shape of a metal bull, inside which victims were to be locked and then roasted alive. Their screams were to play sweet music through flutes placed in the bull's mouth. Phalaris imprisoned and killed Perilaus inside his own creation, an act occasioned, Phalaris explains, by his anger at the man's cruelty in even conceiving of such a fearsome machine. He claims that the inventor deserved to experience the effects of his own imaginings.

To a modern reader perhaps unfamiliar with the horror associated with Phalaris's memory, Lucian's one-sided presentation may seem convincing. We have to assume, however, that to Lucian's contemporaries the elaborate defense was a demonstration of the orator's ingenuity and flexibility rather than a reinterpretation of history. Listeners or readers would be forced to admire the verbal skill of the presentation, even though its argument would be unlikely to win them over. Readers might also reflect on the instability of historical judgments in general. Lucian's text, however, does not suggest that he intended a revision of standard views of Phalaris. Despite the implied call for external moral judgments, the work ultimately leaves the reader within the text, impressed by its author's powers of rhetoric, not outside, attempting a reevaluation of a misunderstood historical figure.

Quite different from the two Phalaris speeches, with their troubling paradoxes, is Lucian's disease eulogy, the *Podagra* (*Tragopodagra*), a mock tragedy on gout. Although generally considered inauthentic, even during the Renaissance, the *Ocypus* (Swift-of-foot), a short companion-play to the *Podagra*, was published in some sixteenth-century editions of Lucian's complete works.[47] Some scholars have suggested that both pieces were composed while Lucian was himself suffering from the disease he eulogizes. Mentioning the possible biographical inspiration, Maurice Croiset praises the wit and mocking good humor of the two works, concluding that there is insufficient reason to declare them apocryphal.[48] Other critics such as Alexis Pierron and Bompaire are quite enthusiastic about the *Podagra*, Pierron calling it the product of a "talent fort distingué" and Bompaire stating that "elle mérite d'être savourée."[49]

In the *Podagra*, the Chorus, characters, and the goddess Gout all use the language of the loftiest of tragic plays. The short drama also contains the paradoxical element of an unpleasant, painful disease being praised and glorified. The words of praise are inspired by pain and fear, not love, but their form remains that of the eulogy proper. The first to speak is a gouty man, who addresses Podagra, tracing her ancestry to one Fury, Megaera, and her attributes to another, Alecto. Declaring that the disease inflicts tortures worse than those invented for such legendary sufferers as Ixion, Sisyphus, and Tantalus, Lucian paints a vivid picture of the effects of the disease, burning and twisting limbs, coursing through the bloodstream until its victim is reduced to a helpless shadow of himself. When he cites Ovid's characterization of the disease as incurable, "tollere nodosam nescit medicina podagram" [medicine does not know how to remove knotty gout], the pathos would seem to be more apparent than the irony.[50] The Chorus now begins to speak, addressing celestial Podagra in terms customarily reserved for the deities of Olympus. They describe their religious ceremony in honor of the goddess, whose rites are performed in spring, when she attacks most severely those mortals who are her priests:

> In these first days of early spring,
> Now that every field is green
> And richly clad with grassy sward,
> While the gentle Zephyr's breath
> Brings every tree her tender leaves,
> While her plaint through homes of men
> The swallow, luckless wife, doth send,
> And the Attic nightingale
> Throughout the woods the whole night long
> Mourns with tears her Itys lost.[51]

Realizing upon seeing his crutch that the gouty man is one of them, the members of the Chorus describe to the newcomer the dignity and noble birth of Podagra, that "unconquered goddess" (l. 85). In a genealogical fantasy similar to the family ancestry traced for the subjects of serious panegyrics, the Chorus outlines Podagra's descent from Ophion, supposed to have lived before Saturn. As the gouty man recognizes his allegiance, the lady herself enters, "staff-supported," singing her own praises, pouring scorn on the useless cures that foolish mortals invent to oppose her. The startling mixture of remedies includes colchicine, still used to alleviate gout, as well as some bizarre concoctions made of plants, metals, various animal organs and excreta, mixed together to the accompaniment of magical chants and incantations. At her bidding, the Chorus sings Gout's praises in the hyperbolic language traditional in invocations to the gods:

> Mighty Maid with heart of steel,
> Goddess dreadful in thy wrath,
> Hear the cries of thine own priests.
> Prosperous Gout, how great thy power!
> (ll. 191–94)

They hail her with a string of elaborate nouns and adjectives incongruous in such a context:

> Bandage-loving Sickbed Queen,
> Speed-impairing Joint-Tormentor,
> Ankle-burning Timid-Stepper,
> Pestle-fearing, Knee-Fire Sleepless.
> (ll. 198–201)

The mockery of doctors begins next, as the customary tragic messenger, here limping, brings on two quack physicians who, refusing to admit the omnipotence of Gout, claim to have an infallible cure. Shocked at such impudence, the goddess asks the two how they dare oppose her, the vanquisher of so many heroes of antiquity. Lucian asserts that various well-known figures were laid low, not in combat, but by Gout's attacks. She, not Paris, destroyed Achilles by way of his heel, and the fates of Bellerophon, Oedipus, and Philoctetes serve to support the same contention. Undeterred, the two doctors maintain that their father, on his deathbed, gave them a cure for gout, the details of which they have sworn never to reveal. The wondrous remedy soon proves its worth as the goddess bids her tormentors do their worst with the rebellious physicians. Their ointment proving useless, the men beg for mercy. After comparing them to other men and women who defied the gods—Salmoneus, Marsyas, Niobe, and Arachne—the Chorus remarks that "men's daring boldness cannot match the wrath of blessed gods" (l. 320). From their fate Podagra bids mortals learn a salutary lesson: "Let all men know that I alone of gods / Do not relent or yield to remedies" (ll. 310–11). Blending and parodying lines taken from the endings of several plays by Euripides, the conclusion advises men to be brave and patient in the face of incomprehensible adversities. Lucian adds to the notion of fortitude the idea of cheerfulness, which can come from acceptance:

> But let those who have gout find relief from their woes
> By being schooled to endure and accustomed to pain.
> In this way cheerfully you who share this our lot
> Will forget all your pain.
> (ll. 327–28)

The importance of good humor was often stressed in later disease encomia. Thus Thomas Francklin's English translation of Lucian (dated 1780) develops the original lines considerably, using the bouncy rhythm to reinforce the jollity:

> Hard is the lot of mortals here below;
> But we some intervals of comfort know,
> For use and patience lessen ev'ry woe.
> Cease, then, my fellow-suff'rers, to complain,
> For the kind goddess may relieve our pain:
> Mean time, be chearful, blith, and gay,
> And let us laugh our pains away.[52]

Since the *Podagra* is unusual among Lucian's mock encomia in having a fully dramatic form, it is important to consider the effect and function of such a presentation. Popular during the Renaissance because of its striking mixture of paradox and parody, the play manipulates in a subtle fashion the ideas of serious tragedy. In place of the incomprehensible and awe-inspiring fate imposed upon some mortals by the gods, Lucian offers us an equally mysterious but exclusively physical affliction, gout. Like the spectator at a regular tragedy, who occasionally believes he glimpses order or seeming reason behind the chaotic events on stage, the reader of the *Podagra* may try to explain the appearance of gout as a punishment for those who have overindulged their senses. Here the suspect *Ocypus* is far more explicit, reiterating ideas that were to be belabored during the fifteenth and sixteenth centuries, when Sebastian Brant described gout as the "rich man's malady."[53] The disease was also often seen as a reminder of divine power, sent to those who, like the quack doctors, believed themselves to be free and independent. But the *Podagra* shows that gout's attacks are too random and too disparate to be explained away by any simple moral truisms. The messenger and the Chorus, all respectful worshipers of the goddess, are nonetheless afflicted by her. In fact, their entire life seems to be spent placating, praying to, and otherwise deferring to the demanding divinity. Obedience to one's fate does not exempt one from it. At best, the torments may be momentarily lightened, but even the humblest sufferers remain marked for life, only slightly less stricken than the rebellious or the ignorant. The *Podagra* is original in suggesting the possibility of momentary relief through involvement in the complex procedure of the poem. As the gouty man or interested reader measures the difference between the truly tragic victim, such as Oedipus, unwittingly involved in murder and incest, and himself, an unfortunate but not tragic mortal, he may gain greater acceptance of his destiny.

The usefulness of the paradox for changing perspectives, inverting habitual modes of thought, and questioning received opinion is also apparent in the shortest of Lucian's mock encomia, the *Muscae Encomium*. This eulogy of a small, insignificant creature is readily recognizable as a skit on the serious panegyric. Critics have reacted variously to the piece. Harmon sees it as a minor piece belonging to the domain of belles lettres, not science, and calls attention to its resemblance to numerous works by Italian poets of the Renaissance on "all manner of things good, bad, and indifferent."[54] Croiset's description is more enthusiastic: "*L'Eloge de la mouche* est la plus finement ciselée de ces trois courtes compositions; l'esprit moqueur y étincelle autant que l'imagination dans les mille facettes du style."[55] While careful to pick out only those aspects of his subject that could be described as attractive, such as the fly's gauzy wings and harmless bite, Lucian did include a number of empirical facts in his encomium. The opening sentence forces the listener or reader to rapidly adjust his sense of relative size, for Lucian meticulously situates the fly in nature's hierarchy, pointing out that while not the largest of creatures, it is not the smallest either. The change in perspective achieved by looking only at small, winged creatures operates throughout the work in a quite disconcerting manner, calling into question our predisposition to use physical magnitude as a factor in judging intellectual development and potential. The technique recalls that of Swift in book 1 of *Gulliver's Travels* or of Voltaire in *Micromégas*. Having successfully increased the stature of the fly, Lucian next reduces and distorts the world of human mythology and history to support his claims. The fly "grows" on the page, taking on human characteristics. First these are physical—four legs only are for walking, while the fly's front legs serve as what Lucian calls "hands," enabling it to eat "just as we human beings do" (4, 85). Next the fly acquires mental qualities of intelligence, strength, and courage until, by a logical progression, we find that the insect needs to be endowed with a soul, the only point that "Plato overlooks in his discussion of the soul and its immortality" (7, 89). The few negative aspects of the fly that receive mention are transformed: thus, its bite and bloodthirstiness are shown to be caused by an insatiable love for, rather than hatred of mankind. It needs to "sip beauty" where it may. Its Latin name, "Musca," derives from that of Myia, a maiden whom Selene is said by Lucian to have turned into a fly as punishment for falling in love with and disturbing Endymion. With a soul and a classical pedigree, the word-picture of the insect is full indeed. A brief reference to dog-flies' hermaphroditism confers sexual completeness as well. Then Lucian declares that he must end, lest his hearers think that he is "making an elephant out of a fly" (12, 95). The final joke, destined to be repeated by many later panegyrists, propels us swiftly back to the larger world and a more "normal" sense of proportion. Herein lies the key to the paradox of the *Muscae Encomium*. A clever rhetorical change of focus, combined with the skillful manipulation of evidence, can indeed make the fly loom as large as the elephant. Only by moving with the final joke back to the world outside the verbal construct can we regain our ability to evaluate worth and size. A panegyric always creates an arranged picture of its subject: acceptance or rejection of its presentation must be based on criteria that lie outside its terms even though they are called up by the text. In concluding so abruptly with the mighty elephant, Lucian reminds the reader that the entire argument of the encomium was based on the acceptance of an arbitrarily adjusted sense of relative size and scale. The art of the paradox constantly calls for the reader to balance the declared subject of the investigation against the ideas evoked by the language of the text but lying in the extraliterary domain.

OTHER CLASSICAL MOCK ENCOMIASTS

Given the range and originality of Lucian's paradoxical encomia, it is hardly surprising that he exerted so strong an influence on the Renaissance revival of the genre. However, four other Greek and Roman writers of mock panegyrics who were to be well known during the Renaissance may be discussed at this point. They are Seneca, Favorinus of Arles, Bishop Synesius of Cyrene, and Emperor Julian the Apostate.

Dating from A.D. 34, Seneca's contribution to the mock encomiastic tradition was his Menippean piece on the deification of the Emperor Claudius. Known as the *Apocolocyntosis*, the work inverts the process of deification of the dead ruler into one of "gourdification," the Latin *cucurbita* meaning *gourd*. Whether we take the idea of the gourd to mean "empty-headed" or infer more scatological intentions from the phallic shape of some gourds matters little. The reasons for its composition have been seen by some in Seneca's desire to revenge himself on the emperor who had earlier banished him and by others in his wish to undermine Agrippina, who sponsored the historical deification of Claudius. These biographical facts may explain why the text is more aggressively hostile to its victim than Lucian was to be in his mock encomia. Even the *Rhetorum Praeceptor*, which appears to have a specific individual rather than a group in mind as its target, is mild by comparison with the Senecan work. These lines illustrate the tone of much of the work:

And he [Claudius] did indeed gurgle his life out, and from then on ceased to have even the appearance of existence. However, he breathed his last while he was listening to some comic actors, so you know I have good reason to be afraid of them. This was the last utterance of his to be heard in this world, after he had let out a louder sound from that part by which he found it easier to communicate: "Oh dear, I think I've shit myself." I rather suspect he did. He certainly shat up everything else.[56]

Reminiscent of Lucian, however, are the jokes about the gods, the description of the arrival in heaven and of the emperor's unprepossessing appearance, the mingling of verse and prose passages, and the insertion of cunningly chosen lines from classical writers. This work continued to be known during much of the Middle Ages, when knowledge of Lucian was lost. The *editio princeps* dates from 1513, and the first annotated edition, by Beatus Rhenanus for Froben, from 1515. The fact that Erasmus included it in the prefatory list of mock encomia he attached to the *Moriae Encomium* indicates how early the identification between the Senecan and Lucianic pieces was made. The strongly vituperative tone and brutal humor of the work on Claudius provided Renaissance writers with a striking illustration of how to insert more overt satire into the ostensibly laudatory mock encomium.

Favorinus, a Greek rhetorician of Gallic birth, was a slightly older contemporary of Lucian. His work is known to us by way of Aulus Gellius's *Noctes Atticae*, popular in the sixteenth century. Favorinus seems to have been a witty, inventive, and hard-working orator, although he was mocked by Lucian.[57] He founded schools of philosophy and eloquence in Ephesus, Athens, and Rome. Believing that rhetorical defenses and paradoxical encomia sharpened his oratorical skills, he wrote both for and against old age. Aulus Gellius notes that when Favorinus composed his eulogy on Thersites he found charming and original things to say:

> But in his eulogy of fever he even produced Plato as a witness, declaring that the philosopher wrote that one who after suffering from quartan ague got well and recovered his full strength, would afterwards enjoy surer and more constant health. And in that same eulogy he made this quip, which, of a truth, is not ungraceful: "The following lines," he says, "have met with the approval of many generations of men: Sometimes a day is like a stepmother, / And sometimes like a mother. The meaning of the verses is that a man cannot fare well every day, but fares well on one day and ill on another. Since it is true," he says, "that in human affairs things are in turn, now good, now bad, how much more fortunate is this fever which has an interval of two days, since it has only one stepmother, but two mothers!"[58]

Philostratus lists three other sophistical exercises—on Gossip, on Gladiators, and on the Public Baths—as "authentic and well written" works of Favorinus.[59] Despite the brevity of these references, Favorinus was regularly mentioned in Renaissance panegyrics, and his witticism about the stepmother and the good and bad days of the quartan fever was elaborated in several later encomia, probably because it was such a striking example of the mock encomiast's fondness for unexpected juxtapositions and metaphors.[60] The quartan fever, which recurs every third day in the ancient and fourth in the modern system of reckoning, is an appropriate disease for paradox. As Favorinus's joke makes plain, we identify its presence by noting the days on which it is absent, even as, in the house of a spiteful stepmother, we learn to appreciate a loving mother.

The second non-Lucianic classical encomium to be of importance to the Renaissance is Synesius's *Calvitii Encomium*, written in the fourth century A.D. The essay was inspired by the bishop's reading of Dio Chrysostom's praise of hair, a large portion of which Synesius quotes within his own work. The *Calvitii Encomium*, Synesius's only ironic eulogy, had a more limited influence than Lucian's works. Nonetheless, it was regularly classified and published with major encomia, for example, in Froben's 1515 edition of the *Moriae Encomium*, which also contained the *Apocolocyntosis*, under the title *De Morte Claudii Caesari*. The three works are printed with extensive commentary and notes by Girardus Listrius and John Free.[61] In the *Rhetorum Praeceptor*, Lucian's speaker had imagined his own opponent. Synesius interpolates an opposing set of ideas formulated not by himself but by a well-known predecessor. The rhetorical challenge is now to defeat in argument another writer, not an invented persona such as Lucian's "second" guide. The vagaries of history have compounded the witty game, for Dio's encomium has survived only in Synesius's text. Thematically, the inclusion of the praise of hair within that of baldness suggests that the two concepts cannot be considered in isolation from one another. Our understanding of baldness proves to be based on a notion of it as the absence of hair, not as a positive and independent attribute.

Just as Lucian was probably suffering from gout when he composed the *Podagra*, so Synesius was likely enough bald when he praised baldness. Having claimed hair to be a sign of strength and virility, Dio quoted various poets who had glorified its beauties. Synesius sets himself to find proof to the contrary. While hair is only dead matter, baldness is a sign of wisdom and learning. Since nature produces fruit only gradually, a bald head is a fruit ripened by the years. Next comes a proof taken from the realm of astronomy: what the Greeks called "hairy stars," comets and the like, are stars of ill omen, destined to burn up and disappear. Considerations of health are invoked: a bald head becomes hardened by exposure to the elements, resulting in a skull less easily broken. Far from being a mark of virility, hair is more becoming to women than to men. Men who have beautiful hair tend to be adulterers, a claim which seems a strange non sequitur but may mean simply that such men are more attractive to women. If tonsuring is an indication of moral strength, how much more blessed are those naturally tonsured by God. Quotations from prose writers and poets, together with a sprinkling of adjusted popular sayings and beliefs, form the bases for Synesius's arguments, and the eulogy ends with the hope that what he has written may benefit other worthy sufferers from baldness, such as statesmen, philosophers, and clerics.

As in the *Rhetorum Praeceptor*, the irony in Synesius's work lies in the fact that baldness, like facile public speaking, can only be understood in reference to its opposite, which is thus enhanced rather than negated by the orator's patient attempts to denigrate it. Synesius begins with the idea of baldness as a negative notion, the absence or loss of hair, then gradually assembles more positive ideas in order to make it comprehensible that men may voluntarily give up their hair when tonsured. Gradually demolishing traditional arguments and popular prejudices, the bishop presents philosophical acceptance of the unavoidable as a humanistic search for the desirable. Nonetheless, as with Lucian's paradoxical encomia, the final spectacle requires a double perspective: the aggrandized fly remains merely an insect from the point of view of the elephant, the phony speaker and the sponger look for acceptance from society at large, and the bishop's defense of baldness does not veil the beauty of Dio's praise of hair, his original source of inspiration.

The last work of antiquity that may be appropriately discussed in this chapter is the *Misopogon* (Beard-hater), by the Emperor Julian (A.D. 331–363). Julian became emperor in 361, on the death of his cousin Constantius, and soon proclaimed the official restoration of the pagan gods. Although he is remembered today chiefly as the Apostate, manuscripts of his orations, letters, and satires survive from the thirteenth, fourteenth, and fifteenth centuries. The *Misopogon* was published in Greek in Paris in 1566 by André Wechel, and there were other editions of Julian's epistles and complete works. Much of what we know about the emperor is derived from the orations and epistles of the sophist Libanius, whose paradoxical works on Achilles, Hector, and Thersites have been mentioned above. Some information is also contained in Julian's own writings. A serious student of rhetoric and philosophy, and a competent soldier and general, Julian composed several straightforward encomia following the traditional rules for the *basilikos logos*, the praise of a leader. Of these pieces, on the Emperor Constantius, on the heroic deeds of the same Constantius, and on the Empress Eusebia, first wife of Constantius, only the last seems to have been sincere in historical terms. The praises of Constantius "were thoroughly insincere, a compulsory tribute to a cousin whom he hated and feared" (1:3). However, despite what external biographical knowledge might suggest, there is no suggestion of irony within the texts of the first two orations. It may well have been too dangerous for Julian to insert any ambiguous passages at a time when he had only just arrived at court and was only surviving there thanks to the protection of Eusebia.

The three serious orations serve to illustrate Julian's familiarity with the techniques of the encomium. In the *Misopogon* he attempts something more original. The latter work was composed after an unsuccessful visit to Antioch, in Syria. Famous for its wealth and commercial strength, the city was not willing to revert to paganism. The school of rhetoric there had been neglected, as had the shrine of Apollo, famous in antiquity. When the new emperor arrived in the city, his austerity and criticism offended the citizens, who made their disapproval abundantly clear. In response, the ruler composed the *Misopogon*, a self-criticism by the author. Sending Libanius as spokesman, the citizens of Antioch eventually sought to make peace with the emperor, but Julian appears never to have forgiven their insulting treatment of him. Even in the *Misopogon*, resentment often breaks through his mask of self-deprecation.

The work has been variously analyzed and judged. Some critics have seen it as the product of deep personal resentment, even the delayed result of childhood deprivations. Several have found its anger and outspokenness astonishing in an emperor. In a recent article arguing that the *Misopogon* shocked contemporary readers less than it does modern ones, Maud Gleason looks for an explanation of this more muted reaction in the social conventions of the day.[62] The popular Kalends or New Year celebrations, which coincided with Julian's visit to Antioch, incorporated a number of public events as well as the opportunity for the populace to feast, make merry, and invert customary social roles and behavior. At such a moment, it would not have been too shocking for an emperor to criticize his unruly subjects by way of an edict posted in a prominent place in the city. Marcus Aurelius, for example, issued a very severe one against the people of Antioch in connection with their support of Cassius.[63] The *Misopogon* is written as if the author were looking at himself from the point of view of a citizen of Antioch. Such an individual might see him as a gnarled, tough, unattractive man, bearded like a goat, his fingers "nearly always black," ill at ease in public, and unappreciative of the finer things of life. His long, lice-filled beard is the most obvious symbol of his unaccommodating and difficult nature. Gleason suggests that the people of Antioch may have mocked the emperor's beard because he cultivated it as a result of his admiration for Marcus Aurelius, who was equally disapproving of popular games and other kinds of frivolity.[64]

The work may thus seem at first to be a traditional *vituperatio*, unusual only in that it turns on the author. However, from the start Julian's self-criticism is two-edged. Listing his own so-called faults, he constantly implicates his readers, the people of Antioch, in complementary faults. His rough and over-masculine nature results from his being unwilling to emulate the Antioch people's "soft and delicate way of living," their "effeminate dispositions" (339a, 2:425). His dirty fingers are "black from using a pen." He is admittedly incapable of spending an entire day at the horse races or the theater: "Sleepless nights on a pallet and a diet that is anything rather than surfeiting make my temper harsh and unfriendly to a luxurious city like yours" (340b, 2:429). A balance of extremes, of luxury and asceticism, is being set up. Gradually the author comes to sound more like Lucian's old-fashioned *rhetor*, ostensibly condemning but indirectly praising his own stern morality. The bitterness is apparent in the following lines:

> And all of you are handsome and tall and smooth-skinned and beard-less; for young and old alike you. . . prefer "changes of raiment and warm baths and beds."
>
> "What then?" you answer, "did you really suppose that your boor-ish manners and savage ways and clumsiness would harmonize with these things? O most ignorant and most quarrelsome of men, . . . you are wrong; for in the first place we do not know what temperance is and we hear its name only, while the real thing we cannot see. But if it is the sort of thing that you now practise, if it consists in knowing that men must be enslaved to the gods and the laws, in behaving with fairness to those of equal rank and bearing with mildness any superi-ority among them; in studying and taking thought that the poor may suffer no injustice whatever at the hands of the rich; and . . . in put-ting up with all the annoyances that you will naturally often meet with, hatred, anger, and abuse; . . . then you yourself have ruined yourself and moreover you are ruining us, who cannot bear in the first place even to hear the name of slavery, whether it be slavery to the gods or the laws. For sweet is liberty in all things!" (342c–343b, 2:435–37)

The moral laziness of the citizens is at least as apparent in this imagined speech as any real sense of guilt in the emperor.

In later passages of two-sided criticism, a discussion of the philosophical and religious differences between himself and the people of Antioch, Julian suggests that they forgive his ineptness even as he forgives their impolite-ness and self-indulgence. In the final paragraphs of the work, he returns to the theme of ingratitude: "Why, I repeat, in Heaven's name, am I treated with ingratitude? Is it because I feed you from my own purse, a thing which before this day has never happened to any city, and moreover feed you so generously? Is it because I increased the register of Senators? Or because, when I caught you in the act of stealing, I did not proceed against you?" (370d, 2:509). As if overcome at the memory of such unwarranted ill treat-ment, the writer abruptly ends his tirade with a return to his original self-critical framework:

> I am myself responsible for all the wrong that has been done to me, because I transformed your graciousness to ungracious ways. This therefore is the fault of my own folly and not of your licence. For the future therefore in my dealings with you I indeed shall endeavour to be more sensible: but to you, in return for your good will towards me

and the honour wherewith you have publicly honoured me, may the gods duly pay the recompense! (371b–c, 2:511)

The *Misopogon* does not always sustain its professed goal of self-criticism, particularly in its sarcastic concluding words. Such varying of authorial postures is found, however, in many Renaissance mock encomia, such as those by Erasmus and Philibert de Vienne. Julian's choice of form for his attack is well suited to his purpose. A direct criticism of the citizens would have been in their eyes yet another instance of his uncouthness and lack of sophistication. By seeming to accept and condone their view of him, he entangles them in the texture of his attack before they fully realize the double-edged nature of the criticism. The elegance of behavior and speech so dear to the citizens is used by the forthright and uncourtly emperor to show their admirers' self-indulgence and superficiality. The implication is that truly polite behavior is not merely a surface veneer, but derives from spiritual decency and intellectual strength. It is appropriate that the gods "recompense" the citizens' insensitivity to the difference between their ruler's grubby exterior and his inner qualities by imposing upon them this public humiliation. Theme and form are thus closely bound up with one another in this highly personal use of a well-established genre.[65]

Most of the works analyzed above as sources of Renaissance mock encomia were in prose. However, later writers such as Erasmus frequently referred not only to Catullus and the *Greek Anthology*, but to Homer's *Batrachomyomachia*, the mock epic depicting a struggle between frogs and mice, to Virgil's *The Gnat* (*Culex*) and the *Garlic Salad* (*Moretum*), and to the Ovidian *Nut* (*Nux*). Not all of these works are nowadays thought to be by the famous authors to whom they were attributed during the Renaissance, but, as was noted above, such doubts had little effect on writers eager to imitate the new genre. In the *Gnat*, a loyal insect awakens from sleep a peasant about to be bitten by a snake. When the ungrateful man crushes the gnat, it appears to him in a dream to demand a proper funeral. The *Garlic Salad* is a lighthearted description of the life of a peasant, and the *Nut* presents the complaint of a nut-tree wounded by stones thrown at it to dislodge its fruit. These pieces all provided Renaissance imitators with examples of what could be done with playful burlesque and lighthearted parody. Their links to the works discussed earlier in this chapter are evident, but they included less mock praise and less satire than the traditional mock encomium. Among verse forms, the mock eulogy was more often close to the verse epitaph, because both relied on praise as an essential technique.

In conclusion, the diversity of the classical encomia was to encourage variety in the sixteenth-century imitations. The later works might be long or short, in verse or in prose, satirical throughout or in only a few passages. In addition, they frequently overlapped with other genres, such as the epitaph. What is beyond doubt, however, is the importance of Lucian.[66] Not only was he the most prolific of the mock panegyrists whose works survived, but his writings and Seneca's mock deification of Claudius encouraged Renaissance writers to move the genre increasingly towards more overt satire, a shift that was to result in some of the finest ironic creations of the period.

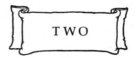

TWO

Erasmus and the
Moriae Encomium

My praise of Folly is not altogether foolish.
ERASMUS

LUCIAN IN THE RENAISSANCE

Lucian was one of the first Greek skeptics to be rediscovered and imitated by Renaissance humanists. Complete manuscripts of his works were available in some circles in Italy perhaps as early as the 1420s and certainly by the 1440s. Many Latin translations followed, some anonymous, others by well-known scholars. The works translated were usually the more rhetorical pieces, such as the *Muscae Encomium, Calumnia,* and *Philopatris* (then thought to be by Lucian), together with some of the moralistic works such as *Charon.*[1] The *editio princeps* of the Greek text appeared in Florence in 1498, and, by the second half of the fifteenth century, vernacular translations of individual works into Italian began to appear. As Robinson puts it, "we can reasonably conclude that certain scholarly circles, or circles with intellectual pretensions, took a close interest in Lucian, that this interest proliferated, and that something like a 'canon' of texts and translations arose."[2]

Recent studies of Lucian's influence on fifteenth- and sixteenth-century French satire have demonstrated how regularly Renaissance humanists and reformers adapted and updated the classical author's satire of his society.[3] Religious superstitions and abuses and the foibles of social climbers and hangers-on were, as was noted in chapter 1, some of Lucian's most frequent targets. Similar figures, suitably modernized, reappear in the later period. But Lucian's chief contribution to Renaissance satire resides less in the choice of victim than in the manner and tone of the attacks. The same groups of people had been criticized during the Middle Ages, but the ironic posture, so typical of Lucian, was not common in medieval times.[4] Although direct vituperation as a mode of criticism by no means disappeared from satire in the Renaissance, a number of writers began to adopt the Lucianic attitude together with the Lucianic topoi.

The precise nature of this authorial stance is explained by Douglas Duncan in a study of Ben Jonson that traces what Duncan calls this "art of teasing" back to the Greek term *spoudogeloion*, associated with Menippus.[5] It is also close to the Latin term *ioco-serius*, used many times by Renaissance authors in connection with mock encomia.[6] Although Lucian was not the only classical writer to employ such an attitude, he was for the Renaissance one of the chief exemplars of its successful manipulation. In his 1605 edition of Lucian, Isaac Casaubon categorized Lucian as a Menippean satirist, one who mixes prose and verse and who on several occasions introduces the figure of Menippus, the detached and ironic Cynic philosopher.[7] In *The Double Indictment*, for instance, Lucian speaks of Menippus as smiling "as he digs his teeth in."[8] The type of the amused observer is also related to the Greek *kataskopos*, "qui du haut d'une montagne ou d'un astre observe (et méprise) les humains."[9] The "down-looker" figure appears in many Lucianic works but is less popular with later mock encomiasts. More important for the latter group is the term *ioco-serius*. As Rinuccio Aretino points out, "What others express seriously in their writings, Lucian put playfully."[10] We can now begin to understand why the Renaissance so regularly applied to Lucian Horace's maxim "ridentem dicere verum / quid vetat?" [What stops a joker from telling the truth? or To tell the truth with a smile / Does aught forbid?][11]

The gradual changes in Lucian's reputation through the ages have been catalogued by Robinson, who shows that Byzantine writers particularly admired and imitated the dialogues, using them to compose attacks on lawyers, doctors, and monks, which intensified the satirical content of the form. The early Italian humanists, especially Leon Battista Alberti, the "Lucianist of the age par excellence," appreciated Lucian for his wit, learning, and philosophy, and believed he had propounded a general ethical system.[12] But it was not until the appearance of the translations by Erasmus and Sir Thomas More that Lucian began to exert a major influence throughout Europe. In the course of the sixteenth century, opinion as to the value of his philosophy and writings became sharply divided. Influenced by the approval of Erasmus, More, Pirckheimer, and Melanchthon, many readers learned to enjoy the Greek writer's clear style, independence of thought in religious and philosophical matters, and witty manner of presenting even the sharpest of attacks.[13] However, his earlier popularity with Byzantine writers did not always serve him well, for he was later criticized by many for works such as the *Philopatris*, which were in fact imitations dating from the Byzantine period.[14] These and certain genuine works of Lucian were seen as scoffing at all things sacred. Despite this resentment, both sides in the sixteenth-century religious disputes quoted Lucian as suited their purposes. By the end of the century, however, those hostile to the Greek writer succeeded in having all his works placed on the Roman Index.[15]

The two literary forms in which Lucian's influence was to be most apparent were the dialogue and the ironic encomium. Ben Jonson, for instance, may well have first become acquainted with Lucian at school in the 1580s, when dialogue books were used to train students in writing. The mock eulogy was practiced by writers as various and wide-ranging as Pirckheimer, Hans Sachs, and Melanchthon in Germany, Ronsard and Du Bellay in France, and More, Jonson, and even Shakespeare in England.[16] Between 250 and 300 printings of works attributed to Lucian appeared before 1550, the Greek text alone being printed in part or in its entirety more than seventy times by the middle of the sixteenth century.[17] The wide tonal variety of Renaissance mock encomia, ranging from the discreetly playful to the overtly critical, is due in part to the authors' contrasting perceptions of Lucian, their chief source.

But the most important translators and popularizers of Lucian were More and Erasmus, who were also established authors in their own right. Erasmus gave us not only his translations but also the most brilliant and influential of all Renaissance mock encomia, the *Moriae Encomium*.

LUCIAN AND ERASMUS

Erasmus of Rotterdam was the paramount Lucianist of the Renaissance. None of Lucian's other imitators was as widely recognized or contributed as significantly to reawakening interest in the classical writer. Erasmus's debt to Lucian has been investigated by many scholars, who have demonstrated that the great humanist was sometimes praised and sometimes attacked because of his Lucianism. Typical of the words of praise are those of the Imperial Councillor Udalricus Zasius, who, in a letter to Erasmus in 1515, remarked that "Lucian, most famous of stylists and satirists, were he alive today, would not dare compete with you on level terms, so shrewdly do you challenge him with your brilliant declamations" (Allen, letter 344, 3:150).[18] Elsewhere in the same letter Zasius praises Erasmus's "elegant translations from the Greek," possibly meaning those of Lucian. A typical criticism, on the other hand, is that voiced by the theologian Maarten van Dorp in a 1514 letter to Erasmus included in many later editions of the *Moriae Encomium*. "In the old days," he chides Erasmus, "everyone admired you, they all read you eagerly, our leading theologians and lawyers longed to have you here in person; and now, lo and behold this wretched Folly, like Davus [in Terence's *Andria*, 663], has upset everything. Your style, your fancy, and your wit they like; your mockery they do not like at all, not even those of them who are bred in the humanities."[19]

Despite the virulence of certain attacks, Lucian's fame seems only to have increased. The extraordinary reputation of Erasmus among his contemporaries, documented in letter after letter of his voluminous correspondence, seems to have guaranteed popularity for any author he admired. He first became acquainted with Lucian when he was struggling to teach himself Greek, a language he had come to believe indispensable both for the theologian and the man of letters. Unfortunately, the scholar then available in Paris as a teacher, George Hermonymus, proved to be neither good at nor even interested in teaching, "talis ut neque potuisset docere, si voluisset, neque voluisset, si potuisset" [the kind of man neither capable of teaching, had he been willing, nor willing, had he been capable], as Erasmus remarks sourly in a 1523 letter to his friend John Botzheim.[20] Erasmus therefore decided to teach himself and by about 1502 was proficient enough to begin translating the sophist Libanius from the original Greek to the Latin so much more familiar to educated readers of the time (Allen, letter 177, 2:73).

Significant so far as the present study is concerned is the fact that some of the first texts he translated were by Lucian (Allen, letter 1, 1:7).[21] We do not know why he began with Lucian, although Robinson speculates that one reason may have been his contact with Janus Lascaris, dedicated humanist and popularizer of Greek writings.[22] The task of translation proved difficult; sadly Erasmus tells John Botzheim, in the same long letter of 1523, that the "epithets" in Lucian have daunted him; he cannot match their "felicitas" in Latin. He refers here not just to Lucian in general, but specifically to the *Podagra*. This candid confession indicates that, not content to translate only the sense of the Greek words, Erasmus strove also to recreate the general tone and stylistic felicity of the work. When the attempt failed, he abandoned the entire endeavor rather than present an aesthetically inadequate rendition of the original. After quoting examples from Homer and Lucian to illustrate his difficulty, he concludes that Latin is incapable of adequately rendering the graces of the Greek: "Latinus sermo nec umbram horum possit reddere" [the Latin language cannot give even an imperfect image of (these graces)] (Allen, letter 1, 1:7).

Despite, or perhaps because of this sensitivity, Erasmus and More produced from 1506 on a series of translations of more than thirty works of Lucian, which were to become the standard Latin versions for about 150 years. "Rapiebantur hae nugae primum magno studiosorum applausu" [At first these trifles were seized upon with great approval by the learned] (Allen, letter 1, 1:8), notes their translator with understandable pride. In fact, the number of printings of the translations only fell off because the translations themselves had so helped to awaken interest in learning Greek that more people could now read the texts in the original language. Erasmus was happy to record the change in his readers' capabilities: "Sed ubi Graecae linguae peritia coepit esse vulgo communis, id quod miro successu factum est apud nos, coepere neglegi; quod ego sane ut futurum sciebam, ita factum gaudeo" [But when skill in Greek began to become widespread, which fortunately happened here, I began to be neglected. This indeed was something I knew would happen, and I rejoiced when it did].

In several of the prefaces to his translations, Erasmus explains his fondness both for Lucian and for individual works, thereby helping in a very direct fashion to influence readers' tastes and opinions. His discussion of his translation of *Somnium* (The Dream, or The Cock), dedicated to Christopher Urswick, could equally apply to the mock encomia. Calling the piece "this little flower of Lucian's," praising its "delightful freshness," Erasmus notes that Lucian possessed to a high degree the gift of combining improvement and entertainment in a single work. "Reviving the sharpness of the Old Comedy, while stopping short of its abusiveness, he shows amazing artistry and finesse in his wide-ranging criticisms, turning up his nose at the whole world, rubbing the salt of his wit into every pore and always ready with a nasty crack on any topic that crossed his path." He concludes that "for profit and pleasure combined, I know of no stage-comedy or satire which can be compared with this man's dialogues." [23] In the same preface he adapts the Horatian maxim mentioned above concerning the scoffer's right to tell the truth smilingly, and applies it to Lucian: "Sic ridens vera dicit, vera dicendo ridet" (Allen, letter 193, 1:426). He even goes so far as to defend Lucian's supposed atheism, on the grounds that those attaching the title to him in antiquity were unfair, being themselves guilty of "superstitious paganism." [24]

It is important to realize that Erasmus consistently found both matter and manner in Lucian, profit and pleasure. *Utilitas* and *voluptas* are the terms used in the preface to *Somnium*, and they are the key to his understanding and appreciation of Lucian. When he came to classify his own works for publication, he offered Botzheim some suggestions concerning both the *Moriae Encomium* and his translations of Lucian. Of the latter he remarked that they belonged with those writings concerned with the teaching of letters, "quae spectant ad institutionem literarum" (Allen, letter 1, 1:38). Another volume was to feature works concerned with moral teaching ("quae faciunt ad morum institutionem"), such as the *Moriae Encomium* and the *Institutio principis christiani*. He then added that several of his translations of Lucian belonged to the second group, even though they had been assigned to the first. This editorial meticulousness mirrors faithfully Erasmus's twofold appreciation for Lucian; he should be read for moral and ethical purport as well as for amusement and literary pleasure.

OTHER SOURCES OF THE MORIAE ENCOMIUM

The idea of praising folly is said to have occurred to Erasmus while he was travelling from Italy to England, where the work was finally written. Cautious by nature, Erasmus appreciated the advantages of the paradoxical encomium, in which an author, covering his satire with a veil of irony, could remain to a substantial extent safe from his enemies. But before analyzing in greater detail the debt of the *Moriae Encomium* to Lucian, we should mention certain other sources closer to Erasmus in time and place. Of considerable importance in connection not only with Erasmus but with the satirical eulogy in general is the question of the influence of medieval literature. In the introduction to his translation of the *Moriae Encomium*, Clarence H. Miller sums up the much debated issue of Erasmus's nonclassical sources. He suggests a complex mingling of the following elements: Sebastian Brant's *Narrenschiff*, the Latin dialogue *Marcolf and Solomon*, Erasmus's personal experience of licensed court fools in England and Italy (More had one, as did Henry VII and Henry VIII), the feast of Fools held at Christmastime in many European cathedrals and churches, the Fasching foolery and carnival in Germany, and, finally, the French *sotties* and *sermons joyeux*.[25] French scholars have discussed the last two of these sources at some length. The matter is explained as follows by Augustin Renaudet, echoing a much earlier statement by Charles Lenient: "Erasme ne conçut pas le premier l'idée de donner la parole à la Folie: dans les Soties françaises, mère Sotte discourait abondamment. Mais il aimait trop Lucien pour ne pas préférer à la satire lourdement didactique du Moyen Age l'éloge ironique de l'absurde."[26] The general consensus that there are resemblances between the medieval works and the *Moriae Encomium* is thus accompanied by an awareness of the important differences between Erasmus and his predecessors. The precise nature of these differences becomes clear if we consider some representative medieval and early Renaissance works containing topoi obviously similar to those found in Erasmus's eulogy.

Of the numerous French sermons joyeux presenting traditional medieval ideas on folly, the following typical example is useful because of its lengthy self-explanatory title:

> Sermon joÿeux et de grande value
> A tous les foulx qui sont dessoubz la nue.
> Pour leur montrer à saiges devenir
> Moyennant ce que le temps advenir
> Tous sotz tiendront mon conseil et doctrine
> Puis congnoistront clerement sans brine
> Que le monde pour sages les tiendra
> Quand ilz auront dequoy notez cela.[27]

The sermon illustrates the idea from Ecclesiastes that the number of fools is infinite, "numerus stultorum est infinitus." Declaring that he intends to list the characteristics of various fools, the speaker, or *sermonneur*, summons Bacchus to assist and support him. Although fools are stupid, he begins, they pretend to resemble Socrates or Virgil, those perfectly wise men.

Fools are, in fact, sociable, pleasure-loving folk, a boon at any banquet. One is reminded here of Lucian's very similar claim with respect to parasites. Next the sermonneur considers women, declaring that the height of folly is to try to keep them virtuous. If Samson, Aristotle, and Virgil were all deceived by females, jealousy is indeed useless. A particularly foolish type of man, therefore, is the nighttime street-roamer, hoping to peep in at his lady's window and serenade her when she is probably busy in bed with another man.

Widening his range, the preacher asserts that all nations are mad in their own way, further proof that fools are numberless. The medieval fondness for lists and categories here takes the form of an enumeration of various follies in different regions and countries. The Lombards, for example, are mad "par force destre saiges," the Germans "par force de boyre," and a similar stereotyped tag is provided for other groups.[28] Then follows a more sharply satirical passage containing, in skeletal form, many of the ideas developed with such devastating effect by Erasmus. A comparison between the following lines, barely more than an outline, and the complex passages of religious satire in the second half of the *Moriae Encomium* will amply demonstrate that the resemblance between medieval works and Renaissance satirical eulogies, where it exists at all, lies in a shared *fonds* of traditional topoi, not in the style or manner of presenting the material:

> Lon a bien veu par plusieurs foys
> De sotz papes et de sotz roys
> Sotz empereurs cardinaux archevesques
> Lon a veu et de sotz evesques
> Abbez curez aussi chanoynes
> ya partout et de sotz moynes
> Sotz gendarmes et chevaliers
> ya par cens et par miliers
> Cordeliers et augustins
> Croisez Carmes et Jacopins.[29]

All the classes of people satirized by Erasmus appear—musicians, doctors, astrologers, writers, geometricians, and many more. The only remedy suggested for the common folly is that each man should try to amass money for himself; he will thus automatically be considered a "saige homme." This parody of the usual moral lesson of the sermon leads the mock preacher to conclude with the de rigueur apology for his words: "Si jay rien dit / C'est tout par jeu" (Bii^v).

French farces on folly differed little in content from the mock sermons, although the dramatic form of the farce was closer to that used by Lucian in the *Podagra*. A typical short farce, entitled *Farce nouvelle tresbonne de folle Bobance*, presents "folle Bobance" and her followers, who are at one point divided up according to nationality, as in the sermon joyeux discussed above.[30] The resemblance between the farce and the *Podagra* is clear as the lady "Bobance," like Gout, summons her fools: "Où estes vous tous mes folz affollez / Sortez trestous & me venez voir" (A.A[r]). Those called come forward, declare themselves her servants, and present gifts. The farces and sermons joyeux share with the satirical eulogy a tendency to parody serious genres or forms of writing, such as the sermon or the mystery play. Their techniques, however, link them most closely with the procedure of the "monde à l'envers," the systematic inversion of customary views described by Mikhail Bakhtin in his work on Rabelais, and associated by him with the notion of the carnival.[31] Distinctions in degree and kind of folly are not discussed in the farces and mock sermons. Rather than stressing the paradoxical praise and glorification of the failing or the need to discriminate between its various degrees of reprehensibility and intensity, the farces focus on folly as the force that levels or inverts the social hierarchy.

Another popular French work using a female figure of Folly similar to Erasmus's Moria is Pierre Gringore's *Les Fantasies de Mère Sote*, published between 1516 and 1551, according to its modern editor, R. L. Frautschi.[32] Exploiting the liberty of speaking as "mère Sote," Gringore applied to his own day twenty-seven tales of antiquity taken from the *Gesta Romanorum*. The term "fantasie" here means a vision of some possible ideal or moral moment, and the work has in fact little but its central figure in common with Erasmus.

The contemporary work most often mentioned as having influenced the *Moriae Encomium*, Sebastian Brant's *Narrenschiff*, incorporates many medieval traditions and attitudes towards human folly. An extremely popular book, it was translated into both English and French soon after its first appearance in Basle in 1494. Eli Sobel believes that Erasmus found many direct suggestions for his encomium in the German work.[33] However, while similarities between the two works are readily apparent, the differences between them are far more important, so much so that A.H.T. Levi, in an introduction to the *Moriae Encomium*, asserts that not much of the Erasmian work comes from the "non-ironic *Ship of Fools* (1494) by Sebastian Brant."[34] The key to these differing assessments lies, as we shall see, in Levi's choice of the word "non-ironic" to epitomize the difference between the two works.

Written in the form of an allegory, the *Narrenschiff* describes a ship (the world) laden with fools (men) on its way to Narragonia, the fools' paradise. The images of the ship and of the journey are not, however, sustained throughout the work, which is in fact a collection of over one hundred short sections or chapters each considering a different type of fool.[35] Like Erasmus in his preface, Brant in his final apology suggests that satirists may well be guilty of the very sins they decry (Zeydel, 362). In chapter 13 of the *Narr-*

enschiff, Venus speaks of her power much as Folly does of hers in the early part of the *Moriae Encomium:*

> Dame Venus I, with rump of straw,
> Fools do regard me oft with awe,
> I draw toward them with a thrill
> And make a fool of whom I will,
> My clients, who could name them all?
>
> (Zeydel, 88)

Among the types of fools attacked by both authors are vain pedants, drunkards, lechers, old men who, despite their infirmities, act like youths, women's fashions, banqueters, cuckolds, jealous husbands, governors, magistrates, doctors, lawyers, gamblers, and pilgrims.

Occasionally, both satirists choose less familiar themes. Brant, for example, criticizes those utter fools, the obsessive builders, who spend their last penny on the construction of unnecessarily grandiose houses until they have nothing left to live on: "The man that is well instructe edyfyeth no gretter werkes than his goodes may extende to, nor than he maye easely perfourme."[36] Brant then adds classical quotations to prove that the ostentatious houses of the rich will all be cast down and destroyed. Here is Erasmus's rendition of the same theme:

> Very like them is the sort of men who burn with an insatiable desire to build, replacing round structures with square and square with round. Nor is there an end to it, nor any limit, until they are reduced to such utter poverty that nothing at all is left—neither place to live nor food to eat. What of it? In the meantime they have passed several years with the greatest pleasure.[37]

We can immediately sense the difference between Brant's sermonizing and Erasmus's lighthearted mockery. Brant's weighty style calls attention to what he sees as a deplorable instance of human materialism and pride. Erasmus's ironic inversions and repetitions ("replacing round structures with square and square with round") imitate the vagaries and caprices of a passion presented as a human foible, not a sin. His final question and answer condone more than they condemn.

When discussing astrologers and scientists, the two authors seem once again close. Brant writes:

> He is holden a foole truely
> The whiche putteth his besy cure
> To calke the sterres in the skye
> And all theyr natures to procure
> In pronostynge as he were sure

Of the tyme the whiche is to come
That he knoweth not all nor some.[38]

Erasmus transforms Brant's cryptic condemnation of the star-gazers into the following mocking portrait:

After them come the philosophers, venerable with their beards and robes, who assert that they alone are wise, all other mortals being mere fleeting shades by comparison. How delightfully they are deluded as they build up numberless worlds; as they measure the sun, the moon, the stars and their orbits as if they were using a ruler and plumb line; as they recite the causes of lightning, winds, eclipses, and other unfathomable phenomena, without the slightest hesitation, as if they were confidential secretaries to Nature herself, the architect of all things, or as if they came to us straight from the council chamber of the gods. At the same time, Nature has a grand laugh at them and their conjectures.[39]

As he did with the builders, Erasmus has here developed the comic, dramatic spectacle afforded by the fool engrossed with his pet hobby-horse. He reminds us of the enjoyment to be found in such activities ("how delightfully they are deluded"), implying that this pleasure, foolish though it may be, is one of the reasons why men cannot easily be sermonized, Brant-style, into mending their ways. Using Lucianic irony to steer her followers away from the more dangerous human failings, Moria provides men with an infinite number of silly but enjoyable pastimes or distractions. Even Nature "has a grand laugh" at the foolish men, rather than condemning them outright. Brant's attitude to such foibles is less tolerant; relatively minor flaws or eccentricities are criticized in terms almost as strong as those employed for serious vices. Undoubtedly, differences in temperament, education, and literary purpose are responsible for many of these distinctions between the two writers, but at least part of the dissimilarity is due to the strong influence of Lucian on Erasmus.[40] Lucian's skill with irony evidently encouraged Erasmus to try his hand at a similar form of satire. The result was a masterly synthesis of learning, wit, and rhetorical brilliance.

The *Moriae Encomium*

Apart from its general tone, the most strikingly Lucianic aspect of the *Moriae Encomium* is, as has been suggested above, its basic form. The mocking praise of a seemingly unworthy subject, here that of folly by herself, resembles that found in the *De Parasito*. Well aware of the long and complex history of this form, Erasmus provides in his preface a list of predecessors, in order to justify what might appear a strange choice of subject. The preface is, in fact, a letter written to his dear friend More, whose name, Erasmus claims, inspired the title of the work. He explains that even the greatest classical writers have not scorned to discuss seemingly trivial or unworthy subjects:

⟨Ages ago Homer amused himself with the Battle of the Frogs and Mice, as Virgil did with the Gnat and the Rustic Salad, and Ovid with the Walnut-Tree.⟩ So too Polycrates ⟨and his corrector Isocrates⟩ both wrote encomia of Busiris; Glauco praised injustice; Favorinus, ⟨Thersites and⟩ the quartan fever; Synesius, baldness; Lucian, the fly ⟨and the art of the parasite. Seneca amused himself by writing an *apotheosis* of Claudius. Plutarch wrote a dialogue between Gryllus and Ulysses. Lucian and Apuleius wrote comic tales about an ass, and some writer or other composed the last will and testament of the piglet Grunnius Corrocotta, which is even mentioned by St. Jerome.⟩ (3)[41]

The importance Erasmus attached to this prefatory list is attested to by the fact that he extended it in the later edition, as indicated by the brackets in the modern text.

Erasmus, however, never leaves humor without a moral. He hastens to make clear that even if for his predecessors such writing was little more than a pleasant diversion from serious studies—and why should not scholars deserve such diversion?—his own satirical eulogy contains far more. Like Rabelais urging his readers to search out the "substantificque moelle," Erasmus explains:

And so, ⟨if they wish,⟩ they can imagine that I was simply playing with pawns for my own amusement or, if they prefer, that I was riding a hobbyhorse like a child. . . . [But] just as nothing is more trivial than to treat serious matters in a trivial way, so too nothing is more delightful than to treat trifles in such a way that you do not seem to be trifling at all. Whether I have done so others will judge. But unless I am completely deceived by "*Self-love*," my praise of Folly is not altogether foolish.[42]

Within the text of the encomium, Erasmus again reminds readers of the source of the work. Folly laments the fact that man is so ungrateful for her many benefits to him that he has never praised her as he should, even though "there has been no lack of speechwriters who have spent sleepless nights burning the midnight oil to work out elaborate encomia of Busiris, ⟨Phalaris,⟩ the quartan fever, flies, baldness, and other dangerous nuisances" (12). This passage is important, first, because the works referred to were to become the standard authorities cited by later mock encomiasts, and second, because the sentence contains a striking double irony. Flies and tyrants were certainly not customary subjects for praise, but neither was folly. Attacking the very genre he is using, Erasmus makes his criticism appear yet more ambiguous by putting the attack into the mouth of Folly, presented as a whimsical, unreliable speaker.

While adopting the overall form of the satirical eulogy, Erasmus does not hesitate on occasion to abandon the eulogistic tone in favor of straightforward criticism. The direct approach is especially evident in the passages on religion, where Erasmus appears to have been particularly anxious that no one should mistake his meaning. The complex nature of the persona Folly, by turns mocking, playful, bitter, and sardonic, is a further Erasmian addition to the genre. A third innovation, the wide range of subjects treated, introduces a diversity similar to that noted in the medieval works and in the *Narrenschiff*, but not found in classical encomia.

By using the self-condemnation type of paradoxical encomium and a speaker other than the author, the cautious Erasmus was able to some extent to forestall criticism. If opponents of Lucian attacked his mockery of philosophers, he could retort that the opinions expressed in the *De Parasito* were not his own, but those of a parasite, a notoriously unreliable character, not to be equated with his creator. This defense Erasmus employed to cover a wider and more dangerous range of criticisms. The advantages of an indirect attack, in which the words spoken belonged, theoretically, not to Erasmus, but to Folly, were considerable. Sir R. C. Jebb explains the strategy: "The popularity of the satire throughout Europe was boundless. The mask of jest which it wore was its safeguard; how undignified, how absurd it would have been for a Pope or a King to care what was said by Folly! And, just for that reason, the *Encomium Moriae* must be reckoned among the forces which prepared the Reformation."[43]

Many of Erasmus's later attempts at defending the work were based on the same disingenuous idea, that the opinions expressed were a mere "lusus ingenii," expressed by Folly, and therefore not to be taken seriously by anyone who did not himself wish to be considered a fool.[44] This argument might have been more convincing if his persona had not so often abandoned her mask of frivolous femininity to speak as her creator had been known on occasion to express himself. Not surprisingly, most of Erasmus's contemporaries discounted his pleas of innocence: the work was attacked, particularly after the appearance of the 1514 edition, by those such as monks and members of religious orders whom Folly had angered by her attitude. Erasmus eventually resorted to other means of defense, such as the approval of his work by churchmen to whom he had sent copies. In the letter to Dorp, he seeks to justify himself as follows: "I have lived in several places since the 'Folly' was published. I have resided in many universities, in many large cities. I was never aware of any theologian who was angry with me, except one or two from that contingent which is hostile to all literary culture."[45] Were it not for fear of annoying less tolerant individuals, he continues, he could provide "a long list of theologians, men celebrated for their holy lives, men of extraordinary learning and of the very highest standing, some of them even bishops, who were never more fond of me than after the 'Folly' was published and who were far more pleased with that little book than I myself" (153).

Erasmus realized that not only would the form and much of the content of his encomium be considered Lucianic, but also its tone: "They will cry out that I am reviving the Old Comedy or imitating Lucian, accusing me of ripping everything to shreds" (2). In fact, the influence of Lucian has more often been discerned in Erasmus's lighthearted irony than in his "ripping everything to shreds," but he was probably thinking here of those who would object on religious and political grounds. Despite these protestations, both his contemporaries and subsequent readers continued to interpret the work in opposing directions. The function of the elaborate effort at self-protection appears therefore to have been chiefly social and political, allowing the satirist to respond to or ignore criticism at will.

Within the text of the encomium, references to and adaptations of works by Lucian are numerous. They have been documented by many editors, who point to the mention of or borrowings from the *Gallus* and *Icaromenippus* as well as from *Navigium* (The Ship), *Alexander*, *Phalaris I*, *De sacrificiis*, *Timon*, *Saturn*, *De saltatione*, and *Philopseudes*.[46] Lucianic characters and gods, Momus, Menippus, Mercury, Misoponia (a term for laziness used by Lucian) also appear. These references are found in the 1511 and subsequent editions. Of Lucian's mock encomia the *Muscae Encomium* is cited by name in the 1510 version of the prefatory letter to More, and the *De Parasito*, as was noted above, was added to the list in 1514. In addition, several passages bear a resemblance to Simon's denigration of normal societal values in favor of more selfish ones. For instance, there is a distinct similarity between Lucian's description of a fine parasite and that by Folly of her followers. Lucian writes:

> First, then, let us strip them to the skin; now inspect your men, sir, one by one, and give them a physical examination. Some of them you can see to be thin and pale through privation, shuddering, and as limp as if they had already been wounded. Pass on, and now see how the parasite looks! In the first place, is he not generous in his proportions and pleasing in his complexion, neither too dark nor fair of skin; and besides, has he not a spirited look, with a fiery glance like mine, high and bloodshot? (285)

Folly describes some of her disciples as follows:

> You see, don't you, how these grave and sober personages who devote themselves to philosophical studies or to serious and difficult tasks

seem to enjoy hardly any youthful years at all; they grow old before their time because they are forever worrying and beating their brains out about knotty problems, so that their vital spirits gradually dry up, leaving them exhausted and juiceless, as it were. My fools, on the other hand, are plump and rosy, with a very well-preserved complexion; they are *as fit as a fiddle*, as the saying goes [lit: as the Acarnanian pigs].[47]

A reference to the cowardice of Demosthenes occurs in a similar context in both works. "And as for the topmost of them [those who attacked Philip in the assembly], the man who was continually talking in the assembly about 'Philip the scoundrel from Macedon, where one could never even buy a decent slave!,' he did venture to join the advance into Boetia, but before the armies joined battle and began to fight at close quarters he threw away his shield and fled," remarks Simon, contemptuous of philosophers (287). Folly takes up the theme: "No, you need thick-skulled, lumbering louts, whose boldness is in direct proportion to their lack of intelligence. Unless someone thinks that Demosthenes made a good soldier: following the advice of Archilochus, he had no sooner caught sight of the enemy than he threw down his shield and ran away—as cowardly in a battle as he was wise in a speech."[48]

Walter Kaiser has shown how close the technical structural divisions of the *Moriae Encomium* are to those of the classical panegyric. He detects a *prooemion, genos, anatrophe, praxeis, synkrisis,* and *epilogos,* of the type approved by Aphthonius, and he finds that Erasmus changed only slightly the divisions recommended by Quintilian, namely, the exordium, narration, partition, confirmation, and peroration.[49] It would be impossible within the limits of the present study to consider in detail the entirety of Erasmus's great work. But in order to show something of the manner in which he made use of classical and religious paradoxes together with the whole gamut of epideictic skills, I shall discuss three representative sections of the work, taken from the beginning, the middle, and the end. The passages selected reflect the general movement of the encomium from the "ioco" to the "serium."

The Latin genitive "Moriae" in the title has several meanings. The encomium is at once a praise of (belonging to) Folly and a praise of (about) Folly. It is also a praise of More, the feminine "Moriae" being similar to the masculine "Mori" of More's Latin name, Morus. The eulogy is formulated by Folly herself in a manner more complex than that used by Lucian in the *De Parasito* and the *Rhetorum Praeceptor*. She begins by noting that her mere appearance on stage has instantly cheered her listeners, who, recognizing her costume, expect to enjoy themselves. Holbein's woodcuts dress Folly in the full regalia of the traditional court jester; her frivolous external appearance is perceived as a true reflection of her personality, not a temporary disguise or posture. The humorous rhetoric harmonizes with the ideas expressed.

She intends to praise herself, Folly continues, since for some unknown reason no writers have yet eulogized her, preferring instead to compose encomia of gods and heroes. The mode of presentation here, of folly by Folly, is the key to understanding the entire passage. It recalls one of the classic paradoxes, that of the Cretan liar, Epimenides, who declared that all Cretans were liars.[50] If he was telling the truth, then he himself provided the exception to the rule and the negation of his own statement. If, on the other hand, he was lying, he becomes the quintessential Cretan liar of the statement, which itself is now false. This paradox is a perfectly circular and thus a continuous argument. The next section of the *Moriae Encomium* again stresses the appropriateness of Folly's praising herself: "who can describe me better than I myself?" (11). But Erasmus's Folly can in fact only accurately portray herself if she is somehow detached from her own essence, since her essence is depicted in this work as marked by childish naturalness, spontaneity, and inconsequentiality. For such a character to give a coherent picture of herself would be to lose the very thoughtlessness she so acutely perceives to be one of her charms. We are thus constantly reminded of the wise Erasmus pulling the strings of his "foolish" spokeswoman.

The next section makes even clearer Folly's conception of herself as an open, extemporaneous speaker, saying whatever is on her mind. The posture of thoughtlessness is soon shown to be in fact the height of artificiality; the supposedly impromptu speech includes a reference to Homer, Latin and Greek expressions, and technical rhetorical terms such as "definition" and "division." Undaunted by such contradictions, the lady claims that "I never wear disguises" (13) and that she has no intention of being a complete fool, i.e., someone who pretends to be wise. Such individuals she christens "foolosophers" ("morosophers" in some translations, a rendering that makes clear the pun on More's name), or wise fools.[51] This complex and difficult notion, the subtlety of which is indicated by the strange hybrid term, highlights the central paradox of Erasmus's panegyric, that only the most consummate wisdom and eloquence can adequately portray total simplicity.

A reflection upon the use of rhetoric occurs in the same section when Folly declares that she ought to copy the rhetoricians who, like those satirized in the *Rhetorum Praeceptor*, sprinkle their speeches with obsolete terms dredged up from old manuscripts. It has often been pointed out that the paragraph is toying with the reader. The first edition of the *Moriae Encomium* contains about a hundred Greek expressions; indeed, the passage condemning such decorations ends with two Greek tags (14). Levi's footnote to the Radice translation explains that "Erasmus is having a joke at his own expense."[52] The Janus-like quality of this entire section is prominent

here, as our attention shifts between the erudite author, apparently depre-
cating intelligence, and the outspoken persona's flow of professedly una-
dorned speech. And yet, on another level, the rhetoric does conform exactly
to what Erasmus seems to be trying to suggest: it both is and is not intelligent and truthful, since it must present a logical impossibility, dramatize in
words a "living" contradiction, a consciously unselfconscious speaker.

The reader must not, however, be moved too close to real folly and madness, or the delicate balance between intelligence and its opposite fails.
Therefore, the lady addresses the audience as "most foolish": her followers,
by being totally subservient to her, become doubly fools, making Folly herself laugh at folly. The notion of Folly's fools cannot but remind us of the
parasite's parasite created by Lucian. The same section of Erasmus's work
presents her family tree, a required part of the serious panegyric. Needless
to say, Folly's ancestors are not noble heroes and ladies but Plutus, all-pow-
erful god of wealth, and Youth, "the fairest, the most charming nymph of
all" (15). The conception of Folly apparently took place when her father was
healthy but drunk. Once again, the passage permits two opposing interpretations. The conception can be seen as a joyful and romantic act of love or
as the sordid result of a drinking bout. The tone of the paragraph, however,
with its Homeric quotes about being "mingled together in passionate love"
and condemnation of the "forbidding bonds of matrimony" (15) inclines us
toward the more favorable view, a good-natured acceptance of the pleasures
of youth and money. But since the presenter of this viewpoint is the lady
Folly, we risk becoming her fond followers if we neglect the satire inherent
in her speech. The child nursed by Drunkenness and Ignorance may make
fools of us all.

The introductory section of the *Moriae Encomium* thus serves to make
clear the importance of rhetoric and the significance of the manner of presentation. It also demonstrates how that very garb may reveal the truth in
ways that go far beyond the manner and matter presented by the orator.
The second passage I have selected for study is taken from the famous central section of the work, which deals with individual groups of fools after
the fashion of the *Narrenschiff*. These portraits form the bridge between
what might be called the social and the religious groups of fools. The section
moves from hunters and gamblers to superstitious believers in the powers
of saints, candles, and material tributes and offerings to the Almighty.[53]

Erasmus's portrait of hunters has been much praised by modern scholars
for its outspoken and vivid picture of the dedication to hunting so prevalent
among the aristocracy of the time. The harsh sarcasm here has little of Folly's customary playfulness: "I imagine that even the dung of the dogs
smells like cinnamon to them" (60). Two facts become obvious in this section. The first is the way in which the elaborate gestures of a ritual, even
the instruments of hunting ("a special blade set aside for that purpose," 60),

serve to mask the brutality of the occasion, transforming an act of mindless bloodthirstiness into a solemn, even elevating social spectacle. "Then, whoever gets a chance to taste some of the beast is quite convinced that he has gained no small share of added nobility" (61). "Only a nobleman," we are told, may perform certain of the stylized gestures of cutting up the carcass. The second important factor is that the language is that of a religious ceremonial, not just of social self-aggrandizement. "Baring his head," "kneeling down," "devout precision," "in just this order" are expressions which lead away from the fields towards a church service, "some new religious ceremony," as Erasmus puts it, making his point absolutely overt. For these men, hunting has become more than a pastime; it is now a form of religion, but a debasing rather than an elevating one. The hunters "lower themselves almost to the level of the animals they hunt" (61), probably because, Erasmus implies, they are foolish enough to believe that mere ritual acts, divorced from any higher purpose, can really move us beyond the world of crude, often cruel deeds.

Alchemists and extravagant house-builders may seem far removed from the John Peel world the hunters delight in, but they all share a loss of purpose in their actions. By insisting on unnecessary and endless additions and modifications, the house-builders destroy the financial foundations of the constructions they so fondly undertake. Their lives inevitably end in total destitution, since the passion for building per se, rather than for building a home, leads them to impoverished homelessness, their sole consolation the imagined houses in which lodge only their minds, not their bodies. The alchemists seeking gold resemble the tireless builders. The real, tangible gold of their family fortune is squandered in the effort to make the same substance by artificial means. As with the builders, hope, in a secular form, consoles them in their failures. Erasmus is equally critical of gamblers who, when their money is gone, remain so enthralled with the procedure of the game that winning is no longer important. Sick and penniless, they still stagger to the tables, although unable to play. They find forgetfulness of their present state only when once again absorbed by the hypnotic click of the dice or flash of the cards whose magic has reduced them to their present state.

Hunters, builders, alchemists, and gamblers share a belief in their ability to transform or control the material world. They seek to alter their lives by the meticulous performance or observance of certain complex but arbitrary types of behavior—carving up dead animals, placing towers and windows, brewing up mysterious chemical ingredients, finding at last a system for "breaking the bank." Every other aspect of life pales before their passionate faith, which is in reality a form of idolatry or superstition. Superstition is thus logically the topic of the next section of Erasmus's eulogy. Here Folly claims as her own all who believe that external forms of religious obeisance—praying to a saint, buying a candle, reciting in a given order a set number of prayers—can obtain for their souls the benefits that can only be won by true faith. In all these instances, Erasmus is careful to point to the merely external, public shows of reverence, never suggesting that when such rituals change men's inner spiritual lives they are without value. Thus, the merchant, soldier or judge who gives money to the church to purify "the whole cesspool of his sinful life" (64) seeks only the freedom to start afresh on a new round of sin. The admirers of saints' lives still cling tenaciously to the pleasures of their own, beseeching the saint to restore their temporarily endangered happiness, rather than to inspire them to become less attached to earthly joys. When her attempt to murder her husband unexpectedly fails, the faithless wife is not contrite and thankful to have been saved from mortal sin, but disappointed at her lack of success (66).

We are thus moved ever closer to a consideration of the nature of true religion in a paradoxical and often mysterious world. Both in the persona of Folly and in his selection of her various followers, Erasmus has shown that for him folly is primarily a social failing. It is quite distinct from those violent, solitary, incommunicable manias he calls true madness, which belong under the aegis of the Furies, not of his laughing lady. His follies manifest themselves in overt actions, presenting themselves constantly for what they are. In the section on the early Christians, Paul and the apostles, Folly declares that Christianity has some kinship with her, and that the disciples in their fervor and disregard for worldly things were sometimes thought to be drunk or mad.[54] She does not unreservedly claim these men for her own, however, and the passage is far more ambiguous than it might appear at first reading. The Christians' form of folly is different from those delineated in earlier sections of the *Moriae Encomium*. These people do not care for wealth or worldly power, turn the other cheek if they are attacked, give away their possessions, and mistrust learning. For Folly, of course, indifference to worldly gratifications and ambitions is a form of advanced foolishness; indeed, finding this conduct odd, she is tempted to see it as madness, outside her sphere, rather than as folly. She compares such conduct to that of the Platonists who, by dint of meditation and effort, transcend the prison of their bodies, moving into the world of ideas and the contemplation of death.[55] Editors of Erasmus are swift to remind us that there are many resemblances between Christianity and Renaissance conceptions of Platonism, and that numerous writers of the period so reduced the difference that Plato's doctrines were sometimes barely distinguishable from those preached by Christ.[56] But we must not forget that in the present text the *rapprochement* is being made by Folly, not by Erasmus, and that the lady has consistently been marked by her inability to distinguish between spiritual and merely material changes. The Platonist who transcends and despises his bodily prison is not really the same as the Christian who believes that he must and will remain in his body, but that religion can ennoble his physical being. The mystery of the sacrament, referred to in this section, epitomizes the Christian's effort to retain the material world of the wafer and the wine, while believing against all the evidence that those objects are somehow no longer merely brute matter. Like him, they have been transformed by the act of faith.

A careful reading, then, of this section of Erasmus's work, with note of who speaks as well as what is said, reveals the danger of simply seeing this section as one in which Erasmus completely drops his mask to speak as he would have "in real life." While Socrates, like David, may in certain ways have been a prototype or forerunner of Christ, to be a Platonist is not synonymous with being a Christian.[57] Only an observer such as Folly, whose understanding of people is based on external mannerisms and foibles, could make such a mistake. In order to remind us once again of his rhetorical vehicle and of its built-in two-sidedness, Erasmus abruptly ends the *Moriae Encomium* with a series of flourishes and quips from his speaker, who begs her listeners to forget and forgive all her inanities, to eat, drink, and be merry.

Despite their brevity, the above analyses may serve to show how much an awareness of the paradoxical encomium as a genre can add to an understanding and enrich a reading of this masterpiece. Although the *Moriae Encomium* was the only work in which Erasmus made extensive and extended use of the genre, he did employ the self-praise technique in his colloquy *Pseudochei et Philetymi,* first published in the 1523 edition of the *Colloquia.*[58] This short piece contains a satirical self-praise by a professional criminal. Maintaining that his profession can be described as both artistic and respectable, Pseudocheus is answered by Philetymus, who calls him a liar and a thief. Pseudocheus follows the rules for encomia by proudly quoting Ulysses and Mercury as his predecessors, recalling Simon's list of classical patrons. He then asserts that his profession is an art, but whereas Simon showed that "parasitic" fulfilled all the conditions of a Stoic definition of an art, Erasmus's character claims to be able to tell lies without Philetymus being aware of it. Accordingly, he calls his interlocutor "vir optime" [best of men] without Philetymus realizing that the crook considers this schoolboy joke a lie so skillful as to prove that deceitfulness is an art. The idea is in fact borrowed not from the *De Parasito* but from the spurious *Pseudosophista,* where one character slips solecisms into a sentence without the other realizing what he is doing. In the Erasmian work, the joke becomes more complicated, since for the teller of lies a gullible listener is indeed "vir optime," the best of men. Pseudocheus's lie is in one sense the truth.

Philetymus next asks for an authority to support the crook's claims to artistry. "Bonam artis partem monstravere tui rhetores" [your rhetoricians have shown a good deal of that art] (320), retorts Pseudocheus, sounding not unlike Simon telling Tychiades that rhetoricians and philosophers are always ready to become parasites, but that the reverse never happens. Seeking to crush his adversary, the innocent man declares that if what the crook says is true, then "artists" are hanged for their artistry every day. Undaunted, the other replies: "Isti non sunt artifices absoluti" [they are not full-fledged artists] (321), recalling Simon's statement that a priori one who lacks food is not a parasite. The chief difference between the two works lies not only in length, but in the tone of moral indignation that pervades the Erasmian dialogue. When the villain describes his unscrupulous methods for extorting money from his victims, Philetymus is horrified and remains so to the end. For him there is to be no conversion to crime as there is to parasitism for Tychiades. Unlike Lucian, Erasmus does not dwell on the difference between what can be proved by logic or argumentation and what is generally accepted as correct by society. The *Colloquia* were intended for use as a schoolbook, and ambiguities in moral stance were hardly appropriate for such readers. Consequently, Philetymus's last words to his shameless companion are "Male sit tibi cum tuis technis et mendaciis. Non enim libet dicere: Vale" [Woe to you with your tricks and lies. I shan't even say 'Farewell'] (324). Unmoved by social rejection, hardened to the judgment of others, the crook replies: "Tu ringere cum tua pannosa veritate, ego interim suaviter agam cum meis furtis ac mendaciis, dextro Ulysse ac Mercurio" [You may continue to carp, with your wretched truth, but I shall in the meantime carry happily on with my thefts and lies, following Mercury and Ulysses] (324).

Although obviously not comparable in importance to the *Moriae Encomium*, this dialogue provides evidence of Erasmus's fondness for the paradoxical type of presentation, and further proof that his chief source in this area was Lucian. On another occasion he made use of the same techniques, not in a complete work, but in a section of a 1525 letter to Pirckheimer. This passage was extracted from its context by Caspar Dornavius and included in his 1619 collection of encomia, the *Amphitheatrum sapientiae socraticae joco-seriae*, as *Podagrae et calculi ex comparatione utriusque encomium*.[59] Gout and kidney or bladder stones (*calculus* in Latin) were frequently associated in literary or quasi-literary works from the Renaissance onwards; in fact, recent studies suggest that there may be medical reasons for what was earlier viewed as an unfortunate but accidental combination of diseases. Erasmus's brief comparison is pithy and to the point.[60] If, he begins, it is possible to compare diseases at all, gout seems to him to be less unkind than the stone, for it is relieved by the jokes, talk, and laughter of friends. Moreover, it does not kill its victims, whereas the stone "non morbus est, sed ipsa mors" [is not a disease, but death itself]. The writer goes so far as to say that it is worse than dying. Not only must one endure the pain of the stone, but, unable to eat much without vomiting, one risks dying of hunger as much as of the disease. The two maladies are alike in one respect, however, in that they are not contagious. Turning abruptly from physical to intellectual considerations, Erasmus declares that if Plato is correct in claiming that philosophy is "mortis meditatio" [a practicing of death], Calculus should rank as high as philosophy, since it enforces just such meditation. Philosophy also claims to teach us not to fear death. Calculus does far more, instilling into the sufferer a longing for death far more acute than any instilled by studying. The stone may be a hard master, Erasmus concludes, but it is teaching man the hardest lesson of all, how to accept death. The letter is too short to qualify as a full-fledged encomium. Its general format suggests a Lucianic basis, but the grudging praise accorded to the lesser of what remain two undoubted evils makes the comparison more hortatory or consolatory than eulogistic or playful.[61] The interest of such an endeavor for Erasmus was probably in exploring the paradoxical way in which a physical weakness can lead to spiritual strength.

Erasmus's translations and imitations of Lucian thus helped introduce the classical writer and, more particularly, the satirical eulogy, to sixteenth-century readers. As Robinson puts it, the mock encomium "became an Erasmian genre."[62] Because of the similarity between certain aspects of their characters, Erasmus was able to appreciate the Greek writer as could few others at the time. His genius enabled him to absorb this influence and benefit from it in order to compose works that contributed both to his own fame and to that of Lucian, their principal source.[63] One wonders if it was not the peculiar brilliance and novelty of the Lucianic paradoxical encomium as a vehicle for philosophic and rhetorical exploration and satire that both fascinated Erasmus the man of letters and unnerved Erasmus the dedicated but generally cautious reformer. The extraordinary and unanticipated success of his own venture taught him never to risk composing another full-length satirical eulogy.

THREE

Other Writers of
Neo-Latin Satirical Eulogies

Contra opinionem omnium.
CICERO

THE ANTHOLOGIES OF MOCK ENCOMIA

Although Erasmus's influence on writers of French satirical eulogies was undoubtedly the most profound of any Neo-Latin writer, the importance of Latin encomia by other Renaissance authors was considerable.[1] The genre enjoyed widespread popularity in most European countries, even though none of the Latin creations attained the fame of the *Moriae Encomium*. Like Fronto and other classical panegyrists, Erasmus's successors explained their compositions as written to while away the time, amuse friends, and demonstrate rhetorical skill.[2] These ancient ideas as to the purpose of the genre and also the topics favored by Greek and Roman writers reappear in the later period. In preface after preface the names of Lucian, Synesius, Favorinus, and others are cited, as authors seek to justify their seemingly frivolous choice of topic. These prefaces are important because rather than in spite of their repetitiveness, in that they demonstrate a clear awareness on the part of their composers of some sort of general or tonal relationship between the (to us) often widely different Renaissance paradoxical creations.

One of the most convenient ways of studying the Neo-Latin encomia is to consult the numerous seventeenth-century anthologies in which they were collected; indeed, the very existence of these often substantial volumes attests to the long-lasting vogue of the genre and to the popularity of certain works. A number of the shorter anthologies, however, contain only writings of the late sixteenth and early seventeenth centuries and therefore remain on the margins of the present study, which focuses primarily on sixteenth-century examples of the genre. Remarkable both for its chronological and thematic range is the lengthy anthology by Caspar Dornavius (1577–1632), the *Amphitheatrum*. Containing the important surviving classical encomia and many Renaissance ones, this volume enables us to understand how an early seventeenth-century editor familiar with a large number of encomia reacted to the genre, and how in many ways his grouping of works resembled those adopted in the present study. The other anthologies, important because indicative of the continuing interest in and demand for such works, contain little not found in Dornavius.[3] I shall therefore refer most frequently to his collection. Published in 1619, the *Amphitheatrum* contains over six hundred encomia, not all of which are truly paradoxical.[4] Most of the major eulogies from Germany appear, as do several from Italy, the Netherlands, and England. Conspicuously absent are the writings of Berni, Ronsard, Rabelais, La Borderie, and Philibert de Vienne. Most entries appear in Latin, but some, such as those of Lucian, are given in both Greek and Latin, while yet others are printed in their original German. The full title of the anthology, *Amphitheatrum sapientiae socraticae joco-seriae*, is explained on the title page:

> Hoc est, encomia et commentaria autorum, qua veterum, qua recentiorum prope omnium: quibus res, *aut pro vilibus vulgo aut damnosis habitae*, styli patrocinio vindicantur, exornantur: opus ad mysteria naturae discenda, ad omnem amoenitatem, sapientiam, virtutem, publice privatimque utilissimum; in duos tomos partim ex libris editis, partim manuscriptis congestum tributumque, a Caspare Dornavio philos. et medico.

> [That is to say, encomia and commentaries by ancient and more recent authors: in which things *commonly held to be either base or harmful* are vindicated and embellished by way of a defense. A work fit for teaching the mysteries of nature, well suited for pleasure, wisdom, and virtue, both public and private. Divided into two volumes, collected and presented partly from published books and partly from manuscripts, by Caspar Dornau, philosopher and doctor.] (italics mine)

The division of the book into two parts, one containing eulogies on topics generally considered "pro vilibus," unworthy, base, and the other on subjects thought of as "pro damnosis," reprehensible, harmful, explains the basis for the groupings. In the first volume Dornavius places works praising animals and insects, with encomia on trees, flowers, and miscellaneous topics such as the lodestone and country life. This volume, the larger of the two, ends with More's *Utopia*.[5] The Lucianic category of the fly has thus been extended to include the entire realm of nature and even More's imaginary world. The second part of the *Amphitheatrum* contains praises of vices or vicious ways of life and of diseases. Thus, Lucian's *Muscae Encomium* and *Iudicium vocalium* (the latter presumably seen as one of the miscellaneous joking works included in the "pro vilibus" category) are found in the first volume, while the *Podagra* and the *De Parasito* appear in

the second, together with eulogies of infamous or unpopular historical figures, such as Isocrates' *Helen* and *Busiris*, and Girolamo Cardano's *Nero*.
This latter group of works has already been shown to be closely related to
the vice encomium.

In addition to the standard encomia, Dornavius includes many pieces that
are not in fact satirical eulogies, such as the encomia on country life by
Virgil and Horace, and Catullus's verses on the death of Lesbia's sparrow.
The latter entries are of particular importance, because they prove that Dornavius recognized the link between the satirical eulogy and the playful epitaph. In many literary epitaphs, the line between the sincere and the ironic
is fine. Laments on dead animals may be intended as jokes or as moments
of gentle badinage to cheer or flatter a grieving pet-owner. Others may be
closer to parody or satire than to true epitaphs. Several such works will be
studied in the chapter on French animal encomia. The same blurring of
generic differences occurs in the mocking epitaph on a human being. The
laments in the *Amphitheatrum* on drunkards and prostitutes, in which the
disreputable life led by these often imaginary characters is jokingly praised,
bear a marked resemblance to the vice encomia on historical individuals and
to the works of ironic advice modeled on the *Rhetorum Praeceptor*. The
mock encomia on people resemble epitaphs in that they recount the details
of an individual life. Those offering ironic advice recall those epitaphs in
which the mores of a deceased individual are mockingly held up as models.
However, despite these convergences, the satirical epitaph, widely popular
during the Renaissance, remains a distinct genre that must be constantly
understood in relation to its serious form. Therefore, although I shall discuss those mock laments which most closely overlap with the satirical eulogy, I shall not provide a full-length study of them here.

Dornavius's reference to Socrates in his title, *Amphitheatrum sapientiae
socraticae joco-seriae* (An amphitheater of mock-serious Socratic wisdom),
may at first seem strange. Discussing the early composers of satirical eulogies, Hauffen notes that Johann Fischart, in *Das Podagrammisch Trostbüchlin* (Consolation for gout) of 1577, also cites Socrates as his predecessor.[6] For similar reasons, as was noted in chapter 1, Cicero and certain Stoics
were often cited in Renaissance encomia as having claimed that seeming
afflictions such as pain, old age, and death were not in fact evil or undesirable.[7] That some philosophers were sincere in defending these paradoxes
seems in no way to have prevented their being quoted by later writers
whose intentions were satiric or playful. In the dedicatory epistle, addressed
to the prince of Silesia, his patient, Dornavius gives a fuller explanation for
his reference to Socrates:

Illustrissime Domine, Socratem accepimus, cum inter auditores consi-
deret suos; non tetrica semper severitate philosophatum, & supercilio

contracto: sed . . . laudasse res, sua natura, parum laudabiles; commendasse alias, quae pretio sane quam exili vulgo habebantur. Industriam eius prudentiamque secuti sunt plurimi.[8]

[Most illustrious lord, we learn that Socrates, when seated with his listeners, did not always philosophize with stern severity and scornful look: but . . . that he praised things not by nature praiseworthy, and commended others commonly held to be of little value. Many have imitated his industry and wisdom in this regard.]

For Dornavius, then, as for his classical predecessors, the paradoxical encomium provided a form of relaxation from more difficult labors, as well as being a useful exercise in rhetoric. The satirical element is not spelled out here, but since the editor included the *Moriae Encomium* and the *Utopia*, and since the other adjective he used to describe his collection was the familiar "joco-seriae," one can infer that he was aware of the more serious possibilities of the genre. This inference is further borne out by the repetition of the quotation from Horace so often cited by Erasmus, More, and other satirists: "Ridentem dicere verum / Quid vetat?"[9] That Dornavius placed this quotation on his title page indicates the domain to which he felt his collection as a whole belonged. Playfulness and lightness of touch, hallmarks of the successful satirical eulogy, do indeed harmonize well with the Horatian rather than the Juvenalian satiric posture.

Having considered in some detail the question of the genre's origins, Dornavius does not rely solely on Socrates in his search for respectable exponents of the mock-serious style. Instead of quoting the more famous classical names, however, he reminds the reader of the many extraordinary and unlikely encomia of which only the titles have survived. Among these are encomia by Cato, Polycrates, Pythagoras, Themiso, Chrysippus, Hesiod, Diocles, Democritus, and many others.[10]

Dornavius's preface to his anthology and Erasmus's to the *Moriae Encomium*, some one hundred years apart in time, thus refer to similar authorities, even though only the names of some are still known. Despite its wide variety of style and affinities with other genres, the Renaissance paradoxical encomium proves a remarkably stable and, to its practitioners, recognizable form.[11] This relative stability means that the categories of eulogy found in antiquity still provide a useful means of grouping encomia.

THE VICE ENCOMIA

Looking first at the vice eulogies, one is struck by the fact that, as Hauffen remarks, no sin has so rich a literature in the sixteenth century as drunkenness.[12] Praises of wine and of Bacchus, often sincere lyrical tributes to the pleasures and inspiration afforded by the fruit of the vine, had proliferated since antiquity. Mock encomia on drunkenness, however, tended to be written by moralists, who perhaps hoped for more success with humor than with exhortations and condemnations. A burlesque praise of this failing, involving a detailed description of its effects, was often intended to put readers on their guard against it.

Appearing in 1519, the earliest of these works, the *Encomium ebrietatis* by Christoph Hegendorff (1500–1540), the Lutheran scholar and philologist, also contained a song vituperating drunkenness, a "Carmen in vituperium ebrietatis."[13] Immediately identifying himself with the tradition of the satirical eulogy, the young author complains that many people will object to his choice of subject, neglecting to note that Favorinus praised the quartan fever and Plutarch lauded vomiting. Mention of the *Batrachomyomachia* and of Isocrates' *Helen* is followed by a perceptive assessment of the brilliance of the *Moriae Encomium*. Hegendorff asserts that in eulogizing folly Erasmus, whom he calls "totius Germaniae incomparabile decus" [the peerless ornament of all Germany], "tanto lepore, tanto eloquentiae apparatu cumulavit ut si nihil librorum vir tantus ad posteros perpagasset hic unus vere divinum arguere posset" [composed with such charm and such breadth of erudition that if nothing else by this great man survived to posterity, this work alone would prove him divine].[14] Beginning his own encomium, Hegendorff celebrates wine as the bringer of joy, the remover of cares, able to make the shy bold and the silent talkative. Basing his defense on the Bible and on Greek myths, he attempts to excuse the love of wine by a comparison with worse sins. He even argues for the benefits of vomiting: "O ingens ebrietatis emolumentum. O ingens remedium quo res & letalis & ipso auditu abominanda, expellitur. Quis nunc non ebrietatis commoda amplecteretur?" [O mighty advantage of drunkenness. O mighty remedy, by which something both deadly and hateful even to hear about, is eliminated. Who would not now embrace the benefits of drunkenness?][15]

Nonetheless, lest anyone should doubt his true opinion on the subject of the bringer of the mighty advantage, Hegendorff later published an *Encomium sobrietatis*.[16] Here, as in his "Carmen in vituperium ebrietatis," he refuted everything he had said on behalf of drinking. Although, in the earlier work, he had claimed that drunkenness was sent to make man more able to bear his troubles, the writer now avers that man was not born for pleasure and thus has no right to seek relief in drinking. Christ taught sobriety; indeed, to gain eternal life we must not shrink from difficulties but be prepared to suffer as Jesus did. Next comes a catalogue of the misfortunes, murders, fighting, and lying that invariably result from drinking. The didactic tone of this work is in marked contrast to that of the preceding encomium, but the author links both efforts in his dedicatory epistle. There he claims that he was merely playing in his praise of drunkenness, obeying the rules for that type of speech: "ebrietatem commendatam reddere omnes nervos contendebam" [I strove with might and main to commend drunkenness]. But he begs the reader not to believe that his praise was written from the heart ("ex animo"). He was merely indulging in a game, a "lusus."[17]

Hegendorff's two pieces are not therefore to be interpreted as traditional rhetorical pro and con exercises, in which the author's own opinions remain ambiguous or veiled. He has a didactic purpose and a clear moral position. His flirtation with the indirect method was an attempt at varying presentation, not at reappraising his own beliefs. The process of developing his defense of drunkenness, however, led to a moral quandary, making necessary the later retraction.

To Hegendorff's arguments Gerardus Bucoldianus, in his long *Pro ebrietate oratio* (1529), added many more.[18] Following the classical rules for encomia, he seeks to provide honorable ancestry for drunkenness in Bacchus, creator of wine, once identified with the sun. Among all nations, wine is considered a strengthener of body and spirit, sharpening the understanding and gladdening the mind. Many men famous for bravery and wisdom have liked to drink. Since sober men as well as drunkards commit crimes, Bucoldianus suggests that intoxication should no more be blamed for crimes than should sobriety.[19] The form of this eulogy is traditional; in the margins of the pages expressions such as "Confirmatio," "Transitio," "Exordium," "Ab Absurdo," "Ab Authoritate Argumentum," and others recall classical rhetorical divisions and arguments.

Another eulogy on the same subject, the *Oratio de laude ebrietatis*, was composed later in the century by Robert Turner, the theologian and philologist.[20] The author claims that the pleasure obtained from drink inspired the political and artistic achievements of the Greeks, Romans, and Venetians. A drunkard is in a unique way a free man, a god, for whereas a sober man will be held responsible for every sin, drunkenness serves as an excuse, protecting the offender from punishment. Drunkards, like fools, can clearly be seen to be happy, sober men miserable. Through sparkling eyes the toper sees the whole world in a rosy light, his shiny red nose providing him with a cheerful appearance and his snoring creating a "harmonia" worthy of the nightingale, "ut cantillantam lusciniam."[21] Turner adds the following invocation: "O pulcherrima voluptatum domina ebrietas, . . . o Dea certe. O suavissima Regina" [O drunkenness, most beautiful mistress of pleasures, . . . o true goddess, o sweetest queen].[22] No one throws strong men to the ground as quickly as drunkenness, personified as a royal conqueror. The boisterous humor and realistic images of Turner's encomium make it one of the best of the group. His enthusiastic, hyperbolical style mirrors the expansive, effusive state of the drunken man. The reader, however, remains amused but ultimately unconvinced, enjoying the flow of words but conscious that they are organized with the care of a sober man: the double paradox of drunkenness, like that of folly, is that only the sober and wise can articulate and truly understand it.

In view of the reputation of the Swiss and Germans as mighty drinkers, it is not surprising that the German Neo-Latin writers were chiefly responsible for the encomia on drinking.[23] In this respect, it is interesting that Turner lived in Germany. The oration on beer by Abraham Werner, however, one of several similar pieces, offers serious instructions on the preparation of beer, a description of its effects, and an expression of gratitude to God for His heavenly gift.[24] Such compositions are but distantly related to the satirical eulogy, as is another group of works, modeled on Ovid's *Ars amatoria*, providing instructions and suggestions for the noble art of drinking. Typical of these *artes* is the *De Arte bibendi libri tres* of Vincentius Obsopoeus (or Opsopoeus), which appeared several times from 1525 until the mid-seventeenth century.[25] The authors of more satiric *artes* may also have had in mind the *De Parasito* or the *Rhetorum Praeceptor*, both of which profess to teach and defend a reprehensible set of skills. The Latin *ars* by Turnèbe, the inspiration for Du Bellay's "Poëte Courtisan," will be discussed in connection with French encomia rather than here, since the fame of the French imitation eclipsed that of its Latin source.[26]

Related to the vice encomia, as well as to the epitaph, are panegyrics on a specific historical or mythological figure renowned for his or her infamous life. Lucian's *Phalaris I* and *Phalaris II* and Isocrates' *Busiris* and *Helen* were the inspiration for Girolamo Cardano's *Neronis Encomium* and for Andreas Arnaudus's various eulogies on unlikely characters.[27] In the *Neronis Encomium*, composed in about 1546 but not published until 1562, Cardano (1501–1576) sets out to justify and excuse the conduct of Nero. So enthusiastic is he in defense of his hero that, as Henry Morley remarked:

> We might be misled by his writing into the belief that he really did take Nero for a great and good man, if we did not know that not a doubt had then been cast on the good faith of those by whom he was originally painted as a monster. In the sixteenth century it would have been almost heretical to separate from Nero seriously the ideas of cruelty and wickedness. . . . Cardan chose Nero for his whitewashing because he was the blackest man of whom he knew.[28]

Morley also notes that, in a work containing horoscopes on various classical and contemporary figures, Cardano provided a very different, and far more traditional view of the emperor. Here the writer spoke in considerable detail of Nero's cruelty to his brother, mother, and wife, as well as to ordinary citizens. The details of the emperor's horoscope, planetary conjunctions and many technical astrological calculations, are used to explain the background to his personality and history.[29] In his eulogy, however, Cardano follows the classical method of selecting and expanding upon favorable facts, such as Nero's strength, energy, and youthful intellectual prowess, while neglecting or glossing over conflicting or less complimentary information. In a recent study, Alfonso Ingegno has commented on Cardano's originality in this encomium. He shows how the writer calls into question normal criteria for judging human behavior. This sense of historical relativity permits Cardano to claim that other emperors were even worse than Nero and that much of Nero's bad reputation came about because, in seeking to defend the little people, he fell foul of those in power, who were then eager to besmirch his name. Many of the emperor's actions were inevitable—Cardano the astrologer reappears here. In short, concludes Ingegno, "Cardano . . . è destinato a ristabilire la verità su Nerone, a liberare la sua figura dalle calunnie che l'hanno oscurata"[30] [Cardano is destined to reestablish the truth concerning Nero, to free him from the calumnies that have darkened his name].

Whereas the *Neronis Encomium* was Cardano's only vice eulogy, Andreas Arnaudus, in France, composed several such works, dedicated to Guillaume du Vair.[31] In the introductory epistle to his *Ioci*, Arnaudus urges du Vair to imitate Agesilaus and Augustus by accepting even these "pauca" as a distraction from more demanding pursuits. Arnaudus's introduction to his *Apologiae*, one section of the *Ioci*, shows clearly his awareness of the link between the paradoxical encomia and Renaissance paradoxes of the type popularized by Lando's *Paradossi*. He writes that "de Baccho, Epicuro, Phalari, Apuleio dicam" [I shall write about Bacchus, Epicurus, Phalaris, and Apuleius], and adds that he will be writing against the opinion of the ages.[32] The methods employed by Arnaudus differ little from those used by classical encomiasts. He even mentions Lucian by name in the apology for Bacchus, a work having obvious connections with the praises of wine and drunkenness.[33] Oratorical devices, alliterations, and puns abound. In the *De Phalari*, modeled on Lucian, he first presents all the usual criticisms of his chosen subject, accumulating facts until we feel that anyone who can find a way of defending such a man is indeed ingenious. As in Greek eulogies, the more unlikely the subject, the greater the credit accruing to the successful orator:

> Eius nomen cuncti horrent. Quid enim horrendum magis, quam hominem homini insidiari? quod atrocius, quam in carcerem detrudere, quaestione affligere, aqua, & igni intercidere, exilio damnare, . . . affigere cruci, vivum cremare, & excoriare . . . ? Haec omnia Phalaris in cives.[34]

> [All shrink at the mention of his name. For what can be more terrible than for a man to lie in wait for another? What more dreadful than to throw in jail, torture, kill by fire or water, send into exile, . . . crucify, burn and flay alive . . . ? Phalaris did all these things to his citizens.]

[56]

The narrator stresses that those the tyrant killed were not rebels or criminals, but people who happened to disagree with him or to have said something negative about him. After this dramatic negative presentation, Arnaudus, burying his tyrant's vices beneath cunningly presented virtues, gradually enumerates more positive aspects of Phalaris. His work, like Cardano's on Nero, deserves comparison with Machiavelli's *The Prince*, for all three writers considered public political conduct apart from traditional religious and ethical norms. However, what became for Machiavelli a fully developed political credo remained for the two Neo-Latin encomiasts an isolated venture into this form of mock encomium. Their chosen topics forced them out of the realm of rhetoric and into that of history, in which they faced the possibility that, in certain political circumstances, some degree of tyranny or absolutism may be inevitable, perhaps even justifiable. These encomia demonstrate the value of the paradoxical mode of enquiry for opening up new ways of viewing historical figures as well as general faults or vices.

Another short paradox by Turner, in praise of debt, is apparently modeled on Rabelais's "Eloge des dettes" in the *Tiers Livre*. The *Encomium debiti, seu Paradoxon, Melius est debere quam non debere* (The praise of debt; or, Paradox, that it is better to owe than not to owe) was included by Dornavius in the *Amphitheatrum* and had been published in the posthumous edition of Turner's works in 1602.[35] The writer makes use of a combination of religious and philosophical arguments. Although his title suggests ironic praise, Turner's tone is serious, recalling at times Odet de la Noue's paradox on the profit of imprisonment to a man's soul, to be discussed in chapter 5. We are urged not to laugh at the title of the work, but to understand that since man is not born for himself but for others, debt must be both a necessary and a desirable fact of life. The author illustrates his contention with a passage recalling the classical fable used by Rabelais to demonstrate the interdependence of the members of the body:

> Oculus videt pedi, pes stat manui, manus tangit ori, os edit stomacho, stomachus digerit corpori, . . . tanto ordine . . . ut videamus, Deum aut nolle hominem esse, aut velle esse debitorem in omnibus partibus, non in singulis tantum.[36]

> [The eye sees for the foot, the foot stands for the hand, the hand touches for the mouth, the mouth eats for the stomach, the stomach digests for the body, . . . in such a well-ordered fashion . . . that we see that God wishes man either not to exist at all or to be a debtor in all things, not just a few.]

Maintaining for a moment this lofty, lyrical tone, Turner mentions the joy of the debtor, reminding his readers that they are all indebted to Christ.

Then, abruptly, he employs a more mundane argument, already used by Berni when, in the plague poem, he notes that in time of plague one need only complain of a headache for all creditors to take to their heels in panic. Pursuing a similar line of reasoning, Turner declares that the debtor is always the master; creditors come to him, begging for money. Furthermore, and here the argument is on the a priori lines of the *De Parasito* or of the dialogue *Pseudochei et Philetymi*, debtors by definition can be neither vicious nor covetous men. Returning to his Rabelaisian inspiration, Turner moves from the microcosm of man to the macrocosm of the universe to explain that the earth and sky are interdependent: "Nam si cogitemus mente ideam mundi extra debitum, nihil praeter odium, invidiam, turbam, cogitabimus" [For if we try to imagine a world without debt, we will find nothing but hatred, envy, and turmoil].[37] Without debt all would be chaos, since every system, large or small, functions on the principle of the interrelatedness of its parts. On the level of the microcosm, Turner repeats his contention that if a man denies the notion of debt, the head might as well deny the use of the feet to the eyes, or the eyes refuse sight to the feet. The paradox ends with the enthusiastic exclamation "O felicem me, omnia debitorem!" a reformulation of Panurge's fervent prayer never to be so unfortunate as to be out of debt.[38]

While simplifying Rabelais's lavish verbal games, Turner retains enough of the tone and substance of the "Eloge des Dettes" to make clear his own chief literary debt. The irony here thus lies in the fact that literary indebtedness is the one kind of borrowing *not* explicitly mentioned in Turner's text. The words glorifying borrowing are themselves in large part unacknowledged borrowings. A new level of paradox is reached as the work on debt proves to be itself a work indebted. However, although he uses a first person narrative voice, Turner, unlike Rabelais, does not present his text as spoken by a coherent fictional character. Panurge as speaker resembles Erasmus's Folly in that the reader, aware of the character's failings, must view with caution much of what is said. Where Folly is inconsistent, Panurge is self-serving. In both cases the reader must consider a larger context in order to assess the worth of the arguments. The larger context for Turner lies outside the text, in his encomium's relationship to its most famous predecessor. This work is one of the most sophisticated instances of the satirical eulogy, in that the genre's constant tendency to reuse its predecessors is now the central focus of the entire work. Only a reader familiar with the background of this genre can understand the subtle humor of the *Encomium debiti*.

The Neo-Latin writers' vice encomia, less numerous and varied than their other satirical eulogies, are marked not only by a consciousness of literary parentage but by an interest in reusing, with subtle modifications, specific arguments and details from earlier works. This deliberate use of the past enables paradoxists such as Turner to make the entire problem of literary indebtedness part of their theme. Previously a prefatory cliché, the mention of worthy ancestry becomes part of the work itself. The list of respected antecedents of the paradoxical encomium serves in some instances as the counterpart of the laudatory description of the noble subject's ancestry in the serious panegyric.

The Disease Encomia

The relative scarcity of Neo-Latin authors' vice encomia is amply offset by the frequency of their disease paradoxes. Although disease encomia in French were relatively rare, authors writing in Latin, particularly in Germany and Italy, produced many interesting works. With the exception of Pirckheimer's *Podagrae laus*, few have been studied by critics, and no extended analysis of the entire group has been undertaken. The chief source of the disease encomia, the *Podagra*, was published several times during the sixteenth century, in the complete works of Lucian and also together with later encomia by other writers. Erasmus's early attempts at rendering the play into Latin have been described above. Pirckheimer's *Podagrae laus* appeared with the *Podagra* in 1529 and again in 1570, this time with an encomium by Christopher Arbaleste of Paris.[39] Michael Toxites, the compiler of the 1570 edition, gave the works the name of "lusus," indicating that he shared the classical view of the genre's ludic function.[40] An interesting blend of literature and medicine was published in Rome by Andrés Laguna, the Spanish Hellenist and translator of Dioscorides.[41] The volume combined Laguna's own *De articulari morbo commentarius* and the *Tragopodagra*, and was a reissue of his 1538 translation of Lucian, published in Alcalá.

The earliest Renaissance gout eulogy, by Pirckheimer, was first published in 1522 as *Apologia seu podagrae laus*, with Lucian's *Calumnia*, and continued to be reprinted in collections of encomia until the middle of the following century.[42] Joel Lefebvre finds Pirckheimer too didactic, less complex, and less fundamentally paradoxical than Erasmus.[43] Pirckheimer does, however, borrow both from Erasmus and from the typical scholastic mock-defense. His Gout, like Erasmus's Folly, speaks on her own behalf before an imaginary jury. First, she sets out to prove that the pain of the disease, of which so many complain, is but the result of the sufferer's overindulgence and unhealthy way of life, and that the suffering is, in any case, not as terrible as those enduring it maintain. Then making for herself various positive claims, she lists her many benefits to mankind.

The first assertion is easily demonstrated by use of Brant's image of gout as the affliction of the spoiled rich. Pirckheimer's lady describes those she attacks, suggesting that "I am present, they wish me away: I am absent, with their vices they call me againe."[44] Claiming not to be as cruel as people say, she reminds her hearers that the attacks of gout are not constant in their severity, and that sufferers are not ostracized but rather cheered and visited by their friends. Gout forces its victims to mend their lives in order to lessen the force of the attacks. People make way in the streets for the gouty, who may sit when others must stand, even in the presence of princes, advantages frequently repeated by later praisers of gout. Although it may be retorted that such concessions are made to the sick person out of pity, not respect, the writer feels that a poor man does not ask *why* a gift has been bestowed upon him, but is grateful for it unreservedly. Being confined to his room protects a man from the dangers of the outside world and encourages study and meditation. Having listed the vices cured by her intervention, the narrator concludes by naming classical sufferers, borrowing many names from the *Podagra*—Priam, Bellerophon, Peleus, Oedipus, Pleisthenes, Protesilaus, Ulysses, and Achilles. Gout then pleads with the judges to find in her favor: "So shall Truth be honoured, your selves for Justice commended, and my Accusers reformed, and my selfe bound incessantly to pray unto the Almightie, that your Honours bee never touched with my disease."[45] The original text of Pirckheimer ended less ironically, with the assertion that the judges, if they remained fair-minded, must find unanimously in favor of Gout. To end a mock eulogy with the hope that readers might *not* ever suffer from the disease praised ensured that everyone would be aware of the writer's true opinion of his subject. The same last-minute twist appears in several of the Pléiade *hymnes-blasons* on insects, as when Ronsard hopes that his friend Belleau may never feel the bites of the insect he has just eulogized. As G. Thompson has pointed out, the *Podagrae laus*, with the exception of the *Moriae Encomium*, is the finest Neo-Latin disease encomium.[46] Pirckheimer's Podagra presents her monologic self-defense and self-praise in the flexible Erasmian manner, passing from the moral to the jocular, the plausible to the preposterous, the logical to the ludicrous. This erudite yet witty work embodies in its own rhetorical procedure the spiritual and intellectual benefits Gout claimed she would bring to her victims. Lefebvre's somewhat harsh judgment surely needs some modification.

The next encomium on gout, by Christopher Arbaleste ("Ballista" in Latin), appeared, as noted earlier, with that by Pirckheimer. A monk and doctor, Ballista was born in Paris, then moved to Strasbourg, where he became involved in the early stages of the Reformation. Little is known of his life, but several of his letters written around the year 1528 survive, as do two editions of his *In Podagram concertatio*, dated 1525 or 1528 and 1570.[47] In the preface, dedicated to the bishop of Sion, Ballista explains that he chose his dedicatee because the bishop suffered from gout, which he bore with great courage. Intended to cheer and amuse the sufferer, the work is not in fact a true satirical eulogy, but a list of cures or "weapons" to overthrow gout.[48] Although more closely related to a medical treatise than to the works of Pirckheimer and Lucian with which it appeared in 1570, the fact that it was included in such Renaissance collections provides yet another illustration of the flexible view of the genre. Ballista lists the causes of gout—heredity, overexercise, the frequenting of such dangerous deities as Venus and Bacchus, idleness, anger, too much blood, even illness and old age. The weapons against the ailment are herbs, such as lemon-mint or colewort; stones, such as jet; sea-bathing; and various potions, such as owl's meat, pig's fat, or the ashes of goat dung. Since other, still less savory recipes were seriously recommended at the time, there is no reason to assume that these suggestions were intended ironically. Ballista proposes bathing the legs in weasels' blood, or applying the grease from a roasted cat. As for the foods recommended to the sufferer, those forbidden seem to outnumber those permitted. Bread and honey are allowed in moderation, but nuts, pepper, onions, garlic, salt, and rich meats are all harmful. A moderate amount of sleep, clear wine, music, and wise, sweet companions are desirable, further "weapons" against the tyrant. The martial metaphor is continued to the end of the poem, the last lines of which, in the English version, run as follows:

> Inough now have we tryed the feelde,
> the Trumpet bids retire:
> Heer stands the bownds of mine exployt
> and end of my desire.[49]

In a sense, the chief interest of this work and of the *Dialogue* that follows lies in their marked difference from the majority of Neo-Latin writings with which they were associated and printed.

The *Dialogue* presents Ballista and Gout. No longer a powerful tyrant, Gout now appears as a sufferer from the disease she personifies, bemoaning her fate in terms similar to those used by Lucian in the *Podagra* and the *Ocypus*. When Ballista tells her that, having deserved a thousand tortures for tormenting the good "Sedunian bishop," she will die painfully, Gout offers to make amends, promising to spare the bishop if Ballista spares her. Never before has the goddess been portrayed in such a humble posture. Ballista declares he will pardon her only if she spares all good and virtuous men as well as the bishop. Whom then, Gout asks meekly, may she attack? In a sudden satirical passage, the narrator tells her she may torment men who fight, rebel, and commit murder, thieves, blasphemers, and pimps, together with warmongering kings and "paunches," unworthy priests grown fat at the expense of their flocks. The last lines exhort Gout to "Forbeare the vertuous and the good, / plague those that wicked be." Once again, the Neo-Latin encomiast moves towards an unequivocal moral stance. Indeed, Ballista does not even go so far as Hegendorff, praising elaborately before refuting convincingly. His title and rhetorical framework are those of the Lucianic paradoxical encomium, but the content of his works on gout is closer to that of the medical treatise and the preacher's homily. The satire takes the form of a direct Brant-style attack, while the praise is conspicuous in its absence rather than its excess.

In 1537, some ten years after this encomium, the German writer Helius Eobanus Hessus (1488–1540) published a Latin translation of a German gout eulogy. Like the *Moriae Encomium*, the *Podagrae ludus* is written in the form of a courtroom defense: "Podagrae velut apud iudicem accusatae defensio" is the revealing title of the first piece.[50] The defense is followed by a judgment on the case, a "Iudicis superacta podagrae caussae Pronunciatio," and a song for a chorus of the gouty, "Cantilenam in Podagram Chorus Podagricorum canit Archilochio. Sicut Gaude visceribus." The use of a poetic form, marked by apostrophes, mythological references, and complex images recalls that of the *Podagra*. However, the later work manipulates a combination of legal and literary procedures, rather than the techniques of classical tragedy. Written in elegiac couplets, it urges the gouty reader to move from resentment and unhappiness towards acceptance and religious faith. As with Pirckheimer, the sufferer's implication in and responsibility for his suffering is constantly recalled, while at the same time the reader-judge is flattered and urged to find in favor of Podagra. The poem suggests that by reflecting on the truths contained in the work, the reader, gouty or healthy, can learn much about the relationship between health and suffering.

Cardano's other satirical eulogy, written during the same period as the work on Nero, is also on gout.[51] Because of Cardano's fame as a doctor, it has sometimes been taken as a serious treatise, instead of what it clearly is, as Morley points out, a satirical eulogy in the best tradition of the genre: "He amused his anxious mind by writing his Encomium on Gout, to whom he was just pledged a subject; thereto incited, perhaps, by the authority of Lucian, among whose works there is a dramatic tribute to the might of the same despot, and throughout Cardan's works it is evident that he read Lucian and liked him."[52] Cardano begins by saying that man should be grateful for the blessings he receives: "Nec quaerendum puto, in gratia compensanda, quis auctor fuerit beneficii, nec quo animo, id contulerit in te, sed quantum per id profeceris" [Nor do I think that in matters of gratitude, you should be concerned about who the author of the benefit is, or in what spirit he helped you, but how you profit from it].[53] This statement, an echo of Pirckheimer, is followed by a list of various encomia, on tyrants, gout, death, and disease, to which the author claims his own does *not* belong. His eulogy is not an "argumentum paradoxum" or show of eloquence and wit, for "Male laudantur ea, quae iuste laudari non queunt" (216) [Those things are wrongly praised which cannot justly be praised]. It has already been shown that to question the sincerity or competence of predecessors while adapting many of their arguments was one of the standard Renaissance ways of creating new insights out of old, pushing further or in a slightly different direction than earlier writers. It is in this spirit that Cardano asserts that gout should be praised as an evil, not as a so-called good. A clue to the Lucianic origin of his essay surely lies in the admiration expressed for "Lucianus ille Samosatensis, vir acer, magnaeque eruditionis" (216) [Lucian the Samosatan, a man of keen mind and great learning].

In the body of the eulogy, Cardano declares that Podagra is the mightiest of her clan, comprised of herself, the diseases nephritis, arthritis, and others. Assuaged by no charm, ointment or incantation, controlled only by God, Gout reveals her generous nature by sparing women, children, and the very old. Like Pirckheimer, Cardano notes that gout prefers the luxurious lifestyle of the wealthy and nobly born. Feeding on the best wines and choicest delicacies, gout also benefits a man intellectually. Many philosophers have been her disciples; for example, "Vir magnae eruditionis Eras. e cubili Podagrae quicquid legi meretur, expromsit: in morbo sanior quam bona valetudine" (217) [Most learned Erasmus composed from bed whatever he wrote that is worth reading].

Great warriors such as Hercules and Antonius Leva (Leyva), doctors, such as G. Budaeus, and many other eminent figures have fallen prey to the conqueror.[54] The mention of Budaeus (Guillaume Budée) refers to his 1539 work *De curandis articularibus morbis commentarius*, in which the liminary verses rashly proclaim that although, as Ovid noted, medicine used to be unable to cure gout, "At Budaeus adest iam divum munere, morbum / Hunc facili & firma qui ratione levat" [The gods have now given us Budaeus, who will relieve us of this illness by an easy but firm method]. Cardano gloatingly describes gout's revenge on the bold rival physician: "Irata sane merito fuit Gugliel. Budeo, qui cum tam publ. conatus sit docere eliminare; ipsum auctorem ita concussit, ut nil integrum ei reliquerit" (217) [Gout was doubtless angry at Gugliel. Budaeus, who had so publicly begun to teach how to eliminate her, for she attacked the author so hard that she broke him utterly]. This sad fate provides an historical equivalent of the painful punishment inflicted on the fictional doctors in Lucian's *Podagra*. Moreover, the pain of gout merely serves to confirm her noble nature, since it is felt only by those of high social status, not the poor and temperate.

The next section of the work resembles closely the gout encomia discussed earlier. Since gout is not contagious, a man's friends will visit him when he is ill; he sits when others must stand, rides when they walk. He becomes "pium, castum, continentem, prudentem, vigilem," a wise counsellor and a cultivated individual (218). Understandably, death loses its horror, becoming "lenissimam & somno simillimam" (218) [most gentle, just like sleep]. Since our whole life, with its evils, vices, and inevitable pain, is a kind of disease, gout is preferable to most types of suffering. Furthermore, the temperance it enforces will clear the mind, purify the body, aid sleep, and encourage longevity. A catalogue of vividly described diseases leads the author to the negative conclusion that since after the age of forty a man cannot hope for freedom from disease, gout remains the best of an undesirable collection of ills.

Like Lucian, Cardano also presents criticism of his initial assertions. This "malevolus calumniator" declares that, far from being a goddess, the disease is a "rem foedam abominandam, morbumque diuturnum atque insanabilem" (219) [a dreadful and abominable thing, a long-lasting and incurable disease]. The narrator recalls that Podagra saved Andrea Doria's life by preventing him from attending a banquet at which his enemies intended to kill him, and that she does not entirely prevent us from acting when necessary: many gout-sufferers have been able to flee from fire or battle just as if they were healthy (219). Such tongue-in-cheek reassurances, telling us more about the human instinct for self-preservation than about the advantages of gout, are typical of Cardano's sharp wit. His encomium resembles the other Neo-Latin eulogies nowhere more than in his claim to originality and novelty of approach. The chief innovation of the *Podagrae encomium* is in the wry comments on Erasmus, Andrea Doria, Budaeus, and Leva, references certain to amuse contemporaries, and an effective way of modernizing Lucian's list of gouty heroes.

A fifth Neo-Latin gout eulogy, the *De Podagrae laudibus oratio* by Joannes Carnarius (the latinized form of Vleeschouwer), was published in 1553.[55] Carnarius was born in Ghent about 1520 and died in 1562, having practiced medicine in Padua, where the work on gout was published. As with Cardano, the fact that the author knew all gout's negative effects seems only to have enhanced the enjoyment of writing an encomium on the disease. Written as a public speech, the oration was actually delivered by its author, if we are to believe the title page of the 1553 edition. The success of this performance, the author explains in a prefatory letter, led him to publish the work. Although Pirckheimer's gout eulogy was well known and had preceded Carnarius's by many years and several editions, and although Cardano's gout work had been composed in about 1546, Carnarius still claims, like Cardano before him, that his oration was a complete novelty and should be commended as such. The *Podagra*, he asserts, was but a distant relative, for in it Lucian attacks gout more than he praises it. The narrator recalls Lucian's statement that gout, born of the Furies, is a stern goddess feared by the gods themselves. He continues: "Quod quam diversum sit a meo instituto, cuilibet nostra legenti facile fuerit videre" (4ᵛ) [How far this is from my own view, anybody reading the present work will be able to judge]. The simultaneous mention and criticism of one's chief source has already been shown to be a popular strategy of the mock encomiast.

Professing on the one hand his complete originality, Carnarius on the other hand expresses eagerness to imitate classical panegyrists such as Lucian and Synesius. He is not interested in echoing the scholastic praises of his own day. In a list similar to that preceding the *Moriae Encomium*, he pays tribute to his classical ancestors, also admitting Erasmus, "insigne nostrae aetatis decus" (6ᵛ) [extraordinary glory of our age], to the group. In the body of his encomium, he utilizes the same arguments as most other gout-praisers, but he follows a more clearly defined and classical plan than some. He first describes the origins and family of his heroine. Gout was not born of the Furies or some other terrible goddess, despite what one "Cynicus temerariusque Sophista quem nulla hominum Deorumve terruit Maiestas" (7ʳ⁻ᵛ) [a Cynic and bold Sophist, who was not overawed by the majesty of men or gods], probably Lucian, dared assert. The child of Venus and Bacchus, born in a luxurious palace, she was nursed by two beautiful nymphs. This image is an Erasmian one. Her kingdom is wherever Venus and Bacchus are, or have been in the past, especially in the homes of princes and prelates. Lucian is here mentioned as having catalogued classical gout-victims. Eunuchs and women were believed by Hippocrates to be spared by gout, but Carnarius asserts that this exemption no longer holds true if the individuals in question are rich and leisured.

Gout, he continues, reminds us of our humanity and humbles our pride by forcing us to confess that there are certain phenomena over which we have no control. Doctors and patients alike should bless gout, the former because even a miser will become generous in his efforts to find relief, and the latter for the temperance the disease enforces. Like the quartan fever in Favorinus's eulogy, gout makes men stronger after the attack than they were before. Some try to deny the divinity of Podagra on the grounds that they have never seen an altar erected to her: Erasmus's Folly had also complained of men's negligence in this respect. Carnarius explains that the luxurious, food-filled houses of the rich are completely dedicated to Podagra, who must therefore be considered beneficent, not pernicious. By enduring gout, one of the mildest forms of mankind's inevitable suffering, we may win heavenly glory. Yet we ingrates try to deny that the source of our beatitude is itself blessed. With this syllogism the author ends his oration, adding a few words of thanks to his listeners for their kind attention. More didactic than satiric, this essay blends the arguments of Lucian, Pirckheimer, and Cardano with a number of points made by Erasmus in favor of folly.

In the early seventeenth century, Joannes Sommer composed a work on gout that was closer to Lucian's mock tragedy in that it had a dramatic form. Entitled *Colicae et Podagrae tyrannus*, it presents Colicus, Colica, Podagra, and two choruses, one gouty and the other colicky.[56] Two different diseases had already been playfully compared by Erasmus, but only in a brief section of a letter. Sommer provides a complete play and offers some lively dialogue. Each group of sufferers asserts that its affliction is the more powerful tyrant. Colicus wonders "quis comparandus est malis nostris dolor?" (457) [what pain can be compared to our ills?], and the gouty chorus chants "tu deorum terror" (459) [thou terror of the gods] to its deity. All declare themselves humble suitors of their respective diseases. The tragedy concludes when Gout and Colic recognize one another as sisters and plan to rule together. The play suggests few possible gains for sufferers, even of the spiritual or intellectual type, and thus well-nigh loses sight of the eulogistic element of the mock encomium. The reader is firmly convinced, however, of the reasons for including the word *tyrannus* in the title.

The popularity of the gout eulogy among Renaissance Neo-Latin writers appears to have been virtually inexhaustible. Also in the early seventeenth century, G. B. Pontanus, in a verse eulogy, uses the well-known arguments, but treats them in a different way.[57] Instead of being dedicated to a friend or patron of the author, his *Triumphus* is addressed humorously to a group of people presented as struggling against gout:

> Admodum Reverendis, illustribus, et eximiis viris, . . . cuiuscunque dignitatis, conditionis, status & eminentiae fuerint, cum Podagra militantibus, salutem & sanitatem precatur. (3)

> [To the most reverend, illustrious and distinguished men, . . . of whatever greatness, condition, rank, or eminence they may be, who do battle with Podagra, I wish safety and health.]

Unlike the encomia analyzed above, the *Triumphus* takes the form of a narrative. Much of the mock-heroic description is a parody of various classical works, and the transporting of the author-hero, enveloped in a cloud, to the scene of the triumph, suggests a medieval romance. The poem begins with a lengthy description of a beautiful valley in which the procession honoring Podagra is to take place. A triumphal arch here extols Podagra's universal sway, not her kind selectivity. Given that Brant and Pirckheimer had characterized gout as the scourge only of the rich and idle, the fact that the disease is now more democratic in her choice of victims is important.

Attacks on doctors, popular with encomiasts from the time of Lucian, are repeated by Pontanus with virulence. The participants in this mock-epic procession reminiscent of book 6 of the *Aeneid* include men, women, and even children from every walk of life. Not all are suffering from gout: some have the colic, others the stone, fevers, intestinal parasites, or hereditary diseases. In short, "Spectaclum superos adeo miserabile movit" (24) [The wretched spectacle was enough to move the gods]. The familiar gouty he-

roes, Ulysses, Priam, Bellerophon, and Achilles, reappear. Even the gods
have sent gifts to placate the goddess, who is borne in on her chariot and
welcomed with songs of praise. Some of the usual arguments in favor of the
disease are repeated in a song reflecting the enjoyment with which Pontanus, like Lucian, plays with well-known epic or tragic passages, adapting
words and phrases readily recognizable to most of his readers:

> Progenies Divum gaude, tuus iste Triumphus.
> Tu populi victrix sine ferro, sanguine, bello,
> Tu disciplinae domina es, foelixque Magistra.
> Tu vera es, vere veri patientis imago.
>
> .   .   .   .
>
> Tu facis indomitos, domitos, stultos sapientes.
> Ex pravis rectos: Nova tu facis omnia sola.
>
> .   .   .   .
>
> Bella premis, pacem firmas, contraria tollis.
>
> .   .   .   .
>
> Tu casta es, nullum occidis.
> (27–29)

[Rejoice, offspring of the gods, this is your triumph. You vanquish the
people without sword, blood or war, you are the mistress of discipline,
the happy teacher. You are true, and truly the image of true patience. . . . You master the unruly, make the stupid wise, the depraved
righteous. You alone make all things new. . . . You stop war,
strengthen peace, remove oppositions. . . . You are chaste, killing no
one.]

Inspired by this song, the narrator begs to compose a poem in honor of the
goddess, who gives orders for him to be taken home to bed, where he exclaims with feeling that "Non est sub caelo maior virtute Podagra!" (33)
[No one on earth is greater in virtue than Podagra!]. Looking back on a long
literary tradition of gout eulogies in antiquity and the sixteenth century,
Pontanus blends the Lucianic Renaissance gout praise with a parody of the
medieval dream structure and of classical epics. His poem thus inserts the
paradoxical encomium into a wider context, even as he places gout beside a
number of other diseases. Implied is a reflection on the complexities of genres as fluid as the mock encomium. The interrelated and yet individual qualities of the various diseases Pontanus lists mirror the interlocking and yet
separate genres with which he is playing in this lively work. In a sense, his
narrative incorporates its own generic history.

Erasmus, Pontanus, and Sommer were not alone in introducing other
afflictions into their encomia, although none received as much attention as
gout.[58] A dialogue by Iacobus Pontanus (not the same as the author of the

Triumphus) was published by Dornavius in the *Amphitheatrum* under the title *Iacobi Pontani de societate Iesu Morbidi duo, & laus Podagrae*.[59] In the work, Calculosus and Podagricus, a man with gall (or kidney) stones and a gout-sufferer, argue as to which of their respective illnesses is the worse. The lighthearted tone of the debate resembles that of the *De Parasito* and the *Podagra*, while ideas common to several Neo-Latin encomia reappear. The gouty man bemoans his fate, declaring that gout was born of Megaera and nursed by Alecto.[60] Quoting the old saw about the incurability of "nodosa podagra," he is interrupted by the man with the stone, who retorts that his disease is far more painful and serious than gout. Calculosus attempts to silence these protests by saying that those who have endured both illnesses have declared gout to be the milder: "comparatione calculi podagram vocant auream," an echo of Erasmus's findings (214). Unconvinced, Podagricus declares that he should be numbered with the dead rather than with the living. Stones, he assures his interlocutor, can sometimes be operated on successfully, but, short of amputating both legs, gout cannot be relieved. Calculosus, having seen a man die from an operation for gallstones, advises against such an attempted cure. Podagricus now exclaims "Et tamen (o stultitiam hominum otio & litteris abutentium) incidi nuper in librum, quo podagra laudabatur" (214) [and yet (o foolishness of men, abusing both leisure and letters), I recently came upon a book in which gout was lauded], indirectly drawing our attention to the dialogue's resemblance to the foolish praises so decried. Defending such encomia, Calculosus lists the familiar blessings of gout: being made way for in the streets, being carried on a litter when others go on foot, and always receiving the best food and drink at feasts.

As Erasmus had noted in connection with folly and madness, the gout-sufferer is freed from the cares of high office and from dangers encountered when venturing abroad. The varying degrees of pain in his extremities enable him to foretell changes in the weather, surely a great boon. Unconvinced, Podagricus paints a vivid picture of this plague of humankind, which "exsorbet nostrum sanguinem, . . . corpus incurvat, oculos hebetat, somnum adimit, hilaritates omnes fugat, manus, digitos, articulos, humeros, membra omnia debilitat atque frangit" (215) [drains our blood, twists our body, weakens our eyes, takes away sleep, drives off mirth, weakens and destroys hands, fingers, joints, shoulders and all our limbs]. This heartfelt rhetoric fails to daunt Calculosus, who assures his friend that "Illa ex inhumanis humanos, ex iracundis mites, ex intemperantibus temperantes, ex libidinosis castos, ex impiis religiosos, ex avaris liberales efficit" (215) [gout makes the inhuman human, the irascible meek, the intemperate temperate, the licentious chaste, the impious religious, the miserly generous]. It is surely better to suffer in the illustrious company of kings, princes and philosophers than "cum plebeis & sordidis mortalibus" [with plebeian and low-born mortals]. The learned Lucian, remarks the narrator, also praised gout (215). By bringing down Achilles, gout took part in the Trojan war, thereby becoming well known to the Greeks. She neither kills her victims nor attacks women, children, or old men, preferring the strong and those of noble birth. Podagricus finally relents, like Tychiades in the *De Parasito*, remarking that the plague, war, drunkenness, folly, death, flies, baldness, and other seemingly unsuitable topics have all been praised in this fashion. Pontanus's reference to authors as diverse as Berni (on the plague) and Erasmus demonstrates his familiarity with contemporary practitioners of the genre. Calculosus closes the dialogue with a saying of Seneca: "Nihil tam acerbum est, in quo non aequus animus solatium inveniat" (215) [Nothing is so bitter that a tranquil mind cannot find comfort in it].[61] The spectacle of two sick men arguing about who is the more afflicted is a macabre innovation in the ironic encomium. Calculosus finds an almost perverse pleasure in forcing his limping friend to admit that he, Calculosus, is the more unfortunate of the two. Unlike Simon, who unwittingly made of Tychiades an admirer and potential rival, Calculosus finds momentary distraction from pain by systematically imposing his own assessment of his suffering upon the victim of another painful disease. This type of pleasure is very different from the elevating one claimed by so many disease-praisers, who suggest that the thought and meditation inspired by being confined to bed could provide a means of moral improvement. Pontanus takes a less sanguine view, suggesting instead that the only momentary escape from the invalid's self-absorption may be that afforded by vanquishing someone as sick as himself.

Pontanus's dialogue is the last extended praise of gout to fall within the period prior to the anthologizing of mock encomia by Dornavius and others. The other disease eulogized in antiquity and therefore likely to be a topic in the Renaissance was the quartan fever. Favorinus's theme was adapted briefly by Ulrich von Hutten who, in two short dialogues employing himself and Febris as speakers, appropriates many of his predecessors' justifications of the fever. In *Febris I*, he pretends to be trying to persuade Febris to attack the cardinal in whose expedition he is participating. Febris retorts that, as a punishment for his extravagant way of life, the cardinal deserves gout far more than fever. The dialogue is primarily a framework for attacks on the cardinal and on religious abuses. Fever remarks, for instance, that monks are not attacked because they have enough diseases already. Among the more general arguments produced are that fever makes sufferers industrious, pious, patient and temperate, sharpening their wits and checking their passions. It is superior to most illnesses in not being fatal and in protecting the body from other infections. Hutten mentions in passing the German fondness for wine, another reason why the temperance enforced by the fever is so desirable. *Febris II* is as much a self-criticism by the author as it is an attack on anyone else. Febris announces that she will transform the portly Hutten into a pale and interesting individual. Thomas Best, in a recent study of Hutten, rightly claims that the two essays provide excellent proof of the fact that Hutten was on occasion a skillful ironist, not the constant producer of biting invective some have believed him to be.[62] The moments of self-mockery provide welcome relief from the aggressiveness of the religious attacks.

However, despite these playful and less serious passages, Hutten's encomia on the quartan fever remain primarily vehicles for religious satire. A more traditional and much-cited encomium on the same fever is the 1542 *Encomium febris quartanae* by Guilielmus Menapius Insulanus, the German scholar.[63] First Menapius discusses the exact nature of the disease, relying on extended quotations from Galen and Hippocrates. After urging his readers to forget their prejudices against the disease in order to listen with an open mind, Menapius attempts to explain why the fever is so long-lived and persistent. The fever's persistence is due, he claims, to the obstinate nature of its mother, the black bile. The assertion used by gout-praisers, that their disease never kills a patient, is next on Menapius's list, although he is forced to admit that the fever can kill if proper care is not taken between attacks. Instead of inserting the usual criticism of doctors, Menapius, a student of medicine but not himself a doctor, assures readers that by following their physician's advice they will certainly recover.

Another advantage of this fever is that it allows several days of freedom between attacks, during which time a sufferer can eat and drink as usual so long as he avoids excess. Undoubtedly the best and mildest of fevers, this one may truly be called blessed, especially as in human life pleasure is always mingled with pain. Adapting Favorinus, Menapius quotes the Greek proverb about days being sometimes kind mothers and sometimes spiteful stepmothers: the advantage of the quartan fever is that the patient can be sure of some days of respite. After listing suitable foods and pharmaceutical cures, Menapius describes the manner in which the fever attacks the various parts of the body, repeating Favorinus's contention that men are healthier after the fever than before. Having traced the origin of the word *febris* by way of numerous quotations, the writer concludes with a criticism of war, praying that all fighting may cease. He asks wise men who have read and enjoyed his encomium to do their utmost to make it widely known as a reward for his efforts. Menapius's goal in this long eulogy seems to have been to intertwine the latest medical advice for curing the fever with more intellectual weapons in case the physical ones failed. His move from the individual's battle against disease to the larger concept of war in general is interesting. The juxtaposition of the disease, over which man has no control, and the war, over which he should have at least some control, moves the reader to consider more carefully his reaction to and possible responsibility for some of life's many adversities.

Hutten and Menapius do not appear to have inspired many imitators, although both were mentioned approvingly by later writers, and the French blason inspired by Menapius will be discussed in detail in chapter 6 below. For other encomia on physical hardships we must turn to France. Jean Passerat, whose eulogies in French will be analyzed later, composed an oration on blindness, elaborating on Cicero's claim that blindness was no real hardship since so many blind statesmen and philosophers had led productive and happy lives.[64] Such an oration, although anthologized by Dornavius and cited by other Renaissance paradoxists, is more philosophical and consolatory than ironical. Another Frenchman, Antoine Hotman, repeated many of Synesius's ideas on the disadvantages of hair, entitling his piece Πωγωνιας, *De Barba, Dialogus* (1586).[65] This dialogue, between Pogonias and Misopogon (the name used by Julian), features quotations from Lucian, Erasmus, and Synesius that indicate that it is in fact a satirical eulogy. Even some of the picturesque chapter headings recall themes developed by Synesius. Hotman is, however, far more in favor of hair than against it, so that what first presents itself as a dialogue rapidly becomes an attack on baldness and shaven heads, the exact opposite of Synesius's work. Synesius's game with Dio's encomium on hair is thus reversed and expanded.

With the works by Passerat and Hotman, this survey of Neo-Latin disease eulogies is complete. The favorite disease, gout, was peculiarly appropriate for such playful works because, although painful and incurable, it was neither fatal nor contagious. Its association with self-indulgent living made it a natural choice for moralists, but because the sufferers could still eat, meditate, enjoy friendship and generally improve themselves, the satire did not have to be too harsh or destructive. It was not unreasonable to claim that the mingled meditation and enjoyment caused by perusing a gout eulogy might be of help to a gouty person. The playful and satiric aspects of the genre could thus both be sustained.

THE ANIMAL ENCOMIA

The animal encomia by the Neo-Latin writers are rarely as long as their works on illnesses. The tendency of the disease encomium to length may be in part the result of the influence of the medical treatise, even as the brevity of the animal eulogies probably owed much to the shortness of Catullus's lines on Lesbia's sparrow and of the *Muscae Encomium*. Apart from its appearance in editions of the complete works of Lucian, the *Muscae Encomium* was published separately on at least two occasions during the sixteenth century. Editors' introductions give us an idea of contemporary attitudes towards the work and, on occasion, towards the genre it exemplifies.

The Lyons editor of Lucian's works, for example, uses the text of the earlier Frankfurt edition, introducing the *Muscae Encomium* as follows: "Declamatio est ex eorum genere quae exercendi ingenii causa tractari solent" [The declamation is of the playful sort often used as a means of training the mind].[66] He mentions the way in which these matters were developed by way of amplifications, and refers quite specifically to Lucian's fear of making an elephant out of a fly.

French reaction to the encomium on the fly can be glimpsed in the Paris edition of 1583 by Filbert Bretin, who clearly had a high opinion of Lucian, for he defends the writer against those who view him as frivolous and atheistic. "Et si nous voulons y prendre garde, nous verrons que plusieurs doctes personnages ont tiré de Lucian, la moelle et methode de leurs ecrits qui sont pour le iourd'huy bien estimez."[67] On the *Muscae Encomium* he makes only a terse comment, less favorable than that of Micyllus, composer of the Frankfurt preface: "C'est une declamation ou harangue, faite pour cause d'exercice d'esprit; encores que le sujet ne soit pas beaucoup utile." The satirical aspect of the fly eulogy either escaped Bretin entirely, or else he may have felt it to be of less interest or importance than the rhetorical one.

An early separate edition of the work in Latin was by Nicole Bérauld, the Greek scholar, friend of Erasmus, and "lecteur royal." Published in 1517, dedicated to Louis de Berquin, the encomium is introduced by Bérauld as "haec Luciani declamatiuncula" [this little declamation of Lucian's].[68] The editor mentions Synesius, Lucian, and Erasmus, as well as Seneca's piece on the deification of Claudius, then repeats Augustine's notion that we should admire small animals as much as large, the ant as well as the elephant. The aspect of the work that Bretin criticized, its lavishing attention on an unimportant topic, had earlier been discussed by Geoffroy Tory, in an edition of the work consisting of a mere sixteen pages, published around 1533.[69] The preface explains Tory's liking for the eulogy:

AUX LECTEURS. S.
Vous avez icy ung petit Oeuvre où est contenu la Description & Nature de la Mousche, Par lequel vous pouvez non seullement cognoistre mainte bonne chose en la dicte Nature dicelle Mousche, Mais y verrez l'excellent Esprit & Sçavoir de l'Autheur Lucian, qui comme ingenieux & parfaict Orateur monstre à tous, Que les Petites choses ne sont à despriser. Et que l'efficace de l'art D'oratorie est de pouvoir faire ample description non seullement d'une grande chose, Mais aussi bien d'une petite. Ce dict Petit Oeuvre n'est à despriser en son invension & Style courant, emplus qu'est le poete Persius en ses Metres, Duquel L'epigrammataire Poete Martial a dit.

Saepius in libro memoratur Persius uno,
Quam levis in tota Marsus Amazonide.

Tory suggests that, in addition to demonstrating rhetorical skill, Lucian wished to show in the fly eulogy that "les petites choses ne sont à despriser." With this interpretation he gives the work a more serious, even a moral purpose, reminding us yet again of Augustine's reverence for all aspects of creation. Tory praises the inventiveness and lively style of Lucian and even, in his opening sentence, implies that, by helping readers understand the nature of the fly, the work has some scientific value.

As has already been suggested, not all Renaissance animal encomia were descended solely from Lucian, since there was a widespread vogue for the Catullan animal epitaph. Other classical sources for animal epitaphs were Martial's poem in honor of the dog Issa, some of Statius's *Silvae*, Ovid's *Amores*, and sections of the *Greek Anthology*.[70] The sixteenth-century poems, of varying length and quality, are sometimes sincere expressions of grief and sometimes pretexts for compliments to friends and patrons. Typical of the latter group are Nicolas Bourbon's epitaphs on his lady's sparrow, which, like the *Epîtres de l'Amant Vert*, portray the intelligent bird as having faded away in sorrow at its mistress's absence.[71] Bourbon's style is closely modeled on that of Catullus; indeed, the title is "Catulli Imitatio." In her study of Catullus's influence on the Neo-Latin writers of the Renaissance, Mary Morrison also mentions Visagier, who parodied Catullus in a work entitled "Ad Perinnam Italam."[72] However, this poem contains too little praise to qualify as a satirical eulogy. More lyrical and tender than Visagier's attack on Perinna, J. C. Scaliger's poem laments the death of a tame thrush, but departs from the satirical eulogy in preferring sentiment to irony or playfulness.[73]

The complexity of sixteenth-century attitudes to animals has been extensively explored by Hélène Naïs in her 1961 study, *Les Animaux dans la poésie française de la Renaissance*. In addition to works imitating Lucian and Catullus, Naïs discusses several other Renaissance genres featuring animals. In the medieval bestiary or *Physiologus*, animals were used primarily for teaching and preaching, as symbols of human vices and virtues. Early zoologists, emblem-writers, composers of epitaphs, and paradoxical encomiasts shared a common heritage of stories about and opinions on animals, derived for the most part from Pliny and Aelian.[74] It is at first surprising to the modern reader to find ironic praises of animals included by the zoologist Conrad Gesner in the *Catalogus* to his monumental scientific work, the *Historiae animalium*. Naïs gives a full description of the works listed by Gesner, which include Pierre Galissard's *Pulicis encomium* and Celio Calcagnini's *Ciconiae encomium*, both satirical eulogies, and Hieronymus Vida's *De Bombycibus*, a nonironic poem portraying in lofty language the life of the silkworm. Catullus, Ovid, Lucian, Virgil, and Homer appear on the list, as does Alciati, because of his emblems.[75]

Gesner's work was continued by the Italian Ulisse Aldrovandi, whose volumes of natural history were to provide yet another readily available source of anecdotes, myths, and fables about animals and insects. Aldrovandi continued the moralizing tendency of the Middle Ages, devoting seven folio pages, for example, to proving the rationality of ants. As George Boas remarks, Aldrovandi's "description of [the ants'] cities and piety to their fellows, a mixture of citation and observation, reads more like a phantasy than like a book in science."[76] This movement between domains is apparent in the *Amphitheatrum*, where Dornavius extracts from Aldrovandi's work several animal anecdotes that he places side by side with regular ironic encomia such as the *Muscae Encomium*. Serious encomia by Aldrovandi on the worm, the ant, the glowworm, the bee, the spider, and even the fly appear. Of the fly, Aldrovandi remarks that such annoying animals are said by Augustine to have been created to quell our pride. The Biblical plagues of rats and flies and a series of legends are recalled to support these claims. As the examples of Gesner and his successsor prove, it was not unusual, throughout the sixteenth century, for a satirical eulogy on an animal to be viewed either as a literary or as a scientific work. A similar phenomenon has already been demonstrated with regard to the disease eulogy as, for example, when Daniel Sennertus used the *Podagra* to illustrate a medical treatise. In understanding the satirical eulogy, it is important to realize that Renaissance writers made less rigid distinctions between so-called scientific and literary writing than do modern scholars. They recognized that a naturalist often composed with great rhetorical skill and care, and that, conversely, many a mock encomiast included realistic and accurate descriptions as part of his portrait. What may appear to be confusion between different realms was not so for sixteenth-century readers. Sennertus's citation of Lucian demonstrated his classical background and eye for vivid description, not his ignorance of other doctors' work.

As Naïs and other critics have shown, also relevant to the satirical eulogy is the complex literary genre of the emblem.[77] This immensely popular genre shared with more scientific works the traditional sources of ideas and attitudes towards animals. Dornavius includes several of Joachim Camerarius the Younger's emblems, which, like the works on nobler animals and attractive flowers, must have qualified for inclusion as "vulgo pro vilibus habitae." Such juxtapositions should not, however, lead us to draw any overhasty conclusions about connections between emblems and mock encomia. The cryptic style of the typical emblem might bring the genre close to that of the epigram and hence, potentially, to that of satire, but in fact its concision was that of the proverb or apophthegm, pithy, occasionally witty, but not a combination of irony and praise. Recognizing some overlap between the paradoxical encomium and the emblem, I believe nonetheless that the differences between the two genres justify separate study of each.

The other popular Renaissance genre resembling the satirical eulogy was the paradox, which will be discussed in detail in connection with the French encomia. The role of the paradox in the development of the animal eulogy is less significant, however, because, unlike the emblem and the epitaph, the paradox does not deal with specific animals. A superficial resemblance to the animal eulogy appears in paradoxes asserting that since animals lead a happier life than men, learning must be an evil.[78] Despite its affinities with and modification by other genres, the Renaissance animal encomium remains recognizably within the mock-epideictic tradition. In prefaces or in the body of their texts, panegyrists continue to describe their descent from Lucian and the other patriarchs of paradoxy. Indeed, one of the first Renaissance revivals of the satirical eulogy in any country was a close imitation of the *Muscae Encomium* by L. B. Alberti (1404–1472), probably composed in 1443.[79] In a letter to C. Landino, the author explains that the idea of the composition occurred to him after reading a translation of Lucian's work sent to him by Guarino da Verona. The enjoyment found in writing his *Musca* enabled Alberti to recover from an attack of fever. The imitation is not slavish, Alberti's tone differing markedly from that of Lucian. He uses classical myths and legends even more extensively than his predecessor, sharing with him only the Homeric references and the story of Myia. Alberti gives the encomium a larger satiric content and some overt moralizing. Describing in comic fashion the social organization of the fly, showing its military efficiency, industriousness, courage, faithfulness, and patience, he transforms the insect into a paragon of morality: "Mitem, pacatam equabilemque vitam ipsi homines ut ducerent persimilem muscis" [Would that men would lead a gentle, peaceful, equable life, as do flies], he sighs.[80] He ends by returning to a playful posture, "Scripsimus haec ridendo et vos ridete" [We wrote these things laughing, and so you too must laugh], thus combining, like so many paradoxists, preaching and pleasure.[81]

Alberti composed another animal eulogy, the *Canis*, at about the same time as the *Musca*. After discussing funeral panegyrics and defending himself for writing one, he praises in exaggerated language his dog's ancestry and birth, glorious life, and untimely death from poison. The work forms a link between two genres, the parody of a panegyric, typified by the *Muscae Encomium*, and the Catullan epitaph in praise of a specific dead animal. His hyperbolical praise of a dog was to be echoed by Bernesque and Pléiade poets alike:

O noster Canis, . . . splendor & ornamentum familiae tuae qui & forma & moribus & virtute nobilissimam vetustissimam ornatissimamque familiam tuam multo nobilitasti; ac longe celeberrimam effecisti.[82]

[O our dog, . . . splendor and ornament of your family, who by your being, conduct, and virtue ennobled and made most famous your most noble, ancient and honored family.]

While sufficiently extravagant to be parodic, the praise in the *Canis* is not completely absurd or paradoxical, since the praise of household pets is not of necessity comical.[83] In the sixteenth century, however, an imitation of the *Muscae Encomium* by Celio Calcagnini eulogized a more obviously humorous subject, the flea. Calcagnini (1479–1541), from Ferrara, also composed one of the most extensive early lists of satirical eulogies. Although his eulogy did not appear in print until 1544, the preface is dated 1519. Dornavius gives the preface in full, but it does not appear in Froben's 1544 edition of Calcagnini.[84] Quoting titles of works by no fewer than thirty-five classical and contemporary authors, Calcagnini repeats the standard names, Lucian, Favorinus, Isocrates, and Homer, but adds some less frequently cited classical authors, Democritus, Pliny, Catullus, Aristophanes, Cato, and Pythagoras, as well as a number of contemporary writers, Erasmus, Guarino, Pandolfo Collenuccio, Alberti, Iacopo Sadoleto, and others. Once again we are struck by the mock epideictic writers' extraordinary catholicity. While ceaselessly proclaiming and tracing their generic family tree, they were with equal regularity adding new and sometimes ill-assorted contemporary names to their genealogies. Catullus's sparrow poems might be related to the paradoxical encomium for one reason and Sadoleto's *Laocoon* for quite another. In this manner, the genre remained both recognizable and yet highly flexible.

Calcagnini explains in his preface that "me non pigeat post tot praeclara nomina Pulicem in argumentum arripuisse. . . . In tenui enim re non tenuis labor" [I am not ashamed after so many famous predecessors to be putting forth an argument in favor of the flea. . . . For a slight thing calls for no slight toil].[85] These elaborate catalogues and self-justifications served a dual function in the development of the newly revived genre. In the first place, they provided the literary authority for indulging in such trivia as a praise of the flea. A genre practiced by Seneca and Plutarch, Calcagnini implies, was ipso facto respectable. In the second place, the lists provided topics and ideas for would-be imitators. Calcagnini's work employs with confidence the familiar stylistic and rhetorical techniques. His eulogy was to be expanded by a Frenchman, Pierre Galissard, also writing in Latin. This, the second *Pulicis Encomium*, was published in Lyons in 1550 by Jean de Tournes, who was, as we shall see, an important publisher of French mock encomia.[86] The author declares that small things deserve our attention more than large, even as in sculpture we admire detail and care such as that shown by the Greek artist Myrmecedes. After reminding his readers of his famous predecessors, Homer and Virgil, he explains that the flea is not born in filth and squalor, but of the dust. Its name, "Pulex," is formed by an analogy with the Latin *pulvis*, or dust. So famous is the insect that all languages have a name for it. Galissard takes this opportunity to demonstrate knowledge of Greek and Hebrew, giving the name for flea in the two languages and quoting authors who use the term. Next he considers the insect's physical appearance, as Lucian had that of the fly: "Tria habet membra praecipua, caput, ventrem, & medium quiddam" [It has three chief members, the head, abdomen, and a sort of middle section].[87] The flea has a long proboscis, like the elephant or the fly, and four "tibia," of which the back two are longer than the front, enabling the creature to jump easily. The author praises his subject's ceaseless energy: "Pulex nullum capit quietem, nullum habet delectumque diei & noctis"[88] [The flea has no rest, and no distraction by day or night]. Having extolled its bravery in terms suitable to a description of battle, Galissard reminds readers that a flea's bite is not nearly so harmful as that of the louse, the "pediculus." He concludes with a resume of his case, reiterating Lucian's wish not to turn a fly into an elephant by too extended a panegyric.

The disparity between highly wrought *forme* and insignificant *fond*, manner and matter, proved constantly intriguing to Neo-Latin encomiasts. The insect eulogy was of course particularly appropriate for the exploration of such contrasts. An encomium similar to that by Calcagnini, Caspar Heldelinus's *Ciconiae encomium*, published in 1534, proclaims its intended use for training the young in rhetoric: "Ciconiae encomium; utilis adcommodataque ratio exercendi iuventutem declamando."[89] In accordance with its pedagogical purpose, the work follows a strict formal plan, including the customary accumulation of quotations and classical references. In 1540 appeared an animal encomium which departed yet further from the Lucianic tradition, bringing serious religious moralizing into the animal eulogy. The full title of the *Aranei Encomion*, by C. S. Curio, makes clear the difference between Curio and Lucian:

Aranei Encomion in quo Aranei erudita natura Rhetorico schemate explicatur: Et in eo loci communes de Ente supremo & unico, de divina Providentia, de spiritus humani perpetuitate, aliisque nonnullis scitu dignis.[90]

[An encomium on the spider, in which the learned nature of the spider is explained by way of rhetorical figures. Containing also commonplaces concerning the supreme, unique Being, divine Providence, the perpetuity of the human spirit, and several other worthy matters.]

The spider is not treated mockingly or playfully, and, despite the seemingly burlesque philosophical claims made in the title, the treatise resembles not parody, but the emblem-book, wherein certain creatures have traditionally been associated with or symbolic of specific human qualities. Curio's work is closer to the parables of the Bible and to Alciati's emblems than to Lucian or Alberti.

The *Amphitheatrum* includes another animal work differing radically from the *Muscae Encomium*, Jeremias Wilde's *De Formica*.[91] This ant eulogy is divided into fifteen chapters, each discussing a different aspect of the insect. Wilde describes the varieties of ants, their mind, seven admirable traits, ethical and economic virtues, and natural and moral utility. Notwithstanding these qualities, Wilde classes ants with the irrational animals, but asserts that they are not thereby prevented from being almost divine, having memory and imagination, if not of ideas, at least of "sensible species." Wilde's and Curio's treatises are borderline cases, hovering between the moralizing or quasi-scientific and the parodic or the burlesque. They are mentioned in the present study because they were so often grouped by contemporaries alongside the more typical mock eulogies.

Schönfeld, publisher of the *De Formica*, had in 1614 printed a book destined to be popular with anthologizers of satirical eulogies, the *Muscae, ex continua cum principe comparatione encomium* by Franciscus Scribanius.[92] This point-by-point comparison between the prince and the fly resembles in some ways the *Muscae Encomium*, including even the ubiquitous formula about making an elephant out of a fly. The work has received little critical attention, despite its obvious interest for those studying Renaissance attitudes to monarchy, but is not sufficiently eulogistic or paradoxical to be analyzed at length in the present investigation.

This study of Neo-Latin satirical encomia would not, however, be complete without mention of the numerous eulogies of objects or abstract concepts, mud, stones, nothing, and something, which appeared at intervals throughout the period. There are also many eulogies on foodstuffs, some apparently sincere or scientific, others more lighthearted in tone. Since the discussions of topics such as nothing were so popular that they provided Rosalie Colie with the point of departure for her study of paradoxy, they will not be discussed in detail here.[93] One of the most famous of such pieces, Passerat's *Nihil*, is a linguistic exploration that lists expressions containing the word *nihil*, then develops ideas about the concept of nothing.[94] Erycius Puteanus, in the following century, was to develop a similar theme, using the shape of the egg, a zero, as a way of formulating various ontological paradoxes.[95] Typical of encomia on foodstuffs was Estienne de l'Aigue's (Aquaeus in Latin) *Encomium brassicarum sive caulium*, a dialogue in which the speakers are Orator, Physicus, and Coquus. Once again the dedicatory epistle refers to predecessors who have sought distraction by praising nuts, flies, baldness, and "id genus minutula," and urges the reader to accept the present game, "lusus noster," in the same spirit as the classical works. Cabbage, explains the writer, may seem an inferior topic for praise but was highly prized in antiquity. His speakers confirm their creator's assertion, explaining the nourishing and medicinal properties of the vegetable. Although the topic is Bernesque and the tone lighthearted, the work uses the conventions of the mock encomium to excuse what remains fundamentally a serious endeavor.

In conclusion, the importance of the little-studied Neo-Latin satirical eulogies cannot be overemphasized. It is relatively well known that mock encomia by major humanists such as Alberti, Erasmus, and Pirckheimer first encouraged the revival of the genre in the Renaissance. But so little attention has been paid to other Neo-Latin eulogies that critics often overlook the fact that more famous vernacular forms of the mock eulogy, such as the capitolo and the hymne-blason, accompanied rather than succeeded the Neo-Latin efforts. Moreover, the early seventeenth-century collectors of encomia discussed at the beginning of this chapter customarily included more encomia in Latin than in other languages. The regular production throughout the sixteenth century of Latin encomia (which often provided the basis for vernacular imitations or adaptations), ensured the genre its continuing wide appeal. The universality of Latin meant that any educated person in Europe could read and understand the references in these pieces.

This sense of a universal tradition may help us understand the Neo-Latin encomiasts' regular reminders of their literary ancestry. Far more frequently than their rivals in the vernacular literatures, they retrace for the reader the history of the genre. Of course, such professions help justify the authors' odd topics. They also become a signal as to the correct interpretation of these sometimes puzzling works. Several writers carried the game of self-justification a step further, as they solemnly protested their difference from rather than their likeness to earlier ironists. Such transparent stratagems merely encourage the reader to study the ensuing works more attentively.

Another reason for these constant reminders of sources may be that, as was noted above, the genre bore a resemblance to and was consequently often influenced by other forms of discourse, the medical and the zoological work, the epitaph, the paradox, and, to a lesser extent, the emblem. When, as sometimes in the "scientific" works, the element to fade was the satiric one, the consequent blurring of boundaries compounded the difficulty of interpreting certain works. The *Aranei Encomion* and Scribanius's *Muscae . . . Encomium*, professedly written within the Lucianic tradition, are but two of a number of borderline works. The very adaptability and similarity to previously established forms that were responsible for the mock encomium's early and widespread revival could also lead to fragmentation and confusion. Authors' sense of this inherent tendency may well account for the anxious tone of many of their assertions of generic strength and purity.

FOUR

The Satirical Eulogy
in Italy

O sacri, eccelsi e gloriosi ghiozzi!
BERNI

THE BERNESQUE WRITERS

As the previous chapter has shown, satirical eulogies written in Latin by Renaissance Italians differed little from those written in Latin by their contemporaries in other countries, largely because all these authors followed the same classical models relatively closely. But during the sixteenth century, Italy also produced vernacular works that employed some of the techniques of native genres to revitalize the classical paradoxical encomium. These modified encomia encouraged in certain French satirical eulogies the development of stylistic and thematic elements that cannot be traced back to classical and Neo-Latin works. The present chapter will discuss first the Bernesque poets' satirical capitoli, then the various means whereby awareness of the Italian revival of the genre spread to France, and finally certain mock-eulogistic prose genres and works popular in Italy and later imitated across the Alps.[1]

The first group of works, the satirical or mocking capitoli composed by the Bernesque poets, Berni, Mauro, Molza, Firenzuola, Grazzini, the painter Bronzino, and others, is related to the satirical eulogy because these verses praise improbable topics—gout, the cough, lies, eels, sausages, pet animals, and so on. The Bernesque writers used their hyperbolical encomia on ridiculous subjects in part to parody the exaggerated expressions with which Petrarchan poets honored their ladies.[2] The varied and uninhibited language of the capitoli violated the restrictions on vocabulary adopted by latter-day imitators of Petrarch. The writers of capitoli found additional inspiration for their play upon language in Burchiello's sonnets, full of fantasy and obscure references.[3] However, Burchiello, the Florentine barber, differed fundamentally from the Bernesque poets in that, although able to write in Latin, he was no humanist.[4] His vivid imagery and biting wit were applied to themes common to Italian burlesque poetry. Two main kinds of work resulted, poems containing grotesque portraits, either attacks on various classes of men or descriptions of decrepit horses and mules, and works relating to some comical or unlikely adventure, a visit to a country inn, a tiresome journey, or a sleepless night. Berni and his friends made use of these popular themes, as had Burchiello before them, but, as humanists, they preferred to mingle classical and popular traditions.[5]

Several editions of Berni's works are available, but few contain the poems of his followers. Giorgio Bàrberi Squarotti's edition of Berni provides biographical, bibliographical, and interpretive introductory sections. The bibliographical section informs us that critical studies of the Bernesque capitoli are few, a scarcity that may be understood by considering a representative critical view of the genre. Thus, for Natale Condeescu, "la satire bernesque se contente de piquer légèrement sans avoir l'air d'y prétendre."[6] The capitoli here are reduced to little more than playful sallies, jokes between friends rather than serious literary endeavors. Considering historical influences, Verdun L. Saulnier stresses the increasing importance of the burlesque element in French writing under the influence of Berni. This "genre parodique," he states, pretends to praise "gravement des objets futiles ou laids, ou inversement."[7] These two interpretations help explain the extensive overlapping of the two genres. They also make manifest the fact that little critical attention has been paid to the details of these poems as literary creations. Critics have primarily been interested in placing them in the correct historical setting and in tracing their influence upon better-known successors. A recent study of the Bernesque poems by Paolo Cherchi, however, takes a very different approach, emphasizing the differences rather than the similarities between Berni and Burchiello. He feels that burlesque poets such as Burchiello, Matteo Franco, Filippo de' Bardi, and others rely for their comedy and parody on the use of archaic or slang elements of the language, and on twisting in a crude or obscene manner traditional lyric themes. The mock encomium, he feels, sets itself up in opposition to an accepted value system. The greatest composers of mock encomia are, he believes, as far removed from Burchiello as Ariosto is from Pulci. The anti-Petrarchan tendencies of Berni's poems are relatively unimportant, since the works are primarily a "negazione di tutta una concezione della produzione e della mimesi artistica" [negation of an entire conception of production and artistic mimesis].[8] The Bernesque encomia are concerned with exploring the sixteenth-century disruption of the medieval balance between res and verba, an imbalance that results in entertainment rather than teaching: "Res e verba sono dunque presenti ma in flagrante contrasto: la cosa è bassa o volgare, lo stile è medio o alto" [Res and verba are therefore present but in flagrant opposition: the object is low or vulgar, but the style is on the middle or high level].[9] According to this interpretation, beneath the capricious, paradoxical style of the capitoli lie some profound metaphysical anxieties. In combining a traditional type of popular poetry with a newly re-vived classical genre, the young Italian humanists created an original and flexible linguistic vehicle. Cherchi's reading of the Bernesque writers pro-vides a valuable antidote to the somewhat condescending tone of so many of their earlier critics.

The range of the capitolo in the hands of Berni and his followers is wide. Not only did they compose more traditional burlesque satirical poems and many pieces that were in fact typical satirical eulogies, but they also wrote capitoli containing either one or the other of the essential features of the satirical eulogy, namely praise and satire, but not both.[10] The affinity be-tween the classical encomium and Italian burlesque writing seems to have encouraged writers to experiment with a greater range of authorial stances. Thus, Grazzini's "Capitolo in lode di Montughi" is apparently a sincere praise of a place, and Berni's "Capitolo di papa Adriano" is a direct attack, not a mocking *vituperatio*.[11] A study of the tables of contents of the various editions of the capitoli indicates not only the lasting popularity of these poems but also how many are satirical eulogies or mock vituperations. In the three-volume edition of 1538, for example, just over half the poems belong to these two categories.[12] Study of the tables of contents also reveals one of the most striking innovations in subject matter attributable to the capitoli, namely, the frequency of poems praising foodstuffs of all kinds, from eels and peaches to beans and salad. In works glorifying more delicate fruits and meats, the satirical element is minimal, the humor lying in the exaggeration of the praise and in the flouting of traditional notions that food, of whatever kind, is not fit material for elegant encomia.

Some of the best poems on food were composed by Berni himself. Apos-trophizing the gudgeon, for example, he begs for grace to praise it fittingly:

> O sacri, eccelsi e gloriosi ghiozzi,
>
> . . . .
>
> datemi grazia ch'io vi lodi alquanto,
> alzando al ciel la vostra leggiadria,
> di cui per tutto il mondo avete il vanto.
>
> (13)

[O sacred, sublime, and glorious gudgeon . . . give me grace to praise you somewhat, raising to the heavens your loveliness, for which you are famed the world over.]

In his capitolo on the eel, the "Capitolo dell'anguille," Berni was to use the same technique, humbling himself before the splendor of his subject as if he were a classical encomiast eulogizing a noble person or place. He stresses the near-impossibility of doing justice to the eel:

S'io avessi le lingue a mille a mille,
e fussi tutto bocca labbra e denti,
io non direi le laudi dell'anguille;

non le direbbon tutti i miei parenti,
che son, che sono stati, e che saranno,
dico i futuri, i passati e' presenti;

quei che son oggi vivi non le sanno,
quei che son morti non l'hanno sapute,
quei c'hanno a esser non le saperanno.

L'anguille non son troppo conosciute;
e sarebbon chiamate un nuovo pesce
da un che piú non l'avesse vedute.
(20)

[If I had a thousand tongues and were all mouth, lips, and teeth, I could not tell the praises of eels. Nor could all my relatives, who are, have been or will be—I mean my future, past and present relatives. Those now alive do not know these animals, those who are dead never knew them, and those who are to come will never know them. Eels are not too well known, and would be called a new type of fish by anyone who had not seen them.]

Berni's style is typified by the above lines, in which words and phrases seem to grow out of themselves, one verb or verbs (here *dire* and *sapere*) leading through a series of linguistic games rather than precise stages of thought to the next. The three-line stanzas lend themselves well to the tri-partite splitting of tenses and historical periods into present, past and future, "son, che sono stati, e che saranno." The three tenses then inspire a further explanation as to exactly why members of the different generations cannot know the glories of the eel. And so on. This type of argument has less to do with logic than with the intrinsic pleasures of language. Classical encomia on the parasite, the fly, or gout referred to and manipulated the paradoxes inherent in the phenomena themselves; Berni, his imitators, and friends developed the paradoxes and amibiguities embedded in the world of discourse.

Mauro's two poems on the bean, "In lode della fava," are constructed in a manner similar to Berni's piece on the eel. It is high time, the poet exclaims, that someone sang the praises of this noble plant, rather than of laurels and vines.[13] Instead of writing pedantically, as Mauro claims scholars do, giving the plant's etymology and history, he intends to describe the vegetable more directly:

La Fava è un legume bianco e nero
Il qual si mangia tutto: & è senz' osse:
E piú diletta chi lo mangia intero.
(1:101ʳ)

[The bean is a white and black vegetable, which is all edible. It has no
bones and is better eaten whole.]

After this seemingly neutral beginning, Mauro rapidly equates his plant
with the moon and then with a phallus. Cherchi points out that such swift
changes in the object referred to by the words are typical of Bernesque techniques. The reader is prevented from moving back from the poetic to the
real world, from locating and identifying once and for all the object praised.
Whether Mauro is praising three objects or none of them is no longer de-
terminable; the only certainty is that his mocking juxtapositions and surprising superimpositions encourage new ways of viewing the objects. The
most simple entities can prove as complex and fluid as the most abstract
philosophical notions: what seemed perfectly neutral and identifiable in the
"real" world now takes on an almost surreal dimension. Herein lies one
explanation for these writers' fascination with encomia on foodstuffs and
small objects, a type of encomium that was to influence the French Pléiade
writers and prove a major Italian innovation in the history of the paradoxical encomium.[14] Although verbal playfulness and experimentation of this
sort had hitherto been rare in the paradoxical encomium, the fundamentally
rhetorical and self-conscious nature of the genre enabled the encomiasts to
incorporate such features readily.

VICE EULOGIES IN ITALIAN

The Italians also produced numerous capitoli fitting more closely into the
three Lucianic categories of encomium. Their vice eulogies, for example,
many of which are by Mauro, may praise debt, lies, and poverty, or vitu-
perate honor. This type of encomium and the work of satiric advice modeled
on the *Rhetorum Praeceptor* were particularly apt vehicles for satire. However, the Bernesque writers did not always develop the satirical aspects of
the genre: Berni even apologized for the harshness of his attack on the
Pope:

San Pier, s'i' dico pur qualche pazzia,
qualche parola ch'abbia del bestiale,
fa'con Domenedio la scusa mia:

l'usanza mia non fu mai di dir male;
che sia'l ver, leggi le cose mie;
leggi l'Anguille, leggi l'Orinale,

le Pèsche, i Cardi e l'altre fantasie:
tutti sono inni, laude, salmi et ode.

(45)

[Saint Peter, if I say anything foolish, any beastly-sounding word, beg pardon for me from God. It was never my custom to say ill. To be sure of this, just read my writings. Read the Eels, the Urinals, the Peaches, the Thistles and my other fantasies. All are hymns, praises, psalms, and odes.]

Mauro, however, does introduce sustained satire into his vice capitoli. Typical is his "In lode de' Frati," which begins, like the *De Parasito*, with a discussion of the *summum bonum* of man. Some people believe this goal to lie in riches, says the narrator, others in power or friendship. It certainly is not found in love, for lovers always experience many troubles for any one small pleasure. The real *summum bonum* is "la vita de Frati" (1:159ᵛ) [the friars' life], not merely because of their certain future bliss but because of the joy of their earthly existence, which the poet sets out to describe. In the first place, a monk's habit is a far more natural and less constricting garment than that of the layman. Monks never have to go to war, are not pestered by creditors, lawsuits or the police, and are always well fed. A picture of jolly, full-bellied monks reminiscent of Lucian's band of plump parasites follows:

In mensa le vivande subit'hanno
Calde e si copiose, & dilicate
Ch'allargar i cordon à tutti fanno.

(1:160ᵛ)

[At table, they get food right away, hot food so plentiful and delicate that all have to let their belts out.]

Monks' fondness for flirting with women who come to them for confession is a commonplace of Renaissance satire; nothing Mauro says approaches the harshness of Erasmus's attacks on monks.[15] Yet his lively and dramatic presentation of the amorous brothers has been seen by Vianey as a precursor of Regnier's hypocrites and even of Molière's Tartuffe.[16] He describes them visiting women and their daughters, talking sagely to them, taking the hand of the most attractive maids. Reasoning devoutly, the friars explain that to hear the truth is nothing unless it is accompanied by good works. The world is deceitful and weak, the women are told. It is better to rely on "uno amor stabile, e fermo" [a stable, strong love].

Et poi si dice come di leggiero
Si pecca, & come fragile è la carne,
Ma che Dio in perdonar non è severo.

Anzi che vuol, che l'uno & l'altro amarne
Debbiamo.

(1:161ᵛ)

[And then they explain that it is easy to sin, and that the flesh is weak, but that God is not severe in pardoning. Rather, He wants us to love one another.]

The satirist concludes that a monastery is really a sea, a "mare," enfolding the women who go there to shed their burden of guilt. The image of water implies also that the monks' absolution not only enables the sinners to wash away their guilt, but also promises anonymity and protection if the fault is repeated. Such wide-ranging powers lead the narrator to wonder whether monks are not in fact gods rather than mortals, and to swear that he would himself willingly enter a monastery:

I Frati, infine son felici in tutto,
Del cielo, e della terra son padroni,
Essi cogliono il fiore, & essi il frutto.

(1:162ʳ)

[In short, the brothers are fortunate in everything, the masters of heaven and earth. They gather both the flowers and the fruit.]

The resemblance between *cogliere*, to gather, and *coglione*, testicle, is not likely to be an accidental pun: monks reap both earthly, female flowers and heavenly fruits, paradise here and hereafter. The paradox of their lives is that the posture, whether genuine or feigned, of striving for that which transcends the mortal and the fleshly proves to be precisely that which enables the friars to enjoy sensual pleasures with impunity. In just this fashion Molière's Tartuffe, whether through villainy or self-deception, almost becomes a wealthy man of property with a beautiful woman at his beck and call. Nor is the speaker of these verses blameless. His evident relish for the seamy details of the decadent monks' life and his jealousy of their pleasures implicates him in their folly.

Although Mauro's poem on the monks contains few of the verbal fantasies and digressions found in so many Bernesque poems, his "Capitolo delle Bugie" [In praise of lies], concerned with the manipulation of words, naturally lends itself to such experimentation. At times the poem recalls Erasmus's description of the self-delusion and flattery that seem necessary to life in society.[17] Mauro begins by saying that he is about to sing of something as universal and eternal as the elements, but which has never been celebrated before:

una certa piana & dritta via;
Che ci conduce alla vita beata,
In nostra lingua detta la bugia.

[86]

> Per la qual vive ogni persona nata,
> Et senza lei morremmo tutti quanti,
> Come muoion le mosche la vernata.
>
> (1:163ʳ)

[A certain flat, straight road, which leads us to the blessed life; in our language it is called the lie, for which everyone lives, and without which we would all perish like flies in winter.]

The boldly stated paradox, that lies are a straight way to a happy life, surprises and intrigues the reader. Mauro goes on to deal with various kinds of lies, from those of poets to those of preachers, lovers, and social climbers. The discussion of the lies necessary to the smooth functioning of society leads to a more extended consideration of the lies writers must tell. Those like Aretino, who speak the truth even though honesty causes them many problems, would do better, the narrator claims, to employ a veil of deceit and indirection, an "invenzion piú arguta & piú sottile" (1:165ʳ) [a keener and more subtle invention]. The word "invenzion" leads to a consideration of imagination and inventiveness, shifting the focus of the poem to literary rather than social "lying." Moving from the white lies of the tactful to the self-serving deceptions of the ambitious, from the fantasies and myths of literature to the euphemisms and deceits of society, Mauro circumambulates his subject, concluding nothing, but suggesting the complex relationships between the various domains and classes of fabrications. Some untruths, he implies, are recognized as such but smooth the path of social interchange. Others, such as those of tyrants and social climbers, are more sinister and reprehensible. Literary "lies" and myths—he mentions Medusa, Scylla, and other monsters—may serve to illustrate certain truths while not themselves being true. The fluidity of this poem mirrors the elusive quality of its subject-matter and thus points to a more general truth about that special form of lying, poetic invention.

Three other poems by Mauro may be discussed at this point: the first two are vituperations of honor and the third is a eulogy of poverty, "la carestia." All three develop the image of the golden age, when artificial concepts of honor did not inhibit sexual activity, and mankind supposedly lived in a state of romantic poverty. The piece on poverty, although a praise of a human misfortune rather than a vice, is clearly a paradoxical encomium, explicitly linked by its author to the long tradition. He claims that his subject will appear a new one, unless the reader recalls what others have written.

> La guerra fu cantata anticamente;
> E un nuovo degno Fiorentin Poeta
> Ha cantato la peste nuovamente.[18]

[War was sung in olden times, and a worthy new Florentine poet has recently sung the praises of the plague.]

Self-justification by way of naming famous ancestors, a characteristic device of the paradoxical encomium, now appears in a capitolo. As arguments on behalf of poverty, Mauro relies chiefly on the types of ideas used in favor of gout: poverty has many beneficial effects on the health of a poor man, no longer able to gorge himself on expensive and unsuitable foods. Like the rich man's disease, poverty makes men meek, pious, and kindly. It relieves the stomach of rich food, providing a better purge than "i bagni di Lucca, ò di Viterbo. / Fà, che Dio sia temuto, & sia pregiato" (1:140^{r-v}) [the waters of Lucca or Viterbo. It makes men fear and esteem God].[19] Mauro next explores the idea that poverty and the ensuing simplicity of life help renew the Golden Age of Saturn, destroyed by the "mondo avaro," the greedy world. Long ago, people lived in security and virtue, feeding simply and never worrying about the morrow: "Era in quel tempo antico ogni huomo buono" (1:141^r) [In that ancient time all men were good]. Clément Marot was to use the identical arguments in his rondeau 60, "De l'Amour du Siecle Antique."[20]

The romantic notion of the Golden Age reminds us of the overall romanticization of Mauro's presentation of poverty. The reader is made acutely aware of the difference between the simple beauty of the literary creation of a well-housed humanist poet and the grim reality of actual historical "carestia." The only poverty that can be eulogized proves to be fictional, not real. In his two capitoli "In Dishonor dell'honore" (or "Del Dishonore"), poems which were later to be translated and imitated, Mauro attacked another contemporary ideal, honor. Some passages may well be sincere attacks on the extremes of Italian respect for honor; such nonironic moments, as was noted in connection with Erasmus, are not infrequent in paradoxical encomia. Mauro's poems, despite their variations in attitude, remain paradoxes, condemning what was popularly considered at the time to be a desirable social value.[21]

Declaring that he would like to banish honor from the world because it imposes artificial restrictions that take away "Tutti i piaceri, e tutti li diletti, / Che per nostro uso la Natura cria" (1:118^r) [all the pleasures and delights Nature created for our use], the poet remarks that the only reason men go to war is that they have been persuaded that this activity is fine and honorable:

> E dicon che'l morir di lancia è bello,
>   O di colpo di stocco, o d'archibugio,
>   Come Fabrizio, Cesare, e Marcello.
> E c'haver ne la schiena un gran pertugio,
>   O nella pancia d'una colobrina,
>   Ti fà gir à le stelle senza indugio.[22]

[They say that dying from a lance wound is fine, or from the blow of a rapier or arquebus, as did Fabrizio, Caesar and Marcellus. And that to have a great hole in your back, or in your belly from a culverin, sends you straight to heaven without delay].

The realistic portrayal of a soldier's death serves to emphasize that this abstract concept may have brutally physical consequences. Not only may honor ruin mental and bodily health, but it also inhibits our natural instincts. Man alone of all animals is foolish enough to impose restrictions upon his love-making. Other creatures know no such constraints and even man, in the Golden Age, behaved more sensibly, sleeping and making love in the open when and where the fancy took him. Nowadays, laments the poet, there is no escaping this importunate honor, which accompanies us "al letto, à pranzo, e à cena" (1:120^r) [to bed, dinner, and supper]. Yet it is but an abstraction, as intangible as gout or the fever. Acquired with great toil and labor, it can be lost in an instant.

In his second poem against honor, Mauro again complains of its inhibiting effects and recalls the idealized simplicity of the age of Saturn. Then men were free from the problems of modern life, "li dottori, & li notai, . . . / La carestia, la fame, & gli usurai, / Et la peste, & la guerra, & li soldati" (1:123^v) [doctors, and lawyers, want, hunger, and usurers, and the plague, and war, and soldiers]. However, much as he professes to resent the power of honor, the poet admits in his closing lines that his fear and respect for the tyrant outweigh all feelings of rebellion:

> Vi giuro à Dio, ch'io non ho pelo adosso
> Che non s'arricci quand'esso mi tocca,
> Et mi trema ogni membro, & nervo, & osso.
> (1:124^r)

[I swear to God that every hair on my back stands up when (honor) touches me. Every limb, nerve, and bone trembles.]

The references to war and the plague, the latter surely a reminder of Berni, enable Mauro to clarify the central paradox of his notion of honor. As concepts, both disease and honor are invisible; yet both can be shown to bring mankind a complex blend of benefits and suffering of a physical as well as a mental sort. Moreover, such are the vagaries of both afflictions, that the cautious and the respectful may as easily be disgraced or infected as the unbelievers or the careless. Yet all these encomia show that we remain fascinated by the invisible presences in our lives, placating them with panegyrics, superstitiously fearful of being the next victim, minds and souls unwittingly elevated by contemplation of the mystery. As the very title of his poem suggests, "In Dishonor dell'honore," the very act of dishonoring honor but extends and ultimately draws attention to the idea Mauro seeks to negate. The word *honor* lurks within the word *dishonor*, and the poet ends by expressing more fear of the notion than when he began his attack.

A similarly elusive concept, debt, is eulogized in a "Capitolo del debito" by Berni, who discusses the *summum bonum* in a pseudo-serious style comparable to that adopted by Mauro in his poem on the "frati." Like Mauro, Berni decides that one of the happiest lives is that of the monk, but he asserts that the ruined debtor has a better life than either the Grand Turk or the Emperor himself:

> Questo è colui che si può dir beato:
> in tutto l'universo ove noi stiamo
> non è piú lieto e piú tranquillo stato.[23]

[It is he who may be called blessed. In all the universe we live in there is no more pleasant or peaceful state.]

To be in debt is an "opra virtuosa," declares Berni, using the terms of formal argumentation:

> Or fatto il presupposito, e concesso
> che'l debito sia opra virtuosa,
> le consequenzie sue vengon appresso.
>
> (146)

[Now if we assume and admit that debt is a virtuous act, the consequences follow therefrom.]

A miser is hated even by his own children, whereas everyone loves a debtor, who is in fact kept alive at the expense of his creditors. After some jibes at priests, proverbially debt-ridden, Berni describes the arrest of a debtor, ironically eulogizing the "gloriose Stinche di Firenze" [glorious prisons of Florence] as a "luogo celestial, luogo divino" (149). To reach a totally paradoxical stage in an argument, here that of wishing to be incarcerated, is common to the mock encomium, and it usually signals either an abrupt change of posture (as in the *Moriae Encomium*) or the end of the work. For the reader, such an impasse serves to recall the limitations of the adapted view of the world that has been developed by the paradoxist. The technique became a stock-in-trade of the French hymne-blason.

The last Bernesque vice praise I shall consider here is Grazzini's "In Lode della Pazzia," a poem with several Erasmian themes. Although this editor of Berni and Burchiello was himself a prolific composer of capitoli, no complete edition of them was produced in his lifetime.[24] Consequently, several poems mentioned by Grazzini are now lost, the work on madness being a rare survivor. The narrator begins his encomium by swearing that if the gods offered to grant him any wish, he would not choose wealth, honors or position, but "di grazia l'impazzare" [please, to go mad].[25] Begging the Muse to unhinge his mind so that he may compose lines worthy of his subject, he lists various types of folly, deciding that although we are all a little mad, only a few in each country are blessed with true madness. To be happy at court, for example, one must be completely mad, a passing jibe which is not developed. All seek the happiness attained only by the fool, untroubled by the anxieties besetting normal people. Incapable of comprehending death, the fool will not be disturbed by the loss of friends and relatives. It becomes clear that Grazzini is referring not to the folly described by Erasmus, the self-love common to all men, but to real madness, that form of folly considered by Erasmus only in one short section of his work. Untouched by the law and convinced that everyone and everything is loving and lovable, Grazzini's madman is oblivious to the weather, plague, war, and his surroundings. In short, he enjoys life to the full, singing and smiling, believing that all are his friends and at his command, "al suo comando."[26]

Madness becomes a refuge against the blows of fortune, the sole source of contentment, that which "senza le mosche doni il mele" [gives us the honey without the flies].[27] However, Grazzini does not follow Lucian and some Neo-Latin writers in suggesting that we should worship folly as a goddess. The capitolo provides no family tree for folly, Grazzini recommending merely that man ask God not for health of mind or body, but for madness. Explaining that although this work may not be a very adequate tribute, he hopes to do better in the future with the aid of folly herself, Grazzini concludes his poem. The notion of madness is ambiguous here, because Grazzini's madman would be unable to appreciate his own felicity. Only the sane can observe and relish the madman's blessed state of tranquility. The madman may indeed be happy, but he can never know it or express it, since to be mad in the terms of this capitolo is to lack awareness of one's state. The final hope for a better performance under the direct control of folly, when such a performance would in fact be impossible, underscores the paradoxical nature of the entire enterprise. Although owing a great deal to Erasmus, Grazzini has concentrated on one contradiction inherent to Folly, the inability of the fool to appreciate the advantages of his condition.

Mauro and another contributor to the Grazzini collection each composed a poem apologizing for laziness, which they presented as a praise of their beds, and similar passages in other pieces seek to excuse individual eccentricities and failings.[28] However, the Italians wrote relatively few capitoli praising human vices and weaknesses or advocating an immoral way of life, as had Lucian in the *Rhetorum Praeceptor*.[29]

DISEASE EULOGIES IN ITALIAN

The next large group of capitoli comprises the disease eulogies and includes the most famous of all Berni's poems, his two encomia on the plague. It has been pointed out that Berni is apparently the only writer to have praised the dreaded pestilence, viewed throughout the centuries with fear and terror.[30] Since the plague was such an unlikely topic for a eulogy, the challenge to the writer was correspondingly greater, as was the glory if he succeeded. Accordingly, Berni sets himself, in his first capitolo, to change our perception of this "fléau de Dieu." The pestilence time is a fine one, he declares, thinning the ranks of scoundrels, enabling worshippers to attend church without being crushed by an unruly crowd. Merchants forget to record debts, and importunate creditors flee in panic if the debtor says his head hurts or his arm aches. The streets are virtually empty, law enforcement weakens, and no work need be done.

Unfortunately, as with Grazzini's portrayal of madness, such advantages are only appreciated by the nonsufferer, who can exploit the situation for his own social and financial benefit. Even Berni does not claim that to catch the plague brings joy. The plague victim's only gain, he asserts, is a swift and peaceful death. Rather than eulogize the illness itself, the poet cunningly focuses on the changes in social conduct brought about when an epidemic strikes. By his choice of a lethal and contagious rather than a noninfectious and nonfatal ailment, he stretches to the limit the framework of the disease eulogy, and is forced for the time being to abandon the traditional ways of praising the disease as a disease. Instead, he portrays the plague *season*, not the plague itself, comparing the period to spring, summer, autumn, and winter in having its own distinct atmosphere. This biased and slanted glorification of "plague-time" serves to satirize stereotyped representations of springtime and summertime.

In the "Capitolo secondo della peste," Berni finally considers the plague not as an event in society that radically alters all men's behavior, but as a disease. He explains that his earlier poem had not said enough about the mighty Plague. She is like a woman, seeking to devour as many victims as possible, a Pandora figure who arouses our curiosity only to destroy us. He imputes the malady to nature who, following her custom of providing a cure for every ill she sends, employs the pestilence to purge the body politic of waste and ill humors, i.e., of criminals, "furfanti." The plague is thus a large-scale emetic, a Gargantuan dose of senna or rhubarb. Moreover, a death of plague is peaceful, undisturbed by lawyers or unwanted visitors. False friends soon disappear, and love relationships are put to the ultimate test. The plague is a modest and discreet disease, attacking the hidden parts of the body, seeking out the vital organs like some celestial bird of prey. It picks our bodies over with the skill of a cook dissecting a carcass—just such a cook as the poet's friend Piero Buffet, to whom the capitolo is dedicated.

Reflecting now on his poem, Berni remarks that in constructing a mighty verbal edifice, an "edificio," to the plague, he has neglected to provide a roof, a task that would call for phrases as lengthy as those in the prayers and psalms of Benedictine monks. Refusing to provide such a roof, he offers instead a final assertion: the plague is an ill sent from God, and he who believes otherwise is a "balordo," a blockhead. This abrupt return to the world of normal reactions, to the common man's feeling that, despite all the arguments, the plague is still the plague, has been shown to be typical of the paradoxical encomium. Berni has shown that the only way to agree that the plague is beneficent would be in some mad sense to believe oneself immune and thus able to profit from it. That final step towards a completely inverted world Berni does not take.

Berni's exploration of the complex nature of the plague thus produces two seemingly contradictory images. The ironic image of wholeness, the plague personified as a dangerous woman, and the equally ironic image of incompleteness, the building without a roof, suggest two possible interpretations of the pestilence. The first metaphor harmonizes the random deaths and outbreaks, seeing in them the consistency and purposefulness of a woman in search of admirers. Such a view implies that there may be a reason even for the most terrible of illnesses. The second image, that of the roofless edifice, contrasts with the first. Explanations and rationalizations of the mystery remain ultimately incomplete and vulnerable. However, this picture is rendered even more paradoxical by the fact that the two images are themselves ambiguous. The suggestion of the mysterious but perceptible divine purpose of the plague is thrown into an ironic light by the perverse nature of the persona chosen to represent the idea, and the edifice, although unfinished, remains a recognizable entity, just as Berni's portrayal of "la Peste" is consistent and convincing. At this point in his poem, when both external unifying figures and internal ratiocinations prove unsatisfactory, Berni turns to God, who alone knows why the plague exists. Berni leaves the completion of his edifice to a "miglior architetto," perhaps God Himself. The conclusion of the capitolo thus contrasts two extremes, the "balordo" who refuses to believe that God sends the plague, and "Dio," using the position of the words at the end of successive lines to draw our attention to the poles between which the two poems have been articulated. Blind faith in the divine purpose of the pestilence may be desirable but, in the face of experience, remains hard to sustain for any but the simple or, perhaps, the thickheaded. And yet prolonged contemplation of the phenomenon does lead the sophisticated poet to God. The educated man may obtain only intermittently the comforting confidence of the "balordo," but he will have achieved more than the fool in one sense, since he will have understood a quite different function of the pestilence, that of plaguing men's minds into activity. Of course, this intellectual plague should not be entirely separated from the physical one, lest we become complacent and indifferent to suffering, or even, as the height of madness, believe ourselves immune to the disease. The poet must never forget that he too may fall victim, a self-inclusive notion that recalls Erasmus's mention of himself in his own eulogy. On the other hand, the poem's images are not to be equated with the real plague, any more than the capitoli are to be read as medical or theological treatises.

In a more traditional disease encomium, on gout, Matteo Francesi, another Bernesque poet, declared that gout is an unrecognized good, not an evil.[31] Doctors claim that it is caused by the body's inability to absorb more than a certain amount of wine and meat. Francesi feels, and modern medicine agrees with him, that gout is hereditary, sent from God, and therefore not to be resisted. Since it is fostered by wine and lechery, it is particularly common in the homes of abbots and priors. Poor working monks, those who fast on more days than are required by the church calendar, are spared. Gout is attentive to our spirit, body, and fortune. The spirit is improved by enforced bedrest and contemplation, the body by the necessity of following a simple diet, and wealth appears to be a *sine qua non* of the illness. Perhaps gout is not in fact an illness, for the gouty are never hospitalized, and no pharmacist stocks a cure for the afflicted. As was noted above, such moves into the absurd, abandoning normal reality, are typically Bernesque. Francesi presents a wide variety of arguments in favor of gout, ranging from the religio-philosophical (God sends the malady, therefore we must not rebel against it) and the moral (gout gives us time to read and meditate) to the comical or ridiculous (gout cannot be so terrible, since no one goes to the hospital with it, and friends continue to visit those who are suffering). In addition to using the lack of medical cures for the gout to argue paradoxically that gout cannot be an illness, Francesi is also interested in satirizing gouty members of religious orders. Combining the preacher's idea of gout as God's punishment and the longstanding popular association of gout with affluent and self-indulgent living, Francesi is able to make a particularly vivid satiric point. The wealthy friars ignore both the teaching of God and their own unfortunate dramatic spectacle—a gouty monk, in the popular view of the day, had ipso facto to be an unworthy monk.[32]

Francesi's other disease capitolo, on the cough, concerns another trying but not lethal affliction.[33] Once again, he claims that the illness is probably sent from God, although one can invite an attack by going outside without wrapping up. The chief benefits conferred by the ailment are that it keeps one awake at night, thereby averting nighttime indigestion and giving the sufferer time to meditate and create poems such as the present one. The work thus forms a perfect ironic circle. The cough keeps one awake; while awake one may as well think and write; a likely topic for a poem at such a time would be the cough, without which one would have been sleeping, not writing. The hyperbolical language used to describe the poem, this "fontana," or "pantanaccio d'eloquenza" [fountain or quagmire of eloquence], of course implies that a more comfortable situation might have been to avoid the cough and write fewer poems.[34] Once again, the reader has been moved into a world of madness, perfectly logical in its own terms, but un-acceptable to normal human beings.

ANIMAL EULOGIES IN ITALIAN

The Bernesque poets are at their most original and varied in the vice and disease eulogies. Their capitoli on animals are primarily parodies of the ex-aggerations of Petrarchan laments. One can also detect the influence of Ca-tullus, as in the case of the Neo-Latin epitaphs. The Bernesque laments were to influence Du Bellay and other members of the Pléiade, particularly their hymnes-blasons. For example, Berni's "Capitolo del Cornacchino" purports to be the lament of Nardino on his little crow, "bel, grazioso e umano" [beautiful, gracious, and human] (16). The grieving owner is pitied even by one of his dogs. The poem incorporates lines parodying Petrarch and Dante is framed by the poet's invitation to enjoy the "piacer del Mag-nolino," Magnolino being an Italian who, as Bàrberi Squarotti explains, found pleasure in doing the opposite of what others found enjoyable. The reader's contrariness lies in his being amused, not touched, by the extrava-gance of the poem's expression of grief, finding pleasure in another's pain. Nardino, the stricken bird-owner, perceives as tragic loss what outsiders may see as a mundane accident. The ironic stance is reinforced by the fact that the crow was traditionally not seen as an attractive bird, a perception which a later French poet, Etienne Forcadel, was to manipulate in a French encomium on the crow.

Closer in topic to Lucian's eulogy on the fly is Bronzino's "Capitolo in lode della Zanzara."[35] It is essential to tell the truth, says the poet, and so he must explain that the mosquito is the best of creatures. This enemy of idleness keeps men awake at night and first taught barbers how to let blood. After some personal reflections, the poem concludes that:

> Quest'Animal in somma mi contenta
> Si stranamente, ch'à tutti i miei amici
> Ne vorrei sempre intorno almanco trenta,
> Per farli destri, & più sani, & felici.
> (2:164ʳ)

[In short, this animal pleases me in such a special way that I would like to bestow at least thirty of them on all my friends to make them nim-ble, healthier, and happy.]

These ironic wishes to friends were to become a characteristic ending of the Pléiade hymnes-blasons. They serve to undercut and bring back to reality the overfavorable picture that has been drawn. Bronzino's friends would certainly prefer thirty lines of poetry about the mosquito to thirty living creatures. This comical and abrupt conclusion forces the reader back out of the circle of madness that the poet has constructed.

The ironic capitoli form the largest group of Italian descendants of the satirical eulogy. Not only did their composers present them as inspired by the classical genre, but Filippo Giunti, publisher of the 1555 edition, makes the link explicit in his preface to the *Secondo libro*. After mentioning Homer and Virgil, he praises Berni, who "per piacere altrui, & per esercitar se stesso, cotante belle & argute poesie ci lasciò di suo, quante hoggi si veggono publicate al mondo per le nostre & per laltrui stampe" [for the pleasure of others and to exercise himself, left us so many beautiful and witty poems, which we now see published by our own and other presses].[36] Like Favorinus and many Neo-Latin encomiasts, the editor stresses the pleasure and intellectual exercise to be obtained from such compositions rather than their usefulness as vehicles for satire. After studying the full range of poetry written within this group, we can see that the Bernesque writers in fact introduced some important new elements into the genre. First, they favored a poetic form rather than the prose one employed in most classical mock encomia. Second, they broadened yet further the subject matter of the genre, only occasionally praising the same disease or object as their predecessors. Third, they greatly extended that encomium's stylistic range, by habitually favoring a style marked by great verbal freedom and variety. The digression, attached to the main topic by some slight metaphoric relationship or highly individual train of thought, became the hallmark of Bernesque writing and exerted an influence on later French poetry.[37] An inevitable result of the rapid change of subject was the equally abrupt change of tone and language. Within a few short pages the loftiest and the most obscene language are juxtaposed. Such rapid changes are helpful to all paradoxical argumentation, which must constantly change direction and tactics if it is not to reach a logical impasse, and they are essential to the Bernesque writings, which habitually construct a circle from which the reader has finally to break out.

The question of these poets' influence on French writers, especially upon the Pléiade, has been much discussed but never conclusively settled. Apart from well-known contacts by way of such authors as Marot and Du Bellay, there are other channels through which knowledge of contemporary Italian fascination with paradoxy passed to France. An important mention of such writing occurs in Castiglione's *Cortegiano* (Venice, 1528), translated into French in 1537 by Jacques Colin, secretary to François I, and published without the translator's knowledge. A year later, a more correct edition by Dolet and Sainct-Gelays appeared in Lyons. This book, whose widespread and long-lasting popularity has been the object of many studies, contains a passage that clearly shows an awareness of the satirical eulogy, perhaps of Bernesque capitoli. Teasing Sir Federico, Lady Emilia urges him to speak, declaring that since people have written on the fly, the quartan fever, and baldness, the noble lord must surely be able to produce a comment or a story. The lady takes for granted that her hearers will understand her references. Like Grazzini, she seems to view the genre as the epitome of intellectual agility, a worthy pastime for cultivated courtiers.[38]

Another link with France appears in the writings of Gabriello Symeoni, an Italian who spent much time in France and commented frequently on French writers and political figures. As their title indicates, Symeoni's *Satire alla berniesca* are modeled on Berni and blend classical and Italian influences. Published in Turin in 1549, only ten years after the appearance of the first, partial edition of the works of the Bernesque poets, these imitations demonstrate how rapidly the earlier pieces became known, since Symeoni felt able to use the term "alla berniesca" in a collection directed mainly at French readers.[39] Dedicated to Henri II, the book contains a poem on the death of François I, others addressed to French dukes and princesses, one to the poet Sainct-Gelays, and another on the exile and death of Clément Marot. The verso of the title page bears a version of the Horatian maxim so often affixed to mock encomia, "Quis vetat dicere verum?" [Who forbids us to tell the truth?] The preface discusses satire, mentioning Persius, Horace, and Juvenal, three classical satirists much admired during the Renaissance.[40] Later in the preface Symeoni even inserts a passage of self-justification by way of classical writers, altogether in the style of the mock panegyrists. Citing Homer, Virgil, and Catullus, he asserts his right to compose lighthearted pieces "per essercitare variamente l'ingegno" [to exercise his mind in various ways]. Passing next to a consideration of Berni, in a poem entitled "Dello stile berniesco," he praises the "gentil compor berniesco" [refined Bernesque style], listing a number of capitoli, particularly those on food.[41] His list may well have furnished topics for later French poems.

In 1567, the French reader was presented with a work in which the resemblance between the classical satirical eulogy and the Bernesque capitolo was even more explicitly noted. Of course, Berni was well known in France by this date. The interest of the passage lies in its composer's assertion that Berni and his friends were in fact reviving a classical genre. The passage appears in *La Pazzia*, attributed to but probably not written by Vianesio Albergati, the papal nuncio, and originally published in 1540, when the Bernesque works were still something of a novelty.[42] *La Pazzia* is an imitation of the *Moriae Encomium*, omitting most of Erasmus's religious satire but expanding his portrayal of social follies, particularly those of women. Whereas Erasmus had justified his topic by citing classical works praising tyrants, agues, and so on, the Italian mentions contemporary works. The French version of *La Pazzia*, entitled revealingly *Les Louanges de la Folie*,

Traicté fort plaisant en forme de Paradoxe, lists the recent pieces as follows: "de nostre siecle se sont encores trouvez de tresnobles esprits, qui ont faict de mesme des jeux de la Prime & des Eschets, des Artichaux, de la Verolle, & plusieurs autres choses moins digne (*sic*) de louange."[43] These additional links, from Castiglione to Symeoni, from Grazzini to the author of *La Pazzia*, helped set up a far more varied family tree for French writers seeking to experiment with the mock eulogy.[44] The diversity of French efforts in the domain cannot but have been encouraged by the variety of contemporary and classical examples which were available by the second half of the sixteenth century.

THE *PARADOSSI* AND THE *SERMONI FUNEBRI*

Although the capitoli were the most numerous descendants of the satirical eulogy to appear in Renaissance Italy, they were by no means the only works to be influenced by the genre. Strangely enough, both other types of literature that show this influence were known to the French by way of the writings of one man, Ortensio Lando, whose *Paradossi* and *Sermoni funebri* were translated into French on several occasions well into the seventeenth century.[45] First published in Lyons, the *Paradossi* must have been available in both French and Italian to any educated Frenchman.[46] Written in prose, they uphold various unlikely causes, such as that it is better to be poor than rich, mad than sane, drunk than sober. They are usually on more abstract themes than the capitoli, lauding conditions rather than objects. A few, such as those condemning Aristotle or the works of Boccaccio, are more specific, approaching the form of a mock *vituperatio*. The original thirty paradoxes were cut to twenty-five by the French translator, Charles Estienne, who omitted the more specific ones.[47] As their topics suggest, some of the essays are in fact classic satirical encomia. Since they closely resemble some later French works and must have been particularly important in France, because of the translations and because the first edition appeared in Lyons, they will be discussed in detail below, together with the works they most influenced.

Like the *Paradossi*, the *Sermoni funebri* appear to have been widely popular, appearing in both French and Latin translations.[48] They have received less critical attention than the paradoxes. Their initial popularity is perhaps best understood in terms of the Renaissance vogue for so many kinds of poems and prose works on animals—blasons, emblems, epitaphs, and so on. Each purporting to be by a different person regretting the loss of a beloved pet, the sermoni consist of eleven laments. A typical example, that "Di Frate Puccio nella morte d'un suo Pidocchio," (The lament of Brother Puccio on the death of his louse) is related to the animal eulogy because of its concern with a small and generally unpopular insect. Bemoaning his lack of eloquence, Brother Puccio prays for inspiration in order to do justice to "l'infinita gentilezza d'un mio Pidocchio."[49] He found his louse in church during the Magnificat: "ritto mi levai, & ecco in sul braccio manco veggo caminar questa Creaturina con un passo lento & grave, che pareva a vederlo l'Abbate di Clugni" (12ʳ) [I stood up, and there on my left arm I saw this little creature walking with a slow, solemn step that reminded me of the Abbot of Cluny]. Its arrival under such auspicious circumstances naturally led everyone to believe that the insect was of divine origin, and Brother Puccio explains that the louse soon became as precious to him as a miser's gold. Having put his small friend in a safe place to grow strong, he fed it for two years on a fanciful diet of "latte di Gallina, col grasso di Zanzara" (12ᵛ) [hen's milk, with mosquito grease]. The growing insect was allowed to wander freely in the monk's cell with two small bells on its feet and a Parisian-made chain around its neck—a caricature of a household pet.

In mock-heroic style, the brother explains to his superiors that this was the dearest friend he ever had, one that never abandoned him either by day or night. The monk-narrator concludes that "sarebbe piu agevol cosa à separare il concavo dal convesso, che noi dua; si di perfetto amore uniti eravamo" (12ᵛ) [it would be easier to separate the concave from the convex, than to part the two of us, so perfect was the love that bound us]. Following the usual practice of the panegyrist, Lando names celebrated friendships, none of which was apparently comparable in depth and constancy to that of Frate Puccio with his louse. Next, in a passage describing ridiculous feats in mock-serious style, the narrator lists the accomplishments of the tiny animal, which, it is claimed, snuffed out the monk's candles, dusted books, and cleaned the cell. In short, "Era il mio Pidocchio la reputatione del monistero, l'essempio della vera Pacientia, & la norma dell'humiltà, che à frati minori si conviene" (13ʳ) [My louse was the reputation of the monastery, the model of true patience and norm of the humility appropriate to Minorites].

All flocked to see this paragon among lice, which was not ashen in color like the lice of Puglia, or black like those of Fiamenghi, or white like those of the Levant, "ma era d'un schietto & vero bigio" (13ʳ) [but of a true clear grey], similar to that worn by the founders of the monk's order. Its attractive mouth, ivory teeth, refined eating habits, and liking for a diet not of human blood but of sugar, dew, balm, and manna suggest a leader among lice who might have turned the species away from its taste for human blood.

Having related the story of his pet's life, the owner now describes its death, a most disturbing event. Although aware that all things must perish, he was not prepared for his louse to be murdered by a jealous monk. Insults are heaped on the murderer's guilty head: "questo rapacissimo Lupo" [this most greedy wolf] will go to hell for his crime. The sermon concludes with the hope that a star may be dedicated to the louse. The brother's meticulous description of his devotion to an unworthy object becomes a caricature of the real monks' excessive attachment to and respect for trivia, the details of ceremonial piety, petty observances, and so on. Brother Puccio so humanizes his louse that it becomes a small monk to him, clad in the colors of the "ordine minore." Consequently, he perceives a human monk as a murderer. In the *Muscae Encomium*, Lucian achieves a similar change of perspective, but applies it to the reader's process of adjusting to the demands of a given text. Lando places this distortion in a religious context, suggesting that the brother's error is but a comical manifestation of one of the constant traps of cell life, the tendency to magnify small events until they can replace the people and events in the larger world outside the monastery. Puccio's companion is thus appropriately described as the "reputatione del monistero."

The style and tone of the sermon on the louse are typical of the *Sermoni funebri*. Lando consistently conjures up whimsical and burlesque qualities, accomplishments, and adventures for the various pets whose loss the owners bewail. Aware of his literary ancestry, he provides a long apology for his choice of material, mentioning all the familiar classical mock panegyrists and a number of writers on medical topics and plants, but no contemporary predecessors.[50] Again we see how broad and yet how stable was the Renaissance concept of the satirical eulogy.

Before concluding this study of the Italian paradoxes, we may mention a few other relevant prose works. Antonio Francesco Doni, editor of Burchiello, was also the author of *L'Asinesca gloria*.[51] This work contains prints of donkeys and people in various situations, and recalls Lucian's and Apuleius's writings on the donkey. The tone is sometimes playful, as when Doni wishes his dedicatee "perpetua Asinità," but is in general part of what Grendler, in his study of Doni, calls "a genre of moral criticism which compared the strong, humble, patient, peaceable, long-suffering, useful, and even musical ass to sinful, weak, and warlike man."[52] Doni includes more social criticisms than had his Spanish predecessors.

Girolamo Bargagli composed a work similar to Doni's, entitled *Il Valore de gli asini*. In their reevaluation of the relative worth and virtues of men and animals, these two works may be compared to Montaigne's *Apologie de Raymond Sebond*. For similar reasons, Giulio Landi's *Lode dell'Ignoranza*, published in 1551, rejects learning and sees ignorance as a prerequisite to holiness.[53] Another famous work of the period that dealt with the same ideas was Agrippa's *De Incertitudine et vanitate scientiarum*.

Aretino's *Dialogues*

Last but not least among ironic prose works in Italy are Aretino's *Dialogues*, first published in 1534 and 1536.[54] The various conversations reveal the secrets of courtesans, nuns, and midwives from the point of view of the women themselves. Like Gnatho the parasite or Lucian's Simon, the speakers seek to make their ways of life seem more attractive and to minimize any flaws. The tone of the speeches is often sarcastic, but always lively and fast-moving. Antonia, Nanna's friend, decides after listening to Nanna's description of the difficult life of nuns and wives that the mother would be well advised to make her daughter Pippa into a prostitute. The prostitute, unlike the wife or the nun, betrays no vows, merely selling what is hers to sell. Antonia's last words might be borrowed from Tychiades: "From what I have understood of your talk, a whore's vices are really virtues" (158). In part 2 of the work, Nanna teaches Pippa the art of being a prostitute. She must be thrifty and neatly dressed to attract the right kind of customer. Her mother teaches her about makeup and about repairing her hymen to seem intact. Advising against gambling, she urges Pippa to accept lovers of various nationalities. The second day's discussion dwells at length on men's betrayal of women. Whores are particularly badly treated by the opposite sex. On the third day the midwife tells Pippa how to be a procuress, a trade that, like many midwives, she practices in addition to her more socially acceptable trade. Being a procuress or bawd takes more brains than being a whore, she tells the young girl. Cleverly, she ennobles the image of the procuress until the following at first inadmissible comparison becomes at least plausible: "A doctor walks with assurance into all houses, and a bawd who knows what she's about does the same. A doctor knows the complexions, poses, faults, bad humors, and illnesses of this person and that, while the bawd knows the frenzies, whims, private parts, and hidden vices of almost everyone" (310–11). The bawd fares very well in this series of comparisons. The satire of inversion here is complex, as the lowest of females manages to equate herself with a usually respected male superior. Aretino's work shocked many contemporaries, in part because of its scatological content, but in part, surely, because he used the techniques of paradox to investigate the roles of the sexes. It is closely related to the Bernesque mock encomium because of its persistent use of what we have called the circle of madness, in which from inside a given argument the claims made are irrefutable.

With this brief study of the Italian satirical encomia of the Renaissance, the present investigation into the background of the French paradoxical eulogy is complete. The Italian authors broadened the range of the genre considerably, chiefly in the area of style and tone, but also by extending yet further the choice of subject matter and pushing to the limit the Erasmian construction of a world of madness which could be used to distort all other worlds. The liveliness and linguistic skill of the capitoli, the comic exaggerations of the *Sermoni funebri,* and the systematic explorations of the *Paradossi* were all much appreciated in France. In France also, the satiric possibilities of the genre were to be pushed farther than had been customary before: Aretino's and Mauro's tough but flexible use of irony was to be matched by several writers across the Alps.

The Vice Eulogy
in France

Donques, si tu es sage, embrasse la feintise.

DU BELLAY

NONCLASSICAL INFLUENCES

The preceding chapters have described the satirical eulogy as a genre that began in antiquity, was revived in the late fifteenth century, and flourished during the sixteenth century. The Renaissance revival was made easier because of resemblances between the classical genre and certain other types of writing, often in the vernacular. For example, the subject matter of much medieval fool literature is related to that of the *Moriae Encomium*, and Burchiello's satiric poetry has much in common with the paradoxical capitoli perfected by Berni. However, despite these convergences with contemporary forms, the sixteenth-century satirical eulogy remains primarily a humanistic and classically oriented genre, ever conscious of its Greek and Latin predecessors. Indeed, the present study's historical approach was adopted precisely because such an awareness was an integral part of the genre itself. The following brief account of related medieval and early Renaissance literary traditions is intended to lead to a better appreciation of the innovative aspects of the French mock eulogy.[1]

The first of these related traditions, that of Christian paradox, is discussed by H. K. Miller in the following terms:

> The tradition of Christian paradox, exemplified in Tertullian's "certum est, quia impossibile est," and that of the "advocatus diaboli" might well have maintained a concern with paradoxical subjects, and with "making the worse appear the better reason" that would provide some continuity between classic practice and the resurgence of interest in the paradoxical encomium that appears during the Renaissance.[2]

It is true that some mock encomiasts, such as Erasmus and Berni, explore religious paradoxes. But whereas the typical Christian paradox concerns theological and metaphysical doctrine and speculation, the paradoxes discussed in the present study are primarily secular and literary, exploring moral, social, and linguistic problems.

In an article on the bestiary, Grover Cronin reconfirms the importance the Church attached to technical ability in upholding the more difficult and paradoxical Christian tenets. He quotes Robert de Basevorn's *Forma Praedicandi*: "Et Leo papa: Haec est virtus eloquentiae ut nihil sit tam exile quod non extollat, nihil tam incredibile quod non dicendo praeornate probabile fiat, nihil tam horridum vel incultum quod non oratione splendescat" [And Pope Leo states: This is the virtue of eloquence, that nothing is so humble that eloquence cannot exalt it, nothing so unbelievable that it cannot be rendered probable by the ornaments of speech, nothing so horrible or uncivilized that it cannot be made to shine brightly in language].[3]

This power of words to make the incredible believable and the ugly attractive, a power appreciated by Christian preachers, closely resembles that sought by classical orators.[4] Indeed, the acceptance of the truth hidden in a paradox could become a test of faith, as Tertullian had suggested. But for the Church, the methods of rhetoric were to be learned in order to present theological matters persuasively. The preacher usually intended what he said to be believed, no matter how strange it might appear. For the classical orator, on the other hand, rhetorical techniques were more often a means of exploring in new ways certain themes and ideas while entertaining an audience. The mock encomiast tended to believe either the opposite or a considerably modified version of what he actually said. The same oratorical strategies can thus serve very different purposes. In studying the satirical eulogy, the question of the writer's goal can never be ignored.

Another flourishing type of medieval writing with connections to the satirical eulogy is the parody, either of Holy Writ or of religious literature and themes.[5] As was noted above, the classical paradoxical encomium arose in part out of a desire to parody the serious panegyric, the *Muscae Encomium* being a good example of this tendency. Similarly, the *Podagra* made fun of classical tragedy, and many capitoli caricatured Petrarchan poems. Parody frequently shares with the satirical eulogy the technique of applying lofty language and elevated ideas to lowly or unworthy subjects. However, the target of parody is customarily some other genre or form of discourse, with which the reader must be familiar if he is to appreciate the finer points of the mocking imitation. The satirical eulogy, particularly in its sixteenth-century form, could satirize a wider, often nonliterary range of topics and contain elements of several different genres and styles within a single work. Noting these complexities, Miller again urges caution: "Finally, the numerous parodies of religious ritual and themes and the Goliardic songs of the late medieval period offer celebrations of the power of gold, of drinking, and of physical love, which, *if they do not fall within our genre*, must at least have helped to establish an atmosphere in which the paradoxical encomium could flourish" (italics mine).[6] These superficial resemblances between medieval parodies and Renaissance encomia will not be discussed in detail.

As was noted in chapter 4, the Italian revival of the paradoxical encomium, in the capitolo, influenced French encomiasts at least as much as did classical and Neo-Latin works. Since this revival did not take place until the 1520s and 1530s, large-scale production of Italianate mock encomia did not occur in France until the 1540s and 1550s. The influence of the Bernesque writers may help explain the fact that in France many satirical eulogies were by poets intrigued by the Italian verse encomia, rather than by prose writers imitating Erasmus and Lucian. Even the imitations of Lando, whose sermons and paradoxes had been in prose, were frequently in verse.

Another important factor encouraging the use of verse rather than prose in French mock encomia was the existence of the native poetic form known as the *blason*, a genre that had an independent development before the revival of the paradoxical encomium but was to change significantly under the influence of the classical genre and the Italian capitolo. There are several short studies of the blason, and Alison Saunders has recently published a more extended analysis.[7] The clearest and most often quoted definition of the form is that composed by Thomas Sebillet in 1548: "Le Blason est une perpétuéle louenge ou continu vitupére de ce qu'on s'est proposé blasonner. . . . Car autant bien se blasonne le laid comme le beau, et le mauvais comme le bon. . . . De quelconque coin soit-il sorty, le plus bref est le meilleur, mesque il soit agu en conclusion: et est plus dous en ryme platte, et vers de huit syllabes: encores que ceus de dis n'en soient pas regettés comme ineptes."[8] The word *blason* originally meant a coat of arms, then was extended to the description of the coat of arms, and finally applied to the description of other objects.[9] Although the earliest surviving blasons generally praise their chosen topic, the blason could in fact be either laudatory or defamatory. Modern critics have invented various subdivisions for the different types of blason: "blasons symboliques," "hymnes-blasons," "blasons satiriques," and so on. Grappling with the problems of classification, Saulnier discerns two distinct trends in the history of the genre after the appearance of the famous *Blasons anatomiques*. First, he points to what he calls the "discours didactique monographique, du genre du *Discours du lacis* ou de la *Bellete* de François de Clary, Albigeois." One form of this type of blason is the hymne-blason. The second broad tendency introduces symbolism and satire into the descriptive blason médaillon. Thus "le *Blason du Bonnet carré* est une charge contre gens d'église et gens de loi," and "le

Blason des Basquines et Vertugalles, les *Blasons du Gobellet* et du *Platellet,* manifestent la même déformation du genre; c'est le médaillon satirique et symbolique.''[10]

In focusing on the descriptive and didactic aspects of the blason, Saulnier's analysis does not do justice to the playful, joking quality of the hymnes-blasons. This neglect is probably due to a failure to appreciate the role of Lucian and of the Italian capitoli in the mid-century flowering of the French genre. Some capitoli were entitled *blasons* when translated or imitated in France, probably because, like the capitolo, the blason tended to be relatively short, monographic, plotless, and rich in a variety of arguments supporting its central thesis. Up to the 1530s, the period of the *Blasons anatomiques,* the writers' opinions were expressed directly rather than indirectly. If a poet approved of his subject, his verses were laudatory; if not, he attacked directly. However, since certain parts and functions of the body were unlikely subjects for praise,—the "cul," the "pet," and the "vesse," for example—"blasonneurs" began after 1543 to use the title *contre-blason,* indicating that the poem was vituperative, not eulogistic. A prolific composer of contre-blasons, Charles de la Huetterie systematically condemned parts of the body praised by Marot and others.[11] By 1547, however, a group of anonymous blasons published in Lyons was clearly ironic, mockingly eulogizing gout and the quartan fever, and attacking honor.[12] Trtnik-Rossettini has demonstrated that the blason against honor is at times a direct translation of Mauro's "Capitolo dell'Onore" and that the origins of the other two poems are Lucianic and Bernesque.[13] From midcentury on, blasons appear that belong to all three categories of eulogy described above in connection with classical and Renaissance paradoxical encomia. In a sense, the poetic genre has been subsumed by the broader category of the satirical eulogy. This shift in the blason demonstrates once again that only by appreciating the complex, often overlapping sources of French mock encomia can we even correctly identify them, much less assess their originality.

Following the order adopted earlier, and considering first the vice eulogies and works of ironic advice, we find in France a varied and extremely individual set of writings. A few were modeled on the *Moriae Encomium* and related works, but many more were influenced by the *De Parasito* and the *Rhetorum Praeceptor.* I shall discuss first those works modeled primarily on the two Lucianic pieces; secondly, those whose themes link them most closely to Erasmus and Brant; thirdly, Rabelais's contribution to the satirical encomium; and, finally, French works influenced predominantly by Italian paradoxical writings. Although these groups are related to one another, the dominant pattern of influence is usually clear and is often acknowledged by the author in question. I will conclude with a discussion of the speeches of Bruscambille, the early seventeenth-century *harangueur.*

Chapter Five

FRENCH IMITATIONS OF LUCIANIC VICE EULOGIES

As Mayer and P. M. Smith have convincingly demonstrated, Lucian's *Rhetorum Praeceptor* and *De Parasito*, mock glorifications of ways of life far from admirable, contributed significantly to the earliest French vice eulogies.[14] Since most of the French works concern some aspect of life at court, Lucian's *De Mercede conductis potentium familiaribus*, satirizing those seeking positions in great houses, was also much referred to and imitated. In addition, the 1540s and 1550s saw the beginning of hostile French reaction to certain of the ideas in Castiglione's *Cortegiano*. Although this portrait of the ideal court lady and gentleman was composed at the request of François I, the royal sponsorship did not prevent increasing numbers of Frenchmen from being profoundly suspicious of the ideas contained in the work.[15] Most of the satires to be discussed in the present section of this chapter use Lucianic irony and indirection to attack either traditional court problems or, more frequently, those caused or thought to be caused by the introduction of Castiglione's teachings. The relation of many of these works to French anticourtier satire in general has been described by P. M. Smith; I shall therefore focus on their place in the history of the mock eulogy as a genre. I will attempt to demonstrate that an awareness of the works' generic history enriches our understanding of the often complex ways in which they functioned.

In a sense, the sixteenth-century court was coming to be perceived as what might be called the home of the satirical eulogy, the breeding ground for that type of verbal disguise known in its negative (usually social) form as flattery or hypocrisy and in its positive (often literary) form as *ironia*. Eustache Deschamps had early provided mock advice on how to succeed at court, noting the need to drink, swear, and deny truth and virtue. Martin le Franc also described decadent courtiers with some irony (P. M. Smith, 52). In 1466, Pierre Michault, in what P. M. Smith calls a "rare" and "unsubtle" use of irony, composed a satirical *Doctrinal du Temps Present*, in which Lady Virtue complained of being neglected by courtiers, who follow instead a new doctrine in which Faulceté, Vantance, and other vices are the teachers (P. M. Smith, 46). The road to success here is taught by grammatical cases, parodying the *Doctrinale puerorum* of Alexandre de Villedieu. Thus, the nominative relates to names and titles, the vocative to forms of address, the accusative to the courtier's constant attacks on his rivals, the genitive to his parents and lineage. The dative is interpreted in a passive sense, as what he expects to be given, while the ablative, predictably, refers to what he can try to take away from others. If challenged about such conduct, the courtier must use the passe-partout excuse, "C'est usance de court." In the introduction to his edition of Michault, Thomas Walton points out that the writer is portraying the courtier of the day "tel qu'il le voyait," only indirectly suggesting a more admirable alternative.[16]

In the anonymous *Dialogue de Placebo pour un homme seul*, a flatterer similar to Terence's Gnatho praises his own skills.[17] The *Farce nouvelle de folle Bobance* contains passages of ironic advice on how to be a follower of luxury, i.e., a courtier.[18] These early satires are not full-fledged mock encomia sustaining an ironic posture throughout, but by 1542, with the publication of Bertrand de la Borderie's "L'Amye de Court," such works began to appear. Sometimes part of the so-called "querelle des Amyes," in which writers argued for and against women, they were also much affected by current discussions of the *Cortegiano*. Indeed, several of the French encomia to be discussed in the present chapter make clear reference to Castiglione's ideal courtiers and ladies. But instead of the direct vituperation or fairly obvious sarcasm of earlier works, the later writers produce a complex and subtle series of attacks that are most fully understood only by reference to their generic antecedents.

In La Borderie's poem, a female speaker seeks to explain and justify what proves to be the selfish and manipulative way of life of a sixteenth-century Simon.[19] The work first appeared in Paris, the Privilège being dated March 9, 1541. No liminary pieces or epistles to the reader precede the decasyllabic verses, which are presented as being spoken by the Amye de Court. Like Simon, the lady is determined to vindicate her way of life and attack those who question her philosophy. Her first targets are Petrarchan lovers, those who babble of Cupid's bow and arrows: "Je croy le tout n'estre que poësie, / Ou pour mieux dire humaine frenaisie," what she goes on to call a "folie ou infelicité" (112). La Borderie's portrait of his court lady apparently deceived some contemporaries into thinking he was seriously advocating her attitudes and views, and it is true that certain statements, if taken out of context, seem very convincing. However, the brief passages that show the Amye in a more favorable light are rapidly invalidated by the surrounding lines revealing her cynicism and greed. Just as Panurge parades both erudition and seeming idealism in justifying what proves to be a selfish and extravagant way of life, so the Amye wishes to turn to profitable material use the fine aspirations of love that she expresses with such confidence. Thus, when she claims that her heart is locked up in a tower called "Fermeté," guarded by "Honneur," "Crainte," and "Innocence" (116), and vows that no man shall win her "place" because "De Dieu la tiens, à Dieu seul la veux rendre" (118), or that "la vertu me conduit pas à pas" (126), she would seem to be less an adventuress than a potential resident of Christine de Pisan's Cité des Dames. But the reader soon realizes that this much-vaunted virtue is adopted for purposes of material gain, not moral improvement. Each flutter of the eyelashes is calculated:

Je mettois peine à porter proprement
Mes blondz cheveux & mon accoustrement.
A posément conduire mes yeux verdz,
Pleins de doulceur, ne peu ne trop ouvers.

(114)

The fight for success is portrayed in military terms, as a battle with the opposite sex. Words such as "guerre," "tour," "assault," "artillerie," "batterie," and "ennemys" punctuate the text at regular intervals. The woman's strategy is to lead men on, then refuse to give herself. In this way she has a greater choice of victims and can enjoy herself far more:

Je retien tout, & personne ne chasse,
Fondant ma gloire & louenge estimee
Sans aymer nul, estre de tous aymee,
Qui est le poinct de mon enseignement.

(115)

Depuis le temps (Dames) que je me hante,
Je me congnoy, de moy je me contente,
Je me sens forte, instruite & bien apprise,
Pour prendre autruy, & n'estre jamais prise.

(121)

Not only does having a large number of suitors amuse and flatter her, but the devoted gentlemen serve a more practical purpose:

J'ay sceu gaigner un grand Seigneur, ou deux,
Pour avoir tout ce dont j'ay besoing d'eux,
Accoustremens, anneaux, chaines, doreures,
Nouveaux habitz & nouvelles pareures.

(122)

As she boasts of her skills, the Amye gradually reveals her tricks and psychological ploys. Simon, the classical parasite, exploited the conventions of hospitality and friendship: the Renaissance lady manipulates the game of love and courtship. Her chief ally in this fight is lady "Dissimulation," who warns of the enemy's tricks. La Borderie provides further clues to interpretation as he uses ironically the words "honneur" and "honneste." Thus, the lady calls "honnestes ornemens" (124) gifts presented in return for promises she never intends to fulfil. Since gifts benefit both the giver and the receiver, she explains that "la vertu, s'ilz la sçavent comprendre, / N'est offensee à donner ny à prendre" (125), a statement masking the fact that this is a one-way arrangement, in which the man gives and the woman receives. She remarks scornfully that the idea that one should not accept presents without giving in return must have been invented by "quelque sotte amoureuse imparfaicte," since jewels can always be returned, but virginity cannot be restored. Rejecting absolutely this "Loy" that "en prenant d'eux, je leur doyve donner" (124), she is determined to enjoy herself with a number of suitors, often with young pages at court, waiting, like a "Lyonne saige" or an "Esprevier rusé," until the choicest victims succumb.

Occasionally, she admits, she has permitted a "survenant" to touch her thigh or breast "mauglré moy" (132), but such activities went no further, and her admirer at court respected her self-control. These dangerous games, however, are not recommended for weaker women. Aware that her beauty and this "plaisant exercice" (138) will not last, she seeks to marry, hoping to find a husband she can love, but prepared to marry a boor if he has the necessary cash. Money can hide all imperfections for the Amye, only poverty being in her eyes a "mal incurable":

> Quant à mary je resoulz donc ce poinct
> De l'avoir riche, ou de n'en avoir point,
> Bien qu'il soit crud, & que ses moeurs perverses
> Du tout je sente estre aux miennes diverses.
>
> (141)

She would try to "domestiquer" her crude man, but if this effort failed, little could be done. Earlier, she had criticized jealous husbands, "gros Veaux de nature brutale" who try to keep their wives away from the court, home of "parfaicte science" (130). In such lines, La Borderie undercuts the elevated neo-Platonic notions of love, often borrowed from the *Cortegiano*, with which his lady baits her hook.[20] And yet the poem unexpectedly ends with a lyrical passage describing the Amye's longing to find true love and fear of the consequences if she fails. This section of the work has been little attended to by critics because it is so different in tone from the remainder of the poem. In the context of the mock encomium, however, the return to a more "normal" point of view is easier to accept. The poignancy of these lines recalls Synesius's obsession with hair or the Emperor Julian's with the conventions of politeness. The Amye's relentlessly calculating actions turn out to be directed to the most sentimental of goals. Unaware of her public spectacle, she does not see what the reader sees, that her cynical wall of protective vanity and suspicion may well be cutting her off from what she most seeks, a happy and romantic marriage.

By means of this cleverly developed paradox, La Borderie shows what can become of the Italian ideals if they are exploited by unscrupulous or selfish individuals. It is worth recalling here that the famous Spanish attack on the *Cortegiano*, Antonio de Guevara's *Menosprecio de Corte*, appeared in French translation in 1542, the same year as the first edition of "L'Amie de Court."[21] But Guevara was interested in the *beatus ille* theme, lauding the beauties of country life and criticizing directly the weaknesses of the court.

La Borderie's way of exploring court abuses was closely linked to his choice of genre. The fluidity and ambiguity of the mock encomium were perfectly adapted to the moral slipperiness of his female character. At every step, the reader has to change perspective, distancing himself from the Amye in order to consider her overall goals and dramatic spectacle. Only thus can he avoid being duped by her clever parroting but underlying exploitation of the ideals of Castiglione. La Borderie's brilliance lies in suggesting, by way of his conclusion, that the Amye is unlikely ever to realize her goal of a happy marriage, since she has come to prefer the narcissistic pleasure of having many suitors to that of improving a true lover by her good influence. In fact, she represents not Castiglione's ideal lady, but one of the types of women he criticizes when Lord Casper launches a vehement attack on those of the fair sex,

> which . . . procure as muche as they can to gete them a great numbre of lovers, and (if it were possible) they would have them al to burne and make asshes, and after death to retourn to lief, to die again . . . . to kepe them still in afflictions and in desire, they use a certein lofty sowernesse of threatninges mingled with hope, and wold have them to esteame a woorde, a countenance or a beck of theirs for a cheef blisse.[22]

By pretending to doubt their admirers' sincerity, such women manage to avoid giving themselves to anyone, their pleasure lying in achieving power and mastery over another. As the Amye puts it, "ne sçauroie plus grand heur demander, / Qu'estre obeie & tousjours commander" (136). Lord Casper's direct attack, which served as a warning parenthesis in the larger context of Castiglione's work, has in the French work become a full-length ironic self-praise in the Lucianic mode.[23]

Among those failing to perceive the irony of La Borderie's poem was Charles Fontaine, who felt obliged to compose "La Contr'Amye de Court," in which a female narrator attacks La Borderie's heroine and defends all unselfish and devoted women.[24] Fontaine cites in full many lines from the poem, pouring particular scorn on the Amye's greed, vanity, and deceitfulness. Interestingly, in the light of La Borderie's conclusion, Fontaine ends with the prayer that the lady may fall in love "sans qu'elle soit aymee."[24] Such a fate has both psychological plausibility and poetic justice, since the lady's self-centeredness could easily prevent her from recognizing or perhaps even attract her to a more cunning deceiver than herself. The defenses of women by Fontaine and others were published together in 1547. The risk of misinterpretation has been shown to be a constant feature of ironic works and to have served as useful protection for cautious writers such as Erasmus.[25] In the case of "L'Amye de Court," the lady perverts the courtly virtue of *dissimulatio*, the tactful self-deprecation Castiglione advised the courtier to practice when in the presence of people less fortunate than he.

Those listening to the Amye may perceive only the surface modesty, un-aware that what is hidden is worse, not better than what is revealed. The overcredulous reader, like Charles Fontaine, risks falling into a similar trap.

The ironic manner of presenting attacks on hypocritical courtiers was widely popular in France, probably because it permitted writers to combine most effectively the matter and manner of their critiques. Insincere flattery, hypocrisy, and the covert pursuit of personal ambition were readily mirrored in the extravagantly eulogistic tones of the mock encomium. In addition, the genre's regular call upon the reader to switch perspectives and consider ultimate purpose in the characters it portrayed made possible some fine explorations of the problems of court life.

A Lucianic court satire that has attracted attention in recent years is Philibert de Vienne's *Le Philosophe de Court*, a 110–page prose work first published in Lyons and presented as a philosophical treatise. Little is known about the author, who was an "advocat en la Court de Parlement à Paris" and must have spent some time in Lyons, where he met Scève and other writers. According to the work's introductory prologue, the *Philosophe de Court* was the outcome of conversations held in Lyons during the winter of 1546–1547. Philibert de Vienne, who often styled himself "L'Amoureux de Vertu," dedicated his prologue to "l'Amye de Vertu." There exists unfortunately no modern edition of the satire, but it is discussed at some length by Mayer, P. M. Smith, and Daniel Javitch.[26] I shall therefore focus on the work's place in the history of the paradoxical encomium.

Sixteenth-century writers, as was noted above, were swift to see how readily classical satire on parasites could be adapted to apply to Renaissance courtiers.[27] Such modernizations, however, were not always presented in the ironic manner employed by Lucian and by Philibert de Vienne. The latter begins his treatise by promising to explain the new *summum bonum*, success at court. In the remainder of the work, as Alfred Cartier puts it, "sous une forme ironique et parfois assez piquante, l'auteur fait l'éloge des qualités, c'est-à-dire des vices indispensables pour réussir à la cour."[28] The encomium is preceded by a revealing liminary sonnet by none other than Maurice Scève, entitled "M. SC. Au Lecteur," which reads as follows:

> Si la Morale est des trois la premiere
> Pour haultement l'Esprit instituer:
> Ne devra donc l'homme constituer
> Son but en elle, & l'avoir pour lumiere?
> Veu que la vie à errer coustumiere
> Ne pourroit trop en moeurs s'esvertuer
> Pour à tout bien ses faitz perpetuer,
> Sans lequel elle est vapeur, ou fumiere.
> Et pour bien vivre, & tresheureusement,

Seroit assez de bien sçavoir sa Court,
Fust au Lettré, Marchant, ou Artisan:
Mais entre tous celuy est seurement
Vray Philosophe, & tresbon Courtisan,
Qui se compose au fil du temps, qui court.

(2)

In the last three lines of this sonnet Saulnier sees evidence of Scève's "dés-enchantement, calme d'ailleurs, sans amertume," while Enzo Giudici judges the prevailing melancholy of the piece to be one of its chief virtues.[29] Although, as Giudici demonstrates, Scève's liminary sonnets do not always sum up the argument of the work for which they were written, his sonnet for Philibert de Vienne contains themes strikingly similar to those found in the work itself. It seems likely, therefore, that Scève was fully aware of the nature of Philibert's treatise, either because he had been present at some of the discussions that inspired it (if we are to believe the prologue as to its origins) or because he recognized the ironic tone of the completed work. His last lines can thus be read as mere bourgeois common sense or as a moment of melancholy sarcasm. Philibert constantly suggests that the courtier should adapt himself to all circumstances, following everything the court finds acceptable and desirable. Similarly, the sonnet asserts that the best philosopher at court is one who "se compose," shapes and fashions his actions and beliefs according to his milieu. The rhyme of "court" and "Court," however, recalls the transitoriness of such stances.[30] The "Courtisan," another rhyme suggests, may come to resemble an "Artisan," tailoring his mental cloth according to the fashionable styles of the day. Wisdom and philosophy become mere crafts and skills, of no more than temporary and utilitarian value, not the selfless pursuit of eternal verities. The paradox suggested by the poem, as by the work, is that at court inconstancy is the highest form of fidelity.

After the prologue, the *Philosophe de Court* offers an introduction proving that "fashion in general and courtly fashion in particular is our true philosophy, since by philosophy we mean a way of life, and not abstract speculation."[31] The first chapter of the work seeks to prove that the new philosophy is none other than the fashion of the court: "Ceste Philosophie morale & nouvelle peult estre ainsi definie, la congnoissance de vivre à la mode de Court" (27). Being a philosophy, its chief concern must be the definition of virtue, a task the author now undertakes:

Vertu est, un vivre à la mode de Court: & est differente de celles des anciens en cela, que leur vertu (comme j'ay dit cy devant) est vivre selon Nature: la nostre est, vivre selon la Court: & tout ainsi que anciennement ilz disoient, que si nous suyvions Nature, et ne feissions autre chose sinon que nostre raison naturelle nous monstre, nous ne

ferions jamais mal: aussi tant que nous suyvrons la maniere de faire de
Court, nous ferons tousjours bien. Car qui seroit le fol qui voudroit
dire une chose mal faite, qu'auroit faite un gentilhomme de Court bien
apris? Appellons nous pas bestes, et Pithaux ceux qui ignorent ou ne
trouvent pas bon une vertu Courtisanne? (31–32)[32]

The cutting sarcasm of the last sentence, conveying the courtier's scornful
rejection of the fools who believe that virtue can exist anywhere but at the
court indirectly calls attention to the limitations of his views. The sudden
"nous," uniting the reader with the arrogant courtier, in fact underlines the
need to remain detached from the proud "philosophe de court." Understanding of the entire work will depend on sensitivity to this initial and
regularly repeated distancing procedure, for if we once accept that the
"nous" includes ourselves, we are forced to agree with the remainder of
Philibert's conclusions. The need for cautious reading is as great here as in
"L'Amye de Court."

The involvement of the reader in the writer's stance becomes yet more
evident when Philibert explains how easy it is to become skilled in this new
art, once a few minor qualms have been laid aside: "Si tost que ces petites
estincelles de vertu sont ainsi esteintes, & que nous nous abandonnons à
suyvre la mode de Court, nous devenons incontinent grans maistres, tant
somes (sic) dociles à apprendre le mal (comme dit le bon Juvenal).—Quoni-
am dociles imitandis / Turpibus ac pravis omnes sumus" (26). A small ad-
justment to or compromise with accepted standards of good and evil can
eventually warp our entire judgment and discernment.

After discussing Virtue, the author considers Prudence, or Wisdom, essential to the perfect courtier, and lists such fashionable requirements as
fencing, singing, and dancing. Wisdom will determine how much should be
sought in each area, the courtier needing neither too much nor too little
skill in any domain: "Et pource que vertu est la mediocrité entre deux vices,
quand on congnoistra les deux extremitez, facilement on trouvera le my-
lieu, qui est vertu" (42).[33] What is needed in the courtier, says the author
with evident disdain, is "la science de quelques lieux communs des artz libe-
raux meslez & fricassez ensemble, dont on puisse s'ayder en tous propos,
& à fin d'avoir matiere pour rencontrer, & deviser de toutes choses, & non
plus" (41). The two dangerous extremes of knowledge, to be avoided at all
costs, are "Temerité" and "Curiosité."[34] At this point in his narrative, Philibert de Vienne criticizes various characters other than courtiers. These
sketches, which resemble those composed by Erasmus and other praisers of
folly, satirize astrologers, alchemists, and magicians, among others. The
"curieux," those who delve too deeply into an area of learning, form the
first group, and are presented as court killjoys, similar to Lucian's dull philosophers and Erasmus's feasting bores (*Moriae Encomium*, 39):

Nous appellerons en nostre Philosophie Courtisanne le Curieux, celuy qui se rompt la teste es artz, & sciences, qui ne servent de rien à l'instruction de nostre vie, selon vertu, c'est adire, selon la mode de Court. . . . On en peult voir beaucoup de telz au jourdhuy, comme ceux qui marchent encor par les passees des anciens sages, & veulent attaindre ceste vertu vraye, & parfaite, comme ilz l'appellent, qui est si hault logee, & en un lieu tant difficile. Vous les verriez à la Court plus mornes, plus tristes, plus melancholiques, ilz ne mengent que à leurs heures, ilz ne parlent sinon quand il leur plait, ilz ne riroient pas pour le Pape, ilz ne veulent estre subjetz à Prince ne seigneur tant grand soit il, ilz trouvent mauvais tout ce que les autres font, brief ilz ne plaisent à personne. (46–47)

The "curieux," continues the author, are not appreciated by others as were those famous and more jovial members of society, Menippus and Rabelais's Frère Jean des Entommeures.[35] Indeed, a new Diogenes would probably be set upon by the court pages. Whereas Lucian and Erasmus had stressed philosophers' social ineptness and lack of jollity, Philibert mocks their moral rigidity—"ilz ne veulent estre subjetz à Prince ne seigneur tant grand soit il." These remarks render the portrait of the "curieux" more ambivalent and disquieting than Lucian's caricature of bearded and quarrelsome philosophers. The reader is being brought to view as boring fools men who prize liberty and knowledge and cling to ideals despite pressure from society.

Propounding a philosophy of gentlemanly moderation, Philibert next considers legal and moral justice. Moral justice, basic right and wrong, is the ideal goal, but has long since abandoned this earth, leaving behind but a poor compromise, legal justice, either commutative or distributive. Showing professional knowledge in his familiarity with Aristotle, the author asserts that justice in the courtier consists merely of the outward appearance: "Il suffit envers nous, que la mine soit bonne soubs laquelle celuy qui le plus subtilement trompe son compaignon est le plus sage" (97), as he puts it later in the work. Justice here, of the external, legal kind, is thus quite different from inner moral rectitude, the goal of ancient philosophers. Commutative justice concerns contracts, titles, and obligations. For the new court philosopher, justice consists most fundamentally in not being proved guilty. So long as the judge cannot convict you, any crime is permissible: "Lhomme seroit il pas bien de son païs, cestadire, nyais, simple & beste, qui ayant locasion de tromper honnestement son compagnon, ne le trompe pas? cela ne sentiroit pas son Philosophe, ne sa Court" (55). The use of *ironia* here, already noted in the "L'Amye de Court" in connection with the same concept, that of honesty, becomes even more overt in the next sentence: "Generalement, & cest un grand poinct de ceste vertu, il est permis, tromper, brouiller, chiquaner, faire du pis que on peult, moyennant que le Juge ny puisse mordre" (55). In this philosophy, crimes committed with arms are more excusable than those committed without, since the former usually occur in duels defending the courtier's honor or can at least be disguised beneath "semblable couverture" (56). Stretching to the limit the notion of commutative justice, Philibert formulates an elaborate defense of the court-ier's obligation to fight for this extremely suspect and violent form of honor:

> Et ne peult on si peu blesser l'honneur d'un gentilhomme ou autre Courtisan, quil n'y gise un combat (il se entend en deffault de preuve) tellement que pour un desmentir il est permis, & peult on justement tuer un homme: car vanité & menterie est la plus grand playe que lon sçauroit point faire à nostre honneur. En quoy lon peult voir quel es-time nous faisons de l'honneur: veu que cela nous est permis pour le defendre, que les anciens & les loix mesmes ont permis pour defendre la vie. Et non sans cause: car l'honneur & la reputation sont la fin de nostre vertu, sans lesquelz, nostre vertu ne seroit rien. (57)

Indifferent to other offenses, the court philosopher seeks redress only for crimes endangering his reputation. The impeccable logic of these proposi-tions recalls Scève's sonnet, where the premise was formulated that only the surface composition, not the inner person, counted at court. In such circumstances, an affront to or breach of the honorable surface would indeed be tantamount to physical murder in a normal context and should, logically, receive similar punishment. Trtnik-Rossettini remarks that in general the French were wary of satirizing duels, perhaps because the "point d'hon-neur" was so recognizable a mark of the gentleman that criticisms risked provoking dangerous reactions. Philibert's strong condemnation is there-fore yet more noteworthy. At one stage he writes that all else, even family and religion, must be subservient to honor, "car lhomme n'est magnanime, qui prefere telles petites choses à ces grandes richesses dhonneur" (83).[36] The new philosopher begins to sound like a caricature of Christ's disciples, also summoned to leave family for a higher ideal.

The second type of justice, the distributive, concerns the distribution of worldly goods and honors, the "recompense de vertu" (60). Generosity is here of great importance, since it is by being generous that one acquires a good reputation at court. But, like Lucian's *rhetor*, one must pick with care the objects of such generosity, bearing in mind their possible usefulness in building one's reputation. Unpublicized or overgenerous acts of kindness are a dangerous waste of time, since to be poor and virtuous is by no means as desirable as some may claim. The remaining sections of the *Philosophe de Court* deal with prodigality versus "Taquinerie" or stinginess, and with magnanimity, temperance, and "Bonne Grace," terms borrowed from the *Cortegiano* and applied ironically or in a distorted form to the new philosopher.[37] Gradually, the French writer brings out the potential weaknesses of the Italian philosophy, portraying its generous ideals as utilitarian, self-serving, and dilettantish. A striking example of such distortion is the down-to-earth demonstration of the practical advantages of "Bonne Grace": "Vous voyez de noz gentilz hommes avoir plus d'honneur avec les marchans, & les contenter mieux de paroles: que les autres incivilz & rustiques en leur baillant argent" (95). On occasion, words, the currency of the fickle court, may delude even those whose livelihood depends on their ability to distinguish between promises and performance.

Although certain passages in the book, as in the *Moriae Encomium*, are direct attacks, the basic framework remains that of the vice eulogy. Pretending to explain and defend an important new philosophy, Philibert de Vienne furnishes ample indication of a contrary, more "normal" attitude to the views presented. Indeed, from the start, in his prologue, he warns his reader to look beyond the text's superficial meaning:

Donques congnoissant vostre tant bonne affection, & à fin de vous mettre hors de ceste prison, & tenebres miserables d'ignorance, je vous ay escrit ce petit livret, assez rude et impolit toutesfois, comme d'un homme allant par païs: par lequel vous verrez en brief ce qui m'ha tousjours semblé de la Philosophie, en laquelle posoient les anciens le Bien souverain: puis comme en ce temps elle est desguisee, & fondee sur les opinions des hommes, non sur Nature: apres cela vous trouverez assez amplement (& non pas tant encore que jeusse bien voulu) ce que je sens de ceste nouvelle Philosophie, qui est la mode de vivre de ce temps: en escrivant laquelle je n'ay peu que je n'aye fait le Democrite, & usé de faceties. (11–12)

In the sixteenth century, as was noted earlier, Democritus was automatically associated with a joking type of satire, and the term "faceties" in this paragraph, together with the parenthetical aside, all suggest an ironic presentation.[38] On occasion the irony is that of simple inversion, as when adverbs such as "justement" and "honnestement" qualify verbs such as "tuer" and "tromper." Elsewhere the irony extends to an entire passage, as in the section on the new philosopher's way of keeping promises:

Encores diray je ce mot avant que passer oultre, que la loyauté nest point tant requise en nostre Justice envers nos semblables ou inferieurs, comme en celle des anciens, qui en font son fondement: car il suffit tenir sa parole en tant que le Juge nous y peult contraindre: hors le danger de procès, ce nest que braverie de bien promettre: tellement que on dit en communs proverbes, Promesse de gentilhomme, Eaubeniste de Court. (57–58)

In this manner, the *Philosophe de Court* skillfully combines elements of the *Rhetorum Praeceptor* and the *De Parasito*. The narrator is sometimes at one with the "philosophe," using the inclusive "nous" to implicate the reader in his views, and sometimes more detached, employing the pronoun "on." Occasionally the mask of approval drops completely, permitting more overt criticism, as in the attack on things Italian that ends with the words, devastating in the context: "Brief ilz naissent au païs Courtisans" (108). A comparable shift from positive to negative presentation occurs in Lucian's *Rhetorum Praeceptor*, when a single narrative voice is responsible for articulating two opposing points of view. The themes of the French work, however, are closer to those of the *De Parasito*, the courtier's accommodations and compromises with truth being similar to Simon's social machinations. Philibert de Vienne's innovation is that he is presenting what he calls a philosophy, not an art. What for Simon is a readily teachable set of practical skills, easily learned and applied once certain foolish prejudices are destroyed by his arguments, becomes in the French work a new form of morality, as Scève was the first to point out in his introductory sonnet. The Renaissance courtier was not always totally dependent on a patron for food and lodging, as was the classical parasite, although the French court was rapidly becoming the chief source of favors and benefices. But the courtier's undoubted psychological subservience was ultimately more dangerous. If the corruptible, ever-changing world of the court is accepted as some sort of stable absolute, source of an eternal *summum bonum* as admirable as that of the most ancient of philosophical creeds, the courtier's narrowness of vision and arrogance become natural and comprehensible. Philibert de Vienne composed much more than an ironic *ars*. Like Machiavelli in the same century, he provided a new insight into the all-encompassing, self-serving doctrines that made possible the smooth functioning of Renaissance court life. As Daniel Javitch puts it, "Philibert's anticourtliness was so radical for his time that he needed to be unusually equivocal."[39] For him, as for Erasmus, the shifting perspectives that were characteristic of the satirical encomium made it a natural choice of genre. Moreover, for Philibert, the very nature of his chosen genre became part of his theme. The link in the courtier between external mannerisms and mores and the psychological implications of such postures parallels the link in the mock encomium between the playful, rhetorical posture of the author and his often serious underlying purpose. The difference lies in the fact that the courtier is unaware of this relationship between external form and inner goal, and thus becomes an artisan, not a philosopher, whereas the writer and the reader must remain alert to the need to relate means and ends, joking exterior and inner moral purpose.

The next important French vice eulogy, Du Bellay's "Poëte Courtisan," is a companion-piece to his translation of Turnèbe's *De nova captandae uti-*

litatis e literis ratione epistola of 1559.[40] Clearly influenced by the *Rhetorum Praeceptor*, the Latin work also imitates elements of the *De Parasito* and of the satirical eulogy in general. The poem is thought by many critics to be directed at Pierre de Paschal, contemporary of the Pléiade poets, who promised but never delivered a work eulogizing his most important contemporaries.[41] Other critics believe the target to be Sainct-Gelays. Turnèbe begins by suggesting that the would-be writer choose Apollo and Mercury as guides. As the poem progresses, the god of poetry is gradually forgotten in favor of the wily Mercury, and by the end of the work the reader is urged only to "auspice Mercurio." In a sense, the entire poem can be seen as an explanation of this shift. The recommendations are extremely concrete. Instead of concentrating on learning, the aspiring court writer should aim to deceive and push himself forward. To do this, he needs to go to Italy and become as Italianate as possible. Turnèbe in 1559, like Philibert de Vienne in 1547, already manifests much of Henri Estienne's anti-Italianism.[42] Praising other scholars only in order to be praised himself, the student must gain the protection of the ladies, especially of those with pretensions to learning. He must write a few small trifles, but on no account ever publish his work. By restricting himself to criticizing others, he may pass for a connoisseur in literary matters. Publication, if and when risked, must be anonymous: only if the work is a success should the poet admit to authorship. It is best to talk a great deal about future works but never to let them be seen. Turnèbe's poet, like Lucian's newfangled orator, is totally preoccupied with his external social spectacle, wishing to appear to others as an artistic, intelligent, and productive writer: in the undiscriminating court world, Turnèbe implies, one can be as successful playing the role of a good writer as by actually studying and working. As in Lucian, the new court poet does not question the intrinsic worth of the old ideal of the writer; rather than devoting his creative skills to producing a work of literature, he diverts his energies into manufacturing a socially respectable persona.[43]

The mock encomium's tendency to self-reflection is much in evidence in this work, since it is a poem about how to become a poet. However, since the narrator of the poem is clearly not following his own advice about never publishing and avoiding study and hard work, the reader is immediately made aware that this is an ironic presentation. There is a further ambiguity in Turnèbe's conclusion, since only history can ultimately decide whether the criticism is itself a fine work of literature independent of any personal and local quarrels or yet another example of court infighting.

Under the penname of I. Quintil du Tronssay, Du Bellay translated Turnèbe's satire as the "Nouvelle maniere de faire son profit des lettres," which he published with the "Poëte Courtisan" in 1559. Admiring Turnèbe, probably approving of his attack both on Italianism and on bad court poets, he first translated, then, in an independent poem, expanded his predecessor's ideas. The translation remains reasonably close to the original, only moderating mention of certain churchmen. But in the "Poëte Courtisan," many of the additions to Turnèbe are derived directly from Lucian, reinforcing the Lucianic tone of the resulting poem. The first piece of advice the narrator offers his would-be poet is not to work too hard. We recognize Lucian's picture of the old-fashioned type of public speaker for whom "hard work, scant sleep, abstention from wine, and untidiness are necessary and indispensable" (4:147). Du Bellay writes:

> Je ne veulx que long temps à l'estude il pallisse,
> Je ne veulx que resveur sur le livre il vieillisse,
> Fueilletant studieux tous les soirs & matins
> Les exemplaires Grecs & les autheurs Latins.
>
> (6:131)

Given the long years members of the Pléiade devoted to studying the classics, such lines, an inversion of the Horatian maxim repeated in the *Deffence*, must have struck Du Bellay's friends as especially comical. Both Du Bellay and Lucian profess to feel that ignorance is an asset, an impressive physical appearance being far more important than the quality of the speeches and works produced. Chamard points out that Du Bellay's ironic portrait of the "catareux, maladif & debile" serious scholar resembles that drawn of himself by Ronsard (131). The self-inclusive thrust is plain here, just as when Lucian in the *Rhetorum Praeceptor* inverts the sensible advice given to him by Paedeia. "Soit la seule court ton Virgile & Homere" (133), declares Du Bellay's narrator, echoing Lucian's "As for reading the classics, don't you do it" (4:157). Both are suggesting that in the demotic world of popular oratory or court success, there is no need to strive for more than the surface appearance of the literary training traditionally expected in both poet and speaker. In Du Bellay's case, this rejection represents a rejection of beliefs fundamental to the humanists, for whom history and the study of earlier authors was crucial.

The court poet of Du Bellay and Turnèbe, like Philibert's philosopher, is far subtler in dealing with enemies than Lucian's speaker, encouraged to slander and mock rivals, even to accuse them of plagiarism. Du Bellay's poet must never forget that he is first and foremost a courtier, and that any newcomer to the court will be either a fool or a wise man. If the new arrival is a fool, the poet must seek his company, for he himself will appear brilliant beside the weak rival. If, on the other hand, he proves to be a wise man, the poet must befriend him, control his every move, and praise and patronize him, so that any honors the other gains will seem to be due to the friendship of his self-appointed guide. What is ironically underscored here is the fact that if all court life is a series of postures, the genuine article may be indistinguishable from the fake. Only over a period of time will the falseness of the pretender become apparent, as he fails to produce anything of value. With an awareness of the double perspective required of readers of satirical encomia, we may be more easily made aware of the need to distinguish between outward form and inner purpose.[44]

Du Bellay was not the only author to attack phony court poets: Ronsard, in "La Promesse" of 1563, gives an ironic account of how he was told to become a courtier.[45] Even closer to Lucian is Jean de la Jessée's "Le Poëte courtisan," a poem presented in autobiographical form, in which the narrator complains that the many hours he has spent studying have brought him no recognition at court.[46] Fortunately, a charming "Nymphe" has now taught him a better path to success. Fortune and Favor are more important to the rising court poet than talent, travel, and experience. A "Meçenas" is as essential as elegant dress (1437). The lady guide, predictably named "la Court," urges him to flatter the great and follow her (1440). He must write a short "chanson facile," not a "longue Aeneïde" (1439). Having at last found a patron, the narrator ends with the wish that his friend Guy de la Val, to whom the poem is dedicated, may have the same success. At intervals, the poet's feelings about his now compromised morality and standards become plain, as when he exclaims in a parenthesis "(Las! voyez à quel poinct la science est reduicte!)" (1438). This sad chronicle of the gradual commercialization of an aspiring poet has a melancholy personal tone not found in the "Poëte Courtisan" of Du Bellay, in which the narrator remains hostile and distant to the end, never himself accepting the new methods for achieving success. However, we cannot quite rest with La Jessée's conclusion, for despite everything the writer remained independent and free enough to publish a poem complaining of his own lack of freedom. The wistful remark that "Belle chose est Sçavoir, belle chose est Avoir," nicely mirrors the tension between the constraints of the patronage system and the artist's longing for full freedom of expression.

Vianey compares the ironical approach of Du Bellay's "Poëte Courtisan" with that of certain sonnets in the *Regrets*:

Le *Poëte Courtisan* se rattache donc beaucoup moins à la *Deffence*, qu'aux sonnets CXXXIX–CLIV des *Regrets*, qui sont une satire de l'hypocrisie et de l'ignorance de la Cour. Et dans les sonnets comme dans la pièce en alexandrins, c'est le même genre de satire: la satire ironique qui loue ce qu'elle veut condamner. . . . On doit se garder de croire que le *Poëte Courtisan* soit simplement une satire personnelle contre Mellin de Saint-Gelays. Ce qui fait la valeur de cette pièce, c'est sa portée. C'est qu'elle attaque avec une merveilleuse justesse tous ceux pour qui la littérature n'est qu'un jeu frivole et un moyen de parvenir.[47]

It is certainly true that these sonnets show how suited to Du Bellay's temperament and circumstances was the satirical eulogy cast in the form of ironic advice on how to succeed. Indeed, his gift for sustained irony was appreciated by his contemporaries as early as the 1550s, when Antoine Fouquelin, in his *La Rhétorique Françoise*, dedicated to Mary, Queen of Scots, quoted lines from Marot, Ronsard, Belleau, and Du Bellay to illustrate tropes such as metonymy, metaphor, synechdoche, and irony.[48] In the section on "Ironie," he refers at some length to Du Bellay:

> La seconde espece de Trope est apellee Ironie, quand par le contraire le contraire est entendu: c'est à dire quand on usurpe quelque mot, le contraire du quel nous voulons signifiér. Les François la peuvent apeller simulation & dissimulation, la quelle se peut entendre, tant par la pronuntiation, que par la nature de la chose de la quelle on parle. Car si elle repugne à ce qu'on dit, il est manifeste, qu'on dit d'un & entent d'autre. . . . Aucunefois l'Ironie est multipliee & continuee, comme au discours sur la louenge des vertus, & divers erreurs des hommes, par du Bellay.[49]

Elsewhere he repeats that in irony "par la negation l'affirmation est signifiee" (10ᵛ). It hardly seems likely that Fouquelin was alone in so reading Du Bellay: as a theorist seeking readily acceptable models of each figure of speech, he would not be looking for borderline illustrations of his various points. His good judgment in selecting such an outstanding group of contemporaries remains impressive. He goes on to quote lines 115–144 of Du Bellay's "Discours sur la louange de la vertu & sur les divers erreurs des hommes," dedicated to Salmon Macrin, explaining his selection as follows:

> Auquel exemple, ces mots là, divine ruse, loüable envie, belle chose & singuliere, heureuse poursuitte, & autres semblables, sont usurpez pour leurs contraires, c'est à dire sotte ruze, envie digne de vitupere, vilaine chose, malheureuse poursuitte, &c. [50]

Fouquelin rightly perceives these verses to be satirical yet cast in the form of praise. The poem is none other than a rudimentary mock encomium, indirect criticism of the familiar target, the courtier:

> C'est une divine ruze
> De bien forger une excuze,
> Et en subtil artizan,
> Soit qu'on parle ou qu'on chemine,
> Contrefaire bien la myne
> D'ung vieil singe courtizan.
>
> C'est une loüable envie
> A ceux qui toute leur vie

> Veulent demourer oyzeux,
> D'ung nouveau ne faire conte,
> Et pour garder qu'il ne monte,
> Tirer l'eschelle apres eux.[51]
>
> Ce sont beaux motz, que *bravade*,
> *Soldat, cargue, camyzade*,
> Avec' ung brave *san-dieu*:
> Trois beaux detz, une querelle,
> Et puis une maquerelle,
> C'est pour faire ung Demy-dieu.[52]

The term "artizan" in the first stanza recalls Scève's sonnet for Philibert de Vienne, which used the same word in a similar context and also rhymed it with "courtizan." Du Bellay spells out in some detail what he means by the artisanal quality of the contemporary courtier. His courtier is knowingly false, indicated by terms such as "forger," "excuze," and "contrefaire." The second stanza echoes Lucian's advice to the aspiring modern orator to trick and undercut all rivals, while the third focuses on the fashionable expressions, often of Italian origin, adopted by many French courtiers of the day but despised by others. Du Bellay's sonnet 139 of the *Regrets* employs a comparable technique of sarcastic advice to instruct an outsider on the way to behave at court:

> Si tu veulx vivre en Court (Dilliers) souvienne-toy
> De t'accoster tousjours des mignons de ton maistre.
> Si tu n'es favory, faire semblant de l'estre,
> Et de t'accommoder aux passetemps du Roy.
> Souvienne-toy encor' de ne prester ta foy
> Au parler d'un chascun. . . .
> . . . .
> Faisant ce que je dy, tu seras galland homme:
> T'en souvienne (Dilliers) si tu veulx vivre en Court.[53]

Jean de la Taille later wrote a very similar sonnet ironically praising the courtier as a "galland homme," but his structure was based on a series of highly questionable premises introduced by the repeated use of "si":

> Si piaffer, si faire bonne mine,
> Faire trotter un dé, & en tout lieu
> Une querelle, une carte, un sang-dieu
> Porter long poil fait à la Sarrazine:
> Si retrousser son feutre à la mutine,
> Faire vertu & du vice & du jeu,
> Si se moquer des lettres & de Dieu,
> Rire & gaudir d'une grâce badine:

> Si sçavoir bien violer & voler,
> Habler, morguer & pezer son parler,
> Trancher du brave & faire rien qui vaille,
> Bref, si tel art fait les hommes galands,
> Je suis d'avis qu'au rang des plus vaillants
> Tu sois le prime, & que l'ordre on te baille.[54]

The gradual development of this sonnet towards its caustic climax is similar to Du Bellay's use of the form. The grammatical structure of the poem expresses the idea already found in a more fully developed form in the *Philosophe de Court*, namely, that much anticourtier literature of this period was based on the notion of a complete system, an *ars*, which could be learned at will by those ready to abandon traditional standards and values. La Taille makes the point by saying that if a certain group of acts is what makes a man "galland," then the addressee of his sonnet is indeed "galland." In moving from a list of external postures to the idea of an entire philosophy, Philibert de Vienne suggests that, when considered in their entirety, the apparently superficial and unrelated details of courtiers' amoral behavior point to the overall loss of purpose that makes of them a caricature of ancient philosophers.

In general, however, the sonnet was not the form most favored by writers of satirical encomia. Perhaps this was due to the brevity of the form: most paradoxical eulogies relied on the gradual accumulation of details rather than the rapid sketch and quick final thrust of the satirical sonnet. Moreover, most anticourtier sonnets so thinly disguise their contempt that the ostensible praise, a key ingredient of the true mock encomium, well-nigh vanishes. Long before his conclusion, Jean de la Taille's true opinion of such gallant courtiers is obvious in such lines as "se moquer des lettres & de Dieu," and "ne faire rien qui vaille." The resulting poems are subtilized vituperations rather than true ironic encomia.

A longer work related to success at court, a topic of enduring interest to writers still caught up in a system of patronage, is the "Médecin Courtizan," also of 1559. The plan and style of the poem have led some critics to attribute it to Du Bellay, but P. M. Smith has shown that the author was Jacques Grévin, physician and poet.[55] Like the "Poëte Courtisan," the "Médecin Courtizan" begins by advising against long hours of study. The court being the center of power, one must concentrate on wooing those who hold the key to a successful career:

> Que nous sert plus longtemps racourcir nostre vie
> Epluchants les secrets de la Philosophie?
> Que sert, pour le plaisir de ces menteuses Seurs,
> Acravanter nos ans de cent mille labeurs.
> (100)

The court poet is advised to disregard Homer and the classics: the court doctor is told to practice "sans Hippocrate et sans un Galien" (102):

> Il ne te fault longtemps remascher le laurier;
> Il ne te fault veiller, ainsi que l'escolier,
> Jusques à la minuict.[56]

Like Lucian's orator, the doctor must have a stock of obscure Latin words with which to dazzle his hearers. The appearance of a "sçavoir pedantesque / Un peu entremeslé de la langue Tudesque" (102) will impress all patients. The "langue Tudesque" was presumably to be adopted because of its frighteningly obscure and therefore impressive sounds.

Ignoring subjects most physicians study, relying on his wits to extricate him from awkward situations, the new-style doctor concocts elaborately named brews from a few simple substances. The author here repeats a traditional jibe against doctors, recommending his pupil to cultivate bad handwriting, far more impressive to the layman. Thus armed, the new physician may begin work at court. If no other diseases occur, he will at least be certain there of a never-ending supply of patients suffering from venereal diseases. Like the quacks in Lucian's gout tragedy, the recruit should claim to have a secret ointment. He may inspect his patients' excreta and check their diet, but he must take care that his ignorance of what truly ails them and how to cure it is never discovered.

The poem ends as the narrator explains that he composed the work in order to ensure greater success at court for his Italian doctor friend Dordonus, to whom the work is dedicated. This passage adapts that part of the *Rhetorum Praeceptor* in which the newfangled speaker pours scorn on the old-fashioned, difficult road to fame. The French narrator declares that his poor friend has misguidedly been struggling to achieve both knowledge and success at court. Such aims form a contradiction in terms, doomed to failure. Only by following the methods described earlier in the poem can the situation be rectified. This poem provides another excellent example of the Pléiade writers' fascination with the effect of various forms of court corruption upon men of principle and sincere ambition. The mock eulogy is an appropriate vehicle, because in an age when successful cures were as much a matter of good luck as good medicine, the external mannerisms of a doctor might be just as successful with patients as the cures prescribed by physicians who had studied for many years. Success at court can thus be divorced from serious training and knowledge. The reader is left in a quandary, unable ever to be certain that he has placed his medical trust worthily.

This sense of verbal disguise, artifice, and hypocrisy as dominant features of the contemporary court is neatly summed up by Jean de la Taille in "Le

Courtisan retiré" of 1574. Developing the notion of the court as the place for the inversion or distortion of truth, he writes:

> car s'il est gracieux
> On le nomme flatteur: si grave, glorieux;
> Si gaillard, eventé: s'il parle peu, ignare;
> Si vaillant, estourdy; si ménager, avare.[57]

Nowhere is Du Bellay's mock advice on denigrating the virtues of potential rivals better illustrated than in these few terse lines. The problem now becomes how to tell the really unworthy individual from the good one slandered by those jealous of his virtue. There is a risk of total confusion. The answer would seem to be that only by taking a long-term view that evaluates actions and results, rather than mere words, can such discriminations ever be made.

Also in the second half of the century, Jean Vauquelin de la Fresnaye's "Satyre à Jean Antoine de Baïf," modeled on Sansovino's second satire, ironically urges Baïf to follow and adapt to the demands of the court, not the Muses.[58] Later in the period, Guillaume du Buys's long *Discours de la Noblesse* (1583) recommends swearing as one of various prerequisites for popularity at court—others are arrogance and laziness—while Tahureau's *Dialogues* of 1565 repeat in a similarly sardonic manner many of the above criticisms and precepts.[59]

A later court satire making use of Lucianic methods is Artus Thomas's *L'Isle des Hermaphrodites*, published in 1605 but describing the "mignons" at the court of Henri III. This Lucianic allegorical journey is discussed in detail by P. M. Smith, who notes Thomas's frequent use of irony.[60] In the laws of a strange imaginary island the narrator presents an ironic version of Castiglione's ideas. By developing *ad absurdum* the Italian precepts, utilitarianism, dilettantism, and self-seeking behavior can be recommended. Smith feels that Thomas may have known the *Philosophe de Court*, and it is true that both works provide a detailed picture of court corruption. Thomas shows how easily the new attitudes can be seen as a coherent system by making them literally that, the laws of an independent country. Philibert de Vienne employed the notion of a philosophy to point to the same idea. Thomas's inverted system only works in a purely imaginary island, whereas Philibert's can be supported only by focusing on the process of courtliness rather than the product.

With the exception of the *Isle des Hermaphrodites*, however, the passages of ironic advice by other French writers are in general less extensive and all-pervasive than those in the full-length works discussed earlier in this chapter. Nonetheless, they serve to complete the picture of the Lucianic vice eulogies of the French Renaissance, and help explain why a way of life marked by linguistic and moral trickery was so appropriately satirized by the techniques of the paradoxical encomium. The two-sidedness of some attacks is here more than just the hallmark of the genre as a whole. It is the inevitable outcome of the invidious position of financial dependence combined with intellectual resentment so vividly expressed in La Jessée's "Poëte courtisan."

The major French mock encomiast remains nonetheless Du Bellay, whose criticisms of foolish or immoral ways of life were not confined to general types of men, whether poets or physicians. Another of his attacks on various forms of ignorance was his ode "A Bertran Bergier, Poëte dithyrambique," which appeared with his only disease encomium, the "Hymne de la Surdité," in the *Divers Jeux rustiques* of 1558.[61] For all its apparent simplicity and good humor, the ode has been variously interpreted, because at times Du Bellay seems to be seriously advocating greater spontaneity in poetry.[62] An attentive reading, however, suggests serious limitations in the type of spontaneity practiced by Bergier.

The ode is placed in the collection after the playful animal eulogies on Peloton and Belaud, immediately after that on the abbé Bonnet. Of the four pieces, that on Bonnet is the most overtly satiric. However, no one individual has ever been identified as the target for this portrait of a dirty, garlic-smelling "plaideur" whose only lost argument was against the god of death. Bergier, on the other hand, had been a friend of Du Bellay since their days at the Collège de Coqueret and was the subject of poems by both Ronsard and Baïf. For the hard-working Pléiade members, Bergier seems to have represented a living paradox, a poet of great naturalness and verve, expert at onomatopoeic verse, but temperamentally averse to the labor and classical studies undertaken by his friends.[63] Du Bellay's choice of the ode, one of the more learned forms revived by the Pléiade, to describe this most deliberately unlearned of poets is the first incongruous element to strike the reader. The poem is relatively long, one hundred lines in octosyllabic quatrains rhyming *aabb*. The short lines give speed to the ode, mirroring Bergier's method of composition. First Du Bellay refers to Hesiod, "Ascrée," who became a poet immediately after having "songé en Parnasse, / Et humé de l'eau de Pegase" (5:117). Never having had to travel as far as Parnassus to achieve his metamorphosis into a poet, Bergier is ahead even of Hesiod. He has nothing to do with the complexities of versification studied by rhetoricians, but, like Orpheus, Hesiod, and Musaeus, relies on a "franc naturel mouvement" for his inspiration. Not until the Latin writers, with their "fascheuses" *Aeneids* and *Thebaids*, were poets forced to toil over their verses. The irony of these lines puzzles Saulnier, who, while admitting that Ronsard also had some harsh words for the *Thebaid*, cannot but add that no matter what he may say here, "l'oeuvre de Du Bellay est plaine (*sic*) de reminiscences de Virgile."[64] In the context of the mock encomium, however, the reference is less puzzling. Du Bellay is using paradoxical argumentation to explore a disquieting but charming exception to the rules of humanistic study whereby he and most of his Pléiade friends lived.

Entering into the specifics of Bergier's verse, Du Bellay writes as follows:

> Premier tu feis des dithyrambes,
> Lesquelz n'avoient ny pieds ny jambes,
> Ains comme balles, d'un grand sault
> Bondissoient en bas & en hault.
>
> Tu dis maintes gayes sornettes,
> Sur le bruit que font les sonnettes,
> Accordant au vol des oyseaux,
> Les horloges & leurs appeaux.
>
> Apres en rimes heroiques
> Tu feis de gros vers bedonniques,
> Puis en d'autres vers plus petis
> Tu feis des hachi-gigotis.
>
> Ainsi nous oyons dans Virgile
> Galoper le coursier agile,
> Et les vers d'Homere exprimer
> Le flo-flotement de la mer.
>
> Que diray-je des autres graces,
> Que les Dieux comme à pleines tasses
> Ont verse dessus toy, à fin
> D'en faire un chef d'oeuvre divin?
> (5:121–22)

The energy and good humor of these lines echo the qualities of Bergier's poetry that his friends appreciated. But the somewhat comical words and phrases such as "hachi-gigotis," "sornettes," and "ny pieds ny jambes" begin simultaneously to suggest a less lofty aspect. The image of the "pleines tasses" of divine gifts sounds as indiscriminate and uncontrolled as it is bountiful. Considering now the physical appearance of his friend, Du Bellay compares the bearded man's "grave port honorable" to that of a king. Having so ennobled Bergier, the poet imagines a possible court role for him:

> Si les Roys avoient cognoissance
> De toy & de ta suffisance,
> Sans toy ilz ne prendroient repas,
> Et sans toy ne feroient un pas.

Car quand il te plaist de bien dire,
Tu dis mille bons mots pour rire,
Serenant de ton front joyeux
Tout soing & chagrin ennuieux.
(5:122–23)

From being a descendant of the most admired Greek poets, Bergier has now become almost a buffoon or court jester, loved, like Falstaff, because of his ready wit and good humor. But whereas Prince Hal eventually rejects the fat knight on moral grounds, Du Bellay expresses no such reservations. The irony of his portrait seems to be due rather to the hesitation someone of his training must have felt with regard to so untutored and undisciplined a talent as that of Bergier. The poem's professed admiration for simplicity is thus undercut first by its form, that of the erudite ode, then by its repeated use of learned classical references, and finally, by the overall tone of the description of Bergier's verses.

Bergier, the natural poet, could do no more in his poems than reflect the universe around him in the most literal manner, by way of onomatopoeia. This talent was also that stressed by Baïf in his poem on the writer. What Bergier lacked was the training and discernment necessary to enable him to transform the base world of mere sound into something more profound. It is notable that this ode appears in the same collection as that containing the "Hymne de la Surdité," Du Bellay's most extended investigation of the world of sound. The Bergier ode is a rarity among mock encomia in that it praises ironically a living person. When eulogizing named individuals, writers normally chose dead people or legendary figures. Perhaps for this reason, it is the kindest of Du Bellay's ironic encomia and belongs in the present group because of its manipulation of and reference to so many of the arguments used in other praises of false roads to success. Because there appears to have been no element of calculation or egotism in Bergier, he is mocked in a rather gentle fashion. Quite as much mocked, indeed, are Du Bellay's own fondness and reverence for hard study and long years of training. This move to include a reflection upon the writer of the encomium within the encomium was to be repeated in several later French eulogies.[65]

In France, the mocking praise of an individual as opposed to a type (poet, doctor, court lady) usually took the form of the epitaph, whose relationship to the standard mock encomium has been discussed in connection with the Neo-Latin authors. Like them, the French found inspiration in Catullus and in the *Greek Anthology* and also profited from the rich native tradition inspired by Villon. Pietro Toldo remarks that at this time, "les testaments et les épitaphes burlesques sont à l'ordre du jour."[66] Thus Tabourot collected a number of them in the *Bigarrures* with the following comment: "L'on m'a rapporté qu'un jeune docte personnage en a colligé trois volumes, y comprins les non imprimez qu'il a peu rechercher. Le premier livre est des antiques monumens, le second des vers, Et le tiers, des François. Mais je luy conseille d'adjouster un quatriesme des follastres Epitaphes, car ils seront aussi curieusement recherchez que les autres."[67]

Castiglione's courtiers, whose interest in composing elegant mock encomia was noted earlier, might also have enjoyed the game described later in the century by Girolamo Bargagli in his *Il Dialogo de' Giuochi* of 1572: "An amusing game is that game of Epitaphs, where each chooses a person to write his epitaph."[68] Most Renaissance mock epitaphs on people are far more satirical, even crude, than those on animals, which will be studied in a later chapter. They deal with drunkards, "maquerelles," prostitutes, and other real or imaginary individuals. Since all cannot be considered here, I propose to develop further the picture of Du Bellay as a mock encomiast by considering his "Epitaphe de l'abbé Bonnet," already mentioned in connection with the ode on Bergier.

The poem is yet another investigation of an individual's lack of formal learning, although in this case the court in question is the law court, not that of kings. Beginning with the time-honored words "Cy gist" (here lies), the epitaph in a sense brings back to lie before us on the page this indefatigable "plaideur." Like Bergier, Bonnet despised formal learning:

> Bonnet fut un Docteur sans tiltre,
> Sans loy, paragraphe & chapitre.
> Bonnet avoit leu tous autheurs,
> Fors poëtes & orateurs:
> D'histoires & mathematiques,
> Et telles sciences antiques,
> Il s'en moquoit: au demeurant,
> De rien il n'estoit ignorant.
> (5:112)

In the world of legal learning, Bonnet represents the same paradox as Bergier in the world of poetry. Since, as Saulnier points out in his edition of the *Divers Jeux Rustiques*, the word "orateurs" should be taken to mean "prosateurs" (111), Du Bellay is implying that his expert "plaideur" was untrained in areas traditionally revered by the humanists. And yet, he continues, "De rien il n'estoit ignorant." The remainder of the poem explains exactly what Bonnet did know. First, he was learned in an "occulte Caballe," not, the narrator hastens to add, of the "defendu" variety. His particular skill lay in foreseeing the future, predicting major events such as wars and the death of princes, everything, in short, but his own demise. This power was based on his studies of astrology. In Hebrew and the "Caldaïque" tongues he was well versed, but of the more traditional Latin he "n'entendoit ny A ny B" (5:113). His own speech was a strange mixture of French,

Italian, and "Savoysien." A keen alchemist, Bonnet spent his fortune "pour multiplier tout en rien" (5:113).[69] Nonetheless, he still claimed to possess two containers of jewels and precious stones. A jack-of-all-trades and a quack doctor, he was a frequenter of "monstiers," and an ardent pursuer of legal cases. Physically, he is compared to a series of animals: the comparisons are not flattering:

> Bonnet portoit barbe de chat,
> Bonnet estoit de poil de rat,
> Bonnet fut de moyen corsage,
> Bonnet estoit rouge en visage,
> Avecques un oeil de furet,
> Et sec comme un haran soret:
> Bonnet eut la teste pointüe,
> Et le col comme une tortüe.
>
> (5:114)

Always shabbily dressed in the same dirty old clothes, he rode an ancient mule, very different from the attractive imaginary creature Belleau was to offer his friend Simon Nicolas in "Le Mulet."[70] Bonnet's diet of raw onions, "porreaux," and "aulx" perfumed both the man and his room. He was also a heavy drinker. Here Du Bellay refers for the second time to the abbé's inability to protect himself:

> Bonnet en tout se cognoissoit,
> Bonnet de tous maulx guerissoit,
> Et si n'usoit que d'eau de vie:
> Mais la mort, qui en eut envie,
> Tellement ses forces ravit,
> Que son eau rien ne luy servit.
>
> (115)

The punning on "eau de vie" and "mort" underlines the main theme of this poem, the way in which everything this man does ultimately fails him.

Bonnet's chief expertise, however, lay not in alchemy or medicine, but in the law. Beside this expert pleader, declares the narrator, the greediest of courtiers seeking benefices was a mere novice. The description of Bonnet's cunning tricks and delaying tactics is reminiscent of that contained in Gringore's "Blason de Pratique":[71]

> Pour bien emboucher un tesmoing,
> Et pour bien s'ayder au besoing
> D'une vieille lettre authentique,
> Pour trouver quelque tiltre antique,

Pour rendre un proces eternel,
Pour faire un civil criminel,

. . . .

Il n'estoit qu'un Bonnet au monde.

(116)

The epitaph ends as the poet notes that, plead though he may, Bonnet is unlikely to be able to persuade Rhadamanthus to change the sentence of death passed on him.

As well as being a vivid Bernesque portrait of the physical appearance of an unattractive character, Du Bellay's epitaph suggests why Bonnet remains such an unappealing even though clever person. By continually stressing that death undercut every one of the man's endeavors, the poet is not merely making the traditional trite point that all must die, a fact that might tend rather to evoke some sympathy for Bonnet. Instead, he stresses that the abbé's skills were all ones that seek in some way to transcend or obviate the normal laws of life and tendencies of the material universe. Astrology claims to know the future, alchemy to alter the very nature of matter, and the quack doctor seeks a miracle cure. Even in the law, Bonnet sought a kind of godlike control, to "rendre un proces eternel." He becomes a burlesque Prometheus, eager to outwit the gods. As such, he is appropriately pictured at the end as pleading in vain before the classical god Rhadamanthus.

Bergier's poetic and intellectual limitations, although obvious, seemed to pose an intriguing challenge rather than a serious threat to the learned Du Bellay. For Bergier was not selfish, pretentious, or ambitious, not a despicable "poëte courtisan" feigning gifts he did not have in order to achieve wealth and power. What he clearly did possess was fullness of personality, social skill, and charm. He could thus not altogether ironically be compared to a king. Bonnet, on the other hand, compared by Du Bellay to predatory animals such as the rat, the "furet," and the cat, has a sinister and altogether unpleasant aura. His neglect of the central subjects of humanistic learning revered by the Pléiade (Latin, Greek, "poëtes et orateurs") is paralleled by his neglect of his own physical appearance. The purpose of learning as a means of developing and expressing the nobility and beauty of the self, whether internal or external, has totally eluded him, lost in his endless futile experiments and plots to control the outside world. This loss of a sense of higher purpose eventually leads him to squander a large amount of money (alchemy), fail to foresee his own death (astrology), and probably help to bring the latter about by excessive drinking ("eau de vie"). Bergier and Bonnet are both ignorant in important areas, but the unspiritual abbé becomes a creature of prey, unattractive to human beings, whereas the "poëte dithyrambique" remains a pleasant companion even for monarchs.[72]

What links Bergier to Bonnet is thus their insensitivity to or failure to develop one part of their being. Scorning the lessons of humanism, with its emphasis on the development of the whole person, Bonnet never realized that his unattractive exterior constantly worked against the goals of social manipulation and control that he was seeking to attain. On the other hand, not realizing that it takes both subtlety and complexity to convey simplicity, a paradoxical truth embodied in the very texture of Du Bellay's ode, Bergier was limited in the intellectual domain. His friends were therefore justified in parodying his verses. Reading these two poems as mock encomia has enabled us to see the relationship between them and to understand the appropriateness of Du Bellay's choice of genre. The very switching of perspectives that has time and again been shown to be an integral part of the process of this genre is what Bonnet and Bergier fail to achieve.

ENCOMIA ON THE THEME OF FOLLY

French Renaissance vice encomia modeled closely on classical works frequently concentrated on current figures, in particular those seeking power of some sort at court. Traits of Lucian's parasite and rhetorician and of Terence's flatterer were adapted and modernized, enabling French writers to create an important group of satires. We can now pass from direct imitations of classical vice encomia to those influenced chiefly by the earliest major Renaissance mock encomium, the *Moriae Encomium*, and by the related work of Brant. Immediately recognized as a classic of the genre, Erasmus's great satire was frequently cited alongside Favorinus, Lucian, and Synesius in the customary prefaces to editions.[73] Both Erasmus and Brant were translated into French, Rivière's rendition of Brant dating from 1497, that by Drouyn from 1498. Erasmus's encomium first appeared in French in 1520. On occasion, as Charles Béné has demonstrated, one can trace in later French satires elements of both Erasmus and Brant, for example in Rabelais's *Tiers Livre* and Louise Labé's *Discours d'Amour et Folie*.[74] Important also in the context of the present study is the way in which both Drouyn and Rivière stress in their introductions that the *Nef des Fous* is hiding a serious intent beneath its seemingly frivolous exterior. Drouyn explains that "le sens littéral n'est pas le principal de la matière," and that the reader must move beyond the exterior folly of the work to look for the "sens moral" within. Failure to look below the surface is like trying to "menger les amandez sans casser."[75] Erasmus issues the same warning to his readers, and the notion also resembles the Horatian "ridentem dicere verum" the saying so popular with Neo-Latin encomiasts.[76] Thus, although French translations of the *Narrenschiff* remain basically within the medieval didactic tradition, Béné feels that they are beginning to move towards the idea of the difference between container and contained later used by Rabelais in the Silenus box and "substantificque moelle" images.

In about 1550, another French work on folly appeared in Lyons, the city that Condeescu notes to be of great importance in the publication of satirical writings in the sixteenth century.[77] Surviving in only one example, the *Triumphe de haulte folie* is closely related to another mock triumph, that of Dame Vérolle, a much-feared figure.[78] The idea of a triumphal procession or entry recalls Lucian's gout tragedy, and Montaiglon believes there could have been actual carnivals in which such personifications of disease and vice appeared.[79] "Folie" here heads the procession, summoning all fools to join her. "Folz et folles de tous estas, / Venez tous generallement," she declares, much as did Folly in the farces discussed in connection with Erasmus. A list of fools follows, some of whom are mentioned by name. Volupté, Sot Desir, Folle Bobance, and Oultrecuidance are among the personified vices, while the classes or groups of people include lovers, usurers, jealous husbands, gossips, "plaideurs," "maquereaux," and misers.[80] Mentioned by name are Cupid, Venus, Domitian, and, interestingly, Nero. Nowhere than in the following self-portrait of the wicked ruler can we see better the prevailing view of him and thereby appreciate to the full the innovative quality of Cardano's *Neronis Encomium* for the Renaissance reader:

> Je suis Néron, de tous pires le pire;
> Le bon Seneque, mon maistre, feiz morir,
> Rome brusler en tenant son empire;
> Par cruaulté, qui noblesse empire,
> Je feiz ma mere, comme tyran, ouvrir,
> Sang des martyrs sur la terre courir.
> Le premier fuz persecutant Eglise.[81]

The inclusion of Domitian and Nero shows that folly in this work refers to outright depravity as well as to Erasmus's less culpable foolishness. Appropriately, therefore, the procession ends with the appearance of Death, who, after promising to carry off all men, urges them to beg for mercy. The closing lines plead with the reader to remember Christ, expect Death, and fear the Last Judgment. Although the *Triumphe* contains some ironic elements, it thus remains more overtly didactic and serious than the Lucianic *Moriae Encomium*. In fact, it is more serious in tone even than the other mock triumph, of Dame Vérolle, to be discussed in chapter 6 below.

A more playful treatment of the topic of madness is found in the *Louanges de la Folie, traicté fort plaisant en forme de paradoxe*, a translation by Jean du Thier of the Italian *La Pazzia*.[82] Du Thier at first claims to have no predecessors: the importance of Erasmus is thereby denied, although the work that follows proves to be derived in large part from the *Moriae Encomium*. However, the French and Italian writers turn not to a religious perspective at the end of their essays but to a criticism of those who use bad Latin or reject Latin in favor of the vernacular, and of those who, thinking themselves most "sages," are the biggest fools of all. In addition, the narrators constantly refer to themselves using the first person pronoun, a stylistic shift that results in a different tone from that of Erasmus's laughing persona. To include themselves within the circle of folly, they complain about personal problems of health and family, remarking that only folly keeps them writing. Whereas Erasmus's conclusion implies that the paradoxes of human thinking can be somehow subsumed within the realm of religious faith, du Thier and the author of *La Pazzia* remain with the world of language and personal idiosyncracies and vanities. To believe we can transcend our vehicle, language, their conclusion suggests, is indeed to be the biggest fool of all. What has sometimes been classified as a mere translation of Erasmus thus proves to be making a very different final point from that made by Moria.

Lando's praise of madness, later translated by Estienne into a French *Paradoxe*, will be discussed below, but a less well known work on folly, which apparently existed in French, is known to us only in its English translation of 1576.[83] Entitled in translation *The Mirrour of Madnes; or, a Paradoxe maintayning Madnes to be most excellent*, the work provides no details of the original author. The translator, James Sandford, dedicates his work to Sir Arthur Champernon. His dedicatory epistle discusses the power of nature, "mistresse and lady of living thinges," over all our actions, but complains that nature has been perverted by love of money. A poem to the reader follows, containing the type of self-justification offered by so many mock encomiasts:

> Reprove me not, though fame by me enlargement take
> This trifling toy, this mery jeste, for solace sake,
> Compiled was in foraine speache, I pardon crave,
> If any bee, whom I herein offended have.
> For Cynicke like the Authoure here, with skoffes doth barke
> At mens madde deedes, which vainely bent no reason marke.
> Wherefore in earnest some wil take, that which in jeste
> Is meant of me, in doing so, they do not best.
> (A.iii^r)

After recommending his efforts to the reader, Sandford concludes with the device "Tutto per il Meglio."[84] This type of prefatory poem leads us to wonder about the genuineness of the *Mirrour* as a translation, for Sandford seems in a way to be using his so-called original writer as yet another protective device for himself. Renaissance satirical eulogies were so frequently translated that the translators' self-deprecating verses or epistles could serve indirectly to call attention to the more daring aspects of what was being presented. The *Mirrour of Madnes* begins with a discussion of the *summum bonum* that resembles passages in the *De Parasito*, the *Philosophe de Court*, and Berni's capitolo on the plague. The supreme good proposed in the English work is madness; the entirety of the piece is an attempt to justify this initial notion.

First, the author reviews various chief aims proposed by philosophers such as Zeno, Cicero, Aristotle, Plato, and Epicurus, the last of whom is here said to have asserted that man's main end in life lay in wine, food, fine clothing, sleep, and love. After a fine description of the food, drink, and clothing of the period comes a list of famous epicureans, Sardanapalus, Heliogabalus, and Nero. Their pleasure is in fact madness, declares the narrator, but since, when moderately taken, pleasure is usually held to be beneficial, one can infer that madness should be similarly viewed.

The next section of the work contains an ironic attack on the Pope, deemed by the author the most excellent subject on earth, "in somuche that hee is able to dispence with the Newe and Olde Testamente, and to call thinges which are not, even as though they weere, & of nothing to make something, and to create his creatoure" (B.5ᵛ). The doctrine of transubstantiation is discussed at length as a particularly mad claim, a "solemne Madnes."

From religion, the text passes to warfare, famous warriors such as Hannibal and Caesar being named and their road to power described. Surrounded by the blood, torn bodies, and cries of the wounded, these men triumphed by the sword, by murder and crime. Although war brings fame and peace, both eminently desirable, it is also madness. The logical conclusion is that madness must be "most excellente" (Cʳ). The same form of proof by elementary syllogism is next applied to love: "All fire is madnes in his operation, every love is a fire, therefore every Love is madnes" (C.vvvvᵛ). Politian, Petrarch, Castiglione, and Ovid are among the writers on love mentioned in a section whose tone is generally misogynistic. After deciding that both fantasy and study are madness, the work ends with the hope that all will honor madness, since, as Cicero put it, "to bee a mad man is to bee a wise man" (D.2ʳ).

The writer has shown that philosophy, religion, bravery, and love, man's highest aspirations, can by a simple verbal operation be equated with madness. At this point the meaning of the title becomes clearer. The medieval *speculum stultorum* furnished the reader with a caricatured but still recognizable image of the world's fools; the French-English paradox uses its repetitive argumentation to form a mirror that distorts man's ideals and intellectual endeavors. The lengthy attention given to religious matters, particularly to the doctrine of transubstantiation, is important. Whereas the transformed wine and wafer can by an act of faith elevate man to the religious sphere, the lack of such a sense of direction permits reversion to madness. The paradoxes of religion lead to a clear goal for the believer but to folly for the skeptic who sees them as no different in kind from any other of the world's mysteries.

The exploration of madness continued to attract mock encomiasts, and the early seventeenth century saw the publication, in the *Cabinet satyrique* of 1618, of "Les Foux," a poem by Adrien Montluc, comte de Cramail, extracted from the *Ballet de sept fols et de sept sages*.[85] The emphasis of this poem is on the vanity of human wishes, their ultimate futility, rather than on their intrinsic ridiculousness, the element stressed in most earlier mock encomia. The work thus becomes more of a sermon than a satirical eulogy. The author attempts nonetheless to maintain the humorous Erasmian posture, claiming that only in our mode of dress and in our "barbe" do we differ from one another. All other desires—for wealth, fame, wisdom, or sex—are alike in futility. Those commonly believed to be mad are in fact less mad than they seem: "Et la sagesse et la folie / Leur tiennent bonne compagnie" (357). In a second, shorter poem on the same topic, he claims that men become mad for love of women and that the "fou" fears neither battle nor death. Asking the reader not to take offense at these statements, the narrator, like the creator of Moria before him, claims that his words, being those of a "fou," should offend no one.

Finally, we may note that Charles Béné has suggested that the entirety of Rabelais's *Tiers Livre* is a "nouvel Eloge de la Folie," in that it caricatures (in Panurge's various consultations) so many of the classes of people—poets, doctors, lawyers, and so on—mocked earlier by Erasmus.[86] Rabelais's ironic tone brings his work closer to that of Erasmus than to that of Brant. In addition, Béné points out that many aspects of the *Quart Livre*, *Gargantua*, and *Pantagruel* are related to the *Moriae Encomium*. *Pantagruel* caricatures the foibles of jurists and "faux savants." *Gargantua* mocks theologians, medieval-style educators, monks, pilgrims, and soldiers. In the *Quart Livre*, a boat closely resembling contemporary woodcuts of the fools' ship of Brant appears, while the strange residents of the countries visited during the voyage are readily recognizable distortions of various human faults— the "chicanous," the "Papefigues," the dwellers on the island of Messer Gaster, of the Andouilles, and of Quaresmeprenant. However, this generalized sense of irony and of human folly does not mean that *Gargantua* and *Pantagruel* can be seen in their entirety as paradoxical encomia. The most classic paradoxical encomium in Rabelais's works is Panurge's "Eloge des Dettes." The section on pantagruelion, despite some playful moments, is fundamentally too serious to qualify as a mock praise.[87] Although paradoxical encomia not infrequently contained serious moments, even Erasmus succeeded in preserving his framework of ironic self-praise, his Moria rapidly retreating to a playful posture after her serious discussion of religious folly. Accordingly, while agreeing with a number of recent critics as to the presence of mock encomiastic tendencies in most Rabelaisian works, I shall discuss in detail only the eulogy so named by its author. Because the idea is also found in Berni, the discussion of the praise of debts will provide a transition to the third group of French vice encomia, those influenced chiefly by Italian models.

RABELAIS'S "ELOGE DES DETTES"

When the *Tiers Livre* was published in 1546, the "Querelle des Amyes," in which "L'Amye de Court" (1542) played such an important part, was already some years old. Although part of the *Tiers Livre* is linked to this famous argument for and against women, Michael Screech and others have stressed that the work is concerned both with the function of rhetoric and with the growing differences between Panurge's and Pantagruel's attitudes to life in general and religious matters in particular. The praise of debts plays an important role in preparing the reader for the divergent views and contrasting personalities of the *Tiers Livre*'s two chief protagonists. The eulogy is contained in chapters 3 and 4 of the work, chapter 5 being a refutation by Pantagruel of Panurge's thesis. Although the presentation of first one and then the other side of an argument dates from classical times, Condeescu believes Rabelais might also have been familiar with Bernesque works of this type. He had been in Italy just before composing the *Tiers Livre* and had not previously introduced into his works any full-length formal paradoxes.[88] One can also perceive in the pair of speeches traces of medieval "débats." However, while Panurge's arguments are clever but ultimately sophistical, Pantagruel's are usually declared by critics to reveal Rabelais's "true" opinions.[89] The praise of and subsequent attack on debts do not therefore form one of the more or less equally balanced pairs found in the work of Grazzini or Berni. Instead, a highly inventive but formally typical paradoxical encomium is followed by a straightforward, nonironic refutation.

Abel Lefranc suggests that the inspiration for the praise of debts may have been provided by some lines in Isaac Habert's *Songe de Pantagruel*:

> Ilz sont tenus me rendre la somme
> Quant on verra content estre tout homme,
> Et quant mourra du monde l'heresie
> Ou bien d'un gras moine l'hypocrisie.
> Ou quant prelatz n'auront qu'ung benefice
> Et que puny sera tout malefice;
> *Quant on verra mettre fin aux proces,*
> Et qu'on verra, sans querelle et exces,
> Vivre le monde, *et en tranquillité*
> *Quictes debteurs et estre en liberté.*[90]

These lines are similar to the passage at the beginning of chapter 4 of the *Tiers Livre*, in which Panurge is imagining an improbable but marvelous future world:

> Entre les humains paix, amour, dilection, fidelité, repous, banquetz, festins, joye, liesse, or, argent, menue monnoie, chaisnes, bagues, marchandises troteront de main en main. Nul proces, nulle guerre, nul debat; nul n'y sera usurier, nul leschart, nul chichart, nul refusant. Vray Dieu, ne sera ce l'aage d'or, le regne de Saturne, l'idee des regions Olympicques, es quelles toutes autres vertus cessent, charité seule regne, regente, domine, triumphe? Tous seront bons, tous seront beaulx, tous seront justes. O monde heureux! O gens de cestuy monde heureux! (51–52)

But although certain details of the two passages are similar, their purposes are quite different. The lines in the *Songe* are satirically saying that the money will never be returned, an equivalent to the English "month of Sundays." Panurge's enthusiastic vision, on the other hand, represents what this incorrigible spendthrift would really like to see happen in the world. The joke lies in the fact that the hopeful reference to the "aage d'or," usually an image of bliss in a vague sense, must here be realized in the most literal manner.

Closer in tone to Rabelais is the Erasmus of the *Moriae Encomium*. Like his contemporaries, Rabelais would have known Lucian directly, but cannot have failed to be impressed also by the brilliance and success of Erasmus's modernization of Lucianic techniques and topics. The manipulation of mythology and history, the alternating bursts of ironic and serious lyricism, and the satire on philosophers all find a counterpart in the praise of debts. In almost every paragraph of Rabelais's encomium, for example, are quotations from or adaptations of classical writers and mythology. Often such reminiscences are presented in novel and comic contexts, as when Panurge gives details of his debt-free world:

> Un monde sans debtes! La entre les astres ne sera cours regulier quiconque. Tous seront en desarroy. Juppiter, ne s'estimant debiteur à Saturne, le dépossedera de sa sphaere, et avecques sa chaine homericque suspendera toutes les intelligences, dieux, cieulx, daemons, genies, heroes, diables, terre, mer, tous elemens. Saturne se r'aliera avecques Mars, et mettront tout ce monde en perturbation. Mercure ne vouldra soy asservir es aultres, plus ne sera leur Camille, comme en langue hetrusque estoit nommé. Car il ne leurs est en rien debteur. Venus ne sera venerée, car elle n'aura rien presté. (46)

This playful and irreverent attitude toward the gods is thoroughly Lucianic, as is the ending of the same chapter, a "revision" of Menenius Agrippa's tale, already repeated by Erasmus, about the revolt of the various parts of the body against one another.[91]

On several occasions in the encomium Rabelais modernizes Lucian's attacks on sophists and philosophers of earlier times by having Panurge quote and distort the works of Ficino, Hippocrates, and other respected authorities. When taken out of context, the lyric energy of many of these arguments, like those of the Amye de Court, may seem persuasive. But the reader knows that such moments are typical of paradoxical reasoning and that their lucidity and good sense are likely to be undermined or called into question by a larger context or opposing argument. Panurge's entire speech is no more than an elaborate defense of his selfish and extravagant way of life. The noble tone of some of his declarations is thus constantly thrown into comic perspective by the reader's mental image of the bankrupt but loquacious Panurge confronting the sober, thoughtful Pantagruel. Small wonder that Panurge has been compared to Falstaff and, like him, studied separately. Florence Weinberg calls this self-defense a "sham Dyonisiac fever which Pantagruel rapidly deflates."[92] However, we must not forget that although he lectures Panurge sharply about his thoughtless ways, Pantagruel does not cast him off, as Hal does Falstaff. On the contrary, he follows and guides him step by step through the marriage quest that forms the ostensible subject of the *Tiers Livre*. Even at the end of the *Quart Livre*, when Panurge's abject fear has led him to emerge from his hiding place covered in his own excrement, the ever-patient Pantagruel merely laughs, then tells his foul-smelling follower to wash, calm himself, and put on clean linen. This tolerant behavior is easier to understand from the point of view of paradox, finely poised between good and evil, but for the most part suspending ultimate decisions and judgments. But once again, in the praise of debts as in the exploration of the mirror of madness, the need for a sense of the purpose of rhetorical display becomes evident. The notion of the golden age can become a true ideal or an excuse for chronic extravagance. All such goals must be contextualized in order to be properly understood and evaluated. Failure to take into account the larger setting of Panurge's speech, and to realize that the wily speaker is roundly condemned by Pantagruel, may lead to acceptance of the clever rhetoric. Awareness of the need for a wider interpretation, a need common to all mock encomia, thus enriches our reading of Rabelais's creation.

Rather than devote more space to this already much-discussed work, I shall consider here another French encomium on debt. Annibal de l'Ortigue, who also composed disease encomia, and whom Condeescu believes to have been influenced by the Bernesque writers, published in 1617 "La Felicité du debteur."[93] The poem begins as follows:

> Il me prend une extreme envie
> De faire voir l'heureuse vie,
> Les plaisirs; et les voluptez
> Des personnages endebtez.
>
> (144)

Personal reasons for pleading on behalf of debt are explained only later, when the author addresses a friend imprisoned for debt and urges him to accept his plight cheerfully. He claims that borrowing is a necessity, as when captains borrow from merchants in order to be able to go to war. A description follows of "Sergens" surrounding a debtor's house at night in order to drag him off to prison. Usually, the debtor escapes under cover of darkness. Hoping for repayment, creditors court the debtor as if he were a prince. Having nothing for them to take, he need never fear burglars. If he finally does end up in prison, he is fed and lodged at his creditors' expense, guarded and protected as securely as any prince. The narrator is sure that his imprisoned friend will now agree that there is nothing so fine as to "Debvoir & ne payer personne" (149).

This brief analysis shows that, despite its topic, the seventeenth-century work is closer in tone to the Bernesque capitoli than to Rabelais. The writer has so rationalized the notion of debt that he urges his friend, already in prison and therefore well aware of the disadvantages of such a state, to be happy about his fate. The context here is not the larger written work, as it was with the *Tiers Livre*, but the extraliterary world of creditors and debtors. To accept the arguments of the poem is to imprison oneself mentally just as firmly as the poet's friend is imprisoned physically. Once again, the ambiguity inherent to this genre is essential to an understanding of the theme being explored.

THE ITALIAN INFLUENCE

The two groups of Italian works to exert the greatest influence on the French vice eulogy were Ortensio Lando's *paradossi* and the Bernesque *capitoli*. Since the *paradossi* appeared in many French cities in the numerous editions of Charles Estienne's free translation, whereas the *capitoli* were not translated into French in their entirety during this period, we may consider first the former group, the paradoxes.[94] Estienne habitually cut and adapted Lando's text, so that the resulting essays, although not original, are different enough from their source to be considered a separate force in arousing French interest in the genre. They were probably more important in this respect than the Italian originals. All were satirical eulogies, but only those

of particular importance in tracing the development of the paradoxical encomium in France will be discussed here.[95] This section will conclude by
considering some original French works linked in topic and tone to Estienne's essays.

It is important first of all to attend to the manner in which Estienne presents his adaptations. Like most mock encomiasts, he is anxious to make his
intentions absolutely clear. In the 1553 Poitiers edition, he reiterates the
phrase derived from Cicero about the paradox being "contre la commune
opinion" ("fuori del comun parer" in Italian), then adds. "En quoy toutesfois je ne vouldrois que tu fusses tant offensé, que pour mon dire ou conclusion, tu en croye antre chose que le commun. Mais te souvienne, que la
diversité des choses resjouit plus l'esprit des hommes que ne fait tousjours
& continuellement voir ce qui leur est commun & accoustumé."[96] Protected
by this Erasmian wish for nothing more harmful than diversity and entertainment, Estienne, like so many others before him, feels free to insert some
paragraphs of sharp criticism into his creations.

The fifth paradox bears a title that links it to the Erasmian tradition:
"Pour le sot. Qu'il vault mieulx estre sot, que sage" (49–61). The author
remarks that the theme has already been dealt with by two excellent advocates, almost certainly Erasmus and perhaps Grazzini or the author of the
Italian La Pazzia. Estienne proposes merely to fill in the gaps left by his
predecessors. Madness, he begins, is surely one of the pleasantest states;
indeed, philosophers used to say that in order to be happy one had merely
to be able to "contrefaire le sot" (50). This contention is illustrated with a
tale of a man who, believing that all the ships arriving in Dieppe were his
own, would make plans for them, arranging imaginary voyages, an idea that
may derive from Lucian's Navigium, in which Adimantus thinks that a ship
in the harbor belongs to him.[97] But whereas Lucian emphasized the folly of
such wishes, Estienne stresses the happiness to be obtained from these states
of delusion. When the brother of the man of Dieppe finds a doctor to cure
him, the man is far less content.[98]

Similarly, thanks to folly, at this point equated with imagination, poor
men can fancy themselves kings and popes. Estienne tells of a "lacquaiz"
who would shut himself up once a day and make believe he was the Pope
(51). What is more, when imagining one holds high office, one enjoys all
the advantages of power with none of the accompanying difficulties and
responsibilities. Even Solomon and the seven sages of Greece ("ceste men-
teuse & ambitieuse Grece," remarks the author) experienced moments of
folly (53). The following paragraph is remarkable in that it condenses all
the major Renaissance arguments in favor of insanity or folly:

> Le sot, ne se sent espoinct de tant d'esguillons de fortune: ne cherche
> combats à oultrance; n'a plaid, ne procès, ne querele pour acquerir ou

debatre son bien: n'a tant de peine à faire la court pour entretenir les
uns & les autres: ne se rend (pour la misere de deux ou trois escuz)
bouclier à dix mille boulets d'artillerie, mosquettes ou harquebouzes:
ne se rompt le col à courir en poste, offices, benefices, ou confiscations:
ne languist à la poursuitte de l'amour ou faveur des dames: ne paye
taille ne tribut: Finablement, n'est aucunement subject à personne, &
vit en plaine franchise & liberté. Il luy est permis & licite, de dire ce
que bon luy semble, touchant le faict des princes, & personnes privees:
sans que pour cela il en tombe en aucun danger de prison ou punition
corporelle: & n'ha aucun besoing de rhetoricque artificiele, pour se
faire attentivement ouyr, & donner à un chascun le joyeulx passetemps
de ses risees.[99]

In short, fortune protects fools so well that they often live longer than the
wise. Having completed his list of the physical advantages of madness as
providing protection from war, litigation, and social responsibility, the paradoxist turns to literature, in particular poetry. "Sottie" and poetry are
closely linked, he asserts, since both presuppose a "fureur divine": "Chascun sçait, que le poëte qui plus en a, est estimé des plus excellent" (57).
Great men such as Plato and great nations such as France are all a little mad.
In a list of various mad nations the author combines satirical jibes with
compliments to Italian cities such as Siena, Modena, Parma, and Verona,
whose admiration for folly is equaled by their beauty and wealth. Estienne
here omits the names of friends to whom Lando pays compliments, but he
concludes with some nationalistic digs at the foolish Germans and praises
the inventor of Tarot for making the Fool a major figure. Unlike Erasmus,
he does not venture to discuss religious folly. The chief paradox underlying
his presentation is the sense in which all the practical advantages listed depend upon the continuing existence of so-called sane people to judge the
fool foolish and duly permit him his special license and exemptions. Without such protection, the type of fool presented in most of this paradox would
perish by the wayside. It is also likely that such compassionate sane people
would have a sense of the religious dimension of folly, and that this open-
ness of mind would account for some of the special consideration they accord the fool. Estienne's inclusion of contemporary figures and references
distinguishes him from Erasmus, who prided himself on criticizing no one
by name except himself. By incorporating the realm of history as well as
that of the background of the genre he was manipulating, Estienne provided
slightly different grounds for refutation or for stepping outside the framework of the arguments. His public could decide either that his use of the
previous arguments was unsatisfactory or that the historical instances he
cited were somehow unconvincing or inappropriate. In either case, the
reader was forced outside the immediate text.

Estienne's characteristic technique is thus to recombine and compress earlier arguments, sometimes achieving slightly different effects from the new juxtapositions. The passage concerning the fool's exemption from the horrors of war is strongly voiced but appears more innocuous for being placed between more abstract and general phrases about the "esguillons de fortune" and the "amour ou faveur des dames." The interspersion of strong and mild comments is frequent in the *Paradoxes* and enables Estienne to introduce new passages of his own in a less provocative manner.

A second related paradox is "Pour le Chiche" (170–76), which sets out to praise a way of life not normally sought after or desired. The piece proves to be a eulogy of temperate living, justified, interestingly enough, by the argument that intemperance causes gout. Another familiar illness mentioned in the same context is the quartan fever. The French are urged to imitate the frugal existence of the recluses and philosophers of ancient times and to forget the rich dishes they so enjoy. This paradox is perhaps less obviously "contre la comune opinion" to the diet-conscious modern reader than to the reader of Estienne's day. Another of his essays, however, entitled "Pour les biberons. Que l'ebrieté est meilleure, que la sobrieté" (68–76), returns to the main current of Neo-Latin encomia on vice. The Bible, says the writer, tells us that wine was sent to gladden men's hearts, a claim repeated by Homer, Horace, and Plato. Truth lies in wine, not, as Democritus asserted, at the bottom of a well. Water, "ce fadde brevage" (70), destroys a man's virility and strength. Having criticized a "mal croyant humaniste" who, despite the authority of Scripture, attacked wine, the narrator provides a somewhat confused list of famous topers, from Noah and Hector to Pindar and Agamemnon. The Tartars and the Germans, as well as the peoples of Greece and Italy, have all been or still are wine-lovers, and numerous are the medical treatises advocating this drink. The author ends what he calls one of his most enjoyable discussions by urging men to flee sobriety, which "rend les personnes, melancolicques, & de si petite force & courage" (76).

These paradoxes on wine and madness follow the general pattern of the classical mock encomium, citing famous names, adapting and reinterpreting authoritative texts, stressing the universality of the new "ideal," and calling for the reader's benevolence and willingness to be amused. We realize how well established the form and even the details of the arguments have become as elements of Erasmus, Berni, and others are combined to create new and often vivid effects.

Estienne does not always take Lando as his basis; the "Paradoxe que le plaider est chose tresutile, & nécessaire à la vie des hommes" seems to have been his own invention.[100] Here, like Erasmus's Moria, the narrator addresses the reader as if he were pleading a case in court, a posture particularly appropriate in the present instance. The chief focus is on the fact that the litigant in a court case has to curry favor with important people so that they will help him win. The question of intrinsic right and wrong is not even considered. What does occur is that the person pleading his case must become polite, courteous, and energetic: "De lourdault en peu de temps il est devenu gentil, de recluz privé, de presumptueux affable, de desdaigneux doulx & humain, de mespriseur familier & reverend" (a.iii^r). He must learn to speak carefully and effectively in order to advance his case: "Tous ses propos n'estoyent que monsieur & madame, vostre treshumble & tres-obeissant: toutes ses contenances n'estoyent, que la jambe en arriere, le bonnet au poing, la teste panchée" (a.iii^v–a.iiii^r). He must become stronger physically, since he must run from office to office without showing signs of fatigue or irritation. Since jargon is as necessary in the legal world as it is in the sciences, he must also become intellectually adept. Although Estienne briefly presents an opposing view of Procès as a kind of monster, a Hydra ruining families, he asserts that this endless multiplication should be seen as beneficial, comparable to the increase of corn at harvesttime.

The pace of Estienne's prose in this paradox nicely mirrors what seems to be one of his chief points: that the man involved in a lawsuit frequently allows it to take over his whole life (as do some of the characters in Dickens's *Bleak House*). A litigant's every action and word will be calculated in terms of its likely effect upon his suit. Forgotten is the original reason for the case and the danger of allowing it to dominate existence. When the title of the paradox tells us that "plaider" is useful and necessary "à la vie des hommes," it is thus underlining the fact that litigation may so encompass its victim's life that even legal victory would become a kind of defeat. The process of the "procès" becomes an end in itself; the reader wonders what the pleader would do with himself if his suit were ever settled.

An even more self-defeating human activity, war, is considered in the nineteenth paradox, "Pour la guerre. Que la guerre est plus à estimer, que la paix" (1553 ed., 138–44). The essay proposes to counter the arguments of authors such as Erasmus who have written in praise of peace. In peacetime, the narrator explains, all military discipline, long recognized as essential for the maintenance of empires, is lost. Most statues of classical figures show their subjects in military uniform, the Carthaginians' esteem for warriors being especially famous. Because it is an honor to bear arms for Christ, all men respect the knights of Jerusalem and Rhodes. Moreover, the bravest fighters become a menace in times of peace, when they have nothing to occupy them. The Romans rightly called war Bellona, for she is indeed "belle," those who suggest that the name was intended ironically being entirely mistaken. The Bible relates many bloody battles: indeed, God was called the "Lord of Hosts" by the children of Israel, and Christ told his disciples to sell their mantles to buy swords. Checking the pride and insolence of the rich, war "sert à esveiller & aguiser les esprits des hommes, &

rendre leurs corps plus robustes, legiers, patients, & endurciz à tout mal & fortune" (143). It should therefore be preferred to peace, "bien grandement louee, & à haulte voix exaltee" (144).

It becomes clear that Estienne's paradoxes operate chiefly by manipulating the realm of "commune opinion." The truisms of popular philosophy and superstition, together with the ideas of previous paradoxical writers, are collected to form, not a fount of eternal human wisdom, but a set of ambiguous data to be reorganized at will for either defense or attack. Since many of the arguments used to flout what is presented by the text as common opinion come in fact from the selfsame area of common opinion, the entire notion of a general consensus is thrown into question. Nonetheless, despite the demonstrable two-sidedness of received opinion, these pieces are still recognizable as paradoxes. Common opinion is constantly subject to questioning and to being undercut, but the accumulated weight of centuries will still tend to bring the scales down on one side or the other. The paradoxical and foolish nature of certain human activities, of the litigant or of the fighter, for example, is made apparent in Estienne's works, but the reader does not believe that the author seriously advocates war or litigation. Estienne's careful projection of himself and the reader into unusual points of view suggests a genre so advanced that it can now begin to warn against the absolute authority of its own hard-won tradition.

In view of the many editions of the *Paradoxes*, it comes as no surprise to find that there are several other French works whose allusions, themes, and sometimes style are in the same vein. In 1544, a year after Lando's original *Paradossi* appeared, one of the earliest French vice eulogies, or eulogies on an undesirable activity, was published in Paris by Chrestien Wechel. Philibert de Vienne, author of the *Philosophe de Court*, almost certainly composed an epistle published in the same work, and its author, Claude Colet, also published with de Tournes in Lyons. We can therefore reasonably suppose that Colet was aware of the classical and probably the Italian paradoxical traditions. His work, entitled the *L'Oraison de Mars aux Dames de la Court*, was republished by Wechel in an expanded version in 1548. Colet, from Champagne, styled himself "l'Amoureux de Vertu" and often used the device "Tout pour le mieulx," occasionally rendering this in Italian as "Tutto per il meglio."[101] Since the same device also appears in the English translation of the *Mirrour of Madnes*, it is possible that Colet composed that satirical encomium, but a translated device is scant evidence of authorship.

In addition to Lando's work, Colet may also have known the praise of war by Thomas Lineus, the *Oratio in laudem belli*, discussed above with the other Neo-Latin encomia.[102] But whereas Lineus specifically mentions Polycrates, Favorinus, Synesius, and Erasmus in his introduction, placing himself firmly within the tradition of the mock encomium, Colet cites no predecessors, referring in his introductory epistle only to an earlier poem of his own against war. These lines he had not dared publish at the time, fearing the opposition of the "ministres de Mars et aultres lesquels ne se delectent et prennent plaisir qu'en rapines, embrasementz & saccagementz de villes & chasteaulx, violements de femmes, forcements de filles, pillages d'eglises & toutes aultres manieres d'inhumanités nouvellement excogitées, & dont le recit seul causeroit une horreur & frayeur auz escoutans."[103] Given these views, one wonders how the author will manage to defend Mars. He also promises a *Response* of the ladies to the god of war, which is printed immediately after Mars's speech on his own behalf. Colet thus makes clear his true opinion of war, "ceste infernale furie," as he names it in the same introduction (5).

The reader duly forewarned, the author launches into his defense, placed into the mouth of Mars. The god complains that all the ladies criticize him, seeking to drive him from the land. He admits candidly that he is

> de visage terrible,
> Aux paovres gens le plus souvent nuysible,
> Les yeulx flambans & la main equippée
> De pots de feu, d'armures & d'espée,
> Tousjours sanglante & de meurdres pollue.
>
> (9)

Returning to the military point of view, Mars explains that he does not in fact break the laws, for he is the son of Justice and was created by Jupiter to fight the giants. Unfortunately, Justice, his mother, was forced to flee from earth to heaven, giving rise to the idea that Mars is always found in the company of Discord and Ambition. The friend of kings, ready to protect the good and punish the wicked, the god claims that he helps preserve the diversity and individuality of nations, causing cities to be strong and magistrates safe.

Moving from the social to the academic and literary realm, Mars declares that the arts and sciences are full of arguments and contention. Colet here has the chance to poke fun at a wide range of people, "Sorbonistes," grammarians, lawyers, and historians. He pays particular attention to squabbles among different religious orders and groups:

> Entre praelats & entre les chanoynes,
> Et entre abbez, le couvent & les moynes,
> Officiauls, vicaires, promoteurs,
> Inquisiteurs, clercs, laics, accusateurs,
> Entre mondains & entre reguliers,
> Entre Augustins & entre Cordeliers,

> Se trouveront trop plus de differents,
> Que n'en avoyent les chevaliers errants.
>
> (13)

The very complexity of this catalogue suggests part of the reason for the endless conflicts between the opposing groups of churchmen and women. Just as marked by conflict is the layman's world of marriage. In short, concludes the god, "rien n'est sans moy" (14). Job found life a battle, Christians are bidden to fight, and the entire universe is marked by conflicting forces as the winds, planets, and stars move in contrary directions. Within the microcosm of man occurs an endless struggle between mind and body, good and evil desires. Since nature provides animals with claws, horns, and stings with which to fight, war must be part of the order of the universe. To those who retort that man, being born "nud," seems destined by nature for peace, not war, Mars replies that man, being much cleverer than other animals, can invent his own weapons.

Abandoning his defensive strategy of explaining the world as it is, the author now attacks, calling into question popular logic. If war is indeed so terrible, he asks, why are such splendid triumphs granted to victors and why is history full of tales of battlefield exploits and glories? Mars and Minerva are appropriate companions, prudence and courage both being essential in war. Dead soldiers are honored and praised, their death being decreed by God, not by Mars. Since death is inevitable, a glorious end in battle is surely preferable to a lingering one from some painful disease. Soldiers must be strong, temperate, and hard working, following the example of Alexander, Pompey, and Hannibal. Men unskilled in arms are considered cowards: even some women, notably Semiramis, Cleopatra, and Xenobia, have led armies into battle. Shifting to the contemporary scene, Mars tactfully assures his hearers that the valiant François I is fighting a just war and is sure to win. The customary compliment to the patron or monarch is placed here in a curious context, but one typical of the strategies of the satirical encomium. Begging the world to excuse the roughness of his speech, Mars explains that he must leave in order to supervise and favor the French cause. The sudden incursion of contemporary history into the paradoxist's world of reorganized mythology and selective logic explains the abrupt end of the oration. The author's evident preference for peace is confronted with the need to justify the national war effort and placate the king. Mars is about to abandon fiction for faction, and the delicate balancing of opposing points of view tilts towards political apologetics.

Whereas de l'Ortigue introduces another dimension into his apology for debt by referring to his imprisoned friend in the world outside the poem, Colet refers to the realm of national history. Both works make the satirical eulogy's customary switch to another frame of reference, another set of values. Our final assessment of the war poem must depend on whether the work suggests that in the campaign led by François I, the end, peace and victory, justifies the means, the dreaded war. It seems to me that the matter remains unresolved, the bulk of the poem taking a strong stand against war, and the surprise ending presenting a more ambivalent view.

Colet's highly original treatment of the paradox of war is more extensive than anything attempted by Estienne and seems to have found no imitators. More popular in France was the theme of imprisonment, developed in Estienne's paradox 18, "Que la prison est chose salutaire & profitable." Since paradoxes on debt often dealt with being in prison, there is sometimes a close relationship between works on the two topics. Estienne's essay was imitated in verse by Jean de la Jessée in 1583. Discussing both works, and the capitoli on similar themes by Lando, Bronzino, and G. F. Ferrari, Trtnik-Rossettini shows that what have been taken in the La Jessée poem to be personal reminiscences of Italy were in fact borrowings from the *Paradossi*.[104] A comparison suggests that La Jessée was probably using Estienne's rendition of the *Paradoxes*, since he includes Estienne's mention, not found in Lando, of the prisons of France and rearranges the first sentence of the text in a manner similar to that of Estienne. Developing the first half of Estienne's paradox, the general arguments in favor of prison, he cuts considerably the exempla, the list of famous people whose character was improved or life saved by being behind bars.

Both French writers begin in a similar fashion, whereas the Italian paradox 19, entitled "Meglio è d'essere in prigione, che in libertà" (1543 ed.), uses a different introduction. The most precious things, assert Estienne and La Jessée, are always kept locked away. As Estienne puts it, "Si les biens enfermez & recluz es estroittes maisons sont de plus grand pris & requeste, & en plus grande diligence conservez, que ne sont les desployez & exposez à l'arbitre de ceulx à qui touche la volonté d'offencer autruy: J'ay bien grande occasion d'affirmer que la prison soit meilleure, que la liberté" (1553 ed., 132–33).

The point is made here by a simple logical development, rendered plausible by the author's glossing over the reason for the concealment. The phenomenon is indeed the same for the jewels as for the prisoners, but the purpose, here unmentioned, is radically different. Also suppressed is the fact that one of the items hidden is an inanimate object, the other a living, freedom-loving human being. La Jessée renders this notion:

> Si les biens, & Joyeaus, es maisons recellez,
> Sont beaucoup moins communs, & de plus chere garde,
> Que ceus que le Vulgaire es boutiques regarde
> A l'oeil, voire au pouvoir, d'un chascun estallez:

> Qui ne croira, je vous suplie,
> (Si l'imprudence, & la folie,
> N'enchantent par trop ses espris:)
> Qu'il vaut mieus estre en asseurance
> Dans une close demeurance,
> Que vivre au large, & n'estre pris?
> (230)

The chief addition here is the parenthetical remark about "folie." It draws attention to the fact that most people believe the exact opposite of what is stated here, feeling that only a madman would prefer to be locked up in prison, even if that word has now been replaced by the more innocuous "close demeurance." The paradox begins to imply that we are being frightened by mere words, whereas the truth, as the writer puts it, is that "Ne doivent soubs correction ces paroles de prison & prisonnier, tant offencer les aureilles d'aucunes personnes" (133). La Jessée, once again, is more dramatic:

> Ce mot de chartre, serf, esclave,
> Offance en vain l'enfleure grave
> De quelque titre, ou dignité.
> (230)

Reflection, both writers note, will remind us that all men are prisoners of their sinful bodies until released by death:

> Qui fut la cause pour laquelle le sainct Apostre de Dieu, demandoit à haulte voix, Qui seroit celuy qui le delivreroit de ceste mortelle prison? il entendoit la prison de ce corps charnel, laquelle ne me semble de rien moins utile à la vie de l'homme, qu'est la prison de pierre, qui luy sert de vray rampart & sauvegarde, à l'encontre de touts les dangers qui le peuvent journellement assaillir. (Estienne, 133)

> Voyla pourquoy Saint Paul crioyt à haute voix,
> Qui me delivrera de ma prison mortelle?
> Entendant les travaus, la peur, & la cautelle,
>
> Du corpz fresle, & charnel, asservy sous ces loix:
> C'est vrayment un monçeau de terre,
> Qui (comme un tombeau) l'Ame enserre,
> Luy servant de Fort, & rempart.
> (La Jessée, 231)

While the prose work here moves logically from the traditional Christian and Neo-Platonic image of the body as the fleshly prison of the aspiring soul to the more positive image of it as the protective ramparts of the soul's fortress, the poem at this point almost loses sight of its professed aim, to defend the notion of prison. La Jessée's additional images of the body as a tomb and a heap of earth cause the negative impression to outweigh the positive one. The poem ends by saying that prisoners all pray devoutly and are free from sin and danger. As the poet begs to stay pure, to be free from evil at all costs, the notion of a literal prison fades. Estienne, on the other hand, stays resolutely with the idea of a literal prison, and concludes that since being in prison confers so many benefits, we should pray to God to be put there.

These two works use different processes to make a similar point: to lose the sense of the spirit is to lose the ability either to avoid going to prison or, once there, to transcend and benefit from it. The paradox is further complicated by the suggestion that the positive image of prison evoked by the poet's words, may lead us to forget the very real difference between freedom and jail.

The poet's hesitation with regard to prison as a real entity reappears in "La Contreprison. Stances." Here La Jessée takes a very different point of view, but one that is understandable given the difficulty he experienced in seeking to remain with the paradox of prison.[105] The prison is now the physical jail, which the incarcerated narrator compares to hell, much as Clément Marot had done many years before. There is surely some self-mockery in the following lines:

> J'estime fol cestuy-la qui me dit
> Qu'il s'y conforte, affine & enhardit,
> Franc de peril, & ferme de courage:
> En sa prison se plaise qui voudra,
> Captivité jamais ne me plaira:
> Il n'est que d'estre un Oyseau de boscage!
> (1:237)

La Jessée here draws attention to what he himself has done in the past, namely, attempted to blur the distinction between a real and a spiritual prison. And yet such blurring was facilitated by the very conventions of the satirical eulogy, which encouraged linguistic explorations of this type. Once again, the genre is coming to include consideration of its own procedures.

An autobiographical treatment of the theme of prison was undertaken by Odet de la Noue in 1588, after spending seven years incarcerated in the Château of Tournay. Once again the publisher was Jean de Tournes of Lyons. This *Paradoxe, que les adversitez sont plus necessaires que les prosperitez* was translated into English in 1594 as *The Profit of Imprisonment, A Paradox*.[106] Despite its title, indicating its adoption of an attitude "contre la commune opinion," the work is primarily a philosophical meditation, "a paradox against libertie," describing the author's feelings and aspirations during his captivity. Ideas similar to those found in earlier encomia reappear but are presented in a very different fashion. The tone is elevated, as the prisoner asserts that man, unlike animals, must seek what is spiritually good. He must train his children for the war against evil, understanding that God and His Son are our only helpers in the struggle. Adversities are not only inevitable, but are more desirable than prosperity, no adversity being more desirable than prison. Such a claim may seem paradoxical, he writes, but is less so than many others, such as that a man can relinquish wealth and yet be happy. The narrator expresses pleasure at being in jail, where he can read, play music, sing, and study, far from the vanities of the outside world. Whereas Estienne and Lando present individual cases of reformed or happy prisoners, enabling the reader to accept the possible social utility of prison, and La Jessée poeticizes the notion of prison in a mingling of Christian and Neo-Platonic imagery, Odet de la Noue becomes his own exemplum and authority. He eulogizes and defends at length the state of captivity, his tone that of the confession rather than of the exercise in rhetoric. The paradox is presented as actually proven by individual experience, not as a momentary exploration of an unusual point of view. In both title and content, the work is closer to the stoic paradoxes discussed in connection with Cicero than to the more playful mock encomium.[107] Even in its own terms, however, the reader cannot but be aware that he is being offered a highly selective view of Renaissance prison life. Only aristocratic and wealthy captives such as Odet de la Noue would be able to read, sing, and meditate tranquilly in their cells. This simultaneous acceptance of a paradoxical position and awareness of other points of view that call it into question have been shown to be typical of the paradoxical encomium. Colet moves the reader out to François I's real-life battles; Odet de la Noue introduces the autobiographical dimension.

Estienne's "Pour le Chiche," discussed above, or Francesi's "Sopra lepiteto della Povertà" or another Estienne piece, "Pour le Desmis de ses estats" may have provided inspiration for Jean Godard's "La Pauvreté" of 1594.[108] Francesi's poem makes the point that the real pauper is the greedy man, who never has enough. Since all of us have both gifts and defects, we should accept our lot. His conclusion, however, is less confident: "Ma infin chi nasce ricco ha gran vantaggio" (2:47ʳ), and the most positive adjective he applies to poverty is "timida." Godard's poem, longer and more personal than either of its predecessors, is dedicated to Audebert Heudon, who, with his brother Jean, was a close friend of Godard. The brothers both composed liminary verses for Godard's collection and had poems dedicated by him to them. Godard begins "La Pauvreté" by explaining that he sings only of what he knows well: "Aussi veux-je à ce coup chanter la Pauvreté, / Laquelle est prest de moy & la tousjours esté" (303). Since poverty prevents the poet from presenting Heudon with a rich gift, he offers him this poem, which, if Godard becomes famous, will one day be of value. The irony here is that the only real gift conferred by poverty may be the poem lauding it. The notion of the poem as a gift to a benefactor or friend is frequent in the Pléiade hymnes-blasons, as will be seen in the discussion of French animal encomia. But there the poetic mule or frog is offered as a verbal representation of the real thing. Godard is far from wishing to present poverty to his friend; indeed, his professed admiration for this state does not prevent him from hoping that poverty may soon leave him. However, aware that the number of poor men has always been large, he is prepared to be patient.

When Jupiter sent Pandora's box, continues the poet, he enclosed in it all the diseases and vices. "Plaisir" and "Paresse" between them made "Pauvreté," a lady who has not left men since and whose virtues are now described. Fleeing luxury and jewels, this virtuous woman lives on bread and water, and humbly salutes all who pass by. But no one notices her. Such sardonic comments again suggest the problems rather than the advantages of poverty; the narrator does not find consistency of attitude easy to maintain. "Paresse" may indeed be poverty's mother, he continues, but the daughter does not love her mother, preferring to work hard for anyone who will employ her. Envying no one, she lives simply, as men used to in the "vieux siecles passés," which are described in terms echoing Mauro. In those days, men were virtuous and poor, sometimes visited by the gods, as were Philemon and Baucis. People should respect, not despise Poverty, for she is "sage & prudente, accorte, & avisée" (309). In a further mythological development, the poet explains that when "Memoire" gave birth to the Muses, she decided that Poverty should bring them up humbly. The Muses therefore decided that no one should follow them if he did not first dedicate himself to poverty and honesty. To be rich, especially at court, one must be a hypocrite, an impossible sacrifice for a true poet. Having obeyed the wishes of the Muses in this respect, the narrator is himself almost destitute. He nonetheless bravely assures his friend that a "denier" from a poor poet is worth more than an "escu" from a rich man. Classical examples of people who refused or renounced wealth complete the defense, which ends with a more playful *envoi*, similar to those found in Pléiade hymnes-blasons.[109] As a reward for his literary efforts, the narrator begs poverty to spare his friends:

> Escoute ma requeste ô sainte Pauvreté
> Ne te monstre jamais farouche ny cruelle
> Ny à mes deux Heudons, ny à mon Pimpernelle.
>
> (320)

The poet asks poverty not to free him altogether, but to loosen the chains with which she binds him. He would like to live in "honneste Pauvreté" rather than "nécessité" (320). Given more financial security, he would sing of Francus, who came to Gaul and gave his name to France.[110]

In an age when most authors still needed patrons, Godard stresses the connection between money and creativity. Although the ability to write well cannot be bought—the Muses prefer a state of simplicity and poverty—the starving man may not write at all. Too much wealth is probably undesirable, but as the poem ends and the writer addresses a living friend, the natural human desire for money and security returns. Various epic possibilities and possibilities for epics are inseparable from the need for a steady and lasting source of income. Godard's initial literary paradox, relating poetry in a general fashion to a personification of poverty, gradually moves towards the real world of poor writers and their friends. The process of grappling with poverty has produced rich verse, the wealth that poverty can confer.

In addition to the paradox by Estienne, we find several other French works on the theme of drunkenness. There were a number of epitaphs on drunkards, such as that by Forcadel, "De Guyon Precy, somellier de Bacchus," which lauds the late drinker's "nez precieux" and ends with the suggestion that a "treille" should grow over his tomb.[111] Once again, the work was published in Lyons by Jean de Tournes, together with Forcadel's *Encomies*. Ronsard's "Folastrie 8" (1553) imitates the slurred speech of Thenot, a drunkard.[112] The longest French work to deal playfully with the vice of drunkenness was the *Discours de l'Yvresse et Yvrongnerie* by Jehan Moussin, dated 1612.[113] A liminary acrostic on the author's name calls this an "oeuvre paradoxal." Almost four hundred pages long, the *Discours* is not humorous throughout. It contains mock encomiastic sections such as the chapters entitled "Des louables effects du vin," "Que le vin tient le premier rang entre tous les aliments," and "Que le vin est un aliment vrayement salutaire & medicamenteux," but it also presents ways of avoiding drunkenness and a daunting list of the unpleasant effects of the condition: double vision, vertigo, and amnesia. It deserves more extended study.

Estienne's paradox on lawsuits is a likely source for a 1598 poem by Passerat, the "Divinité des Procés." Trtnik-Rossettini was unaware of any predecessors for the poem: "Passerat n'imite personne, sa pièce est tout à fait originale. Seule l'idée de diviniser le procès peut passer pour bernesque et autoriser à ranger cette satire dans le groupe des plaidoyers burlesques."[114] In fact, Passerat could have found inspiriation not only in Estienne but also in the much earlier "Blason de Pratique" by Gringore and in the similar "Description de Procés et de sa figure."[115] However, the "Blason" and the "Description" are direct attacks, with only traces of irony, whereas Estienne's paradox employs a jocular tone similar to that adopted later by Passerat. The "Blason de Pratique" presented an imaginative vision of an allegorical figure, a personification of Pratique, elsewhere referred to by the author as Procés. The concept of justice becomes a single animal combining traits of the donkey, the goat, the hog, the monkey, and other creatures. The corruption of the law is thus rendered in striking physical terms. The implication is that the machinery still functions and has some vague unity, but the grotesque unity and chaotic functioning of a monster. We recognize Pratique when we find it in society because it has one constant characteristic, that of being everywhere debased. The details of the beast's behavior are carefully chosen to apply principally to physical corruption and laziness. The monster is happy when offered good wine, is an ardent womanizer, and will say nothing unless given money. This poem is a blason in that it is a description of a single phenomenon, but the entity described is as much imagined by Gringore as existing in the real world. The allegory is evident but forms an integral part of what the writer seeks to suggest about his topic. The actual practice of the law of his day resembles for him a kind of living allegory, in this case a uniformly deformed creature.

Estienne, however, attacks indirectly rather than directly, an innovation continued by Passerat, who deifies lawsuits much as earlier encomiasts deify gout. Declaring that at such a time of crisis the topic is too dangerous, the narrator begins by refusing to discuss religious matters. He proposes instead to consider a topic closely related to religion, namely "Procés." On this religious parallel rests the remainder of the poem. The mysteries of God and of Procés, Passerat declares, are equally difficult to understand. Both must be treated with reverence and ceremony, since both can suddenly change their opinions. Thus, having favored Troy for ten years, the gods suddenly gave victory to the Greeks, just as lawyers may attack one another all day in court and make merry together in the evening. Both Procés and the gods make men pay dearly for their favors. The following passage resembles Estienne's picture of the changes wrought in a man by Procés:

> Avant que par Procés soit riche une partie
> Il se faut coucher tard, & se lever matin,
> Et faire à tous propos le diable Sainct Martin:
> Remarquer un logis, assieger une porte,
> Garder que par derriere un Conseiller ne sorte,
> S'accoster de son Clerc, caresser un valet,
> Recognoistre de loing aux ambles un mulet,
> Avoir nouveaux placets en main & en pochette,
> Dire estre de son cru tout cela qu'on achete
> A beaux deniers contans: bref, il faut employer
> Possible & impossible à Procés festoyer.
> On n'ose dementir des Dieux les saincts oracles:
> Ny l'arrest des Procés. Les Dieux font des miracles
> Les Procés que font-ils? Les plus gouteux troter,

> Galoper les boiteux, pour les solliciter,
> Les rendants au besoin prompts, dispos, & habiles.
>
> (1:66–67)

Like Gringore's monster, Passerat's Procés demands sacrifices but accepts only the choicest offerings. Now the mythological element is developed as Passerat lists the characteristics of Procés. It has the wiliness of Mercury, the eternal youth of Apollo and Bacchus, and the changing form of Proteus: "Vous le pensez civil, il devient criminel: / Vous l'estimez finy, le voilà eternel" (70). One of the talents Du Bellay attributed to the abbé Bonnet was precisely his ability to prolong cases indefinitely. In this Lucianic mock deification, Passerat vividly illustrates the superstitious awe and fascination inspired in the layman by the processes of the law. Underlining the mysterious, unpredictable nature of lawsuits, his poem at the same time suggests that, like gods, "Procés" have a clear identity and appear to be working towards a discoverable and recognizable end. The old device of personification thus takes on new depth and subtlety. Procés here has lost a sense of function; instead of leading to justice, it becomes synonymous with the pursuit of money and social prestige.

Passerat gives somewhat different treatment to the theme of trials and lawsuits in a poem published in his *Recueil des oeuvres poétiques* of 1606, in the *Labyrinthe d'Amour* of 1610, and reprinted in the *Cabinet satyrique* of 1618. Sometimes entitled "Comparaison de la femme au Procés," the sonnet claims that women and lawsuits are alike in that both talk endlessly, are wily, changeable, confusing, and expensive. Furthermore, both believe they are always right. In the 1606 version used in Blanchemain's edition, the ending runs as follows:

> L'une attize le feu, l'autre allume les flames:
> L'un aime le debat, & l'autre les discords:
> Si Dieu doncques vouloit faire de beaux accords,
> Il faudroit qu'aux procés il mariast les femmes.[116]

This ending suggests that the solution to the problem of disharmony lies in having the two discordant forces negate one another in marriage. A different but equally mocking ending is found in the *Cabinet satyrique* version of the poem:

> Tous deux sont d'une humeur de difficile accez:
> Qui courtise une femme et poursuit un procez
> Peut s'assurer qu'il fait son purgatoire au monde.[117]

The joke in this comparison lies in the narrator's initial posture of innocence with regard to his connection with both women and lawsuits. The first part of the sonnet treats both as external phenomena over which the hapless man has no power. The last lines here, with a twist worthy of Du Bellay, make plain that the man "fait son purgatoire." He is implicated both in initiating the lawsuit and in beginning his courtship of the woman. The problem is that without a sustained sense of ultimate purpose he may lose himself in the day-to-day difficulties of the lawsuit or the courtship. This poem cannot, however, be called a true mock encomium in any of its versions, since it contains only criticism, not praise.[118]

We have now seen that the *Paradoxes* and *Paradossi* inspired more French vice eulogies than did the Bernesque capitoli. However, the latter works did not lack imitators, as Trtnik-Rossettini shows in discussing the interesting series of works inspired by two poems by Mauro. The first French imitation, in 1547, was one of the three anonymous blasons published by Jean de Tournes in praise of gout and of quartan fever, and against honor. The third blason owes most to Italian sources: Mauro's "Capitolo in dishonor dell'Honore al Prior di Iesi," and "Del Dishonor al medesimo," which appeared in the 1542 edition of the Bernesque writers' works, *Tutte le opere del Bernia*. These capitoli may also have influenced the famous passage in Marot's third "Epître du coq à l'âne," on the disadvantages of honor on the battlefield.[119]

Consideration of honor was a popular theme at the time, the *Philosophe de Court* being one of the more extended treatments. Whereas the blasons on gout and the quartan fever seem to have been the only full-length mock encomia in verse on these two diseases composed in French in the sixteenth century, satirical writing on honor, bane or glory of the courtier's existence, was frequent. Later on, the same arguments are repeated in a dramatic setting by Falstaff, who, on the battlefield of Shrewsbury, reflects ruefully on the inability of Honour to mend the physical injuries suffered in its defense, and on the ease with which it is irretrievably lost:

> Well, 'tis no matter, honour pricks me on. Yea, but how if honour prick me off when I come on, how then? Can honour set to a leg? No. Or an arm? No. Or take away the grief of a wound? No. Honour hath no skill in surgery then? No. What is honour? A word. What is in that word honour? What is that honour? Air. A trim reckoning! Who hath it? He that died a-Wednesday. Doth he feel it? No. Doth he hear it? No. 'Tis insensible, then? Yea, to the dead. But will it not live with the living? No. Why? Detraction will not suffer it. Therefore I'll none of it. Honour is a mere scutcheon—and so ends my catechism.[120]

Of course, the larger world of the play contradicts Falstaff's bold claims. So far is honor from being a mere scutcheon, the lowliest form of heraldic ensign, that Falstaff's dishonorable behavior on the battlefield leads to his very real disgrace.

Trtnik-Rossettini provides a detailed comparison between the Lyons blason and Mauro's two poems. Unlike Pietro Toldo, she believes that the blason captures the Bernesque spirit better than Amadis Jamyn was to do in his "Elegie de l'Honneur": "L'anonyme français, tout en voyant, comme Mauro, dans l'honneur la cause des différents maux qui affligent l'humanité, ajoute cependant des détails originaux et conserve l'allure du paradoxe bernesque."[121]

In beginning his first capitolo, Mauro asserts that the topic has never before been treated. Although most men revere it, he would prefer to banish honor from the world because it forbids the enjoyment of the sexual pleasures so natural to man and even seeks to convince us "che'l morir di lancia è bello." Surely it is far better to lead a peaceful life than to die in battle. The narrator sees himself as the defender in particular of women, whose right to sensual enjoyment he champions. His beloved is so hard-hearted only because she follows the tyrant honor as a blind person does his dog. Like an invisible disease, honor gradually destroys us, until we are prepared to die for its sake. The first poem ends with a renewed plea for support from the ladies. The second considers the primitive golden age, when the concept was unknown. All human laws making men work, fight battles, and restrict their love-making can be traced back to some rule of honor's endless code. The poet's chief scorn is reserved for the knightly "point d'honneur," cause of so much useless bloodshed at the time.

Trtnik-Rossettini sums up the poem as follows: "Mauro fait ainsi apparaître la décadence des moeurs dans l'Italie du seizième siècle, l'absence de principes moraux, le cynisme, l'indifférence envers la patrie et l'avidité de jouissances."[122] The matter is more complicated than this historical analysis would suggest, for *honor* lurks in the word *dishonor*, and the writer remains fascinated by that which he so cynically denigrates. Mauro undercuts his posture of indifference by admitting at the end of the capitolo that despite his professed scorn he remains terrified of honor. In developing this latter notion considerably, the French poet alters the balance of the entire poem.

The full title of the anonymous French work is "Blason Declamatoire au Deshonneur de Honneur," a close equivalent of Mauro's "In Dishonor dell'honore." The poem is presented as an intellectual exercise that will lead us to appreciate the unchangeable but mysterious nature of God's wisdom. The writer proposes to demonstrate that man may question everything, "fors divine science" (11). The intangibility of honor is first underlined; it is but a word, "et pour autant chose plus que frivole" (11). A kind of malady, it blights our lives in much the same way as a physical disease such as fever or gout. Although the immediate source for these lines is Mauro, the passage gains added resonance from the fact that these same afflictions are the topics of the two other blasons in the collection. The ironic assertion that honor is a form of disease is reinforced by the poem's position between a pair of mock encomia on physical illnesses.

The French writer's first departure from Mauro's arguments concerns the origins and gradually increasing power of honor. Introduced when Adam and Eve sought to conceal their nakedness with the "Figuier," honor in the "beaux siecles dorés" did not prevent men from enjoying the pleasures of love:

> Alors Amans avecques leurs Amyes
> Sans d'Honneur crainte, ou d'aucune infamie
> Par champs, par boys, par montaigne, ou valee
> S'entredonnoyent l'un l'autre l'accollee.
>
> (13)

As time passed, honor grew from a "Gars" to a tyrant, "le pire des pires" (14). Using the customary mock-encomiastic technique, the poet rewrites history. Honor, he asserts, was the reason for the death of Abel, the fame of Nimrod as a hunter, the building of the tower of Babel, and the creation of countless false gods and idols. It even led to the invention of the various arts and to the divisions among "escoles." These sweeping assertions are not explained, but the lines in general seem to equate honor with ambition or personal pride. Even noble souls, this passage concludes, are often corrupted by the tyrant ideal. Cain, presumably, is to be viewed as such a man.

Returning briefly to the sexual barriers raised by honor, the author wonders how many abortions have been performed in order to maintain a respectable facade. Heresy, treachery, theft, and conspiracy frequently result from our attachment to this concept, which can even trick us into believing that death in battle is glorious. The following lines seem to be an attack on Machiavellian politics:

> Mais n'ha il pas une plus grande erreur?
> Disant qu'on doit, & peult sa foy faucer
> L'homme, qui veult regner, ou s'avancer?
>
> (15)

The suggestion here is that for different people there are different rules concerning what is honorable. Most men are taught that it is ignoble to betray their "foy." The blasonneur asserts, however, that an ambitious monarch or leader may be persuaded to break his word, presumably because he has in mind some more important consideration, such as his own political future or the good of his realm. This notion of a nonabsolute honor seems to be part of the author's presentation of the gradual evolution of honor through the ages.

Its originality is further illuminated when the poet dismisses in three lines the "inhumains" Greeks and Romans, capable of destroying themselves or members of their own families to preserve honor. The danger to families had been mentioned earlier in connection with Abel, although the biblical murder was that of an honorable man by a dishonorable one. The famous Greek and Roman murderers, on the other hand, killed family members whom they believed to have disgraced the shared family name. In the case of suicide, the action was taken by noble men who felt that only in death could their integrity be preserved.

After a passing mention of Lucifer's fall, also blamed on honor, the poet returns to the theme of unnecessary sexual restrictions:

> Bref il leur fait si honteuses molestes, [aux femmes]
> Que plusieurs ont regret de n'estre bestes
> Pour prendre, ainsi qu'elles, sans deshonneur
> Leurs appetitz, desirantes qu'Honneur,
> Et ses respectz, vraye gehenne mortelle,
> Fut forbanny de l'humaine cervelle.
> (15)

Demanding absolute marital fidelity and refusing recognition to illegitimate children, honor may eventually make marriage almost impossible. It is the thorn in every rose of pleasure; the writer laments, echoing Mauro:

> Quon ne sçauroit à rien faire, ou entendre,
> Aller, venir, manger, dormir, & boire,
> Ou damp Honneur ne survienne en barboire.
> (16)

In short, it demands more love and respect even than God: "Et plus, que Dieu, veult qu'on l'adore, ou prise" (16). This startling line, not found in the Italian poem, completes in a dramatic manner the portrait of honor's evolution, from its beginning with Eve's fig leaf to a superhuman, omnipresent force. The conclusion drawn by the poet is that this new religion, rather than elevating man, has degraded him. The cuckold's horns, legendary signs of disgrace, are but one of a number of far more serious metamorphoses "Horribles plus, que celles là d'Ovide" (17). Men become foxes, pigs, wolves, and dogs at the false god's bidding. This passage is connected to those deploring the deceptions, duels, murders, and other crimes performed in the name of honor. At this stage of the poem, the reader must feel that the treacherous idol should be overturned, its powers destroyed. In debasing and animalizing its followers, honor has achieved precisely the opposite effect of that sought by traditional religions.

Yet all this chaos is brought about by no more than a "vent mobile," swiftly lost and rarely regained. The term "vent" emphasizes honor's elusiveness and also the sense that it is but a word, a breath of wind, like Falstaff's "air." But despite this seven-page tirade, the poet reaches a conclusion that echoes that of Mauro:

> Quoy que ce soit tant la finesse, & ruse
> De cest Honneur me fait craindre & m'amuse,
> Que toutesfois, qu'il vient au devant moy,
> Tremble de peur, & suis en tel esmoy,
> Que tous plaisirs je laisse pour le suyvre,
> Aymant plus tost mourir, que sans luy vivre.
>
> (17)

The word "amuse" here should be taken in the sense given by Cotgrave of "stay, hold, or delay from going forward," not in the sense of "to entertain." We may view these lines as a final albeit reluctant acceptance of the need for social conformity. Such a view would seem to be valid in the case of Mauro's conclusion, but does not, I believe, do justice to the tone of the last couplet of the blason. Mauro emphasizes that he obeys the god out of fear ("mi trema ogni membro, & nervo, & osso" [1:124^r]), but the blasonneur goes further, claiming to prefer death to life without honor. In so doing, he makes more apparent the logical impasse to which his paradoxical reasoning leads. For he implies that, despite all, there remains some positive motivation behind the return to honor. The poem encourages the reader to recognize as snares many false forms of honor, but these debased forms never seem to efface all of honor, even as the word *honneur* remains visible within the word *deshonneur*. Indeed, each new attack on the concept seems but to elevate it yet further, until it finally achieves the status of a divinity, beyond the reach of mere words. Similarly, behind Falstaff's battlefield tricks lies the desire that his prince should believe him a worthy warrior, capable of slaying Hotspur in a fair fight. While the manifestations of honor in the blason's postlapsarian world may fall so far short of the ideal as almost to contradict it, the would-be rebel retains an uneasy sense of the lofty purpose behind the irksome, seemingly unnecessary constraints and rules. A principle of the honor of honor remains, deriving either from religion or from a secular moral sense of the need for the concept in the maintenance of law and decency in society.

The fact that the very terms of many attacks tend to be borrowed from the domain of the object or concept attacked has already been noted in connection with Synesius's encomium on baldness, which included within its text Dio Chrysostom's praise of hair. For all Synesius's rhetorical skill, baldness remained the absence of hair, not a positive attribute: the author finally voices regret at his hairless state. Similarly, the blasonneur can never escape his fascination with his subject, despite all attempts at denigrating it. This eventual return to the fold and departure from paradoxical investigation and hesitation are completed in the short "Chanson sus" that closes the de Tournes collection. Also anonymous, the poem is a lament over the "grande guerre, qu'un chacun ha contre soymesmes" (28). After seven stanzas of seven lines each, the eighth stanza cites Job and St. Paul as having also longed for an end to man's eternal struggle against his baser passions and instincts. The poet begs God, "qui seul les deffaitz reffait" (30), for deliverance from this long battle in which, as his introductory stanza had put it, "mon grand ennemy, las, c'est moy" (28).

In the same year and, yet again, from the de Tournes press, appeared Noël du Fail's *Les Propos rustiques*.[123] These contain some criticism of Castiglione and also an attack, in chapter 6, on honor as a barrier to love. The title of this chapter is revealing: "La difference du coucher de ce temps, & du passé: & du gouvernement d'Amour." In the old days a simple "bouquet" or "ruban" were sufficient gifts for ladies. Jealousy was unheard of, as was all the elaborate ritual of service, sighs, and sonnets. Similar ideas appear in Tahureau's *Dialogues*, in Marot's rondeau 60, "Au bon vieux temps," and in the poem by Victor Brodeau often printed with that by Marot, "De l'Amour du Siecle Antique."[124] Chronologically, the next attack was that by Philibert de Vienne, and then, in 1575, Amadis Jamyn published yet another poem on the topic, the "Elegie de l'Honneur."[125] Trtnik-Rossettini shows that, in imitating Mauro, Jamyn concentrates on the love problems caused by ladies' attention to honor, and neglects his predecessor's references to battlefield honor and to the chivalric "point d'honneur." This omission was perhaps due to the fact, noted earlier, that French writers were in general reluctant to attack the latter custom. Trtnik-Rossettini calls Jamyn's poem "une pièce froide et abstraite" and moves from this statement to a general conclusion concerning French adaptations of the capitoli: "On voit que les Français n'étaient pas doués pour les paradoxes bernesques et que tout en les traduisant et en les imitant, ils s'éloignaient du genre."[126] Surely the above study of the Lyons blason suggests that some French writers at least were "doués pour les paradoxes bernesques."

A more successful imitation of Mauro, according to Trtnik-Rossettini, is Regnier's "Satyre VI," written in Rome between 1604 and 1605 and published in 1608. It seems to derive nothing from Jamyn or from the Lyons blasons.[127] To these poems must be added one more vituperation of honor, by Gilles Durant.[128] Trtnik-Rossettini does not mention either Du Fail or Durant in her study. Like Jamyn, Durant focuses in his "Contre l'honneur" on the image of the "siècle d'or," when "ce vain tiltre d'Honneur" was unknown to man (147ʳ). In those days, people made love happily in the grass, their motto seeming to be "s'il te plaist, il t'est permis." Nowadays, this "nom plein d'imposture" (148ᵛ), inhibits sexual freedom and ruins the pleasures of "nostre siècle." Jamyn's and Durant's poems are part of the Renaissance literature idealizing country as opposed to court life. They make use once again of the myth of the Golden Age developed with such feeling by Panurge.[129] But what Panurge exploits in seeking to justify his extravagance, Jamyn and Durant manipulate in order to win over their ladies. All three confuse means and ends. Panurge is no more likely to persuade Pantagruel to agree to his view of the world than are the poets' ladies to succumb to this type of invitation to bed. The ultimately preposterous nature of both sets of arguments becomes a call to the other, better point of view, whether from the upright Pantagruel or the moral ladies. Inherent in the presentation of the paradox is its own negation.

BRUSCAMBILLE'S STAGE PARADOXES

In the early seventeenth century, the Bernesque satires enjoyed a renewal of popularity in a very different form, the dramatic works of Bruscambille, also known as Deslauriers. At the beginning of this period, Bruscambille was harangueur at the Hôtel de Bourgogne:

> Venu à Paris en 1606, il entre à l'Hôtel de Bourgogne comme harangueur: avant le spectacle ou en intermède, il débitait des morceaux de son cru, "satires bernesques," d'après des modèles italiens sur des sujets généraux de politique ou sur des points d'actualité. Comme il s'adressait au parterre, ses boniments étaient souvent bouffons, trop souvent orduriers. Il vivait encore en 1629.[130]

In his article, "Bruscambille et les poètes bernesques," Joseph Vianey sets out to show exactly what the actor owed to Italian predecessors.[131] He notes that, after a marked decline in popularity during the years following its Pléiade development in the hymnes-blasons, the Bernesque eulogy was revived, in this very different form, by Bruscambille. After describing the subjects treated by Bruscambille, Vianey discusses his use of Italian techniques, which mix "des bouffonneries vulgaires et des réflexions sérieuses, des comparaisons triviales et des images précieuses."[132] As has been shown above, these claims concerning the novelty of Bruscambille's Italian inspiration need qualification. Hymnes-blasons and other works inspired by the Pléiade continued to be written throughout the sixteenth century, and the sequence of poems on honor owes much to Mauro. Moreover, Bruscambille's speeches are related not only to Italian works, but also to the tradition of French farce, and to stylistic techniques found in much earlier French writing, as Barbara Bowen and Robert Garapon have shown in recent studies.[133] In Vianey's view, Bruscambille succeeded with Bernesque writing where Ronsard and the Pléiade failed because he recaptured the essential feature of the capitolo, the fact that it was written for oral delivery. He adds that Bruscambille stripped the Bernesque poetry of much of its elegance and fine language in order to adapt it for his less educated audience. John Lough has shown, however, that we must be wary of too lightly dismissing early seventeenth-century audiences as solely made up of the lower classes.[134] Bruscambille in fact includes a number of Latin and Italian quotations and at least as many double meanings and sexual innuendoes as the capitoli.[135] Some of his speeches can stand comparison with many of the better known mock encomia and provide a useful corrective to attempts to dismiss French skill at Bernesque writing.

When published, the harangues were frequently entitled "paradoxes," a fact significant in itself and indicative of the wide popular knowledge and acceptance of the term and its accompanying literary techniques. A short edition containing only a few pieces appeared in Rouen in 1610, and several others were published throughout the century. Referring to the 1615 and 1629 editions, I shall focus on those "prologues" closely related in topic and treatment to the Bernesque and Lucianic paradoxes. In the 1615 edition, one notices immediately a "Paradoxe sur la prison," which contains some familiar arguments in a more playful form than usual. Bruscambille asserts that "la prison est l'azille sacré de la Vertu, le domicille des bonnes moeurs: bref que les privileges des Prisonniers [sont] sans nombre."[136] In what he terms his "Primo Capitulo," a title borrowed from Italian, he explains that prisoners are exempt from paying taxes and fighting wars. The "Secundo Capitulo" explains that prisoners are so carefully looked after that they are harder to approach than princes. Prison improves both general health and the complexion. In addition, it affords time to read and meditate. Every one of these arguments had been used in earlier mock encomia: Bruscambille's originality lies in the dramatic spectacle his choice of form offers the viewer. Even in the printed text, some of this energy and feeling of spontaneity is retained. In addition, the reader-spectator cannot but enjoy the Panurge-like sangfroid and wit with which even the most outrageous arguments are advanced.

Other paradoxes in the first edition of Bruscambille speak in favor of winter, of pedantry, of "la Chicane," of the bottle (i.e., drinking), and of spittle. The 1629 edition contains several new pieces on old topics. One in favor of ignorance, entitled "Paradoxe, *Nihil scientia peius, aut inutilius*" (86–90), derives much from Lando, Montaigne, and Agrippa. In a by-now familiar image, the speaker asserts that one of the boasts of rhetoric is to disguise the truth, making white appear black. He next lists various arts and sciences, concluding, like Montaigne in the *Apologie pour Raymond Sebond*, that all are ultimately vain. Next in this edition comes a paradox entitled "*Egestas nobilissima*" (91–95), in which the orator shows that poverty is the mother of invention and that the poor need never fear robbers. After this brave speech come three less noble ones, "Qu'un pet est quelque chose de corporel," "Qu'un pet est spirituel," and "Qu'un pet est chose bonne." Only Eustorg de Beaulieu had previously treated this topic at such length.[137]

A noteworthy prologue in the context of the present study is the one "des Cocus, & de l'utilité des Cornes" (224–33). The many French encomia on this topic will be discussed in the following chapter, since the joke for French writers seems usually to have consisted of taking as a physical infirmity what was in fact a moral one. Like others before him, Bruscambille stresses the attractiveness of the curved shape of the horn. The new moon and several signs of the zodiac are horned, as is that fabulous and attractive creature, the unicorn. The very name "cocu" is a charming one, conjuring up an image of one of spring's most delightful birds. Many other pieces in this edition of speeches are on topics related to those found in full-length Renaissance encomia. Thus, we find prologues on madness, on the "Galeux," on cowardice, on the misery and then on the excellence of man, in praise of big noses, honor, beards, cabbages, and fleas. In the same volume appears a "Prologue en faveur du Mensonge," which proves to be similar to Mauro's capitolo. "Je soustiendray que le mensonge est fort utile & necessaire à l'homme," declares Bruscambille, "& que l'une des plus belles vertus qui le rende aujourd'huy recommendable, est de sçavoir mentir parfaitement" (113). The latter statement recalls many other attacks on court hypocrisy and makes apparent the special quality of the paradox in its stage form. Any paradoxical assertion gains added resonance from the dramatic spectacle, sometimes the dramatic irony, of the speaker imagined as addressing it to an audience. The traditional other point of view always called for by the paradox is here presented in the very person of the harangueur. The sight of Bruscambille elaborating his long paradox on the advantages of being able to tell perfect lies must have brought home the point to his audience. Like the Cretan liar of the ancient paradox, he is at once undercutting and confirming what he is saying about lies.

Former civilizations, he continues, in a brief moment of harsher satire, all realized the value of lying, for they invented gods in order to control the populace. Kings and rulers are obliged to use lies, as are merchants if they are to sell anything. On the deceits of lovers the speaker could write an entire book, so necessary are they to the maintenance of love's illusions. As he puts it, in a none too subtle image: "Les Amoureux, sur lesquels je pourrois estendre mon discours, mais un grand Volume n'y suffiroit pas, ne moüilleroyent pas si aisément l'anchre de leurs desirs au Havre tant desiré de tous les Amants, s'ils n'employoient le vent d'une infinité de menteries pour y parvenir" (116–17). The theme of lovers' deceits is developed at length in the *Moriae Encomium*, but not in such crude language. Courtiers and doctors are two more groups of people forced to lie, while Aristotle and Plato, teachers of rhetoric, indirectly approved of the art, "Car n'est-ce autre chose l'art de Rethorique, sinon l'art de bien mentir" (121). Once again, attention is drawn to the sight of the rhetorical expert praising the tricks of his own craft, challenging his hearers to judge for themselves the paradoxical truth he is articulating. The peculiar nature of such postures is reinforced by the fact that this prologue is one of the few to be followed immediately by another praising the exact opposite, truth. If truth has no need of eloquence, says the speaker, it must follow that eloquence serves the cause of lying, since it would otherwise have no function at all. Bruscambille's reader-listener is thus constantly encouraged to delve beneath and think about the implications of the polished surface of his speeches.

The inventiveness and general knowledge of the harangueur are remarkable, and the speeches deserve far more extended study than they can be given here. They demonstrate that the genre was by now so well known to the general public that the speech-maker could toy not only with the various traditional arguments but also with the entire genre and with its habitual exploitation of the game of literary lying. The sophisticated awareness of generic history manifest in these speeches serves to confirm Lough's claims about the differing social classes who attended seventeenth-century theater performances and to explain why the harangues were published so many times. Bruscambille brought the history of the paradoxical encomium full circle, from the speeches of Lucian and other classical orators to this French oral revival so many centuries later. Awareness of Bruscambille's close links to the literary genre of the mock encomium as well as to earlier forms of French theater may explain why his works survived when, as Bowen explains, many farces did not.[138] In fact, the harangues were being anthologized at precisely the time when the mock encomium in general was being so collected, as we have seen in chapter 3 above. In view of the extensive and profound uses to which English dramatists such as Jonson and Shakespeare put the paradoxical encomium, as Brian Vickers and others have demonstrated, we should attend more closely to this striking instance of French stage paradoxy.[139] A modern edition of Bruscambille is long overdue.

The works studied in the present chapter form one of the richest and most varied groups of satirical encomia written in Europe during the sixteenth century. Most of the Neo-Latin encomiasts sought consciously to revive and later to develop further what they presented to the reader as an ancient classical genre. The Italians brought humor, fantasy, and a host of burlesque and poetic elements into what had hitherto been a prose-dominated sphere. But only in France did a number of major satirists exploit and develop so widely and self-confidently the varied possibilities of the genre. These writers benefited greatly from the efforts of both their Italian and Neo-Latin precursors. Less preoccupied with self-justification and historical precedent than were the majority of Neo-Latin writers, they were freer to develop more fully the playfulness and irony appreciated by the Italians. In addition, in the dominant target for Renaissance satire, the court, the mock eulogist found a unique opportunity to blend the theme and form of his satire. As gout rapidly became the favorite disease for mock encomia, so court hypocrisy of one kind or another was the most frequent butt of the vice eulogies. The two groups of works dominate their respective categories in a manner which at first seems surprising, but which becomes understandable when one is aware of the history of the genre and of the times to which they belong.

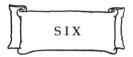

SIX

The Disease Eulogy in France

I will turn diseases to commodity.

FALSTAFF

As was shown above, Lucianic disease encomia were widely popular with Neo-Latin writers of all nationalities. French writers took the praise of disease in a somewhat different direction. Although there were some notable imitations of classical and Italian disease encomia, French satirists were equally interested in praising physical peculiarities and eccentricities. Since the influence of previous encomia is apparent in both these areas, it is important to consider what editions of earlier works were available to the French before passing to a consideration of French efforts in this category of eulogy.

So far as the *Podagra* is concerned, both it and, on occasion, the *Ocypus* appeared in various editions of Lucian. Editors such as Bretin seem to have read the play chiefly as a satire on doctors' arrogance, although mention was also made of the work's parodic nature.[1] In addition to the *Podagra*, Synesius's *Calvitii Encomium* was a much-published source of inspiration for praisers of physical infirmities. Between 1515 and 1522, Froben published several editions of the work, as translated by John Free, the fifteenth-century English humanist.[2] Froben customarily printed Synesius's eulogy with the *Moriae Encomium*, probably indicating that he viewed the two works as belonging to the same genre. Synesius's works also figured in the libraries of Montaigne and Théodore de Bèze.[3] French awareness of Italian disease capitoli has been discussed above. Another disease eulogy available to French readers was Pirckheimer's *Podagrae Laus*. André Pasquet's preface to Tabourot's *Les Bigarrures* (1583) specifically mentions "Pikemerus" in its self-justificatory list of predecessors.[4] We can conclude that the various editions—the Neo-Latin work was reissued in 1529 and 1570—must have been well known, although there does not appear to have been a French translation. Finally, Menapius's *Encomium febris quartanae* seems also to have been appreciated in France.[5]

In chapter 4, it was pointed out that disease encomia frequently make reference not only to other literary sources but also to current medical theories about the malady being praised. Since the composers of such encomia were often either doctors or patients, they had firsthand knowledge of their topic. As W.S.C. Copeman has demonstrated, beliefs about the origins, nature, and treatment of gout, that popular butt of satirists, remained remarkably constant for many centuries.[6] The satirical eulogist's traditional fondness for repeating standard arguments is thus reinforced by the continuity of medical and popular ideas about gout. French physicians such as Fernel, Paré, and Rondelet may have disagreed about details of treatment or nomenclature, but a study of their writings shows that medical, popular, and literary perceptions of the malady were closely related. All believed gout to be hereditary, but aggravated by self-indulgent and licentious living. They hesitated between their conviction that gout was incurable (Ovid's "tollere nodosam nescit medicina podagram") and the medical man's natural hope that all problems might prove to be curable. Their treatises therefore tend to move somewhat uneasily from exhortations to patients to moderate all fleshly appetites and to pray for God's mercy to confident descriptions of ancient or recently discovered cures.[7]

New editions of works on gout were of wide interest. Thus Demetrius Pepagomenus's thirteenth-century treatise on the topic was translated into French by Fédéric Jamot, himself a doctor, in 1567, and reprinted in 1572. Its publication in French was apparently something of a literary event, for it was heralded by such writers as Remy Belleau and Jacques Grévin. With several others, these two men composed effusive odes to be included with the liminary verses praising the author's and translator's efforts.[8] The work's full title in French is typical of heavy-handed Renaissance attempts to cover all eventualities when discussing complicated illnesses: "Traicté de la Goutte, contenant les Causes & Origine d'icelle, Le moyen de s'en pouvoir preserver Et la sçavoir guerir estant acquise."

French Works on Gout

French literature of the sixteenth century abounds in references to gout, but, so far as I have been able to ascertain, only one full-length gout encomium survives. This work, a blason, will be discussed below. Its originality may be better appreciated, however, by considering some more traditional and popular references to the illness. In French farces, for example, a character such as "Maistre Mimin le gouteux" could be introduced as a figure of fun.[9] Audiences or readers would immediately realize that he was satirized because to be gouty was automatically to be self-indulgent. Earlier, the theme of gout was a recurrent one in the poems of Eustache Deschamps, who suffered from the disease as well as from the "gravelle." Both afflictions he treated by abstinence. In one of his letters, he tells an unfortunate "nouvel marié gouteux" to refrain from sexual activity if he wishes to relieve his condition.[10] Rabelais, in the *Tiers Livre*, affectionately refers to his readers as "Goutteux tresprecieux," when they are not "Beuveurs" and "Verolez" of equal price.[11] "Goutteux" here can mean those who drink and those who have gout, a useful doubling of meaning.

Antonio de Leyva, the unfortunate gouty general mentioned by Cardano, was the subject of an epitaph by Sainct-Gelays portraying him as too lame even to flee before the enemy, a clever inversion of the usual joke that gout was not so crippling that men were unable to run if necessary:

> Sous ce tombeau gist une sepulture,
> J'entens un corps servant de monument;
> Car il n'avoit d'humaine creature
> Proportion, chaleur, ne mouvement.[12]

The Spanish soldier reappears in the Lyons blason on gout. That the omnipotence of the illness extends even to medical men is noted in a humorous manner in the *Podagra* and in more respectful tones in Cardano's account of the aggrieved deity's devastating revenge on the presumptuous Budaeus. Montaigne makes regular mention of gout, as well as of his kidney stones, in the *Essais* and the *Journal de Voyage*.[13] Jean de la Jessée, that prolific composer of mock encomia, seeks to punish an interfering old "bigotte" by wishing that she may suffer from, among other diseases, "auz piez la goute."[14] Passerat bewails his own gout in a short poem of 1583 punning on the many meanings of the word gout:

> Plus de six mois y a qu'il pleut ou qu'il degoute,
> Sans qu'on voye un seul jour le ciel clair & ouvert:
> C'est pour quoy je ne puis si bien estre à couvert
> Que je ne sois contraint d'en sentir quelque goute.[15]

Halfway between Lucian's mock reverence and the solemnity of most Renaissance doctors' treatment of the gout is a poem by René Bretonnayau entitled "Les Goutes." In the margin of the Bibliothèque Nationale edition of the poem, which appeared with another Bretonnayau work, "La Génération de l'homme," a later reader has added the succinct comment "sans cure." Gout, the author declares, is a "tiran inexorable," "enragee, horrible, abominable, / Invincible, & qui fait trembler mesme les dieux."[16] The afflicted author, himself a doctor, begs this hard-hearted deity born of Bacchus and Richesse to recognize his awed respect for her power and deign to lighten his torments. Although so-called cures are listed and may serve to alleviate the attacks, only God can completely remove this affliction. Pliny's account of a gouty man cured upon falling into a bin of grain is cited as one such miraculous recovery. Although making use of the exaggerated language associated with Lucian's gout tragedy, this poem is in fact the rueful recognition by a doctor of his own limitations.[17] The two French works in which gout is treated either humorously or satirically are the 1539 *Le Triumphe de très-haulte et puissante Dame Vérolle, Royne du Puy d'Amour* and the 1547 "Blason de la Goutte," one of the three anonymous Lyons blasons, the first of which, on honor, is discussed above.[18] The *Triumphe*, which will be discussed in more detail in connection with other works on the disease which forms its chief topic, lists "la Goutte" as a character in the triumphal procession honoring the "Vérolle." Gout and venereal disease are related because both are believed to be the result of intemperate living. The personified Gout speaks, much as had Podagra:

> En ce triumphe prens mon lieu
> Avec la Diette ma grant mere
> Je suis la Goutte de par dieu
> Aux ungs rudes (*sic*), aux aultres amere
> Et ny a Virgille, ou Homere
> Par qui je puisse estre ravye:
> Quant je tient (*sic*) compere, ou commere
> C'est à la mort, & à la vie.[19]

The reference to Virgil and Homer, suggesting that even great writers cannot charm gout away, is an important variant on the usual attacks on the powerlessness of doctors, because it reflects on one of the most frequent claims of disease-praisers, that their works could indeed to some extent dispel the pain of illness. The Paris edition of the *Triumphe* also includes, in the section containing the poem called the "Pourpoint," a short poem attacking the "ord vaisseau" from whom the writer claims to have caught the "vérolle." As a result of this attack, he complains that "la goute me tue & affolle."[20] A final message urges the reader not to be scandalized by the crude language of the work. Instead, he should learn to laugh at the world's folly and to avoid "paillardise."

The *Triumphe* is related to works such as the *Podagra* and the *Moriae Encomium* in that it applies solemn or grandiose terminology to a topic not generally thought to deserve such language. The element of incongruous self-praise is equally apparent. But the French work on gout that is most obviously a satirical eulogy is one of the three anonymous blasons published by Jean de Tournes in Lyons in 1547. In fact, two of these three poems are on diseases popular with mock encomiasts, since in addition to the blason on gout, there is one on the quartan fever. Although she has clearly demonstrated the debt these pieces owe to Italian capitoli, Trtnik-Rossettini has not considered them in terms of the paradoxical encomium as a genre.[21] The third poem, vituperating honor, owes much to Mauro, but the disease blasons are less directly inspired by their Italian predecessors. Aretino's "Capitolo della Quartana," for instance, is quite unlike the Lyons poem, while the blason on gout resembles the *Podagra* and Neo-Latin gout praises as much if not more than it does Francesi's "Lode delle Gotte."[22]

The full title of the blason on gout makes apparent its burlesque nature: "Louange de la tresfroide, tres-chaude, inexorable, & tresredoutable Dame, la Goutte."[23] Written in decasyllables, the poem begins as the writer declares that the enforced abstinence of sufferers from gout has inspired him:

> De reciter plus de louange d'elle,
> Que Lucian en ce beau dialogue,
> Où il la met au ranc, & catalogue
> Des Dieux trescraintz, recitant plusieurs preux
> N'estre famés, que pour estre goutteux.
>
> (3)

The presentation of a disease as a powerful goddess is immediately familiar. Personification is peculiarly appropriate for conveying the sense in which the attacks seem at times to the afflicted to be controlled and directed by an external power bent on vengeance or punishment. After a passing mention of gout's selectivity, for she spares women and the virtuous, the blasonneur reminds the reader of the disease's incurability, reiterating the Ovidian claim.

The next passage in the blason is one for which I have found no precedent in previous gout eulogies. The source of the malady is traced back to the circumcision of Abraham. Gout marks her elect as indelibly as does the ancient rite or as did the angel who, in struggling with Jacob, marked "the hollow of his thigh."[24] The idea that gout is a kind of external brand making visible to others that the bearer belongs to a particular group of people is implicit in Francesi's picture of the gouty monks. But whereas the Italian writer suggests that gout betrays something the monk would prefer to hide, his fondness for luxurious living, the blasonneur treats the "signe" of gout as a matter for almost religious pride. Only in this manner, it is asserted, can the sufferer prove himself one of the "vrays esleuz," the "vrays Israël-ites" whose election by God is marked upon them by the angels. By comparing gout to circumcision the poet suggests that man may come to accept certain forms of pain as a way of raising himself above ordinary mortals.

The religious imagery and transformation of the gouty man into a kind of priest figure belonging to an elite group continue as the poet addresses the goddess directly:

> O caractere indelibile & cher!
> O *sainte* Goutte indigne d'attoucher
> Fors delicatz, & qu'on doit dorlotter
> Sus coussinetz, & en douceur frotter,
> Et dyaprer, comme un *reliquiaire*:

Ou autrement elle peult grand mal faire.
Car c'est (pour vray) un *sacrement* tresdigne.

(4, italics mine)

The traditional claim made on behalf of gout, that she does not attack women, takes on a different dimension in this context. Instead of being a sign of the goddess's merciful nature, as was usually asserted, it becomes proof that she seeks a band of strong men who, once converted to her cause, can become loyal priests. Indignantly, the narrator explains that true gout has nothing to do with the "raige enragee," the illness that attacks the "impudicz." We may see here a reference to some form of venereal disease, perhaps syphilis, which can eventually attack the joints. The name "Goutte," on the other hand, is said by the poet to be related to "Artique" and "Sciatique," "Noms derivans de tous biens & sçavoirs." The parallelism is presumably based on the similarity between the words *art* and *artique*, *science* and *sciatique*. This section of the poem concludes with another declaration that gout is "tressainte & Angelique," seeking only her disciples' "ayse, & proffit" (5). The link between the material world of pain and swollen joints and the spiritual realm of religion and meditation has thus been carried through into the very etymology of the words describing the various types of gout.

The blasonneur next explains, as had Francesi before him, that gout does no harm to man's chief blessings, "de l'esprit, de fortune, & du corps." Like Francesi's sufferers, or like the happy debtors in Berni's capitolo on debt, the gouty man is always surrounded by well-wishers. This statement is another instance of reinterpretation of the truth. The reader realizes that the debtor is so accompanied only because no creditor wants harm to befall him before he has repaid his debt, and that the gouty man's visitors are happy to visit him because his affliction is not contagious. Few would call if he had the plague: indeed, Berni's plague poem had recommended complaining of symptoms of the plague precisely in order to be rid of creditors.[25] As if in recognition of gouty men's superiority, people make way for them in the streets:

> quand dans la chaire à bras
> Portés en Ducz, faisant des Fierabras,
> Il fault qu'honneur chacun aux goutteux face,
> Soit en l'Eglise, en maison, ou en place.
>
> (6)

Those making way for the patient may even, suggests the narrator, credit him with as much intellectual as physical weight. This passage serves as a humorous reminder that gout is a very visible, but also a "safe" disease. The sufferer does not have to retreat from his fellow men, but can remain in their midst, showing them how he copes with pain. As for the patient's enforced avoidance of the excesses of "Venus, & de table / Cela leur est (peult estre) profitable." The "peult estre" seems at first an odd interjection, but serves as a reminder that not all react courageously to their trials, despite the noble birth and powerful social position of most victims. The poet passes over the opportunity for social satire Francesi grasps at this point. Instead, he details the different kinds and levels of benefits conferred by his new divinity. First among these is a purely physical one, the freedom to take life easily:

> O comme au lict ses possesseurs esgaye,
> Tresexcusés pour affaire, qu'on aye,
> De n'en bouger: où le sain malheureux,
> Dormant à l'ayse, encor tout sommeilleux
> Sort de son lict pour courir & baller.
>
> (7)

The next advantage of gout concerns a more significant realm of activity: the varying degrees of pain in his joints enable a gout victim to foretell changes in the weather "mieux, qu'un grand Astrologue." Again, the almost religious nature of the affliction is underlined. Furthermore, gout forces her elect to lead a sober life, thereby encouraging them to cultivate "bon corps, & bonne ame." Surely, therefore, she must be viewed as a "tresadmirable dame," raising our thoughts heavenwards. There follows a list of famous gout-sufferers, the first of whom is not a classical or mythological figure, but the familiar "feu Antoine de Leve:"

> Assis en chaire, & ne bougeant d'un lieu,
> Craint des Soudars, plus obey, qu'un Dieu:
> Qui aux assaux, & mirables victoires
> Ha plus acquis à son Cesar de gloires,
> Que maintz Ducz sains. Car en sa providence
> Plus de force eut, qu'en son Ost de puissance.
>
> (7)

Because Leyva, one of Charles V's most successful generals, helped defeat the French at the battle of Pavia (1525), he would have been well known in France. In a discussion of his career, Brantôme mentions Leyva's gout, and it has been shown that Rabelais entitled a book in the library of Saint Victor the *Entrée ès terres du Brésil* in order to mock the general's desire to invade Provence.[26] I have already quoted the hostile epitaph on him by Sainct-Gelays.[27] The unusually favorable portrait found in this Lyons blason can perhaps be explained by the poet's wish to stress the beneficial transformations brought about by gout. Instead of gout, it is now her famous disciple, Leyva, who is "plus obey, qu'un Dieu." Having accepted the necessity of being carried into battle, rather than riding, he has turned a disability into an advantage. As the rhyme makes plain, his thoughtful "providence" has become a more powerful force than the solely physical "puissance" of the "Ost." The French poet has gone far beyond Cardano in using his contemporary example.

An even more effective illustration of the transforming powers of gout is provided, according to the blasonneur, by the gouty Roman emperor Severus, who is reported to have remarked, when pardoning a group of conspirators, that the head, not the feet, rules a man.[28] This statement might seem to call into question the importance of gout, but the poet interprets it as a reflection of the goddess's worth, "Dont dire fault, que sa suave oppresse / Mere est (pour vray) de toute gentillesse" (8). By first understanding and striving to control his own feelings of pain and resentment, the emperor learned that the best way to control others is to temper firmness with compassion. Gout thus becomes a mother figure, whose "suave oppresse" teaches men the way to "toute gentillesse."

Her kindly nature even influences her treatment of the sufferer's body. Gout lessens the force of other diseases, such as the quartan fever, and does not affect "coeur, langue, ou chef," the "membres hautains," but renders the rest of the body incapable of such vain activities as running and dancing. The disciple can devote all his mental energies to religious and philosophical meditation. Moreover, this change of direction is brought about not merely by the blocking of other paths, such as those leading to the ballroom and the tavern, but by a more positive impetus:

> elle rend les espritz plus adroitz
> Pour artz apprendre, & justice, & tous droitz:
> Foy observer, exercer charité:
> Dompter la chair, despriser vanité.
>
> (8)

These improvements are of course those traditionally associated with the effects of religious faith.

So great a degree of moral and religious transformation of pain has now been achieved that the poem might seem to have moved beyond the need to discuss disease at all. In a sudden twist typical of paradoxical writing, the poet returns to a consideration of gout as a disease, one that we all at first hope to cure completely by medical means. He notes that if the gouty man observes a sufficiently "povre" regimen, he may well free himself entirely from his "gouttiques douleurs." Like most other gout-praisers, from Lucian to Ballista, the blasonneur recommends patience and abstinence as the best weapons against the tyrant. He cites the case mentioned by Pliny of a man who was cured of gout by a fall into a bin of "froment," but does not go so far as so suggest, as did Bretonnayau, that this unexpected recovery was due to divine intervention.[29] Great men are exhorted not to complain of their afflictions. Domitian's baldness, Caesar's nightmares, and Severus's gout should serve as reminders of shared humanity, not as pretexts for self-pity. Let them recall, says the poet,

> Leurs grandz honneurs, triumphes, & victoires,
> Sans estre ingratz de ce bien, qu'ilz sont hommes
> Subjetz aux maux, ainsi que tous nous sommes.
>
> (9–10)

No longer a divinity, the gouty man must now view as a "bien" his inevitable human weakness. Since we can never know perfect happiness or freedom from adversity, it is foolish to make "tant d'Agios pour la Goutte."[30] This passage differs from that concerning Leyva and Severus in being a defense by negatives, not positives. The moment of controlling the flesh and despising worldly vanity has passed, to be replaced by renewed anxiety about the ability even of great men to sustain such a lofty state of mind and body. The alternative now offered is therefore to accept gout not as a good, but as a relatively bearable instance of life's many and unavoidable ills.

The poet's conclusion, adapted from Francesi, is at first presented firmly: "Je vous dis d'abondant, / Qu'en Goutte n'ha ne mal, ne maladie: / Mais dons divins, quoy qu'on murmure, ou die" (10). This assertion is said to be borne out by the fact that "Medecins," "Drogueurs," "Charmeurs," and "saccageurs de vie & de santé" stock no cure for gout. Such a statement, claiming that if there is no antidote there is no disease, too obviously flouts known experience to be taken at face value. The absence of a cure proves only the inadequacy of medical knowledge, not the nonexistence of the disease. But the poet, pushing his argument *ad absurdum*, tells the sufferer: "Garde la donc, & guerir n'en demande / Celuy, à qui par grace Dieu la mande" (10). The favorable presentation of gout has moved from a defense back to a panegyric. Pain has once again been so distanced that the reader is placed in the ridiculous position of being exhorted to long for gout's continuance rather than its alleviation or cure. Even the most fervent of the goddess's disciples might hesitate to beg for such a boon.

The last four lines of the blason are set in larger type than the remainder of the poem. The fact that they contain a series of puns on the word *goutte* is thus made doubly prominent. The lines run as follows:

> Fin des goustz goustés de la Goutte,
> Qui, quand en degouttant degoutte,
> De gouste un trop meilleur gouster,
> Que Goutte au vin me fait gouster.
>
> (10)

The various words based on *goutte* can mean *to drip, to disgust, to taste*, or *to enjoy*. The chief source of the joke, medically speaking, is that the origins of gout were believed by many physicians to lie in a dripping of liquid into the joints. Hence the use of the Latin *gutta* (drop), to designate the disease.[31] The reader of the blason is struck both visually and linguistically by the forms of the word *goutte*, repeated nine times in this quatrain. Gout, at first presented by the blasonneur as an external sign conferred upon a group of "esleuz," is gradually transcended as the poem proceeds. Now we are reminded in a most obvious manner of the persistence of this most public disease. The pleasure of playing with words, with the "goustz" of "Goutte," may indeed have replaced the now-forbidden pleasures of wine. But the gout-laden foot of this page provides a salutary and humorous corrective to anyone naive enough to suppose that the inspiration for all this clever paradoxy is anything other than a painful and incurable disease. The blason has proposed various ways of coping with pain, even of achieving moments of resignation and contentment. But Gout's priests cannot for long elude her power. The verbal drunkenness, like that of wine, will pass, leaving the sufferer yet more acutely aware of his vulnerability. The Lyons blason on gout thus varies earlier arguments on behalf of gout by concentrating chiefly on the gouty man's function and actions in society. As one marked for life by his disease, he can become gout's respected disciple, like Leyva or Severus, or a weak and complaining victim, forever making "tant d'Agios pour la Goutte."

With the exception of this long poem, the literature of the French Renaissance does not contain any instances of extended ironic praises of gout. Not until the early seventeenth century do we find another, freer translation of the *Podagra* and not until the eighteenth century do new paradoxical encomia on the disease appear. In Copeman's "golden age of gout," the renewed vogue for such works is readily understandable: indeed, two French encomia on the subject, by Louis Coquelet and Etienne Coulet, appeared within a few years of one another in the late 1720s.[32]

THE QUARTAN FEVER

The second Lyons blason concerns the quartan fever, praised in classical times by Favorinus. As was noted in discussing Menapius's work, fevers of all sorts were the subject of numerous treatises throughout the Renaissance. Balthasar Conradinus, Thaddaeus Dunus, Fernel, Paré, Rondelet, Valla, and others made minute discriminations between the different kinds of fevers, their symptoms, and, where possible, modes of treatment.[33] Montaigne declared that one of the achievements of philosophy is that it can "apprendre la fain et les fiebvres à rire."[34] Parts of the Lyons blason on the quartan fever are based on current medical ideas, but the poem is derived as much from literary as from then current "scientific" sources.

The introductory lines are of interest in that they refer to the author's own earlier blasons. He becomes, in a sense, his own authority:

> Pour avoir fait au deshonneur d'Honneur
> Blasonnements, aussi en la faveur
> De la grand'Goutte, *à tort dite* incurable,
> Je veux aussi à l'exemple notable
> Des plus sçavans Modernes, & antiques,
> Canonizer par raisons autentiques
> La Quarte icy, l'engin exercitant.
> Car Phavorin jadis en feit autant:
> Puis Menapie, Encomiaste exquis,
> En dit maints loz: & duquel ay enquis
> Maints argumens pour former sa louange.
>
> (18, italics mine)

Addressing all "febricitans," the poet criticizes their belief in the severity of their affliction:

> A telz propos je vous peux contredire,
> Qu'il n'y ha mal (au vray) pour mal receu,
> Si ainsi n'est par opinion creu,
> Au dire au moins d'aucuns philosophans.[35]

The line of attack here is slightly different from that followed in the gout blason. In the earlier work, it was admitted that gout involved suffering, but the claim was made that if publicly endured and accepted, the pain could be rendered more tolerable. Quartan fever, on the other hand, was not usually a lifelong or fatal illness. Its defense was based primarily on its most striking characteristic, that of being absent for more days than it is present.

But first the poet questions the very name of the malady. It should never have been called a fever, for it has nothing to do with "ferité" or even "ferveur," terms that might appear to be linked with it.[36] Not meriting the epithet of "fiere," it is the mildest of fevers, a "gratieux tourment," a "douce langueur," and a "purge salutaire."[37] Turning next to his own historical situation, the blasonneur remarks that in recent times people have observed an increase in the severity of the disease. This change he attributes to "aucune insolence / Faite au manger, ou en quelque autre affaire" (19). If it is not prolonged by the patient's intemperance, the fever will, however, gradually subside. All other fevers are more dangerous than the quartan, particularly since it strikes in winter, the safest season for such diseases. A fever caught in the summer will be aggravated by the heat, whereas we willingly remain indoors when it is cold outside, "demenans près du feu chere lie." The illness begins to resemble a state of health, in which "à toute heure est loysible / De s'esventer, manger, boire, & courir" (20). In a sense it is even superior to normal health, for it can drive off other fevers from which the patient was suffering previously. This may lead doctors, continues the poet, to wish that their patients may catch the "Quarte," driving off a greater with a lesser ill. The "Quarte," a disease, now becomes not a goddess, as had been the case with gout, but a force having "puissance / Plus grande assez, que l'hautaine science / Des Medecins" (21). This paradoxical image of a disease as a kind of doctor is the second recurrent theme of the blason. It suggests the way in which the disease contains the elements of its own "cure," or at least can teach us how to tolerate it.

Another boon is the fact that because of its characteristic pattern of attacks at regular intervals, the "Quarte" can never be wrongly diagnosed or incorrectly treated. Indeed, on days between bouts of fever, "on joue, on rit, on s'esbat," whereas with most illnesses the suffering is so constant that "rien, que mort, on n'attend, ou demande" (22). Surely, the narrator suggests, it is better to contend with a known but intermittent ill than to face one of life's countless disagreeable surprises. That the fever is not very severe is proved by the fact that even "enquartenez" are expected to appear before a judge if summoned to do so. In short, we can lead much the same life with the fever as without. Even exercise is deemed beneficial, whereas sufferers from other diseases are forced to modify and restrict their activities drastically.

Despite their professed admiration and desire for the disease they were eulogizing, most writers, as has been seen above, include in their works either a section discussing the cure for the illness or some recommendations as to how best to cope with its attacks. The French poet follows this trend but introduces a note of sardonic humor into his description of the process:

> Car simple peur, leger ou grand exces,
> Maints ont gueriz, & guerissent assez,
> Voire à simple eau d'un simple distillee
> Souventesfois elle s'en est allee.[38]

Continuing this quasi-scientific discussion of how to cure a disease whose very reality he had previously questioned, the narrator now relates a personal experience. He explains that in 1545, the year of the composition of the blason, he, although not a physician, cured several cases of quartan fever in patients for whom qualified doctors were too expensive. The cure was achieved by administering "de ladite eau," that said earlier to have been distilled from a "simple." Since the promise the blasonneur makes to describe this brew is never fulfilled, we must look elsewhere for what he may mean by a "cure."

The answer will be found in the gradually unfolding procedure of the blason, as the poet explains that the "humeur melancolique," cause of the fever, makes a patient "Doct, & prudent, en tout ingenieux" (24). It strikes only those strong enough to withstand it; the very old, like the very young, usually escape. The reader has been maneuvered into the familiar paradoxical situation of asking to have the "quarte"; "tresjoyeux ilz sont un peu l'avoir, / Comme à purger faisant meilleur devoir, / Que nul bolus, ou pillule, ou breuvage" (26). And yet health still remains the ideal; the fever is to be welcomed only as a means of attaining this ultimate goal:

> Donc pour un peu, qu'elle peult tourmenter,
> Ne vault il mieux la Quarte supporter
> Pour puis avoir santé perpetuelle,
> Qu'estre en danger d'un grand meschef sans elle?
> (26)

Not only does the fever eventually strengthen the body, it also transforms the personality:

> Tristes espritz fait devenir joyeux,
> Vivre en espoir, rejouvenir gens vieux,
> Extenuant humeurs melancoliques,
> Qui rendent gens bien souvent fantastiques.
> (27)

Once again a disease is pictured as a kind of healer, a cure for other maladies. "Gens enquartenés" are urged to accept their sufferings with "joye & patience," secure in the knowledge that, if careful, they will enjoy

> une convalescence
> Trop plus utile, & salubre, & durable,
> Que si n'eussiez eu la Quarte louable,
> Et plus facile à guerir, qu'on ne dit,
> Si lon sçait bien ce, qu'à sa cure duit.
> (27)

Thus ends the second blason. While the gout poem seeks to investigate the best way of living with what was almost always an incurable illness, the poem on the "Quarte" continually stresses that the fever is both curable and physically beneficial. The goddess Gout, after branding her followers with the external signs of fleshly overindulgence and weakness, then gives them the chance to achieve moral and spiritual superiority and strength; Severus and Leyva typify this process. The quartan fever functions and is presented differently. A serious but not necessarily incurable illness, it is characterized by the intermittence of its attacks and by the fact that it was commonly held to strengthen and cleanse the body of the survivor. The idea of a disease whose presence is identified by the number of days on which it is absent is at first sight as strange as that of a disease being a kind of cure. Yet each of these propositions holds an element of truth, presented playfully by the poet in the form of interlocking paradoxes. The allegedly effective "simple" is of course never found, for the writer is a paradoxist, not a doctor. His claim to have cured some sufferers is not the main point made in his poem, but a short section in a wide-ranging investigation into the positive and negative aspects of this peculiar type of fever. The power of the "Quarte" should not be disregarded, but the conclusion cautiously suggests that by pondering "ce, qu'à sa cure duit" a fever-sufferer may learn what might be termed a healthy way of coping with what nonetheless remains a disease. This changed state of mind and body, a combination of mental agility and physical moderation, has been described in and illustrated by the very procedure of the blason, a kind of intellectual "simple," which may encourage reflection and broaden the reader's understanding of the mysterious nature of disease.

The Triumph of "Dame Vérolle"

Like the blason on gout, that on the quartan fever seems to have been the only full-length humorous treatment in French of its particular disease. We may therefore turn back and examine more closely the 1539 *Triumphe de très-haulte et puissante Dame Vérolle*. Montaiglon, the modern editor of the work, discusses the possible attribution of the piece to Rabelais but reaches no conclusion. The poem is preceded by a prose dedication and two tales tracing the origins of the disease. These tales, once thought to be by Jean Lemaire de Belges, are not so attributed by Montaiglon. Since the work bears no resemblance to Bino's capitolo on the "Mal francese," there seems no reason to suppose any detailed Bernesque influence. The idea of deifying or aggrandizing a personified disease was commonplace by this time. The name "dame Vérolle" appears even in poems that do not pretend to be praising the disease, as when François Habert calls the "lady" a "vieille interdicte" for attacking one of his friends.[39]

The dedication of the *Triumphe* is headed "Martin Dorchesino à Gilles Meleanc son amy et Cousin Salut." It describes the way in which the Romans used to accord triumphal processions to victorious generals such as Scipio Africanus and Julius Caesar. These ancient triumphs, the author continues, are as nothing compared to that which should be held to honor a certain noble lady:

> Mais quant je considere quels ilz ont estez, ne meritent quon en face sinon bien petit destime, fors paradvanture celluy d'une grand Dame nommée Vérolle. Laquelle issant en gros equipage bellique du Puydamours son royaulme & pays, a couru & faict ses fors exploitz de guerre

par tout le Monde: & a vaincu à peu de gens jusques à aujourduy plus
d'ennemis, que ne feirent oncques tous les plus excellentz Capitaines
qui furent jamais. (iv)

So successfully has "la Vérolle" conquered the world that a friend of the
narrator's has recently commissioned a painting of her.[40] The *Triumphe* is
intended as a consolation for sufferers, who may find relief in the knowledge that others share their plight. For the miseries of venereal disease, it
seems, jokes and laughter are the best medicine. As the text of the work
begins with some pages of prose, we rediscover the *raison d'être* so often
cited for paradoxical encomia on disease:

> Or doncques, . . . iceulx pauvres Verollez par le moien de la raillerie
> et joyeulx mots quilz en dient commodement font moindres entre eulx
> les fortes passions veroliques. . . . Jescay que lesditz verollez trespre-
> cieux comme dit maistre Alcofribas Nasier en ses Pantagruelines hys-
> toires entre eulx de telle guerre [genre] de parler se plaisent et font
> feste.[41]

After the reference to Rabelais comes a discussion of the birthplace of the
"Vérolle," a matter much debated at the time by doctors, scholars, and popular writers. Even the various names given the disease, "mal français,"
"mal de Naples," "mal d'Italie," indicate, in addition to their obvious chauvinism, a genuine scientific uncertainty that even modern research has not
completely dispelled. The composer of the *Triumphe* supplies various stories and conjectures concerning the origin of the mighty conqueror. These
speculations include the two full-length stories. Then the triumphal procession begins: "Le Triumphe verolique commence à marcher par ordonnance
de Ranc en ranc ainsi que verrez le tout bien en ordre" (xlii). Other figures
joining the parade are the "seigneur de verdure," "la gorre de Rouen," and
a group of musicians.[42] Scatological puns and double meanings abound. After the appearance of "la Goutte," a relative of "dame Vérolle," the lady
herself arrives in her chariot, declaring:

> Du puy d'amours je suis reyne & princesse,
> Tesmoing Venus & Cupido aussi.
> La plus grand part du monde en grant humblesse
> Rend lhonneur deu à mon triumphe icy.
>
> (lxxv)

The mock-heroic style of the lady's boastful introduction of herself exactly
parallels that of gout in the *Podagra*.

Her retinue includes mythological figures (Cupids), personified abstrac-
tions ("Volupté"), and representatives of various groups such as soldiers
and lackeys. In his edition of 1874, Montaiglon claims that the work may

well have been composed to be recited during an actual procession of carts in Lyons (32–42). Such a parody of classical triumphs and medieval and Renaissance royal entrées would surely have delighted spectators. Venereal disease, relatively new in Europe at the time, was a frequent topic of speculation and discussion, but most analysis was either medical, describing symptoms and treatment, or philosophical, conjecturing as to the reasons for this latest sign of God's anger and power. The *Triumphe*, on the other hand, cleverly revitalizes and modernizes the medieval carnival tradition discussed earlier in connection with the farces on folly. Both folly and venereal disease are readily presented within the structure of a procession, the former because of the interrelatedness of man's many kinds of folly, and the latter because Dame Vérolle was associated with other kinds of disease—gout, itching, loss of hair—all of which are represented or referred to in the *Triumphe*. This similarity between folly and the "vérolle" is underlined on a practical level by the fact that the same woodcuts served to illustrate the triumph of folly after being used for that of "vérolle." Although the reasons for this double usage may have been largely economic (such reuse was not uncommon at the time), there was certainly no strain or difficulty involved in the transition from one mock-heroine to another.[43]

THE "HYMNE DE LA SURDITÉ"

There appears, however, to have been little attempt to introduce extended satire into works praising the power of Dame Vérolle. Sometimes crude in tone, they contain few of the learned allusions and adaptations of mythology found in Neo-Latin and Pléiade mock encomia. One of the finest examples of the latter group is Du Bellay's "Hymne de la Surdité," written in Italy in the last months of 1556 and first published as the last poem in the *Divers Jeux rustiques* of 1558. It was shown in discussion of the vice eulogies that this collection of poems includes a number of satirical encomia. The "Hymne de la Surdité" is thus no isolated example of the genre in the writings of Du Bellay.

The title "Hymne" is probably borrowed from Ronsard, who had published his hymns in 1555 and 1556. These long, philosophic, epic or mythological poems, composed primarily in alexandrines, treated such lofty persons and themes as King Henri II, Justice, Heaven, and Demons. Their style was very different from that usually employed by Du Bellay, who in the first sonnet of the *Regrets* (1558) professes his aims to be less elevated:

> Je ne veulx point fouiller au sein de la nature,
> Je ne veulx point chercher l'esprit de l'univers,
> Je ne veulx point sonder les abysmes couvers,
> Ny desseigner du ciel la belle architecture.

> Je ne peins mes tableaux de si riche peinture,
> Et si hauts argumens ne recherche à mes vers:
> Mais suivant de ce lieu les accidents divers,
> Soit de bien, soit de mal, j'escris à l'adventure.[44]

Du Bellay took the Ronsardian hymn as a structure within which to present a wide-ranging picture of deafness, a topic his own hearing problems made of great interest to him.[45] Since satirical eulogists had from the earliest times tended to select for ironic praise diseases from which they themselves suffered, Du Bellay was following a well-established precedent. However, he succeeded in making his hymn one of the most successful and original French encomia on disease.[46]

He begins with lines in praise of Ronsard, to whom he dedicates the hymn but to whose gifts he modestly refuses to compare his own. Commenting on the unprofitability of the poet's calling, he briefly criticizes the laziness of priests and prelates:

> Bien ay-je, comme toy, suivy des mon enfance
> Ce qui m'a plus acquis d'honneur que de chevance:
> Ceste saincte fureur qui, pour suyvre tes pas,
> M'a tousjours tenu loing du populaire bas,
> Loing de l'ambition, & loing de l'avarice,
> Et loing d'oysiveté, des vices la nourrice,
> Aussi peu familiere aux soldats de Pallas,
> Comme elle est domestique aux prestres & prelats.[47]

Modesty does not prevent him, however, from inserting a few lines of self-praise, put in the mouth of those who "trop me favorisent." These readers, states the poet, still addressing Ronsard:

> Au pair de tes chansons les miennes authorisent,
> Disant, comme tu sçais, pour me mettre en avant,
> Que l'un est plus facile & l'autre plus sçavant,
> Si ma facilité semble avoir quelque grace,
> Si ne suis-je pourtant enflé de telle audace,
> De la contre-peser avec ta gravité,
> Qui sçait à la doulceur mesler l'utilité.[48]

Whatever their differences, the two poets share two important characteristics, their love of sincerity and their deafness. It is for this reason that the hymn is dedicated to the "Vandomois." The poet next declares that he is not one of those who "d'un vers triomphant / Déguisent une mouche en forme d'Elephant," using the glories of verse to disguise a fly as an elephant (29–30). This proverb, it will be remembered, appeared both in the *Muscae Encomium* and in the *Moriae Encomium*, both of which were likely to be

familar to readers of Du Bellay's hymn.[49] Nor will he, the narrator continues, join those who seek to praise folly or the plague, a probable reference
to Berni and Erasmus.[50] The fact that Du Bellay was able to allude so casu-
ally and fleetingly to these two works, giving no details of authors or exact
titles, shows how widespread knowledge of the genre must have been by
the 1550s. It is in marked contrast to the laborious self-justification and
detailed lists of predecessors found in early Neo-Latin encomia. Du Bellay
is thus professing to dismiss a genre his verses will persist in conjuring up,
even as our appreciation of the so-called advantages of deafness will prove
to be based on the premise of having once been or of still being able to hear.
In exactly the same way, Synesius's praise of baldness was dominated by
the concept of baldness as the absence of hair rather than as the presence of
some desirable attribute as yet to be explained. Synesius's attempt to deco-
rate the bald page with sparkling verbal threads is comparable to Du Bellay's
creation of a hymn full of harmonious verses celebrating a world devoid of
sound.

In the *Muscae Encomium*, Lucian portrays the fly in an almost scientific
manner. Du Bellay, relying for his information on Paré, provides a similarly technical description of deafness, in a complicated twenty–line passage
that has been qualified as "assez obscur."[51] This part of the hymn seems far
less off-putting when it is understood as that common device of the panegyric, the detailed but selective presentation of the phenomenon being
praised. Du Bellay does not, however, pursue this part of his argument to
its logical conclusion, namely, that to be born deaf is the best fate, or that
one should seek like the Stoics to transcend the mortal world altogether. He
is interested in the person who has once heard normally but becomes deaf
as the result of illness or accident.

The central part of the poem is a schematic dialogue, the first section of
which opposes a series of "si" clauses listing the pleasures of sound to qual-
ifying "aussi" clauses recalling the disadvantages of hearing. *If*, for example, the deaf man is deprived of the joy of sweet music, he is *also* spared the
pain of hearing false notes. And so on. It is interesting to note here that
Bronzino, the painter, also composed a capitolo criticizing excessive noise.
In his "Capitolo de' Romori," the ailing poet complains bitterly of the din
that prevents him from resting peacefully in his room. He is so disturbed by
the sounds of various animals that he declares himself forced to recover fast
in order to escape from his room. The poem ends as Bronzino announces a
forthcoming poem on church bells, the "Capitolo contro à le Campane,"
which, like the previous one, is an attack on noise, specifically, that of
church bells.[52] Du Bellay's criticism of noise is more complex, part of an
elaborate defense of deafness, not a direct attack. This difference in the underlying framework of the French hymn means that the reader is constantly
called upon to adopt a dual perspective, at once inside the poem, agreeing

with the poet's irritation at unwanted sounds, and outside it, seeing the ways in which its own procedure suggests more positive aspects of the world of sound.

After the "si-aussi" series of arguments, the poet moves to a new pattern. The various objections to deafness, introduced by "mais," are answered by a succession of sardonic comments. *But* the ladies do not look kindly upon a deaf suitor. Happy is he who does not have to fear women's mockery, retorts the narrator. *But* he is never invited to the council chambers of the great. How dearly are such favors bought! Rhetorically, these two sections oppose positive and negative arguments but invert the order of presentation of pros and cons. The result is a verbal balancing act, mentioning but swiftly negating all likely objections, another typical procedure of the paradoxical encomium. The contre-blason, the lines stressing the disadvantages of deafness, are encased within and to a large extent neutralized by more favorable notions.

Du Bellay next presents a positive, even lyrical picture of Ronsard, happy in his semideafness, without which he would be a harrassed courtier, not a poet communing with the spirit of nature on the banks of the river, undisturbed by barking dogs. Yet the portrait of Ronsard is full of words referring to noise: "cry," "aboy," "bruit," "chant," "harmonie," and what the poet calls a "tintin," his verses echoing the muted sound still audible to the two men. This undercurrent of sounds gradually becomes an internal music, discreet but distinct. Partial deafness changes a crashing waterfall into a tinkling stream, helping the poet to transform crude decibels into melodious vocables. The humming in his ears enables him to listen to the perfect music of the spheres, inaudible to ordinary men, weighed down by the "lourde masse" of their mortality. Partial deafness thus comes to confer, paradoxically, a selective but improved kind of hearing, somewhat as the quartan fever for the Lyons blasonneur led to an improved kind of health. By virtue of this transforming power, deafness must be viewed as a goddess bestowing mingled pleasure and pain upon her followers.

The argument moves a stage further as Du Bellay voices his regret at his return to partial hearing: "Las, feusse-je aussi sourd, comme j'estois adonc!" (190). "Adonc" refers to the time when he would not have heard "trois marteaux tumbans sur une masse / De fer estincelant" (187–88), probably during his first illness in 1549. In a series of conditional verbs, the next thirty lines present a fuller development of the "si" clauses employed earlier. If he were once again deaf, the poet declares, he would be spared various disagreeable noises. At this point occur the strongest passages of criticism of life in Rome. The attack on the warlike Pope Paul IV, "ce bon Pere Sainct," is all the more devastating for being presented within the conditional structure, that of a fruitless wish. Short parenthetical remarks reinforce the posture of wistful nostalgia and seemingly benign detachment with which the poet laments the necessity of hearing so many criticisms of the pontiff:

> Et n'orrois dire mal de ce bon Pere Sainct
> Dont ores *sans raison* toute Rome se plaingt,
> Blasmant sa cruauté et sa grand' convoitise,
> Qui ne craint (*disent-ilz*) aux despends de l'Eglise
> Enrichir ses nepveus, & troubler sans propos
> De la Chrestienté le publique repos.
> (201–6, italics mine)

That Du Bellay's contemporaries, like those of Erasmus, read these lines as ironical is borne out by Henri Estienne's marginal note of explanation: "Contre le Pape, sans faire semblant de rien."[53]

At the climax of this section of the poem, the narrator's enthusiasm for his theme leads him to wish not only for deafness, but even for blindness:

> O bien heureux celuy qui a receu des Dieux
> Le don de Surdité! voire qui n'a point d'yeux,
> Pour ne voir et n'ouir en ce siecle ou nous sommes
> Ce qui doit offenser & les Dieux & les hommes.
> (221–24)

The writer is here reconciled not merely to his current affliction, but to the possibility of a new illness, one of which he has no personal experience.[54] As was noted in discussing the Lyons blasons, such extreme moments of paradoxical reasoning cannot long be sustained. In the present instance, the satirical attack suddenly ends, to be replaced by a memorable portrait of "saincte & alme Surdité" enthroned in a cavern, the quietness of which is made more complete by the "cheutes du Nil" which "tempestent à l'entour." Accompanied by "Estude," "Melancholie," "Jugement," and "les Discours," watched over by the "Ame imaginative," the goddess is described as the "nourrice de sagesse" and of "raison" (180–95). This striking apotheosis, inspired in part by Ronsard's "Hymne de la Philosophie," is followed by the request for a reward found in so many serious and mock encomia.[55]

> Donq', ô grand' Surdité, nourrice de sagesse,
> Nourrice de raison, je te supply, Déesse,
> Pour le loyer d'avoir ton merite vanté
> Et d'avoir à ton loz ce Cantique chanté,
> De m'estre favorable, et si quelqu'un enrage
> De vouloir par envie à ton nom faire oultrage,
> Qu'il puisse un jour sentir ta grande deité,
> Pour sçavoir, comme moy, que c'est de Surdité.
> (243–50)

These lines again draw attention to the world of sound, in particular that beautiful realm of the sung word, the "Cantique." Here Du Bellay suggests something about the hymn as a literary genre. The printed hymn, as practiced by Ronsard, lay on the borderline between the sung (and heard) and the written (and unheard, or mentally "heard"), even as the two friends' malady held them suspended between sound and silence. Just as the traditional paradox, such as that of the Cretan liar, is never resolved, so Du Bellay's hymn does not rest with total deafness, but constantly uses sounds, words, and ideas that recall the world of hearing. In deifying the goddess of deafness, the poet in a sense grows deaf to his own poem of beautiful sounds. The world of poetic sound, however, must be used with great care, as the ode on Bertran Bergier, part of the same Du Bellay collection, makes plain. One of Bergier's most serious limitations was his passion for indiscriminately portraying in verse the world of sound. Because of these intertextual echoes and juxtapositions, Du Bellay's title, "Hymne de la Surdité," becomes one of the most paradoxical and resonant of all titles for mock encomia.

Later Developments: Beards, Horns, and Scratching

The brilliance of this hymn might have been expected to inspire imitators, but it is not until the early seventeenth century that we find another poem in French offering a comical presentation of a physical affliction. The work, "Le Delice des galleux," is by Annibal de l'Ortigue, who composed the "Felicité du debteur" discussed in chapter 5.[56] "La Galle" here refers to the rash or irritation symptomatic of early syphilis rather than to scabies, the term's more general meaning. The expression "la gale de Naples" occurred in the "Pourpoint" that accompanied the *Triumphe de Dame Vérolle*.[57] It is defined by Montaiglon as "la Vérole." Godefroy shows that the term can also mean "réjouissance, plaisir."[58] It does not require much imagination to guess the use to which this convenient double meaning will be put by de l'Ortigue.

The poet waxes lyrical over the joys to be obtained from scratching:

> C'est un merveilleux delice,
> C'est une agreable lice,
> C'est un esbat gracieux
> Plus grand qui soit sous les Cieux
> Que d'estre attaint de la galle,
> Nulle volupté n'esgalle:
> Celle d'un galleux parfaict.
>
> (184–85)

The terminology of love is thus applied to one of love's least desirable after-effects. Continuing in the same vein, the narrator declares that if theologians understood the pleasure to be obtained from scratching, they would forbid such self-indulgence. If it is true that Paradise is most easily reached by way of affliction, the "galleux" may never attain the longed-for goal, for his state can in no way be classified as suffering. On the contrary, the scratcher prefers his itchy skin to the ambrosia of the gods or to any kingdom that might be offered him. A less ecstatic note creeps in, however, as we are told that "La galle est un don du Ciel, / Pleine de fiel & de miel" (186). In tracing the etymology of the term from "galant," de l'Ortigue links it also with "galanterie." Explaining how and when it is caught, he concludes that the Muses are "galleuses comme nous" (192). The poet's topic and his chosen form, the mock eulogy, here combine in a fine moment of ironic self-reflection: if anyone has rendered the Muses "galleuses" it is surely the poet who has used the resources of the loftiest poetry to eulogize scratching.

A group of works less pornographic in tone concerns the beard. The "Blason des barbes de maintenant," the first in the series, was published several times in the sixteenth century.[59] In his article on the blason, Robert Pike shows that the advantages and disadvantages of beards were frequent topics for discussion in sixteenth-century France.[60] Participants in the controversy could draw on Synesius, on the *Misopogon*, and on editions of the *Ecloga de calvis*.[61] Among the Bernesque writers, the prolific Grazzini composed a capitolo on beards, "In Lode delle Barbe," dedicated to a male friend. In a prose introduction, he remarks that of the two differences between men and women, modesty prevents him from naming the first, while the second is the beard. He suggests that Mazzuoli, his friend, should grow a beard in order to resemble the sages of ancient Greece. The beard is the "primo onore," the "ornamento principale" of the face, the distinguishing mark of biblical figures since the time of Adam. The poet playfully lists the various styles of beards:

> Le barbe son di più fatte maniere,
>   e rade e folte e lunghe e larghe e corte
>   e tonde e quadre e rosse e bianche e nere.
> Sonne delle diritte e delle attorte,
>
>   .   .   .   .
> e'n altri modi, come dà la sorte.[62]

[Beards are of all sorts, sparse, thick, long, wide and short, round, square, red, white and black. They are straight, twisted, . . . and of other sorts as chance determines.]

[188]

The narrator would put up with any illness, "la peste, il canchero e la tossa" [the plague, cancer, and the cough], even the fever, the "febbre repentina," rather than the "pelatina" (the French "pelade"), which could rob him of his beloved beard. The fact that the likely cause for "la pelatina" was an attack of venereal disease means that the underlying sexual theme has been maintained throughout the poem. The traditional notion of the beard as a sign of virility is given added poignancy by the Renaissance anxiety as to the probable reason for loss of hair. Mauro prefers death to dishonor: Grazzini chooses extinction rather than impotence.

Returning now to the "Blason des barbes de maintenant," we should note that Montaiglon speculates that it may have been composed much earlier than the edition he reprints, perhaps around the time when François I grew a beard to hide a scar. Discussions of beards were also related to discussions of tonsuring. The French Catholic jurisconsult Antoine Hotman, brother of the well-known Protestant propagandist, François Hotman, composed a dialogue on beards that dealt with the significance of such observances.[63] The "Blason des Barbes de maintenant" is a straightforward poem of condemnation, rather than a mock vituperation or ironic praise. However, its playful tone and passages of vivid description link it to the more ironic blasons. It consists of a description of the new French mania for beard-growing. More than two dozen different types of beard are listed. Even the "hideux barbaulx paysant" has apparently acquired the habit, for he

> tort la gueulle et fait la mine.
> Sa barbe [est] plaine de vermine,
> De morpions, de poux et lentes
> Sans repos, et puces groulantes.
> Mais sans cesser sa barbe frotte;
> Il la desmesle, il la descrotte;
> Il la secoue, puis il la tire;
> Il la retord, puis il la vire;
> Il la resserre, et puis l'espart;
> Chascune main en tient sa part.
> (214)

The blasonneur is of the belief that priests should not be bearded like soldiers. In discussing these lines, Pike quotes a document of 1556 granting the architect Pierre Lescot permission to become canon of Notre Dame "avec sa barbe."[64] The blasonneur declares that only those who have vowed for religious reasons not to shave, such as "chartreux, convers, anachorites," should be permitted beards (220). A further exception is to be made in the case of great "seigneurs d'authorité," provided that the beard is not "trop exquise." In terms of the history of the blason, it is interesting that the word *blason* for this writer could still signify a poem of direct condemnation, even though, since the appearance of the "blasons du corps féminin" in the 1550s, the term *contre-blason* had been frequently used for derogatory blasons and would have been more appropriate here. If the work originally appeared earlier than the "blasons du corps féminin," this question would of course be resolved. After some lively and picturesque verses describing various kinds of beards and expressing the hope that someone pluck them out "poil à poil" from their wearers, the poem ends with the firm statement that it is "une grande folie / D'estimer un homme à sa barbe," and that a man should "sortir de la case / Le pied ferrat, la barbe rase" (221).

The poem elicited an immediate response from an indignant "barbu," who, in a "contredict," answered the various statements made by the earlier writer:

> Apres avoir le Blason entendu
> D'un barbiton et tout son pretendu,
> En m'esbatant j'ay voulu m'entremettre
> A briefvement luy respondre par metre.[65]

The above lines are taken from the author's dizain "Aux Lecteurs." The verb "s'esbatre" was frequently used by poets of the sixteenth century to lead readers towards a playful interpretation of a given work.[66] Relating the works to the paradoxical encomium, it suggests that neither the defense nor the condemnation of beards should be taken too seriously.

Sygognes composed a poem on the same theme. In a Bernesque style similar to that of Regnier, Motin, and their contemporaries, he uses mock-heroic language to present his somewhat mundane topic:

> Barbe, des barbes la merveille,
> Barbe qui n'a point de pareille,
> Reine des barbes, en effect,
> Je veux que ma Muse feconde,
> Fasse cognoistre à tout le monde
> Le bien que ton maistre te fait.[67]

This poem follows the mock encomium's technique of bestowing exaggerated praise on an unworthy object. The interest in discussing beards and hair persisted well into the seventeenth century. Jean de Schelandre (1585–1655), the Calvinist poet and soldier whom Charles Asselineau compared to Agrippa d'Aubigné, produced several pages of "Stances en faveur d'une barbe blanche" as early in his life as 1608.[68] In 1621, Synesius's *Calvitii Encomium* inspired a long imitation by Jean Dant, entitled "Le Chauve ou le mespris des cheveux."[69] In his epistle to the reader, Dant states that although he has read Synesius's work recently and will refer to it, his own composition is no mere piece of plagiarism. He intends to cover the matter more thoroughly than had the balding bishop. The resulting work, no less than 196 pages of prose, accordingly both elaborates and adds considerably to the ideas found in Synesius. Its very prolixity makes it typical of many seventeenth-century mock encomia, which sometimes made up in length for what their works by now lacked in originality.

Following the French tendency to praise physical peculiarities and eccentricities rather than actual diseases, another early seventeenth-century poem concentrates on the nose, in a manner reminiscent of certain sixteenth-century blasons on the "corps feminin," one of which presented the nose as "joliet, poly, bien façonné, / Ne court, ne long, ains proportionné."[70] Eustorg de Beaulieu, author of this 1537 blason, stresses that the nose is clean, sweet-smelling, and delicate. Indeed, a person without a nose would be a "marmot," not a human being. Another early blason on the nose, by J. N. Darles, appeared in several editions of the *Blasons anatomiques* from 1537 on. These and other laudatory blasons inspired a number of contre-blasons on the same topic, one by Charles de la Huetterie and another, longer one by Jean Rus. The latter poem, entitled the "Contreblason du Nez," was published in 1540.[71] The contre-blasons spare no revolting details, are not satirical encomia—far from it—and therefore do not resemble Dolce's "Capitolo del naso," published in Grazzini's edition.[72] Dolce endeavors to show that a long nose, like a bald head, is a highly desirable attribute. He justifies his claim by listing famous long-nosed individuals—Dante, Nebuchadnezzar, Ovid—and explaining the advantages of such appendages. In France, however, even blasons on such unlikely topics as "Le C.N." and "Le Pet" may be nonironic and descriptive. Title alone is no sure guide to an ironic encomium.[73] But one long anonymous poem describing an unpleasant nose does come closer to that genre. Entitled the "Anatomie d'un Nez à la mode. Dedié aux bons buveurs," it is a Bernesque piece concentrating on the most grotesque aspects of a diseased and swollen nose.[74] However, it lacks the Italian poets' lightness of touch and is more closely related to Sygognes' poem on the beard and to writings by Regnier and others on articles of clothing belonging to the courtier.[75] These works are blason-like descriptions used for overtly satirical purposes. By describing items such as the sword, breeches, and stockings of the courtier, the poets indirectly suggest the owners' vices and weaknesses. For instance, the courtier's sword, rusted in its scabbard, calls attention to his cowardice. Two anonymous blasons of an earlier period, the "Blason du Gobbellet" and the "Blason du Platellet," use a similar process of external description to satirize aspects of the religious conflicts of the time. All these works are presented as mocking encomia. Thus Sygognes' satire "Le Pourpoint d'un Courtisan" is presented as follows:

> Sus Deesse aux dents veneneuses,
> Chantons les louanges fameuses,
> De ce pourpoint rapetassé.[76]

The ensuing poem, however, like the others in this group, is a vituperative contre-blason rather than an ironic poem of praise. Although related to the mock encomium, these works will therefore not be studied in detail here.

The French, like the Bernesque writers before them, seem to have enjoyed "praising" that legendary physical affliction, the horns of the cuckold. Remy Belleau and the little-known Caye Jules de Guersens each composed poems on the theme. Both treat their topic primarily as a physical affliction rather than as a moral dilemma. For this reason the works may be considered disease rather than vice encomia. The French poets may have known a capitolo on horns by Grazzini, in which he declares them to be without doubt the finest of attributes.[77] Jupiter, he continues, took on the horns of a bull in order to woo Europa. Horn is one of the most useful of substances, able to be fashioned into all manner of articles. The new moon is horned in shape, and even the venerable Moses is sometimes pictured with horns on his head. We should not put horns on drawings of the devil. Finally, the best months of the year are represented by the animals Capricorn and Taurus.

A French work on horns that remained linked to an Italian one was *Le Monde des cornuz,* a section added to the 1580 edition of Gabriel Chappuis's translation of Anton Francesco Doni's *I Mondi celesti.*[78] This work was a series of visions of imaginary worlds such as "Le Monde des sages et fols." The long section on horns, attributed to one "F.C.T.," consists of a dialogue between Momus, Jupiter, "le fol," and "le sage." The Menippean *Monde des cornuz* contains a variety of poems and conversations on the subject of horns. Women are to blame for the difficulties of men, and many tales of deceitful wives are narrated. A short play, *De L'Avare cornu,* is included and in another passage a "cornu" defends his state. Moses wore horns, the "cornu" explains, Apollo's rays are the equivalent of horns around his head, noble animals such as bulls are horned, and so are many useful objects. The horn of plenty, the cornucopia, completes the picture of completeness and fulfillment. We recognize immediately elements of Grazzini's poem and will meet many of the same claims in other French works on this topic. The basic strategy is to ignore the unfortunate moral reasons for the imaginary horns in order to concentrate on the virtues of horns as physical objects. This selective refocusing of the reader's attention mirrors the willful blindness of the deceived husband, prepared not to see what others see so clearly about his marriage, and gives added resonance to this group of encomia. The very same arguments in favor of cuckoldry are used by Bruscambille in one of his speeches, described in chapter 5 above.

The first extended French encomium on horns, that by Remy Belleau, appeared in his *Petites Inventions* of 1578.[79] It is in fact an hymne-blason, with mythological references and a playful envoi. The poet begins by wondering who first imagined that horns were undesirable. Jupiter did not scorn to wear them and the invention of the horn of plenty proves that there is no intrinsic stigma attached to the substance. Jason's precious fleece came from a horned animal, and several creatures in the Zodiac have horns. Mythology abounds in tales of Pan, fauns, and satyrs, while tragedy, most noble of genres, is associated with the goat. Bows and other useful objects are horn-shaped, and the hats worn by members of various professions are given the name "cornettes" because of their shape. Like Rabelais, who took Panurge's idea of debt to a universal level, Belleau writes:

> Bref je croy que la terre basse,
> Et tout ce que le ciel embrasse
> N'est qu'une composition,
> Qu'une certe confusion
> De cornes mises en nature,
> Non les atomes d'Epicure.
> (87)

After listing illustrious horn-bearers, the narrator addresses the "compere" for whom the poem is intended. Be content and keep your "plumage / Et ce bonnet empanaché," he tells him:

> Puis que vous l'avez attaché
> A vostre front si proprement,
> Vivez Compere heureusement.
> (87)

The poem thus begins and ends with the comical figure of the cuckold. The choice of horns to represent this state is appropriate because they are something everyone can see except the man who wears them. What in an animal is a sign of strength and sexuality becomes, paradoxically, when imagined on a human brow, a sign of impotence and weakness. The "mari complaisant" is a far cry from Jupiter the seductive bull. This point relates to Belleau's sardonic conclusion, which suggests that the man, whether by complacency or passivity, is in part responsible for his cuckolded condition, "vous l'avez attaché."

The second poem on horns is that by Caye Jules de Guersens, from Normandy, who, with J. C. Scaliger, took lessons from Turnèbe.[80] Since de Guersens, born in about 1543, refers in "A la Louange des cornes" to his youth ("mon imbarbu menton"), we may infer that the poem was composed in the 1560s. This eulogy differs from that by Belleau in being full of recondite, even obscure allusions. Although it refers to the horns of the cuckold, they are not, as for Belleau, the point of departure for the entire poem, merely a passing mention. De Guersens begins instead with a justification for his subject. Since the traditional sources of poetry are all in some way connected with horns, he explains, an obvious choice for a poem must be the praise of these appendages:

> Si du docte coupeau le front audacieux
> D'une corne jumelle avoisine les cieux;
> Si du volant destrier la corne talonniere
> Fit saillir du rocher la source qui premiere
> Abreuva les neuf soeurs de ses prophetes eaux,
> Et si des lauriers vers cornus sont les rameaux;
> Si encore souvent les mieux disantes muses
> Soufflent dans les cornets, enflent les cornemuses,
> Voire si tous les lieux d'où se puisent les vers
> Sont des cornes issues ou des cornes couvers.
> Estant vrai que l'effect à sa cause retire,
> Que puis-je faire mieux que des cornes escrire?
>
> (108)

Moving now to a universal level, the poet declares that before God created the earth it was "une masse cornue," surrounded by the horned figures of the Zodiac. Even the sun's rays are not straight, "ains cornes rayonnantes." The horned shape is undoubtedly the finest, a fact proved by the beauty of the crescent moon.

Again developing a notion used by Belleau, de Guersens remarks that were he not so young, he would put forward a bold new theory about the true nature of the sky:

> Que l'essence du ciel, tout telle qu'on la voit,
> Ne tient rien de la terre, et que l'air, ne la flamme,
> Ny l'eau n'ont peu ourdir une si belle trame.
> Moins encore faut-il croire legerement
> Que nostre rond soit basti d'un cinquieme element;
> Nostre oeil en sera juge, il n'est besoing de preuve
> Où le sens plus aigu si clairement se treuve;
> Nous le voyons de corne, il est corne partout,
> Corne parfaicte en soy, corne qui n'a de bout.
>
> (109)

The dome of the sky is nothing more or less than the inside of a giant horn. Anything horn-shaped or even curved, like the sky, can be introduced as evidence to support this theory.

The next section describes various gods who have had or adopted the outward form of an animal. Once again, Jupiter's metamorphoses provide useful illustrations. Egyptian deities such as Isis and Osiris, the first of whom at one stage became a cow and the second of whom is often pictured as a bull, are cited next, followed by the satyrs and fauns mentioned by Belleau.

As the last lines of this section show, some of these references are quite obscure:

> Les cornes de Cippus le firent nommer Roy,
> L'Hebrieu estoit cornu quand il donna la loy:
> Hercule nous ouvrit, Jupiter a plantée (*sic*)
> La corne d'Achelois, la cornée d'Amalthée.
>
> (111)

Since so many gods have worn horns, it is incomprehensible to de Guersens that men still dread them. In their incongruous mixture of exotic mythology and popular superstition, the following lines are typical of the poem as a whole:

> O corne! qui des dieux va eslevant le front,
> D'où vient le peu d'honneur que les hommes te font?
> D'où vient, corne, d'où vient que ta pointe honorée,
> Au Lybique desert chez Ammon adorée,
> Est blasmable entre nous, et que le moindre hommet
> Se sent deshonnoré, te portant pour armet?
> Belle corne, est-ce pas nostre foible nature
> Qui ne peut supporter la divine encorneure
> D'une chose si rare? Ainsi le chassieux
> Se fasche du soleil qui luy touche les yeux;
> Ainsi le degouté rejette la viande,
> Ainsi le cerveau creux s'ennuie de la bande
> Des mignons de Phoebus, quand d'une masle voix
> Ils marient un vers au vent de leur haubois.
>
> (110)

From horned gods the poet passes to objects made of horn or having some connection with it. The list ranges from hunting horns to knife handles. Anything can be included if it has a curved shape or if its name implies some connection with the word *corne*. Thus the stone cornelian is dedicated to deceived husbands. "Cornoüaille," "corail," and "cornette" are all discussed. Most of us are "cornus" in one sense, whether or not we are cuckolds, because we have a double "cornée." Let us therefore not fear to fulfil what is so clearly our destiny. The poem ends with a discussion of the significance of the word *pan*, which can either mean "all" or can refer to the god who was one of the most famous wearers of horns. The universality of the horn is thus conclusively and finally demonstrated.

"A la Louange des cornes," with its complicated mythological allusions, seems at times to be almost a parody of Pléiade themes and terminology. But such moments of near-parody are not sufficiently sustained for one to feel confident that this was in fact the purpose of the poem. What is indisputable is the author's interest in linguistic exploration. Since the cuckold's horns are but an imaginary attribute, a picturesque image for a familiar problem, the writer is led to explore other related images—the crescent moon, the curved sky, and so on. At times the idea of horn as a physical substance predominates, as in the mention of knife handles. At others, the curved shape rather than the composition of the horn is stressed. The intricate procedure of the poem serves to build an elaborate protective dome of mocking language over the unfortunate cuckold's intangible affliction.

Closely related to the two formal encomia on cuckoldry are three poems by Jean Passerat. A cynical view of the cuckold is taken in the first two short pieces:

DES COCUS

Qui est cocu, & n'en croit rien,
Je le pren pour homme de bien.
Qui le sçait, & semblant n'en monstre,
Pour homme accort passe à la monstre.
Qui à son front taste s'il l'est,
Je le pren pour maistre Benest.

QUATRAIN
D'UN COCU DE BIEN

Qu'on ne s'en moque desormais:
Pour cocu qu'on ne le diffame:
Car le bon-homme n'en peut mais,
Et ne l'est que de par sa femme.[81]

The first poem suggests that ignorance, whether real or feigned, is a less foolish reaction to wifely deceit than suspicion or jealousy. The ironic title of the second poem, "D'un cocu de bien," points to the implication of the entire quatrain, that the wife's extramarital activity probably results from frustration at her husband's complacent bonhomie. The désabusé tone of both stanzas recalls that of the end of Belleau's encomium, "vivez Compere heureusement." The husband seeking only a quiet life had better content himself with no more than that. His wife's passion will be bestowed elsewhere.

The third poem by Passerat of interest here is entitled "Elegie sur le reproche de Cocuage, & sur la jalousie." In it the poet declares that cuckoldry, being no crime, deserves no public reproach. Since a husband cannot really lose his wife (presumably in the Renaissance legal sense of the term), his worry is unnecessary. The poem then praises love, even adulterous love. Women like to inspire admiration, from whatever quarter; men should therefore try not to feel jealous. The speaker concludes with the hope that his own faith may be rewarded by fidelity on the part of his wife. These three poems are more ambiguous in their so-called praise than the works by Belleau and de Guersens. They are of interest in that they focus as much on the husband's implication in his wife's actions as on the traditional moralist's blame of the erring woman.[82]

The last work to be discussed here is a short poem published in *Les Muses gaillardes* of 1609, a collection that also included Belleau's "Les Cornes." Entitled "Louange de la bosse en faveur d'une maistresse," the work's most interesting feature in the context of the present discussion is that the writer uses the arguments that Synesius had invented in praise of a round, bald head and that Belleau and de Guersens had repeated in favor of cuckoldry in order to praise the beauties of a lady's round back:

> Quiconque dit que ma Nymphette
> Porte une eschigne contrefaite,
> Est un vrai baudet & ne sçait
> En quoy consiste le parfait.
> Se void-il rien en tout ce monde
> De parfait qui n'ait forme ronde?[83]

Just as the eulogies on horns list curved objects, so the author of this poem reminds his readers of various circular objects, sky, sun, and full moon. All animals have some curved limbs, as do trees, whose seeds and fruits are also round. Such evidence suggests that it is better to have a hunchback than a straight one, and with this brave conclusion the work ends. Its strategy is to find attractive curves in the natural world and then to imply that since some curves are perceived as beautiful, all should be so viewed. The reader is encouraged to forget that a curved back is a divergence from the customary norms of human beauty, whereas a round apple represents the norm. Like the cuckold poems, the work on the "bosse" functions by manipulating and confusing what are in fact different categories of moral and aesthetic judgement.

This somewhat grotesque effort to "straighten" our view of the curve is the last French disease eulogy I shall discuss. The disease encomium in France followed a different path from that taken by Neo-Latin writings in this category. Moral and social issues remained of constant importance, even in purportedly descriptive pieces such as "Les Cornes." The rhetorical, recreational aspect of the genre was thereby diminished, as was the preoccupation with citation of previous authorities for purposes of self-justification. In the unjustly neglected Lyons blasons and in the masterly "Hymne de la Surdité" we see the full flowering of the genre in French—elusive and self-aware, forever playing with multiple perspectives and challenging the reader's desire for a clear conclusion. In toying with the overlap between the physical and the spiritual domains, these works are certainly related to vice encomia. But their point of departure is a physical one, either a literal illness, such as gout, or an imaginary physical impediment, such as horns. In this respect, the disease praises move closer to the animal encomia, the subject of my final chapter.

The Animal Eulogy
in France

Je meurs quand je repense à luy.
GILLES DURANT

The Mock Encomium and the Animal Epitaph

The third type of mock encomium, that on animals, in France frequently moves beyond itself toward either parody or a close intermingling with related genres. Some mock encomia do sustain their characteristic blend of praise and play, balancing inner and outer perspectives, but others subordinate these features to those typical of other forms. The history of the animal encomia centers upon two poetic forms, the epitaph and the blason. Hélène Naïs has demonstrated that editions of the classical playful or ironic works on animals by Catullus, Ovid, Statius, and writers included in the *Greek Anthology* were numerous.[1] It is therefore not surprising that many of the Renaissance works were in verse, even though Lucian's *Muscae Encomium*, sometimes published separately in France, was in prose.[2]

The animal epitaph showed two distinct tendencies in the sixteenth century. The first was to imitate a classical or Neo-Latin predecessor or an earlier French writer such as Marot or Jean Lemaire de Belges. The second was to move away from the epitaph-compliment, the "pièce de circonstance" written for a specific individual or occasion, in order to introduce more seemingly personal details and reminiscences, often comical or absurd, presented by way of the hyperbolical or grotesque language found in the Bernesque epitaphs and the *Sermoni funebri*. Both these types of praise moved consistently towards parody. The animal blasons were a development of the earlier, serious blasons but differed from them in being more humorous and ironic in attitude. By analyzing how French writers manipulated the various types of animal encomium, we may better understand the reasons for the eventual fragmentation of the genre as an independent literary form.

The first important French poems to contain the combination of fantasy and humor typical of the animal encomium were not, technically speaking,

[199]

epitaphs, since they were written as if spoken by the animal in question. However, the animal, a parrot, was in fact dead when the poems were composed, and in many ways the works resemble epitaphs, both in content and function. Written in 1505 and published in 1511, the two poems are Jean Lemaire de Belges's *Epîtres de l'Amant Vert*.[3] They deal with a specific pet, Marguerite d'Autriche's parrot, killed by a dog while she was away. Seeking to console and distract the bird's mistress, his own recently widowed benefactress, Jean Lemaire transforms the bird's prosaic fate into a poetic suicide occasioned by its being abandoned by Marguerite. The way in which the parrot describes its devotion to Marguerite, its adherence to the rules of courtly love, and tragic, but willing death, have been much discussed and admired.[4] The author succeeds in combining pathos, even nobility of expression, with moments of pure fantasy and imaginative wit. Thus, the Amant Vert decides to die:

> Par ainsi doncq à ung cueur hault et fier
> On ne sçauroit son propos empeschier:
> Car moins griefve est la mort tost finissant
> Que n'est la vie amere et languissant.
>
> (15)

He espies an old mastiff,

> Qui ne mengea depuis hier au matin,
> A qui on peut nombrer toutes les costes,
> Tant est haÿ des bouchiers et des hostes.
>
> (15)

Deciding to throw himself into the mouth of the waiting dog, he remains aware of poetic vraisemblance, telling the hungry beast:

> Attens ung peu, vilaine creature,
> Tu jouÿras d'une noble pasture;
> Attens ung peu que ceste epistre seulle
> J'aye achevée, ains me mettre en ta gheulle;
> Si saouleray ton gosier mesgre et glout,
> Et tu donras à mon dueil pause et bout.
>
> (15)

The idea of the parrot solemnly telling the mastiff to wait for him to finish his farewell poem calls attention to the artificiality of so many postures of love poetry but does not go so far as to parody or undercut the human lover. The poem's rueful irony reminds us that, given the difference in social station, there was probably as little likelihood of a love relationship between Marguerite and Jean Lemaire as between the lady and the parrot. Nonetheless, the writer manages to convey a sense of affection, of a genuine desire to please and console. When scholars note that the queen was so delighted with the first epistle that she encouraged the poet to compose a second, and that Anne de Bretagne learned the poem by heart, we do not feel that the ladies were being deceived by false praise. Although it plays with the conventions of much court writing of the period, the *Epître* is not a caricature or parody. A true mock encomium, it manipulates a traditional genre, here the Petrarchan love poem, without seeking to destroy it. The devotion of the *Amant Vert* remains touching and sincere, representing the poet's own respect for his gracious and cultivated patron. The poet is extremely skillful throughout the two epistles at suggesting an identification between the ostensible narrator, the parrot, and the real one, himself.

Although the parrot-narrator is obviously not yet dead, these poems resemble animal epitaphs of the time in that they use subtle badinage enlivened with classical and mythological references as a means of complimenting or consoling the owner. Mentioning in his *Seconde Epître* Catullus's sparrow, Virgil's gnat, and other famous literary creatures, Jean Lemaire blends lyric and epic elements identical to those used by composers of epitaphs on animals.

Among the earliest works to be entitled "épitaphes" by their authors is Clément Marot's "Du Cheval de Vuyart" (composed in about 1531). Like Jean Lemaire's parrot, Vuyart's horse tells of a life of devotion to its owner. It then describes its untimely death, providing a vivid image of its "viste virade" and "pompante pennade," but ending with a sexual joke unimaginable in the context of the *Epîtres de l'Amant Vert*:

> Mais mon Maistre cher
> N'a permis seicher
> Mon los, bruit & fame;
> Car jadis plus cher
> M'ayma chevaucher
> Que fille ne femme.[5]

The same comparison between a horse and a woman had been made by the little-known poet Pierre Danche, in the envoi to his "Blason de la Femme":

> Gentil Prince pour vostre esbatement
> Si vous trouvez ung tel appoinctement
> Au petit pied jambe grassette et ronde
> Montés dessus et picqués hardiment,
> Parfaicte en bien seroit la plus du monde.[6]

Dedicated to powerful men (Vuyart was "secrétaire du duc de Guise"), these poems flatter their dedicatees by pointing out the pleasure to be derived from control over others, whether women or animals. Their jocular, man-to-man tone suggests that pets and women are extensions of the male owner's ego. As the master enjoys control over his pets and his women, so the poet finds satisfaction in determining the verbal presentation that is to represent for posterity the essence of the chosen subjects. Many later sixteenth-century animal epitaphs and blasons developed this theme of service, either of the robust, sexual variety typified by the horse-woman poems or, more frequently, of a delicate, playful sort.

The latter type of relationship is portrayed in two poems by Melin de Sainct-Gelays published in 1547, the first of which was entitled "Epitaphe de la belette d'une damoiselle."[7] Whereas Marot had concentrated on the power of the master to confer immortality on his animals by encouraging writers to eulogize the departed creatures, Sainct-Gelays compliments the owners by detailing the departed animals' quaint tricks and winning ways. In the epitaph on the weasel, for instance, the poet relates the life of the animal, which, treated like a pet dog or cat, was allowed into every room in the house and hunted for birds' nests in the garden and nearby woods. The jealousy between the weasel and the household dog, a rival for the lady's affection, often led to fights that the narrator describes in terms perhaps intentionally reminiscent of Homer's battle between rats and mice:

> L'un couroit, l'autre alloit après,
> Et l'autre le suivoit de près,
> Se mordant col, cuisse et oreille;
> Oncques ne fut guerre pareille.
>
> (1:54)

That the weasel is a projection of the lover's desire is made plain when the narrator explains that the animal slept in its mistress's bed, a privilege envied by many men. When it was eventually killed by an envious "fouine," a stone marten, the weeping members of the household buried it at the foot of a cypress tree. In mentioning a dog, a weasel, and a stone marten in his poem, the author is referring to animals whose relationships to mankind range from that of the traditionally domesticated and faithful dog, through the here tamed but still aggressive weasel, to the totally wild and fierce stone marten, jealous of the weasel's new status. There is constant movement between the poet's and the lady's efforts to domesticate and humanize the wild creatures and nature's attempts, eventually successful, to reclaim her own. Part of the charm of the weasel for the lady seems to be its wild energy and boldness; its innocence gains it entry to her bed. As the poet remarks, "O sage et heureux animal, / S'elle eust sceu le bien et le mal!" (1:55). The domesticated dog and respectful lover can but envy this good fortune. The poem is thus a skillful blend of the Catullan sparrow epitaph, with its erotic undertones, and the more lyric laments of the *Greek Anthology.*

Sainct-Gelays's other epitaph is what Blanchemain has dismissed as a "paraphrase languissante" of Catullus (1:60). By bearing in mind some of the complexities of the animal epitaph discussed above, we may arrive at a more positive reading of the piece. Following the general plan of the Latin poem, the "Epitaphe du passereau d'une damoiselle" provides a detailed description of the physical appearance and talents of the bird. The lines are put into the mouth of the bird's mistress, not of the bird itself or of the mistress's human admirer. Like Catullus's sparrow poems and many other Sainct-Gelays pieces, this epitaph is sexually suggestive. The mistress even refers coyly to the bird's "petit je ne sçay quoy / Que je tastois du bout du doy" (1:60). Blanchemain here notes with irritation that "Il faut toujours que notre diable d'abbé de cour mette de la sensualité partout, même quand il s'agit d'un passereau" (1:61). Such comments neglect the likelihood that one of the attractions of such poems was precisely that sensuality in the context of a pet animal could be presented as innocent and charming, rather than threatening or dangerous. Giving a detailed description of her small bird, the lady declares her intention to have its portrait painted:

> Son petit corsaige joly
> Son petit bec si bien poly,
> Sa petite teste follette
> Eveillé, comme une bellette,
> Ses plumettes si bien lissées
> Ses jambettes tant deliées.
>
> (1:59)

Naïs believes that such references to portraits echo the "rivalité entre peintres et poètes pour s'acquérir les bonnes graces des Grands en peignant ou en chantant leurs animaux favoris" (496). Whether or not this statement is historically accurate, it is surely evident that the poet is here reflecting on the role of the writer or artist in presenting the world of nature, whether in words or paint. Depending on the precise dates of composition, Sainct-Gelays's mention of the "bellette" may be a reference to his own epitaph on the animal, a subtle reminder of his demonstrated skill in this type of writing. Such self-conscious presentation, typical of the mock encomium, forces the reader to make comparisons and consider earlier instances of the genre in order to interpret and assess each new manifestation. The owner's longing to immortalize her sparrow resembles the poet's desire to give lasting significance to the fleeting specifics of life.

These early French animal epitaphs were as important for later French writers on animals as the classical sources. In fact, Henry Guy points out that "Jean Lemaire de Belges et les poètes de la première moitié du XVIe siècle ont donné à ces bagatelles une importance et une étendue qu'elles n'avaient nullement dans les textes latins et grecs. La Pléiade, à cet égard, s'est accommodée au goût français, et . . . Ronsard et Joachim du Bellay

. . . ont travaillé selon la méthode de leurs prédécesseurs immédiats."[8] The most common subject for later animal epitaphs was the dog. The list compiled by Paul Laumonier shows that some poems, such as those by Ronsard, Jamyn, Passerat, and Desportes on Madeleine de l'Aubespine's dog, Barbiche, even concerned the same animal and involved the writers in overt rivalry with one another.[9] In such "pièces de circonstance," the grief sometimes appears strained, but there is little justification for viewing the works as outright parodies of serious epitaphs, particularly since such a purpose might have endangered the poet's standing with the patron for whom the work was composed.

Typical of the dog epitaphs, Ronsard's piece on "Courte, chienne du Roy Charles IX" praises the intelligence of Courte, as shown in her various accomplishments:

> Courte estoit pleine, grosse & grasse,
> Courte jouoit de passe-passe,
> Courte sautoit sur le baston,
> Courte alloit dans l'eau, ce dit-on,
> Comme un barbet, lequel aporte
> A son maistre la cane morte.
>   (14:110–11)

Completely devoted to her master, in this respect a lesson to the king's subjects, the dog finally died when parted from him. This image of the abandoned pet pining for the master is similar to that noted in the Amant Vert poems. Even in death, however, poor Courte still served her owner, for the king had a pair of gloves made of her skin: "Courte ainsi morte & vive a faict / A son Roy service parfaict" (112).[10] This final illustration of the dog's total devotion to her master pushes the poem towards the grotesque, to the edge of parody. The reader wonders if the king's subjects are expected to give up their skins as well as their lives for their sovereign, or whether the poet's desire to flatter the monarch has got the better of him. Perhaps the answer is merely that modern readers may be more sentimental about animals than were their Renaissance forebears. We cannot decide such matters with any confidence, and the fact that we cannot highlights one of the central problems of the animal encomium, its tendency to move imperceptibly from irony to parody. In the case of the Ronsard poem, his hovering on the brink of the absurd may be interpreted positively as a deliberate posture designed to underscore the artist's control over his material, but this type of reading is not feasible in some later animal works.[11]

Although not an epitaph, Ronsard's "Prosopopée de Beaumont levrier du Roy, & de Charon," has an underworld setting that relates it to the second Epître de l'Amant Vert. Reminiscent at times of Lucian's Mortuorum Dialogi, it consists initially of a conversation between Beaumont and Charon, in which the dog flatters his master, Charles IX of France (14:114–20). Once conveyed to the other bank, Beaumont meets Courte, subject of the earlier Ronsard poem, who asks for news of France. The remainder of the work portrays Beaumont happily chasing deer through the woods as he did when alive. Nonetheless, he would like to return to earth, the animal says, even as a lowly "mastin," so greatly is life to be preferred to death. Abandoning the epitaph-compliment and indirect exhortation to the king's subjects, this poem concludes with a lyrical celebration of the beauties and pleasures of life. The playful tone of the beginning of the poem vanishes as, once again, Ronsard's genius pushes him beyond the bounds of his chosen genre. Time and again, later writers of animal encomia found themselves moving away from irony either towards lyricism and sentiment, or, alternatively, towards parody and caricature.

As the sixteenth century progressed, the various Italian works on animals, in particular the Bernesque parodies of Petrarchan laments, became popular in France. Two important changes in the epitaph resulted. First, its hyperbolical language became on occasion so extreme as to move into the realm of outright parody. Second, instead of being the doted-on pet of a beloved mistress or respected patron, the animal might now be presented as belonging to the narrator of the epitaph. These modifications are related to one another. When the animal did not belong to the composer of the lament, some sense of restraint or even of detachment was maintained, but when the animal was presented as the narrator's own, the latter often expressed himself more effusively. Illustrative of this contention are Du Bellay's three animal epitaphs in the *Divers Jeux rustiques* of 1558. Two concern dogs and one a cat. The first is a translation of Andrea Navagero's Latin lament on a shepherd's brave dog, the "De obitu Hylacis canis pastorici," first published in 1530. Probably using the later Paris edition of 1547 or 1548, Du Bellay lengthens slightly the original and replaces the Latin proper names with appropriate French ones. Entitled an "Epitaphe," the poem is part of the group entitled "Voeux rustiques," instances of what Saulnier calls a "vogue . . . assez peu durable."[12] It resembles the epitaphs of the *Greek Anthology*, and is a precursor of the later hymnes-blasons, which contained similar wishes or "voeux," sometimes in the quasi-religious sense of an offering of thanks to or a request for favor from the gods. But such wishes became increasingly playful, as for example when Ronsard hoped that the ant being eulogized would not bite a friend sitting beneath a tree with a lady friend.

Du Bellay's second animal epitaph, the "Epitaphe d'un petit chien," is shown by Saulnier to have been the "fruit d'un petit concours poétique de du Bellay contre Olivier de Magny," in which each poet lamented the death of what scholars believe was Jean d'Avanson's dog.[13] It is similar to the pieces by Sainct-Gelays and Ronsard discussed above. His third animal epitaph, the "Epitaphe d'un chat," also combines description of the animal's physical appearance and clever tricks with sorrow at its death. However, the grief over the death of Belaud the cat, presented as having belonged to the narrator, is far more intense than that expressed for the dog. This change of emphasis alters the effect of the resulting poem, which begins in a dramatic fashion:

> Maintenant le vivre me fasche:
> Et à fin, Magny, que tu sçaiche'
> Pourquoy je suis tant esperdu,
> Ce n'est pas pour avoir perdu
> Mes anneaux, mon argent, ma bource:
> Et pourquoy est-ce donques? pource
> Que j'ay perdu depuis trois jours
> Mon bien, mon plasir, mes amours:
> Et quoy? ô souvenance greve!
> A peu que le cueur ne me creve
> Quand j'en parle ou quand j'en escris.
> (5:103–4)

One of the strange facts to come to light in studying this work is that some of its most poignant passages are close imitations of an Italian capitolo on the death of a cat by Francesco Coppetta, the "Canzone nella perdita d'una Gatta."[14] Although the reader may feel moved by the emotion expressed in the epitaph on Belaud, as by that in many later French poems about the narrators' own pets, we must understand that such expressions of acute grief became so conventionalized that it is difficult to judge of their "sincerity."

A brief comparison between the French and Italian poems will demonstrate this point in connection with Coppetta and Du Bellay. Coppetta declares that his cat, a female, was more useful to him than any other animal he possessed. Like Du Bellay, he laments his loss in exaggerated terms:

> Chi mi t'ha tolto? ò sorte empia, & fatale
> Destinata al mio male,
> Giorno infelice, infausto, & sempre amaro,
> Nelqual perdei un pegno (ohime) si caro
> Che mi sarà cagion d'eterne pene.
> (2:24ʳ)

[Who took you from me? O wicked and inevitable fate, destined for my misfortune, unhappy, ill-omened, and forever bitter day on which I lost a pledge so dear (alas) that it will be a cause of my eternal grief.]

After another page repeating, with variations, his expressions of deep grief, Coppetta considers the cat's noble ancestry. He sees the dead animal in imagination everywhere:

> & dico qui prima s'assise,
> Ecco ov'ella sorrise,
> Ecco ov'ella scherzando il pie mi morse.
>
> (25ʳ)

[And I say, here is where she first sat, there where she smiled, and over there where she playfully bit my foot.]

The cat's many accomplishments include pulling off Coppetta's gloves for him, performing tricks, and most important of all, protecting him at night from rats. Echoing classical epitaph conclusions, he hopes that Jupiter, who has so unjustly seized his pet, will make of it a new star, or rather a pair of stars, one for each glowing eye. This poem seeks to recreate in words the beloved animal; its detailed description gives it a blason-like quality. Coppetta constantly stresses the role of the writer in conferring immortality on these household pets known only to a few individuals but treated in the poems as if they were world-renowned heroes. The twist at the end, the hope for not one star of immortality, but two, moves towards a whimsical stance. By pushing to the point of absurdity the traditional wish for permanence, it confers a more self-aware and playful perspective on the entire poem.

In one of the veiled references beloved of mock encomiasts, Du Bellay admits that his cat is more Italian than French in coloring: "Ny tel qu'en France on les void naistre / Mais tel qu'à Rome on les void estre" (5:104). This Italian coloring is of course as much verbal, in the borrowed details of the poet's epitaph, as it is physical, in the dead Belaud's outward appearance. While repeating Coppetta's praise for his cat's rat-catching abilities and his own wish for death now that he is alone, Du Bellay does not copy the Italian poem slavishly.[15] Thus, he develops in an unusual fashion the notion of the cat as the protector from rats. When Belaud was alive, the narrator explains, "si dextrement les happoit, / Que jamais un n'en eschappoit" (109). Now that the "seure garde" has been killed, the rats have become so bold that they gnaw at "les vers que j'escris" (109), threatening his ability to preserve in words Belaud's memory. In this way the poet ironically calls attention to the writing process and to the variables of literary history.

Certain details provided by the French narrator are not found in Coppetta; they serve to complete a vivid picture:

> Mon-dieu, quel passetemps c'estoit
> Quand ce Belaud vire-voltoit

Follastre autour d'une pelote!
Quel plaisir, quand sa teste sotte
Suyvant sa queuë en mille tours,
D'un rouet imitoit le cours!
Il s'en faisoit une jartiere,
Et monstrant l'estomac velu
De panne blanche crespelu
Sembloit, tant sa trongne estoit bonne,
Quelque docteur de la Sorbonne!
(5:106–7)

The impression here is of a personal recollection, but we have already seen that the work is in fact a tissue of borrowed and orginal elements. The simultaneously general and yet individual quality of these two poems reflects something about death in general: the loss is both personal, in the sense that only the individual's family may feel or even be aware of it, and yet also universal, in that any reader can sympathize with the private grief. This dichotomy is less prominent in a serious epitaph on a famous public figure, who may be mourned even by those who did not know him, but is obvious in the case of a domestic pet. The somewhat contrived quality of some parts of the works, such as the notion of Jupiter's creating twin stars in memory of the animals, reminds us that the entire endeavor is the poet's own commemorative star. Such moments of self-reflection also help to pull the works back from the edge of parody.

In some works, however, the convention of extreme grief in the formulation of epitaphs on animals belonging to the narrators of poems does move into parody. An example is an epitaph on the pig, Claude de Pontoux's long "Elegie sur la mort d'un couchon nommé Grongnet," which appeared in his *Oeuvres* of 1579.[16] In *The Politics and Poetics of Transgression*, Peter Stallybrass and Allon White demonstrate very clearly that in the sixteenth century a work in praise of a pig undoubtedly represented a deliberate flouting of common opinion.[17] In his introduction, Pontoux, an admirer and imitator of Ronsard, dilates upon but does not explain his grief. Du Bellay and Coppetta had employed the same delaying tactic to intrigue the reader. Pontoux presents a dramatic picture of distress:

Ha Gaulard, c'est faict de ma vie.
Elle est de-ja demi ravie.
Mon amy Gaulard, je me meurs,
Je voy les filandieres Soeurs,
Je voy ceste fatale parque,
Je voy Charon, je voi (*sic*) sa barque

. . . .

O le mal'heur! ô l'amertume!
J'ay le coeur plus dur qu'une enclume

Je ne desire aucunement
Sinon de mourir vittement.
(315–16)

Eventually the stricken man explains the reason for his despair, which is that his little pig, Grongnet, "mourut seul en un coignet / Dessouz mon lict, ô quelle perte!" (317).

Since Pontoux translated the *Sermoni funebri* into French, it is possible that he knew Coppetta's poem on the cat. He was certainly aware, from the *Sermoni funebri*, of the long Italian heritage of playful works on animals. Accordingly, he describes his pig as being of noble birth:

> Grongnet fut le plus beau Couchon
> Qui naquit jamais dans Branchon
> Dans Porlan, dans Bay, dans Baudreire
> Dans Chenauve, ni dans Plombeire.
>
> (317)

This enumeration of places continues for several lines, parodying the blasons and other poems which described the virtues of a series of towns, wines, and so on. Every detail of the pig is described, from its feet, mouth, snout, teeth, and alabaster skin to its adorable curly tail, which "sembloit la crosse d'un Abbé" (320). Its eyes, like those of Coppetta's cat, should be made into stars. The image of the pig's small eyes as stars highlights the parodic nature of the entire work, an aspect further developed when the narrator remarks that pig's flesh provides one of the most delicious of meats. As was noted in connection with the king's dog, Renaissance owners expressed no sentimental remorse about putting their dead pets to continuing use, but this remark concerning the pig combines with several others to convince us of its mocking intent.

For the narrator moves on from the taste of pig's flesh to consideration of some of its habits when alive. Although some may object to his praising a pig on the grounds that "il n'est honneste / De louer une sale beste" (321), he claims that his animal was not dirty, but had the most refined habits. He is, however, hard pressed to defend Grongnet's fondness for eating all manner of filth. By citing some tales from Galen, Hippocrates, and contemporary life proving that it is not wrong to eat human excreta, the narrator seeks to counter this criticism, which in any case pales to insignificance when set beside the incomparable virtues of Grongnet. Sometimes the two of them would sing together, and they regularly shared a bed, which the animal never soiled, "Au moins que l'aye aperceu" (325), as the narrator notes with the same mock-serious meticulousness found in Coppetta. Although the owner frequently teased his pet, its only offense had been to bite its master as he sought to make it drop a stolen partridge wing. The grieving owner would gladly suffer a hundred bites if his pet could be returned to life. The dead animal is to be buried with the following inscription: "Cy gist Grongnet que l'on veit estre / Le plaisant mignon de son maistre" (328). In its hyperbole, grotesque details, and deliberate repetitiveness, this bizarre epitaph shows clearly the influence of the Italian animal works but pushes their playfulness beyond the two-sided stance of the mock encomium into the realm of parody. Images such as that of the master sleeping with the pig or of the pig biting its own master undercut both the owner, who, like a fond parent, excuses the overindulged animal, and the genre that has developed towards these extreme expressions of grief. The dominant impression remains that of the pig degrading the master rather than of the master ennobling the pig, as had been the case in earlier animal encomia.

Pontoux was not alone in playing with this constant tendency of the realistic specifics of the animal eulogy to undermine the narrator's desire to elevate his subject matter. In 1594, Gilles Durant, sieur de la Bergerie, published a poem on the death of an ass, a work variously entitled the "Regrets funebres sur la Mort d'un Asne ligueur" and "A sa Commere, sur le trepas de son Asne qui mourut de mort violent durant le siege de Paris, mil cens quatre vingts dix."[18] Here again is the deep sorrow professed by Du Bellay and Pontoux, although in this case the animal is not the narrator's:

> Je meurs quand je repense à luy;
>
> . . . .
>
> Je pers le sense & le courage
> Quand je repense à ce dommage.
> (214ʳ)

The Ligue cost the ass its life, but it died a noble death:

> Pour le moins il eut ce bonheur
> De mourir dans le lit d'honneur,
> Et de verser son sang à terre
> Parmy les efforts de la guerre.
> (215ʳ)

In a rapid switch from the elegiac to the practical, the poet explains that the dead animal was sold to a butcher for "trente escus d'or sol," and that its flesh was probably later marketed as veal or mutton, a fate praised in lofty terms:

> De ceste façon magnifique,
> En la necessité publique,
> (O! rigueur estrange du Sort!)
> Vostre Asne, ma Commere, est mort.[19]

The notion of imitation veal and the reference to the price of meat degrades both the dead animal and the supposedly grieving owner. Even the sum specified, "trente escus," recalls in burlesque fashion the treachery of Judas. The king's acceptance of gloves made of Courte's skin, although unpalatable to the modern reader, resulted from his affection for this particular animal, not from a desire for financial gain. In a sense, Courte continues to be part of her master's life. The butchered donkey, on the other hand, is only incorporated into others' bodies when they believe it to be something other than it is. To present such an end as "magnifique" is to parody poems like that of Ronsard. The donkey meat is marketed as something finer than it is, and the entire poem is a parody of the nobler version of its own genre.

On occasion, as in earlier mock eulogies, later encomiasts make their ironic or parodic intentions plain. Vincent Denis's "Epitaphe du petit chien Lyco-phagos," for example, published in Paris in 1613, declares in some liminary verses:

> Arrière pleureux Heraclite!
> Nous ne pleurons pas comme vous;
> Nos pleurs sont ris de Democrite,
> Car pleurer, c'est rire, chez nous.[20]

In general, however, poets could by this time rely on the public to understand their meaning without stating it so overtly.[21]

THE HYMNES-BLASONS

In a sense the animal epitaph is a kind of blason, an attempt to prolong or represent in words a life unkindly cut short by the Fates. Du Bellay makes this resemblance explicit in sonnet 60 of the *Regrets*, probably addressed to M. d'Avanson, the dedicatee of the collection and owner of the dog that was the subject of one of Du Bellay's animal epitaphs. The poet explains that he has not dealt in his works with gold, heaven, demons, and so forth (a clear reference to Ronsard), but that:

> d'un petit Chat j'ay fait un petit hymne,
> Lequel je vous envoye: autre present je n'ay.
>   Prenez le donc (Seigneur) & m'excusez de grace,
> Si pour le bal ayant la musique trop basse,
> Je sonne un passepied ou quelque branle gay.[22]

The statement that the poet does not wish his "petit hymne" to be taken too seriously moves the work closer to the animal hymne-blason, to be discussed below, than to the regular epitaph. This overlap between the two animal genres sometimes extends to the imagery: as we saw above, Marot in epitaphs and Danche in a blason both make use of the same sexual double entendre. However, in being concerned with an animal, Danche was exceptional among early blasonneurs, who usually wrote about the female body or other topics that could readily be presented in groups or lists of short individual poems—wines, towns, household objects. Not until the vogue of the Pléiade poems that modern critics have called the *hymnes-blasons* do we find a substantial number of blasons on animals, often on small or insignificant ones.

The name *hymne-blason* was first coined in a work on Remy Belleau published in Budapest in 1917 by Alexandre Eckhardt, who believed these poems to be first and foremost translations or imitations of the Bernesque capitoli.[23] In fact, their debt to Italy is often less significant than Eckhardt suggests, for their inspiration was as French as it was Italian. Unlike Eckhardt, Laumonier remarks that to discuss the Bernesque element in the hymnes-blasons "nous entraînerait trop loin."[24] This is to go too far in the other direction. Marcel Raymond stresses the fact that Ronsard and his friends were primarily revitalizing the French tradition of the blason, which they sought to ennoble in poems like the "Grenouille," the "Freslon," and the "Fourmi" by Ronsard, and the "Papillon" by Belleau.[25] Trtnik-Rossettini sums up the hymnes-blasons as follows:

> En fait, Ronsard, aidé peut-être par les recherches voisines de Baïf (*Laurier*), se contente de hausser jusqu'au lyrisme le blason bernesque et marotique; il interpelle les Muses et les Dieux, il mêle des vocables savants aux mots du terroir, enfin, après la dédicace où le nom du blasonné est dix fois martelé, il introduit au centre du poème un mythe, une fable qui ont pour mission de voiler des vérités avec de la "poésie."[26]

Naïs comments on the Renaissance fondness, not only in the hymnes-blasons, but also in other literary creations, for invented legends and tales from mythology rather than scientific facts. Even in the major Pléiade hymnes-blasons on animals, "l'animal disparaît souvent sous un fatras d'ornements poétiques qui n'ont plus guère de rapports avec lui" (555).

What these critics fail to mention, however, is the Lucianic influence on the blason. The Lyons blasons of 1547 mention Lucian by name as a source, and the "Hymne de la Surdité" includes well-known Lucianic images. The playful use of mythology and the ironic tone of many Pléiade hymnes-blasons are due as much to Lucian as to the capitoli. Moreover, since the capitoli were themselves much affected by Lucian, the Greek writer's influence becomes once again a mixture of the direct and the indirect. Given this widespread awareness both of Italian and of classical mock encomia, it is not surprising that a more flexible and complex approach to description is evident in the hymnes-blasons.

Entitled either "hymnes" or "blasons," the hymnes-blasons did not have the elevated tone and subject matter deemed by the Pléiade appropriate to the hymn, although there was ambiguity in Ronsard's attitude to certain of his serious hymns.[27] In the case of the blason, the refusal to use the word as title was perhaps due to the Pléiade poets' scorn for the minor native genres, seen as popular and low, not noble, an attitude made most evident in Du Bellay's *Deffence*. Nonetheless, certain of Ronsard's hymnes-blasons, for example, "Le Houx" (1555), do contain references to the genre:

> Mais moi, sans plus, je veux dire
> En ces vers, d'un stille doux,
> Le nouveau *blason* d'un Houx.
> (6:136, italics mine)

The newness here was presumably inherent in the "stille doux" and in the choice of a tree as the subject of the poem, not in the details of nomenclature. "Blason" for Ronsard evidently described his poem, even if such was not its title. Similarly, in the "Elegie du Verre," also part of *Les Meslanges*, Ronsard writes:

> Il me sufist si l'honneur d'un seul verre,
> Lequel tu m'as pour estraines donné,
> Est dînement en mes vers *blasonné*.[28]

The gift referred to here came from Jean Brinon, dedicatee of this and several other hymnes-blasons, and longtime friend of the Pléiade poets. The homophonic "vers" and "verre", the word and the object represented, are typical of the blason-writer's way of calling attention to his recreation in words of a material object. They remind us that, in representing the "verre," the "vers" can move its chosen topic either up or down, ennoble or degrade it by way of the poet's craft. Du Bellay uses the verb "blasonner" in a similar context in the conclusion to his epitaph on Belaud:

> Que pleust à Dieu, petit Belon,
> Que j'eusse l'esprit assez bon,
> De pouvoir en quelque beau style
> *Blasonner* ta grace gentile,
> D'un vers aussi mignard que toy.
> (5:111)

In both these cases the poets may have had in mind a poetic description rather than the traditional French blason, but their association of a certain style with this verb suggests at the very least an awareness of their relationship to the older genre.

In 1551, a few years before the appearance of the most famous hymnes-blasons, Etienne Forcadel, scholar, lawyer, and poet, published an interesting and closely related poem.[29] This appeared in a collection containing six eulogies, five of which are primarily descriptive and serious, closely related to the eulogistic form of the blason and similar in tone to Ronsard's serious hymns. One poem, however, the "Encomie du Corbeau," is more ironic. In order to praise a bird not usually thought of as attractive either to look at or to hear, Forcadel must seek out unusual arguments.[30] He begins by declaring:

> Je pretens avoir peu d'estime,
> Pour coucher icy dans ma ryme
> Le los qui est dû au corbeau.
> Tant il est doux, tant il est beau,
> Que plustot envieux seroit
> Quiconque ne le priseroit,
> Que benin qui sa grace monstre.
>
> (250)

The exaggerated language of these lines emphasizes their disingenuousness and suggests that the exact opposite may in fact be true. Forcadel follows the customary plan of the animal praise, a description of the physical appearance of the bird, then of its attributes, physical and mental, embroidered by various classical and other references. Finally, he praises one of the most unattractive aspects of the bird, its voice:

> Loüons sa voix de bassecontre,
> Celle voix, dy je, qui fait rendre
> Ce que l'homme luy veult apprendre.
> Qui salua par mots humains
> L'empereur second des Romains.
> L'aigle n'eut pas cest avantage.
>
> (250)

Arguing in this way for the raven's superiority over the eagle, usually viewed as the king of birds, the narrator marvels at its glossy plumage, smooth as jet or velvet. In a Lucianic adaptation of authorities, he claims that Noah sent a raven, not a dove, out of the ark to see if the waters of the Flood had subsided. It became both hoarse and black in serving humanity, since when sent out to survey the flood it cried "Noë, Noë, / Tant qu'encor en est enroué" (251–52). As a sign of grief at losing sight of the ark, it turned black and has remained both hoarse and black ever since. This ingenious reinterpretation confers on the bird an almost human sense of loyalty. Nonetheless, to use the beauties of the poet's voice to mask the ugliness of that of the raven comes perilously close to self-parody. The "Encomie du Corbeau" thus provides both an illustration, by way of its use of mythology and the resources of rhetoric, of what could be done with this mixed genre, and a warning, in its bathetic "Noë, Noë" cry, of the delicate line the blasonneur must tread between the sublime and the ridiculous. The dog can be raised up to become fit clothing for a monarch, but the pig can bite its owner, and the embellished crow may croak too loudly at the reader.

Most of the Pléiade hymnes-blasons were written between 1554 and 1556, not long after the publication of the capitoli, and while Du Bellay, one of the form's chief exponents, was living in Italy. The first to appear in print, "Le Laurier" and "Le Meurier," were in fact by Jean Antoine de Baïf, not Ronsard, Du Bellay, or Belleau, so often associated with the genre.[31] The laurel, most literary of plants, was an obvious choice for a poetic blason. These two poems are not, however, ironical, but directly laudatory, in the older tradition of the blason as "perpétuéle louenge."[32] The other poems on trees by Pléiade members and their followers imitate the tone of those by Baïf. Later, Belleau's poems on precious stones also praise their chosen topics directly. From the start, therefore, one group of hymnes-blasons follows the older blason tradition of straightforward praise while another group, concerned with animals, usually adopts a playful or even a mocking tone. Most of Ronsard's hymnes-blasons antedate the "Hymne de la Surdité," the most markedly satirical of the entire group, but the earliest animal hymns make a clear move toward badinage and indirection, usually in the last lines, or envoi.

In Ronsard's "La Grenouille," for example, part of *Le Bocage* of 1554, the narrator declares that the frog is a "Déesse" who never suffers from thirst, even in the hottest of summers: " (Hé Dieu que je porte d'envie / Aus felicités de ta vie.)"[33] Christening the frog the "Roine des Ruisseaus," he describes how its croaking frightens away much bigger animals. Even the greedy heron cannot digest it, so well do the gods protect it from harm. The frog has various medicinal uses, and its croaking is commonly thought to presage good weather. Instead of a long, wearisome life, it has six months of carefree bliss, earned as a reward from the gods for having roused them when the giants were invading Olympus.

In recognition of his eulogy, the encomiast begs the frog not to disturb Belleau as he works or sleeps, a request that contradicts his earlier positive statements about its voice, but a familiar device in mock eulogies for drawing attention to irony or an ambivalent attitude. Having lulled the reader into a fictive world of beautiful croakings, the poet now reminds him of the raucous sounds of frogs in nonfictive gardens. Poems may swallow up frogs, but frogs may drown out soft poetic music. We may recall here Belleau's title, *Petites Inventions*, for the collection in which so many of his hymnes-blasons appeared. As personal creations at once related to but not bound by the extraliterary world, such portraits can be varied or undercut at will. Ronsard's mythologized picture of the frog is never long permitted to distract us from its less glamorous characteristics. The play of poetic fancy here draws attention to itself in a very clear manner, but falls short of self-parody. On the contrary, it seems rather to assert once again the author's power over his material.

This dual perspective, in which the poem's mythological fantasy is ironically questioned at the end, reappears in Ronsard's "Le Freslon." The heart of the piece is a tale of "freslons" stinging Silenus's donkey, jolting it into sudden motion that saves the rider from capture by the "Indois."[34] The portrait of the heroic wasp is vivid and dramatic:

> Là, sur tous un frellon estoit
> Qui brave par l'air se portoit
> Sur quatre grands ailes dorées :
> En maintes lames colorées
> Son dôs luisoit par la moitié.
> Luy courageus, ayant pitié
> De voir au meillieu de la guerre
> Silene, & son asne par terre,
> Piqua cet asne dans le flanc
> Quatre ou cinq coups jusques au sang.
>   (6:90–91)

The military language here ("brave," "courageus," and "piqua") makes the wasp, rather than Silenus, the hero of the adventure. Such an inversion of the normal hierarchy echoes Lucian's conversion of the fly into an elephant. But the change in the Ronsard poem is moral rather than physical. The picture is further complicated by the fact that Silenus was himself an ambiguous figure, a satyr and drunkard but also the source of wisdom to whom Plato compared his master, Socrates. Such complexities prevent the reader from drawing any hasty conclusions about the poem. The result of the wasp's sting is described in a way that draws attention to the donkey rather than to its rider:

> L'asne, qui soudain se reveille
> Dessous le vieillard, fist merveille
> De si bien mordre à coups de dens
> Ruant des pieds, que le dedans
> Des plus espesses embuscades
> Ouvrit en deus de ses ruades.
>   (6:91)

This mock-heroic narrative, with the wasp the courageous warrior, the donkey the energetic battle steed, and Silenus the beneficiary of the animals' action to save him, concludes with lines reminiscent of the envoi of "La Grenouille":

Or vivés bienheureus Frellons:
Tousjours de moi vos aiguillons
Et de Belleau soient loing, à l'heure
Que la vandange sera meure.
(6:92)

These more personal, less "noble" lines refer us to the world outside that of epic battles, where stings are a painful inconvenience, not a spur to heroism. The balance of perspectives in this poem is delicate, and its inversion of roles is not a straightforward one. For the donkey's "courage" derives from an instinctive reaction to pain and fear, not from the moral fortitude of the ideal knight, and the wasp's "bravery" is that of a predatory insect, not an epic warrior.

In some poems, Ronsard mentions not only his friends' names but other related works: thus, in "Le Fourmi," he refers to the "Grenouille" and the "Freslon," meaning his two poems, as gifts offered by him to Belleau. In an extended effort at self-justification, he explains, following Virgil, that "On n'aquiert pas petite gloire / A traicter bien un oeuvre bas" (6:93). Furthermore, it is important to strive for variety in poetry, since no single note, however fine, should be sounded for too long. Readers unwilling to accept such poetry are urged to go away and peruse Scève's already proverbially obscure *Délie*.

In the eulogy proper, the narrator describes a long line of ants, burdened with spoils, crawling back to their nests, well-organized societies. A traditional biblical comparison between mankind and the ant is used to urge the French to profit from the example of these orderly and industrious insects. The narrator next claims that ants are one of the poet's most reliable sources of images and comparisons, and he ends with a reference to their proverbial meteorological gifts:

Que dirai plus? Vous avisés
Les vens que vous profetisés
Plus d'un jour devant leur venüe:
La Nature vous est connüe,
Et toutes les saisons des cieus:
Bref, vous estes de petis Dieus.
(6:97)

The argument has now been taken to the edge of paradox, if not beyond; from being some of the smallest of God's creatures, the ants have become small gods themselves. As in Lucian's *Muscae Encomium*, the chain of being has been momentarily inverted. As ever, such moments of extreme paradox are brief, the above passage being followed by an envoi of the by-now familiar type:

Or, gentils Fourmys, je vous prie,
Si un jour Belleau tient s'amie
A l'ombre de quelque Fouteau,
Sous qui sera vostre troupeau,
Ne piqués point la chair douillette
De sa gentille mignonnette.

(6:97)

The final lines turn on the noble fiction created in the poem. In so doing, they remind us that the poet's imagination, aided by the wealth of legend, parable, and fable surrounding a given creature, may enable him to construct a complex and moving tribute to an animal, but that such a structure is as delicate as the skin of Belleau's beloved. The animal blasonneur is forever moving between the pole of epic or lyric grandeur and that of burlesque or parodic humor. This is why so many poets were attracted by the genre, but also why so few achieved the results they sought.

Another well-known animal poem by Ronsard, "Le Chat," dedicated to Belleau, is a most original defamatory blason. Grazzini had written a capitolo against dogs, but the two works are not alike except insofar as they deal with a personal phobia.[35] Since both attack their chosen subject, they are not satirical eulogies. At times, Ronsard also criticizes dogs, as when he threatens a dog whose barking awakened the parents of his lady companion. Warning the noisy animal that, had it been more discreet, it would have been made a "chien immortel" in one of his poems, he now offers only threats. Such self-inclusive irony reminds us of the poet's favorable hymnes-blasons, making the lines an inversion of an inversion, undercutting what was already an ironic form. Once again, attention is being drawn to the writer determining the positive or negative presentation of material. The poem thus becomes a mocking reflection on the entire endeavor of the hymnes-blasons.[36]

Belleau's hymnes-blasons on animals contain almost as much mythology as Ronsard's and even more meticulous description. For example, in "Le Papillon," dedicated to Ronsard, he writes:

Est-il *peintre* que la Nature?
Tu contrefais une *peinture*
Sur tes aelles si proprement,
Qu'à voir ton beau bigarrement,
On diroit que le *pinceau* mesme
Auroit d'un artifice extreme
Peint de mille & mille fleurons
Le crespe de tes aellerons.
    Ce n'est qu'or fin dont tu te dores
Qu'argent, qu'azur dont tu *colores*
Au vif un millier de beaux yeux,

> Dont tu vois: & meritois mieux
> De garder la fille d'Inache
> Qu'Argus, quand elle devint vache.[37]

The compressed mythological references in the last six lines of this passage are typical of the procedure of the Pléaide blasonneurs. From the notion of "beaux yeux," the poet moves to Argus "Panoptes," of the one hundred eyes, who was ordered to guard Io, beloved of Zeus, after the jealous Hera had persuaded her errant husband to deliver Io, disguised as a heifer, into her keeping. When Hermes killed the vigilant Argus, Hera placed his one hundred eyes in the tail of the peacock, her chosen bird. This entire development by Belleau is based on the physical resemblance between the butterfly's multiple "eyes," probably those on its wings, and the "eyes" on a peacock's tail. The development is itself a "beau bigarrure." This type of elaborate artistic manipulation brings to mind Naïs's remarks, cited earlier, concerning the rivalry between poets and painters with regard to portraiture. Despite the reference to the "vache," however, there is little overt irony in this piece, which is primarily an instance of the verbal gilding of a creature already commonly held to be attractive. The creator's role is nonetheless emphasized, since the poet has sought, not to make the ugly admirable, but to make the pretty beautiful.

Belleau's most interesting hymne-blason from the point of view of the present investigation is his "Le Mulet," also published in the *Petites Inventions* of 1556.[38] The poem was dedicated to his friend Simon Nicolas, "Secrétaire du Roy," who was supposedly suffering from the quartan fever, a topic popular with mock encomiasts. Belleau explains that Nicolas is obsessed with the desire to have a mule, preferably one from the king's own stables. It would be wonderful if the monarch were to present Nicolas with such a gift, but the poet notes sardonically that "aisément on ne tire rien / Des grans, qu'on ne l'achepte au double" (108). To resolve this difficulty and satisfy his friend's craving, he offers Simon a poetic mule.

The point of departure of this poem is thus the perennial and practical one of poets' and courtiers' requests to their sovereigns. But this pragmatic impetus is soon abandoned as the narrator explains that the mule he is sending will be an imaginary one, endowed with all possible virtues. I offer you, he writes to Simon, punning on the resemblance between *panser*, to groom, and *penser*, to think,

> Le mien qui pensé de la main
> Ne mange n'avoyne, ny foin,
> N'estant que l'image & la feinte,
> L'attente & l'esperance peinte
> D'un Mulet.
> (109)

This animal, groomed or created by the poet ("engraissé de mon stile"), is easier to care for than a real one, but it remains in the poem only the "feinte" and "attente" of a mule. Once again, a simultaneous inside and outside perspective is called for to understand the subtlety of the piece. The language of painting ("image," "peinte") reappears in the context of verbal description. Belleau's beast is fearless and gentle, worthy of the "celeste Asnon" associated with the youth of "pere Bacchus." This passage leads to a short contre-blason asserting that the mule is not one of the typical thin, bad-tempered asses. The negative portrait within the positive one draws attention to the fictive quality of both good and bad creatures, since the undesirable animal is at least as believable an invention as that offered to Nicolas:

> Il n'est de ces mulets hargneux,
> Acariastres, & peureux,
> Ruans, mordans, tousjours en rage,
> A qui faudroit plus de cordage
> Pour tenir la teste et les piez,
> Qu'à cent navires bien armez:
> Longs d'echine comme une barque,
> Eflanquez, à qui l'on remarque
> Fort aisement par le travers
> Des costes, ce grand univers.
>   (110)

Given that there is as much detail and vividness in the Italianate satirical portrait as in the laudatory one, it is appropriate for the blason to end with a reminder that both are fictive creatures. Since one of the most troublesome symptoms of Nicolas's illness is his state of semidelirium, the narrator suggests that his friend load his fever, and with it his imaginings, onto the back of the proffered mule, which will then depart, carrying away the disease. The last line of the poem reads, "Et chez toy n'habite jamais" (111). A sufferer originally depicted as marked by the fanciful wish for an animal from the king's stables is presented with an imaginary realization of his wishes. The result is to be regained health and sanity, but, paradoxically, loss of the imaginary mule that is to carry off the fever. The aim of the poem is to restore a man's ability to distinguish between controllable poetic daydreaming, an example of which is the present blason, and the obsessive hallucinations induced by fever. In this most purposeful of hymnes-blasons, Belleau's humor is kind, his language relatively simple, and the mythological embroidery minimal. As was shown in the chapter on the Italian mock encomia, there were several literary works on the donkey during this period.[39] The originality of "Le Mulet," as of Ronsard's "Le Fourmi," lies in its manipulation of the traditional tropes and images to show the need for awareness of the two-sided quality of elements of the natural world, their potential for noble and delicate, but also for comical and "low" verbal representation.

In this way, the hymnes-blasons gradually became what might be called word-objects, to be given and received by a group of cultivated and sophisticated friends. Indeed, some became almost an "in-joke," their composers sharing both the poems and the ironic, self-aware attitude with which they were written. Even "Le Mulet," exceptional in having a deeper purpose closely related to its form, operates on the edge of parody. Nonetheless, there are a number of imitations of these Pléiade works after a lapse in the 1560s. In 1576, for example, Pierre de Brach composed a longer version of Ronsard's "Le Freslon," making his debt apparent by first asking himself if he dare write on a subject previously treated by the "grand Vandomois tant vanté." He decides to be brave, since "Couhart est celui qui refuse, / Et qui n'ose une trait décocher / Lorsqu'il voit un meilleur archer."[40] De Brach does not copy all the details of Ronsard's poem, but his overall plan is the same, and he too, at the end of his blason, begs the wasp not to sting his friend. Since de Brach's poem lacks the vitality and richness of the Ronsard work, the final sting for the reader is likely to be that provided by comparing the earlier to the later poem.

In 1578, François de Clary published *La Bellete*, praising a live weasel, not, as had Sainct-Gelays, a dead one. This difference enables the poet to combine the specificity of most animal epitaphs with the more generalized quality of the hymne-blason. The first lines refer not to contemporary writers, but to classical sources, Virgil and Catullus, upon whom he calls for inspiration:

> Affin que, comme sur la lyre
> L'un a faict son Mouscheron bruire,
> L'autre son Passereau chanté,
> Ainsi je dise ta beauté
> Et la façon mignardelette
> De laquelle, gente Bellette,
> Tu t'estudies à chasser
> Le soing et le triste penser.[41]

Citing both an epitaph and a narrative poem as predecessors, the writer demonstrates once again the Renaissance fondness for playing with the possibilities of related genres. Following the plan of the animal hymne-blason, describing how the weasel's antics dispel his moments of depression, the poet relates the story of the origin of the weasel. When Galanthis was transformed into a weasel at the request of the ever-jealous Juno, Jupiter ensured that the animal would be both agile and beautiful.[42] Ovid stated that Hecate made it her attendant and that Hercules erected a sanctuary to her. The weasel in the present poem is beautiful, agile, and capable of many tricks, such as waking its master in the morning by ringing a small bell, chasing troublesome flies, and even "studying" his books with him. Although the poem is less mocking in tone than some Pléiade hymnes-blasons, the odd mixture of mythological invention, hyperbolical language, and specific details places it firmly in the tradition of the playful hymnes-blasons. An instance of the deliberate shift to an unromantic point of view occurs when the poet describes the "senteur" with which the animal, skunk-like, can destroy a poisonous snake such as the "basilisque."[43] This moment, like Forcadel's "Noë, Noë," threatens to drag the poem down from its mythological heights. But the contrast is less jarring than in the eulogy on the raven, where it provides the foundation for the entire defense of the bird. Here, it serves more as one of the fleeting references to a less romantic world that are found in the majority of Pléaide hymnes-blasons.

Other hymnes-blasons related to the more famous Pléiade ones were Jean de la Jessée's "L'Abeille" of 1583 and Jacques Peletier du Mans's "L'Alouete." The former work is of interest because its author, whose poems on prison have already been discussed, was an active composer of mock encomia of all sorts. Peletier's "Le Fourmi" is more directly laudatory, a traditional moralizing comparison between man and the ant with little of the self-inclusive irony that marked Ronsard's poem of the same name.[44]

THE FLEA ENCOMIA

Also linked to the hymnes-blasons and their descendants is an important series of French poems on animals, one later quoted by Dornavius, entitled *La Puce de Madame des Roches*. The volume was published in 1583 at the instigation of the lawyer and humanist Etienne Pasquier, and the lady referred to in its title was Catherine des Roches, the beloved of Caye Jules de Guersens, author of "A la Louange des Cornes."[45] A bold creature, the flea jumped out from the bodice of Catherine's dress in full view of a group of distinguished lawyers gathered at the home of Catherine and her mother during the "grands jours" in Poitiers. Thus inspired, the visitors gallantly composed a series of short works in French, Latin, Greek, Italian, and Spanish, blessing and praising the flea for its good fortune and fine judgment. Since their verses about the event were published with the others, Catherine and her mother apparently joined in the fun.

Before discussing this volume, an extreme form of "pièce de circonstance," it should be noted that many other flea poems already existed, not only in the Italian and Neo-Latin traditions, but also in French and German. Marcel Françon has described a number of these earlier works, from the learned classical pieces influenced by the *Metamorphoses*, the *Culex*, and the *Greek Anthology* to the popular "débats."[46] One of these is the *Procès des Femmes et des Pulces,* dated about 1520 and consisting of 176 lines divided into octaves, the "huitains" of Villon. Angry because the biting fleas prevent her from sleeping, the woman vows to revenge herself by crushing them. With the beginning of the fleas' self-defense, the poem takes on the form of a medieval debate. It is, however, a humorous one, a "facétie," as Montaiglon, its modern editor, calls it.[47] The work was one of those which inspired the best-known German example of flea-literature, Fischart's *Flöh Hatz,* a popular and bizarre collection of prose and verse writings about fleas. Fischart's imitation of the French poem ran to more than four thousand lines and included additional writings on mosquitoes and other insects. Since there was often confusion in the Renaissance between "culex" and "pulex," the introduction of other insects into the anthology is not surprising.[48]

Françon shows that Ronsard plays a major role in the growth in popularity of the flea topos in love poetry. In the *Folastrie VI* of 1553, the narrator longs to become a flea in order to be at liberty to wander at will over his lady's body.[49] At night, however, he would want to regain his human shape. This theme of the flea-man-lover was to be popular in France and in England, where it was exploited by Thomas Watson, William Drummon, John Donne, and others. French poets, however, had a built-in linguistic advantage in this literary effort: the resemblances between the words "puce," "pucelle," "pucelage," "dépuceler," and so on made possible a range of verbal games less easily rendered in other languages. The English, for instance, had to rely on puns on "flea," "fly," and "flee," which were more difficult to blend with the love schema.

Imitating these Ronsardian love games and yet subtly diverging from them is the "Hymne de la Puce" of François de Chantelouve.[50] The flea has awakened the narrator, we are told, in order to urge him to write a hymn in its honor. Accordingly, he begins:

> Petite puce! puce! ô combien à bon droict!
> Ton bel honneur chanter un Pindare devroit,
> Un Horace, un Ronsard en ces excellents hymnes
> Devroit crier bien hault tes louanges divines.

Like Ronsard, this narrator asserts that the flea's greatest good fortune is its freedom to explore a woman's body. Gradually, the flea itself takes on the qualities of a woman; its dress is described as "plus noir que l'ebene," and it is even addressed by the human admirer as "quelle beauté!" The poet would like to be transformed into a flea in order to gain access to his lady's bedroom. Rather than bite her, however, he would talk quietly to her and fall asleep on her breast. To die in such a place would be true bliss.

After narrating the customary legends concerning the insect's early history, the poem concludes in a more practical vein:

Je te salue ô puce, & si dedans mes vers
J'ay bien haut ta louange apprins à l'univers,
Permets en ma faveur que jamais je ne sente
Pour troubler mon repos ta piqueure cuisante
Et que la marguerite estant dedans le lict
Ne soit de ton piquon offencée la nuict.

This ending, typical of the Pléiade hymne-blason, reminds the reader that he has become entangled in the poet's lyric creation. Not only has he first accepted the familiar identification between flea and man, but he has then been manipulated into confusing an insect with a woman, forgetting less agreeable concerns such as the insects' bites and the lady's reluctance. Abruptly switching perspectives and separating the two creatures, the ending restores lover and lady to their own beds and to the rather less romantic wish for uninterrupted, if solitary sleep. In moving toward the more humorous ending of an animal hymne-blason, the poet is distanced from the identification between himself and the flea. The final image thus creates a very different effect from that conveyed by the erotic suggestiveness of Ronsard and Donne. This difference brings the hymn far closer to the tradition of the mock encomium we have been tracing in the present chapter.

Despite these other efforts, the *La Puce* collection was the most extensive grouping of flea works collected in France in the sixteenth century. It appeared at a time when the various popular and learned trends were sufficiently well established and familiar to readers for the contributors to the volume to be able to play with and reflect upon them. Bringing together prose and verse, the Poitiers writers are constantly aware of their literary heritage. I believe that while the love motif of the volume has already been amply discussed, the importance of the work in the history of the mock encomium repays further study. In this way we may better be able to explain the concluding work in the collection, a prose piece probably by Pasquier that does not even mention the work's professed raison d'être, Catherine's bold flea.

Before considering that final work, a look at three other pieces in the collection may enable us to understand how they toy with their own generic history. The first, by Barnabé Brisson, the Paris jurisconsult, appeared in two versions, one Latin and one French (by Pasquier), the latter of which will be examined here. It mentions Homer's frogs and "souris," Catullus's "vers mignard" on the sparrow, the "petit coussin" immortalized by Virgil, and, finally, an anonymous work on the flea. The present poet's endeavor is deemed superior to those of its famous predecessors:

Mais cela n'egalle point
Nostre Pucette, qui point

Cette charnure marbrine
De la docte Catherine.
(9ᵛ)

The poem thus focuses on the transforming power of the writer. But whereas poets of old immortalized their subjects in words, the flea is ennobled merely by having had the good fortune to bite the "charnure marbrine" of Catherine. The marble-white flesh thus becomes a living "temple de memoire" in which the poet would be happy to make his own "tombe." This conceit, with its Catullan sexual undertones, epitomizes the procedure of Pasquier's entire volume. The contributors all wished to transform a mundane, even embarrassing incident into complimentary literary creations that would demonstrate both poetic skill and a desire to please a learned society lady. In expressing their thoughts in the playful form of the mock encomium, they remind us nonetheless of the comedy of the entire business. The lofty poetic fiction and the humble reality remain ultimately distinct from one another. As was shown in connection with Bruscambille, a more theatrical notion of the mock encomium as a performance piece or word-object had entered the genre by the end of the sixteenth century. The *La Puce* collection shares this sense of public spectacle, but is different in that it is a group publication. The total "event" of this volume is greater than any of its contributing parts, for its appearance signals a general level of sensitivity to the mingling of literary-historical and social sophistication that had become characteristic of the genre at this stage of its development.

Proof of the awareness of genre with which the pieces were composed may be found in a second contribution to the volume, the "Pulex." The author, Joseph Scaliger, incorporates not only a mention but even textual echoes of his predecessor, Catullus:

Pulicelle niger, nigelle Pulex,
Incitatior hoedulis petulcis,
Delicatior hinnulis tenellis,
Docti passere nequior Catulli,
Stellae blandior albula columba.
(14ʳ)

[O black little flea, o little black flea, swifter than a frisky small goat, softer than a tender young stag, more licentious than the learned Catullus's sparrow, more charming than Stella's white dove.]

Equally self-conscious and replete in intertextual references is a third poem, by R. Chopin, in which the narrator imagines himself reproached for making so much of this "vermiculum" [grub]. It is as if he were making "ex musca Elephantum," he continues. After all, mortals scorn this dust-born creature and girls seek to crush it beneath their nails. But, he answers himself, "muscas Lucianus, apes Maro laudibus ornat" [Lucian praised flies and Virgil bees] (13ʳ).[51] Chopin thus recalls for his audience not only the *Muscae Encomium* and the mock eulogy in general, but also Lucian's ever-popular closing remark about the fly and the elephant. Although the amount of praise or mockery contained in the des Roches poems varies considerably, by so regularly referring to their generic family tree, the authors provide a clear signal that the works are to be taken playfully, and that their moments of self-parody are deliberate, not unconscious. In taking this step towards rhetorical self-reflection they also, like François de Chantelouve, move back from the amorous social game being played with Catherine. This more literary and rhetorical emphasis makes more understandable the fact that the des Roches ladies were willing to take part in the enterprise.

The closing work in the *La Puce* part of the collection, the prose "Louange de la Puce," demonstrates most clearly these claims. Lachèvre argues convincingly that the composer of the piece was none other than Pasquier himself, summing up the overall effort of the group and, in a sense, providing an envoi for the volume.[52] The inspiration given for this composition is far closer to that given in classical mock encomia than to that related to Catherine: "Il n'y a pas long temps que je dis en quelque compagnie, par maniere de moquerie, non autrement à bon, que je voulois escrire quelque chose en l'honneur de la Puce, à fin d'exercer ma veine & façoner mon stile à l'imitation de Lucian, qui en a fait autant à l'endroit de la mouche" (57ᵛ). This remark demonstrates the planned quality of the volume as a whole; we cannot be sure here which came first, the writer's desire to "exercer [sa] veine" or the incident with Catherine's flea. The "Louange de la Puce" follows closely both the plan and the text of the *Muscae Encomium*, rather than that of the Catullan poems on Lesbia's sparrow or the other classical pieces on animals. Lucian had begun: "The fly is not the smallest of winged creatures, at least in comparison with gnats and midges and things still tinier. On the contrary, she is as much larger than they as she is smaller than the bee" (1:83). The French narrator brings in the opposite end of the animal scale, the elephant, rather than a slightly larger animal within the same relative scale, such as the bee: "La Puce est le plus petit de tous les animaux, comme au contraire l'Elefant est le plus grand, je parle des terrestres. Quelque rongneux m'objectera que le ciron est encore plus petit: je luy respond que de cirons & morpions ne se doit faire mention entre gens d'honneur et reputation" (57ᵛ). By combining Lucian's concluding image with his beginning one, the narrator retains the more human sense of scale that Lucian initially tries to make the reader forget. In addition, the French writer includes his own persona, "je luy respond," "je parle," and so on, placing the man-sized, ironic figure firmly within his text. The quibblings over unimportant details such as the smallness of "cirons" and "morpions" as compared to fleas are of course traditional techniques of the mock encomiast.

When describing the legs of their respective insects, both writers anthropomorphize their subject, Lucian by pointing out that "though she has six feet, she walks with only four and uses the two in front for all the purposes of hands" (1:85), and Pasquier by adding details concerning the length of the various legs: "Or de ces six pieds les deux de devant sont plus courts que les quatre autres: & de ces deux là elle se sert comme de mains" (58ʳ). The heroic courage of their subject is given particular praise. Lucian says that Homer likens a hero's spirit to that of a fly, rather than to that of a leopard, boar or lion: "Even if she is kept away, she does not desist, but is eager to bite. So outspoken is he in his praise and fondness for the fly that he mentions her not merely once or twice but often: in consequence, references to her enhance the beauty of his poems" (1:87). The French writer adapts these lines slightly in order to praise the flea:

> Discourons de sa hardiesse: . . . On a beau la serrer sous le doit, la rouller sous le pouce, si une fois elle peut eschaper de vos serres, elle retourne plus furieuse que devant à l'écarmouche, enragée de vous mordre: & ne vous laissera jamais en paix que premierement elle ne soit soullee de vostre sang. Un tygre, un lion, un liepard en feroient ils d'avantage? Et toutefois vous me confesserez que ce sont bestes de grand cueur & pleines de vaillance. La mouche donc ne sera rien au prix de nostre Puce, encores que Homere l'usurpe souvent en ses comparaisons, & magnifiquement luy attribue la force & la hardiesse. (59ʳ)

This type of mock-heroic presentation resembles that employed by Ronsard in "Le Freslon," but, unlike his predecessors, Pasquier regularly deflates his portrait. His style at times resembles that of Rabelais, mentioned by name in the text, for he addresses and includes the reader ("vous confesserez," "nostre Puce"), resorts to vivid or grotesque details ("on a beau la serrer sous le doit, la rouller sous le pouce"), and adopts in general a tone of jocular bonhomie. He often includes moments of self-mockery, as when, after the introductory sentence quoted above, we read, "Je pense que mesdames les puces en ont senti le vent: car depuis ce temps là elles n'ont cessé de me mordre, tant le jour que la nuit" (57ᵛ). "Ce temps là" is the moment he decided to compose his encomium. Having dismissed other small insects as unworthy of discussion among "gens d'honneur & reputation," the author calls the flea "ô chose excellente, & vrayement digne d'estre canonizee, voire dis-je consacree, par tous les temples & chappelles du monde" (57ᵛ–58ʳ). The notion of deification, much used in mock encomia on disease, reminds the narrator that the ancient Egyptians deified the ibis, because "il a enseigné aux Apothicaires à donner des clysteres" (58ʳ). Fleas deserve a similar honor, since they are "si aspres à nous saigner, que le plus souvent elles nous ennuyent" (58^v), a comment probably closer to the narrator's true feelings about his topic.

Everything about the flea's physical appearance, from its size to its color and the number of its legs is praised and justified with reference to Homer, Plutarch, and even Rabelais. Popular sayings, such as that "à la saincte Luce le jour croit du saut d'une Puce" are explained as being to the flea's credit:

> Je vous demande prend on les mesures du temps, ou d'autres choses, sinon de celles qui sont les plus signalees & excellentes? Exemple, le cours du soleil est la mesure de l'annee, le cours de la Lune est celle du mois: de mesme le saut de la Puce est la mesure de l'accroissement du jour saincte Luce.[53]

This reinterpretation of popular wisdom is similar to that noted in connection with the *Paradoxes*. At every step the reader is drawn in, encouraged to agree with the claims made: "Vous noterez bien ce trait, Messieurs, comme faisant fort à la cause" (59^v). By this lawyerlike procedure, found in so many mock encomia, the writer drives home his points. Obviously, a special type of reader was needed to understand the esoteric games being played with familiar or adapted traditions. Indeed, the interplay of the texts involved in the formulation of the defense becomes a pleasurable part of the reading process.

The work ends with a lengthy explanation of the brevity of the flea's life, a fact mentioned by Lucian only in passing:

> Au reste quant à ce qu'on pourroit objecter qu'elle est de courte vie (aussi est il vray qu'elle ne passe volontiers l'Automne) cela est leger & facile à refuter: & tourne plus tost à sa gloire, qu'à son vitupere. Car je soutiens que la briefveté de sa vie ne vient point d'autre cause, sinon pour autant qu'elle se jette ainsi à tout propos, à cors perdu, & la teste baissee, au milieu des dangers. Ces grans guerriers coustumierement ne vivent pas long temps, & ordinairement ne portent pas la barbe grise, "Turpe senex miles." (60^{r-v})

Quoting a statement by Homer that the mighty Achilles was short-lived, the writer abruptly concludes with the words "Et plus n'en dit le deposant." After the Greek and Latin citations and complicated mythological embroidery, the shortness of the flea's life is mirrored in the abrupt conclusion of the work. The legalistic terminology of the ending, linking the text to the tradition of Erasmus and Pirckheimer, also serves as a reminder that most of the contributors to the des Roches collection belonged to the legal profession. For them, the mock eulogy seems to have afforded many pleasures. In the first place, it enabled them to show off their forensic skills in a playful context that demonstrated social flexibility and good breeding. Secondly, it permitted an illustration of the shared literary competence that made social interchanges of this sort possible. Finally, Pasquier's concluding piece, which moves back from the extraliterary incident towards the best-known classical example of the animal mock encomium, situates the entire enterprise firmly within the literary tradition chronicled in the present study.

In the French animal encomia, the satirical eulogy's multifaceted nature was developed with great subtlety. The short, self-contained works came to represent the small creatures being described and "offered." But the modest size or unworthiness of the subjects immediately called attention to the paradox underlying the writers' efforts. The tension between external and internal viewpoints, sometimes less prominent in other types of mock encomia, was therefore difficult to avoid. As a result, this group of encomia contains some of the most finely balanced examples of the genre. Encomia such as that by Pontoux, however, illustrate the tendency of the mock eulogy in general and the animal encomium in particular to slip towards fragmentation, self-parody, or dispersal and appropriation by other genres. The animal encomia provide an appropriate conclusion because they suggest how the types of formal mock encomiastic writing described above passed from the mainstream of literary history. For many years they provided a fruitful way of exploring the challenging area of paradoxical argumentation, but gradually, as authors' sense of their own dramatic spectacle moved them closer and closer to parody, the word-objects became too trite or self-mocking to serve as genuine gifts or tributes. The form that, for a period, subsumed and manipulated history for its own literary and social purposes became a mode appropriated by quite different literary genres.

Conclusion

"In tenui enim re non tenuis labor," wrote Celio Calcagnini in the preface to his *Encomium Pulicis*. "And yet I am apt to believe I have not praised folly in a way altogether foolish," claimed Erasmus in the prefatory letter to the *Moriae Encomium* some forty years earlier.[1] I have sought to explain why so many Renaissance writers were willing to devote so much "labor" to such slight subjects as the flea, gout, and folly, in the belief that in so doing they were not altogether foolish.

Their fascination with this type of writing seems to have been due in large part to the multifaceted quality of the mock encomium, its simultaneous fluidity and recognizability, two features that permitted a great variety of development while providing a measure of protection for the satirists' bolder statements. The rhetorical challenge and the generally learned and humanistic aura of the genre were further attractions. The mock encomium provides a perfect illustration of the fact, noted by several critics, that in the Renaissance a rigid system of genres "never existed in practice and barely even in theory."[2] In the mock eulogy a series of complex intertextual references combined with the well-known Renaissance habit of citing approved predecessors to create a body of works clearly related but having only minimal shared characteristics. Manipulation of this small but crucial common heritage was for its practitioners an integral part of their purpose, not an unfortunate derivative moment in otherwise original creations. On the contrary, they wished their readers to use familiarity with past mock encomia in order to interpret new ones.

The three different types of encomium, vice, disease, and animal, developed in rather different ways. The vice encomium proved particularly suitable for anticourt satire: Philibert de Vienne, Du Bellay, and others transformed Lucian's parasite into a Renaissance courtier and unmasked the language of praise. Those praising madness shed light on both the positive and negative aspects of folly, and the praisers of disease suggested a dialectical relationship between the sick and the healthy person, the observer and the sufferer. Those who mockingly eulogized small animals and insects implied new perspectives, whether inverted or distorted, thereby pointing to different ways of understanding the hierarchies of being in the human and animal kingdoms.

All three groups of encomia call for constant shifts in attitude, for a reading stance at once inside and outside the work in question. Thus, Lucian first involves the reader in a highly selective view of the fly's relative size, then distances him by recalling the mighty elephant. Having engrossed the reader in her presentation of Christian folly, Moria abruptly takes her leave, bidding her audience eat, drink, be merry, and forget what she has said. After glorifying the plague for several pages, Berni concludes that it is a "mal che manda Dio" and that to believe otherwise is to be a "balordo." Challenging and intriguing when well executed, these constant shifts can also be confusing. Instead of showing the fruitful and thought-provoking "doubleness" so important to paradox, they sometimes indicate a loss of control or even an unconscious drift towards parody. This latter tendency is often found in the animal eulogy in France, practiced in the latter part of the century by the Pléiade poets and their followers.

The vogue for composing paradoxical encomia as independent works seems largely to have passed by the end of the Renaissance. Although still popular in England in drama, in most of Europe the traditional type of mock encomium was preserved chiefly by way of editions and anthologies of older works. The existence of a series of these anthologies, mostly of and by Neo-Latin writers, proves that the genre was by that time sufficiently recognizable to be deemed collectable and sufficiently popular to be worth publishing. Unlike the first Renaissance practitioners, the anthologizers of encomia did not always feel called upon to explain their choice of works or to justify their decision to undertake a collection. In general, they seem confident that mock encomiastic writing would be readily understandable and of interest to their readers.

This decrease in the numbers of new encomia has been attributed to the growth of the scientific spirit and to the lessening of interest in rhetorical figures of wonder and mystery such as the paradox. Other critics have disputed such a conclusion.[3] The analyses in the preceding chapters have shown that from the start this genre was marked by features that readily led to disintegration and dispersal—fluidity, closeness to other genres, and lack of a fixed form or length. When practiced by the earlier humanists, enamored of classical literature and anxious to make a place for themselves in the humanistic literary world of the Renaissance, the genre flourished as a clear and deliberate revival. However, as the classical genre became more fully absorbed into the vernacular literatures, its structural links with the classical encomium frequently diminished. For irony, whether that of the trope of inversion or the more pervasive irony of posture typified by Socrates, need not take the form of a coherent, structured encomium. Later writers seem to have taken the spirit of the mock encomium, its blending of praise and satire, into forms very different from the classical one—into the epitaph, the blason, the Bernesque capitolo, the stage harangue, and so on. As a result, fewer and fewer works could be seen in their entirety as mock encomia, but more and more contained a part or parts that linked them to the long tradition. Panurge's praise of debts, a section of the larger whole of the *Tiers Livre*, is an early instance of this tendency. I believe that this shift, amply documented in the preceding pages, provides an explanation for the later development of the mock encomium that is based on the internal dynamics of the form. Such an explanation precedes and may be a preliminary to decisions about the influence of larger forces such as the growth of the scientific spirit.

In an essay on the interrelatedness of eighteenth-century literary forms, Ralph Cohen asserts that mixed forms are not necessarily "forms of disorder."[4] This contention is surely borne out by the mixed history of the mock encomium. By suggesting that a genre always functions in relation to other genres in the same historical period, Cohen seeks to broaden the notion of genre. A further distinction helpful in the present context is that which Cohen makes between "form" and "mode." In the context of the pastoral, for example, a pastoral form would be a specific "Pastoral" by, say, Pope or Phillips, whereas pastoral as a mode can apply to "different poetic kinds— to 'Lycidas,' a pastoral elegy, to drama, *As You Like It*, to prose fiction, *Arcadia*, to selected features of the pastoral form such as descriptions of shepherds or nature."[5] In these terms, the earliest revivals of the classical mock eulogy were closer to the idea of "form," that is, they retained the pattern of a classical encomium and were extremely concerned with self-justification and generic authority. Later, the inherent fluidity and ambiguity of the mock encomium drew it to other forms and other forms to it. The results of this cross-fertilization were particularly dramatic in the case of the blasons, both the hymnes-blasons of the Pléiade and the Lucianic Lyons pieces.

The crossing of boundaries and the mixing of forms are not of course unique to the mock encomium. They are, however, particularly frequent in this type of writing. We find in analyzing these works that the other perspective evoked by the text is frequently an extraliterary one, as in the case of Simon the parasite and the Amye de Court. To evaluate these speakers' arguments, which conserve perfect internal logic and consistency, the reader has to turn to a set of values evoked by but somehow outside the immediate bounds of the text.

This delicate balance of viewpoints is called for even more obviously in later works such as the hymnes-blasons, the *La Puce* collection, and the Bruscambille speeches, all of which seem not merely to elicit but even to make a theme of and toy with multiple points of view. When Ronsard and Du Bellay develop word-objects as gifts, when the entirety of the des Roches anthology represents a shared group project, and, in particular, when Bruscambille embodies on stage the phenomenon found hitherto only on the printed page, the genre, while enriched, is stretched to the breaking point so far as its links with the early sixteenth-century revival are concerned. In this sense, it truly moves beyond and outside itself.

In my view, it was not the oft-cited frivolousness but the strength and richness of this genre that were responsible for its eventual dispersal into other forms. At one point or another, it attracted virtually every major writer of the Renaissance: only the most superficial of readers would believe its practitioners' disingenuous explanations of their fascination as the shamefaced momentary lapses of weary scholars and humanists. On the contrary, there was real excitement in this form, real challenge in its multiple shifts and self-reflections. For these reasons it flourished, but for the same reasons it was gradually appropriated by quite other forms eager to exploit its manifold possibilities. In passing out of widespread use as an independent *form*, however, it became a *mode* that enriched European literature from Fielding and Swift to Fontenelle and Voltaire.

Notes

Complete publishing details for all works cited are in the bibliography. To clarify the discussion in the notes, the dates of pre-nineteenth-century editions have been included after first mention. Unless the note concerns the publisher or place of publication, other publishing details are omitted. For nineteenth- and twentieth-century editions and works of criticism, the author's name and the title (usually in shortened form) are given at first mention, with author's name and short title as needed thereafter. Works cited from the Loeb Classical Library Series carry the indication "Loeb CLS." Section number as well as volume and page number is given in Loeb citations.

PREFACE

1. Quoted by Arthur F. Kinney, "Rhetoric and Fiction in Elizabethan England," 387.
2. Rosalie Colie, *The Resources of Kind*, 9.
3. Heather Dubrow, *Genre*, 10.
4. Arthur Stanley Pease, "Things Without Honor," 42.
5. Colie explains the fascination of paradox: "Operating at the limits of discourse, redirecting thoughtful attention to the faulty or limited structures of thought, paradoxes play back and forth across terminal and categorical boundaries— that is, they play with human understanding, that most serious of all human activities" (*Paradoxia Epidemica*, 7).

CHAPTER ONE

1. Theoretical treatises relating to this type of writing that were frequently cited in the Renaissance were by Aristides, Aphthonius, Menander (*On Epideictic Oratory*), Quintilian (*Institutio oratoria*, especially 2.7.1–8), and the *Rhetorica ad Herennium* associated with but not by Cicero. On the serious panegyric as practiced by Claudian in late antiquity, see Alan Cameron, *Claudian*. See also the study by O. B. Hardison, Jr., *The Enduring Monument*, especially 29–32.
2. Theodore C. Burgess, *Epideictic Literature*; Adolf Hauffen, "Zur Litteratur der ironischen Enkomien"; and Pease. The first section of the present chapter owes much to these critics. See also George Kennedy, *The Art of Rhetoric*.
3. On Erasmus, see Sister Geraldine Thompson, C.S.J., "Erasmus and the Tradition of Paradox." On Shakespeare and paradoxy, see Brian Vickers, "*King Lear* and Renaissance Paradoxes." On Lucian in the Renaissance, see, among others, Mayer, "Lucien et la Renaissance," and Robinson, *Lucian*. On Ben Jonson, see Douglas Duncan, *Ben Jonson*. Further study of Renaissance paradoxes in relation to

Lucian is found in A. E. Malloch, "Techniques and Function." Mayer's Ph.D. thesis, "Satire in French Literature," also contains much valuable information on this matter. His most recent book, *Lucien de Samosate*, brings up to date and completes the study begun in his dissertation.

4. Critics often use the terms *satirical eulogy* and *ironic* or *paradoxical encomium* interchangeably, largely, one suspects, for the sake of stylistic variety rather than in conformity with conscious distinctions between the expressions. Thus Henry Knight Miller explains that "I have taken as synonymous the terms 'paradoxical encomium,' 'pseudo-encomium,' 'ironic encomium,' and 'mock encomium.' " Some refinement of this system may be desirable, Miller agrees, but he finds that such a distinction "introduces more problems than it solves." "The terms as I use them," he continues, "all imply that the author intended to praise an object or idea that he actually considered not entitled to that honor" ("The Paradoxical Encomium," 145 n. 1). G. Thompson, discussing the genre, shows that a third factor, that of parody, further complicates definitions: "Parody is not always panegyric, nor mock panegyric always parody; neither is necessarily satiric" ("Erasmus and the Tradition of Paradox," 42). Since the purpose of the present work is to explain and show the value of a belief in the simultaneous recognizability and amorphousness of the genre, I shall retain the customary gamut of terms, except when a work is given another generic title such as *blason* or *epitaph*.

5. On the various types of epideictic literature, see *The Cambridge History of Classical Literature*, vol. 1, *Greek Literature*, especially "Oratory," by George Kennedy, 500. See also George Kennedy, *The Art of Persuasion in Greece*, especially "Epideictic Oratory," 152–203.

6. See the works by Cameron and Hardison, described above, and also Gregory Nagy, *The Best of the Achaeans*, 222–42.

7. Dio Chrysostom, "The Twenty–Third Discourse," in *Discourses*, 11, Loeb CLS, 3:283–84. See also Pease, 27.

8. Burgess, 122. Such a plan is not dissimilar to that of the Pindaric ode. The encomium is not historical, but openly partial and selective.

9. H. K. Miller, 146.

10. See Aristotle, *The Nicomachean Ethics*, 8.2.8, Loeb CLS, 383. The statement continues, "The sophists wish to show their cleverness by entrapping their adversary into a paradox, and when they are successful, the resultant chain of reasoning ends in a deadlock: the mind is fettered, being unwilling to stand still because it cannot approve the conclusion reached, yet unable to go forward because it cannot untie the knot of the argument." The quotation from Lucian is from *Charidemus*, 14, Loeb CLS, 8:487. Also quoted by Burgess, 159 n. 1.

11. See Burgess, 162. Poverty praises herself by claiming to be the driving force that makes men work and produce goods for others to buy (*The Plutus*, 581–609, Loeb CLS, 3:409–421). As in many Renaissance encomia, gout is here associated with wealth. On Athenian audiences, see Maurice Croiset, *Essai*, 22. Robinson notes that our scanty information about these audiences comes chiefly from Philostratus, who stated that spectators were used to live performances and complex literary references such as are found throughout Lucian (*Lucian*, 61). This familiarity with a wide range of earlier literature obviously enabled Lucian's hearers to appreciate his

parodies to the full. Their general literary background and experience were related to their age of archaism and imitation. As Robinson puts it, it was almost unthinkable to express an idea in a form that owed nothing to tradition (*Lucian*, 5–6). Lucian's genius lay in making a virtue of this necessity.

12. Pliny, *Natural History*, 20.33.78, Loeb CLS, 6:47. The references to other works on plants are in the same edition.

13. Quintilian, 3.7.28, Loeb CLS, 1:478.

14. See Celio Calcagnini's preface to his *Encomium Pulicis*, published in his *Opera aliquot* of 1544, for Cato and Pythagoras, and Dornavius's 1619 preface to his *Amphitheatrum* for all three authors. These prefaces are discussed further in chap. 3. Lando cites all three names once again (see chap. 4, n. 50).

15. On the early use of mock-epideictic writing as a safety valve, Barry Baldwin says,

> It is probable that the popularity of mock panegyrics was an intellectual safety-valve for some. When Favorinus extolled Fever or Thersites, Fronto Smoke and Dust, and Lucian the Fly, they were discreetly making mockery of a very necessary element in their lives. The satirist needed patrons as much as the courtier. Lucian baited his victims without mercy, but had also to bait his hook for patrons. (*Studies*, 80)

Pease sums up succinctly the varied reasons for the mock encomium's popularity, attributing it to "the search for a form combining brilliancy and safety, the striving for novelty by the path of paradox, the sophistic desire to present effectively the inferior side of a case, the tendency of the age toward greater realism and the consequent exploration of the undiscovered possibilities of the commonplace, and, finally, a real scientific interest in the microscopic" (33). He discusses also the development of other genres concerned with the "little," but is careful to distinguish these other genres from the paradoxical encomium (32). He notes that later classical writers such as Pliny often defended themselves for lavishing attention on the smallest parts of creation. Even St. Augustine could be used as an authority in this context during the Renaissance: "The smallest [animals] are most admired, for we are more amazed at the work of tiny ants and bees than at the huge bodies of whales" (*The City of God*, 22.24, Loeb CLS, 7:335; cited by Pease, 32).

16. Isocrates, *Helen*, 13, Loeb CLS, 3:67. Exactly the same criticism was repeated during the Renaissance; for example, Gabriel Harvey in 1593 wrote scornfully: "They were silly country fellowes that commended the Bald pate, the Feauer quartane; the fly, the flea, the gnat, the sparrow, the wren, the goose, the asse; flattery, hypocrisie, coosinage, bawdery, leachery, buggery, madnesse itselfe. What Dunse, or Sorbonist cannot maintaine a Paradoxe?" (quoted by H. K. Miller, 156 n. 65).

17. Polybius, *The Histories*, 12.26^b-d, Loeb CLS, 4:395–97.

18. *The Rhetorica of Philodemus*, p. 304, quoted by H. K. Miller, 147. Pease quotes the words of Socrates in Plato's *Phaedrus*:

> But if I tried to persuade you in all seriousness, composing a speech in praise of the ass, which I called a horse, and saying that the beast was a most valuable possession at home and in war, that you could use him as a mount in bat-

tle, and that he was able to carry baggage and was useful for many other purposes—

PHAEDRUS: Then it would be supremely ridiculous. (260B-C, Loeb CLS, 515)

Renaissance joking portraits of mules are discussed in chap. 7 below. Miller comments,

> The paradoxical encomium carries to its logical conclusion the implication of sophistic rhetoric that truth qua truth is not the end of rhetoric, that, morally neutral, its end is persuasion, and its materials are the "proofs" that human ingenuity can invent—and apply to man's natural and unchanging passions.
> . . . On the other hand, the paradoxical encomium appealed to, and perhaps in its own small way helped to create, flexible minds. By placing in a new context persons or objects traditionally seen in a contrary light, it established ironic tensions that evoked not only laughter, but thoughtful laughter. (172)

It is noteworthy, however, that in his *Rhetorica* Philodemus concentrated on *epideixis*, verbal display, removing Aristotle's judicial and forensic oratory. The Roman emperor Julian, whose *Misopogon* will be discussed below, noted that rhetoricians have as much freedom as poets with facts: "Fiction is denied them, but flattery is by no means forbidden, nor is it counted a disgrace to the orator that the object of his panegyric should not deserve it. . . . Orators, again, assert that the advantage of their art is that it can treat a slight theme in the grand manner . . . in short, marshall the power of words against that of facts" ("Panegyric in Honour of Constantius," in *Orations*, Loeb CLS, 1:7). Volume and page numbers for subsequent quotations from Julian will be given in the text.

19. Pease, 37.

20. Philostratus the Elder, *Epistolae*, 16, quoted by Pease, 36. A more serious praise of hair was that contained in the *Golden Ass* by Apuleius, see *The Metamorphoses or Golden Ass*, 8–9, pp. 54–56.

21. The term *adoxography* is much used by Pease, who discusses its origins (28 n. 1). In adoxography, he explains, "the legitimate methods of the encomium are applied to persons or objects in themselves obviously unworthy of praise, as being trivial, ugly, useless, ridiculous, dangerous, or vicious" (29). The corresponding form of the ψόγος is the blame of that which is admittedly "beautiful, great, valuable, or otherwise excellent" (29 n. 1).

22. Fronto, *The Correspondence*, Loeb CLS, 1:45–49. On Appion's speech in the homilies, see Pease, 36.

23. Quintilian deals at length with praise and blame in book 3 of the *Institutio oratoria*. In the *Institutio oratoria* 3.7.19, Loeb CLS, 1:473, Quintilian notes that Thersites was a typical subject for vituperations.

24. Philostratus, *The Life of Apollonius of Tyana*, 4.30, Loeb CLS, 1:417.

25. Plato, *Symposium*, 177, Loeb CLS, 5:97: "And again, pray consider our worthy professors, and the eulogies they frame of Hercules and others in prose,—for example, the excellent Prodicus. This indeed is not so surprising; but I recollect coming across a book by somebody, in which I found Salt superbly lauded for its usefulness, and many more such matters I could show you celebrated there."

26. See Mayer, *Lucien de Samosate*, 105: "A de très rares exceptions près, tous

les éloges satiriques de la Renaissance ont pour sujet une maladie, un animal petit et insignifiant ou bien un vice." See also Olga Gewerstock's study, *Lucian und Hutten.*

27. See A. M. Harmon's introduction to the *De Parasito,* Loeb CLS, 3:235, and Baldwin, 70 n. 54.

28. Typical of such doubts as to authorship are those expressed by Filbert Bretin in discussing the *Ocypus* in his 1583 edition of *Les Oeuvres de Lucien:* "Icy a esté laisse une autre Tragedie manque, imparfaite & pleine de fautes infinies, ditte Ocipe, ou Pied-leger: qui encores ne ressent rien qui soit de son Lucian" (696). Despite a promise to publish this work with other "oeuvres bastardes & attribues," Bretin does not in fact print it (see also below, n. 47). Modern scholars have also contested the attribution of the *Culex* to Virgil and of the *Batrachomyomachia* to Homer, but, yet again, the Renaissance accepted the traditional attributions of these two pieces, which were also much cited by Renaissance mock encomiasts. See Robinson, *Lucian,* 241, for classification of the *Ocypus* with those now known to be "definitely" spurious.

29. The debate continues. See, for example, Baldwin, 4–5: "Internal evidence would lead me to support the rejection of the *Cynicus* and the *Philopatris,* whereas I would return an open verdict on, say, the *Ocypus* and the *Epigrams.* Beyond this, I do not see that we can reasonably go." Bretin would not have been best pleased. On the *Philopatris* debate, see Robinson, *Lucian,* 73–75, who states that the work was probably composed in the eleventh century but was often believed during the Renaissance to be by Lucian. It caused its supposed author many difficulties with critics who saw it as anti-Christian. It was placed on the Catholic Index in 1559 (Robinson, *Lucian,* 98).

30. Robinson, *Lucian,* 140. Robinson explains that in this type of satire the alazōn unwittingly betrays himself to the audience as he delivers what is formally a mock encomium of his own vices (35). Mayer uses the term *témoin domestique,* ("The Genesis of a Rabelaisian Character," 229). On the "récit-aveu," see Mayer, "Monologue ou récit-aveu."

31. Gnatho, the parasite in Terence's *Eunuchus,* was also viewed in the Renaissance as a typical "self-denouncer." See Pauline M. Smith, *The Anti-Courtier Trend,* 106, and Mayer, *Lucien de Samosate,* 53–55. A major Renaissance use of this technique was in the *Epistolae obscurorum virorum,* discussed below in chap. 3.

32. *De iis qui mercede conducti degunt,* Loeb CLS, 3:413–81. The apology was in the *Apologia,* Loeb CLS, 6:191–213. Baldwin reminds us to be cautious in guessing which Lucianic works were autobiographical (7). Similarly, G. W. Bowersock writes, "Outside Lucian's own works and a wretched derivative notice in a Byzantine lexicon, there is no evidence for Lucian's existence at all" (*Greek Sophists,* 114). Cf. Robinson, *Lucian,* 4, 65–66. Bowersock does not express much enthusiasm for Lucian: "Perhaps Lucian, prolific as he was, was not very important; his Greek and his wit adequately explain his survival" (114).

33. Lucian, *Timon,* Loeb CLS, 2:325–93. Robinson (*Lucian,* 18) notes that the portrait of the new type of rhetorician contains characteristics found in many of Lucian's villain figures—effeminacy, drunkenness, ignorance, and deceitfulness.

34. Lucien Bompaire, *Lucien écrivain,* 607–10. On Socrates, see Bompaire, 609, and the discussion in chap. 2 below. Cf. Robinson, who states that in the *De Parasito*

"the Socratic method becomes in part the subject while the bulk of the structure is purely rhetorical" (*Lucian*, 11). The work is both a parody and a paradoxical encomium: "In general, . . . the humour derives quite simply from the incongruity of associating a serious philosophical method with an extremely frivolous subject. It does not constitute any kind of critique of philosophy. Like the pastiche-parody in *Lexiphanes* it is merely amusing. . . . overtly *l'art pour l'art*" (27). Thomas Francklin, an English translator of Lucian, likes the piece and is well aware of its irony: "Under the Mask of a grave and laboured encomium on the Art or Mystery of Parasitism, universally practiced in Lucian's time, and not uncommon in our own, we have here a severe Satire on the Professors of it" (*The Works of Lucian* [1780], 2:251). The reader failing to smile at the work, he concludes "must either have no risible muscles, or knows not how, or when, to make use of them." William Tooke, the enthusiastic editor of a handsome two-volume edition of the works in 1820, admires the dialogue as "one of the most ingenious of our author's productions," but fears that many of the contemporary references contained in the work must escape modern readers (*Lucian of Samosata*, 1:142n). The present analysis of Lucian's work seeks to restore more depth to the *De Parasito*, in particular by focusing on its structure.

35. Lucian, *De Parasito*, Loeb CLS, 3:235.

36. See Harmon, introduction to the *De Parasito*, 235. It is not certain who first used this definition of the word *art*, but it is certainly the orthodox Stoic one and is often quoted by Sextus Empiricus. Quintilian defines it in a similar fashion (*Institutio oratoria*, 2.27.41, Loeb CLS, 1:344–45). In this section of the work, Quintilian considers whether or not rhetoric is an art and what are its goals: "ille ab omnibus fere probatus finis observatur, artem constare ex perceptionibus consentientibus et coexercitatis ad finem utilem vitae, iam ostendemus nihil non horum in rhetorice inesse" (344). For subsequent quotations from the *De Parasito*, section and page numbers from the Harmon Loeb translation will be given in the text.

37. For another use of Tychiades, see Lucian's *Philopseudes* (The lover of lies) and Robinson, *Lucian*, 51. My discussion of the *De Parasito* owes much to Mayer, "Rabelais' Satirical Eulogy," and his *Lucien de Samosate*, 105–109.

38. For this colloquy, see Erasmus, *Opera Omnia*, ed. L. E. Halkin et al., I–3, 320–24.

39. "I have prayed to compose a lucubration for Helen's adulation and my own delectation," quoted in the introduction to Isocrates, *Helen*, Loeb CLS, 3:57. On Gorgias, see H. D. Rankin, *Sophists*, 35–45. Rankin points out that Gorgias described his *Helen* as a *paignion*, a piece of light amusement, but that despite this modest disclaimer the author was in another sense "a prime exponent of responsibility." Gorgias was seeking to persuade the Greek states to feel guilt at their internecine quarreling and unite instead against Persia (Rankin, 44). Similarly, Isocrates declares: "I perceive that I am being carried beyond the proper limits of my theme and I fear that some may think that I am more concerned with Theseus than with the subject which I originally chose" (*Helen*, 29, Loeb CLS, 3:77).

40. Erasmus, *The Praise of Folly*, ed. and trans. Clarence H. Miller, 4. Except where otherwise indicated, subsequent quotations will be taken from this edition, with page numbers given in the text.

41. Hegendorff's work is discussed in detail in chap. 3 below.

42. *De Parasito*, 307. Note also the study of this theme in the Renaissance by Mayer, *Lucien de Samosate*, 56–74.

43. Lucian, *Rhetorum Praeceptor* (A professor of public speaking), Loeb CLS, 4:133. Page numbers for subsequent quotations from this edition will be given in the text.

44. In interpreting this work, one must be aware that it presents one speaker, not two. The second speech is also put into the mouth of the original, old-fashioned speaker. Robinson, *Lucian*, 8 and 35, discusses the work almost as if there were two speakers, and Baldwin, although less clear on the matter, seems to adopt the same view when he mentions "two professionals" and a "second speaker" (34). Pages 151 and 171 of the Loeb edition of the *Rhetorum Praeceptor* clearly mark the beginning and end of an interpolated speech delivered by a single speaker. Mayer's discussion of the piece implies that the interpolated speech represents the thrust of the entire work (*Lucien de Samosate*, 54–55). William Tooke's 1820 translation of Lucian calls the *Rhetorum Praeceptor* "an ironical school for orators," a "half laughing and half bitter and biting satire" (2:496).

45. Baldwin, 71.

46. On this identification, see Bompaire, 128; Graham Anderson, *Lucian*, 68; and Baldwin, 34. On the work itself see Jennifer Hall, *Lucian's Satire*, 252–58, and C. P. Jones, *Culture and Society*, 108.

47. The *Podagra* and *Ocypus* are omitted from the edition of the *Works of Lucian* by H. W. Fowler and F. G. Fowler. Baldwin is not inclined to attend to the *Podagra* very fully, either: as he puts it, "The logical place for Lucian's gout is in a footnote" (9 n. 9). Robinson refers to the work as "(probably) pseudonymous" (*Lucian*, 98). The play is included in William Tooke's 1820 translation of the works (2:735–49), with the more charitable comment that in this composition Lucian, "on some favourable day, sought to beguile the tedious hours of a poor creature lying bound by the Gout on his couch." (2:735n). In an earlier English translation by Gilbert West, himself a gout-sufferer, the *Ocypus* and the *Podagra* are spliced together into a single play (in *Odes of Pindar* [1749], 229–257). Providing yet another instance of the mingling of the literal and the literary with regard to diseases, the bookseller who sold the translation also offered to sell "a Sovereign Remedy for the Cholick, Gravel, and Stone" (on a note inside the cover of the volume in the British Library). Michael Vascosanus included the *Ocypus* in his 1546 edition of the works of Lucian, but called it a "poema imperfectum & mendosum" (314), a description comparable to that of Bretin. William Tooke, however, refused to attempt a translation because it had been almost unanimously pronounced spurious. In the 1871 translation of the *Podagra* by the gouty Reverend Symeon T. Bartlett, the *Ocypus* is also attacked as a "much inferior, and perhaps, a frigid imitation by some other hand" (3). This translation is graced with these liminary verses:

> The French have taste in all they do,
> Which we are quite without;
> For nature, which to them gave goût
> To us gave only gout.

The desire to amuse a suffering friend or distract oneself from pain is apparent in the 1780 translation of the *Tragopodagra* by Thomas Francklin, dedicated to the Vicar of Charing, Kent, one of the "chief priests" of the goddess gout:

> This is a Kind of Dramatic Interlude, or Mock-Heroic Poem, containing a fine burlesque Imitation of the Greek Tragedians, together with a most spritely and severe Satire on the Empirics of his Time, who, like the boasting Pretenders of our own, were perpetually finding out Cures for a Distemper which the Experience of Ages had already proved to be incurable. . . . The whole is so well written, and with such infinite Humour, that, with all the Disadvantages of a Translation, I defy any Gouty Man, if the Fit is coming on, to read it without trembling, or, if it is going off, without laughing. (*The Works of Lucian*, 2:577)

On Lucian and doctors, see Baldwin, 40 n. 91, J. D. Rollestone, "Lucian and Medicine," and H. Crosby, "Lucian and the Art of Medicine." The edition of Lucian's works published by James Woodward in London in 1711 displays considerable British chauvinism in presenting the gout tragedy. The translator, one "J.P.," declares that in addition to mocking the "swelling fustian of the ancient tragedies," the play serves still "for a Satyr upon the Modern German Doctors and Mountebanks" (188). Attitudes to Lucian's gout plays thus remain remarkably constant through the ages.

48. Croiset, 84.

49. Alexis Pierron, *Histoire*, 540, and Bompaire, 646.

50. See Ovid, *Epistulae ex Ponto*, 1.3.23, in *Tristia. Ex Ponto*, Loeb CLS, 282.

51. Lucian, *Podagra* (Gout), 44–53, Loeb CLS, 8:329. Line numbers for subsequent quotations from this edition will be given in the text.

52. *The Works of Lucian*, 2:588.

53. Sebastian Brant, *Narrenschiff*, trans. Edwin H. Zeydel, 229. See also *Das Narrenschiff*, ed. Manfred Lemmer, 172, l. 70. The comment occurs in chap. 67 of the work, entitled "Nit wellen ein nar syn," "Not wishing to be a fool."

54. Lucian, *Muscae Encomium*, Loeb CLS, 1:81. Section and page numbers for subsequent quotations from this edition will be given in the text.

55. Croiset, 44. The other two compositions referred to are *Philopatris* and *Hippias*. In his 1820 translation, William Tooke mentions the "urbanity and grace" of the composition but feels it could have been better. He profits from the chance to insert a few lines of congratulation to his age on its scientific prowess. Lucian is praised for doing the best he could to describe his small subject, but "as without the microscope and the unwearied industry of a Leuenhoeck, Reaumur, Roessler and others who have employed nearly the whole of their lives in the observation of insects, it was not possible to know more of it, it stands to reason, that neither the defects of his description, nor the errors that then generally passed current for truth (for instance, the notion, that flies proceeded from the putridity of animal substances as well as from procreation) are to be laid to his account" (2:265n). Francklin, in his edition, was more enthusiastic, noting that "even an Encomium on a Fly by Lucian is not without Merit." Lucian is praised for using a "tolerable Degree of accurate Observation" to immortalize his "diminutive Hero," and for playing with "much Humour" with the "Doctrine of Plato" (*The Works of Lucian*, 2:346). Robinson, explains that this work is a typical "logos epideiktikos," or speech apportioning

praise or blame. He states that "none of these works seems more than at best ingenious," but that Lucian "has the virtue of taking elements which had previously been considered only as preparation towards proficiency in the three divisions of formal oratory, and raising them to the status of art forms in themselves" (*Lucian*, 7). He notes that the fly work is chiefly designed to exploit "the gap between a concept of normality which writer and audience share and what passes for normality within the text" (*Lucian*, 20). Later the piece is described as "merely an ingenious description of the physical qualities and life style of the fly, in which an essentially trivial subject is raised in status by as many comparisons made to its advantage as the rhetorician can manage" (*Lucian*, 90). Bompaire analyzes in some detail the plan of the work, its ordering of *topoi*, before concluding: "L'ouvrage de Lucien est élégant et assez spirituel, mais d'une élégance et d'un esprit qui ne sont pas d'une autre qualité que ce cadre, typiquement rhétorique" (284). My own analysis seeks to qualify the above comments.

56. Seneca, *Apocolocyntosis*, sec. 5, p. 35. On Menippean satire, of which the Senecan piece is an example, see Dorothy Gabe Coleman, *Rabelais*, especially 85–109.

57. See Ludovic Legré, *Un Philosophe provençal*, 331. See also Bompaire, 476. Favorinus was mocked in Lucian's *Eunuchus* (see Jones, *Culture and Society*, 94).

58. Aulus Gellius, *The Attic Nights*, 17.7.3–5, Loeb CLS, 3:251–53.

59. Legré, 334.

60. For example, it was used by G. Menapius Insulanus (discussed in chap. 3 below), by Erasmus in the *Moriae Encomium*, and in the anonymous blasons published in Lyons (discussed in chap. 6 below). Synesius was mentioned by name in prefaces and texts by Lando, Hegendorff, Dornavius, Carnarius, T. Lineus, A. Pasquet, and, indirectly, in Castiglione's *Cortegiano*. These writers and works will be also discussed below. In classical times, fever (Febris) was not necessarily a sinister figure, as P. T. Eden's edition of Seneca's *Apocolocyntosis* makes plain: "*Fever* was however not a literary fiction but an authentic and established *numen* of Roman religion, which aimed at securing a right relationship with all supernatural powers by encouraging the beneficent and vice versa" (88).

61. On Listrius, see below, chap. 2, nn. 37, 52. On Synesius, see William Saunders Crawford, *Synesius the Hellene*; Alice Gardner, *Synesius of Cyrene*; Christian Lacombrade, *Synésios de Cyrène*; and James Carpenter Nicol, *Synesius of Cyrene*. Synesius's hymns and essays were translated into English by Augustine Fitzgerald in 1930 as *The Essays and Hymns of Synesius of Cyrene*. Volume 2 contains *A Eulogy of Baldness*, 243–74. On Dio, see C. P. Jones, *The Roman World*. Jones does not mention the praise of hair, but only the encomia on the parrot and the gnat, both of which have been lost. Another classical paradoxical work frequently referred to by Renaissance encomiasts was Cicero's *Paradoxa Stoicorum* of ca. 46 B.C. See Elbert N. S. Thompson, *The Seventeenth-Century English Essay*, chap. 8. The first of many Renaissance editions of the *Paradoxa* was Mainz: J. Schoeffer, 1465. In his Loeb Classical Library translation, H. Rackham says that Cicero viewed these pieces as "amusing popularizations of the recondite teachings of the Stoics" (252). On the influence of the Ciceronian paradoxes during the Renaissance, see Quirinus Breen,

"The Antiparadoxon," 39. Breen states that the pieces are a kind of "playful exercise." The six paradoxes maintained by Cicero were the following:

1. That only what is morally noble is good.
2. That the possession of virtue is sufficient for happiness.
3. That transgressions are equal and right actions equal.
4. That every foolish man is mad.
5. That only the wise man is free, and that every foolish man is a slave.
6. That the wise man alone is rich.

Cicero also discussed ways to cope with pain and death throughout the *Tusculan Disputations*. In the *De partitione oratoria*, 21.71, part of the Loeb volume of the *Paradoxa stoicorum*, he discusses literature of praise and blame, stating that it "does not establish propositions that are doubtful but amplifies statements that are certain, *or advanced as being certain*" (365, italics mine). At times in the preface to the *Paradoxa*, he sounds remarkably like Tertullian, cited in chap. 5 below: "Sed nihil est tam incredibile quod non dicendo fiat probabile, nihil tam horridum tam incultum quod non splendescat oratione et tamquam excolatur" (*Paradoxa*, Preface 3, 254–56). However, Cicero's writings in this area were in general more philosophical and consolatory than playful or ironic. Noteworthy, nevertheless, is his oft-cited remark about paradoxes being "admirabilia contraque opinionem omnium" (*Paradoxa*, Preface 4, 256), a comment which was later widely applied to all kinds of paradoxes, whatever their tone. See also A. Leigh DeNeef, "Epideictic Rhetoric."

62. Maud Gleason, "Festive Satire," especially 118–19. On the world of the panegyrists, see Sabine MacCormack, *Art and Ceremony*. MacCormack discusses at length the custom of the *adventus*, the emperor's ceremonial arrival in a city, and notes that such public occasions were part of what Gibbon referred to as the "splendid theatre" of late Roman life. Julian's inversion of the tradition of the panegyric seems even more original when contrasted with its serious predecessors.

63. Gleason, 116.

64. Gleason, 117, explains that Julian had a "well-known preference" for Marcus Aurelius, who affected an "old-fashioned beard." In feigning to hate his own beard, Julian was also adopting an ironic posture towards what beards commonly signified in his day.

65. An English writer of paradoxes who took the emperor as his unlikely subject was Sir William Cornwallis, who composed a piece called "The Prayse of the Emperour Iulian the Apostata: His Princely vertues and finall Apostacie," transcribed from the original manuscript by R. E. Bennett under the title "Four Paradoxes." The paradoxes were apparently composed about 1600. All are well within the mock-encomiastic tradition. One states that "a great redd nose is an ornament to the face," another "that it is a happiness to be in debt," and a third that "miserie is true Felicitie." Bennett believes Cornwallis's praise of the French "Pockes" to have been influenced by a Spanish work.

66. Were it not for the fact that his works were only rediscovered in the early nineteenth century, Marcus Cornelius Fronto, Latin rhetorician and tutor to the emperor Marcus Aurelius, would deserve a place in the present study. Fronto wrote encomia on sleep, dust, smoke, and carelessness. He also laid down rules for such writing, providing us with excellent evidence of the persistence and continuity of

identity of the genre. Such "nugalia" were to be written as a pleasant form of relaxation, but Fronto also felt that they provided good training for the higher branches of rhetoric:

> Anyone who practises this kind of composition will choose out an abundance of thoughts and pack them closely and cleverly interweave them, but will not stuff in superfluously many duplicate words, nor forget to round off every sentence concisely and skillfully. . . . But the chief thing to be aimed at is to please. For this kind of discourse is not meant as a speech for the defence in a criminal trial, nor to carry a law, nor to hearten an army, nor to impassion the multitude, but for pleasantry and amusement. ("Eulogy of Smoke and Dust," 3, in *The Correspondence*, Loeb CLS, 1:41)

From this statement we might conclude that Fronto thought only of the amusement to be found in composing paradoxical encomia, but he adds, "The topic, however, must everywhere be treated as if it were an important and splendid one, and trifling things must be likened and compared to great ones. Finally, the highest merit in this kind of discourse is an attitude of seriousness" (3, 1:41). The Latin term here is *adseveratio*. To speak in an apparently serious style of something not customarily so treated is typical of the Lucianic encomium, and the following rule of Fronto's is equally applicable to Lucian's writings: "Tales of Gods or men must be brought in where appropriate; so, too, pertinent verses and proverbs that are applicable, and ingenious fictions, provided that the fiction is helped out by some witty reasoning" (3, 1:41–43). Much of the *De Parasito* makes use of "mendacia" of the type described here. On Fronto, see also Dame Madeleine Dorothy Brock, *Studies in Fronto*, 118–22, Martin Lowther Clarke, *Rhetoric at Rome*, 132, Baldwin, 44–45, and Edward Champlin, *Fronto and Antonine Rome*.

CHAPTER TWO

1. In addition to the works on Lucian mentioned in chap. 1, n. 3, the following are helpful: Natale Caccia, *Note su la fortuna*; Douglas Duncan, *Ben Jonson*; Martha Heep, "Die Colloquia familiaria"; Guido Manacorda, "Notizie intorno alle fonti"; Harold Andrew Mason, *Humanism and Poetry*; Mayer, *Lucien*, 30–33; Robinson, *Lucian*; P. M. Smith, *The Anti-Courtier Trend*, 18–21; Linton C. Stevens, "The Reputation of Lucian"; Craig R. Thompson, *The Translations of Lucian*. On the earliest Renaissance editions of Lucian, see Mayer, *Lucien*, 15 and Robinson, *Lucian*, 81. Other translations of Lucian are listed by Mayer in Appendix B of "Satire in French Literature," and by Mason, *Humanism and Poetry*, 67–72.

2. See Robinson, *Lucian*, 82. Robinson dates the *editio princeps* to 1496 (*Lucien*, 95), but Mayer gives 1498 as the date (*Lucien*, 31).

3. See Manacorda, Robinson, "The Reputation of Lucian," and Jean Plattard, *L'Oeuvre de Rabelais*, 205: "Dans la guerre de brocards, que les humanistes entreprenaient contre l'ignorance et la superstition, Lucien était regardé comme un guide et comme un champion." Cf. also Caccia, 11, and Mayer, *Lucien*, *passim*.

4. Robinson, *Lucian*, 68–81, attends carefully to the pre-Renaissance manifesta-

tions of irony, while noting that these are the exceptions rather than the rule. See also Vladimir R. Rossman, *Perspectives of Irony*. After an introductory chapter, "Towards a Definition of Irony," Rossman discusses irony of words, of episodes, and of entire works in a number of French medieval writings.

5. Duncan, 5.

6. Duncan notes that Lucian achieves a delicate balance between the joking and the serious elements of this term (25). Eunapius, in the fourth century, "unhinged" this balance by speaking of Lucian as "a man who made serious efforts to be funny," suggesting thereby a kind of irresponsibility in Lucian's criticisms. Although some critics accepted this view of Lucian, Duncan asserts that it was not shared by Erasmus or More. The present chapter seeks to corroborate this assertion.

7. Duncan, 9. On Menippus, see Coleman, 84–109.

8. Robinson, *Lucian*, 9, discusses this remark.

9. Bompaire, 327, and Duncan, 15. Duncan (236 n. 7) admits to having some "misgivings" about using the term, preferring the term *episkopos*, but he nonetheless follows Bompaire's use of *kataskopos*. Cf. the beginning of Samuel Johnson's "The Vanity of Human Wishes": "Let observation with extensive view, / Survey mankind, from China to Perú," in *Poems*, 91.

10. Cited by Robinson, *Lucian*, 83. Guarino, in a dedicatory letter for his *Muscae Encomium*, comments on the linguistic merits of Lucian, the worth of his knowledge, and the forcefulness of his attacks on vice (Robinson, *Lucian*, 83).

11. The quotation is from Horace, *Satires*, 1.1.24–25, Loeb CLS, 6. Erasmus's adaptation of the quotation in discussing the *Gallus* is discussed below. See also More, in his *Apology* (1533): "They reprove that I bring in among the most earnest matters, fansies and sports, & merie tales. For as Horace sayeth, a man may sometimes saye full soth in game" (quoted by W. G. Crane, *Wit and Rhetoric*, 19). A. R. Heiserman points out the same notion elsewhere in More in "Satire in the *Utopia*," 163. See chap. 3 below for Dornavius's use of the expression in the title page of his *Amphitheatrum*. The first translation quoted in my text is that of Duncan, the second that of *The Correspondence of Erasmus*, trans. R.A.B. Mynors and D.F.S. Thomson, in *Collected Works of Erasmus*, 3:115 (letter 337 in the numbering of *Opus epistolarum Des. Erasmi Roterodami*, ed. P. S. Allen, H. M. Allen, and H. W. Garrod). When quoting Erasmus's letters in English translation, I shall use the Mynors and Thomson edition, using the abbreviation *CWE* and giving volume and page numbers in the text after the citation. Latin quotations from letters not yet published in this edition will be from the Allen edition. They will have the indication "Allen," the volume, and the page number in parentheses and will be followed by my own translations.

12. Robinson, *Lucian*, 86. Alberti's encomia are discussed in chap. 3 below.

13. As will be seen, Pirckheimer's *Apologia sive Laus Podagrae* was to be extremely popular. Hauffen claims that it was second only to the *Moriae Encomium* as a model of the ironic eulogy (179). See G. Thompson, "Erasmus and the Tradition of Paradox," 44–46. In this article, Pirckheimer's eulogy is given moderate praise, but the critic feels that Lady Podagra is, in the last analysis, "less satisfying than is Moria" (46).

14. See Robinson, *Lucian*, 73–76. Another amusing misunderstanding cited by Robinson concerns Luca d'Antonio Bernardi da San Gimagnano, teacher to Ficino, who took *Philosophers for Sale* as a serious exposition of the various philosophies. Lucian in fact satirizes in this work (83–84).

15. Typical negative views would be those expressed by J. C. Scaliger and Etienne Dolet concerning Lucian's religious attacks (Duncan, 44). Worried about Lucian's effect on young minds was Sir Thomas Elyot: "It were better that a childe shuld never rede any parte of Luciane than all Luciane" (*The Boke named the Governour*, 1:58). Cf. Duncan, 79. Joannes Vulteius, in his *Hendecasyllaborum libri quatuor* (1538) writes "In quendam irreligiosum Luciani sectatorem," who denies Christ and risks damnation (10ʳ). Elsewhere he attacks again, in a poem entitled "In Luciani simium" (30ᵛ–32ʳ), declaring that the sinner referred to in the poem will go to hell. Vives also recommended only selected readings from the Greek author and showed strong moral opposition to Lucian's habitual innuendo and irony (Duncan, 80). More information on this matter can be found in C. R. Thompson. Micyllus (Jakob Moltzer), a Frankfurt editor of Lucian, in 1538 urged a more balanced view of the writer (Duncan, 82). In Elizabethan England, the term *Lucianist* was to become one of abuse, as Duncan points out, citing a poem by John Weever of 1600, "A Prophecy of this present year 1600." Lines 1–2 run as follows: "Then cease fond satyres, quipping epigrammatists, / Sly scoffing critics, jeering Lucianists" (*Tudor Verse Satire*, 137). Robinson charts the Greek writer's gradual transformation into an English gentleman in the works of Dryden and others (*Lucian*, 66–68). A French writer whose contribution to the tradition of the mock encomium will be studied below was Bruscambille, who says of Lucian in one of his theatrical harangues: "Et venez ça, qui voudroit oster l'impieté & dangereux termes contenus au livre de Plaute, Porphire, Lucrece, Lucian, & autres qui ont guerroyé nostre Christianisme" (*Oeuvres* [1629], 65). For further details, see below, chap. 5, n. 136.

16. Hans Sachs's contribution to ironic literature was his *Ein gesprech der Götter ob der . . . Kranckheyt des Potagram oder Zipperlein*, first published in 1544; see Gewerstock, 37. Melanchthon contributed translations of the *Calumnia* and of the *Encomium Demosthenis*, as well as his own works in praise of the violet and the ass, printed by Dornavius in the volume described in chap. 3 below.

17. On the number of translations, see Robinson, *Lucian*, 81 and 95, and Mayer, *Lucien*, 33. Mayer counts over 189 complete or partial Greek and Latin editions alone between 1470 and the middle of the sixteenth century.

18. On Erasmus's reputation, see Preserved Smith, *Erasmus*, chap. 8. For further instances of the way in which his contemporaries viewed him, consider the greeting of Zasius in a letter of 1514: "Farewell, glory of the world, and not the German world alone, for you are the shining light of all living men" (*CWE*, letter 303, 3:17). Heinrich Bebel (1472–1518), lecturer in rhetoric and poetry at Tübingen and teacher of Melanchthon, is equally enthusiastic: "I believe you are the one person to whose gifts, with your many-sided learning and your exceptional skill in both ancient tongues, all other living men must yield; so that, being far in advance, as you are, not only of all Germans but of the French and Italians as well, you can be equated as a man of letters with the famous names of antiquity and must be enrolled among

their number" (*CWE*, letter 321 [dated 1515], 3:58). See also the compliments of Hegendorff, described in chap. 3 below.

19. Allen, letter 304, 3:19. In his translation, Clarence H. Miller sums up as follows the criticism of the *Moriae Encomium*:

> Later assailants of the *Folly* [later than Dorp, that is] . . . ignored the literary character of the work entirely. They picked various sentences out of their context and labelled them blasphemous or heretical. A flagrant example is Cousturier's contention that Erasmus was blasphemous because he made Folly claim that the invention of sciences was due to her: "for God is the lord of sciences, but Erasmus attributes the invention of them to Folly, therefore he has blasphemed against God." . . . In 1543 the Sorbonne officially condemned the *Folly*. From then until the end of the century it was included in at least fourteen indices of forbidden books, in France, Spain, and Italy. The opprobrium heaped on the *Folly* by Erasmus's enemies shows that they took it anything but lightly. (xii–xiii)

20. Allen, letter 1, 1:7. On Hermonymus, see Henri Auguste Omont, "Georges Hermonyme de Sparte." On the whole matter of Renaissance humanists learning Greek, see the two articles by Linton C. Stevens, "The Motivation" and "How the French Humanists Learned Greek." Knowledge of Greek came to be a matter of prestige, the mark of the aristocrat (see Stevens, "The Motivation," 125). See also Paul Oskar Kristeller, *Renaissance Thought*, "The Humanist Movement." The *CWE* translation does not place the letter to Botzheim out of chronological order (in vol. 1), as Allen does. The translation not yet having reached the year 1523, I return to the Latin text here. The fullest recent study of Erasmus's skill and importance as a translator is that by Erika Rummel, *Erasmus as a Translator*.

21. In fact, before his first published translations of Lucian, Erasmus translated not only from Libanius, but also from Euripides (see Rummel, chap. 2). On a completed Renaissance translation of the *Podagra*, by the Spaniard Andrés Laguna, see the article by Michael Zappala, "Andrés Laguna." See also below chap. 3, n. 41 and chap. 4, n. 32.

22. Robinson, *Lucian*, 95. Some of the translations were undertaken in collaboration with More, others were not. On Lascaris, see "Lascaris," in Peter G. Bietenholz, ed., *Contemporaries of Erasmus*, vol. 2. Erasmus explains that Lascaris helped him prepare the Aldine edition of his *Adagiorum Chiliades* (Allen, 1:523), the preface to which is dated 1513. Lascaris also taught Greek to Guillaume Budé (see *CWE*, letter 403, 3:273). In 1518 (*CWE*, letter 836, 5:413), Erasmus writes to Lascaris about finding a Greek professor for the Collegium Trilingue at Louvain. Although he does not invite Lascaris to apply, modern editors feel that may have been the underlying intention of the letter. A 1519 letter to Erasmus from Petrus Mosellanus (*CWE*, letter 911, 6:222) says that surely Erasmus will not limit his friendship to people such as Budé, Lascaris, Reuchlin, Bembo, and others, but will listen also to "ordinary people." There exists, however, no series of letters between Erasmus and Lascaris comparable to those surviving for so many of Erasmus's friends.

23. Translated by Duncan, 28.

24. Duncan, 29. Pirckheimer used his prefaces to Lucian for polemical purposes

during the Reuchlin controversy concerning the study of Hebrew (see Robinson, *Lucian*, 97). See below, chap. 3, n. 95, on the *Epistolae obscurorum virorum.*

25. xviii–xix. Miller has recently completed the edition of the *Moriae Encomium* that forms volume IV-3 of the *Opera omnia* of Erasmus.

26. Augustin Renaudet, *Préréforme et humanisme*, 606–7. See also Charles Lenient, *La Satire*, 14. Lenient is typical of earlier scholars who credit Erasmus with having almost singlehandedly reintroduced irony into European literature (13). Another such critic is J.A.K. Thomson, *England und die Antike*, 67. G. Thompson, like other more recent scholars, is more cautious:

> Erasmus has been credited with having reintroduced irony into European literature—a questionable tribute surely: one has but to think of Chaucer's Pandarus or Pertelote or Skelton's Parrot among many such early or contemporary ironic creations to counter the notion. But it is true that the delight of Erasmus's satiric writing comes often enough from its ironic ingenuity, though this is not at all the unique or even the prime cause of the endurance of his work. (*Under Pretext of Praise*, 7).

27. Bound in the *Collection of French Farces*, British Library. This farce was published in Lyons, n.p., n.d.

28. For another list of fools divided according to nationality, see Nigellus Wireker's *Speculum stultorum*, which appeared in the 1470s. See also the discussion of the *Mirrour of Madnes* in chap. 5 below. Du Bellay treats the entire process of national stereotyping with great humor in the *Regrets*, sonnet 68, when he refers to his hatred for "l'yvrogne Thudesque," but ends by implicating himself in irrationality by his exaggerated scorn for "un sçavoir pedantesque" (Du Bellay, *Oeuvres poétiques*, ed. Henri Chamard, 2:104–5. Except where otherwise indicated, the Chamard edition of Du Bellay's works will be used throughout the present study. Page and volume numbers will be given in the text). On pp. 69–70 of the C. H. Miller translation of the *Moriae Encomium*, Erasmus also indulges in this form of list.

29. *Collection of French Farces*, section entitled "Pro secunda parte." This farce also appears in E.L.N. Viollet-le-Duc, *Ancien Théâtre français*, 2:216.

30. Lyons, n.p., 1500, number 40 of *Collection of French Farces*. Reprinted by A. E. Picot in *Recueil général*, 3:235–39.

31. Mikhail Bakhtin, *Rabelais*, 11.

32. *Pierre Gringore's "Les Fantasies de mère Sote,"* ed. R. L. Frautschi. The *Jeu du Prince des Sotz et Mère Sotte* in *Oeuvres complètes de Gringore*, ed. Charles d'Héricault and Anatole de Montaiglon, 1:201, contains a "cry" summoning male and female fools to come forward and see the show. The audience is clearly meant to feel implicated in the dilemma of the figures in the performance. The same edition of Gringore lists other works providing catalogues of fools (1:201 n. i). Compare also the varied kinds of people referred to in *Le Ris de Democrite*, translated from Fregoso's Italian original by Michel d'Amboyse (1547). See below, chap. 5, n. 38, for more on this work, and chap. 2, n. 42, for more on Democritus.

33. Eli Sobel, "Sebastian Brant." Sobel claims, probably correctly with regard to northern Europe, that Brant's creation was "the most famous book of its time" (429). On Brant, see also Dorothy O'Connor, "Sebastian Brant en France," and Fedor Fraustadt, *Uber das Verhältnis*. Joel Lefebvre, in *Les Fols et la Folie*, chap. 2,

discusses Brant and Erasmus. He stresses the continuity in both authors of certain ideas, for example that of carnival, but adds that Erasmus represents a more advanced stage of literary creation. The present chapter seeks to demonstrate that a major element in this advance is the Lucianic one. On the *Narrenschiff*, see also Klaus Manger, *Das "Narrenschiff*," a study with an extensive bibliography.

34. *The Praise of Folly*, trans. Betty Radice, introduction and notes by A.H.T. Levi, 39.

35. Another strange quirk in the history of the mock eulogy is that the 1520 French translation of Synesius's encomium on baldness, by G. Hallouin, used plates from the G. de Marnef *Nef des Fols* of 1498, which in turn had come from the Basle edition of 1497 by B. de Olpe. The reuse of plates was frequent at the time but is particularly interesting in the context of a genre whose very essence is the art of obvious but creative borrowing.

36. Sebastian Brant, *The Shyppe of Fooles*, trans. Thomas Watson (1517), chap. 15: "Of fooles makynge edyfyces."

37. 61. The division of the work into sections, or chapters, was customary in editions and critical studies since the 1765 edition by A.-G. Meusnier de Querlon. More recent editors have discarded the system. In discussing Erasmus it must also be recalled that many older editions of the *Moriae Encomium* do not distinguish between the first edition of 1511 (Paris: G. de Gourmont) and the often substantial additions Erasmus made in 1514 and 1516. For this reason I have chosen to analyze passages little changed from one edition to another. On the important additions to the religious passages at the end of the work see Michael Screech, *Ecstasy*, and Jean Boisset, "*L'Eloge de la Folie* et les études bibliques d'Erasme," 149–65. Boisset notes the importance of the notion of ecstasy for Erasmus and wonders if he may not have based his comments on an actual ecstatic experience of his own, prior to the composition of the *Moriae Encomium*. Boisset stresses that the 1514 text became more satirical and aggressive than the earlier one of Gourmont. The first version had more unity and laid greater emphasis on the passages concerning religious ecstasy. Since my own concern is with Erasmus as a satirist, my reasons for using an edition with the later additions are obvious.

Among the many other articles and books on the encomium are the following: Jacques Chomarat, " 'L'Eloge de la Folie' et Quintilien"; Lynda Christian, "The Metamorphoses of Erasmus' 'Folly' "; J. Austin Gavin and Thomas M. Walsh, "The *Praise of Folly* in Context"; Jozef Isevyn, "Die *Stultitiae Laus* des Erasmus"; David W. Kay, "Erasmus' Learned Joking"; Lefebvre; Clarence H. Miller, "Some Medieval Elements"; Wayne Rebhorn, "The Metamorphoses of Moria"; John Rechtien, "A 1520 French Translation of the *Moriae Encomium*"; Genevieve Stenger, "The 'Praise of Folly' and its Parerga"; Barbara Swain, *Fools and Folly*; Richard Sylvester, "The Problem of Unity"; Winfried Trillitzsch, "Erasmus und Seneca"; Enid Welsford, *The Fool*; William Willeford, *The Fool and His Scepter*; and Kathleen Williams, ed., *Twentieth Century Interpretations*. The recent study of the *Moriae Encomium* by Zoja Pavlovskis, *The Praise of Folly*, adopts an attitude to Erasmus's achievement similar to the one formulated here.

38. *The Shyppe of Fooles*, trans. Watson, chap. 63.

39. 85–86. The Levi notes to the Radice translation point out that Erasmus is less

harsh in his criticisms of lawyers and doctors than were many of his contemporaries, perhaps because "both legal and medical studies were being renewed by Erasmus's humanist contemporaries" (151 n. 98). To the philosophers ("scientists" in some translations) Folly shows no mercy. Later in the same paragraph they are portrayed as using the language of the scholastics, also despised by the humanists.

40. Sobel, 439–40, tries to narrow the gap between Brant and Erasmus, but still comes to the conclusion that "there can never be any doubt as to which is the greater and more readable piece of literature." This attempted rapprochement does insufficient justice to both writers, and points once again to the dangers of comparisons by way of subject-matter alone.

41. 3. Single pointed brackets here refer to the edition of 1514. The care with which Erasmus adds to his list of predecessors indicates a continuing preoccupation with the history and background of his chosen form. The pig testament, a third century A.D. school exercise, was often quoted by panegyrists (see below, chap. 3, n. 42). On Glauco, see Plato, *The Republic*, 2.10, Loeb CLS, 1:145.

42. 3–4. The whole matter of the difference between the "forme" and the "fond" was of constant importance for the mock encomiasts as they balanced *festivitas* and seriousness. Indeed, their appreciation for the Horatian image of the smiling speaker of truth was the reason for the title of the present study. Another favorite image was that of Socrates the ironist, hiding great wisdom beneath his legendarily unattractive exterior. Erasmus used the image in his letter to Dorp in 1515: "I at least had the modesty to shield myself with the mask of Folly when I set out to do something improper; just as Plato's Socrates covers his face when he proclaims the praises of love, so too I assumed a mask to play this part" (Miller, 145). A third much-used image, discussed by Erasmus in the *Adagia* (3.3.1) and brilliantly developed by Rabelais, was that of the Silenus box, foul on the outside and fair inside. A fourth was the figure of Democritus the smiling philosopher. Democritus was usually contrasted with Heraclitus, who wept at men's follies. Erasmus called More "another Democritus" (Duncan, 60). Cf. above, n. 32 on *Le Ris de Democrite*, and chap 5, n. 38.

43. Sir R. C. Jebb, *Essays*, 336. Cf. Lenient: "Pour un homme prudent comme Erasme, jaloux de son repos autant que de sa liberté, la Folie avait un grand privilège, celui d'être irresponsable; sa marotte lui servait de laissez-passer. S'emporter, murmurer, gronder, était chose monotone et compromettante; les prédicateurs y suffisaient. Au lieu d'attaquer en face les abus et les sottises, il trouva plus piquant de les glorifier, en les plaçant sous le patronage de la Folie" (15).

44. Erasmus's 1515 reply to Dorp explains that it is a piece of erudite joking. Less familiar with the classical inspiration of Erasmus's witticisms, we tend nowadays to see more of the serious undertones and less of the playful, epideictic quality of the *Moriae Encomium*.

45. 153. Duncan (28) recalls that Erasmus felt safe in presenting his translations of Lucian to members of the church such as the Bishop of Chartres and the Archbishop of Canterbury; to the latter he described them as "nugas sane, sed literatas." Another term he used to describe this type of work was *declamatiuncula* (see below, chap. 3, nn. 16, 68. The full title of Galliot du Pré's 1520 Paris translation of the encomium suggests how well aware were early readers of the dual purpose—plea-

sure and profit—of the ostensibly joking work: *De la declamation des louenges de follie stille facessieux et profitable pour congnoistre les erreurs et abuz du monde.* The recognition of "erreurs et abuz" is at least as prominent here as the "stille facessieux." We may compare this perception with that of White Kennett, translator of a popular English version of Erasmus:

> Satire and Panegyrick, distant be,
> Yet jointly here they both in one agree.
>
> . . . .
>
> Folly by Irony's commended here,
> Sooth'd, that her Weakness may the more appear.
>
> . . . .
>
> Though Folly Speaker be, and Argument,
> Wit guides the Tongue, Wisdom's the Lecture meant.
>
> (xiii–xiv)

Kennett's original title of 1683—*Witt against Wisdom*—is revealing. He explains it further in his preface: "It is apparent, that . . . our Author, Archer like, shoots just contrary from where he pretends to aim, and makes a compleat Satyr against Fools of what he entitles a Panegyrick upon Folly" (A2ʳ). In his 1549 edition of the *Moriae Encomium*, Sir Thomas Chaloner gives the work equally high praise, noting that "the reader havyng any considerance, shall soone espie, how in every mattier, yea almost every clause, is hidden besides the myrth, some deaper sence and purpose" (*The Praise of Folie*, trans. and ed. Sir Thomas Chaloner, 1549, A.3ᵛ). Clarence Miller edited Chaloner's edition in 1965. In another famous letter, to Ulrich von Hutten, Erasmus claimed that More had persuaded him to write the *Moriae Encomium*, like training a camel to dance, "ut camelus saltarem" (Allen, letter 999, 4:16).

46. These references are explained in the Levi notes to the Radice translation of the *Praise of Folly*.

47. 22–23. Miller notes that the Acharnian (Acarnanian) pigs are mentioned in Erasmus's *Adages*. Levi (81 n.27) points out that Horace uses the words *plump* and *glossy* to describe himself as a pig from the herd of Epicurus (*Epistles*, 1.4.15–16).

48. 36. On Archilochus, see Plutarch, *Lives*, 855a, and *Moralia*, 239b (Miller, 36 n. 1). Erasmus may have had in mind here the section in the *De Parasito* in which Simon asks who would be the better soldiers, well-fed parasites or emaciated philosophers. Manacorda notes that pedants and philosophers were frequently equated during the Renaissance (753–54).

49. Walter Kaiser, "The Ironic Mock Encomium," in Williams, 78–91. Kaiser's analysis does not, however, distinguish between the structure of the 1511 and the 1514 editions. He is generous in crediting Erasmus with inventing "a new kind of irony" (80), by which the mocker is mocked. Another famous analysis of the work is Johan Huizinga's, in his *Erasmus of Rotterdam*, chap. 9, "The Praise of Folly," 69–78.

50. On this paradox or tautology, see Colie, *Paradoxia epidemica*, 6–7.

51. *The Praise of Folly*, trans. Radice, 68.

52. *The Praise of Folly*, trans. Radice, 69. Nowhere is Erasmus's learned joking, the "lusus ingenii" described above more apparent than in these quotations from

other languages. As was noted earlier, so obscure did many of these references seem even to his contemporaries, that the 1515 edition was expanded with notes by Erasmus's pupil Girardus Listrius (Lister), who explained that such joking was clear proof of intelligence. See Gavin and Walsh. Aristotle also discussed the function of learned joking (Duncan, 7). On Renaissance notions of improvisation, see Terence Cave, *The Cornucopian Text*, chap. 4, "Improvisation and Inspiration," especially 127.

53. The progression is described by Pavlovskis, chap. 9. She explains that the series of portraits moves from the active (the hunters) to the sedentary (the gamblers), from the relatively harmless to the utterly destructive. She notes a general "aura of addiction" in the individuals satirized in these passages, and states that the presentation of this series of dreamers leads Erasmus easily to the passages on men's gullibility in religious matters (173).

54. See Screech, *Ecstasy*, 72–75.

55. *Meditation* for Erasmus was a strong term, meaning a kind of profound preparation for and "practicing" of, in this case, death (see Screech, *Ecstasy*, 83, quoting Erasmus's 1534 *On Preparation for Death*).

56. See *The Praise of Folly*, ed. Hoyt Hopewell Hudson, xxii: "With this zeal for what he called 'the philosophy of Christ' went an acceptance, in some measure, of the Christianized Platonism which had been arrived at by some of the Italian thinkers of the preceding generation." On Erasmus's admiration for Plato, see P. Smith, 336 and Screech, *Ecstasy*, 35 and 64.

57. On Socrates, see above, n. 42, and Screech, *Ecstasy*, 35, 41, 67, 76, 79, and 105. On this distinction between Erasmus and Plato, see Miller, xvii: Folly's "inconsistent and contradictory use of Plato should remind us that we are not justified in accepting Folly's view as identical with Erasmus' even though it closely resembles what Erasmus says in the *Enchiridion*. . . . The experience of the book is to play off one irony against the other, not to imagine that Erasmus is simply propounding straightforward Platonism."

58. Quotations from this dialogue will be taken from Erasmus, *Opera omnia*, I-3, 320–24. On the colloquy see also Mayer, "Rabelais' Satirical Eulogy," 151–52, to which my own analysis owes much.

59. See Allen, letter 1558, 6:47–48, and Dornavius, *Amphitheatrum*, 2:202. Pirckheimer and Erasmus both suffered from gout and the stone, and their correspondence contains frequent references to the two diseases. In letter 1440 of 1524 Erasmus specifically mentions Lucian's remark that in spring the devotees of the goddess Podagra must pay her tribute. He regrets in particular the fact that, because of his illness, Pirckheimer is unable to write letters (Allen, letter 1440, 5:442).

60. G. Thompson, *Under Pretext of Praise*, 177 n. 27, also discusses this comparison.

61. Erasmus composed a serious encomium on medicine, the *Encomium medicinae*, composed for a physician friend to deliver in Paris. Written in 1499, it was published in 1518 and is reprinted in Erasmus, *Opera omnia*, I-4, 145–87. On Erasmus's legendary skill as a letter writer, see Judith Rice Henderson, "Erasmus on the Art of Letter-Writing," in *Renaissance Eloquence*, ed. James J. Murphy, 331–55. Henderson discusses Erasmus's *Libellus de conscribendis epistolis* (1521),

in which 66^v of this early, pirated edition, on the "epistola invectiva," states that "non odiosum modo, sed & ridiculum ostendemus. Multam ironiam adhibebimus." Such a remark suggests how carefully Erasmus chose the tone for Moria's criticisms.

62. *Lucian*, 109.

63. Froben's publishing together of Lucian, Erasmus, and Synesius is discussed in chap. 1 above. Duncan notes that part of Erasmus's *Ciceronianus* employs "the common Lucianic device of ridiculing an abuse through the self-revelation of the principal speaker" (41). The section referred to is that in which Nosoponus the Ciceronian tells of the years of toil he has put into his three dictionaries of Ciceronian vocabulary and usage. The later sections of the work are more serious. Erasmus did compose a straightforward panegyric, that on Archduke Philip of Austria, but not, apparently, with much pleasure. As Betty Radice puts it, he "certainly did not enjoy writing the *Panegyricus*" (*CWE*, 27:3). In a letter to Colet, Erasmus states that "I do not remember ever doing anything more unwillingly; for I saw that this kind of thing could not be handled without some flattery" (*CWE*, 27:3). This reluctance is in marked contrast to the ease and enjoyment with which he composed his famous mock encomium.

CHAPTER THREE

1. To the authors to be discussed in some detail in the present chapter, we must add the name of Henry Cornelius Agrippa, whose *De incertitudine* of 1526 (published 1530) exercised an extremely important influence on ironists such as Montaigne. On Agrippa, see Charles G. Nauert, Jr., *Agrippa*; Barbara C. Bowen, "Cornelius Agrippa's *De Vanitate*"; and E. Korkowski, "Agrippa as Ironist." An older study is that of Henry Morley, *The Life of Henry Cornelius Agrippa von Nettesheim*. Nauert argues strongly that Agrippa's work should not be interpreted as a mere "jeu d'esprit," any more, I would add, than should most mock encomia.

2. Of course, many Renaissance encomia were serious satires, as we have seen with Erasmus. The profession of frivolity was usually no more than a protective device. On Neo-Latin poetry of this period, see D. Murarasu, *La Poésie néolatine*.

3. For a detailed list of the encomia included in these collections, see my thesis, "The Satirical Eulogy," appendix, 380–84.

4. The 1619 edition was printed by André Wechel in Hanover.

5. As far as I know, Dornavius is the only anthologizer of paradoxical encomia to have included the *Utopia*.

6. See Fischart, *Johann Fischarts Werke*, ed. A. Hauffen, 3:4.

7. See above, chap. 1, n. 61.

8. 2^r. Dornavius studied medicine at Basle and was successively rector of the college of Gorlitz (1608) and of Bethuen (Byton) in Silesia, then doctor to the princes of Brieg and Lignitz. In addition to the *Amphitheatrum*, he published a smaller volume of eulogies, the *Encomium scarabei* (1617); *Homo Diabolus* (1618); *Ulysses scholasticus* (1620); and the *Invidiae encomium* ([1614] and 1626). On the frequent use of the title *theatrum* see the article by Walter J. Ong, "Commonplace Rhapsody," 114.

9. *Satires*, 1.1.24. See above, chap. 2, n. 11.

10. 2ʳ. The *Larousse universel,* under "Eloge," mentions an encomium by one Claude Bigothier, entitled *De rapina seu raporum encomium* (1540), which is now "excessivement rare." There is an 1891 edition by Joseph-Philibert Brossard.

11. On sixteenth-century attitudes to generic classification, see Colie, *The Resources of Kind.*

12. Hauffen, 174: "Kein Laster hat im 16 Jahrhundert eine so reiche Litteratur als die Trunksucht." Drunkenness was also treated playfully in the Middle Ages, for instance in the *Missa potatorum,* part of which is a version of the Lord's Prayer. The parody contains lines such as "ne nos inducet in ebrietatem," and, later on, the words:

> Ave, color vini clari,
> Salve, sapor sine pari,
> tua nos inebriari
> dignetur clementia.

The work is quoted in Paul Lehmann, *Die Parodie,* 249–50. Filippo Beroaldo (Beroaldus) (1453–1505) came closer to the mock encomiastic tradition in his *Declamatio ebriosi, scortatoris, & aleatoris* (1513). In the preface, Beroaldo calls the piece a "dialogum festivissimum," and begs his dedicatee, the Bishop of Bratislava, "libellum hilaritudinis plenum hilari fronte suscipito" (139ʳ). In the debate, a drunkard argues with his two brothers over which of them deserves to inherit from their father. The piece is presented as if the characters were pleading on their own behalf before a court, and contains an obvious element of paradoxical self-praise.

13. The *Biographie universelle,* under "Hegendorff," explains that Hegendorff embraced the Reform in its early stages. Apparently he read his game on drunkenness to his friends in 1526. He held the chair of law at Frankfurt-on-Oder, then the chair of literature at Lüneburg. In the context of the present study, it is of interest to note that he translated the *Muscae Encomium.*

14. *Encomium ebrietatis,* A2ᵛ.

15. *Encomium ebrietatis,* Bʳ.

16. N.p., n.d. In a letter appended to his *Encomium ebrietatis* (1519), Hegendorff suggested a more traditional rhetorical balancing of favorable and negative arguments: "Id quod olim & a veteribus factum est qui in utramque partem res ipsas vertere consueverant & a Fabio Quintiliano diligenter preceptum est quo Themata ipsa in utramque partem torquere addiscamus, quod ego in ebrietate vituperanda declamatiuncula quadam aliquando exhibebo." He adds that he praised drunkenness "iocandi gratia." Erasmus called the *Moriae Encomium* a "declamatiuncula" (see above, chap. 2, n. 45, and below, n. 68). However, the number and seriousness of the charges Hegendorff levels against drunkenness far outweigh those he produces in its favor.

17. Hegendorff also composed an *Encomium somni* (1519). Although the work is bound with a series of medical tracts in a British Library collection, it is in fact a typical mock encomium, referring specifically to Hegendorff's two other such works. Sleep, like Folly, is personified and speaks in her own defense. She also puts in a good word for her creator: "Nihil stulticia erit si Ebrietatis Encomium quis audierit. Nihil erit Calvitii Laus si quis bullatas ebrietatis nugas legerit." A marginal note here provides the probably unnecessary indication that Synesius is the praiser

of baldness referred to. Claiming Night and Lethe as her parents, Sleep explains that she alone enables mankind to lay aside all cares and passions. The brief work ends with a short poem in which Endymion calls on Sleep. Every other line of the piece begins with the words "Somne veni." The effect is undoubtedly soporific, whether deliberately or not one cannot be sure.

18. Bucoldianus (Bucholds) was a German philologist and physician of the first half of the sixteenth century who wrote a number of works on medicine and on oratory.

19. Crimes committed by drunkards were often mentioned by critics of the vice. Scévole de Sainte-Marthe, in a poem "Contre la Gourmandise," wrote: "O sale Ebrieté, seule peste de l'ame, / Et des mechancetez nourrice plus infame" (from *Les Oeuvres* [1600], here quoted from *Les Satires françaises*, ed. Fernand Fleuret and Louis Perceau, 2:205). "Les goutes douloureuses" are mentioned as one of the unfortunate effects of "orde Gourmandise" (206). Hegendorff dwells at length on the social ills caused by intoxication.

20. Turner was born in Barnstaple and studied at Oxford. In 1586 he became doctor in theology at the university of Ingolstadt and, later on, Canon of Breslau. He held the chair of Latin language at Graz until his death. The "Oratio de laude ebrietatis" is number 6 of Turner's *Orationes XIV*, published in 1584.

21. Turner, *Oratio*, 86. The comical appearance of the snoring drunkard was a popular theme of certain French poems (see below, chap. 5, n. 111, and chap. 6, n. 75).

22. *Oratio*, 86.

23. Compare Du Bellay, *Regrets*, sonnet 68 (in *Oeuvres poétiques*, ed. Chamard, 2:104), which lists the traditional faults of various nations, discussed above. Sonnet 135 of the *Regrets* notes how much he was forced to drink while in Switzerland: "Ilz boivent nuict & jour en Bretons & Suysses" (2:161).

24. *Oratio de confectione eius potus, qui . . . Cerevisia vocatur* (1567).

25. J. Camerarius composed a liminary sonnet for the volume. Obsopoeus translated some of Lucian's works as early as 1527, and also wrote other *artes*, which appeared in print until well into the seventeenth century, as in the edition *De Arte Bibendi libri quatuor* (1648). The latter volume contains, in addition to the works named in the title, an *Artis amandi, dansandi practica*. In the dedication to yet another work, Obsopoeus calls drunkenness a "foedum vitium" (*Rapsodia in ebrietatem*, [1527?], Aii), and wonders why writers do not seek to show the horror and degradation brought about by drinking. Obsopoeus translated the *De Parasito* in *Luciani Samosatensis Opera* (1543 and 1549).

26. A Latin court satire marginally related to our theme is the play *Lucianus aulicus* of 1534. This two-act play by Jean Plaisant (Placentius) presents its protagonist Chremes and a cook from whom he hears about the ways of the court. To be a "Lucianus aulicus" he must learn to sit at table and be a good guest. (See Paul Bahlmann, *Die lateinischen Dramen*.) Other anti-court satires derived from the *De Parasito* that are mentioned by Bahlmann are the *Acolastus* of Gulielmus Gnapheus (1525) and Alberti's *Servus*, a didactic piece on the life of the slave. The latter writer's *Momus* praises vagabonds. Robinson, *Lucian*, 89–95, discusses these works. Mayer cites separate editions of the *De Parasito* in Louvain by R. Rescius and

J. Sturmius in 1530 and by Rescius alone in 1555 ("Satire in French Literature," appendix).

27. *Helen* appeared as early as 1510 under the title *Isocratis oratio de laudibus Helenae*. The oration forms part of the *Herodoti Halicarnassi Thurii Historiae*. The *Busiris* was not published in separate editions but in the collected works and orations of Isocrates, for example that by Aldus Manutius (1513), 21^r–23^r.

28. Henry Morley, *Jerome Cardan*, 1:302–3.

29. *Hieronymi Cardani. . . . Libelli duo* (1543). The section of the book entitled *Geniturae LXVII* contains the horoscopes. Number 40 is that of Nero.

30. Alfonso Ingegno, *Saggio sulla filosofia di Cardano*, 185. The *Neronis Encomium* and the *Podagrae Encomium* were both composed around the year 1546. The *Neronis Encomium* does not seem to have been widely published until the seventeenth century, when it appeared in several collections of paradoxical encomia. It first appeared in the *Somniorum Synesiorum . . . libri IV* (1562). Dornavius includes it in the *Amphitheatrum*. On Cardano, see Alan Wykes, *Doctor Cardano*. On Nero, see chap. 5 below in the discussion of the *Triumphe de haulte Folie*. A different strategy for defending Nero was adopted by John Hall in his 1650 *Paradoxes*, intro. Don Cameron Allen, 14. Hall says that had it not been for Nero, "Rome had never known Nero's golden house." This defense forms part of his first paradox, entitled "That an absolute Tyranny is the best Government."

31. Andreas Arnaudus, *Ioci* (1600, republished Avignon, 1605 and Paris, 1609). Arnaudus died ca. 1615.

32. Arnaudus, *Ioci*, 145.

33. Arnaudus, *Ioci*, 157.

34. Arnaudus, *Ioci*, 191–92.

35. *Amphitheatrum*, 2:175–76, and Turner, *Posthuma* (1602), 148–58.

36. *Amphitheatrum*, 2:175.

37. *Amphitheatrum*, 2:176.

38. A prose Neo-Latin encomium on an unfortunate human pursuit was Thomas Lineus's *Oratio in laudem belli* (1531). The author's real name was Thomas Vlas (1505–1579). According to the Belgian *Biographie nationale*, he was a great admirer of Erasmus, for whom he composed a total of four epitaphs. A humanist and jurisconsult, he taught Roman law at the University of Louvain, and lived in Bois-le-Duc. The encomium on war was written to be delivered "in postremo Cameracensi concilio," i.e., after the Treaty of Cambrai, the Paix des Dames, concluded in 1529. Lineus refers to his work as "ludicrum," and cites Polycrates, Favorinus, Synesius, and Erasmus as his predecessors. In his "Argumentum" he explains that "Nobis autem consilium non fuit quemquam petulantius laedere, sed delectare," and adds that he did not permit himself as much freedom of expression as did "Moria," because of the delicate and overimpatient ears of his contemporaries. His arguments on war resemble those employed later by Claude Colet, who used the same publisher, Wechel. To avoid repetition, I shall discuss only Colet's work in chap. 5 below.

39. *Tragoedia Luciani cui titulus est Podagra* (1529). The edition also contains two medical works on gout and related diseases, by A. C. Celsus and Georgius Valla. The mingling of serious and comic discussions of illness has already been shown to

be frequent in editions of disease encomia, and was probably one reason for the frequent misinterpretations of some such works. Valla (1430–1490), for instance, wrote numerous books, several of which were on medicine, and he held the chair of eloquence in Venice. A true Renaissance man, he was interested in and able to write on virtually any subject. The Pirckheimer work first appeared in 1522 under the title *Apologia, seu podagrae laus.* On Pirckheimer, see Niklas Holzberg, *Willibald Pirckheimer.*

40. *De podagrae laudibus doctorum hominum lusus* (1570). This edition contained the gout works of Lucian, Pirckheimer, and Ballista.

41. 1551. On Laguna and Erasmus, see Zappala.

42. The first edition contains a dedication dated 1521, in which Pirckheimer quotes several predecessors from the standard list: "sed & exemplum habeo, cum quidam tyrannidem, alius febrem, ille calvitiem, hic vero stulticiam laudaverit." His encomium was printed several times in the sixteenth century (see nn. 39 and 40 above, then by Dornavius and also in some of the later anthologies. In 1617, it was translated into English under the title *The Praise of the Gout; or, The Gouts Apologie, A Paradox, both pleasant and profitable. Written first in the Latine tongue, by that famous and noble Gentleman Bilibaldus Pirckheimerus Councellor unto two Emperours, Maximilian the first, and Charles the fift: And now Englished by William Est, Master of Arts.*

> Omne tulit punctum, qui miscuit utile dulci,
> Lectorem delectando, pariterque monendo.
> (Hor. de art. Poet.)

This Horatian maxim about mingling delight and warning is of course close to the other popular one about the joker being permitted to tell the truth. Both were to be staples of prefaces of mock encomia. In the *Nugae venales* of 1642, for instance, the preface quotes Horace as justification for what it calls a "Thesaurus ridendi & jocandi." In the same volume we find the *Pugna porcorum* of Johannes Placentius, the idea of which must derive from the *Batrachomyomachia*, but which is singular in that each word of the text begins with a *p*, as each word of the *Ecloga de calvis* did with a *c* (see below, n. 65). Another familiar work in the same collection is the testament of the pig mentioned by Erasmus. For further discussion of the Pirckheimer work, see G. Thompson, "Erasmus and the Tradition of Paradox," 44–46.

43. Lefebvre, 270.

44. *The Praise of the Gout,* 8.

45. *The Praise of the Gout,* 37.

46. See G. Thompson, "Erasmus and the Tradition of Paradox," 46.

47. The other edition is described in note 40 of this chapter.

48. The English version of Ballista's encomium appeared in London (1577), under the title *The Overthrow of the Gout,* trans. B.G. (perhaps Barnaby Googe). The translator does not appear to have known much more about his source than we do, for he mistakenly asserts that the original was dedicated to "a great Phisitian in Fraunce" rather than to a bishop. He is less enthusiastic about Ballista as a writer: "The verse in Latin is not very eloquent, and therfore no mervail though the translation be rude and unpleasant," (A.ii^v). Another work that emphasizes fighting

rather than praising the disease is Donatus Antonius Ferrus's *De podagra enchiridion* (1585). The title is an echo of Erasmus's *Enchiridion militis christiani*.

49. *The Overthrow of the Gout*, C.vʳ.

50. Helius Eobanus Hessus, *Ludus Podagrae* (1537). The preface is dated 1534. In this edition, a fine introductory plate depicts the gods Jupiter, Neptune, and Pluto dominated by a regal figure wearing a crown and bearing a banner with the words "Solvere nodosam nescit medicina podagram" on it. On the next page appears a group of sufferers with canes, surrounded by sayings such as "cursi vetans," "lectigrada," "genufraga," and "talorum tortrix," echoes of Lucian's epithets. The figure of gout is presented as "hec unica calamitas nostra." Hessus is said by Louis-Gabriel Michaud in the *Biographie universelle ancienne et moderne* to have died of gout. On Hessus, see Carl Krause, *Eobanus Hessus*. Krause follows Eobanus Hessus himself in thinking that the cause of his illness was consumption.

51. Morley feels that in composing his encomium Cardano may have had in mind Alciati, a good friend who suffered greatly from gout.

52. H. Morley, *Jerome Cardan*, 1:302–3. The genre of the work was misunderstood as recently as 1946, when James Eckman wrote: "But Cardan's fame was not always thus happily preserved. One of his pieces on gout was reprinted in 1644 in a little book of ridiculous or silly writings by various men " ("Jerome Cardan," 70n). Eckman might also have mentioned the *Amphitheatrum* and the 1638 edition of the anthology to which he refers. The latter was entitled *Dissertationum ludicrarum et amoenitatum scriptores varii editio nova et aucta* (1644). For the adoption of Cardano's work by a more serious-minded medical writer, see Joannes Loselius the Elder's (Loesel's) *De podagra tractatus* (1639). The 1639 edition is a revised one, but the 1638 edition, presented as "Rostoch: typis haeredum Richelianorum," does not include the work by Cardano.

53. *Amphitheatrum*, 2:215. The following quotations are taken from the *Amphitheatrum*, 2:215–19. Page numbers for subsequent quotations will appear in the text.

54. Leva, or Leyva (1480–1536), the Spanish soldier, was captain general of Italy in 1553 and saved the duchy of Milan for the Emperor on the death of Francesco Sforza. See also *La Grande Encyclopédie*, under "Leyva, Antonio de": "Leyva, qui souffrait de la goutte, se faisait porter en litière sur les champs de bataille." Cf. the reference to him in one of the Lyons blasons, discussed in chap. 6 below.

55. *De Podagrae laudibus oratio*, habitae in celeberrimo gymnasio Patavino, a Ioanne Carnario Gandensi, in initio lectionum, III Idus Novemb. 1552 (1553). Page numbers for subsequent citations from this work will be given in the text. It was translated into German by Johann Fischart (see n. 58 below).

56. *Colicae et Podagrae tyrannis*, part of *Iani Pannonii . . . Poemata* (1619). Page numbers for subsequent quotations will be given in the text.

57. *Triumphus Podagrae*, in gratiam, et favorem omnium, cum ea conflictantium accurate conscriptus, & heroico carmine adumbratus (1605). Page numbers for subsequent quotations from this edition will be given in the text.

58. Apart from the Neo-Latin gout eulogies, there is also Fischart's German *Podagrammisch Trostbüchlin*, published in 1577 (see *Johann Fischarts Werke*, ed. Hauffen, vol. 3). In the same volume appeared a German translation of Pirck-

heimer's gout eulogy, given as *Lob des Podagrams*. Fischart's collection was inspired, he informs us, by numerous classical and contemporary writers. In addition to the customary sources in Lucian, Synesius, and Erasmus, Fischart lists Pirckheimer, Carnarius, and Cardano among contemporary, and Claudian and Petrarch among earlier writers. Claudian was very popular throughout the Renaissance; several of his short poems on animals such as the porcupine, the phoenix, and the cramp-fish were selected by Dornavius (602, 603, 613, and 623 in the *Amphitheatrum*). The poem Fischart refers to is Claudian's epigram,

> *In podagrum qui carmina sua non stare dicebat*
> Quae tibi cum pedibus ratio? quid carmina culpas?
> scandere qui nescis, versiculos laceras?
> "claudicat hic versus: haec" inquit, "syllaba nutat";
> atque nihil prorsus stare putat podager.
> (*The Works of Claudian*, Loeb CLS, 2:186)

See also *Johann Fischarts Werke*, ed. Hauffen, 3:iv, and the study by Cameron. Fischart mentions Petrarch because, in a letter, he quoted the tale of Podagra and the spider, sometimes given as Podagra and the flea. The tale of Aranea and Podagra was also related by Pantaleon Candidus (the Austrian Weiss, 1540–1608). Since Dornavius included the tale with the gout encomia, Fischart was evidently not alone in seeing a resemblance between the tale and the paradoxical encomium. Candidus's version of the story was republished in the section "De Reptilibus" in his *Centum et Quinquaginta Fabulae de Diis*, part of the *Delitiae poetarum germanorum*, ed. G.A.F.G. (Janus Gruterus) (1612), vol. 2, pt.1. Ballista, Iacobus Pontanus, and Hans Sachs are also mentioned by Fischart, as are the Stoics. On Sachs's Lucianic dialogue of 1544, between Podagra and the gods, see chap. 2, n. 16.

59. Dornavius, *Amphitheatrum*, 2:214. For subsequent quotations from Pontanus (1542–1626), the philologist and humanist, page numbers from Dornavius's edition will be given in the text.

60. *Amphitheatrum*, 2:214. Contrast this view with that of Carnarius, described earlier in this chapter.

61. Mention of the *Podagra* occurs in the most unlikely places. In a medical treatise by Daniel Sennertus, Professor of Physic at the University of Wittenberg, there are several references to the mock tragedy (*Institutionum medicinae libri V*, [1628]). Sennertus's work appears to have been popular, for it was reprinted a number of times and translated into English as late as 1676 under the title *Practical Physick*, by H. Care. The subtitle is revealing in the present context: "Five Distinct Treatises of the most Predominant Diseases of these Times." The diseases are scurvy, dropsy, fevers and agues, French pox, and gout. Sennertus describes diseases of the joints as maladies that "take" the various limbs. Thus, Chiragra is the taking of the hand, Gonagra of the knee, and Podagra of the foot. The English translation explains this strategy as follows: "In regard that these members are in this Disease as it were taken, and by it ensnared, and held fast: even as by *Lucian* (in his *Tragopodagra*) the Gout is brought in thus speaking: 'By the most of Men I am called Podagra, / being the taking, and deteining of the Feet' " (2–3 of the section entitled "A Treatise of the Gout").

Two further references to Lucian occur later in the work: in chap. 3, on the "Signs Diagnostick" of the gout, "all which *Lucian* in his *Tragopodagra* hath very elegantly described" (55), and in the section on "Mitigaters of Pain": "The Pain in this Disease for the most part is a most grievous Symptom, and which is most troublesome to the sick parties, and which they most of all Curse and Bann, (as *Lucian* hath it in the beginning almost of his *Tragopodagra*)" (82). Reference to Lucian by a medical man such as Sennertus provides interesting proof of the fame of the Greek writer's powers of accurate observation and vivid description. Yet later in the century, Benjamin Welles, in his *A Treatise of the Gout* (1669), remarked that he did not wish to praise gout as did "Cardan," or publish "Consolations instead of Cures," as did Sennertus, but to offer real cures. As proof he referred readers to the many gouty patients who had recovered under his care. The picturesque cures include the use of a liquid concocted from red snails and of an ointment made by cutting up live frogs.

62. Thomas Best, *The Humanist Ulrich von Hutten*, 71–75. Best asserts that Hutten was quite capable of caricaturing himself and his own wishes as well as those of others. Hutten's *Febris I*, (dated 1515?) appears in the *Opera poetica* (1538). Both dialogues were published several times in the early part of the century, and both are in the *Amphitheatrum*. Hutten also composed a serious work on another disease, the "morbus gallicus," *De Guaiaci medicina et morbo gallico liber unus* (1519). There are numerous Neo-Latin works on venereal disease, but most are serious studies. They were sometimes anthologized, as in the collection *De Morbo gallico omnia quae extant* (1566). This volume, several hundred pages long, contains, in addition to some little-known works, Fracastoro's poem on the disease, *Syphilis, sive morbus Gallicus*, first published in Verona in 1530. A recent edition of it is by Geoffrey Eatough. Other editions of this most popular work are listed in *Bibliography of the Poem "Syphilis sive Morbus Gallicus,"* ed. L. Baumgartner and J. F. Fulton. The authors call the poem a "poetical expression of terror and ominous forebodings" (26). Only in some French works was dame Vérolle treated in a humorous manner reminiscent of that found in encomia on gout and the fever. On Hutten, see also Gewerstock.

63. Menapius was evidently interested in such matters from a more serious point of view as well, for he also wrote a work on curing the quartan fever, which was published together with the fever encomium but antedated it by a year. The eulogy was reprinted in the seventeenth-century collections of encomia and translated into French as late as 1728 by one Gueudeville. It was published togther with an encomium on gout by Etienne Coulet, a seventeenth-century writer, who introduced his work as follows:

L'Eloge de la Goute, Ouvrage Héroïque, Historique, Politique, Comique, Critique, Satirique, Ironique, Véridique, & autres Epithètes en *ique*.

The translation of Menapius is presented in less comical, more paradoxical terms:

L'Eloge de la Fièvre Quarte Où il est doctoralement prouvé

    I. Que ceux qui ont le Bonheur d'avoir cete Fièvre, ne peuvent trop s'en féliciter.

II. Que ceux qu'elle n'a pas encore honoré de sa visite, ne peuvent la souhaiter avec trop d'ardeur. Traduit du Latin de Guillaume Menape. En son vivant, Docteur en Mèdecine (apparemment).

> Cherche qui veut.
> Trouve qui peut.
> Par Monsr. Gueudeville
> (1728).

At the end of his preface, Gueudeville urges readers "quoi qu'en dise Maitre Guillaume," to beware of the quartan fever. "Je la conois mieux que lui," he adds cryptically (12). See also below, chap. 6, n. 32.

64. Passerat's encomium appears in the *Amphitheatrum*, 2:262 and in the *De caecitate oratio* (1597). On Cicero see above, chap. 1, n. 61.

65. Also known in the Renaissance was a short verse work by the monk Hucbald of St. Amand, the *Ecloga de calvis*, a poem in defense of baldness in which every word begins with the letter C (see Maximilian Manitius, *Geschichte der lateineischen Literatur*, 591). See below, chap. 6, n. 61, for a discussion of the article by Daniel Sheerin, "A Carolingian Cure Recovered," and see n. 42 above on the *Ecloga*. Much of the literature on baldness was written by supporters or opponents of tonsuring, sometimes seen as a form of voluntary baldness. See chap. 6, n. 69, for the *Le Rasibus* debate. See also Alfred Liede, *Dichtung als Spiel*.

66. *Luciani Samosatensis opera quae quidem extant, omnia*, trans. I. Micyllus (1549), introduction. The introduction is in fact the same as that of the Frankfurt edition by Christianus Egenolphus Hadamarius (1543), 255. Possibly it was written by Micyllus, the translator, since introductions by other writers such as Erasmus, More, Pirckheimer, and Melanchthon, are attributed to their authors. In his 1583 edition of the works (*Les Oeuvres*), Bretin did not use this introduction.

67. The short liminary verse that Bretin translates from the Latin of Micyllus is particularly appropriate for Lucian's satirical works:

> Lucian, qui sçavoit la sagesse et la sottie
> A escrit tout cecy, d'un sage entendement:
> Ores que les mortels, qui jugent sottement,
> Cuideront que ce soit une badinerie.
> Car il est tout certain, que l'homme estant en vie
> N'a ferme opinion ny ferme jugement;
> Et ce que l'un aura louangé hautement
> L'autre l'estimera une vray' moquerie.
> (A.ii)

68. *Muscae Encomium Luciani* (1517). Erasmus uses the word *declamatiuncula* to describe the *Moriae Encomium*. See Paul van Tieghem, *La Littérature latine de la Renaissance*, 4:364:

> Erasme range lui-même son *Eloge de la Folie* parmi les "déclamations," . . . Il veut parler de ces exercices d'éloquence sur des thèmes fictifs souvent bizarres et paradoxaux, sur des maux ou des infirmités dont on s'amusait à prononcer un pompeux et plaisant éloge, bâti sur les arguments les plus subtils, et paré de

toutes les élégances de l'élocution; éloge de la surdité, du pou, des rats, de la
boue, de la goutte, de l'ivrognerie, de Néron, de l'Enfer . . . et d'autres plus
malodorants ou plus scabreux; pour ces éloges, et en général ces déclamations,
on ne se servit, longtemps encore après Erasme, que du latin. Il dit lui-même
avoir composé cette "declamationnette" comme il l'appelle (declamatiunculam)
d'abord, dans sa tête, à cheval.

The continuing use of Latin for such encomia has been amply demonstrated in the
present chapter. So far as the reference to Augustine is concerned, we may recall
Erasmus in the *Moriae Encomium* remarking that "the life of flies and little birds"
is more attractive than that of domesticated, trained animals such as the horse: "So
certain is it that the creations of Nature are in every way more joyous than the
fabrications of artifice" (Miller, 53).

69. *La Mouche de Lucian et la Maniere de parler et de se taire* trans. Geoffroy
Tory ([1533]).

70. On Martial, see the *Epigrams*, trans. Walter C. A. Ker, Loeb CLS, 1:98. The
poem in question is not a true epitaph, since the dog in question is not dead. Her
master, loving her dearly, has her portrait painted so that when she does die he will
be able to remember her. The poem is marked by the gentle mocking tone characteristic of the Pléiade hymns-blasons:

> Issa est passere nequior Catulli,
> Isse est purior osculo columbae,
> Issa est blandior omnibus puellis,
> Issa est carior Indicis lapillis,
> Issa est deliciae catella Publi.
> (1.109.1–5)

On Statius, see the Loeb edition of the *Silvae*, trans. J. H. Morley, 1:113, for a
typical half-serious, half-playful elegy on a parrot:

> Parrot, prince of birds, glib-tongued favourite of thy master, parrot that clev-
> erly dost mimic human speech, who has cut short thy chatter by so sudden a
> stroke? Yesterday, hapless one, thou didst join our feast, though doomed to die,
> and we saw thee plucking the dainties of the table and moving from couch to
> couch till after midnight. . . . Empty is that happy cage, and silent the chatter-
> ing of that lordly abode. (2.4)

Ovid also wrote a poem on a dead parrot (*Heroides and Amores*, 2.6, Loeb CLS).
The piece is similar to those by Catullus and Statius. The *Greek Anthology* contains
a number of sepulchral epigrams, such as nos. 195 and 196, Loeb CLS, 2:111–13.
Some of these are in fact not epitaphs, but love poems. A true epitaph on a cicada is
no. 200, by Nicias: "No longer curled under the leafy branch shall I delight in sending forth a voice from my tender wings. For I fell to the . . . hand of a boy, who
caught me stealthily as I was seated on the green leaves" (2:113). No. 204, on a
partridge, is by Agathias Scholasticus: "No longer, my poor partridge, exiled from
the rocks, does thy plaited house hold thee in its light withes; no longer in the shine
of the bright-eyed Dawn dost thou shake the tips of thy sun-warmed wings. Thy
head the cat bit off, but all the rest of thee I seized from her, nor did she satisfy her

wicked jaws. Now may the dust lie not light on thee but heavy, lest she drag thy corpse from the tomb" (2:115).

The two parts of this epitaph are in marked contrast with one another, the first being lyrical and the second realistic. The inversion of the usual wish that the earth lie lightly on the body it covers brings to the piece a discordant, almost burlesque note, one Renaissance writers were often to imitate. On the *Greek Anthology*, see James Hutton, *The Greek Anthology*.

71. This poem, entitled "Catulli imitatio," appears in Book 4 of the *Nugae* (1533). It is quoted here from the 1538 edition entitled *Nugarum libri octo*, 226–27. Another is "De passerculo mortuo Rosae puellae," (1538 edition, bk. 1, 80–81). Yet another Bourbon epitaph is influenced by Clément Marot's "Du Passereau de Maupas" (*Les Epigrammes*, ed. Mayer, 183). Entitled by Bourbon "De passere mortuo Lampadis puellae, ex vulg. Maroti," it explains that love killed the sparrow in annoyance at being unable to soften the hard heart of the bird's mistress (1538 edition, bk. 5, 197, "Carmen lxvii").

The Neo-Latin epitaphs were gathered together several times, as were the satirical eulogies, in the seventeenth century. Janus Dousa the Younger published *Orationes funebres in obitus aliquot animalium* together with his own *In Laudem umbrae declamatio et carmen* (1591). Dousa published other collections of mock encomia (see my "The Satirical Eulogy," Appendix B, 380–86). See chap. 7 for a discussion of the many versions of Lando's and Pontoux's Italian and French epitaphs. Another similar collection, by Franciscus Swertius, was entitled *Epitaphia ioco-seria* (1645). The title page to Dousa's 1591 edition carries two biblical quotations related to the mock-eulogistic genre:

> In multa sapientia, multa est indignatio. Vidi cuncta quae fiunt sub sole, & ecce universa vanitas, & afflictatio spiritus, & infinitus stultorum est numerus.
>
> Moritur doctus similiter ut indoctus.
>
> Et cognovi quod non esset melius nisi laetari, & facere bene in vita sua.

These quotations are ascribed to "Ecclesiastes, cap. 1, 2, and 3." The work reappeared in 1645. The use of the adjective *ioco-serius* in the context of the epitaph clearly links the genre to the satirical eulogy. This collection groups many epitaphs from various countries. The works are presented in the original languages. On p. 224 of the collection begins a section called *Epitaphia animalium*, which includes the Grunnius Corrocotta piece on the pig and some French works such as "De la Barbiche de Madame de Villeroy."

Mock epitaphs were also discussed by Iacobus Pontanus in his *Institutio poetica* of 1604. He says that although it may seem strange to joke and laugh in such situations, it happens regularly. We should imitate Martial, sparing the person but blaming the vices. Those who may be so dealt with are "scortatores, avari, ebriosi, maledici, superbi, decoctores, usurarii, haeresiarchae, proditores" (here cited from the 7th edition [1624], 540).

72. Mary Morrison, "Catullus," 380. Morrison explains that Visagier was in fact combining parody of Catullus 2 and 3 and Catullus 42, a threatening letter to a courtesan who refused to return the poet's correspondence. He demanded the return of the sparrow, stolen by Perinna, and alternated between a kind of blason of the bird and abuse of the girl.

73. J. C. Scaliger, *Poematia*, 316, quoted in Morrison, 380. Typical of the piece are lines such as the following:

> Dulci Turdule docte gutturillo
> Asperas animi levare curas,
> Cantillans modulos minutiores:
> Condite mihi pectoris medullas
> Cantiuncula ut inquietiore
> Oblitus veterum miser malorum
> Mentis improbus acquiescat aestus.
> Da mihi blandula murmurilla mille, . . .
> Dulci Turdule docte gutturillo.

74. Naïs stresses the importance of Pliny for Renaissance ideas about animals: "Il ne faut pas oublier qu'au XVIe siècle toute connaissance zoologique commence par lui. C'est bien souvent à travers lui seulement que les lecteurs moyens ont pu avoir une idée de l'oeuvre d'Aristote" (58).

75. Naïs, 118–39. On Alciati, see below, n. 77.

76. George Boas, *The Happy Beast*, 47–48. Another early zoologist discussed by Boas is Pierre Gilles, whom Pantagruel saw under the sea inspecting the urine of a fish, a joke on the empirical method favored by Gilles (40 n. 82). Although a founder of modern medicine, Gilles was sometimes uncritical of his examples, stressing rather the usefulness of animal behavior as a model for that of men. Medieval attitudes towards animals persist within the new discipline: "It apparently did not occur to these earlier zoologists that their subject was justified if it increased human knowledge" (Boas, 47).

77. On the emblem in general, see G. H. Dexter, *La Perrière*, and Elbert N. S. Thompson, *Literary Bypaths*. *The Latin Emblems*, a handsome new edition of Alciati's emblems, with translations, was completed recently by Peter M. Daly and Virginia W. Callahan. The second volume of this edition, entitled *Emblems in Translation*, is by Peter M. Daly and Simon Cuttler.

78. Boas discusses at some length what he calls "theriophily," admiration for animals and their way of life, He uses the *Apologie de Raymond Sebond* by Montaigne and similar works to demonstrate the usefulness of such attitudes for social satire. On occasion, however, he feels that such paradoxical assertions were little more than literary flourishes.

79. The text of the *Musca* is given in L. B. Alberti, *Opusculi inediti*, ed. Cecil Grayson, 45–62. The work is discussed briefly by Girolamo Mancini, *Vita di Leon Battista Alberti*: "Lo scritto è una parafrasi, o, per dirlo cot vocabolo talvolta ripetuto dall'Alberti, un 'esornazione' dell'*Encomio della Mosca*, col quale Luciano beffò le ciarle dei rètori, e i magnificatori delle inezie, se non che nel commentare i concetti del filosofo greco non mise in dubbio l'immortalità dell'anima" (258). Mancini dates both encomia to about 1443 and states that the *Canis* was influenced by an earlier Greek work. On Alberti in general, see the study by Joan Gadol, *Leon Battista Alberti*.

80. *Musca*, ed. Grayson, 52.

81. *Musca*, ed. Grayson, 62.

82. *Leonis Baptistae Alberti Opera* (1500), 45ʳ. The first edition appeared in Venice in 1472.

83. Two other fifteenth-century Italians may be mentioned here, since extracts from their works are reprinted by Dornavius. They are Angelo Poliziano (1454–1494) and Giovanni Gioviano Pontano (1426–1503). Pontano's poems on the dog, on begging, on the nightingale, and other topics appear in the *Amphitheatrum*, as do Poliziano's pieces on the gnat, the dog, and on dreams.

84. The 1544 edition was that of Calcagnini's *Opera aliquot*. The *Pulicis encomium* is 405–8.

85. *Amphitheatrum*, 1:21. Although most of the names in this list are by now familiar, the large number of contemporary authors included is unusual. Sadoleto's *Laocoon* was generally published with his *Curtius*, as in the edition of 1532, *Curtius, eiusdem Laocoon*. Pandolfo Collenuccio, who translated Plautus and several other authors, was compared to Lucian by Beatus Rhenanus in the preface to the 1511 edition of Collenuccio's *Apologi quatuor*, an edition that contained both the *Bombarda* and the *Misoponus*, the works mentioned by Calcagnini.

86. Little is known about Galissard. La Croix du Maine remarks only that he was "Pierre Galissard, docteur en théologie, de l'Ordre des Frères prêcheurs d'Arles, en Provence." (*Les Bibliothèques françoises*, 2:282). De la Monnoye writes in this volume that Araqueus, as Galissard styled himself, probably means that "il étoit né 'aux Arqs,' marquisat en Provence, près de Draguignan." See also Alfred Cartier, *Bibliographie des éditions des de Tournes*, ed. Marius Audin, 1:294.

87. Galissard, *Pulicis Encomium*, 20. Guarino da Verona (1374–1460), friend of Alberti, also composed a *Muscae Encomium* inspired by Lucian (see Robinson, *Lucian*, 81–83).

88. Galissard, *Pulicis Encomium*, 20.

89. Heldelinus also published a translation of Lucian's *Juppiter Tragoedus*, in 1532.

90. There is a second edition in Basle in 1544, by Oporinus, the same publisher as for Menapius's work on the fever, in 1542. On Curio, (1503–1569), philologist and "littérateur," see Markus Kutter, *Celio Secondo Curione*, 92–97. Kutter explains that the *Aranei Encomion* expressed Curio's reformist religious speculations.

91. *De Formica, liber unus* (1615). On Wilde, see also Boas, 48–50.

92. The full title was *Muscae principatus, hoc est, Muscae, ex continua cum principe comparatione, encomium* (1614).

93. Colie, *Paradoxia epidemica*, viii–ix.

94. The 1587 edition contains a French translation as well as the Latin original. Alberti also wrote on *Nemo* between 1507 and 1509.

95. Colie, *Paradoxia*, 224–26. The most brilliant Neo-Latin work related to the self-denouncer type of satire is the *Epistolae obscurorum virorum* (trans. Francis Griffin Stokes), in which the purported writers of letters attacking the humanists in the Reuchlin controversy betray their pettiness, immorality, and poor Latin. As the "obscure men" labor to write correct letters according to accepted precepts and to help fight their enemy, Hebrew scholar Reuchlin, they give away at every turn their ignorance and clumsiness. On Renaissance letter-writing, see Henderson, 342–43.

The brothers are perfect inside witnesses, as described in chap. 1 above. The pleasure of the game is increased for the reader familiar with Neo-Latin mock encomia because the "writers" refer to Hutten, to Helius Eobanus Hessus, and to Erasmus, whose *Moriae Encomium* they roundly condemn.

CHAPTER FOUR

1. To discuss in detail here the widespread Italian influence on France at this time would be superfluous, but for lists of Italians in France, French in Italy, and descriptions of relevant works and translations, the following are helpful: Joseph Blanc, *Bibliographie italico-francaise universelle*; N. N. Condeescu, "Le Paradoxe bernesque"; Francesco Flamini, "Le lettere italiane in Francia alla corte di Francesco I" and "Le lettere italiane in Francia nei secoli del Rinascimento"; Henri Gambier, *Italie et Renaissance poétique*; Henri Hauvette, *Un Exilé florentin . . . Luigi Alamanni*; Manacorda; Carlo Pellegrini, "Relazioni," a study that has an extensive bibliography; Auguste Emile Picot, *Les Français italianisants* and *Les Italiens en France au XVIe siècle*; Edmé-Jacques-Benoît Rathéry, *Influence de l'Italie*; and Trtnik-Rossettini, *Les Influences*. See also J. Vianey, *Mathurin Regnier*.

2. See Trtnik-Rossettini, 34–35:

Berni n'avait pas seulement l'intention de faire rire le public. Il avait un but satirique: railler la poésie pétrarquiste. Les imitateurs de Pétrarque, avec leurs éloges outrés des beautés de leurs dames et de tous les objets qui les entouraient, leurs comparaisons ridicules, faisaient rire même les contemporains. A ces éloges et à d'autres célébrant avec autant d'exagération les grands seigneurs, Berni opposa ses éloges bizarres où l'on peut voir les premiers germes d'une critique du pétrarquisme dont on ne saurait dire si elle était tout à fait consciente.

3. Burchiello's sonnets were edited by Grazzini (Il Lasca) in 1552, as *I Sonetti del Burchiello et di messer Antonio Alamanni*. Alamanni was the Florentine exile studied by Hauvette (see above, n. 1). He may thus have helped bring knowledge of Burchiello to France.

4. See the Grazzini edition described below, n. 13, 5ᵛ–6ʳ, for a poem in Latin that begins "Quem queritis."

5. Trtnik-Rossettini, 34, makes clear Berni's debt to Burchiello. The poet was ready to acknowledge the influence, as in the sonnet beginning "S'i avessi l'ingegno del Burchiello," in Berni, *Rime*, ed. Giorgio Bàrberi Squarotti, 157. Except when otherwise indicated, quotations from Berni will be taken from this edition, with page numbers given in the text. In the "Dialogo contra i poeti," Berni mentions Lucian by name as having made fun of the gods (*Opere*, ed. Eugenio Camerini, 39).

6. Condeescu, 31.

7. Du Bellay, *Divers Jeux rustiques*, ed. Verdun L. Saulnier, xxxvi. On Berni, see also R. B. Ogle, "The Bernesque Satire," and Anne Reynolds, "Francesco Berni." Reynolds stresses the paradoxical nature of Berni's works.

8. Paolo Cherchi, "L'Encomio paradossale nel manierismo," 374.

9. Cherchi, 373.

10. Grazzini, a poet as well as the editor both of Burchiello and Berni (see above, n. 3), composed classically influenced works both for and against topics, such as thought, or individuals, such as Cicero (in 1534). In addition, he produced a number of traditional mock encomia having no opposing counterparts. On the author, see Grazzini, *Le Rime burlesche*, ed. Carlo Verzone, ix–cxvii, and Robert J. Rodini, *Antonfrancesco Grazzini*.

11. See *Le Rime*, 564–66. In this edition the poem in entitled simply "A M. Baccio Davanzati," but in the edition of Grazzini by Raffaello Fornaciari, *Scritti scelti*, 215–17, the poem has the more descriptive title. The Berni is on pp. 37–45 of the Bàrberi-Squarotti edition.

12. For lists of the contents of several of these editions, see my thesis, "The Satirical Eulogy," 152–53 and 386–92.

13. The collection of capitoli edited by Grazzini in two volumes in 1552 and 1555 was rather complete. The first edition of Berni, in 1538, did not contain all his works. Bàrberi Squarotti uses the 1934 E. Chiòrboli text (based on the 1537 and 1538 Navo editions published in Venice). When quoting Bernesque writers other than Berni and Grazzini, I shall use the 1552 and 1555 Grazzini edition (*Il primo libro* and *Il secondo libro*), giving the volume indication 1 or 2 and page numbers in the text. Condeescu notes that the popular 1542 edition *Tutte le opere* could be found in many Renaissance libraries (31). Mauro's poem is here quoted from 1:101^r.

14. Most of the French poems on foodstuffs were considerably later, for instance those by Saint-Amant on "Le Melon" and "Le Fromage." On Saint-Amant, see Richard A. Mazzara, "Saint-Amant and the Italian Bernesque Poets," and the edition of *Oeuvres poétiques* by Léon Vérane. See also Ronsard's "La Salade" (in *Oeuvres complètes*, ed. Paul Laumonier, 15:76–84). This edition will be used in citing works by Ronsard). The poem was part of the *Sixiesme Livre des Poèmes* of 1569. See also "L'Hymne du Formage," by Annibal de l'Ortigue, in his *Poèmes divers* (1617), 176–84.

15. Manacorda, 740–41, stresses that in comparison to several other contemporary works, Mauro's criticisms here are good-natured and mild, unlike the harsh attacks by Folengo, Cingar, Poggio and others. He also notes that Benedetto Varchi attacked begging bags in a mocking capitolo, "In lode delle Tasche," (1:87^v–89^v). Attacks on articles of clothing seen as epitomizing a reprehensible way of life reappeared with Regnier, Motin, and Sygognes in France, where they were used to present anticourtier satires. For Erasmus's feelings on monks, see Miller, 98–101. Robinson, *Lucian*, 80, discusses the virulent Byzantine attacks on monks, typified by *Mazaris' Stay in Hell*.

16. Vianey, *Mathurin Regnier*, 54–55. Pages 50–62 are a general discussion of the Bernesque poems.

17. See Miller, 68 and 70-71.

18. Mauro refers to Berni's poems on plague and Homer's *Batrachomyomachia*.

19. As was noted in chap. 3, Cardano observed the same improvements in connection with gout.

20. The Marot poem is also related to attacks on honor, discussed below in chap. 5. The rondeau appeared in 1538 in *Les Oeuvres* (see Marot, *Oeuvres diverses*, ed. Mayer, 129).

21. See also P. M. Smith, *The Anti-Courtier Trend*, 144.

22. 1:118v. In the third "coq à l'âne," Marot was to repeat the idea of the folly of death on the battlefield. See also below, chap. 5, n. 99.

23. 146. For the French encomia on debt, in particular that by Rabelais, see the discussion in chap. 5 below.

24. See Grazzini, *Le Rime*, capitolo 1, "Le Stampe," ix–lv. Since the sixteenth-century encomia on madness customarily listed so many human vices and failings among the features of folly they wished to eulogize, the encomia on madness will be discussed with the vice rather than the disease eulogies.

25. Grazzini, *Le Rime*, 560. As Thomas F. Crane shows, in his *Italian Social Customs*, 150, poems upholding paradoxes would have been very popular at this time. Indeed, many of the then current society games and debates recall topics explored in satirical eulogies. In Innocenzio Ringhieri's *Cento Giuochi liberali et d'ingegno* (1551), "Giuocho della Pazzia," one question put to the players is "S'egli è meglio nelle cose del mondo l'esser savio, ò stolto" (116ʳ). Other games with familiar titles are the "Giuoco del Savio," the "Giuoco dell'Invidia," the "Giuoco della Gelosia," and the "Giuoco de Nasi." Admiration for playful argumentation as a social game reappears in the *Cortegiano*, discussed below.

26. Grazzini, *Le Rime*, 562.

27. Grazzini, *Le Rime*, 563.

28. "In Lode del caldo del letto," 1:69ʳ–71ʳ and Mauro, "In lode del letto," 1:149ᵛ–52ᵛ.

29. In prose, however, we can see distinctly Lucianic features in the *Dialogues* of Aretino (1496–1556), discussed below. As Manacorda points out in a side-by-side comparison, these discussions are influenced by Lucian's *Dialogues of the Courtesans* (750). Another work that at first sight might seem to belong in the present study is Giulio Landi's *Lode dell'Ignoranza*.

30. Thus Sir Raymond Henry Payne Crawfurd writes that Berni "must surely stand alone among writers as one who would hug the pestilence to him as a friend" (155). Most Renaissance works on the plague were medical and moralizing. See Thomas E. Keys, "The Plague in Literature." The famous physician Ambroise Paré composed a *Traicté de la Peste* (1568). The piece was reissued in his *Les Oeuvres* (1628). His attitude is typical of his age: "Peste est une maladie venant de l'ire de Dieu, furieuse, tempestative, hastive, monstrueuse, & espouvantable, contagieuse, terrible, appellee de Galien beste sauvage, farouche & fort cruelle, ennemie mortelle de la vie des hommes, & de plusieurs bestes, plantes, & arbres" (816). This string of adjectives is reminiscent of Lucian's epithets for his gouty goddess. Paré takes the attitude that one can try to avoid the plague or attempt a cure, but that if these two tactics fail, as they probably will, one must simply accept the will of God. In Italy, Michele Mercati published the *Instruttione sopra la peste* (1576) and Guillaume Bunel, earlier in the period, produced a poem about the plague, "Oeuvre excellente et à chascun desirant soi de peste preserver" (1514). This poem, sixteen pages of decasyllabic lines, contains neither mockery nor praise. An epidemic in 1506 had killed three thousand people in the Toulouse area. Bunel, a doctor, offers advice in the wake of this disaster. First sufferers should seek out a good Catholic doctor. Next, sexual continence is advised, although marital sex is permitted after midnight

when the digestive processes are complete. Avoid drains, be hygienic, burn pleasant-smelling woods, and, if possible, flee:

> Le remede preservatif,
> C'est s'en aller en grant espace
> Et estre bien tost fugitif,
> Et tard retourner quoi qu'on face.

We must be submissive to God, accepting the trial He has chosen to send. (Quotations here are taken from the fascinating anthology of works by medical men compiled by Pascal Pia, *Le Bouquet poétique*, 26.) Jacques Peletier du Mans also composed a work *De peste compendium* ([1560?]). The startling originality of Berni's approach becomes yet more evident. On the Bernesque disease encomia, see my " 'Let Us Laugh Our Pains Away.' " The discussion of Berni's and Francesi's disease capitoli is adapted from this article.

31. "Capitolo in lode delle gotte," 2:47^r–49^v.

32. A further example of the Renaissance ability to work in various literary domains is Andrés Laguna's publishing in Latin of his own medical work, *De articulari morbo commentarius*, and Lucian's *Podagra* (1551). The work by Laguna was later translated into Italian by G. M. Scotto as *Il Rimedio delle podagre* (1552). Even in this serious work on gout, we find humor, as the writer claims that a gouty Franciscan found relief by swimming in "mosto" (must). After bathing in this brew, and "forse ancora orinato," he gave it "alli poveri suoi fratelli" (*Il Rimedio*, 15). The chief recommendations are moderation in sexual activity and caution in all things. When in doubt, Renaissance doctors seem to have recommended sexual abstinence for everything from the plague to the gout.

33. "Capitolo della tossa," 2:53^v–55^r.

34. Agnolo Firenzuola, another Bernesque poet, composed a capitolo on thirst, which can be seen as a physical affliction, but not a disease (1:213^v–16^r). Aretino composed a poem on the quartan fever, "Capitolo della quartana," *Il secondo libro*, 119^v–22^v.

35. 2:159^v–64^r. On Bronzino, see the edition of the *Opere* by Andrea Emiliani, 169^v–76^r.

36. 2:ii^v–iii^r.

37. For a fuller study of Berni's imitators, Molza, Mauro, Tansillo, and others, see Andrea Sorrentino, *Francesco Berni*, especially chap. 10. Carmelo Previtera, *La Poesia giocosa*, sternly dismisses the entire Bernesque tendency in Italian poetry. Condemning its triviality, banality, and vulgarity, he continues that "ci domandiamo con meraviglia come mai un soci forte sequela di scempiaggini abbia potuto recare diletto e suscitare un cosí forte interesse" (335). The present chapter attempts to answer Previtera's question.

38. *Il Libro del Cortegiano*, ed. Giulio Preti, 2.17.134, mentions the mock encomia. On the publication of the work, see V. L. Bourrilly, *Jacques Colin*, 1:51.

39. *Le Satire alla Berniesca* (1549). On Symeoni (or Simeoni), see A. Renucci, *Un Aventurier des lettres*.

40. See Trtnik-Rossettini, 10–13 and *passim*, and cf. P. M. Smith, *The Anti-Courtier Trend*, 13–21.

41. The relevant lines from Symeoni run as follows:

Chi dice ch'el gentil compor berniesco
Non è il piú bel che si leggesse mai
Sta dell'ingegno & del giuditio fresco
(a.iv^r)
Per che lasciando a parte imperii & Regni
Hanno fatto immortai fino all'anguille,
L'ago, il forno, le pesche, i vetri, e i legni.
(b^r)

The authorship of the titles mentioned is as follows: Berni ("l'anguillo," "l'ago," and "le pesche"), Della Casa ("il forno"), Firenzuola ("Del legno"), and, perhaps, Grazzini ("i vetri"). If Symeoni is indeed thinking of Grazzini in referring to "i vetri," the passage would provide further proof that Grazzini's capitoli were known well before their publication.

42. *La Pazzia* was written some time after 1530 (see the *Dizionario biografico degli Italiani*, 1:623). There were editions in 1541 and 1543 and another in about 1550 (n.d.) The French translation, *Les Louanges de la folie*, by Jean du Thier, (cited here from the Lyons, 1567 edition), is discussed in chap. 5 below. An earlier French edition appeared in Paris in 1566. Brunet (*Manuel*) mentions another Paris edition of 1566. Paul F. Grendler, *Critics*, Appendix 5, 253–54, lists editions of the work and discusses its themes. Benedetto Croce studied the relationship between the *Moriae Encomium* and *La Pazzia* in his article "Sulle Traduzioni e Imitazioni Italiane." He notes the popularity of Erasmus's praise of folly in Italy, in particular the Aldine edition (1515) and the 1518 Giunti one in Florence. As an example of Italian appreciation of the work, he quotes from Paolo Giovio, writing in Italian in 1558. The *Moriae Encomium* is said by Giovio to have been the work that spread Erasmus's fame worldwide, and to be an imitation of the "pungenti satire" of Lucian (412). However, he feels the work is unworthy of a man of the church, because the author seems to be making fun of the "cose di Dio" (Croce, 413). Croce also notes the influence of Erasmus on Tommaso Garzoni (1549?–1589), the eccentric and precocious author of *La Piazza universale*, which appeared first in 1587. A modern edition of Garzoni's *Opere* was published by Paolo Cherchi. I use here the version found in the *Opere de Tomaso Garzoni da Bagnacavallo* (1617). The work, over four hundred pages long, is divided into sections, each headed with the name of a different profession or type, on the lines of the *Narrenschiff*. In his preface, Garzoni refers to Apuleius, Plutarch, Lucian, Pythagoras, Diocles, Virgil, Homer, and Il Vida ("scaccheida"), and concludes that he indeed has the right to praise folly: "ben potrò io formare una Piazza di gente nobile" (10^v). Croce, not an admirer of the piece, calls it a "mediocrissima rifrittura del libro di Erasmo in languida e scolorita prosa" (414). The *Moriae Encomium* was translated into Italian by 1545. Another interesting Italian work on folly was the *Mondi celesti* of Antonfrancesco Doni (see below, n. 51). Among the various fictive worlds is a realm called the "Mondo de Pazzi," in which Momus is mentioned by name and the tone is clearly Lucianic. The full title of the overall work in the Gabriel Giolito edition (Venice, 1562) is as follows: "Mondi Celesti, Terrestri, et Infernali, de gli Academici Pellegrini; Mondo Piccolo, Grande, Misto, Risibile, Imaginato, de Pazzi, & Massimo, Inferno, de gli Scolari, de Mal-

maritati, delle Puttane, & Ruffiani, Soldati, & Capitani poltroni, Dottor cattivi, Legisti, Artisti, de gli Usurai, de Poeti & Compositori ignoranti."

43. *Les Louanges de la folie* (1567), 2ᵛ. For a detailed comparison of the two works, showing that the author of *La Pazzia* must have been working from the Latin, see my thesis, "The Satirical Eulogy," 192–207. The antifeminist satire in both the original and the translation is strikingly vehement and extensive. There is, for example, a long attack on women who seek to be "sçavantes" (the term appears in the French text, 9ᵛ). Another Italian work on folly to be translated into French was Antonio Maria Spelta's *La Saggia Pazzia* (1607). This became *La Sage-folie* in French (translations by L. Garon and Jean Marcel appeared in 1628, 1649, and 1650 [Marcel] and 1635 [Garon]), and *Sapiens stultitia* in German (1615). Divided into chapters, each concerning a different type of madman, the work closely resembles the *Moriae Encomium*. The idea of wise folly (already mentioned by Erasmus) seems to have been common in the early seventeenth century. Gaspar Ens composed a Μωροσοφια : *id est Stulta sapientia* (1620), a distant descendant of Erasmus's great work, but influenced more recently by Spelta. The Ens edition also contains Grunnius Corrocotta's last will of the pig, referred to by Erasmus and others.

44. One more link between Berni and a major French satirist may be seen in Du Bellay's translation of Berni's ironic "Chiome d'argento," as "O beaux cheveux d'argent," sonnet 91, *Regrets*, in *Oeuvres poétiques*, ed. Chamard, 2:122.

45. On Lando, see Grendler, 222–39, a list of Lando's printed works. See also Ireneo Sanesi, *Il cinquecentista Ortensio Lando*.

46. The first edition was entitled *Paradossi, cioè, sententie fuori del comun parere* (1543). The first French edition was *Paradoxes, ce sont propos contre la commune opinion*: debatus, en forme de Declamations forenses: pour exerciter les jeunes advocats, en causes difficiles (1553). This stress on the usefulness of paradoxes for legal training goes directly back to antiquity.

47. The two paradoxes omitted by Estienne were nos. 27 and 29 in the Lyons edition, "Che l'opere del Bocaccio (*sic*) non sieno degne d'esser lette, ispetialmente le dieci giornate," and "Che Aristotele fusse non solo un'ignorante, ma anche lo piú malvagio huomo di quella età." The fascination of such works lies in part in what their omissions tell us about contemporary preferences and tastes.

48. Brunet, *Manuel* and *Supplément*, lists a number of French editions from 1553 to 1651. The Latin edition is interesting. In the volume *I. Dousae filii caelestium liber primus*, ed. G. Canterus, appear *Orationes funebres in obitus aliquot animalium* (1591). Closer inspection proves that the *Orationes* are dated 1590, not 1591, and are in fact a double translation, derived from Claude Pontoux's French translations of the Italian works, *Harangues lamentables* (1570). The complexities of Renaissance borrowings are endless (on Pontoux, see below, chap. 7). In 1616, Daniel Heinsius was to select only a few of the sermoni for inclusion in an edition of some of his own mock eulogies such as the *Laus pediculi*, and some serious pieces. Heinsius's *Laus pediculi* was translated into English by James Guitard in 1634 as the *Laus pediculi; or, an Apologeticall Speech*. Its playful intent is indicated by its dedication to "the Worshipful Masters and Wardens of Beggars Hall."

49. *Sermoni funebri de vari authori nella morte de diversi animali* (1548), 11ᵛ. Page numbers for subsequent quotations from this edition will be given in the text.

50. Lando's list of predecessors is the longest of any yet mentioned in this study. Another Italian author, Celio Calcagnini, mentions thirty-five writers. Lando's list seems to have daunted all translators, for it appears in none of the foreign editions. Entitled "Apologia di M. Ortensio Lando ditto il Tranquillo per l'Authore," it explains that although many will condemn the author for not attending to more serious matters, such as medicine, art, or theology, in so doing they attack also his lofty predecessors. Among those listed, with details of what they praised, are Synesius, Dio Chrysostom, Homer, Virgil, Polycrates, Isocrates, Glauco, Favorinus, Lucian (for the *Muscae Encomium* and the *De Parasito*), Seneca, Plutarch, Apuleius, Themiso, Hippocrates, Democritus, Diocles, Cato, Pythagoras, Musaeus, and Asclepiades (34ʳ–35ʳ). Many of the works listed concern plants. Lando adds that the present author (himself) deserves praise because he has elevated these "humili creature" (36ʳ) and shown both erudition and knowledge of nature's secrets. He defends himself angrily against those he calls "mordaci sicophanti."

Giovanni Battista Pino published around 1535 a *Ragionamento sopra dell'asino*, notes Grendler, who adds that Lando wrote a mock funeral oration on the death of an ass and that Adriano Banchieri (c. 1567–1654) composed a work citing Doni called *La Nobiltà dell'asino* (1592) (78).

51. *L'Asinesca gloria dell' Inasinato academia pellegrino* (1553). Doni translated More's *Utopia* into Italian in 1548. On Doni, see *Opere di Pietro Aretino e di Anton Francesco Doni*, ed. Carlo Cordie, 2:582–96. In the Grazzini edition of the Bernesque poets there is a capitolo by M.B. on the ass, "Capitolo in lode dell'Asino," which refers as follows to Berni and other predecessors in the genre:

> Queste son cose degne & immortali,
> Et non cosaccie, che certi han lodato
> La Peste, il mal Francese, & gl'orinali.
>
> . . . .
>
> Che s'un'Asin volevano lodare,
> Sarebbe ogn'un di loro immortalato
> (2:174ʳ)

As did other writers of the period, this poet praises the donkey's patient, hard-working nature, its pleasant coloring, reminiscent of a monk's habit, and ability to speak, unique among animals, demonstrated in the story of Balaam's ass.

52. Grendler, 61.

53. Grendler, 158, reminds us not to confuse Landi with Lando, as some critics and cataloguers have done.

54. My quotations will be taken from the translation by Raymond Rosenthal, *Aretino's "Dialogues."* Page numbers for subsequent quotations will be given in the text. On Aretino, see also the introduction by Francesco Flora to his edition of the works, *Tutte le opere*. Francesco Coppetta also wrote for and against "La Sodomia" (see Abd-el Kader Salza, *F. Coppetta dei Beccuti*, 75, a discussion of Coppetta's defense of his love for "Alessi," a young man). These poems were dated around 1548. It would seem that the pro and con stances in the two pieces were related to the poet's need to protect himself from criticism of his homosexual relationship. Using the familiar claim of earlier paradoxists, he could assert that his two pieces were merely traditional rhetorical exercises, not to be taken seriously. Robinson, *Lucian*,

65, discusses the likely influence of Lucian on Alciphron's *Letters of the Courtesans*. It is worth recalling that Agrippa's *De incertitudine* also had a section on the art of the procuress.

CHAPTER FIVE

1. On these medieval forms, see Maximilian Manitius.

2. H. K. Miller, 151.

3. Grover Cronin, 195.

4. Synesius and Erasmus are but two of the major mock encomiasts to have been directly or indirectly connected with the church.

5. On this and other types of paradoxy, see Lehmann, who discusses medieval parodies of religious liturgy, erotic parodies on grammatical treatises, and student drinking songs. See above, chap. 3, n. 12, and Robinson, *Lucian*, 76–77.

6. H. K. Miller, 151.

7. Alison Saunders, *The Sixteenth-Century Blason Poétique*. See also D. B. Wilson, *Descriptive Poetry in France*. For lists of other studies, see Annette Tomarken and Edward Tomarken, "The Rise and Fall," 160–61; Alison Saunders, "Sixteenth-Century Collected Editions," 153–68; Paul L. Jacob, "Les Blasons anatomiques"; and Robert E. Pike, "The 'Blasons,' " 223–42. One of the most detailed discussions of the blason from the linguistic point of view is that by Enzo Giudici, *Le Opere minori di Maurice Scève*, 65–83. Giudici also discusses the related verb *blasonner*, which, like *blason*, could have a positive or a negative meaning.

8. Thomas Sebillet, *Art poétique françoys*, (originally Paris: Abel l'Angelier, 1548), ed. Félix Gaiffe, 169–70.

9. Giudici, 69 n. 9, and *Oeuvres de Coquillart*, ed. Charles d'Héricault, 2:147.

10. Saulnier, *Maurice Scève*, 1:76. See also my thesis, "The Satirical Eulogy," 216–22. Scholars and editors frequently neglect the Lucianic, ironic type of blason. Thus Dominique Martin Méon, a nineteenth-century collector of blasons, wrote of the genre: "Le mot BLASON est employé dans le même temps en deux sens opposés, blâme et éloge" (*Blasons*, "Avertissement"). The present chapter will seek to show how our understanding of the sixteenth-century blason is enriched by an awareness of irony and indirectness of presentation. On the "Platellet" and the "Gobellet," see Saunders, *The Sixteenth-Century Blason Poétique*, 231–33.

11. For a study of the earliest editions of the *Blasons anatomiques* containing the contre-blasons, see Saunders, "Sixteenth Century Collected Editions," 351–68.

12. *Blasons, de la Goutte, de Honneur, et de la Quarte* (1547). See also my essay, "The Lucianic Blason."

13. Trtnik-Rossettini, 168–74 and 181–93. Since the three Lyons blasons are so closely related to the Italian capitoli, they provide a perfect illustration of the claim made above, that some capitoli are called *blasons* in French. As Trtnik-Rossettini puts it in discussing the Bernesque poets: "Ainsi les éloges grotesques des poètes italiens devaient rappeler aux Français les 'blasons' de leur tradition littéraire dont la vogue continuait encore au XVIe siècle, et qu'on préférait peut-être aux paradoxes bernesques si difficiles à imiter"(165).

14. P. M. Smith, *The Anti-Courtier Trend*, especially part 1, "Sources and Mod-

els"; Mayer, "Lucien et la Renaissance," 5–22; Mayer, *Lucien*, 53–55, 105–9, and 215–17; and Robinson, "The Reputation of Lucian," 385–97. P. M. Smith (32) shows that the *Rhetorum Praeceptor* also influenced Francesco Sansovino's second satire, in *Sette libri di satire* (1560), 169ᵛ–75ᵛ.

15. See P. M. Smith, *The Anti-Courtier Trend*, 60. Page numbers for subsequent quotations from this book will be given in the text in this chapter.

16. Pierre Michault, *Le Doctrinal du temps présent*, ed. Thomas Walton, xlvii.

17. *Dialogue de Placebo pour un homme seul*, in *Recueil de farces*, ed. Leroux de Lincy and Francisque Michel, vol. 1, no. 13, 11–15. The word *blason* is here used in a negative sense, in the lines "Placebo fait les gens cornuz / Par son salacieux blason."

18. *La Farce nouvelle de folle Bobance* (ca. 1500), in *Recueil général des Sotties*, vol. 1, no. 9, 256, and cf. P. M. Smith, *The Anti-Courtier Trend*, 83. "Bobance" is related by Cotgrave to excessive spending, luxurious living, and pride (Randle Cotgrave, *A Dictionarie*, reproduced from the first edition [1611], under "bobance").

19. *L'Amie de Court* (1542). All quotations are taken from the 1547 edition contained in the *Opuscules d'Amour* by Héroët, La Borderie, and others (in which the title is spelled "L'Amye"). Page numbers for subsequent quotations will be given in the text. The work is discussed by Mayer, *Lucien*, 201–5. The 1547 edition was reissued by Michael Screech in 1970 from the British Library copy. In his edition of Antoine Héroët, *Oeuvres poétiques*, Ferdinand Gohin feels that this 1547 edition was "imprimé avec grand soin" (lix). On the "Querelle des Amyes," see Screech, "An Interpretation of the Querelle des Amyes."

20. Gohin notes that La Borderie seems to be attacking works other than the *Cortegiano*, but in fact borrows many details of court ladies' behavior from Castiglione. These borrowed elements, however, are ironically condemned even as they are seemingly justified. As the critic puts it, "L'exagération des traits et l'effronterie des aveux semblent toujours faire tourner l'apologie en satire" (xxv–xxvi). The tentativeness of Gohin's formulation here suggests that he does not fully appreciate the irony of "L'Amye." Similarly hesitant is Abel Lefranc, who dismisses the poem as "un commentaire en vers, assez maladroit, de cette partie du *Courtisan* qui préoccupait tant l'opinion" (Rabelais, *Tiers Livre*, ed. Abel Lefranc, xlviii). Subsequent quotations from the *Tiers Livre* will be taken from this edition, with page numbers after the citation. The love aspect of the *Cortegiano* may have been the first to be attacked in France because some of those chapters of the book circulated in manuscript form before the work as a whole was published.

21. Once again, Lyons was the place of publication for a major satire. The *Menosprecio de Corte* was published there by Etienne Dolet. On the prepublication circulation of the manuscript of the *Cortegiano* in France, see P. M. Smith, *The Anti-Courtier Trend*, 124.

22. This quotation is taken from Thomas Hoby's translation, *The Book of the Courtier* (1561), here quoted from the edition by Walter Raleigh, 285. See also 286–87 of the same edition.

23. Given L'Amye's materialism, willingness to sell herself for money, and blind admiration for the court, we may see her as the ultimate embodiment of an older French satirical image of the court as a prostitute. This image is vividly formulated

in *Le Curial*, the title of works by Pierre Gringore and Alain Chartier discussed by P. M. Smith, *The Anti-Courtier Trend*, 7. Smith also discusses La Borderie's poem (125–34).

24. *Opuscules*, 200. Richard L. Hawkins, in his *Maistre Charles Fontaine Parisien*, agrees that "L'Amye de Court" is indeed a satire, even though Fontaine was unaware of this fact. That the poem was often published together with Guevara's attack on court life suggests that most contemporaries read the French work in this way. Such grouping is not conclusive evidence, however, for, as with the *Opuscules d'Amour* collection, serious and ironic works could be published together if their themes were similar. Tone was not always the determining factor. See Colie, *The Resources of Kind*, especially chap. 3, "Inclusionism."

25. For other confused interpretations, see below, n. 28.

26. See Mayer, " 'L'Honnête Homme' "; "Satire in French Literature," 61–107 and 410–15; and *Lucien*, 207–16; and also P. M. Smith, *The Anti-Courtier Trend*, 138–47. The work was first published in 1547 by the indefatigable Jean de Tournes, who seems to have been fascinated by the satirical eulogy. Subsequent quotations will be from this edition, with page numbers given in the text. It was republished in 1549 (see Mayer, " 'L'Honnête Homme,' " 197 nn. 7, 15), and translated into English in 1575 by George North, as *The Philosopher of the Court*. See also my article, "Philibert de Vienne." Another recent study, from the comparative point of view, is that by Daniel Javitch, "*The Philosopher of the Court*." Javitch studies the differences between the French original and the English translation of the *Philosophe de Court*.

27. See Mayer, "Lucien et la Renaissance," 10, and Manacorda, 733–37.

28. Alfred Cartier, "Louise Labé," 329–30. P. M. Smith notes that Toldo and Saulnier suggest that Philibert de Vienne intended a serious imitation of Castiglione (*The Anti-Courtier Trend*, 138 n. 2). The present analysis, like that of Smith, seeks to demonstrate that such is not the case. Toldo's remarks appear in his "Le Courtisan dans la littérature française." Saulnier's comments are found in his *Maurice Scève*, 1:322–24 and 377, and 2:139–41 and 167.

29. Saulnier, *Maurice Scève*, 1:324. Giudici, 27 n. 17. See below, n. 94, for Scève's translation of the *Paradossi*.

30. The use of the "court / court" rhyme for a very similar purpose occurs in sonnet 144 of Du Bellay's *Regrets*, (in *Oeuvres poétiques*, ed. Chamard, 2:168):

> Gordes, je sçaurois bien faire un conte à la table,
> Et s'il estoit besoing, contrefaire le sourd:
> J'en sçaurois bien donner, & faire à quelque lourd
> Le vray resembler faulx & le faulx veritable.
>
> Je me sçaurois bien rendre à chascun accointable,
> Et façonner mes moeurs aux moeurs du temps qui court:
> Je sçaurois bien prester (comme on dit à la Court)
> Aupres d'un grand seigneur quelque oeuvre charitable.

The tone of this poem recalls that of the satirical eulogy. Similarly, in the "Poëte Courtisan," Du Bellay writes (*Oeuvres poétiques*, ed. Chamard, 6:131): "Toy donc' qui as choisi le chemin le plus court / Pour estre mis au ranc des sçavants de la court," lines that recall the final rebuke in the *Rhetorum Praeceptor*: "You took the road that was easy and downhill" (4:171). Since, therefore, it seems likely that Scève in this sonnet was demonstrating his understanding of Philibert de Vienne's ironic purpose, we should reconsider Saulnier's interpretation of the sonnet as preaching "une morale de l'accommodement social" (*Maurice Scève*, 1:323) and temper Giudici's disappointment with the piece (26).

31. Mayer, " 'L'Honnête Homme,' " 199.

32. For this type of exaggerated mock rejection of normal attitudes, cf. Mauro on those who object to lying: "Quel che non è buggiardo è un huom da poco, / un ignorante, una persona vile, / Da men d'un mulatier, da men d'un cuoco," discussed in chap. 4 above.

33. P. M. Smith, *The Anti-Courtier Trend*, 144, shows how sharply Philibert de Vienne here attacks what he viewed as Castiglione's dilettantish attitude to the acquisition of fashionable skills. On Philibert as a precursor of the "juste milieu" notion that formed the basis of seventeenth-century "honnêteté," see Mayer, " 'L'Honnête Homme,' " 214–16, and Du Bellay's "Poëte Courtisan," discussed below.

34. See P. M. Smith, *The Anti-Courtier Trend*, 145.

35. See Mayer, "The Genesis of a Rabelaisian Character," 219–29.

36. See Trtnik-Rossettini, 185. Despite this reticence with regard to the duel, a number of French satirists did attack honor in general. Two modern studies of the "point d'honneur" are Ellery Schalk, *From Valor to Pedigree*, and François Billacois, *Le Duel*. Some of the Renaissance works criticizing honor are studied below.

37. Mayer, *Lucien*, 214.

38. The French version of Antonio Fregoso's *Le Ris de Democrite* also appeared in 1547, that vintage year for satire. The accompanying *Le Pleur de Heraclite* also describes a voyage, but presents it as an elegiac lament. The misfortunes of man are stressed, and the conclusion is that all is vain save virtue.

39. Javitch, 124. A later work that may owe something to Philibert de Vienne is Louis le Caron's *Dialogues* (1556). Here, the chief attack on Castiglione is contained in the dialogue "De la vraie Sagesse, & des Louanges de la Philosophie," a discussion between a courtier and an author. "Vraie Sagesse" proves to be a satirical personification of the doctrine of "honnêteté." Since the court is the seat of all virtue, other ideals are to be condemned, and one must adapt to the opinions of the "multitude." However, le Caron is so anxious to make plain his disapproval of this doctrine that the technique of mock praise is replaced by a generalized sarcasm.

40. Du Bellay, *Oeuvres poétiques*, ed. Chamard, 6:113. Turnèbe's poem appeared anonymously in Paris (1559), dedicated to Leoquernus (i.e., Léger Du Chesne, the author's friend, also a poet). Du Bellay's rendition appeared ostensibly in Poitiers but probably in fact in Paris in 1559. Page numbers from the Chamard edition will follow quotations from the poem in the text. Turnèbe's appreciation for the nuances of irony is attested to in his comment on Quintilian, whom he edited (*Commentarii*, 1556, 8:112ᵛ): "Significat ironiam multis modis fieri, ut per sarcasmum, asteismum, antiphrasim; tamen quod attinet ad personam, ironiam positam esse in laudis simulatione aut vituperationis: quanquam id in rebus etiam intelligi potest." The idea of simulating praise applies perfectly to Turnèbe's attack on the would-be writer.

41. Charles Fontaine, Pierre de Paschal, and Melin de Sainct-Gelays have all been suggested as contenders for the dubious honor of being the target of this satire. See my thesis, "The Satirical Eulogy," 241 n. 1. To the discussions by Clément, Hawkins, and Vianey described there may be added R. V. Merrill, "Lucian and Du Bellay's *Poëte Courtisan*." Merrill explains that since Erasmus and More did not translate the *Rhetorum Praeceptor*, the work retained a certain novelty for Frenchmen. Both P. M. Smith (*The Anti-Courtier Trend*, 116) and Merrill believe that Du Bellay knew the Lucianic work from another source than Turnèbe. Only in this way can they account for Du Bellay's extra borrowings from the classical text. On Paschal, see also Pierre de Nolhac, *Ronsard et l'humanisme*, 324–29.

42. P. M. Smith (*The Anti-Courtier Trend*, 122 and 202) charts the gradual focusing of French anticourt satire on Italy during this period. Traditional criticism of court flatterers, found since the late Middle Ages, now takes on a distinct anti-Italian bias. Flattery is seen as a specifically Italian art, part of a larger system of dubious morality. Other court vices such as atheism, libertinism, and homosexuality also came to be viewed as of Italian origin.

43. See Du Bellay, *Oeuvres poétiques*, ed. Chamard, 6:131 n. 2, and P. M. Smith, *The Anti-Courtier Trend*, 93 and 111, for criticism of French courtiers' philistinism and ignorance by Olivier de Magny and Estienne Jodelle. Certain of these characteristics seem to have been selected by Lucian as typical signs of the parvenu (Robinson, *Lucian*, 18–19).

44. The "Poëte Courtisan" must soon have been seen as a major work, for Gilles Corrozet include it in his *Le Parnasse des poètes françois modernes* (1571). Since Corrozet died in 1568, compilation of the collection must have taken place within ten years of the appearance of the satire (Du Bellay died in 1560).

45. See Manacorda, 737. The ironic tone of Ronsard's poem resembles that of the anonymous *Doctrine des servants en court* (n.d.) (reprinted in Montaiglon, ed., *Recueil de poésies françoises*, 4:32–35).

46. Jean de la Jessée, *Les Premières Oeuvres Françoyses* (1583), 2:1427–1441. Page numbers for subsequent quotations will be given in the text. Cf. P. M. Smith, *The Anti-Courtier Trend*, 19–20. On the same theme, La Jessée's "L'Ingratitude," not a mock encomium, in *Le Premier Livre des discours poétiques*, bemoans his poverty and begs his prince to protect him (*Oeuvres*, 2:1404–1408).

47. Quoted by Chamard in his edition of Du Bellay, 6:129 n. 1.

48. On Fouquelin (or Foquelin or Foclin), see Walter J. Ong, "Fouquelin's French Rhetoric." Ong states that Fouquelin's appears to have been only the second French rhetoric to appear, Fabri's *Le grant et vray art de pleine Rhétorique* (1521) being the first. Fouquelin was able to use verse quotations as well as prose because he pigeonholed verse within rhetoric by a system of counting syllables. His work appeared again in 1557, but, according to Ong, was never really popular. Although the vernaculars were gaining ground in the sixteenth century, conscious attempts to encourage their use, such as this one by Fouquelin, were more often than not ineffective: "Fouquelin's vernacular program was doomed, on the pedagogical horizon, to an immediate and protracted eclipse" (142).

On *ironia*, see Norman Knox, *The Word Irony*. In the preface to his *Satira seconda*, Sansovino uses the term in an extremely clear fashion. Summing up the argument of his poem, he states: "Riprendendo coloro che attendono alle cose della Poesia, dimostra *per Ironia* che le virtù sono hoggi in poco prezzo, & che esaltano solamente coloro ch'attendono al ventre, all'avaritia, e alla lussuria" (*Sette libri di Satire* [1560], 169ᵛ, italics mine). Sourly, the poet notes that "Hoggi chi scrive è favola alla gente" (170ᵛ). By compromise and flattery, however, "sarai Filosofo e Poeta" (172ʳ). The word *Filosofo* in such a context recalls Philibert de Vienne.

49. Fouquelin, *La rhétorique Françoise* (1557 ed.), 8ᵛ–9ʳ. Note the recurrence of the term *dissimulation*, discussed above in connection with La Borderie and Philibert de Vienne.

50. Fouquelin, 9ᵛ–10ʳ. The Du Bellay poem is from *Oeuvres de l'invention de l'autheur* of 1552, (in *Oeuvres poétiques*, ed. Chamard, 4:145–56). Rabelais's use of these forms of irony by opposites is discussed in chap. 6 below.

51. Fouquelin, 149–50. On the image of the "singes de Court," see below, chap. 7, n. 13.

52. Fouquelin, 152–54; Du Bellay, *Oeuvres poétiques*, ed. Chamard, 4:149–54. Deriving from the Italian words *bravata, soldato, carica* and *camiciata*, the first four of the five terms singled out for attack are obviously linked to Du Bellay's anti-Italianism as well as to a general dislike of false protestations of bravery.

53. *Regrets*, in *Oeuvres poétiques*, ed. Chamard, 2:164–65, and cf. also sonnet 145 of the *Regrets*, 168–69, in which the sarcastic impatience with virtue resembles that found in the attacks on honor to be discussed below:

> Tu t'abuses (Belleau) si pour estre sçavant,
> Sçavant & vertueux, tu penses qu'on te prise:
> Il fault (comme lon dit) estre homme d'entreprise,
> Si tu veulx qu'à la Court on te pousse en avant.
> Ces beaux noms de vertu, ce n'est rien que du vent.
> Donques, si tu es sage, embrasse la feintise,
> L'ignorance, l'envie, avec la couvoitise:
> Par ces artz jusqu'au ciel on monte bien souvent.

54. *Oeuvres de Jean de La Taille*, ed. René de Maulde, 3:ix–x. The poem is number 8 of de la Taille's *Sonnets satyriques* and was published by him three times in 1574.

55. "Le Médecin Courtizan" (1559). Page numbers for quotations here come from the edition by Montaiglon, *Recueil*, 10:96–109. The matter of attribution is discussed by Montaiglon on p. 97, but was settled by P. M. Smith, "Jacques Grévin et le Médecin Courtizan."

56. 102. On some of the details of the "Médecin courtizan," see Mayer, *Lucien*, 222–24.

57. Quoted by P. M. Smith, *The Anti-Courtier Trend*, 166. The poem appears in the René de Maulde edition, *Oeuvres*, 3:xxxiii–li. The lines cited (xxxiv–xxxv) are an adaptation of Guevara. The same type of inversion was noted by Isaac Habert, *Les trois Livres des Météores* (1585), 6ʳ. Isaac was the nephew of François Habert, the "Banny de Liesse." The poem is entitled "Louange de la vie rustique," and is part of the writer's *Bergeries*:

Le vertueux en Court est nommé vicieus,
Le sçavant ignorant, le bon malicieus,
Le modeste poltron, vaillant le temeraire,
Propre leur est tout mal, tout bien leur est contraire.

58. Jean Vauquelin de la Fresnaye, "Satire à Jean Antoine de Baïf" (quoted by P. M. Smith, *The Anti-Courtier Trend*, 163). On Sansovino's suggestions for worldly success, see above, n. 48. Similarly, Charles Fontaine uses irony to recommend following money, not knowledge, in the *Ruisseaux de Fontaine* (1555), 108–9:

En tout honneur, & excellence
Quiconque veult aller avant,
Quiere l'argent, non la science,
Les lettres n'aille poursuyvant,
Mais l'argent noble aille suyvant:
L'argent fait les gens savans, pource
Qu'aujourd'huy l'homme est fort savant
Qui fait force escus en sa bourse.

The title notes that "L'auteur donne conseil selon le temps, *par ironie toutesfois*" (italics mine). Earlier in the century (ca. 1530), a similar comment on the power of money was expressed by the blasonneur Pierre Danche in his ballad "Argent prend villes & chateaux," printed in the collection *La Fleur de toutes joyeusetez* (n.d.). Danche is ultimately less cynical than Fontaine, for his refrain reminds readers that whatever, rightly or wrongly, money can buy, it can never buy health, youth, or paradise. Equally ambivalent towards money was Ronsard, whose "Hymne de l'Or" of 1555 has provoked a modern critical controversy. Maurice Verdier, "A Propos d'une controverse," describes the debate between Jean Frappier and Bernard Weinberg as to whether the poem is to be taken literally or not. Frappier believes it is intended seriously, but Weinberg disagrees, seeing the piece as paradoxical and sometimes comic. In England, Richard Barnfield, a popular poet, published in 1598 "The Encomion of Lady Pecunia; or, The Praise of Money," in which he cited Erasmus's praise of folly and claimed that his own choice of topic had "never beene written on before" (see the reissue in *Illustrations of Old English Literature*, ed. J. Payne Collier, vol. 1, no. 7, i). Barnfield's poem is very like a Pléiade hymne-blason, with personification, mythological references, invented stories, and even a final invocation to Pecunia:

I crave no more but this for my good-will,
That in my want thou wilt supply me still.

Another poem on this popular theme was "Le Debat de l'Homme et de l'Argent," which is reprinted in Montaiglon, ed., *Recueil*, 7:302–29. According to Montaiglon, the piece was presented as a translation from an Italian work, and appeared in three editions but with no date of publication. Its basic theme is that of the refrain of the rondeau that follows it, "Qui a argent heureux se peult tenir." All serve a rich man and pay him honor. He can build "maisons" and "chasteaulx" and, in conclusion, "malgré tous fera à son plaisir" (329). The debate itself concludes more moderately, as the narrator urges readers to "Amasse donc et despens par raison; / Par tel moyen l'argent est tousjours bon" (328).

59. Tahureau, "Premier Dialogue du Democritic," in *Les Dialogues* (1565), 102–3. Tahureau speaks of "ceste dissimulation courtisanne," and quotes again the *Discours* to Macrin in which Du Bellay says that to succeed at court one must be "Aveugle, muet & sourd." For Guillaume du Buys, see his *Les Oeuvres* (1583), 3ʳ. On Tahureau, see also Emile Besch, "Un moraliste satirique et rationaliste," and the recent edition by Trevor Peach, *Poésies complètes*. On du Buys, see Louis-Alexandre Bergounioux, *De Quercy en Cornouaille*.

60. P. M. Smith, *The Anti-Courtier Trend*, 196. Smith notes that attacks on homosexuality at court went back at least as far as Deschamps, and that a frequent model for such criticisms was Juvenal's attack on Rome under Domitian (see the discussion below of *Triumphe de haulte Folie* for Domitian as a stereotypical villain).

61. Du Bellay, *Divers Jeux rustiques*, in *Oeuvres poétiques*, ed. Chamard, 5:117–23. See the analysis by Mayer, *Lucien*, 112–21, which considers carefully the attribution to Bergier (or Berger) of various minor poems. Mayer does not, however, discuss the difference in tone between the Bergier poem and most of Du Bellay's satires. The present chapter seeks to account for the more affectionate attitude adopted in the former work.

62. *Divers Jeux rustiques*, ed. Saulnier, xii. Saulnier sees the ode as a panegyric on burlesque poetry. This interpretation makes the poem either a momentary aberration or joke on the part of Du Bellay or a form of condescension to the "low" genres. Such a reading does insufficient justice to the fullness and paradoxical nature of Du Bellay's portrait. As in earlier references to Du Bellay, quotations will be given from the Chamard edition, with page numbers in the text.

63. Baïf's poem on Bergier stresses his facility with words and sounds (in the *Passetems*, see Jean [Jan] Antoine de Baïf, *Euvres en rime*, ed. Charles Marty-Laveaux, 4:348–50). Baïf's tone is similar to that of Du Bellay. He even selects the same sounds as having been imitated in words by Bergier—bird song, the sound of knives manipulated by "le cuisinier," and clocks:

> Soit les horlogins apeaux,
> Soit le triquetrac encores?
> Triquetracant un vers ores,
> Ores le carillonant,
> L'achigigotant de sorte,
> Le tintant, ou de main forte
> Au bedon le bedonnant.
> ("De Bertrand Bergier," 349)

Charles Marty-Laveaux, in his *La Langue de la Pléiade*, part of *La Pléiade françoise*, 1:53, questions the attribution to Bergier of the "Dithyrambes à la Pompe du Bouc de E. Jodelle, Poëte Tragique," some lines of which are certainly in the style of Bergier as portrayed by Baïf and Du Bellay:

> Evoé mes entrailles sonnent
> Sous ses fureurs qui m'epoinçonnent,
> Et son esprit de ce Dieu trop chargé

Forcene enragé,
Iach ïach Evoé,
Evoé ïach ïach.
   Que l'on me donne ces clochettes,
Et ces jazardes sonnettes,
Soit ma perruque decorée
D'une couronne coulevrée:
Perruque lierreporte,
Que l'ame Thracienne emporte
Deça dela dessus mon col.
Iach ïach Evoé,
Evoé ïach ïach.

Laumonier attributes these lines to Ronsard (*Oeuvres complètes*, 5:53). Here they are quoted from 5:65–66. Volume and page numbers from this edition will be given in the text for subsequent quotations from Ronsard. Du Bellay dedicates two other poems to Bergier, an "Ode pastorale" in the *Oeuvres de l'invention de l'auteur* (*Oeuvres poétiques*, ed. Chamard, 4:184–88) and a piece in the *Vers lyriques* (*Oeuvres poétiques*, ed. Chamard, 3:26–29).

64. *Divers Jeux rustiques*, ed. Saulnier, 120 n. to ll. 45–48.

65. On this matter, see also Michael West, "Skelton and the Renaissance Theme of Folly." West quotes Erwin Panofsky as having remarked that "the discovery of ironic value in that formerly despised figure the fool, most strikingly exemplified by Erasmus's *Moriae Encomium* (1512) in contrast to Sebastian Brant's *Narrenschiff* (1494), is one of the hallmarks distinguishing the Renaissance from the Middle Ages" (23). He notes, citing Enid Welsford, that the court fool's role sometimes overlapped with that of the court poet, a situation very evident in the case of Bergier. Trtnik-Rossettini believes that the author had not forgotten the principles of the *Deffence*, but had "quelque peu assoupli sa jeune intransigeance" (88). It is good for poetry to be natural rather than laborious, but there are limits: "Il se moque donc d'un poète comme Bertrand Bergier qui s'abandonne à l'instinct naturel, jusqu'à composer des poésies ridicules, bien que parfois amusantes" (89).

66. See Pietro Toldo, "Etudes sur la poésie," 217, and François Villon, *Le Testament*, in *Les Oeuvres*, ed. Louis Thuasne, 81–82.

67. Etienne Tabourot, *Les Bigarrures du Seigneur des Accords* (1583), 2:217[r–v].

68. Mentioned by T. F. Crane, 166 n. 3. See also Michele de Filippis, *The Literary Riddle*. For Marot's many epitaphs, some mocking, some serious, see Clément Marot, *Oeuvres diverses*, ed. C.-A. Mayer, 195–238, and for others, see my "The Satirical Eulogy," 256, and below, n. 111.

69. The same attitude to alchemy and the same sardonic image of reverse multiplication appear in Du Bellay's "Discours sur la louange de la vertu," cited above in connection with the epitaph on Bonnet:

C'est ung heureux advantage,
Qu'ung alambic en partage,
Ung fourneau Mercurien:
Et de toute sa sustance

Tirant une quinte essence,
Multiplier tout en rien.
(*Oeuvres poétiques*, ed. Chamard, 4:152, italics mine)

70. Trtnik-Rossettini, 176 n. 3, notes that the description of the abbé's clothes owes much to Berni's poem on "Mastro Guazzaletto."

71. On this blason, see Tomarken and Tomarken, 145–46, and chap. 6 below. There are plaideurs in the procession in the *Triumphe de haulte Folie* discussed below.

72. Helen O. Platt finds the figures of Bonnet and Bergier strange and contradictory, "Structure in Du Bellay's *Divers Jeux rustiques.*" When studied from the point of view of the paradoxical encomium, the two poems become less puzzling. Mayer discusses the Bergier poem in his *Lucien*, 112–21, and concludes that it is one of the finest poems of the French Renaissance, "un des meilleurs legs que Lucien ait donnés à la littérature française; avec l'*Hymne de la Surdité* et les sonnets satiriques des *Regrets* cette ode assure à Du Bellay une place parmi les meilleurs poètes satiriques français" (121).

73. For instance, by Hegendorff, discussed in chap. 3 above.

74. Charles Béné, " 'Folie' et 'Sagesse,' " especially 8.

75. Cited by Béné, 9. On the question of reason and madness, see also the series of articles *Folie et déraison à la Renaissance.*

76. See above, chap. 3, n. 9, and chap. 2, n. 11.

77. Condeescu, 51.

78. *Le Triumphe de Haulte Folie* ([ca. 1550]). Page numbers from the 1873 edition by Anatole C. de Montaiglon will be given for subsequent quotations.

79. See *Le Triumphe de haulte et puissante Dame Vérolle*, ed. Montaiglon, 33. See also the colloquium *Folie et déraison à la Renaissance*, for an article by Hyacinthe Brabant, "Les Traitements burlesques de la folie au XVIe et XVIIe siècles," 124.

80. Although, as was noted in connection with the Italian encomia, Aretino's dialogues of 1534 and 1536 contained several sections ironically praising the skills of ways of life not usually deemed praiseworthy, the French do not seem to have borrowed many specific ideas from these conversations. A piece by Motin, however, published in *Le Cabinet satyrique* of 1618, (ed. Fernand Fleuret and Louis Perceau, 1:14–29), bears the title "L'Hymne du Maquerellage" and does seem reminiscent of Aretino. The use of the title "Hymne" for an ironic work echoes Du Bellay. Most French writers attacked "maquereaux" harshly, their position here among the "foux" in the *Triumphe de haulte Folie* being a relatively mild form of criticism. Motin adapts the notion of universal folly, substituting for it the playful claim that all men are in some sense "maquereaux" because directly or indirectly they assist love. Doctors help by selling beauty potions, preachers by attracting people to church, where assignations can be made. Most artisans labor to make their customers look more attractive, and similar claims can be made for other groups. Gradually "le Macquerellage" (*sic*) (19) becomes the governing soul ("âme") of the world (19). Those who deny their involvement in this activity are either liars or madmen. The poem's final lines contain a satirical dig at German drinking habits, as the work is dedicated to courtiers "Qui, sans foy, sans âme et sans honte, / Du maquerellage

(*sic*) font gloire, / Comme les Allemans de boire"(20). In conclusion, those who blame the art of the "maquereaux" are deemed the true fools.

81. ix. On Nero as the archetypal tyrant, see Baldwin, 28 n. 38. For another negative Renaissance image of the emperor, see Jean de la Jessée, who wrote:

Execrable Neron, vray Monstre de Nature,
Qui vilain adjoustas forfait sur forfaiture!
Et qui non contanté d'occire au mesme lieu
L'Apostre Pierre, & Paul, deus ministres de Dieu!
Incesteus, matricide, & plein de vitupere,
Pollus, tüas, honnis, Agrippine ta mere,
Fis mourir ton Seneque.

("La Jeunesse bien-nee," in *Discours VIII*, 1583 edition of *Oeuvres*, 2:1500–1)

82. See above, chap. 4, n. 43.

83. The work is in the Lambeth Palace Library, bound with other writings in a volume entitled *A Knowledge for Kings*. For the title, cf. Nigellus Wireker, *Speculum stultorum*, above, chap. 2, n. 28. Page numbers in the text refer to this London edition of the *Mirrour*.

84. This device will be discussed below in connection with Claude Colet.

85. *Le Cabinet satyrique*, ed. Fleuret and Perceau, 1:355–57.

86. Béné, 10. See the colloquium *Folie et déraison à la Renaissance*, for a discussion by Marcel de Grève of Rabelais's use of paradox: "Le Discours rabelaisien, ou la raison en folie," 149–59.

87. Even Judge Bridoye's use of dice to decide difficult cases had serious support at this time; see J.D.M. Derrett, "Rabelais' Legal Learning," and Michael Screech, "The Legal Comedy of Rabelais." Similarly, Condeescu notes that Calvin approved of loans and the movement of capital (39). François Dumont makes a similar point in "Les Dettes de Panurge," even claiming that Panurge's encomium may have been meant seriously by Rabelais, who, he asserts, believed in an interrelated world. On Rabelais as a paradoxist, see Deborah Losse, *Rhetoric at Play*; François Rigolot, "Le Fol Eloge de la Folie" and "Rabelais et l'éloge paradoxal." In the latter of these two articles, Rigolot emphasizes that paradox appealed to Rabelais's artistic temperament because it enabled him to move "entre l'éloge et la raillerie"(196). Rabelais's praise of codpieces is related to ironic encomia on articles of clothing, to be discussed in the disease chapter, below. Mary Ragland also discusses the classification of the "Eloge des dettes," in *Rabelais and Panurge*, 76–78. She notes the encomium's connections with various popular genres, and shows how later critics have identified it variously as a paradox, a panegyric, and a piece of pure lyricism. She herself sees Panurge as a paradoxical character, a childlike person whose function is to expose and oppose fallacies in traditional concepts. Mayer discusses the praise of debts in "Rabelais' Satirical Eulogy," 147–55. See also W. M. Frohock, "Panurge as Comic Character"; Coleman, 115–21; Michael Screech, *Rabelais*; Verdun L. Saulnier, *Le Dessein de Rabelais*; Michel Beaujour, *Le Jeu de Rabelais*; Mario Rocques, "Aspects de Panurge," 120–30; Ludwig Schrader, *Panurge und Hermes*; and Abel Lefranc, "Le Tiers Livre du 'Pantagruel' de Rabelais," in *Grands Ecrivains de la Renaissance*, 251–303. Raymond La Charité calls Panurge's idea of an indebted world "an endearing physiological-economic system," in "Rabelais: The Book as Therapy," 12.

88. Condeescu, 37. Condeescu even wonders if Rabelais met Lando through Gryphius the printer.

89. Cave, 189, sees the praise of debts as the beginning of the image of Panurge as a "professional subverter of productive systems. He is a master of dissipation; and, of course, of rhetoric."

90. Quoted from Rabelais, *Tiers Livre*, ed. Lefranc, lx–lxi. The italics are Lefranc's.

91. On the source of this story, see Louis Thuasne, *Etudes sur Rabelais*, 70:

L'origine de ce long paradoxe de Panurge à la louange des debteurs et emprunteurs (*Pantagruel*, III, 3–5) est, d'une part, un passage de l'*Eloge de la Folie* qui se termine par une allusion à l'apologue de Menenius Agrippa [trans. Miller, 40], de l'autre, et surtout, un extrait du traité *Lingua* [1525] dans lequel Erasme, tout en étant surpassé, dans ce duel littéraire, par Rabelais, physiologiste et médecin de profession, doublé d'un écrivain de génie, n'a pas moins donné, dans une forme excellente, une description magistrale de l'économie du corps humain, dans laquelle il a su éviter la sécheresse, tout en restant clair et précis.

Montaigne, "Le Profit de l'un est dommage de l'autre" (in *Essais*, ed. Albert Thibaudet, 1:xxii), also addresses the question of our mutual indebtedness. On Rabelais's skill with medical language, see Michael Screech, "Medicine and Literature." The relationship between the body and its members is also the basis of St. Paul, I Corinthians 12:12–27.

92. Florence Weinberg, *The Wine and the Will*, 53. Like Losse and others, Weinberg notes the constantly paradoxical nature of Rabelais's humor. He propounds, she claims, a "sobria ebrietas," seeking the reform, not the destruction of the Church. In a sense, our inevitable human folly, a state of disease, is a boon, for it leads us to seek a cure, found in religion. Similarly, La Charité, "Rabelais: The Book as Therapy," 13, notes that for Rabelais disease generates art, and the book is a form of medication, for laughter leads to health.

93. De l'Ortigue's poem appears in the 1617 *Les Poèmes divers*, 144–49, described above, chap. 4, n. 14. Page numbers for subsequent quotations from this edition will be given in the text. See Condeescu, who calls de l'Ortigue "un des meilleurs bernesques français" (44).

94. As noted above, chap. 4, n. 46, the title page of the 1553 edition states that these pieces are debated in the manner of legal disputes, as a means of training "jeunes advocats." In a preliminary list of editions of Estienne's *Paradoxes*, I found twenty editions between 1553 and 1638 ("The Satirical Eulogy," 393–94). The first edition appeared in Paris, published by Charles Estienne. It was reissued twice in the same year and then published in Poitiers in 1553 by Jan de Marnef. Quotations here are from the latter edition, with page numbers in the text. Marcel Tétel points out likenesses between Lando and Rabelais, noting that Scève translated several of Lando's paradoxes in 1547, before the French edition appeared and only a year after the appearance of the *Tiers Livre* (*Rabelais et l'Italie*, 26–31).

95. An interesting discussion of the function and value of paradoxes appeared much later, in 1638, under the title *Paradoxes ou les opinions renversées de la pluspart des hommes. Livre non moins profitable que facetieux* (Rouen: Jacques Cail-

lové). The definition remained standard into the eighteenth century, as we see in yet another anonymous treatise, in fact by the abbé André Morellet, the *Théorie du paradoxe* (1775), 10: "C'est une opinion contraire à l'opinion commune & generale. De là, deux genres de Paradoxe, celui qui est opposé à l'opinion commune fausse, & celui qui est opposé à l'opinion commune vraie." In the classical tradition, the anonymous author reminds us of the "grande & importante verité" that "il n'y a point d'objet qui ne puisse être vu de plusieurs manieres. L'assertion la plus vraie a un côté foible, & la proposition la plus fausse un côté vrai" (13–14). The presenter of paradoxes in this work bears a marked resemblance to Lucian's unscrupulous new-style orator. He is told to be bold and outrageous, rude and evasive, to accept what is in doubt, and to conclude without proving his points. He must have, in short, as the "secret de l'art," the "courage de la honte"(15). Caligula and Nero are given as instances of people who can be paradoxically praised, Leibniz, Montesquieu, and d'Alembert as respected figures who can be ironically vituperated.

96. A.ii. The expression "contre la commune opinion" also appears in the French translation of Agrippa's *De incertitudine*, entitled *Declamation sur l'Incertitude, Vanité, et Abus des Sciences* ([trans. L. de Mayerne Turquet] 1582). The Latin original appeared in 1530 but was composed in 1526. After the title in the French version comes an explanatory passage: "Oeuvre qui peut proffiter, & qui apporte merveilleux contentement à ceux qui frequentent les Cours des grands Seigneurs, & qui veulent apprendre à discourir d'une infinité de choses *contre la commune opinion*" (italics mine). Agrippa's attack on the various follies of men and women owes much to Erasmus and Lucian. He mentions Lucian, Apuleius, and Momus in his dedicatory letter and prologue. But the element of praise is minimal, the work being more a satire than a mock eulogy. Part of his satire was translated as *Paradoxe contre l'amour* (1603). Both prostitution and pimping are seen as arts (chaps. 63 and 64), as is "l'art militaire" (chap. 79).

97. Lucian, *The Ship, or The Wishes*, in *Works*, Loeb CLS, 6:445.

98. One of Estienne's most frequent techniques in adapting Lando was that of "gallicizing" elements of his text. The Italian work at this point referred vaguely to "Sicillia"; Estienne situates the episode firmly in Dieppe. A similar cure for an imaginary illness, with similar regrets on the part of the man cured, is related by Montaigne, *Essais*, ed. Thibaudet, 2:12.

99. 55–56. Cf. Marot on dying for honor's sake in the third "coq à l'âne," composed in 1536 and first published in 1539 (see Marot, *Oeuvres satiriques*, ed. Mayer, 134).

100. Published in 1554. The same publishers produced several small volumes of individual paradoxes, all bound together in the British Library volume. Although Estienne's name is not given in this edition, all except one of the pieces printed are identical to the earlier ones of Estienne and are preceded by his preface to the reader. The first three are the same as the first three in the 1553 edition (on poverty, ugliness, and ignorance), then comes the new one, on lawsuits, followed by the next three from the 1553 edition (on blindness, madness, and "Pour le desmis de ses estats"). With these the collection ends.

101. Alfred Cartier stresses that in general in the sixteenth century Lyons was the "capitale de la Pensée française" (*Bibliographie des éditions des de Tournes*,

1:9). Safely removed from the Sorbonne, Lyons was a haven for publishers of works that might never have appeared in Paris. On this matter, see also A. F. Johnson, *Selected Essays*, and A. Stegmann, "Un visage nouveau de l'humanisme lyonnais." Stegmann stresses the importance of those he calls the "traducteurs polygraphes" of Lyons. We may wonder if one of these men was responsible for Jean de Tournes's blasons. Colet published a liminary "dizain" in Gilles d'Aurigny's *Le Tuteur d'Amour* (1547), using the same device, "tout pour le mieux," and, in another prefatory poem, was addressed as "poète sçavant, son frere d'Amytié" by d'Aurigny. It would seem, therefore, that he was based primarily in Lyons, not Paris. On Colet and Philibert de Vienne, see my article, "Philibert de Vienne," 704.

102. See above, chap. 3, n. 38. Both works were published by Christian Wechel.

103. Colet, *L'Oraison de Mars*, 3–4. Page numbers for subsequent quotations from this 1544 edition will be given in the text.

104. See La Jessée, *Oeuvres*, 1:230–34, and Trtnik-Rossettini, 193–95.

105. *Oeuvres*, 1:234–38.

106. Trans. Josuah Sylvester. On Odet de la Noue, see G. Pourtalès, "Odet de la Noue." In the seventeenth century, two encomia remarkably similar to that of Odet de la Noue were composed by other equally noble prisoners. These pieces were entitled *A Paradox against Liberty* (1679) and *A Paradox against Life* (1681). They were presented as having being composed by "The Lords in the Tower."

107. See Cicero, *Paradoxa stoicorum* discussed above, chap. 1, n. 61. Since Cicero called his pieces "admirabilia contraque opinionem omnium," he was probably responsible for the Renaissance use of this definition.

108. Francesi, 2:45^r–47^r. Estienne, 62–68. Godard's poem appeared in *Les Oeuvres de Jean Godard parisien* (1594), 2:303–19. It will be quoted here from the edition *Meslanges poétiques* (1624), with page numbers after the citation. Robinson (*Lucian*, 125) discusses a sixteenth-century Spanish work praising poverty, *El Crótalon*, probably by Cristóbal de Villalón. The work borrows from Lucian's *The Cock* to present a dialogue between Micilo (Micyllus) and a cock. The cock at one point asserts that the "misery of the rich outstrips the discomforts of the poor." The final chapter praises the blessings of poverty.

109. These envois are discussed in detail in chap. 7 below.

110. Godard composed a tragedy and a "Discours poétique" called *La Franciade* and dedicated to Ronsard (181–82).

111. *Poésie d'Estienne Forcadel* (1551), here quoted from the later edition *Oeuvres poétiques* (1579), 205. The reference to the "treille" is on p. 206. Cf. also below, chap. 6, n. 75. François Habert composed some epitaphs on drunkards, which appeared in his *Le Combat de Cupido et de la Mort* (ca. 1550).

112. Ronsard, *Oeuvres complètes*, ed. Laumonier, 5:47–52. Ronsard's interest in rendering the drunkard's strange sounds may be related to his fascination with Bergier's onomatopoeic verse.

113. Jehan Moussin, *Discours de l'Yvresse et Yvrongnerie* (1612). A work listed in the catalogue of but apparently lost from the Bibliothèque de l'Arsenal in Paris is the *Discours de l'ivresse et la maniere de carouser* (1612).

114. 196. French litigiousness was also decried by Jean de la Jessée in an epigram "De la France malade": "La France a deux grandz excez: / Quelz sont-ilz? Guerre,

& Procès" (in *Oeuvres*, 1:407) Passerat's poem appeared in *Les Poésies françaises de Jean Passerat*, ed. Prosper N. Blanchemain, 1:65–71. A French work urging avoidance of lawsuits was *Le Moyen d'éviter procès*, by Jean Figon de Montelimar (1574), who warns readers that lawsuits and debts are costly and disapproved of by God. A modern study of the matter is that by Charles Tilly, *The Litigious French*. Most of these poems spell *procès* with an acute accent, as *procés*.

115. Tomarken and Tomarken, 145–46, discuss these poems' place in the history of the blason.

116. *Poésies françaises*, ed. Blanchemain, 1:72, entitled "Sonnet."

117. *Cabinet satyrique*, ed. Fleuret and Perceau, 1:369.

118. A French paradox not directly related in topic to Estienne's collection but bearing the title *paradox* is the *Paradoxe apologique* by Alexandre de Pont-Aymery (1596), which claims to demonstrate faithfully that "la femme est beaucoup plus parfaicte que l'homme en toute action de vertu." Given the title of the work and the virulence of some antifeminist works of the sixteenth century, one might expect to find here an ironic encomium. But the author is at pains to stress in his preface, dedicated to the Duchesse de Reths, that what others might take as a paradox is for him the truth. The tone and arguments of the ensuing essay do not lead us to believe that the author is providing anything other than the faithful demonstration his title promises (cf. Agrippa, above, n. 96).

119. The following analysis is adapted from my article, "The Lucianic Blason" 223–27. Page numbers from this edition will be given in the text for quotations from the three blasons, in this chapter and in chap. 6.

120. *King Henry IV, Part I*, ed. A. R. Humphreys, 5.1.129–41. On this topic, see G. A. Borgese, "The Dishonor of Honor." Borgese is not enamored of the mock eulogy, which he refers to as "the genus—so desperately comic that it impresses us with a nearly tragic boredom" (44). He believes that Falstaff's attack is a "paraphrase of Tasso's words transmitted to Shakespeare through the channel of Daniel's translation" (51).

121. 174. See also Toldo, "Etudes sur la poésie," 263.

122. 170.

123. See Noël du Fail, *Les Propos rustiques*, ed. Arthur de la Borderie, 42–50. Also discussed by P. M. Smith, *The Anti-Courtier Trend*, 137–38.

124. See Marot, *Oeuvres diverses*, ed. Mayer, 129.

125. *Les Oeuvres poétiques*, (1575), 105ʳ–106ᵛ. See also Amadis Jamyn, *Les Oeuvres poétiques*, ed. Samuel M. Carrington, 2:81–85. On Jamyn, see also Theodosia Graur, *Un Disciple de Ronsard*, 60: "En général, il semble que l'amoureux d'Oriane prenne au sérieux, bien plus au sérieux que ne l'avait fait le poète italien, les accusations portées contre l'honneur; le *Capitolo* de Mauro se transforme chez lui en une *Elegie*."

126. 186.

127. However, in "Satyre VI," Regnier does place himself explicitly within the classical tradition of playful verse so often cited by mock encomiasts:

> Ha! Dieu pour quoy faut-il que mon esprit ne vaille,
> Autant que cil qui mist les Souris en bataille.

Qui sceut à la Grenoüille apprendre son caquet,
Ou que l'autre qui fist en vers un Sopiquet.
(*Les Satyres du Sieur Regnier* [1609], 53)

128. Gilles Durant, *Les Oeuvres poétiques du Sieur de la Bergerie* (1594), 147ʳ–148ᵛ. Quotations refer to this edition, with page numbers in the text. See chap. 7 below , for discussion of Durant's verses on the deaths of a donkey and of a sparrow.

129. On the myth of the Golden Age, see Harry Levin, *The Myth of the Golden Age*. Graur remarks that Jamyn was attacking honor chiefly in order to convince his lady love to be kind to him (60). Much of this literature was derived from Guevara (see P. M. Smith, *The Anti-Courtier Trend*, 35 and 100–3). Honor did have some defenders: Peletier composed a seventeen–page encomium on the topic, dedicated to Scévole de Sainte-Marthe (in *Louanges* [1581]). Earlier, Lancelot de Carle, Bishop of Retz and friend of Ronsard and Du Bellay, composed a flowery blason praising honor, first published with the earliest editions of *Les Blasons anatomiques du corps femenin* (see Saunders, "Sixteenth-Century Collected Editions," 355).

130. *Dictionnaire de biographie française*, fasc. 29, 574.

131. Joseph Vianey, "Bruscambille." On Bruscambille, see also Henry Lyonnet, *Dictionnaire des comédiens français*, under "Bruscambille," and Francis Bar, *Le Genre burlesque*. In studying the language of Bruscambille, Bar singles out the technique of "fausse précision"(366), favored by Rabelais and by the harangueur, as a typical device of burlesque writing. See also Condeescu, 46–47, and Tomarken, "The Joys of the Cuckold."

132. Vianey, "Bruscambille," 572.

133. Barbara Bowen, *Les Caractéristiques essentielles*, and Robert Garapon, *La Fantaisie verbale*.

134. John Lough, *Paris Theatre Audiences*, 10.

135. Bruscambille does not include any Greek quotations and claims not to know more than two words of Greek, given as "*anechou quai apechou*: c'est à dire, qu'il faut desormais devenir patiens" (*Oeuvres* [1629], 75). His style is frequently reminiscent of that of Rabelais in its repetition, invention of new words, and accumulation of dazzlingly complicated sentences. The following is a typical example of the speaker's ability to sound like the master of ceremonies at a Victorian music hall:

Messieurs, & Dames, je desirerois, souhaitterois, voudrois, demanderois, & requerrois desiderativement, souhaitativement, volontativement, demandativement, & requisitativement, avec les desideratoires, souhaittatoires, & volontatoires, demandatoires, & requisitatoires, que vous fussiez enluminez, irredifiez, & esclarifiez, pour pouvoir penetratoirement, secretatoirement, & divinatoirement, *videre, prospicere, intueri & regardere* au travers d'un petit trou qui est en la fenetre du buffet de mes conceptions, pour voir la methode que je veux tenir aujourd'huy à vous remercier de vostre bonne assistance & audience, laquelle vous continuerez, s'il vous plaist, à une petite farce gaillarde que nous vous allons representer. (*Oeuvres* [1629], 135)

These lines were also praised by Bowen, *Les Caractéristiques*, 174.

136. *Facecieuses Paradoxes de Bruscambille, & autres discours comiques* (1615). Page numbers and date will follow quotations from this edition in the text. The 1629

edition, the full title of which is *Les Oeuvres de Bruscambille. Contenant ses Fantasies, Imaginations & Paradoxes, & autres discours Comique (sic)*, will be that most often quoted here, with page numbers and date. For a complete bibliography of Bruscambille, see Georges Mongrédien, *Bibliographie*.

137. See Tomarken and Tomarken, 140–41, for a full analysis of "Le Pet."

138. *Les Caractéristiques*, 172.

139. Vickers, "*King Lear*," On Jonson, see Duncan. See also A. Sackton, "The Paradoxical Encomium." Another work related to the vice encomia is the *Satyre Ménippée*, the famous anti-Ligue satire of 1594, composed by a group of writers. In this work (to which Passerat, Durant, and Rapin, who will be discussed below, in chap. 7, contributed), two charlatans ironically sing the praises of "Catholicon." A burlesque description of the opening procession of the 1593 "Etats généraux" and of the tapestries draped in the assembly hall completes the satirical portrait. Various speeches in the work are forms of unconscious self-betrayal by an inside witness, similar to those described above in chap. 1 in connection with Lucian and the *De Parasito*.

CHAPTER SIX

1. See above, chap. 1, n. 28, for Bretin's highly critical view of the *Ocypus* as a "tragedie manque." Micyllus (Moltzer) was no kinder: "Poema imperfectum & mendosum est, &, ut Erasmus addidit, ne micam quidem Luciani salis habens" (1546), 314.

2. Born in London, John Free died in Rome in 1465. See Rosamund Mitchell, *John Free*. Free studied with Guarino and was later made Bishop of Bath by the Pope. Admiring Free's elegant Latin, Mitchell notes that his translation aimed at being an independent work of art, not a slavish rendition of the original.

3. Probably in an edition by Adrien Turnèbe, of whom Montaigne speaks approvingly in *Essais*, 1:xxv. Turnèbe also edited Cicero's *Paradoxa stoicorum*.

4. Tabourot, *Les Bigarrures*, ed. Guillaume Colletet. The work was first published Paris, 1583, and reprinted in 1584, 1585, 1586, and 1588. The preface, by André Pasquet, refers not only to Pirckheimer, but also to the *Muscae Encomium*, to Favorinus, Synesius, Erasmus, Glaucon (on injustice), Virgil, Homer, Hesiod, and Cardano (on Nero). Ronsard and Belleau are mentioned for their hymnes-blasons, and *Gargantua* and *Pantagruel* appear. So also does the *La Puce* collection of 1583, celebrating a flea that appeared on the bosom of Catherine des Roches (see below, chap. 7). Tabourot was thus remarkably up to date in his list of predecessors. He may also have been the first to classify the hymnes-blasons with the mock encomia.

5. So far as I can ascertain, Menapius's encomium was not translated into French until 1728, as *L'Eloge de la fièvre quarte* (see above, chap. 3, n. 63). But this widely-traveled scholar's work must have been known in Latin soon after its publication in 1542, since the unknown Lyons blasonneur refers to its author as an "Encomiaste exquis" as early as 1547.

6. See W.S.C. Copeman, *A Short History of Gout*, 87: "The method of treatment generally advocated during the eighteenth century was still essentially that

employed by Greek and Roman physicians." See also Ralph H. Major, *A History of Medicine*, 167 and 206.

7. See Copeman, 65–79, and Ernest Wickersheimer, *La Médecine*, 318–22. There was in fact a decrease in the effectiveness of treatment of gout between the seventeenth and early nineteenth centuries, largely due to Thomas Sydenham (1624–1689), who rejected the use of purges, particularly colchicum, one of the few successful ancient ways of combating the disease. A classical medical description of gout by Hippocrates and a literary one by Lucian thus bear a striking resemblance to their later equivalents in, say, Paré and Pirckheimer. Typical of the many famous doctors writing on gout and related diseases were Jean Fernel (1497–1558), physician to Henri II, Ambroise Paré (1507–1590), himself a sufferer from gout, and Guillaume Rondelet (1507–1566), the Montpellier friend of Rabelais and chronicler of marine life. Fernel, in his *Universa medicina* (1574, first published 1567), devotes an entire section to the various types of gout, considered under the general heading of arthritis. Paré, in *Les Oeuvres* (first published in 1575), discusses gout at length in book 18. He calls it a "maladie articulaire, dicte vulgairement Goute," and suggests various treatments. Later in life he grew more cautious, calling the malady the "opprobrium medicorum" (see Copeman, 55). Rondelet, in his optimistically entitled *Methodus curandorum omnium morborum corporis humani* (1609), describes arthritis/gout succinctly: "Arthritis, articularis morbus ab articulis dicitur, a Barbaris gutta, quod existiment esse defluxionem guttatim factam" (cap. 81, p. 601). A less well-known medical writer, Hieronymus Sachetus Aelianus (Hieronimo Sachetto), in his *De podagricis & arthriticis morbis retractatio* (1586), also equates gout and arthritis, as does Franciscus India, in his *De Gutta Podagrica . . . libri duo* (1600). The association of medical and moral perceptions of disease in general and gout in particular is continued in the seventeenth century in Pierre Sordes's *Discours de la Goutte* (1626), which states unequivocally that gout is the way in which "Dieu nous exerce à une patience, la plus forte vertu de l'ame; & d'autant qu'elles [les gouttes] sont plus douloureuses d'autant plus elles nous font aspirer à une meilleure vie, & respirer apres nostre souverain bien" (3). In short, the pangs of gout are the "verges du Ciel."

8. Demetrius Pepagomenus, doctor to the emperor of Constantinople, Michael Paleologus, seems to have composed his treatise for his royal patron, probably a gout-sufferer. Pepagomenus, like others, associates gout and "calculus," the stone. His treatise was published in Latin and Greek (1558), then translated by Jamot (1567). The odes by Belleau and Grévin adopt the traditional view of gout as the punishment of "luxure," greed and drinking. The "Preface du Traducteur" echoing Favorinus, declares that nature is not "maratre." We bring our troubles upon ourselves by intemperate living. Galen and Hippocrates are cited as authorities, as is the sixth-century Alexander Trallianus, whose *Libri XII* were published in 1548 in Paris by Robert Estienne (a corrected version of the earlier Leyden [1504] and Basle [1533] ones). Pepagomenus continued to be cited as an authority on gout, for instance, in J. Freind's *Histoire de la médecine* (1727), 412–14 (a translation from Freind's original English by the same Etienne Coulet who composed his own *Eloge de la Goute* [see below, n. 32]).

9. Maistre Mimin appears, for instance, in the British Library collection of farces

discussed in connection with the *Moriae Encomium* above. His complaints are like those of sufferers in all gout encomia:

> "He dieu helas mauldicte goutte
> Que tant mon povre cueur desgouste
> Fault il que par toy cy je meure."
> (*Farce nouvelle tresbonne & fort joyeuse*)

Although Mimin is clearly a comic figure, the resemblance between the farce and the full-length mock encomia is a limited one.

10. Eustache Deschamps, *Oeuvres complètes*, ed. Le Marquis de Queux de Saint-Hilaire, vol. 8, poem 1408. Deschamps writes that gout is frequently caused by the need to drink and overindulge in order to succeed at court (cf. P. M. Smith, *The Anti-Courtier Trend*, 46). The satirical presentation of gout became more frequent in the sixteenth century, as when Pierre de Boaistuau, influenced by Piccolomini and Guevara, remarked that one leaves the court "les piedz pleins de gouttes" and "les reins pleins de gravelle," *Théâtre du monde* (1561), 44ᵛ. This is the same combination of illnesses as that lamented by Deschamps.

11. Rabelais, *Tiers Livre*, ed. Lefranc, 5: "Bonnes gens, Beuveurs tresillustres, et vous Goutteux tresprecieux, veistez vous oncques Diogenes, le philosophe cynic." Similarly, in the prologue to *Gargantua*, we read: "Beuveurs tres illustres, et vous, Verolez tres precieux,—car à vous, non à aultres, sont dediez mes escriptz" (ed. Lefranc, 3). Jean Mottron studies these Rabelaisian epithets in his *Rabelais*. The term "pauvres Veroles precieux" is used by Noël du Fail in his *Baliverneries* of 1548; see the edition of the *Propos rustiques* by J. Marie Guichard. Du Fail devotes an entire section of his work to gout, relating legends about "ceste mechante maladie" and explaining why she inhabits "les cours des grands seigneurs" while the spider prefers those of the poor (116–21). The *Propos rustiques* first appeared in Lyons in 1547, and were published by Jean de Tournes, who in the same year published the blasons on gout, the quartan fever, and against honor. In the early seventeenth century, the anonymous *La fameuse Compagnie de la lesine*, translated from the Italian (1604), claims to teach how to "espargner, acquerir, & conserver." It claims that gout attacks chiefly the rich in order to encourage them to save their money rather than spend it on gout-producing luxury (47ᵛ).

12. Melin de Sainct-Gelays, "Epitaphe d'Antoine de Lève," in *Oeuvres complètes*, ed. Prosper N. Blanchemain, 1:119. See below, n. 27. Sainct-Gelays ends his poem with an oblique attack on the Emperor Charles V, who was *not* too lame to flee.

13. In the *Essais*, Montaigne refers to the illness fourteen times; see Roy E. Leake, *Concordance des Essais*, 570.

14. La Jessée, *Oeuvres*, 1:367. The poem, "La Bigotte," is part of the *Troisiesme Livre des meslanges*.

15. Passerat, "Quatrain sur sa goutte, l'an 1583," in *Les Poésies françaises*, ed. Blanchemain, 2:143. The connection between gout and "gutta," a drop, is being manipulated here, as elsewhere (see below, n. 31).

16. René Bretonnayau, *La Génération de l'homme* (1583, 151ᵛ). Since La Jessée, Passerat, and Bretonnayau all published works on gout in the same year, we may

wonder if this period, rather than the eighteenth century, should be dubbed the "golden age of gout" (see Copeman, chap. 6).

17. On Pliny, see below, n. 29. Bretonnayau appears to have had a fondness for expressing medical ideas in formal verse—he generally used alexandrines—for he also composed a bizarre work entitled "Les Hemorrhoïdes," published in the same collection as "Les Gouttes." Such a title might suggest an ironic intent, but the writer provides no indication that his lengthy and detailed description is not intended seriously. He contends that piles are nature's way of purging the body of poisonous humors. His unusual but prolix poem thus deserves mention but not further study here. Both his poems, which reflect the fund of ideas common to professionals and laymen, were reprinted by Pascal Pia in *Le Bouquet*. The French poem on the plague by the doctor Guillaume Bunel was discussed above, chap. 4, n. 30. Its advice to readers to flee from the scene of the epidemic was the course of action followed by Montaigne in 1585. Another interesting French work on the plague is the *Remède très utile contre la Peste* (ca. 1530), see *Recueil*, ed. Montaiglon, 12:252–59. While offering stock ideas about how to avoid the plague and professing to give advice, the work is in fact a satire in which the human body represents the body politic. The "Membres principaulx" are the ruling classes, the "Chef" is the King, the "Membres menuz" the lower classes. The "Peste" itself is war and taxation. The chief cause of this plague is the "Chef" (255). The *Remède* boldly declares that the "Membres principaulx" must be cured before the lower limbs can recover.

18. *Le Triumphe de tres-haulte et puissante Dame Vérolle*, ed. Montaiglon, in *Recueil*, 4:214–83. Montaiglon issued a separate edition of the work in 1874. Page numbers will follow subsequent quotations from this edition in the text. His edition is based on the first edition, that of 1539. The anonymous author is identified in the title only as "L'Inventeur de menus plaisirs honnestes." For the Lucianic presentation of a disease as a figure in a procession, see the *Triumphe de haulte Folie*, discussed in chap. 5 above. Another edition of the Dame Vérolle triumph (1540) contained the *Pourpoint fermant à Boutons*, an independent work in which gout and venereal disease are once again linked. The *Pourpoint*'s subtitle was the *Déclinaison casuelle de la grosse Vérole*, and it was probably first published in Angers in 1533 (see *Le Triumphe*, ed. Montaiglon, 1874, 46). The work follows a grammatical format of declensions. Similar to it is *La Patenostre des Verollez*, in *Recueil*, ed. Montaiglon, 1:68–72. This verse parody of the Lord's Prayer ends each stanza with a line from the prayer. The writer puns on "goutte" and on the fact that doctors "ne voyent goutte" when it comes to finding a cure (68). He longs for the "fievre quartaine," which would give him "deux jours" of respite from pain. The Lord is not portrayed as being particularly sympathetic to these sufferers:

> Mais tu t'en ris et nous escouttes,
> Et nous souffrons en ce martyre
> (Des) rognes, chancres, gales et gouttes,
> Tant qu'en la fin nous fauldra dire:
> *Fiat voluntas tua.*
> (69)

Clément Marot also juxtaposes gout and venereal disease, in the fourth "coq à l'âne": "Les gouttes viennent en saison / Quand la verolle a faict son cours" (*Oeu-*

vres satiriques, ed. Mayer, 148). Falstaff takes advantage of his own gout and pox to justify his cowardice, remarking that "A good wit will make use of anything; I will turn diseases to commodity" (*Henry IV, Part II*, ed. Humphreys, 1.2.249–50).

19. lxiv. The idea of a disease in a triumphal procession is picked up by Hans Holbein in a 1545 woodcut "Der Triumph des Arztes." In this print, Doctor Jacobus Castricus, framed by a triumphal arch, rides in a fine chariot. Under the horses' hooves, personified diseases such as the fever and the plague are being crushed. The figure of Death is at his feet. The horses are led by ladies named after various medicinal herbs—Melissa, Mentha, Arthemisia, and so on. See Willehad Paul Eckert and Christoph von Imhoff, *Willibald Pirckheimer*, 193. This Triumph motif has already been noted in chap. 3 above, in connection with G. B. Pontanus.

20. The complaint runs: "A cinq cens dyables la vérolle / Et l'ord vaisseau où je la prins" (1539), xcvi. The same "huictain" was reprinted in Paris in 1543 in *La Fleur de poésie françoyse* (like the 1539 edition, Paris: Alain Lotrian), 27, and in the *Courtizan amoureux* (1582). The writer complains of losing his teeth as a result of the "vérolle." Treatment for the disease was usually by guaiac (lignum vitae), mercury, or heat treatments. In Eustorg de Beaulieu's *Les divers Rapports*, first published in Lyons (1537), a "paovre Verollé" complains of his treatment by means of heat and a hot bed. As a result, he is burning "pis que alumete" (ed. M. A. Pegg, 144). Rabelais's references to the various unpleasant sixteenth-century treatments for venereal diseases are discussed by Mottron.

21. Trtnik-Rossettini, 166–75.

22. This capitolo is discussed in chap. 4 above.

23. *Blasons* (de Tournes), 3. Page numbers will be given in the text for subsequent quotations from this edition.

24. Genesis 32:24–32.

25. See Berni, "Capitolo primo della peste," ll. 103–5, in *Rime*, ed. Bárberi Squarotti, 129.

26. See Pierre de Bourdeille, seigneur de Brantôme, *Vies des grands capitaines*, ed. J.A.C. Buchon, vol. 1, under "Dom Anthoine de Lève." Brantôme says that the general was "goutteux, podagre, maladif, tousjours en douleurs et langueurs: il combattoit porté en chaire comme s'il fust esté à cheval." He then wonders "Qu'eust il faict s'il fust esté bien sain et dispos de ses membres?" On Rabelais's ironic comment on Leyva's abortive attempt to invade Provence, see Marcel Françon's "L'Invasion de la Provence . . . (suite)," 51, and "Sur l'Invasion de la Provence de 1536." Montaigne mentions Leyva in *Essais*, ed. Thibaudet, 1:xi.

27. Cf. above, n. 12.

28. Severus (A.D. 146–211) was admired for his cunning by none other than Machiavelli.

29. Pliny, *Natural History*, 22.57, Loeb CLS, 6:119–21.

30. "Agios" in this context means "simagrées, actions et paroles vaines" (see Huguet, *Dictionnaire*, under "Agio").

31. See above, nn. 15 and 18, and also Cotgrave, *A Dictionarie*, under "goutte." Cotgrave quotes a French proverb, "A la goutte le médecin ne voit goutte," which he translates "(As they find [by the little helpe they find] that have it, and take

Physick for it)." Punning on the various meanings of the word *goute* was thus widespread. Copeman, 1, calls gout a "lay colloquialism" from the Latin *gutta* (drop).

32. The play, composed in alexandrines, was *La Goutte, tragédie nouvelle* (1605). The two eighteenth-century encomia are: Louis Coquelet, *Eloge de la Goutte* (1727) and Etienne Coulet, *Eloge de la Goute*. See above, chap. 3, n. 63.

33. Balthasar Conradinus's work, *Febris miscellanea ungarica* (1574), was edited by Michael Toxites, who was also responsible for the 1570 edition of Pirckheimer, Lucian, and Ballista's works on gout.

Thaddeus Dunus, born in 1523 in Locarno, fled to Zurich to escape religious persecution. A friend of Conrad Gesner, he died at an advanced age in the early seventeenth century. His *De Hemitritaeo sive de febre semitertiana libellus* is contained in a volume published in 1555. Jean Fernel's *Febrium curandorum methodus generalis* was published in 1577. Paré devoted several chapters of *Les Oeuvres* to fevers. His ideas resemble those found in other writers. Of the quartan fever he remarks that it consists of a series of "accez" by which nature seeks to rid itself of the "humeur qui luy est fascheux & moleste" (1575 ed., 220). Caused by an excess of "suc melancholic," it is frequent in autumn, in part because of the dryness and coldness of that season. In its favor he notes, as had mock encomiasts, that it prevents many other maladies such as epilepsy and melancholy. He proposes cures by way of mild medications, warm white wine, and "eau de vie." His minute discriminations lead him to discern what he calls a "fievre quarte intermittente bastarde" (215). Fortunately for poetry, the Lyons blasonneur, no doctor, was less meticulous about nomenclature. Dudley Wilson, in *French Renaissance Scientific Poetry*, 159 n. 7, notes that Ronsard suffered from quartan fever in about 1568. In "La Salade," Ronsard calls the illness "Cette execrable horrible fiebvre quarte / Qui me consomme & le corps & le coeur / Et me fait vivre en extreme langueur" (*Oeuvres*, ed. Laumonier, 15:78, ll. 34–36). Wilson adds that it is par excellence the "melancholy fever" (159 n. 7).

Rondelet's contribution to the study and treatment of fevers is contained in his *Methodus curandorum omnium morborum*, discussed above, n. 7. Georgius Valla (1430–1490) translated *Alexandri Aphrodisaei de febrium causis*, of which there is a Lyons edition of 1506. His *De evitanda podagra* was published with Lucian's *Podagra* and Pirckheimer's encomium in Lyons in 1529, another example of the Renaissance mingling of the medical and the literary (see above, chap. 3, nn. 39 and 61).

34. Montaigne, *Essais*, ed. Thibaudet, 1.26.195. Alfred Glauser asserts that Montaigne's attitude to medicine was essentially paradoxical. Alfred Glauser's *Montaigne paradoxal* has an entire section entitled "Maladie et médecine paradoxales" (99–104). Montaigne, says Glauser, "fait l'éloge paradoxal de la pierre." The essayist's fight with and contemplation of disease produced complex and subtle reflexions. Literature became a way of calming pain: "Sur les sujets les plus graves, la pensée devient frivole; elle endort les maux, s'amuse pour les supprimer" (101). In short, "sans le goût du paradoxe, cette oeuvre [*Les Essais*] n'existait pas" (153). Glauser's claim serves to remind us of the importance of paradoxes of all sorts for Montaigne.

35. 19. The last line here subtly recalls the notion of common opinion (cf. above, chap. 1, n. 61).

36. 19. If correctly printed, this use of the term *ferité*, from the Italian *ferita* [wound] would be one of the earliest in French. For its use by Estienne, see his *Deux Dialogues*, ed. P. M. Smith, 67 n. 16. Estienne and Le Plessis used the term in 1553. However, given the kind of verbal parallels the poet seems to be setting up, we should perhaps read *fierté*, pride.

37. 19. For Paré's notion of the fever as a kind of purge, see above, n. 33.

38. 23. The efficacy of fear as a cure had already been sardonically noted by Cardano.

39. François Habert, *Le Combat de Cupido et de la Mort*. Habert styles himself the "Banny de Liesse," and was, as his poem on poverty indicates, poor for most of his life (1520?–1562?). The poem mentioned here is his "Exclamation contre Dame Vérolle que les aucuns appellent le Mal Italique, & les aultres le mal Françoys, Au moyen d'un sien amy par elle rudement traicté." Habert is at least less chauvinistic about the place of origin of the disease than Bino had been in his capitolo on the illness, entitled "In lode del Malfrancese" (in Grazzini, ed., 1:167ᵛ–71ʳ). The joking tone and stress on the transformations brought about by venereal disease brings Bino's poem close to that of Habert. Like writers discussing many illnesses, he claims that venereal disease prevents the attacks of other maladies. His tone is, to say the least, ambivalent:

> Tu i pazzi savi fai, & belli i brutti,
> Liberi i servi, & i poveri ricchi,
> Giovani, i vecchi & tanti altri bei frutti.
>
> Per nostro ben prego Dio che t'appicchi,
> A chi ti cerca, & in lui come un'ago,
> Come un chiodo t'infilzi & ti conficchi.
> (1:171ʳ)

40. Playful or ironic portraits will be frequently mentioned in connection with animal epitaphs and encomia, discussed in chap. 6 below.

41. viii–ix. Rabelais's fondness for this type of ironic juxtaposition has been noted above. The narrator of the *Triumphe* states that he wishes to present the "verollez" with a "pourtraict" of "celle qui les a vaincuz."

42. As Marot puts it, "Il n'est crotte que de Paris, / Ne verolle que de Rouen" (*Oeuvres satiriques*, ed. Mayer, 167). Montaiglon notes a similarly resigned French proverb, "crotte de Paris et vérolle de Rouen ne s'en vont qu'avec la pièce" (*Recueil*, 4:219). Cardano discussed cures in his *De Radice Cina, et Sarza Parillia*, part of the 1564 edition of the French physician Auger Ferrier's *De Pudendagra lue Hispanica, Libri duo*. On Fracastoro's *Syphilis*, source of the name of one form of venereal disease, see above, chap. 3, n. 62. Paré devotes book 18 of his *Oeuvres* to the topic. See also, above, n. 20.

43. See Montaiglon, ed., *Le Triumphe de haulte Folie*, (originally Lyons: Anthoine Volant, ca. 1550), 6. The popular association between gout and the "pox" was graphically expressed by Falstaff in the same scene in which he talks about turning diseases to commodity: "A pox of this gout! or a gout of this pox! for the one or the other plays the rogue with my great toe" (*Henry IV, Part II*, 1.2.244–46).

44. Du Bellay, *Regrets*, in *Oeuvres poétiques*, ed. Chamard, 2:52, sonnet 1.

45. On Du Bellay's deafness, see the anonymous article, "La Surdité de Joachim du Bellay," 10. After his two–year illness in 1549, the poet was never really well. Irritable and oversensitive, he grew increasingly deaf from 1552 on. Later in life he communicated with his friends in writing. Gladys Dickinson, *Du Bellay in Rome*, 9, describes the difficulties caused the poet in Rome by his deafness. She states that he was stone deaf by 1560. The "Hymne de la Surdité," as the text of the poem suggests, falls in the years between the onset of Du Bellay's affliction and his eventual total deafness.

46. For a sober appreciation of the poem, seemingly oblivious to its frequently ironic tone, see Jean-Marc Bernard, "Les *Jeux rustiques* de Joachim Du Bellay." This fine hymn, says Bernard, is "tout composé de beaux vers didactiques, de beaux vers dorés, d'un ton soutenu et comme gonflé par le lyrisme intérieur" (412). Du Bellay's portrait of deafness is found to resemble that of Melancholia by Dürer. Trtnik-Rossettini focuses on the paradoxical nature of the poem, calling it "le plus original de tous les paradoxes français de cette époque." She believes it to be the only Renaissance French mock encomium on a disease, since "le Blason en l'honneur de la goutte ne peut pas être considéré comme une satire paradoxe proprement dite" (181). While the amount of satire in Du Bellay's poem is certainly greater than that in the works on gout and the quartan fever, the latter two poems surely deserve the place given them here in the history of the paradoxical encomium.

47. Du Bellay, *Divers Jeux rustiques*, in *Oeuvres poétiques*, ed. Chamard, 5:185, ll. 7–14. Line numbers for subsequent quotations from the "Hymne" will be given in the text. Much of the discussion of this "Hymne" is adapted from my article, "Mock Epideictic Literature."

48. 16–22. Note Du Bellay's use of the familiar Horatian quotation about the mingling of tones, "qui miscuit utile dulci" (*Ars poetica*, or *Epist. ad Pis.*, Loeb CLS, 343–44). Du Bellay's constant tendency to a more negative self-evaluation and manner of presenting himself than is found in Ronsard has been discussed by François Rigolot, *Le Texte*, 212–19.

49. For use of the same proverb in the sonnets, see Du Bellay, *Regrets*, sonnet 143 (in *Oeuvres poétiques*, ed. Chamard, 2:167): "Bizet, j'aymerois mieulx faire un boeuf d'un formy, / Ou faire d'une mousche un Indique Eliphant." For the idea of turning black to white by linguistic tricks, see *Regrets*, sonnet 182 (in *Oeuvres poétiques*, ed. Chamard, 2:196):

> Je ne suis pas de ceulx qui robbent la louange,
> Fraudant indignement les hommes de valeur,
> Ou qui changeant la noire à la blanche couleur
> Sçavent, comme lon dit, faire dun diable un ange.

This image is closely linked to Du Bellay's general condemnation of hypocrisy at court. Clément Marot had earlier used the black-and-white image not to discuss verbal disguise but to stress the need for the poet to vary his tone:

> voulentiers, qui l'Esprit exercite,
> Ores le Blanc, ores le Noir recite,
> Et est le Painctre indigne de louange,
> Qui ne sçait paindre aussi bien Diable qu'Ange.

These lines appear in the "Epître xxxix," a self-defense for his blason on the "laid Tetin," and they reflect the traditional interest in arguing for and against the same subject (Marot, *Les Epîtres*, ed. Mayer, 215). Marot urged writers to compose poems attacking the parts of the body they had previously praised, but without praising the "honteux" parts of the anatomy (216). The difference between Marot's and Du Bellay's use of this black-and-white image reflects the difference between the straightforward descriptive blason and its ironic, Lucianic form.

50. Du Bellay might have had in mind Grazzini's "Capitolo della Pazzia," given that the reference to "la peste" is surely to Berni. The anonymous *La Pazzia*, discussed in chap. 4 above, also antedates the French hymn. However, in view of the universal fame of Erasmus's work, it seems most likely that Du Bellay was here referring to the *Moriae Encomium*, as Saulnier asserts (*Divers Jeux rustiques*, ed. Saulnier, 177 n. 32).

51. Du Bellay, *Oeuvres poétiques*, ed. Chamard, 5:187 n. 1. For Paré as a likely source here, see Saulnier, ed., *Divers Jeux rustiques*, 178. The sixteenth century was an important one for research on the ear. Bartolomeo Eustachi (ca. 1500–1574) and Gabriello Falloppio (ca. 1523–ca. 1562) both published on the subject and were active in Italy in the 1550s when Du Bellay was in Rome.

52. Bronzino, in Grazzini, ed., 2:152^r. The second poem is 2:153^r–159^v. Belleau also composed a poem, "Sur l'Importunité d'une cloche," (in *Oeuvres poétiques*, ed. Marty-Laveaux, 1:111–15). In the poem, part of the *Petites Inventions* of 1556, the narrator criticizes the bell's noisiness, especially as it disturbs his friend Nicolas, suffering from a "mal de teste" (113). Nicolas's attack of quartan fever, pretext for the composition of Belleau's "Le Mulet," is also mentioned in the poem (114). The attack ends with the wish that the bell may fall and break. In a later poem the poet adopted a very different attitude to sound. In "Le Sifflet," part of the *Seconde Journee de la Bergerie* (in *Oeuvres poétiques*, ed. Marty-Laveaux, 2:130–32), he declares that the world consists of a kind of "sifflet," not the atoms of Epicurus. Sounds are necessary for a variety of reasons—to wake and entertain us, and to rouse lovers, servants, and dogs. "Le Mulet" is discussed in chap. 7 below.

53. Many of Estienne's handwritten notes, discovered by Saulnier in an edition of the works of Du Bellay in the Bibliothèque municipale of Lyons (see *Divers Jeux rustiques*, ed. Saulnier, lxv), were reproduced in his introduction (here, 185).

54. The theme of the possible advantages of blindness is touched on in *La Récréation et passetemps des tristes* (1595), in an anonymous poem, "Du Bien qu'un aveugle pense avoir":

> Celuy qui souffre mal des yeux,
> Souffre aussi grief desplaisir,
> Et n'a à l'advis de plus vieux
> Rien ne voyant qu'un seul plaisir,
> Qui est de n'avoir le loisir
> De voir malheur et maux infames,
> Et singulièrement les femmes.
>
> (78)

The misogynistic tone of this poem is typical of the entire collection. The same poem appeared earlier, also anonymously, in the 1551 *Louange des femmes* (Lyons:

n.p.) and the 1573 edition of *La Récréation et passetemps des tristes*. It is quite different in tone from the Stoic paradoxes discussed in connection with Cicero.

55. See *Divers Jeux rustiques*, ed. Saulnier, 187. The address to a personified and sanctified being is similar to that by Ronsard at the end of the "Hymne de la Philosophie" (*Oeuvres complètes*, ed. Laumonier, 4:266–67).

56. Annibal de l'Ortigue, *Poèmes divers*, 184. Cf. above, chap. 5, n. 93, for Condeescu's praise of de l'Ortigue. Page numbers for subsequent quotations from this edition will be given in the text.

57. Discussed above, n. 18.

58. Littré also defines "la gale de Naples" as "mal vénérien" (*Dictionnaire*, under "Gale." Cotgrave gives definitions for *galle, galleux,* and *galler,* all terms related to severe types of itching. The term *la pelade* refers to the loss of hair often associated with venereal disease. In a lengthy discussion of *la pelade* (*Oeuvres complètes*, 19.690), Paré repeats the picturesque suggestion of Rondelet that one boil a mole (*taupe*) and make of it an ointment to restore the hair. Du Bellay's sonnet 86 (*Regrets*, in *Oeuvres poétiques*, ed. Chamard, 2:118) states that

> Voila de ceste Court la plus grande vertu,
> Dont souvent mal monté, mal sain, & mal vestu,
> Sans barbe & sans argent on s'en retourne en France.

The idea reappears in sonnet 94 of the *Regrets* (ed. Chamard, 2:126):

> Heureux qui sans soucy peult garder son tresor,
> Sa femme sans souspçon, & plus heureux encor'
> Qui a peu sans peler vivre trois ans à Rome!

Chamard's note to these lines again cites Paré: "L'alopecie est cheute du poil de la teste, & quelquesfois des sourcils, barbe, & autres parties, dite vulgairement la pelade. . . . Or, pour la corruption des humeurs qui alterent la vapeur & matiere dont les cheveux sont engendrés, vient alopecie: ce qui procede du vice de tout le corps, comme l'on voit en la maladie Neapolitaine, autrement grosse vérolle" (*Regrets*, 2:126 n. 1). Venereal disease and "la gale" continued to be associated in two seventeenth–century mock "testaments." Both appear in the 1618 *Cabinet satyrique*, ed. Fleuret and Perceau, 2:256–58 and 1:252–55. The first the "Testament d'un vérolé, Satyre," is by Z. Blénet, and the second, with the same title, is by Sygognes and had first appeared in 1617. In both, the speakers bequeath symptoms of their illness to those who tormented or infected them.

59. "Le Blason des barbes de maintenant," in *Receuil*, ed. Montaiglon, 2:210–22. Page numbers will be given in the text for subsequent quotations from this edition.

60. Pike, 239.

61. Daniel Sheerin explains that the *editio princeps* of the eclogue, ca. 1496 (Mainz: Peter von Friedburg) was followed by other editions in 1505, 1507, 1510, 1516, and 1519. Hucbald's poem intrigued later readers largely because every word in it began with the letter *c*. Since in some editions the poem runs to six sides in length, it was certainly a linguistic *tour de force*. The British Library has an edition of 1552. It was also reprinted in the early seventeenth-century anthologies of mock encomia described in connection with Dornavius.

62. Grazzini, *Le Rime burlesche*, ed. Verzone, 479.

63. Antoine Hotman (1525?–1596), Πωγωνιας, *sive De Barba, Dialogus*, see above, chap. 3, n. 65. According to the *Nouvelle Biographie universelle*, this work was often attributed to Antoine's more famous brother.

64. Pike, 240.

65. Anon., *La Response et contredict d'un barbu* (1551). The work is extremely rare.

66. See my article "Clément Marot," 45–48, for a discussion of Marot's "En m'esbatant je faiz Rondeaux en rime," the "Petite Epistre au Roy" (in *Les Epîtres*, ed. Mayer, 97).

67. The poem (originally 1614) is entitled "Satyre contre la barbe d'un Courtisan." Here quoted from the *Cabinet satyrique*, ed. Fleuret and Perceau, 1:520.

68. On Jean de Schelandre (the name was an anagram of Daniel d'Anchères), see Charles Asselineau (the friend and editor of Baudelaire), *Notice sur Jean de Schelandre*.

69. Jean Dant, *Le Chauve ou le mespris des cheveux* (1621). In 1680 appeared an anonymous burlesque dialogue, *Le Rasibus*, which mocks the Capuchins' desire to keep their beards and criticizes as effeminate those who curl their beards. The work concludes with a group of poems with titles such as "Le Capucin rajeuni," "La Déroute des Barbes," "Epitaphes des Barbes," and a parody of the Lord's Prayer, "Le Pater Noster des Capucins," in which each phrase of the prayer introduces lines begging God to preserve the Capuchins' beards.

70. Eustorg de Beaulieu, *Les Divers Rapports*, ed. Pegg, 289.

71. See Saunders, "Sixteenth-Century Collected Editions," 351–68. Beaulieu's and Darles's blasons appeared in the earliest editions of 1537, whereas the contre-blasons did not begin to appear until the 1543 Paris edition by l'Angelier. Jean Rus's poem was first published around 1540 in Toulouse by Guyon Boudeville and was reprinted in the nineteenth century, in the *Oeuvres de Jean Rus*, ed. Philippe Tamizey de Larroque, 23–26. On nose-literature in general, see Ugo Viviani, *Nasuti*.

72. Dolce, "Capitolo del Naso," in 1:194^r–97^r.

73. I have sought to show elsewhere that certain French blasons are borderline cases so far as ironic presentation is concerned. Beaulieu's "Le Pet," for example, proves to be so ironic that we can readily understand why the term *contre-blason* came to be used for poems with a directly rather than indirectly critical point of view. See Tomarken and Tomarken, 139–63.

74. The poem is also reprinted by E. Fournier in *Variétés*, 5:133–46.

75. Etienne Forcadel's epitaph on Guyon Precy (*Poésie d'Estienne Forcadel*, 181–82), also stresses the beauties of his drunkard's "nez precieux." Rabelais's fondness for the adjective "precieux" in an ironic context was noted earlier in this chapter. Sygognes' *Satyre contre le nez d'un courtisan* appeared in the *Cabinet satyrique* of 1618, ed. Fleuret and Perceau, 1:517–18. It was first published in the *Recueil des plus excellans vers* of 1617 and in Tabourot's *Les Bigarrures* of 1614. It speaks of the nose as a "Nez à peindre, nez à escrire, / Nez qui me faict mourir de rire" (518). The words *peindre* and *rire* place the poem firmly in the tradition of the playful blason. An epitaph on the nose appears in *Les Satyres . . . du sieur Regnier* (1617), 230–31. The poem is not by Regnier. It begins "Cy gist un nez le plus estrange,"

and describes a swollen, smelly, colorful nose. Also published in the early part of the seventeenth century was "Le Nez," by Jean Auvray, a surgeon and lawyer who died in 1623. Auvray's works alternated between strong religious faith and equally strong epicureanism (see F. Lachèvre, *Les Recueils collectifs*, 79–84). The poem first appeared in 1623, then was reprinted in *Le Banquet des Muses ou les diverses satires du sieur Auvray* (1628). It sounds in parts like a forerunner of the famous passage in *Cyrano de Bergerac*:

> Ce grand Nez sert en mainte sorte,
> De verroüil à fermer la porte,
> De bourdon pour un Pelerin,
> De javelot, de hallebarde,
> De pilon à broyer moustarde,
> Et de claquet pour un moulin.
> Il sert aux Massons de truelle,
> D'un eventail à Damoiselle,
> De besche pour les Jardiniers,
> De soc pour labourer la terre,
> D'une trompette pour la guerre,
> Et d'astrolabe aux Mariniers.
>
> (*Le Banquet*, 45)

76. Included in Regnier, *Les Satyres et autres oeuvres folastres*, 110^r–10^v. But this poem, like similar ones by Regnier, Motin, and others, abandons the element of mock praise in favor of direct criticism. One might call them *blasons-médaillons*, using Saulnier's term (*Maurice Scève*, 76), but of the negative variety, not the positive. On the blasons on the "Platellet" and the "Gobellet," see Montaiglon, ed., *Receuil*, and chap. 5, n. 10. On Rabelais and the codpiece, see above, chap. 5, n. 87.

77. Grazzini, *Le Rime burlesche*, ed. Verzone, 618–21.

78. Doni's work appeared in Lyons: Estienne Michel, 1580. The French version was entitled *Les Mondes celestes*. On Doni himself, see Grendler, 49–65.

79. Belleau, *Oeuvres poétiques*, ed. Marty-Laveaux, 1:83–87. Page numbers for subsequent quotations from this edition will be given in the text. The 1578 edition appeared after the poet's death in 1577, as part of *Les Odes d'Anacréon teien, poète grec*. Eckhardt, *Remy Belleau*, 137, notes that Belleau's poem on horns seems influenced by Robert Estienne's *Thesaurus*, because it makes use of certain obscure Latin meanings of *cornu* listed by Estienne.

80. We know little about de Guersens, although Lachèvre and the *Nouvelle Biographie universelle* provide some information, as do La Croix du Maine and Du Verdier. Born in Normandy, he seems, with J. C. Scaliger, to have taken lessons from Turnèbe. An excellent linguist, he fell in love with Catherine des Roches, heroine of the flea poems to be studied in the final chapter of this work. Rejected, he eventually married another. He lived in a milieu and at a time when Ronsard's style was influential and the writing of playful encomia much enjoyed. For details, see George E. Diller, *Les Dames des Roches*, 28–35. Guersens's poem first appeared in *La Muse folastre* (1607). Other editions were Lyons, 1611, and Rouen, 1615. Citations, with line numbers in the text, are from the 1611 edition reprinted in 1864 in Brussels. A similar poem, published in the 1615 edition, *Le Premier Livre*, 59^r–62^r,

the "Consolation pour les Cocus," urges despondent cuckolds to put aside their distress. They will never lack for anything, since a wife's lovers will always protect her deceived husband, and the wife will also wish to please him in order to preserve her public reputation. He will be adored "comme un saint" (60ᵛ), an expression that recalls the respect accorded those other false goddesses, folly and gout. Even if the husband is a kind of martyr, there is still no need for worry. Since God loves martyrs, the man should in fact thank his wife for placing him in this happy state. Another poem, "La Louange des cornes," attributed to C. Brisard, appears in *La Muse folastre*, 1615 edition (*Le Second Livre*, 7–13). More playful than de Guersens's work, it asserts that nothing is more attractive than the horn of plenty or than Jupiter's horned disguises. Since young people will perforce be young, we should not resent this inevitable sign of their activity:

> O cornes tiltres d'honneur,
> Cornes tesmoins d'un bon heur,
> Cornes que chacun salue
> Quand on les voit par la rue.
> (13)

81. Passerat, *Poésies françaises*, ed. Blanchemain, 2:137.

82. Passerat, *Poésies françaises*, ed. Blanchemain, 1:120. Passerat's interest in this topic must have been considerable, for his "Metamorphose d'un homme en oiseau" describes a jealous old man turned into a "cocu" by his young wife, who left him for another "nest" (ed. Blanchemain, 1:33–37). In revenge, cuckoos now lay their eggs in other birds' nests, but, regretting their original faithless mates, always ask, in a last vestige of human speech, "qu'Où?" The irrepressible author ends "Heureux ceux-là qui ont ce privilege!" (37), referring to the privilege of relieving grief by laying one's eggs elsewhere. The role of the two sexes is confused here. Who is laying the eggs, the male or the female? Or is the poet thinking merely of fertilization, in which case the male has taken over the role of the adulterer? Nonetheless, the general drift of the poem remains clear enough.

The number of poems on cuckoldry might suggest to sociologists an outbreak of extramarital activity in this period. Motin wrote "Contre un cocu jaloux," first published in the *Recueil des plus excellans vers* of 1617, and reproduced in *Le Cabinet satyrique*, ed. Fleuret and Perceau, 1:301–4. The poet mocks the man's blindness but sardonically urges him to remain oblivious: "Bien, vous estes cocu, mais ne pensez pas l'estre, / Car l'estre et le penser c'est l'estre doublement" (304). Sygognes, ever alert to human foibles, also has a piece in the *Cabinet satyrique*, 1:296–98, "Stances sur la crainte du cocuage." We are told, he writes, that it will be done unto us as we do to others. Since all men have been guilty of cuckolding someone, have "—tu quelqu'une," as the poet coyly puts it, they must expect like treatment. In the previous century, just after the publication of Belleau's poem on horns, Forcadel included a short work "De n'estre jaloux," in his *Oeuvres poétiques*, ed. Marty-Laveaux, 149. He urges men not to be jealous, since such passion is useless. Many are jealous for no good reason, while others are confident even though all their friends know that they are deceived.

Finally, the question of cuckoldry received paradoxical consideration in England, by R[obert] Heath, in *Paradoxical Assertions* (1659). These Lando-type paradoxical essays were presented by their author as "ioco-seria" (cf. Dornavius's title). One is entitled "Why Cuckolds are said to wear Horns?"; others come directly from Lando, such as "That Imprisonment is better than Liberty," while some are unabashedly sexist: "Why a fair Woman is said to be a Fish below?". At least one reveals some unpleasant prejudices: "Why Jews are said to Stink Naturally."

83. *Les Muses gaillardes*, collected by A.D.B., probably Antoine du Brueil, n.d., n.p. [1609?], 150. On this collection, see P. L. Jacob, "Les Muses gaillardes.'

CHAPTER SEVEN

1. Homer's *Batrachomyomachia*, a parody of epic battle scenes, was cited in many Neo-Latin mock encomia and imitated by Elisius Calentius in Latin under the title *De Bello ranarum et murium, libri III* (part of the *Opuscula Elisii Calentii* [1503]). Eliseo Calenzio was born in Puglia in the middle of the fifteenth century. Separate editions of his poem appeared in 1511, 1512, and 1517. It was translated into French in 1532 and was also placed on the Index. The poem is not, strictly speaking, an animal eulogy but resembles one in that it describes creatures not usually considered worthy of serious consideration. Paul Lacroix (pen name of P. L. Jacob) praises it as a "chef-d'oeuvre de satire allégorique" (*La Bataille fantastique*, ed. Lacroix, vii). The two kings, a rat and a frog, may represent Charles VIII of France and Frederick, king of Naples, asserts Lacroix, who discusses possible attribution of the piece to Rabelais. Seven French editions are listed by Lacroix, who reprints the 1559 edition. The introduction to the work mentions writings frequently listed in prefaces to mock encomia, Virgil's "petites mouches" and Diocles' "grands louanges" on "Raves." Furthermore, the justification offered for treating such humble matters echoes that proposed by many mock encomiasts: "Je cognois plusieurs non de petite estime, delaissees aucunes fois les choses graves, avoir traité des negoces de petit pris, et valeur" (*Bataille*, 7). As in the *Muscae Encomium*, the burlesque element is prominent. This manner of presenting an imitation of Homer shows once again the flexibility with which Renaissance writers viewed the mock encomium. An element of praise combined with an element of irony or satire was sufficient to link a work to the broad tradition.

2. Much of the background to the present chapter comes from Naïs, *Les Animaux*, a work that discusses at length the classical editions of works on animals. Page numbers will be given in the text for subsequent citations from Naïs in this chapter.

3. Jean Lemaire de Belges, *Les Epîtres de l'Amant Vert*, ed. Jean Frappier, 15. Page references for subsequent quotations from this edition will be given in the text.

4. See, for example, *Les Epîtres*, ed. Frappier, xix–xxv. François Rigolot devotes a lengthy section of his *Le Texte* to Jean Lemaire de Belges and the *Epîtres*. He comments on what he aptly calls the "vaste panorama intertextuel de l'ornithologie" which is presented in the second poem, when the parrot visits the underworld (86).

5. Published first in *La Suite de l'adolescence clementine* (n.d.). Here quoted from Clément Marot, *Oeuvres diverses*, ed. Mayer, 226. The 1824 edition of Marot

quotes Pasquier's remarks about the poem's evocation of the horse: "Vous voyez un cheval bondir sur le papier, et estre mené à courbettes, tantost au galop, tantost au trot, tout ainsi que s'il estoit en plein manége, piqué par un escuyer," cited in *Oeuvres complètes de Clément Marot*, 517 n. 1.

6. Pierre Danche, *Les trois Blasons*, (n.d.), 4ᵛ. This comparison becomes a cliché. Thus, the *Cabinet satyrique*, ed. Fleuret and Perceau, 1:368, contains a "Comparaison de la femme au cheval." Women and horses should resemble one another in having a small head, large eyes, a wide brow, and strong thighs. They should be obedient to men, having "le montoir doux, la descente benigne." The only difference between them should be that the one bears a man on its back, the other on her front. This piece is one of a series of comparisons in which women are likened to trials, the moon, and demons. The group is preceded by Motin's "Contre les femmes." For a discussion of Danche, see Saunders, *The Sixteeenth-Century Blason Poétique*, 43–46. In another brief epitaph, entitled "De Frere André, Cordelier," Marot also uses the verb "chevaucher" in speaking of women: the dead man will be missed by the ladies because he "les chevauchoit / Comme ung grand Asne desbaté" (*Oeuvres diverses*, ed. Mayer, 200).

7. Melin de Sainct-Gelays, *Oeuvres complètes*, ed. Blanchemain, 1:53–57. Volume and page numbers for subsequent quotations will be given in the text. The poems were first published in Lyons by Pierre de Tours. To Blanchemain's mention of Navagero and Scaliger we may add Nicolas Bourbon, whose Catullan "De passerculo mortuo Rosae puellae" appeared in his *Nugae* (1533), viʳ. The sparrow continued to be a popular subject for epitaphs. Gilles Durant, sieur de la Bergerie, has a poem "Sur le Trepas du Passereau de Catin," *Livre II des Odes*, in *Les Ouevres poétiques*, (1594), 166ʳ–167ʳ. The same poet's playful "Contre une arondelle" (165ᵛ–66ʳ) attacks the bird for awaking him in the morning when he was busy with Catin, his beloved.

8. Henry Guy, "Les Sources françaises de Ronsard," 249. Another fascinating early Renaissance poem on a parrot is John Skelton's "Phyllyp Sparrowe" (about 1505), presented as an elegy by the bird's owner, Jane Scrope. It combines the mythological references found in Jean Lemaire de Belges with a far more Catullan sensuality. See *The Poetical Works*, 1:51–94.

9. See Paul Laumonier, *Ronsard poète lyrique*, 265. Laumonier agrees with Guy as to the continuity between the Pléiade and their predecessors in this domain: "Ils avaient une fois de plus, en dépit de leurs principes, continué l'oeuvre de l'école précédente" (265), i.e., that of Marot, Sainct-Gelays, the "rhétoriqueur" Jean Bouchet, and Jean Bonnefons (see Laumonier, 265 n. 5). Scaliger composed a Latin epitaph on the death of a dog Adamas, and Alberti's *Canis*, one of the earliest Renaissance animal encomia, also concerned a dog. Grazzini wrote a *canzone* "Nella morte d'un cane di M. Pandolfo de Pucci" (*Opere burlesche*, ed. Verzone, 155–58), and Belleau later composed an "Epitaphe de Travail," about a brave watchdog and loyal sheepdog (*Oeuvres poétiques*, ed. Marty-Laveaux, 2:112–16). Annibal de l'Ortigue, discussed in earlier chapters, contributed a poem on "La Mort de Florentin petit chien pelé" (*Oeuvres*, 431–34). In an odd combination of humor and pathos, the narrator claims that the dog was at once "rogue" and "delectable," that it died for love of another dog, Turquette, and managed to bite Charon on its way to Hades.

The goddess Diana herself begged for it to be made into a star. The playful, more familiar posture of the poet is reminiscent of that found in Du Bellay's animal epitaphs.

10. There may have been a reason other than mere sentiment for the king's decision to make a pair of gloves of Courte's skin. One of the *Sermoni funebri*, on a dog, explains that boots of dogskin protect against Podagra, while dogskin gloves ward off gout of the fingers, Chiragra (the lament "Del Burchiello nella morte d'un suo cane detto Lionzo" in *Sermoni funebri de vari authori* [1548], 15ᵛ).

11. Margaret de Schweinitz writes of Ronsard's poem: "Célébrant la chienne du roi, Ronsard demeure un peu plus élégant que Du Bellay, moins marotique, et somme toute, dans un badinage de ce genre, moins charmant," *Les Epitaphes de Ronsard*, 107. The present analysis suggests that charm was only one of Ronsard's goals in the poem.

12. Du Bellay, *Divers Jeux rustiques*, ed. Saulnier, xxix. On Du Bellay's abilities as a translator, see Michel Glatigny, "Du Bellay traducteur." Glatigny notes that Du Bellay was a subtle and inventive translator, ever seeking concision and vividness of expression while modernizing certain antique details. In a more recent essay, Geneviève Demerson even suggests that at times Du Bellay seems more at home in Latin than in French ("Joachim Du Bellay traducteur de lui-même"). Platt also discusses the "voeux" group of poems, which she sees as paralleling the "Hymne de la Surdité" in the overall structure of the collection. Both plead for things beyond man's control, such as immortality; both address beings superior to Du Bellay (the gods and Ronsard). But the "Hymne" is nobler in tone and more complex than the "voeux," and is also, Platt feels, more original. Furthermore, the "Hymne" wishes paradoxically for an undesirable gift (deafness), unlike the more normal wishes of the "voeux." For Platt, the animal epitaphs serve to demonstrate spontaneous and natural love as opposed to the formalized, codified love behavior of humans.

13. Du Bellay, *Divers Jeux rustiques*, ed. Saulnier, 99n. A playful epitaph by René Bretonnayau, the doctor whose alexandrines on hemorrhoids have been discussed above, concerns the monkey. In "Le Singe," the deceased monkey chides those who mock its death (*La Génération de l'homme* [1583], 181ʳ). The clever creature, loyal and brave, could tell its master's friends from his enemies, had attractive fur and teeth, and was a nimble dancer. The customary mythological adornment asserts that the first monkey lost its tail for stealing the rib from Prometheus when he was making Eve from Adam. This poem is interesting historically because it cites, not the familiar classical predecessors, but Du Bellay's poems on Belant and Pelotan (*sic*) as authorities.

Another poem on the monkey, in *La Muse folastre* (1615), *Le Second Livre*, 79–82, concerns a monkey-like human being, not a real animal. This "singe" is portrayed as a greedy, dirty, tricky magician fond of astrology. Cf. Du Bellay's reference to "vieux singes de court" who follow and mimic their royal masters (*Regrets*, sonnet 150, in *Oeuvres*, ed. Chamard, 172), and cf. above, chap. 5, n. 51. The dedication of Aretino's *Dialogues* is also "to his darling monkey" (ed. Rosenthal, 11).

14. Ed. Grazzini, 2:24ʳ–26ᵛ. Page numbers for subsequent quotations from this poem are given in the text.

15. Yvonne Niord, "A Study of the 'Imitation' of Italian Writers," notes further

points of similarity between the two poems. Both writers use the image of the glove as their cat unsheathes its claws, regret that their cat had no offspring, and tease the reader with a similar minute attention to detail on matters concerning which no one could correct them. Du Bellay, recalling one trick of Belaud's, adds "que j'aye souvenance" (*Divers Jeux rustiques*, ed. Saulnier, 109), while Coppetta remarks " (s'io non fallo)" (24ʳ). The *Sermoni funebri* also contain a short lament on a cat (26ʳ–27ᵛ), which bears some resemblance to Du Bellay's epitaph. This noble and irreplaceable cat caught mice and kept its owner's feet warm in winter. An earlier cat poem, by Jean Molinet, focused less on the cat as an animal and more on its usefulness for criticism of religious abuses. The poem, "Le present dung cat nonne," parallels a cat and a canon; aspects of the one serve to satirize the other:

> Ce cat nonne hante entre gent
> Il va piedz deschaulx sur les fentes
> Et ne manie point d'argent
> Son pourchas vault mieulx que ses rentes.
>
> . . . .
>
> Ce cat nonne devot et saige
> Sendort en disant ses patenostres
> Et de sa patte son visaige
> Lave aussi bien que lung des nostres.
> (Jean Molinet, *Les Faictz et dictz* [1537], cxvii)

Later in the century, Annibal de l'Ortigue, whose dog epitaph was mentioned above, n. 9, composed a cat poem remarkably close to that by Du Bellay, the "Epitaphe de Matou le plus illustre des Chats" (*Oeuvres*, 435–44). Descended from the cat in Noah's ark, Matou was a champion rat-killer whose skill at tormenting mice is vividly portrayed. The same details of behavior appear: the cat chases its tail, singes its fur by lying too close to the stove, does not scratch its master, fights dogs, and comes from a "race Royalle," not from a family of "Matous de village" (442). Its death is compared to that of Pyrrhus killed by the Theban women. It should be made into a star to replace the "chien d'Esté" (444).

16. *Les Oeuvres de Claude de Pontoux gentilhomme Chalonnois docteur en medecine* (1579), 315–28. On Pontoux and Ronsard, see Raymond, *L'Influence de Ronsard*, "Deuxième Partie," 32–26.

17. Chap. 1, "The Fair, the Pig, Authorship." For another pig poem, see note 38 below.

18. Gilles Durant, sieur de la Bergerie, *Les Meslanges poétiques*, 214ʳ–216ʳ (part of *Les Oeuvres poétiques*, 1594). This poem was often published with the *Satyre Ménippée* as an anti-Ligue work.

19. 215ᵛ. The exaggeration of this poem is similar to that found in a poem in *L'Espadon satyrique de Claude d'Esternod* (1619), ed. Fleuret and Perceau, entitled "Sur la Mort d'un perroquet que le chat mangea" (60–67). Professing to be as angry at the parrot's death as he would be if his own father had been killed, the poet concludes with an extended attack on the guilty cat. The link with Jean Lemaire is evident in the topic, while the grotesque exaggeration recalls the Bernesque capitoli.

20. Reprinted by Edouard Fournier, *Variétés*, 4:255–71. Here p. 255. Lycophagos is translated into French by the author as "Mange-loup." The dog worked

turning the spit over the fire in the kitchen of a Paris college. Fournier points out that even Racine composed an epitaph on a dog, while at Port-Royal (*Variétés*, 4:258 n. 1). In Denis's poem the speaker is Courtault, the canine workmate of Lyco-phagos.

21. Some later French epitaphs were openly pornographic; the "Epitaphe du chien Trigalet," which appeared in the collection by François Béroalde de Verville entitled the *Muses incognues* (1604) describes the death of a dog from trying to "faire le gaillard":

> Ainsi pour avoir trop esté
> Prodigue de sa charité
> Pendant sa plus foible vieillesse
> Il est mort au cul d'une vesse.
> (1862 ed., 40)

Baïf also composed a joking epitaph, not crude even though far from sentimental (*Euvres en rime*, ed. Marty-Laveaux, 4:259–61). The dog in Baïf's poem never had a name, was ugly and scruffy, but was nonetheless the envy of more attractive animals because it was loved by a "belle damoyselle." This is a variant on the epitaph-compliment, in that the dog's only positive attribute is its ability to win the love of the lady. Passerat's "Le Chien courant," on the other hand, is a lengthy praise of hunting dogs. It explains how to select and care for them, but has nothing to do with the playful eulogy (*Les Poésies françaises*, ed. Blanchemain, 1:5–15). A late example of the epitaph-compliment, which appears in the *Muse folastre*, pushes the form to its limit. The "Raillerie sur la mort d'un Counin," professedly lamenting the death of a lady's pet, is so exaggerated in its grief that it claims the "counin" was its lady owner's everything, even father and mother (*Premier Livre*, 64–66). The proximity of the word "counin" to "con," and the title "Raillerie" make plain the poem's double entendre.

22. Du Bellay, *Regrets*, sonnet 60, in *Oeuvres*, ed. Chamard, 2:98–99. Given the countless serious funeral orations composed on the deaths of famous and not-so-famous people of the sixteenth century, composers of mock elegies and epitaphs did not have to turn to antiquity for inspiration. For a study of these works, see Christine Martineau-Génieys, *Le Thème de la mort*. The serious praise of a ruler, modeled on the classical *basilikos logos*, was also widely practiced in England, for instance by Thomas Chaloner in his *In Laudem Henrici Octavi* on Henry VIII, recently edited and translated by John B. Gabel and Carl C. Schlam.

23. Eckhardt, 134–40. Eckhardt shows that Belleau was the most prolific blasonneur of all the Pléiade poets. Even the *Amours et nouveaux eschanges de pierres precieuses* "ne sont en dernière analyse qu'un recueil d'hymnes-blasons" (140). On the *Petites Inventions*, see also Marilynn Roach Cloutier, "Remy Belleau's 'Petites Inventions' of 1556," a generic and stylistic study of the collection. So popular do Belleau's hymnes-blasons appear to have been that his "Papillon" received the opposite fate of most poems of the day, being translated into Latin (by Etienne Tabourot in 1565). Conversely, Belleau translated Passerat's "La Cigale" from Latin into French (*Oeuvres poétiques*, ed. Marty-Laveaux, 2:110–12). Tabourot also published Ronsard's "Fourmy."

24. Laumonier notes that this was the first time Ronsard used the term *blason* to describe one of his works (*Ronsard poète lyrique*, 139 n. 3).

25. Marcel Raymond, *L'Influence de Ronsard*, 1:168.

26. Trtnik-Rossettini, 177. According to Laumonier (in Ronsard, *Oeuvres complètes*, 6:136 n. 2), Baïf's *Le Meurier* was dated 1552, and is thus earlier than *Le Laurier* of 1553.

27. See above, chap 5, n. 58.

28. Ronsard, *Oeuvres*, ed. Laumonier, 6:165, italics mine. Laumonier notes that the source of this poem is Bino's "Capitolo del Bicchiere" (*Secondo Libro*, ed. Grazzini, 122ᵛ–25ʳ).

29. *Poésie* (1551). Quotations, with page numbers given in the text, will be taken from the edition by Françoise Joukovsky, *Oeuvres poétiques*. Joukovsky stresses the link between the poem on the crow and the blason, of which it is an inversion. She is not particularly enthusiastic about the genre as a whole: "Ces poèmes appartiennent à la tradition du blason, dont l'intérêt peut sembler restreint" (69). The present study seeks to suggest that these works are of more interest than Joukovsky believes. On Forcadel (1534–1579), see also Charles Oulmont, "Estienne Forcadel."

30. The traditional view of the "corbeau" was that it was a cunning scavenger and bird of ill omen. Forcadel himself adopted such an attitude in one of his "Complaintes" (part of the *Oeuvres poétiques*, 193–97). The piece is entitled "Sus la mort d'un perroquet." Lamenting the death, the poet wonders why the "corbeaux dissoluz" were not taken instead, those birds "Qui vivent maints ans revoluz / Sans mestier autre que rapine" (194). Similarly, in *Les Dictz des bestes et aussi des oyseaux* (n.d.), here quoted from Montaiglon, ed., *Recueil*, 1:256–64, there is a short speech by the raven:

> Subtil je suis en tous mes faictz
> De mal faire souvent m'avise.
> Le regnard et moy avons paix;
> Plusieurs sont plains de grant faintise.
> (262–63)

Du Bellay takes a similar view:

> Et qui pourroit, bons dieux! se contenir de rire
> Voyant un corbeau peint de diverses couleurs,
> Un pourceau couronné de roses & de fleurs,
> Ou le protrait (*sic*) d'un asne accordant une lyre?
> La louange, *à qui n'a rien de louable en soy*,
> Ne sert que de le faire à tous monstrer au doy,
> Mais elle est le loyer de cil qui la merite.
> (*Regrets*, sonnet 183, in *Oeuvres*, ed. Chamard, 2:197, italics mine)

Montaiglon republishes Antoine du Verdier's *Les Omonimes* (1572), in which we read: "Le flatteur de court est pire que le corbeau: / De ceux qui sont vivants il mange le corps beau." Passerat, in his "Elegie sur la Mort d'une linote," yet another bird epitaph (*Les Poésies françaises*, ed. Blanchemain, 2:115–16), refers to the "Corbeau mal-plaisant." Jean Lemaire de Belges (in the *Seconde Epître*, ed. Frappier, 25), mentions the "corbeaux vilains" in the underworld. Belleau's epitaph on Travail, the shepherd's dog (*Oeuvres poétiques*, ed. Marty-Laveaux, 2:116), also stresses the raven's scavenging nature: "Je veux bastir ta sepulture, / Travail, pour n'estre la pasture / Des loups gourmans ou des corbeaux." Naïs, 232, notes that French poets of the period use the names "corbeau" and "corneille" interchangeably. Usually the image is of a black bird of ill omen, be it rook, crow or raven (374 and 443). Ronsard, she adds, uses the "corbeau" to represent bad poets in "Le Houx" (221). Jean de la Jessée took "un noir corbeau" as his *devise*, to show his state of grief. Only in Jean Lemaire's animal paradise of the *Seconde Epître* do we find another flattering reference to this bird as "le corbeau que Pline tant extolle" (ed. Frappier, 33). This reference is to Pliny, *Natural History*, 10.60.121–22, in which a raven saluted by name the emperor Tiberius as he arrived at the forum each morning (trans. H. Rackham, Loeb CLS, 3:371). So popular did this bird become with the people that when a neighbor of its owner killed it, the bird was carried in a solemn funeral procession to the pyre and the killer was "made away with." The bird's gift for imitating human speech, the characteristic alluded to by Forcadel, seems therefore to have been the only trait mentioned with praise at this time.

31. Baïf, *Euvres en Rime*. ed. Marty-Laveaux, 2:43–55.

32. Thomas Sebillet, *Art poétique françoys*, ed. Félix Gaiffe, 169.

33. Ronsard, *Oeuvres complètes*, ed. Laumonier, 6:83. Pontus de Tyard also composed a poem on "Les Grenoilles" (*Les Oeuvres poétiques* [1573], 158). In this piece, a rough crowd of onlookers is turned into frogs for having mocked the daughter of Ceos. Unlike Ronsard, the narrator is hostile to the frogs.

34. Ronsard, *Oeuvres complètes*, ed. Laumonier, 6:90–91. Laumonier finds no clear antecedents for this dramatic scene, and suggests that it was Ronsard's own creation. If true, this fact underlines the poet's belief in the suggestive qualities of even the most seemingly ordinary elements of the extraliterary world.

35. Grazzini, "In dispregio de'Cani," in *Le Rime burlesche*, ed. Verzone, 598–602. Grazzini attacks dogs in general, not one particular specimen. Flies, "zanzare," wolves, and serpents are bad, he remarks, "Ma certo, i più dannosi e i più villani / che vivin sotto la cappa del sole, / sono i malnati e maladetti cani" (599). Dogs are noisy, vicious, sometimes rabid. They tear up everything, even the books of Petrarch and Burchiello, an interesting combination of authors. Ronsard's "Le Chat" is in the *Sixiesme Livre des Poèmes*, ed. Laumonier, 15:39–47. Naïs, 595, states that Ronsard "ne suivait aucun modèle littéraire." The narrator fears cats because of their gloomy prowling ways and general demeanor. He believes they have the gift of prophecy and will bring him bad luck. Naïs remarks that Paré and others at the time thought that cats carried a kind of poison (594 n. 122) and wonders if some such superstition may explain Ronsard's dislike.

36. Ronsard, "Folastrie V," in *Oeuvres complètes*, ed. Laumonier, 5:35–38. Cf. Tomarken and Tomarken, 159: "These poems were most lively when most concerned with themselves as poetic constructs making use of their predecessors' efforts."

37. Belleau, *Oeuvres poétiques*, ed. Marty-Laveaux, 1:50, italics mine.

38. Much of the discussion of "Le Mulet" is adapted from Tomarken and Tomarken, 157–58. Trtnik-Rossettini notes that the description of the unattractive mule is derived in large part from Berni (176 n.3). Belleau's poem is found in *Petites Inventions*, in *Oeuvres poétiques*, ed. Marty-Laveaux, 1:108–11. Page numbers for subsqequent quotations from Belleau will be given in the text. In the 1628 edition

of the collection *Le Banquet des Muses*, there is another eulogy of an imaginary animal, this time a pig. Unlike the encomium by Pontoux, which claims to mourn an actual animal owned by the narrator, the later poem is entitled "Le Pourceau imaginaire" (41–45). The narrator thanks his lady for the "don precieux et rare" of an "admirable Pourceau." The poem blends contemporary history and classical myths concerning Hercules, Adonis, and others. The fictive pig never bites or is bad-tempered. Its flesh is sweet, not polluted: even Jews would be able to eat it. There is a lengthy mention of Rabelais's Frère Jean. In a moment of almost surreal humor, the ending combines the themes traced in the present chapter: the pig's flesh, states the narrator,

> se gardera plusieurs yvers
> Sans autre sel que mes vers,
> Car la faux du temps jamais n'uze
> Le gentil labeur de la Muse.
>
> (44)

No butcher is needed to kill it or labor to utilize all its parts. In conclusion, there is with this animal no risk that "un Ramonneur . . . / En pisse jamais sur l'andouille" (45). The striking quality of this poem lies in the jarring juxtapositions between the crude details of the physical realm and the lofty world of poetry and mythology. However, the contrast, lacking the thematic purpose that gave unity to "Le Mulet," seems almost a caricature of the earlier poem.

39. See above, chap. 4, n. 51. Catherine des Roches, to be discussed below in this chapter, also composed a poem on a donkey called Grisette (in *Secondes Oeuvres de Mes-dames des Roches de Poictiers* [1583]). See also Diller, 83. Barthélemy Aneau took a less favorable view of the donkey, calling it a symbol of "sottise" and "ardeur amoureuse" (*Decades de la description, . . . des animaulx* [1549], "Decade quinte," dizain 8, ll. 9–10).

40. *Les Poèmes de Pierre de Brach* (1576), here 34^v–35^r. In the same collection (59^r–64^v) is a more overtly laudatory and descriptive hymne-blason, an ode on "Le Canarin," one of *Les Amours d'Aymée* (19^r–64^v). See also the reedition by Reinhold Dezeimeris. In this poem the idea of the joke-object holds true, as de Brach says in conclusion: "De ce payment que j'envoye / A mon Raymond, son coussin / Lui payant d'un canarin" (64^v). We are told that Raymond had composed verses in praise of the "coussin." The canary poem is a return gift. The Lucianic link is also made clear, as the poet refers to the idea of using a "vers triomphant" to make "d'une mouche un elephant" (59^v).

41. *La Bellete, par François de Clary, Albigeois* (1578), quoted from Montaiglon, ed., *Recueil*, 8:258–69, here p. 260. In calling the poem a "blason de fantaisie" (259), Montaiglon adds one more category to the genre's subdivisions. On Renaissance identification of the "belette" with the "putois," see Naïs, 244, and Clary's mention of its "senteur" (269).

42. The source of this story is Ovid, *Metamorphoses*, 9.306, Loeb CLS, 2:23. When Alcmene was about to give birth to Heracles, son of Zeus, her friend Galinthias, or Galanthis, distracted the avenging goddesses long enough for the birth to take place.

43. *La Bellete*, 269.

44. The insect poems appear in Jean de la Jessée, *Les premières Oeuvres françoyses* (*Troisième livre*, 1583 edition, 1:328–33), Jacques Peletier du Mans (*L'Art poétique* [1555], reprinted in *Oeuvres poétiques*, ed. Léon Séché, 160), and *Euvres* (1581), 35ᵛ. Jean de la Jessée's poem tells man to learn from the bee a lesson in industry, cooperation, and organization. Princes should model their conduct on that of the bee. The poem has none of the two-sidedness of Ronsard's hymnes-blasons. Another bird hymne-blason (in addition to that on the "linote" referred to in n. 30 of this chapter) is Jean Godard's "La Perdrix" (under the initials "LDLF") in *Meslanges poétiques* (1624), 279–88. This very Ronsardian piece presents the story of Daedalus's nephew Talos who, when thrown off a cliff by his jealous uncle, was turned by the gods into a partridge (in Latin, *perdix*, the name by which Talos was also known). Note also Passerat's "Le Cerf d'Amour," in *Les Poésies françaises*, ed. Blanchemain, 1:16–20 (part of the 1606 *Recueil des oeuvres poétiques*).

45. *La Puce de Madame des Roches*, ed. Jacques de Sourdrai (1583). Page numbers for subsequent quotations from this edition will be given in the text. On the des Roches ladies, see Diller. On Pasquier, see L. Clark Keating, *Etienne Pasquier*.

46. See Marcel Françon, "Un Motif." On the connection between the *La Puce* collection and John Donne, see David Wilson, " 'La Puce' de Madame Desroches." For other discussions of flea-literature, see Saunders, *The Sixteenth-Century Blason*, 257–59, and my article, "Flea Encomia." Saunders describes the early "Blason de la puce faict sur le parve pulex" ([1537], derived in large part from Virgil's *Culex*), the earliest French work of this sort on the flea. A later flea poem, by Guy de Tours, published in 1598, was little more than a pretext for a description of the beauties of the writer's beloved (Saunders, 258). As such it was in the tradition described by Françon. A more critical attitude to the flea is adopted by Guillaume de la Perrière, who in his 1536 *Théâtre des bons engins* compares flatterers to fleas because both are parasites (cited by P. M. Smith, *The Anti-Courtier Trend*, 79). In *Les Muses gaillardes*, the poem "D'une Puce" is closer in theme to the des Roches collection. The narrator wishes to become a flea in order to have the right to sleep with his lady. Having once gained access to her body and made her confess the anguish of having "la Puce à l'oreille," the lover dreams of regaining his human shape (*Les Muses gaillardes*, ed. Antoine du Brueil [1609], 2d ed., 45ᵛ–47ʳ). On the expression "la puce à l'oreille," see below, n. 53. Finally, Motin is credited with a flirtatious poem entitled "La Chasse de la Puce sur la belle Uranie," (*Le Cabinet satyrique*, ed. Fleuret and Perceau, 1:88–91). The piece is actually by Raoul Fornier. The quatrain that opens the anthology assures the reader that "Je veux mourir s'il ne s'esclate / De rire et ne pleure des yeux" (ed. Fleuret and Perceau, 1:14). As in many poems in the *Cabinet*, the humor is sexist, ending with the lines "Ca! mon ame, ça! mes amours, / Qu'à ce coup je vous depucelle!" (91). Such puns would be inappropriate to the social context of the des Roches anthology.

47. *Recueil*, 10:70.

48. On Fischart, see *Johann Fischarts sämmtliche Dichtungen*, ed. Heinrich Kurz. For the French original, see Montaiglon, ed., *Recueil*, 10:61–74. Fischart translated *Gargantua* into German. See Florence M. Weinberg, *Gargantua in a Convex Mirror*. There were seven editions of his *Flöh Hatz* between 1573 and 1610. On the confusion between "culex" and "pulex," see Françon, "Un Motif," 321–23.

49. Ronsard, ed. Laumonier, 5:38–41.

50. François de Chantelouve, *Tragédie de Pharaon et autres oeuvres poétiques* (1576), no pagination. Much of my analysis of this poem is taken from my study, "Flea Encomia." The identification between the lover-admirer and the flea was popular in early seventeenth-century painting (see John Moffitt, "La Femme à la puce," an article focusing on the 1625–1630 painting by Gerard Honthorst known as the *Merry Flea Hunt*).

51. The idea is repeated in a couplet on p. 44^r of the collection: "Quis neget ex musca vos condere posse Elephantum, / Funditis Aonios qui tot pro Pulice versus." The work even contains a kind of contre-blason by N. Rapin (53^r–55^v), entitled "La Contre-Puce de N. Rapin." Attacking the flea, this poem refers indirectly to Lucian, stating that poets who have sung on the flea "t'ont fait un grand Elefant, / Par leur invention gentille" (53^r). Rapin makes explicit the playful intention of the entire "recueil":

> Ceux qui t'elevent jusqu'aux cieux
> Toutesfois ne t'ayment pas mieux
> Que moy qui te blasme & despite.
>
> (53^v)

What these writers did, asserts the poet, was to "vanter / Le mal contre la conscience" (53^r). Since he is himself incapable of such deception, he proposes ways in which men can rid themselves of fleas. Clean clothes and bedding will probably drive away the bloodthirsty insects. Failing that, we should drink ourselves into a stupor so as to be oblivious to the creatures' bites. The Renaissance predilection for the fly-elephant comparison is attested to in two recent essays, the first by Richard Lemay, "The Fly against the Elephant," and the second by Marjorie Boyle, "The Fly to the Elephant," which forms the prologue to her *Rhetoric and Reform*, 1–4. Lemay shows that when Flandinus disputed the famous Pomponazzi concerning fate and the immortality of the soul, he compared himself to a fly taking on an elephant. Boyle picks up Erasmus's description of himself as a fly in comparison to the mighty Luther, the "elephant" of the image. She shows that although the elephant had very positive symbolic connotations in the Renaissance, the fly image was not nearly as negative as Erasmus's joke seemed to make it. Indeed, "with this modest topic of the fly, Erasmus hoped to shame the elephant [Luther] into softening his hide, muting his trumpet, and reducing his pretentious weight" (3). Erasmus is once again exploiting the ironic ambiguities of one of the images most clearly associated in the Renaissance with the Lucianic mock encomium.

52. Frédéric Lachèvre, *Bibliographie des recueils collectifs*, 18. Pasquier also composed a playful encomium called "Le Raisin," part of the second section of the des Roches collection, *Divers Poèmes*, dated 1582 but bound with and running on from the 1583 volume.

53. 58^v. The author reexplains in similar fashion the popular phrase "avoir la puce à l'oreille"; cf. Rabelais, *Tiers Livre*, chap. 7, when Panurge has a flea-shaped earring made. For a modern study of this and other expressions, see Claude Duneton, *La Puce à l'oreille*, 48–49. See also Moffitt, 101.

CONCLUSION

1. On the frequent use, especially in courtroom situations, of the humility *topos* so evident in Erasmus's statement, see Richard J. Schoeck, "Lawyers and Rhetoric in Sixteenth-Century England," in *Renaissance Eloquence*, ed. J. J. Murphy, 290. Schoeck is referring to Brian Vickers's study of Sir Francis Bacon.

2. Colie, *The Resources of Kind*, 114.

3. Colie, *Paradoxia Epidemica*, moves outside the literary form to the larger notion of the growth of the scientific spirit. Frances Yates questions her conclusion in a review article, "Paradox and Paradise," 28.

4. Ralph Cohen, "On the Interrelations of Eighteenth-Century Literary Forms," 67.

5. Cohen, 49.

Bibliography

I. Reference Works

Blanc, Joseph. *Bibliographie italico-française universelle ... 1475–1885.* 2 vols. Milan: J. Blanc, 1886.

Les Bibliothèques françoises de La Croix du Maine et de Du Verdier. 6 vols. Paris: Saillant et Nyon, 1772–73.

Biographie nationale. 29 vols. Brussels: H. Thiry-Van Bouggenhoudt, 1866–.

Biographie universelle ancienne et moderne. 45 vols. Ed. Louis-Gabriel Michaud. Paris: A. T. Desplaces, [1843–65].

Brunet, Jacques. *Manuel du libraire et de l'amateur de livres.* 6 vols. Paris: Firmin Didot, 1860–65.

Brunet, Jacques, and Pierre Deschamps. *Supplément au Manuel du libraire.* Paris: Firmin Didot, 1878–80.

The Cambridge History of Classical Literature. Vol. 1, *Greek Literature.* Ed. P. E. Easterling and B.M.W. Knox. Cambridge: Cambridge University Press, 1985.

Cotgrave, Randle. *A Dictionarie of the French and English Tongues.* 1611. Reprint, with introduction by William S. Woods. Columbia: University of South Carolina Press, 1950.

Dictionnaire de biographie française. Ed. M. Prevost and J. Balteau. Paris: Librarie Letouzey et Ane, 1933–.

Dizionario biografico degli Italiani. Ed. Alberto M. Ghisalberti. Rome: Instituto della Enciclopedia italiana, 1960–.

La grande Encyclopédie. 32 vols. Ed. MM. Berthelot et al. Paris: H. Lamirault, 1886–1902.

Huguet, Edmond. *Dictionnaire de la langue française du 16e siècle.* 7 vols. Paris: Champion, 1925–35; Didier, 1944–67.

Larousse, Pierre. *Grand Dictionnaire universel du XIXe siècle.* 17 vols. Paris: Larousse, 1864–90.

Littré, Emile. *Dictionnaire de la langue française.* 4 vols. Paris: Hachette, 1863–69.

Montaiglon, Anatole C. de, and J. de Rothschild, eds. *Recueil de poésies françoises des XVe et XVIe siècles.* 13 vols. Paris: P. Jannet, 1855–78.

Nouvelle Biographie universelle. 46 vols. Paris: Firmin Didot 1852–66.

II. Classical Works and Renaissance Translations

Apuleius. *The Metamorphoses or Golden Ass of Apuleius of Madaura.* Trans. H. E. Butler. Oxford: Clarendon, 1910.

Aristophanes. *The Plutus.* Trans. Benjamin Bickley Rogers. Loeb Classical Library,

1924. Reprint. Cambridge: Harvard University Press; London, Heinemann, 1963.

Aristotle. *The Nicomachean Ethics*. Trans. H. Rackham. Loeb Classical Library, 1926. Reprint. Cambridge: Harvard University Press; London: Heinemann, 1962.

Augustine, St. *The City of God*. 7 vols. Trans. William M. Green. Loeb Classical Library. Cambridge: Harvard University Press; London: Heinemann, 1957–72.

Aulus Gellius. *The Attic Nights*. 3 vols. Trans. John C. Rolfe. Loeb Classical Library. London: Heinemann; New York: Putnam's, 1927.

Cicero. *Paradoxa stoicorum*. Mainz: J. Schoeffer, 1465.

———. *Paradoxa stoicorum*. Trans. H. Rackham. Loeb Classical Library, 1942. Reprint. Cambridge: Harvard University Press; London: Heinemann, 1960.

———. *Tusculan Disputations*. Trans. J. E. King. Loeb Classical Library, 1927. Reprint. London: Heinemann; New York: Putnam's, 1960.

Claudian. *The Works of Claudian*. 2 vols. Trans. Maurice Platnauer. Loeb Classical Library, 1922. Reprint. Cambridge: Harvard University Press; London: Heinemann, 1963.

Dio Chrysostom. *Discourses*. 5 vols. Trans. J. W. Cohoon and H. Lamar Crosby. Loeb Classical Library, 1940. Reprint. Cambridge: Harvard University Press; London: Heinemann, 1961.

Fronto. *The Correspondence*. 2 vols. Trans. and ed. C. R. Haines. Loeb Classical Library. London: Heinemann; New York: Putnam's, 1919–20.

The Greek Anthology. 5 vols. Trans. W. R. Paton. Loeb Classical Library, 1917. Reprint. Cambridge: Harvard University Press; London: Heinemann, 1960.

Horace. *Satires, Epistles, Ars Poetica*. Trans. H. Rushton Fairclough. Loeb Classical Library, 1926. Reprint. Cambridge: Harvard University Press; London: Heinemann, 1961.

Isocrates. *Busiris*. In *Opera*. Venice, apud Aldum Manutium, 1513, 21ʳ–23ʳ.

———. *Helen*. In *Isocrates*. Trans. Larue Van Hook. Loeb Classical Library, 1945. Reprint. London: Heinemann; New York: Putnam's, 1961.

———. *Isocratis oratio de laudibus Helenae*. Trans. I. Petrus. In *Herodoti Halicarnassi Thurii Historiae*. Paris: apud divi Iacobi Vicum, 1510.

Julian the Apostate. *Orations*. 3 vols. Trans. Wilmer Cave Wright. Loeb Classical Library. London: Heinemann; New York: Macmillan, 1913–23.

Lucian of Samosata. *Apologia*. Trans. K. Kilburn. Loeb Classical Library. Cambridge: Harvard University Press; London: Heinemann, 1959.

———. *Charidemus*. Trans. M. D. Macleod. Loeb Classical Library. Cambridge: Harvard University Press; London: Heinemann, 1967.

———. *De iis qui mercede conducti degunt*. Trans. A. M. Harmon. Loeb Classical Library, 1921. Reprint. Cambridge: Harvard University Press; London: Heinemann, 1960.

———. *De Parasito*. Ed. and trans. A. M. Harmon. Loeb Classical Library, 1921. Reprint. London: Heinemann; New York: Putnam's, 1960.

———. *Luciani Samosatiensis opera*. Trans. I. Micyllus. Frankfurt: apud C. Egenolphum Hadamarium, 1543.

———. *Luciani Samosatiensis opera*. Trans. I. Micyllus. Leyden, 1549.

Lucian of Samosata. *Luciani Samosatiensis opera quae quidem extant, omnia.* Trans. I. Micyllus. Paris: apud M. Vascosanum, 1546.

———. *Luciani Samosatensis opera quae quidem extant, omnia.* Trans. I. Micyllus. Lyons: apud Iohannem Frellonium, 1549.

———. *Lucian of Samosata with the Comments of Wieland and Others.* 2 vols. Trans. William Tooke. London: Longman, Hurst, Rees, Orme, and Brown, 1820.

———. *La Mouche de Lucian et la Maniere de parler et de se taire.* Trans. Geoffroy Tory. Paris: Geoffroy Tory, [1533].

———. *Muscae Encomium.* Trans. A. M. Harmon. Loeb Classical Library, 1913. Reprint. Cambridge: Harvard University Press; London: Heinemann, 1961.

———. *Muscae Encomium Luciani.* Trans. N. Beraldus. Paris, 1517.

———. *Navis seu vota: The Ship, or The Wishes.* Trans. K. Kilburn. Loeb Classical Library. Cambridge: Harvard University Press; London: Heinemann, 1959.

———. *Ocypus.* Trans. Gilbert West. In *Odes of Pindar.* London: R. Dodsley, 1749.

———. *Les Oeuvres de Lucien.* Trans. and ed. Filbert Bretin. Paris: Abel l'Angelier, 1583.

———. *Podagra.* Trans. M. D. Macleod. Loeb Classical Library. Cambridge: Harvard University Press; London: Heinemann, 1967.

———. *Rhetorum Praeceptor.* Trans. A. M. Harmon. Loeb Classical Library, 1925. Reprint. Cambridge: Harvard University Press; London: Heinemann, 1961.

———. *Timon.* Trans. A. M. Harmon. Loeb Classical Library, 1915. Reprint. Cambridge: Harvard University Press; London: Heinemann, 1960.

———. *Tragoedia Luciani cui titulus est, Podagra.* Trans. C. Arbaleste. Strasbourg: per Henricum Sybold, 1529.

———. *The Trago-Podagra or Gout-Tragedy.* Trans. Symeon T. Bartlett. Ryde: H. Wayland, 1871.

———. *The Works of Lucian.* 4 vols. London: James Woodward, 1711.

———. *The Works of Lucian.* 2 vols. Trans. Thomas Francklin. London: for T. Cadell, 1780.

———. *The Works of Lucian.* 4 vols. Ed. H. W. Fowler and F. G. Fowler. Oxford: Oxford University Press, 1905.

Martial. *Epigrams.* Trans. Walter C. A. Ker. Loeb Classical Library, 1919. Reprint. Cambridge: Harvard University Press; London: Heinemann, 1961.

Ovid. *Heroides and Amores.* Trans. Grant Showerman. Loeb Classical Library, 1914. Reprint. London: Heinemann; New York: Putnam's, 1921.

———. *Metamorphoses.* 2 vols. Trans. Frank Justus Miller. Loeb Classical Library, 1916. Reprint. Cambridge: Harvard University Press; London: Heinemann, 1922.

———. *Tristia and Ex Ponto.* Trans. Arthur Leslie Wheeler. Loeb Classical Library, 1924. Reprint. Cambridge: Harvard University Press; London: Heinemann, 1959.

Philodemus. *The Rhetorica of Philodemus.* Trans. Harry M. Hubbell. Transactions of the Connecticut Academy of Arts and Sciences 23. New Haven: Connecticut Academy of Arts and Sciences, 1920.

Philostratus. *The Life of Apollonius of Tyana.* 2 vols. Trans. F. C. Conybeare. Loeb Classical Library. London: Heinemann; New York: Putnam's, 1912.

Plato. *Phaedrus.* Trans. Harold North Fowler. Loeb Classical Library. Cambridge: Harvard University Press; London: Heinemann, 1960.

――――. *The Republic.* 2 vols. Trans. Paul Shorey. Loeb Classical Library, 1930. Reprint. Cambridge: Harvard University Press; London: Heinemann, 1963.

――――. *Symposium.* Trans. W.R.M. Lamb. Loeb Classical Library, 1925. Reprint. Cambridge: Harvard University Press; London: Heinemann, 1953.

Pliny. *Natural History.* 10 vols. Trans. W.H.S. Jones et al. Loeb Classical Library. Cambridge: Harvard University Press; London: Heinemann, 1938–63.

Polybius. *The Histories.* 6 vols. Trans. W. R. Paton. Loeb Classical Library. London: Heinemann; New York: Putnam's, 1925.

Quintilian. *Institutio oratoria.* Trans. H. E. Butler. Loeb Classical Library, 1921. Reprint. London: Heinemann; New York: Putnam's, 1960.

――――. *M. Fabii Quintiliani de Inst. Orat. libros XII commentarii.* 4 vols. Paris: apud Richardum, 1556.

Seneca. *Apocolocyntosis.* Ed. P. T. Eden. Cambridge: Cambridge University Press, 1984.

Statius. *Silvae.* 2 vols. Trans. J. H. Mozley. Loeb Classical Library, 1928. Reprint. London: Heinemann; New York: Putnam's, 1961.

Synesius of Cyrene. *Eloge de la Calvitie.* Trans. G. Hallouin. Paris: P. Vidoue, 1520.

――――. *The Essays and Hymns of Synesius of Cyrene.* 2 vols. Trans. Augustine FitzGerald. London: Oxford University Press, 1926.

III. Neo-Latin Works and Vernacular Translations

Agrippa, Henricus Cornelius. *Declamation sur l'Incertitude, Vanité, et Abus des Sciences.* [Trans. L. de Mayerne Turquet]. Paris: [J. Durand], 1582.

――――. *. . . de incertitudine & vanitate artium et scientiarum.* [Antwerp: J. Graphius, 1530].

――――. *Paradoxe contre l'amour.* 1603.

Alberti, Leon Battista. *Leonis Baptistae Alberti Opera.* Florence: Bartolommeo di Libri, 1500.

――――. *Opusculi inediti.* Ed. Cecil Grayson. Nuova collezione di testi umanistici inediti o rari 10. Florence: Olschki, 1954.

Alciatus, Andreas. *The Latin Emblems.* 2 vols. Trans. and ed. Peter M. Daly and Virginia W. Callahan. Vol. 2, *Emblems in Translation,* by Peter M. Daly and Simon Cuttler. Toronto: University of Toronto Press, 1985.

Aquaeus, Stephanus [Etienne de L'Aigue]. *Encomium brassicarum sive caulium.* Paris: C. Wechel, 1531.

Arnaudus, Andreas. *Ioci.* Avignon: ex typog. J. Bramereau, 1600.

Ballista, Christopher [Arbaleste]. *De Podagrae laudibus . . . lusus.* Strasbourg: apud haeredes C. Milii, 1570. *See also* Pirckheimer, section III.

――――. *In Podagram concertatio.* [Zurich?, 1525 or 1528].

Bibliography

Ballista, Christopher [Arbaleste]. *The Overthrow of the Gout.* Trans. B.G. [Barnaby Googe?]. London: Abraham Veale, 1577.

Beroaldus, Philippus [Filippo Beroaldo]. *Declamatio ebriosi, scortatori, & aleatoris.* In *Varia Philippi Beroaldi opuscula.* Basel: [J. Froben], 1513.

Bigothier, Claude. *De rapina seu raporum encomium.* Ed. Joseph-Philibert Brossard. Bourg-en-Bresse: P. Comte-Milliet, 1891.

Borbonius, Nicolaus, the Elder [Bourbon]. *Nicolai Borbonii nugarum libri octo.* Lyons: apud S. Gryphium, 1538.

———. *Nugae.* Paris: apud M. Vascosanum, 1533.

Bucoldianus, Gerardus [Bucoldz]. *Pro ebrietate oratio.* Cologne: I. Soter excudebat, 1529.

Budaeus, Guilielmus, [Budée]. *De curandis articularibus morbis commentarius.* Paris: apud E. Regnault, 1539.

Calcagnini, Celio. *Opera aliquot.* Basel: per H. Frobenium & N. Episcopum, 1544.

Calentius, Elisius. *La Bataille fantastique des roys Rodilardus et Croacus.* Ed. Paul Lacroix [P. L. Jacob]. Geneva: J. Gay, 1867.

———. *Opuscula Elisii Calentii.* Rome: I. de Besicken, 1503.

Cardano, Girolamo. *Hieronymi Cardani medici mediolanensis, Libelli duo.* Nuremberg: apud J. Petreium, 1543.

———. *Neronis Encomium.* In *Somniorum Synesiorum . . . libri IV.* Basel: per Henricum Petrum, 1562.

Carnarius, Joannes [Vleeschouwer]. *De Podagrae laudibus oratio.* Padua: excudebat Ioan. Baptista. Amycus, 1553.

Collenuccio, Pandolfo. *Apologi quatuor.* Strasbourg: in aedibus M. Schurerii, 1511.

Conradinus, Balthasar. *Febris miscellanea ungarica.* Ed. M. Toxites. Strasbourg: Christian Muller, 1574.

Curio, Caelius Secundus [Coelio Secundo Curione]. *Aranei Encomion.* Venice, 1540.

———. *Aranei Encomion.* Basel: J. Oporini, 1544.

Delitiae poetarum germanorum. 6 vols. Ed. Janus Gruterus. Frankfurt: excudebat N. Hoffmannus, 1612.

Demetrius, Pepagomenus. *Liber de podagra [et id genus morbis].* [Trans. A Turnebus]. Paris: apud Guil. Morelium, 1558.

———. *Traicté de la Goutte.* Trans. Fédéric Jamot. Paris: Ph. G. de Rouille, 1567.

De Morbo gallico omnia quae extant. Venice: apud J. Zilettum, 1566.

Dissertationum ludicrarum et amoenitatum scriptores varii editio nova et aucta. Leyden: apud Franciscum Hegerum, 1644.

Dornavius, Caspar. *Amphitheatrum sapientiae socraticae joco-seriae.* Hanover: typis Wechelianis, impensis Danielis ac Davidis Aubriorum & Clementis Schleichii, 1619.

———. *Encomium scarabei.* Hanover: apud haeredes Iohan. Aubrii, 1617.

———. *Homo-Diabolus.* Frankfurt: imp. J. Thymii, 1618.

———. *Invidiae Encomium.* Gorlitz: Johannes Rhamba, [1614].

———. *Invidiae Encomium.* Frankfurt: impensis Guilielmi Fitzeri, 1626.

———. *Ulysses scholasticus.* Hanover: apud D. et D. Aubrios et Schleichium, 1620.

Dousa, Janus. *See* Lando, section IV.

Dunus, Thaddeus. *T. D. et F. Cigalini J. P. Turriani medicorum . . . item H. Cardani . . . disputationum per epistolas liber unus . . . cui accessit de hemitritaeo sive de febre semitertiana libellus.* Zurich: A. and J. Gesner, [1555].

Ens, Gaspar. Μωροσοφια: *id est Stulta sapientia, itemque sapiens stultitia.* Cologne: Petrus à Brachel excudebat, 1620.

Eobanus Hessus, Helius. *Podagrae ludus.* Mainz: J. Schoeffer, 1537.

Epistolae obscurorum virorum. Trans. Francis Griffin Stokes. London: Chatto and Windus, 1909.

Epitaphia ioco-seria. Ed. Franciscus Swertius. Cologne: apud Bernardum Gualtherum, 1645.

———. *Epitaphia ioco-seria.* Cologne: apud Io. Kakoven, 1645.

Erasmus. *Adagiorum Chiliades tres, . . .* Venice: in aedibus Aldi, 1508.

———. *The Correspondence of Erasmus.* Trans. R.A.B. Mynors and D.F.S. Thomson. In *Collected Works of Erasmus.* Toronto: University of Toronto Press, 1974–.

———. *De la declamation des louenges de follie. . . .* Trans. Galliot Du Pré. Paris: Galliot Du Pré, 1520.

———. *Libellus de conscribendis epistolis.* Cambridge, England: J. Siberch, 1521.

———. *Moriae Encomium; or, a panegyrick upon folly.* Trans. White Kennett. 1683. London: Stephen Austen, 1726.

———. *Opera omnia.* Ed. L. E. Halkin, F. Bierlaire, and R. Hoven. Amsterdam: North Holland Publishing Co., 1969–.

———. *Opus epistolarum Des. Erasmis Roterodami.* 11 vols. Ed. P. S. Allen, H. M. Allen, and H. W. Garrod. Oxford: Clarendon, 1906–47.

———. *The Praise of Folie.* Trans. Sir Thomas Chaloner. London: [T. Berthelet], 1549.

———. *The Praise of Folie.* Trans. Sir Thomas Chaloner. Ed. Clarence H. Miller. Toronto: University of Toronto Press, 1965.

———. *The Praise of Folly.* Ed. Hoyt Hopewell Hudson. Princeton: Princeton University Press, 1941.

———. *The Praise of Folly.* Ed. and trans. Clarence H. Miller. New Haven: Yale University Press, 1979.

———. *The Praise of Folly.* Trans. Betty Radice. Intro. and notes A.H.T. Levi. Middlesex: Penguin, 1971.

Fernelius, Joannes [Jean Fernel]. *Febrium curandorum methodus generalis.* Frankfurt: A. Wechel, 1577.

———. *Universa medicina.* 1567. Frankfurt: A. Wechel, 1574.

Ferrier, Auger. *De Pudendagra lue Hispanica, libri duo.* Antwerp: Ve. M. Nutii, 1564.

Ferrus, Donatus Antonius. *D. A. Ferri de podagra enchiridion.* Naples: apud H. Salvianum, etc., 1585.

Fracastoro, Girolamo. *Fracastoro's "Syphilis."* Ed. Geoffrey Eatough. *ARCA* Classical and Medieval Texts, Papers and Monographs, no. 12. Wolfeboro, N.H.: Longwood, 1984.

———. *Syphilis, sive morbus Gallicus.* Verona, 1530.

Galissard, Pierre. *Pulicis encomium*. Lyons: Jean de Tournes, 1550.

Hegendorff, Christoph. *Encomium ebrietatis*. Leipzig: ex aedibus V. Schumanni, 1519.

———. *Encomium sobrietatis*. N.p., n.d.

———. *Encomium somni*. Leipzig: ex aedibus V. Schumanni, 1519.

Heinsius, Daniel. *Laus pediculi; or, An Apologeticall Speech*. Trans. James Guitard. London: Thomas Harper, 1634.

Heldelinus, Caspar. *Ciconiae encomium*. Basel: apud Henricum Petrum, 1534.

Hotman, Antoine. Πωγωνιας *sive de Barba, Dialogus*. Leyden: ex officina Plantiniana, apud F. Raphelengium, 1586.

Hutten, Ulrich von. *De Guaiaci medicina et morbo gallico liber unus*. Mainz: J. Schoeffer, 1519.

———. *Opera poetica*. [Frankfurt am Main], 1538.

India, Franciscus [Francesco]. *De Gutta Podagrica, Chiragrica, et Arthritica libri duo*. Verona: Societatis aspirantium cura, 1600.

Laguna, Andrés. *De articulari morbo commentarius*. Rome: apud Valerium & Aloysium Doricos fratres Brixienses, 1551.

———. *Il Rimedio delle Podagre, . . . con la Tragopodagra di Luciano*. Rome: G. M. Scotto, 1552.

Lineus, Thomas [Vlas]. *Oratio in laudem belli*. Paris: C. Wechel, 1531.

Loselius, Joannes [Loesel the Elder]. *. . . de podagra tractatus . . . Editio secunda locupletata*. Leyden: ex officina Joannis Maire, 1639.

Menapius, Guilielmus. *L'Eloge de la fièvre quarte*. Trans. Gueudeville. Leyden: Théodore Haak, 1728.

———. *Encomium febris quartanae*. Basel: J. Oporinus, 1542.

Nugae venales. Prostant apud Neminem: sed tamen ubique. 1642.

Obsopoeus, Vincentius [Opsopoeus]. *De Arte Bibendi libri quatuor, et arte iocandi lib. quatuor*. Leyden: ex typographia rediviva, 1648.

———. *De Arte Bibendi libri tres*. Nuremberg: apud J. Petreium, 1525 and 1536.

———. *Rapsodia in ebrietatem*. [Hagenau?]: [J. Secerius?], [1527?]

Passerat, Jean. *J. Passeratii . . . De Caecitate oratio*. Paris: apud Mamertum Patissonium ex officina Rob. Stephani, 1597.

———. *Nihil*. In *Nihil, per Johannem Passeratum; Quelque chose, par Philippe Girard Vandomois*. Paris: Estienne Prevosteau, 1587.

Peletier du Mans, Jacques. *De peste compendium*. Basel: J. Oporini, [1560?].

Pirckheimer, Bilibaldus. *Apologia, seu podagrae laus*. Nuremberg: F. Peypus, 1522.

———. *De Podagrae laudibus doctorum hominum lusus*. Ed. Michael Toxites. Strasbourg: apud haeredes C. Milii, 1570.

———. *The Praise of the Gout; Or, The Gouts Apologie*. London: G.P. for J[ohn] Budge, 1617.

Placentius, Ioannes Leo [Jean Plaisant]. *Lucianus aulicus*. Antwerp: Sim. Cocus excudebat, 1535.

Pontanus, Iacobus [Spanmueller]. *Institutio poetica*. 1604. London: J. Haviland, 1624.

Pontanus a Braitenberg, G. B. [J. B. Pontanus z Praitenberka]. *Triumphus Podagrae*. Frankfurt: typis Wolfgangi Richteri, prostat in officina Nicolai Steinii, 1605.

Rondeletius, Gulielmus [Guillaume Rondelet]. *G. Rondeletii . . . methodus curandorum omnium morborum corporis humani, in tres libros distincta.* Ca. 1545? [Geneva]: apud Iacobum Stoer, 1609.

Sachetus Aelianus, Hieronymus [Hieronimo Sachetto]. *H. Sacheti . . . de podagricis & arthriticis morbis retractatio.* Brescia: ex officina P. M. Marchetti, 1586.

Sadoleto, Iacopo. *Curtius, eiusdem Laocoon.* Bologna: [Ioannes Baptista Phaellus], 1532.

Scribanius, Franciscus. *Muscae principatus, hoc est, Muscae ex continua cum principe comparatione, encomium.* Hamburg: J. Schönfeld, 1614.

Sennertus, Daniel. *Institutionum medicinae libri V.* Wittenberg: apud haeredes Zach. Schureri, 1628.

————. *Practical Physick.* Trans. H. Care. London: for William Whitwood, 1676.

Sommer, Johannes. *Colicae et Podagrae tyrannis. . . .* In *Iani Pannonii . . . Poemata.* 1619.

Swertius, F. See *Epitaphia ioco-seria,* section III.

Trallianus, Alexander. *Alexandri Tralliani Libri XII.* Paris: ex officina R. Stephani, 1548.

Turner, Robert. *Orationes XIV.* Ingolstadt: ex typographia D. Sartorii, 1584.

————. *Posthuma.* Ingolstadt: apud A. Angermarium, 1602.

Valla, Georgius, trans. *Alexandri Aphrodisaei de febrium causis.* Lyons: 1506.

Vulteius, Ioannes. *Hendecasyllaborum libri quatuor.* Paris: apud Simonem Colinaeum, 1538.

Werner, Abraham. *Oratio de confectione eius potus, qui . . . Cerevisia vocatur.* Wittenburg: Io. Schwertel, 1567.

Wilde, Jeremias. *De Formica liber unus.* Hamburg: J. Schönfeld, 1615.

IV. Italian Works

Aretino, Pietro. *Aretino's "Dialogues."* Trans. Raymond Rosenthal. London: George Allen and Unwin, 1971.

————. *Tutte le opere.* Ed. Francesco Flora. Verona: Classici Mondadori, 1960.

Bargagli, Girolamo. *Il Valore de gli asini.* Venice: Giolito, n.d.

Berni, Francesco. *Opere.* Ed. Eugenio Camerini. Milan: Edoardo Sonzogno, 1887.

————. *Poesie e prose.* Ed. Enzo Chiòrboli. Florence: Olschki, 1934.

————. *Il primo libro dell'opere burlesche, di M. Francesco Berni et al.* Ed. Grazzini. Florence: Bernardo Giunti, 1552.

————. *Rime.* Ed. Giorgio Bàrberi Squarotti. Turin: Einaudi, 1969.

————. *Il secondo libro dell'opere burlesche.* Ed. Grazzini. Florence: Bernardo Giunti, 1555.

Bronzino, Angelo. *Opere.* Ed. Andrea Emiliani. Bramante: Busto Arsizio, [1960].

Burchiello [Domenico di Giovanni]. *I Sonetti del Burchiello, et di messer Antonio Alamanni, alla Burchiellesca.* Ed. Antonfrancesco Grazzini. Florence: [I Giunti], 1552.

Castiglione, Baldassare. *The Book of the Courtier.* Trans. Thomas Hoby. Tudor Translations, no. 23. Ed. Walter Raleigh. London: David Nutt, 1900.

————. *Il Libro del Cortegiano.* Ed. Giulio Preti. Turin: Einaudi, 1960.

Doni, Anton Francesco. *L'Asinesca gloria dell'Inasinato academia pellegrino.* Venice: Francisco Marcolini, 1553.

———. *I Mondi celesti.* Venice: Giolito, 1562.

———. *I Mondi celesti.* Lyons: Estienne Michel, 1580.

———. *Opere di Pietro Aretino e di Anton Francesco Doni.* 2 vols. Ed. Carlo Cordie. Milan, Naples: Ricciardi, 1976.

Fregoso, Antonio. *See* Amboyse, section V.

Garzoni, Tommaso. *Opere.* Ed. Paolo Cherchi. Naples: Fulvio Rossi, 1972.

———. *Opere de Tomaso Garzoni da Bagnacavallo.* Venice: Giorgio Valentini and Antonio Giuliani, 1617.

———. *La Piazza universale di tutte le professioni del mondo.* Venice: G. B. Somasco, 1587.

Grazzini, Anton Francesco [Il Lasca]. *Le Rime burlesche.* Ed. Carlo Verzone. Florence: G. C. Sansoni, 1882.

———. *Scritti scelti.* Ed. Raffaello Fornaciari. Florence: Biblioteca scolastica de Classici italiani, 1911. *See also* Berni, section IV.

Lando, Ortensio. *Harangues lamentables sur la mort de divers animaux.* Trans. C. Pontoux. Lyons: Benoist Rigaud, 1570.

———. *Orationes funebres in obitus aliquot animalium.* In *Dan. Heinsii Dissertatio epistolica.* Leyden: Godefridus Basson, 1616.

———. *Orationes funebres in obitus aliquot animalium.* In *I. Dousae filii caelestium liber primus.* Trans. Janus Dousa the Younger. Leyden: apud Fr. Raphelengium ex officina Plantiniana, 1591.

———. *Paradossi, cioè, sententie fuori del comun parere.* Lyons: Gioanni Pullon da Trino, 1543.

———. *Paradoxes, ce sont propos contre la commune opinion.* Trans. Charles Estienne. Poitiers: Jan de Marnef, 1553.

———. *Sermoni funebri de vari authori nella morte de diversi animali.* Venice: Giolito, 1548.

Mercati, Michele. *Instruttione sopra la peste.* Rome: Vincentio Accolto, 1576.

Paradoxes ou les opinions renversées de la pluspart des hommes. Rouen: Jacques Caillové, 1638.

La Pazzia. [after 1530].

———. Venice: Giovanni Andrea Vavassore, 1543.

———. *Les Louanges de la folie.* Trans. Jean du Thier. Lyons: Benoist Rigaud, 1567.

Ringhieri, Innocenzio. *Cento Giuochi liberali et d'ingegno.* Bologna: Anselmo Giaccarelli, 1551.

Sansovino, Francesco. *Sette libri di satire.* Venice: Francesco Sansovino, 1560.

Spelta, Antonio Maria. *La Saggia Pazzia.* Pavia: Pietro Bartoli, 1607.

Symeoni, Gabriele. *Le Satire alla Berniesca.* Turin: Martino Cravotto, 1549.

V. FRENCH WORKS

Amboyse, Michel d'. *Le Ris de Democrite.* Trans. from the Italian of Antonio Fregoso. Paris: Gilles Corrozet, 1547.

Aneau, Barthélemy. *Decades de la description, . . . des animaulx. . . .* Lyons: Balthasar Arnoullet, 1549.

Aurigny, Gilles d'. *Le Tuteur d'Amour.* Lyons: Jean de Tournes, 1547.

Auvray, Jean. *Le Banquet des Muses ou les diverses satires du sieur Auvray.* Rouen: David Ferrand, 1628.

Baïf, Jean Antoine de. *Euvres en rime.* 5 vols. Ed. Charles Marty-Laveaux. Paris: A. Lemerre, 1881–90.

Banquet des Muses. See Auvray, section V.

Beaulieu, Eustorg de. *Les divers Rapports.* 1537. Ed. M. A. Pegg. Geneva: Droz, 1964.

Belleau, Remy. *Oeuvres poétiques.* 2 vols. Ed. Charles Marty-Laveaux. 1878. Geneva: Slatkine, 1974.

Béroalde de Verville, François. *Les Muses incognues.* Rouen: Jean Petit, 1604.

―――. *Les Muses incognues.* Paris: J. Gay, 1862.

Blasons, de la Goutte, de Honneur, et de la Quarte. Lyons: Jean de Tournes, 1547.

Blasons, poésies anciennes des XV et XVImes siècles. Ed. Dominique Martin Méon. Paris: J.-L. Chanson, 1809.

Boaistuau, Pierre de. *Théâtre du monde.* Paris: V. Sertenas, 1561.

Bourdeille, Pierre de, Seigneur de Brantôme. *Vies des grands capitaines estrangers et françois.* 2 vols. Ed. J.A.C. Buchon. Paris: Auguste Desrez, 1838.

Brach, Pierre de. *Oeuvres poétiques.* 2 vols. Ed. Reinhold Dezeimeris. Paris: A. Aubry, 1861–62.

―――. *Les Poèmes de Pierre de Brach.* Bordeaux: Simon Millanges, 1576.

Bretonnayau, René. *La Génération de l'homme.* Paris: Abel l'Angelier, 1583.

Bruscambille [Des Lauriers]. *Facecieuses Paradoxes de Bruscambille, & autres discours comiques.* Rouen: Thomas Maillard, 1615.

―――. *Les Oeuvres de Bruscambille.* Rouen: Robert Sejourné, 1629.

Bunel, Guillaume. *See* Pia, section VIII.

Le Cabinet satyrique. 2 vols. Ed. Fernand Fleuret and Louis Perceau. Paris: Librairie du bon vieux temps, 1924.

Chantelouve, François de. *Tragédie de Pharaon et autres oeuvres poétiques.* Paris: N. Bonfons, 1576.

Clary, François de. *La Bellete.* Lyons: C. Wechel, 1579.

Colet, Claude. *L'Oraison de Mars.* Paris: C. Wechel, 1544.

Collection of French Farces. British Library. C.20.e.13.

Coquelet, Louis. *Eloge de la Goutte.* Paris: Claude Prudhomme, 1727.

Coquillart, Guillaume. *Oeuvres de Coquillart.* 2 vols. Ed. Charles d'Héricault. Paris: Bibliothèque Elzévirienne, 1857.

Corrozet, Gilles. *Le Parnasse des poètes françois modernes.* Paris: Gilles Corrozet, 1571.

Coulet, Etienne. *Eloge de la Goute.* Leyden: Théodore Haak, 1728.

Le Courtizan amoureux. Lyons: Benoist Rigaud, 1582.

Danches, Pierre. *Les trois Blasons.* Poitiers, n.d.

Dant, Jean. *Le Chauve ou le mespris des cheveux.* Paris: Pierre Billaine, 1621.

Denis, Vincent. *See* Fournier, *Variétés*, section VIII.

Deschamps, Eustache. *Oeuvres complètes.* 11 vols. Ed. Le Marquis de Queux de Saint-Hilaire. Paris: Firmin Didot, 1878.

Des Roches, Catherine. *Secondes Oeuvres de Mes-dames des Roches de Poictiers.* Poitiers: pour Nicolas Courtoys, 1583.

Des Roches, Catherine, et al. *La Puce de Madame des Roches.* Ed. Jacques de Sourdrai. Paris: Abel l'Angelier, 1583.

Du Bellay, Joachim. *Divers Jeux rustiques.* Ed. Verdun L. Saulnier. Geneva: Droz, 1947.

———. *Oeuvres poétiques.* 6 vols. Ed. Henri Chamard. Paris: Cornély, 1908–31.

Du Buys, Guillaume. *Les Oeuvres.* Paris: J. Février, 1583.

Du Fail, Noël. *Les Propos Rustiques.* 1547. Ed. Arthur de la Borderie. Paris: A. Lemerre, 1878.

———. *Propos rustiques. . . .* Ed. J. Marie Guichard. Paris: Charpentier, 1856.

Durant, Gilles. *Les Oeuvres poétiques du Sieur de la Bergerie.* Paris: Abel l'Angelier, 1594.

Esternod, Claude d'. *L'Espadon satyrique de Claude d'Esternod.* 1619. Ed. F. Fleuret and L. Perceau. Paris: Librairie du bon vieux temps, 1922.

Estienne, Charles. *Paradoxe que le plaider est chose tresutile, & necessaire à la vie des hommes.* Caen: Martin et Pierre Philippe, 1554. *See also* Lando, section IV.

Estienne, Henri. *Deux Dialogues.* Ed. P. M. Smith. Geneva: Droz, 1980.

Fabri, Pierre. *Le grant et vray Art de pleine Rhétorique.* Rouen: Symon Gruel, 1521.

La fameuse Compagnie de la lesine. Paris: Abraham Saugrain, 1604.

Figon de Montelimar, Jean. *Le Moyen d'éviter procès.* Lyons: Benoist Rigaud, 1574.

La Fleur de poésie françoyse. Paris: Alain Lotrian, 1543.

La Fleur de toutes joyeusetez. N.p., n.d.

Fontaine, Charles. *Ruisseaux de Fontaine.* Lyons: Thibauld Payen, 1555. *See also* Héroët, *Opuscules d'Amour,* section V.

Forcadel, Etienne. *Oeuvres poétiques.* Paris: Guillaume Chaudière, 1579.

———. *Oeuvres poétiques.* Ed. Françoise Joukovsky. Geneva: Droz, 1977.

———. *Poésie d'Estienne Forcadel.* Lyons: Jean de Tournes, 1551.

Fouquelin, Antoine. *La rhétorique Françoise . . . augmentée.* Paris: A. Wechel, 1557.

Freind, J. *Histoire de la médecine.* Leyden: Jean Arningerak, 1727.

French Renaissance Scientific Poetry. Ed. Dudley Wilson. London: Athlone Press, 1974.

Godard, Jean. *Meslanges poétiques.* Lyons: Ambroise Travers, 1624.

———. *Les Oeuvres de Jean Godard parisien.* 2 vols. in 1. Lyons: Pierre Landry, 1594.

La Goutte, tragédie nouvelle. Rouen: Claude le Vilain, 1605.

Gringore, Pierre. *Oeuvres complètes de Gringore.* 2 vols. Ed. Charles d'Héricault and Anatole de Montaiglon. Paris: P. Jannet, 1858–77.

———. *Pierre Gringore's Les Fantasies de mère Sote.* Ed. R. L. Frautschi. University of North Carolina Studies in Romance Languages and Literatures, no. 38. Chapel Hill: University of North Carolina Press, 1962.

Habert, François. *Le Combat de Cupido et de la Mort*. Paris: Alain Lotrian, [ca. 1550].

Habert, Isaac. *Les trois Livres des Météores*. Paris: Jean Richer, 1585.

Héroët, Antoine. *Oeuvres poétiques*. Ed. Ferdinand Gohin. Paris: STFM, 1909.

———. *Opuscules d'Amour*. Lyons: Jean de Tournes, 1547. *See also* La Borderie, section V.

Jamyn, Amadis. *Les Oeuvres poétiques*. Paris: Robert Le Mangnier, 1575.

———. *Les Oeuvres poétiques*. 2 vols. Ed. Samuel M. Carrington. Geneva: Droz, 1973, 1978.

La Borderie, Bertrand de. *L'Amie de Court*. Paris: D. Janot and V. Sertenas, 1542.

———. *Opuscules d'Amour*. Lyons: Jean de Tournes, 1547.

Lachèvre, Frédéric. *Bibliographie des recueils collectifs de poésies du XVIe siècle*. Paris: Champion, 1922.

———. *Les Recueils collectifs de poésies libres et satiriques . . . 1600–1626*. Paris: Champion, 1914.

La Jessée, Jean de. *Les Premières Oeuvres Françoyses*. 4 vols. Anvers: Christophe Plantin, 1583.

La Noue, Odet de. *Paradoxe, que les adversitez sont plus necessaires que les prosperitez*. Lyons: Jean de Tournes, 1588.

———. *The Profit of Imprisonment, A Paradox*. Trans. Josuah Sylvester. London: Peter Short, 1594.

La Taille, Jean de. *Oeuvres de Jean de la Taille*. 4 vols. Ed. René de Maulde. Paris: L. Willem, 1878–82.

Le Caron, Louis. *Dialogues*. Paris: V. Sertenas, 1556.

Lemaire de Belges, Jean. *Les Epîtres de l'Amant Vert*. Ed. Jean Frappier. Lille, Geneva: Droz, 1948.

L'Ortigue, Annibal de. *Poèmes divers du sieur de l'Ortigue*. Paris: Jean Gesselin, 1617.

La Louange des femmes. Lyons, 1551.

Marot, Clément. *Les Epigrammes*. Ed. C.-A. Mayer. London: Athlone Press, 1970.

———. *Les Epîtres*. Ed. C.-A. Mayer. London: Athlone Press, 1958.

———. *Oeuvres complètes de Clément Marot*. 6 vols. Paris: Rapilly, 1824.

———. *Oeuvres diverses*. Ed. C.-A. Mayer. London: Athlone Press, 1966.

———. *Oeuvres satiriques*. Ed. C.-A. Mayer. London: Athlone Press, 1962.

Le Médecin Courtizan, ou la nouvelle et plus courte maniere de parvenir à la vraye et solide medecine. Paris: pour Guillaume Barbe, 1559.

Méon, Dominique Martin. *See Blasons, poésies anciennes des XV et XVImes siècles*, section V.

Michault, Pierre. *Le Doctrinal du temps présent*. Ed. Thomas Walton. Paris: Droz, 1931.

Molinet, Jean. *Les Faictz et dictz*. Paris, 1537.

Montaigne, Michel de. *Les Essais*. Ed. Albert Thibaudet. Editions de la Pléiade. Bruges: Gallimard, 1950.

Morellet, Abbé André. *Théorie du paradoxe*. Amsterdam [Paris], 1775.

Moussin, Jehan. *Discours de l'Yvresse et Yvrongnerie*. Toulouse: Sebastien Philippe, 1612.

La Muse folastre, Recueil des trois livres de. Paris: Jean Fuzy, 1607.

La Muse folastre. Lyons: Barthélemy Ancelin, 1611.

La Muse folastre. Rouen: Claude le Vilain, 1615.

La Muse folastre. [1611.] Reprint. 3 vols. in 1. Brussels: Mertens, 1864.

Les Muses gaillardes. Ed. Antoine du Brueil. Paris: A. du Brueil, [1609?].

Paré, Ambroise. *Les Oeuvres*. 1575. Paris: G. Buon, 1575.

———. *Traicté de la Peste, de la petite Vérolle & Rougeolle avec une bresve description de la Lepre*. Paris: A. Wechel, 1568.

Passerat, Jean. *Les Poésies françaises de Jean Passerat*. 3 vols. Ed. Prosper N. Blanchemain. Paris: A. Lemerre, 1880.

Peletier du Mans, Jacques. *Euvres poëtiques . . . Louanges*. Paris: R. Coulombel, 1581.

———. *L'Art poétique*. Lyons: Jean de Tournes, 1555.

———. *Oeuvres poétiques*. Ed. Léon Séché. Paris: Revue de la Renaissance, 1904.

Picot, A. E., ed. *Recueil général des sotties*. 3 vols. Paris: SATF, 1902–12.

Pont-Aymery, Alexandre de. *Paradoxe apologique*. Paris: Hubert Velu, 1596.

Pontoux, Claude de. *Les Oeuvres de Claude de Pontoux gentilhomme Chalonnois docteur en medecine*. Lyons: Benoist Rigaud, 1579. *See also* Lando, section IV.

Rabelais, François. *Tiers Livre*. Ed. Abel Lefranc. Paris: Travaux d'humanisme et Renaissance, 1931.

Le Rasibus, ou le procès fait à la barbe des Capucins. Cologne: chez Pasquin resuscité, 1680.

La Récréation et passetemps des tristes. Paris: Pierre l'Huilier, 1573.

La Récréation et passetemps des tristes. Rouen: A. le Cousturier, 1595.

Recueil de farces, de moralités et de sermons joyeux. 4 vols. Ed. Leroux de Lincy and Francisque Michel. Paris: Techener, 1837.

Recueil général des Sotties. 3 vols. Ed. Emile Picot. Paris: SATF, 1902.

Regnier, Mathurin. *Les Satyres du Sieur Regnier*. Paris: Toussaint du Bray, 1609.

———. *Les Satyres et autres oeuvres folastres du sieur Regnier*. Paris: Guillaume Loison, 1617.

Remède très utile contre la peste. [ca. 1530].

La Response et contredict d'un barbu contre le blasonneur des barbes de maintenant. Paris: Annet Brière, 1551.

Ronsard, Pierre de. *Oeuvres complètes*. 20 vols. Ed. Paul Laumonier. Paris: Didier, 1914–19.

———. *La Promesse*. [1563].

Rus, Jean. *Oeuvres de Jean Rus poëte bordelais*. Ed. Philippe Tamizey de Larroque. Paris: A. Claudin, 1874.

Sainct-Gelays, Melin de. *Oeuvres complètes*. 3 vols. Ed. Prosper N. Blanchemain. Paris: Bibliothèque Elzévirienne, 1873.

Saint-Amant, Marc Antoine Girard, sieur de. *Oeuvres poétiques*. Ed. Léon Vérane. Paris: Garnier, 1930.

Les Satires françaises du XVIe siècle. 2 vols. Ed. Fernand Fleuret and Louis Perceau. Paris: Garnier, 1923.

La Satyre Menippée de la Vertu du Catholicon d'Espagne. 1593. Ed. C. Read. Paris: Flammarion, 1892.

Sebillet, Thomas. *Art poétique françoys*. 1548. Ed. Félix Gaiffe. Paris: Droz, 1932.

Sordes, Pierre. *Discours de la Goutte*. Lyons: Claude Chastelard, 1626.

Tabourot, Etienne. *Les Bigarrures du Seigneur des Accords*. 3 vols. Ed. Guillaume Colletet. Brussels: Mertens, 1866.

Tahureau, Jacques. *Les Bigarrures*. Paris: Jean Richer, 1583.

————. *Les Dialogues*. Paris: Gabriel Buon, 1565.

————. *Poésies complètes*. Ed. Trevor Peach. Geneva: Droz, 1984.

Le Triumphe de haulte et puissante Dame Vérolle. Ed. A. C. de Montaiglon. Paris: L. Willem, 1874.

————. In *Recueil de poésies françoises des XVe et XVIe siècles*, 4:214–68. *See* section I.

Le Triumphe de haulte Folie. Lyons: Anthoine Volant, [ca. 1550].

————. Ed. A. C. de Montaiglon. Paris: Willem, 1873.

Tyard, Pontus de. *Les Oeuvres poétiques*. Paris: Galliot du Pré, 1573.

Vienne, Philibert de. *Le Philosophe de Court*. Lyons: Jean de Tournes, 1547.

————. *The Philosopher of the Court*. Trans. George North. London: Henry Binneman, 1575.

Villon, François. *Les Oeuvres*. Ed. Louis Thuasne. Paris: A. Picard, 1923.

Viollet-le-Duc, E.L.N., ed. *Ancien Théâtre français*. 10 vols. Paris: Bibliothèque Elzévirienne, 1854–57.

VI. English Works

Chaloner, Thomas. *In Laudem Henrici Octavi*. Ed. and English trans. John B. Gabel and Carl C. Schlam. Lawrence, Kans.: Coronado Press, 1979.

Elyot, Sir Thomas. *The Boke Named the Governour*. Ed. H.H.S. Croft. London: Kegan Paul Trench, 1883.

Hall, John. *Paradoxes*. 1650. Reprint. Intro. Don Cameron Allen. Gainesville, Fla.: Scholars' Facsimiles & Reprints, 1956.

Heath, R[obert]. *Paradoxical Assertions and Philosophical Problems*. London: R. W., 1659.

Illustrations of Old English Literature. Ed. J. Payne Collier. London: privately printed, 1866.

Johnson, Samuel. *Poems*. Ed. E. L. McAdam. New Haven: Yale University Press, 1964.

The Mirrour of Madnes; or, A Paradoxe maintayning Madnes to be most excellent. Trans. James Sandford. London: Thomas Marshe, 1576.

A Paradox against Liberty. London: for James Vade, 1679.

A Paradox against Life. London: for James Vade, 1681.

Shakespeare, William. *King Henry IV, Parts I and II*. Ed. A. R. Humphreys. 1960. Reprint. London: Methuen, 1980.

Skelton, John. *The Poetical Works of John Skelton*. 2 vols. Ed. A. Dyce. New York: AMS Press, 1965.

Tudor Verse Satire. Ed. K. W. Gransden. London: Athlone Press, 1970.

Welles, Benjamin. *A Treatise of the Gout*. London: J. M. for Henry Herringman, 1669.

Bibliography

VII. German Works

Brant, Sebastian. *Das Narrenschiff*. Trans. Edwin H. Zeydel. New York: Columbia University Press, 1944.

——. *Das Narrenschiff*. Ed. Manfred Lemmer. 1962. Reprint. Tübingen: Max Niemeyer Verlag, 1968.

——. *The shyppe of fooles*. Trans. Thomas Watson. London: Wynkyn de Worde, 1517.

Fischart, Johann. *Johann Fischarts sämmtliche Dichtungen*. 3 vols. Ed. Heinrich Kurz. Leipzig: J. J. Weber, 1866.

——. *Johann Fischarts Werke*. 3 vols. Ed. Adolf Hauffen. Stuttgart: Union Deutsche Verlagsgesellschaft, [1894].

VIII. Secondary Sources

Anderson, Graham. *Lucian: Theme and Variation in the Second Sophistic*. Leyden: Brill, 1976.

Asselineau, Charles. *Notice sur Jean de Schelandre poète verdunois 1585–1655*. Alençon: Poulet-Malassis and De Broise, 1856.

Bahlmann, Paul. *Die lateinischen Dramen, von Wimphelings "Stylpho" bis zur Mitte des sechzehnten Jahrhunderts*. Münster: Regensberg, 1893.

Bakhtin, Mikhail. *Rabelais and His World*. Trans. Helen Iswolsky. 1965. Cambridge: MIT Press, 1968.

Baldwin, Barry. *Studies in Lucian*. Toronto: Hakkert, 1973.

Bar, Francis. *Le Genre burlesque en France au XVIe siècle*. Paris: Editions d'Artéry, 1960.

Baumgartner, L., and J. F. Fulton, eds. *Bibliography of the Poem "Syphilis sive Morbus Gallicus" by Girolamo Fracastoro of Verona*. New Haven: Yale University Press, 1935.

Beaujour, Michel. *Le Jeu de Rabelais*. Issoudun: Editions de l'Herne, 1969.

Béné, Charles. " 'Folie' et 'Sagesse' dans la littérature du XVIe siècle." *Studi francesi* 23 (1979): 1–14.

Bennett, R. E. "Four Paradoxes by Sir William Cornwallis, the Younger." *Harvard Studies and Notes in Philology and Literature* 13 (1931): 219–40.

Bergounioux, Louis-Alexandre. *De Quercy en Cournouaille. Guillaume du Buys (1520?–1594)*. Paris: A. Picard, 1936.

Bernard, Jean-Marc. "Les *Jeux rustiques* de Joachim Du Bellay." *La Revue critique des idées et des livres* 21 (1913): 412–15.

Besch, Emile. "Un Moraliste satirique et rationaliste au XVIe siècle, Jacques Tahureau." *Revue du seizième siècle* 6 (1919):1–44, 157–200.

Best, Thomas. *The Humanist Ulrich von Hutten: A Reappraisal of His Humor*. Chapel Hill: University of North Carolina Press, 1969.

Bietenholz, Peter G., ed. *Contemporaries of Erasmus*. 3 vols. Toronto: University of Toronto Press, 1986.

Billacois, François. *Le Duel dans la société française des XVIe–XVIIe siècles*. Paris: Editions des hautes études en sciences sociales, 1986.

Boas, George. *The Happy Beast in French Thought of the Seventeenth Century.* 1933. Reprint. New York: Octagon, 1966.

Boisset, Jean. "*L'Eloge de la Folie* et les études bibliques d'Erasme: quelques réflexions." In *Réforme et humanisme,* ed. Jean Boisset, 149–65. Montpellier: Université Paul Valéry, 1975.

Bompaire, Lucien. *Lucien écrivain. Imitation et création.* Paris: E. de Boccard, 1958.

Borgese, G. A. "The Dishonor of Honor from Giovanni Mauro to Sir John Falstaff." *Romanic Review* 32 (1941): 44–55.

Bourrilly, V. L. *Jacques Colin abbé de Saint-Ambroise (14?–1547).* Paris: Bibliothèque d'histoire moderne, 1905.

Bowen, Barbara. *Les Caractéristiques essentielles de la farce française et leur survivance dans les années 1550–1620.* Illinois Studies in Language and Literature, no. 53. Urbana: University of Illinois Press, 1964.

———. "Cornelius Agrippa's *De Vanitate*: Polemic or Paradox?" *Bibliothèque d'Humanisme et Renaissance* 34 (1972): 249–56.

Bowersock, G. W. *Greek Sophists in the Roman Empire.* Oxford: Clarendon, 1969.

Boyle, Marjorie. "The Fly to the Elephant." In *Rhetoric and Reform: Erasmus' Civil Dispute with Luther,* 1–4. Cambridge: Harvard University Press, 1983.

Brabant, Hyacinthe. "Les Traitements burlesques de la folie au XVIe et XVIIe siècles." In *Folie et déraison à la Renaissance.* Brussels: Editions de l'université de Bruxelles, 1976.

Breen, Quirinus. "The Antiparadoxon of Marcantonius Maioragius." *Studies in the Renaissance* 5 (1958): 37–48.

Brock, Dame Madeleine Dorothy. *Studies in Fronto and His Age.* Cambridge: Cambridge University Press, 1911.

Burgess, Theodore C. *Epideictic Literature.* University of Chicago Studies in Classical Philology, no. 8. Chicago: University of Chicago Press, 1902.

Caccia, Natale. *Note su la fortuna di Luciano nel Rinascimento.* Milan: C. Signorelli, [1914].

Cameron, Alan. *Claudian: Poetry and Propaganda at the Court of Honorius.* Oxford: Clarendon, 1970.

Cartier, Alfred. *Bibliographie des éditions des de Tournes, imprimeurs lyonnais.* 2 vols. Ed. Marius Audin. Paris: Editions des bibliothèques nationales de France, 1937–38.

———. "Louise Labé, le procès Yvard à Genève, et le *Philosophe de Court* par Philibert de Vienne." *Revue des livres anciens* 2 (1917): 329–30.

Cave, Terence. *The Cornucopian Text: Problems of Writing in the French Renaissance.* Oxford: Clarendon, 1979.

Champlin, Edward. *Fronto and Antonine Rome.* Cambridge: Harvard University Press, 1980.

Cherchi, Paolo. "L'Encomio paradossale nel manierismo." *Forum italicum* 9 (1975): 368–84.

Chomarat, Jacques. " 'L'Eloge de la Folie' et Quintilien." *Information littéraire* 2 (1972): 77–82.

Christian, Lynda. "The Metamorphoses of Erasmus' 'Folly.' " *Journal of the History of Ideas* 32 (1971): 289–94.

Clarke, Martin Lowther. *Rhetoric at Rome, a Historical Survey*. London: Cohen and West, 1953.

Cloutier, Marilynn Roach. "Remy Belleau's 'Petites Inventions' of 1556." Ph.D. diss., University of Wisconsin, 1976.

Cohen, Ralph. "On the Interrelations of Eighteenth-Century Literary Forms." In *Selected Essays from the English Institute*, ed. Phillip Harth, 33–78. New York: Columbia University Press, 1974.

Coleman, Dorothy Gabe. *Rabelais: A Critical Study in Prose Fiction*. Cambridge: Cambridge University Press, 1971.

Colie, Rosalie. *Paradoxia Epidemica: The Renaissance Tradition of Paradox*. Princeton: Princeton University Press, 1966.

———. *The Resources of Kind: Genre-Theory in the Renaissance*. Ed. Barbara K. Lewalski. Berkeley: University of California Press, 1973.

Condeescu, N. N. "Le Paradoxe bernesque dans la littérature française de la Renaissance." *Beiträge zur Romanischen Philologie* 2 (1963): 27–51.

Copeman, W.S.C. *A Short History of Gout and the Rheumatic Diseases*. Berkeley: University of California Press, 1964.

Crane, Thomas F. *Italian Social Customs of the Sixteenth Century*. New Haven: Yale University Press, 1920.

Crane, W. G. *Wit and Rhetoric in the Renaissance*. New York: Columbia University Press, 1937.

Crawford, William Saunders. *Synesius the Hellene*. London: Rivingtons, 1901.

Crawfurd, Sir Raymond Henry Payne. *Plague and Pestilence in Literature and Art*. Oxford: Oxford University Press, 1914.

Croce, Benedetto. "Sulle Traduzioni e Imitazioni italiani dell' 'Elogio' e dei 'Colloqui' di Erasmo." *Aneddoti di Varia Letteratura*. Scritti di storia letteraria e politica, 41. Bari: Laterza, 1953.

Croiset, Maurice. *Essai sur la vie et les oeuvres de Lucien*. Paris, 1882.

Cronin, Grover. "The Bestiary and the Medieval Mind—Some Complexities." *Modern Language Quarterly* 2 (1941): 191–98.

Crosby, H. "Lucian and the Art of Medicine." *Transactions of the American Philological Association* 54 (1923): 15–16.

Demerson, Geneviève. "Joachim du Bellay traducteur de lui-même." In *Neo-Latin and the Vernacular in Renaissance France*, ed. Grahame Castor and Terence Cave, 113–48. Oxford: Clarendon, 1984.

DeNeef, A. Leigh. "Epideictic Rhetoric and the Renaissance Lyric." *Journal of Medieval and Renaissance Studies* 3 (1973): 203–31.

Derrett, J.D.M. "Rabelais' Legal Learning and the Trial of Bridoye." *Bibliothèque d'Humanisme et Renaissance* 25 (1963): 11–71.

Dexter, G. H. "La Perrière and His Poetic Works." M.A. diss., University of London, 1952.

Dickinson, Gladys. *Du Bellay in Rome*. Leyden: Brill, 1960.

Diller, Georges E. *Les Dames des Roches*. Paris: Droz, 1936.

Dubrow, Heather. *Genre*. London: Methuen, 1982.

Folie et déraison à la Renaissance. Brussels: Editions de l'université de Bruxelles, 1976.

Dumont, François. "Les Dettes de Panurge." *Etudes d'histoire du droit privé offertes à Pierre Petot.* Paris, 1959.

Duncan, Douglas. *Ben Jonson and the Lucianic Tradition.* Cambridge: Cambridge University Press, 1979.

Duneton, Claude. *La Puce à l'oreille.* Evreux: Stock, 1978.

Eckert, Willehad Paul, and Christoph von Imhoff. *Willibald Pirckheimer: Dürers Freund.* Cologne: Wienand Verlag, 1971.

Eckhardt, Alexandre. *Remy Belleau, sa vie, sa "Bergerie."* Budapest: Librarie Joseph Németh, 1917.

Eckman, James. "Jerome Cardan." *Supplements to the Bulletin of the History of Medicine* 7 (1946): 69–75.

Filippis, Michele de. *The Literary Riddle in Italy to the End of the Sixteenth Century.* Berkeley: University of California Press, 1948.

Flamini, Francesco. "Le lettere italiane in Francia alla corte di Francesco I." In *Studi di storia letteraria italiana e straniera.* Livorno: Raffaello Giusti, 1895.

———. "Le lettere italiane in Francia nei secoli del Rinascimento." In *Varia.* Livorno: Raffaello Giusti, 1905.

Foley, John Miles, ed. *Oral Tradition in Literature.* Columbia: University of Missouri Press, 1986.

Fournier, Edouard, ed. *Variétés Historiques et Littéraires.* 10 vols. Paris: P. Jannet, 1855–63.

Françon, Marcel. "L'Invasion de la Provence et l'allusion au Brésil (suite)." *Bulletin de la société des amis de Montaigne* 24 (1977): 51.

———. "Un Motif de la poésie amoureuse au XVIe siècle." *PMLA* 56 (1941): 307–36.

———. "Sur l'Invasion de la Provence de 1536, et Montaigne." *Bulletin de la société des amis de Montaigne* 23 (1976): 113–14.

Fraustadt, Fedor. *Uber das Verhältnis von Barclay's "Ship of Fools" zur lateinischen, französischen, und deutschen Quelle.* Breslau: R. Nischkowsky, 1894.

Frohock, W. M. "Panurge as Comic Character." *Yale French Studies* 23 (1959): 71–76.

Gadol, Joan. *Leon Battista Alberti: Universal Man of the Early Renaissance.* Chicago: University of Chicago Press, 1969.

Gambier, Henri. *Italie et Renaissance poétique en France.* Padua: Cedam, 1936.

Garapon, Robert. *La Fantaisie verbale et le comique dans le théâtre français.* Paris: Armand Colin, 1957.

Gardner, Alice. *Synesius of Cyrene, Philosopher and Bishop.* London: Society for the Propagation of Christian Knowledge, 1886.

Gavin, J. Austin, and Thomas M. Walsh. "The *Praise of Folly* in Context: The Commentary of Girardus Listrius." *Renaissance Quarterly* 24 (1971): 193–209.

Gewerstock, Olga. *Lucian und Hutten: Zur Geschichte des Dialogs im 16. Jahrhundert.* Germanische Studien 31. Berlin: Emil Ebering, 1924.

Giudici, Enzo. *Le Opere minori di Maurice Scève.* Parma: Guanda, 1958.

Glatigny, Michel. "Du Bellay traducteur dans les *Jeux rustiques.*" *L'Information littéraire* 18 (1966): 33–41.

Glauser, Alfred. *Montaigne paradoxal.* Paris: Nizet, 1972.

Glauser, Alfred. *Rabelais créateur*. Paris: Nizet, 1966.

Gleason, Maud. "Festive Satire: Julian's *Misopogon* and the New Year at Antioch." *Journal of Roman Studies* 76 (1986): 106–19.

Graur, Theodosia. *Un Disciple de Ronsard, Amadis Jamyn, 1540?–93*. Bibliothèque littéraire de la Renaissance, n.s. 18. Paris: Champion, 1929.

Grendler, Paul F. *Critics of the Italian World, 1530–60*. Madison: University of Wisconsin Press, 1969.

Grève, Marcel de. "Le Discours rabelaisien, ou la raison en folie." In *Folie et déraison à la Renaissance*, 149–59. Brussels: Editions de l'université de Bruxelles, 1976.

Guy, Henry. "Les Sources françaises de Ronsard." *Revue d'histoire littéraire de la France* 9 (1902): 217–56.

Hall, Jennifer. *Lucian's Satire*. New York: Arno, 1981.

Hardison, O. B., Jr. *The Enduring Monument: A Study of the Idea of Praise in Renaissance Literature and Practice*. Chapel Hill: University of North Carolina Press, 1962.

Hauffen, Adolf. "Zur Litteratur der ironischen Enkomien." *Vierteljahrsschrift für Literaturgeschichte* 6 (1893): 160–85.

Hauvette, Henri. *Un Exilé florentin à la cour de France au XVIe siècle: Luigi Alamanni (1495–1556), sa vie et son oeuvre*. Paris: Hachette, 1903.

Hawkins, R. L. *Maistre Charles Fontaine Parisien*. Cambridge: Harvard University Press, 1916.

Heep, Martha. "Die Colloquia familiaria des Erasmus und Lucian." *Hermaea* 18 (1927): 1–24.

Heiserman, A. R. "Satire in the *Utopia*." *PMLA* 78 (1963): 163–74.

Henderson, Judith. "Erasmus on the Art of Letter-Writing." In *Renaissance Eloquence*, ed. James J. Murphy, 331–55. Berkeley: University of California Press, 1983.

Holzberg, Niklas. *Willibald Pirckheimer: Griechischer Humanismus in Deutschland*. Munich: Fink, 1981.

Huizinga, Johan. *Erasmus of Rotterdam*. 1924. London: Phaidon, 1952.

Hutton, James. *The Greek Anthology in France*. Ithaca: Cornell University Press, 1946.

Imhoff, Christopher. *Willibald Pirckheimer*. Cologne: Wienand Verlag, 1971.

Ingegno, Alfonso. *Saggio sulla filosofia di Cardano*. Florence: la nuova Italia, 1980.

Isevyn, Jozef. "Die *Stultitiae Laus* des Erasmus und die *De Triumpho St. Libri III* des Faustinus Perisauli." *Menander* 22 (1967): 327–29.

Jacob, Paul L. "Les Blasons anatomiques du corps féminin." In *Recherches bibliographiques sur des livres rares et curieux*, 144–54. Paris: Edouard Rouveyre, 1880.

———. "Les Muses gaillardes." In *Recherches bibliographiques sur des livres rares et curieux*, 204–8. Paris: Edouard Rouveyre, 1880.

Javitch, Daniel. "*The Philosopher of the Court*: A French Satire Misunderstood." *Comparative Literature* 23 (1971): 97–124.

Jebb, R. C. *Essays and Addresses*. Cambridge: Cambridge University Press, 1907.

Johnson, A. F. *Selected Essays on Books and Printing*. Amsterdam: van Gendt, 1970.

Jones, C. P. *Culture and Society in Lucian*. Cambridge: Harvard University Press, 1986.

———. *The Roman World of Dio Chrysostom*. Cambridge: Harvard University Press, 1978.

Kaiser, Walter. "The Ironic Mock Encomium." In *Twentieth-Century Interpretations of "The Praise of Folly,"* ed. Kathleen Williams, 78–91. Englewood Cliffs, N.J.: Prentice-Hall, 1969.

———. *Praisers of Folly: Erasmus, Rabelais, Shakespeare*. Cambridge: Harvard University Press, 1963.

Kay, David W. "Erasmus' Learned Joking: The Ironical Use of Classical Wisdom in the *Praise of Folly*." *Texas Studies in Literature and Language* 19 (1977): 147–67.

Keating, L. Clark. *Etienne Pasquier*. New York: Twayne, 1972.

Kennedy, George. *The Art of Persuasion in Greece*. Princeton: Princeton University Press, 1963.

———. *The Art of Rhetoric in the Roman World 300 B.C.–300 A.D.* Princeton: Princeton University Press, 1972.

Keys, Thomas E. "The Plague in Literature." *Bulletin of the Medical Library Association* 32 (1944): 35–36.

Kinney, Arthur F. "Rhetoric and Fiction in Elizabethan England.' In *Renaissance Eloquence*, ed. James J. Murphy, 385–93. Berkeley: University of California Press, 1983.

Knox, Norman. *The Word Irony and Its Context, 1500–1755*. Durham: Duke University Press, 1961.

Korkowski, E. "Agrippa as Ironist." *Neophilologus* 60 (1976): 594–607.

Krause, Carl. *Eobanus Hessus: Sein Leben und seine Werke*. 2 vols. 1879. Nieuwkoop: de Graaf, 1963.

Kristeller, Paul Oskar. *Renaissance Thought*. New York: Harper, 1961.

Kutter, Markus. *Celio Secundo Curione, sein Leben und sein Werk*. Basel and Stuttgart: Helberg and Lichtenhahn, 1955.

La Charité, Raymond. "Rabelais: The Book as Therapy." In *Medicine and Literature*, ed. Enid Rhodes Peschel, 11–17. New York: Neale Watson Academic Publications, 1980.

Lacombrade, Christian. *Synésios de Cyrène*. Paris: Société d'édition "Les belles lettres," 1951.

Laumonier, Paul. *Ronsard poète lyrique*. Paris: Hachette, 1909.

Leake, Roy E. *Concordance des Essais de Montaigne*. Geneva: Droz, 1981.

Lefebvre, Joel. *Les Fols et la Folie*. Paris: Klincksieck, 1968.

Lefranc, Abel. *Grands Ecrivains de la Renaissance*. Paris: Champion, 1914.

Legré, Ludovic. *Un Philosophe provençal au temps des Antonins, Favorin d'Arles*. Marseilles: Aubertin et Rolle, 1900.

Lehmann, Paul. *Die Parodie im Mittelalter*. 1922. Stuttgart: Anton Hiersemann, 1963.

Lemay, Richard. "The Fly against the Elephant: Flandinus against Pomponazzi on

Fate." In *Philosophy and Humanism: Renaissance Essays in Honor of Paul Oskar Kristeller*, ed. Edward Mahoney, 70–99. Leyden: Brill, 1976.

Lenient, Charles. *La Satire en France, ou la littérature militante au XVIe siècle.* Paris: Hachette, 1866.

Levin, Harry. *The Myth of the Golden Age in the Renaissance.* Bloomington: Indiana University Press, 1969.

Liede, Alfred. *Dichtung als Spiel.* Berlin: De Gruyter, 1963.

Losse, Deborah. *Rhetoric at Play: Rabelais and the Satirical Eulogy.* New York: Peter Lang, 1980.

Lough, John. *Paris Theatre Audiences in the Seventeenth and Eighteenth Centuries.* London: Oxford University Press, 1957.

Lyonnet, Henry. *Dictionnaire des comédiens français. . . .* 2 vols. Geneva: Revue universelle internationale illustrée, 1911–12.

MacCormack, Sabine. *Art and Ceremony in Late Antiquity.* Berkeley: University of California Press, 1981.

Major, Ralph H. *A History of Medicine.* Springfield, Mass.: Charles C. Thomas, 1954.

Malloch, A. E. "The Techniques and Function of the Renaissance Paradox." *Studies in Philology* 53 (1956): 191–203.

Manacorda, Guido. "Notizie intorno alle fonti di alcuni motivi satirici ed alla loro diffusione durante il Rinascimento." *Romanische Forschungen* 22 (1908): 733–60.

Mancini, Girolamo. *Vita di Leon Battista Alberti.* 1882. Reprint. Florence: G. Carnesecchi, 1911.

Manger, Klaus. *Das "Narrenschiff": Entstehung, Wirkung, und Deutung.* Erträge der Forschung, no. 186. Darmstadt: Wissenschaftliche Buchgesellschaft, 1983.

Manitius, Maximilian. *Geschichte der lateinischen Literatur des Mittelalters.* Munich: C. H. Beck, 1911.

Martineau-Génieys, Christine. *Le Thème de la mort dans la poésie française de 1450 à 1550.* Paris: Champion, 1977.

Marty-Laveaux, Charles. *La Pléiade françoise.* 19 vols. Paris: A. Lemerre, 1866–93.

Mason, Harold Andrew. *Humanism and Poetry in the Early Tudor Period.* London: Routledge Kegan Paul, 1959.

Mayer, C[laude]-A[lbert]. "The Genesis of a Rabelaisian Character: Menippus and Frère Jean." *French Studies* 6 (1952): 219–29.

———. " 'L'Honnête Homme,' Molière, and Philibert de Vienne's *Philosophe de Court*." *Modern Language Review* 46 (1951): 196–217.

———. *Lucien de Samosate et la Renaissance française.* Geneva: Slatkine, 1984.

———. "Lucien et la Renaissance." *Revue de littérature comparée* 47 (1973): 5–22.

———. "Monologue ou récit-aveu comme technique satirique." *Studi francesi* 65–66 (1978): 373–79.

———. "Rabelais's Satirical Eulogy: The Praise of Borrowing." In *François Rabelais . . . 1553–1953*, 147–55. Geneva: Droz, 1953.

———. "Satire in French Literature from 1525–1560." Ph.D. diss., University of London, 1949.

Mazzara, Richard A. "Saint-Amant and the Bernesque Poets." *Zeitschrift für Romanische Philologie* 25 (1901): 71–93, 215–29, 257–77.

Merrill, R. V. "Lucian and Du Bellay's *Poëte Courtisan.*" *Modern Philology* 29 (1931): 11–20.

Miller, Clarence H. "Some Medieval Elements and Structural Unity in Erasmus' *The Praise of Folly.*" *Renaissance Quarterly* 27 (1974): 499–511.

Miller, Henry Knight. "The Paradoxical Encomium with Special Reference to its Vogue in England, 1600–1800." *Modern Philology* 53 (1956): 145–78.

Mitchell, Rosamund. *John Free, from Bristol to Rome in the Fifteenth Century.* London and New York: Longmans, 1955.

Moffitt, John. "La Femme à la puce: The Textual Background of Seventeenth-Century Painted Flea Hunts." *Gazette des Beaux Arts* 24 (1964): 99–103.

Mongrédien, Georges. *Bibliographie des oeuvres du facétieux Bruscambille.* Chartres, 1926.

Morley, Henry. *Jerome Cardan.* London: Chapman and Hall, 1854.

———. *The Life of Henry Cornelius Agrippa von Nettesheim, Doctor and Knight, commonly known as a Magician.* 2 vols. London: Chapman and Hall, 1856.

Morrison, Mary. "Catullus in the Neo-Latin Poetry of France before 1550." *BHR* 17 (1955): 365–94.

Mottron, Jean. *Rabelais . . . et les Verollez tresprecieux.* Tours: Arrault et Cie., 1947.

Murarasu, D. *La Poésie néolatine et la Renaissance française des lettres antiques en France (1500–1549).* Paris: J. Gambier, 1928.

Murphy, James J., ed. *Renaissance Eloquence.* Berkeley: University of California Press, 1983.

Nagy, Gregory. *The Best of the Achaeans.* Baltimore: Johns Hopkins University Press, 1979.

Naïs, Hélène. *Les Animaux dans la poésie française de la Renaissance.* Paris: Didier, 1961.

Nauert, Charles G., Jr. *Agrippa and the Crisis of Renaissance Thought.* Illinois Studies in the Social Sciences no. 55. Urbana: University of Illinois Press, 1965.

Nicol, James Carpenter. *Synesius of Cyrene, His Life and Writings.* Cambridge, England: E. Johnson, 1887.

Niord, Yvonne. "A Study of the 'Imitation' of Italian Writers in Joachim du Bellay's Works." Ph.D. diss., University of Wales, 1955.

Nolhac, Pierre de. *Ronsard et l'humanisme.* Paris: Champion, 1966.

O'Connor, Dorothy. "Sebastian Brant en France au XVIe siècle." *Revue de littérature comparée* 8 (1928): 309–317.

Ogle, R. B. "The Bernesque Satire: A Critical Essay." *Symposium* 8 (1954): 309–20.

Omont, Henri Auguste. "Georges Hermonyme de Sparte, maître de grec à Paris et copiste de manuscrits, (1476)." *Mémoires de la société de l'histoire de Paris et de l'île de France* 12 (1885): 65–98.

Ong, Walter J. "Commonplace Rhapsody: Ravisius Textor, Zwinger and Shakespeare." In *Classical Influences on European Culture, A.D. 1500–1700*, ed. R. R. Bolgar, 91–126. Cambridge: Cambridge University Press, 1976.

———. "Fouquelin's French Rhetoric and the Ramist Vernacular Tradition." *Studies in Philology* 51 (1954): 127–42.

Oulmont, Charles. "Estienne Forcadel." In *La Revue des Pyrénées*, 547–83. Toulouse: E. Privat, 1907.

Pavlovskis, Zoja. *The Praise of Folly: Structure and Irony*. Leyden: Brill, 1983.

Pease, Arthur Stanley. "Things Without Honor." *Classical Philology* 21 (1926): 27–42.

Pellegrini, Carlo. "Relazioni tra la letteratura italiana e la letteratura francese." *Letterature comparate*. In *Problemi ed orientamenti, critici di lingua e di letteratura italiana*, ed. A. Momigliano. Milan: Carlo Marzorati, 1948.

Pia, Pascal, ed. *Le Bouquet poétique des médecins*. Paris: Collection de l'écriture, 1933.

Picot, Auguste Emile. *Les Français italianisants au XVIe siècle*. 2 vols. Paris: Champion, 1906–07.

———. *Les Italiens en France au XVIe siècle*. Bordeaux: Imprimerie Gounouilhou, 1902.

Pierron, Alexis. *Histoire de la littérature grecque*. 1869. Reprint. Paris: Hachette, 1950.

Pike, Robert E. "The 'Blasons' in French Literature of the Sixteenth Century." *Romanic Review* 27 (1936): 223–42.

Platt, Helen O. "Structure in Du Bellay's *Divers Jeux rustiques*." *BHR* 35 (1973): 19–37.

Plattard, Jean. *L'Oeuvre de Rabelais*. Paris: Champion, 1910.

Pourtalès, Guy. "Odet de la Noue." *Bulletin de la société de l'histoire du protestantisme français* 67–69 (1918–20): 2–35.

Previtera, Carmelo. *La Poesia giocosa et l'umorismo dalle origini al Rinascimento*. Milan: F. Vallardi, 1939.

Ragland, Mary. *Rabelais and Panurge: A Psychological Approach to History*. Amsterdam: Rodopi, 1976.

Rankin, H. D. *Sophists, Socratics and Cynics*. London: Croom Helm, 1983.

Rathéry, Edmé-Jacques-Benoît. *Influence de l'Italie sur les lettres françaises*. Paris: Firmin Didot, 1853.

Raymond, Marcel. *L'Influence de Ronsard sur la poésie françcaise*. 1927. Reprint. Travaux d'humanisme et Renaissance no. 73. 2 vols. in 1. Geneva: Droz, 1965.

Rebhorn, Wayne. "The Metamorphoses of Moria: Structure and Meaning in *The Praise of Folly*." *PMLA* 89 (1974): 463–76.

Rechtien, John. "A 1520 French Translation of the *Moriae Encomium*." *Renaissance Quarterly* 27 (1974): 23–34.

Renaudet, Augustin. *Préréforme et humanisme à Paris pendant les premières guerres d'Italie (1494–1517)*. 1916. Reprint. Paris: Librarie d'Argences, 1953.

Renucci, A. *Un Aventurier des lettres au 16e siècle, Gabriele Simeoni*. Paris: Didier, 1943.

Reynolds, Anne. "Francesco Berni: The Theory and Practice of Italian Satire in the Sixteenth Century." *IQ* 24 (1983): 5–15.

Rigolot, François. "Le Fol Eloge de la Folie." In *Les Langages de Rabelais*, 162–72. Geneva: Droz, 1972.

———. "Rabelais et l'éloge paradoxal." *Kentucky Romance Quarterly* 17 (1970): 191–98.

———. *Le Texte de la Renaissance*. Geneva: Droz, 1982.

Robinson, Christopher. *Lucian and His Influence in Europe*. London: Duckworth; Chapel Hill: University of North Carolina Press, 1979.

———. "The Reputation of Lucian in Sixteenth Century France." *French Studies* 29 (1975): 385–97.

Rocques, Mario. "Aspects de Panurge." In *Rabelais: Ouvrage publié pour le quatrième centenaire de sa mort 1553–1953*, 120–30. Geneva: Droz, 1953.

Rodini, Robert J. *Antonfrancesco Grazzini*. Madison: University of Wisconsin Press, 1970.

Rollestone, J. D. "Lucian and Medicine." *Janus* 20 (1915): 86–108.

Rossman, Vladimir R. *Perspectives of Irony in Medieval French Literature*. The Hague: Mouton, 1975.

Rummel, Erika. *Erasmus as a Translator of the Classics*. Toronto: University of Toronto Press, 1985.

Sackton, A. "The Paradoxical Encomium in Elizabethan Drama." *University of Texas Studies in English* 28 (1949): 83–104.

Sainte-Marthe, Scévole de. *Louanges*. Paris: Robert Coulombel, 1581.

Salza, Abd-el Kader. *F. Coppetta dei Beccuti poeta perugino*. Turin: Ermanno Loescher, 1900.

Sanesi, Ireneo. *Il cinquecentista Ortensio Lando*. Pistoia: Bracali, 1893.

Saulnier, Verdun L. *Le Dessein de Rabelais*. Paris: Société d'éditions d'enseignement supérieur, 1957.

———. *Maurice Scève (ca. 1500–1560)*. 2 vols. Paris: Klincksieck, 1948–49.

Saunders, Alison. *The Sixteenth-Century Blason Poétique*. New York: Peter Lang, 1981.

———. "Sixteenth-Century Collected Editions of the *Blasons anatomiques*." *The Library* 31 (1976): 153–68.

Schalk, Ellery. *From Valor to Pedigree: Ideas of Nobility in France in the Sixteenth and Seventeenth Centuries*. Princeton: Princeton University Press, 1986.

Schoeck, Richard J. "Lawyers and Rhetoric in Sixteenth-Century England." In *Renaissance Eloquence*, ed. J. J. Murphy, 274–91. Berkeley: University of California Press, 1983.

Schrader, Ludwig. *Panurge und Hermes: Zum Ursprung eines Charakters bei Rabelais*. Bonn: Romanisches Seminar der Universität Bonn, 1958.

Schweinitz, Margaret de. *Les Epitaphes de Ronsard, étude historique et littéraire*. Paris: PUF, 1925.

Screech, Michael. *Ecstasy and the Praise of Folly*. London: Duckworth, 1980.

———. "An Interpretation of the Querelle des Amyes." *BHR* 21 (1959): 103–30.

———. "The Legal Comedy of Rabelais in the Trial of Bridoye in the *Tiers Livre* of Rabelais." *Etudes Rabelaisiennes* 5 (1964): 175–95.

———. "Medicine and Literature." In *French Renaissance Studies*, ed. Peter Sharratt, 156–69. Edinburgh: Edinburgh University Press, 1976.

Screech, Michael. *Rabelais*. Ithaca: Cornell University Press, 1980.

Sheerin, Daniel. "A Carolingian Cure Recovered: Erasmus' Citation of Hucbald of St. Amand's Ecloga de Calvis." *BHR* 42 (1980): 169–71.

Smith, P. M. *The Anti-Courtier Trend in Sixteenth Century French Literature*. Geneva: Droz, 1966.

———. "Jacques Grévin et le Médicin Courtizan." *BHR* 36 (1974): 105–13.

Smith, Preserved. *Erasmus: A Study of His Life, Ideals, and Place in History*. New York: Harper, 1923.

Sobel, Eli. "Sebastian Brant, Ovid, and Classical Allusions in the *Narrenschiff*." *University of California Publications in Modern Philology* 36 (1952): 429–40.

Sorrentino, Andrea. *Francesco Berni poeta della scapigliatura del Rinascimento*. Florence: G. C. Sansoni, 1933.

Stallybrass, Peter, and Allon White. *The Politics and Poetics of Transgression*. Ithaca: Cornell University Press, 1986.

Stegmann, A. "Un Visage nouveau de l'humanisme lyonnais: Paradoxe et humour dans la production des années 1550–1580." In *Colloque sur l'Humanisme lyonnais au XVIe siècle*, 275–93. Turin: Ermanno Loescher, 1900.

Stevens, Linton C. "How the French Humanists of the Renaissance Learned Greek." *PMLA* 65 (1950): 240–48.

———. "The Motivation for Hellenic Studies in the French Renaissance." *SP* 47 (1950): 113–25.

———. "The Reputation of Lucian in Sixteenth-Century France." *Studi francesi* 33 (1967): 401–6.

Stenger, Genevieve. "The 'Praise of Folly' and Its Parerga." *Medievalia et Humanistica* n.s. 2 (1950): 204–48.

"La Surdité de Joachim du Bellay." *La Chronique médicale* 30 (1923): 10.

Swain, Barbara. *Fools and Folly during the Middle Ages and the Renaissance*. New York: Columbia University Press, 1932.

Sylvester, Richard. "The Problem of Unity in the *Praise of Folly*." *English Literary Renaissance* 6 (1976): 125–39.

Tétel, Marcel. *Rabelais et l'Italie*. Florence: Olschki, 1969.

Thompson, Craig R. *The Translations of Lucian by Erasmus and Sir Thomas More*. 1940. Reprint. Ithaca: Cornell University Press, 1958.

Thompson, Elbert N. S. *Literary Bypaths of the Renaissance*. New Haven: Yale University Press, 1924.

———. *The Seventeenth-Century English Essay*. University of Iowa Humanistic Studies, no. 119. Iowa City: University of Iowa Press, 1926.

Thompson, Sister Geraldine, C.S.J. "Erasmus and the Tradition of Paradox." *Studies in Philology* 61 (1964): 41–44.

———. *Under Pretext of Praise: Satiric Mode in Erasmus' Fiction*. Toronto: University of Toronto Press, 1973.

Thomson, J.A.K. *England und die Antike*. Berlin: Bibliothek Warburg Vorträge, 1932.

Thuasne, Louis. *Etudes sur Rabelais*. Paris: Bibliothèque littéraire de la Renaissance, 1904.

Tieghem, Paul van. *La Littérature latine de la Renaissance*. 1940. Reprint. Geneva: Slatkine, 1966.

Tilly, Charles. *The Litigious French*. Cambridge: Harvard University Press, 1986.

Toldo, Pietro. "Le Courtisan dans la littérature française et ses rapports avec l'oeuvre de Castiglione." *Archiv für das Studium der neueren Sprachen und Literaturen* 104 (1900): 75–121.

———. "Etudes sur la poésie burlesque de la Renaissance." *Zeitschrift für romanische Philologie* 24 (1901): 71–93, 215–29, 257–71, 385–410, 513–32.

Tomarken, Annette H.. "Clémént Marot and the Grands Rhétoriqueurs." *Symposium* 32 (1978): 45–48.

———. "Flea Encomia and Other Mock Eulogies of Animals." *Fifteenth-Century Studies* 11 (1985): 137–48.

———. "The Joys of the Cuckold: Bruscambaille and the Tradition of the Mock Encomium." *LittéRealité* 1 (1989): 68–77.

———. " 'Let Us Laugh Our Pains Away': The Italian Bernesque Poets' Encomia on Disease." *Fifteenth-Century Studies* 3 (1980): 211–17.

———. "The Lucianic Blason: A Study of an Edition by Jean de Tournes." In *Literature and the Arts in the Reign of Francis I*, ed. I. D. McFarlane and P. M. Smith, 207–36. Lexington, Ky.: French Forum, 1985.

———. "Mock Epideictic Literature of the Renaissance." In *La Retorica e i generi letterari*. Padua: CLEUP, 1983.

——— [Annette Porter]. "Philibert de Vienne." *BHR* 27 (1965): 702–8.

——— [Annette Porter]. "The Satirical Eulogy in French Renaissance Literature." Ph.D. diss., University of London, 1966.

Tomarken, Annette, and Edward Tomarken. "The Rise and Fall of the Sixteenth-Century French Blason." *Symposium* 29 (1975): 139–63.

Trillitzsch, Winfried. "Erasmus und Seneca." *Philologus* 109 (1965): 270–93.

Trtnik-Rossettini, Olga. *Les Influences anciennes et italiennes sur la satire en France au XVIe siècle*. Publications de l'Institut français de Florence, sér. 1, no. 13. 1958.

Verdier, Maurice. "A Propos d'une controverse sur l'*Hymne de l'or* de Pierre de Ronsard." *BHR* 35 (1973): 7–18.

Vianey, Joseph. "Bruscambille et les poètes bernesques." *Revue d'histoire littéraire de la France* 8 (1901): 569–76.

———. *Mathurin Regnier*. Paris: Hachette, 1896.

Vickers, Brian. "*King Lear* and Renaissance Paradoxes." *Modern Language Review* 61 (1968): 305–14.

Viviani, Ugo. *Nasuti, snasuti, et camusi nell'arte, nella storia, nella letteratura*. Collano di pubblicazioni storichi, artistiche et letterarie Aretine, no. 35. Arezzo: I. Beucci, 1930.

Weinberg, Florence M. *Gargantua in a Convex Mirror: Fischart's View of Rabelais*. New York: Peter Lang, 1986.

———. *The Wine and the Will: Rabelais' Bacchic Christianity*. Detroit: Wayne State University Press, 1972.

Welsford, Enid. *The Fool: His Social and Literary History*. London: Faber and Faber, 1935.

West, Michael. "Skelton and the Renaissance Theme of Folly." *PQ* 50 (1951): 23–75.

Wickersheimer. Ernest. *La Médecine et les médecins en France à l'époque de la Renaissance*. 1905. Reprint. Geneva: Slatkine, 1970.

Willeford, William. *The Fool and His Scepter*. Chicago: Northwestern University Press, 1969.

Williams, Kathleen, ed. *Twentieth Century Interpretations of "The Praise of Folly."* Englewood Cliffs, N.J.: Prentice-Hall, 1969.

Wilson, David. "La Puce de Madame Desroches and John Donne's 'The Flea.'" *Neuphilologische Mitteilungen* 72 (1971): 297–301.

Wison, Dudley B. *Descriptive Poetry in France from Blason to Baroque*. Manchester: Manchester University Press, 1967.

Wykes, Alan. *Doctor Cardano, Physician Extraordinary*. London: Frederick Muller, 1969.

Yates, Frances. "Paradox and Paradise." *New York Review of Books*, 23 Feb. 1967, 26–27.

Zappala, Michael. "Andrés Laguna, Erasmus, and the Translation of Lucian's *Tragopodagra*." *Revue de littérature comparée* 53 (1979): 19–31.

Index

Index

Euripides, 9, 17, 248n.21
Eustachi, Bartolomeo, 298n.51

Fail, Noël du, 161, 292n.11
Falloppio, Gabriello, 298n.51
Falstaff, 128, 139, 156, 160, 167, 288n.120, 294n.18, 296n.43
farces and dialogues, French, 34–35, 107, 162, 165, 168, 275nn.17, 18, 291–92n.9
Favorinus, 38, 49, 145, 237n.15, 290n.4; mocked by Lucian, 21, 243n.57; on quartan fever, 7, 21–22, 38, 53, 65, 69–70, 76, 96, 132, 177, 257n.38, 258n.42, 273n.50
Fernel, Jean, 168, 176, 291n.7, 295n.33
Ferrari, Giovanni Francesco, 148
Ferrier, Auger, 196n.42
Ferrus, Donatus Antonius, 258n.48
fever, quartan and others, 7, 38, 143, 170, 174, 237n.16, 261n.63, 292n.11, 293n.18, 295n.33, 297n.46, 298n.52. See also Lyons blasons, on quartan fever; Favorinus; Hutten, Ulrich von; Menapius Insulas, Guiliemus
Ficino, Marsilio, 139, 247n.14
Figon de Montelimar, Jean, 288n.114
Firenzuola, Agnolo, 80, 270n.34, 271n.41
Fischart, Johann, 51, 233, 259nn.55, 58, 311n.48
fleas, 7, 76–77, 164, 222–29, 230, 237n.16, 260n.58, 311nn.46, 48, 312nn.50, 51, 53; flea literature in England, 223. See also des Roches, Catherine and Madeline
fly, 69, 74, 78, 237n.16; contrasted with elephant by Lucian and imitators, x, 19–20, 72, 77, 78, 183, 226, 230–31, 297n.49, 310n.40, 312n.51. See also Alberti, Leon Battista, Musca; Lucian of Samosata, Muscae Encomium
folly, 34, 35, 90–92, 102, 132–37, 141–43, 182, 192, 230, 237n.16, 249nn.28, 32, 271n.42, 272n.43, 283nn.75, 79, 286n.96, 298n.50
Fontaine, Charles, 110–11, 276n.24, 278n.41, 280n.58
foodstuffs. See eulogy, satirical, on foodstuffs
fools, court, 33, 41, 142, 251n.43, 282n.65
Forcadel, Etienne, 95, 213–15, 222, 300n.75, 308n.29, 30
Fouquelin, Antoine, 121, 278n.48
Fracastoro, Girolamo, 261n.62

Francesi, Matteo, 94–95, 151, 171–73, 175
Francklin, Thomas, 17, 240n.34, 242nn.47, 55
Franco, Matteo, 81
François I (king of France), 96, 97, 147–48, 151, 189
Françon, Marcel, 222, 223
Frappier, Jean, 280n.58
Frautschi, R. L., 35
Free, John, 22, 167, 290n.2
Fregoso, Antonio, 249n.32, 277n.38
Freind, John, 291n.8
Froben, Johann, 21, 22, 76, 167, 254n.63
frogs, 212, 215–16, 217
Fronto, Marcus Cornelius, 7, 237n.15, 244n.66
Furies, 16, 64, 65, 68

Galanthis, 221
Galen, 70, 124, 209, 269n.30, 291n.8
Galissard, Pierre, 73, 76–77, 266n.86
gallstones. See calculus
gambling, 36, 44
Garapon, Robert, 162
Garzoni, Tommaso, 271n.42
genre theory, ix; Renaissance fluidity and development of, xi, 229, 230–33. See also eulogy, satirical; encomium, serious
Germans and drinking, 34, 55, 69, 143, 249n.28, 283n.80
Gesner, Conrad, 73–74, 295n.33
Gilles, Pierre, 265n.76
Giovio, Paolo, 271n.42
Giudici, Enzo, 112, 274n.7, 277n.30
Giunti (printers), 96, 271n.42
Glatigny, Michel, 305n.12
Glauco(n), 38, 251n.41, 273n.50, 290n.4
Glauser, Alfred, 295n.34
Gleason, Maud, 24, 244n.64
Gnapheus, Gulielmus, 256n.26
gnat. See mosquitos
Gnatho (in Terence's Eunuchus), 100, 107, 132, 239n.31
Godard, Jean, 151–53
Godefroy, Frédéric, 187
Gohin, Ferdinand, 275nn.19, 20
Golden Age, myth of, 87–89, 138, 152, 157–58, 161, 289n.129
Gorgias, 4; praises Helen, 6, 7, 11, 240n.39
gout: "cures for," 16–17, 61, 168–69, 242n.47, 261n.61, 291n.7; works on, 7,

Index

money, 85, 90, 104, 134, 151, 155, 280n.58.
  See also debt; poverty
monkeys, 279n.51, 305n.13
monks. *See* religious figures
Montaiglon, Anatole C. de, 133, 180, 181,
  187, 189, 223, 279n.55, 280n.58, 296n.42,
  308n.30, 310n.41
Montaigne, Michel de, 100, 163, 169,
  254n.1, 265n.78, 286n.98, 290n.3,
  292n.13, 293n.17, 294n.26, 295n.34
More, Sir Thomas, 246n.11, 251n.42; as
  dedicatee of Erasmus' *Moriae Encomium*,
  38, 40, 41, 42, 252n.45; as translator and
  admirer of Lucian, 29, 30, 246n.6,
  248n.22, 262n.66, 278n.41; *Utopia*, 50,
  52, 273n.51
Morellet, abbé André, 286n.95
Moria (Folly). *See* Erasmus, *Moriae Enco-
  mium*
Morley, Henry, 55, 62, 259n.51
Morrison, Mary, 73, 264n.72
Moschion, 5
Mosellanus, Petrus, 248n.22
Moses, 19, 195
mosquitos, 7, 95–96, 237n.16, 243n.61,
  266n.83
Motin, Pierre, 190, 268n.15, 301n.76,
  302n.82, 304n.6, 311n.46; "Hymne du
  Maquerellage," 283n.80
Mottron, Jean, 292n.11, 294n.20
Moussin, Jehan, 153
mule. *See* ass
Musaeus, 273n.50
Muses, 90, 123, 125, 152–53, 188, 194
Myia and the fly, legend of, 19, 35

Naïs, Hélène, 73–74, 203, 212, 219, 265n.74,
  303n.2, 309nn.30, 35
Nauert, Charles, 254n.1
Navagero, Andrea, 205, 304n.7
negligence, 7
Neo-Latin mock encomia. *See* eulogy, satiri-
  cal, in Neo-Latin literature
Neo-Platonism. *See* Platonism
Nero, 11, 133, 135, 257n.30, 263n.68,
  284n.81, 286n.95. *See also* Cardano, Gi-
  rolamo
Newton, Thomas, ix
Nicolas, Simon, 130, 219–20, 298n.59
Nigellus Wireker, 249n.28
Niord, Yvonne, 305n.15
Noah, 143, 214, 306n.15

noses, 153, 164, 191, 244n.65, 300n.75
Noue, Odet de la: on prison, 57, 150–51;
  and similar English works, 287n.106
nuns. *See* religious figures

Obsopoeus (Obsopoeus), Vincentius, 55,
  256n.25
Oedipus, 17, 60
old age, 7, 21, 36, 51
Ong, Walter J., 254n.8, 278n.48
Ovid: *Amores*, 73, 263n.70; *Ars amatoria*,
  55; comments on gout, 16, 63, 68, 168,
  171, 259n.50; *Metamorphoses*, 159, 221,
  222, 310n.42; *Nux*, 26, 38, 78; in Renaissance, 73, 135, 191, 199

Pan, 193
Pandora, 92, 152
panegyric, 3, 103, 235n.1, 238n.18, 252n.45,
  254n.63. *See also* epitaphs
Panofsky, Erwin, 282n.65
Paradossi. *See* Lando, Ortensio, *Paradossi*
paradox: in Renaissance and later, 74–75, 79,
  237n.16, 285n.95, 287n.106, 288n.118;
  Christian, 102–3. *See also* Cicero, *Paradoxa Stoicorum*; Estienne, Charles;
  Lando, Ortensio, *Paradossi*
parasitism. *See* Gnatho; Lucian of Samosata,
  De Parasito
Paré, Ambroise, 168, 176, 184, 269n.30,
  291n.7, 295n.33, 296nn.37, 42, 298n.51,
  299n.58, 309n.35
Paris, 17
parody: and animal epitaphs, 76, 208–11;
  and the farce, 34–35; and the hymne-blason, 214, 216, 221, 229; and Italian literature, 81, 95; of medieval literature, 67,
  103–4, 106, 182, 255n.12; of religious
  themes, 103–4, 274n.5, 293n.18, 300n.69;
  and satirical eulogy, 18, 103, 199, 204–5,
  229
parrots, 7, 243n.61, 263n.70, 306n.19. *See
  also* Lemaire de Belges, Jean
Paschal, Pierre de, 118, 278n.41
Pasquet, André, 167, 243n.60, 290n.4
Pasquier, Etienne, 222, 224, 226–29, 304n.5,
  312n.52
Passerat, Jean, 71, 78, 153–56, 169, 196–97,
  204, 290n.139, 292n.16, 302n.82,
  307nn.21, 23, 308n.30
Paul IV, pope: attacked by Du Bellay, 185–
  86

Index

Index